T5-CQG-113

Encyclopedia of Giftedness, Creativity, and Talent

Editorial Board

Encyclopedia of Giftedness, Creativity, and Talent

Editor Barbara Kerr

University of Kansas

VOLUME

2

Los Angeles | London | New Delhi
Singapore | Washington DC

A SAGE Reference Publication

For information:

SAGE Publications, Inc.
2455 Teller Road
Thousand Oaks, California 91320
E-mail: order@sagepub.com

SAGE Publications Ltd.
1 Oliver's Yard
55 City Road
London, EC1Y 1SP
United Kingdom

SAGE Publications India Pvt. Ltd.
B 1/I 1 Mohan Cooperative Industrial Area
Mathura Road, New Delhi 110 044
India

SAGE Publications Asia-Pacific Pte. Ltd.
33 Pekin Street #02-01
Far East Square
Singapore 048763

Printed in the United States of America.

Library of Congress Cataloging-in-Publication Data
Barbara Kerr, editor.
p. cm.
Includes bibliographical references and index.
ISBN 978-1-4129-4971-2 (cloth)
1. Gifted children—Education—United States—Encyclopedias. 2. Creative ability in children—United States—Encyclopedias. I. Kerr, Barbara A.
LC3993.2.E63 2009
371.950973'03—dc22 2008055506

This book is printed on acid-free paper.

09 10 11 12 13 10 9 8 7 6 5 4 3 2 1

Publisher: Rolf A. Janke
Acquisitions Editor: Jim Brace-Thompson
Editorial Assistant: Michele Thompson
Developmental Editors: Carole Maurer, Sara Tauber
Reference Systems Manager: Leticia M. Gutierrez
Reference Systems Coordinator: Laura Notton
Production Editor: Kate Schroeder
Copy Editors: Kristin Bergstad, Robin Gold
Typesetter: C&M Digitals (P) Ltd.
Proofreader: Penelope Sippel
Indexer: Julie Grayson
Cover Designer: Janet Foulger
Marketing Manager: Amberlyn McKay

Contents

Volume 2

List of Entries

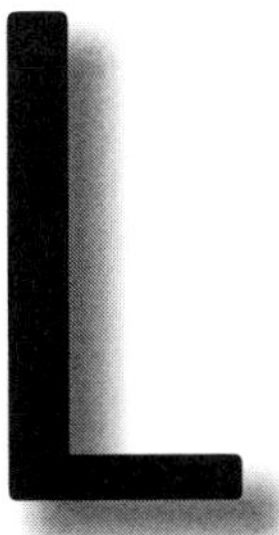

Language Arts, Curriculum

A typical language arts curriculum includes a wide range of receptive and expressive language skills, including reading, viewing, listening, thinking, writing, speaking, and performing. Topics taught within a language arts curriculum generally include grammar, vocabulary, rhetoric, literature, poetry, drama, criticism, research, and journalism. Standards promulgated by the National Council of Teachers of English mention even more language arts topics, including visual language, media techniques, databases, computer networks, and dialects across cultures.

This entry discusses language arts curricular constraints that hinder gifted children and discusses how teachers and parents can accelerate and enrich the language arts experiences of gifted children. The curricular and instructional strategies in this entry capitalize on various characteristics of gifted children, including strong curiosity, heightened concern with justice and fairness, advanced powers of reasoning, and tendencies to question authority. Although the strategies are listed under language arts areas, a reading strategy might include writing elements, and a grammar strategy might include reading elements. Many gifted children learn best when employing multiple aspects of language arts simultaneously.

Curricular Constraints

The language arts curriculum can be a source of frustration for gifted children. The spiral nature of the curriculum requires teachers to revisit language arts concepts introduced in prior years. A gifted child who learns how to use commas in first grade may have to listen to comma usage rules repeated in five or six subsequent grades. A gifted child who reads voraciously from an early age may find that spelling and vocabulary tests lack challenge. Novels assigned to an entire class are often below the reading level of gifted students.

Teachers' good intentions and school districts' textbook adoptions can add to the frustration felt by gifted language arts students. Teachers who lack knowledge about the needs of gifted children might believe that a basic enrichment section of a spelling book, which includes adding "er" suffixes to the regular spelling words, is sufficient differentiation. Long after a particular gifted child has mastered the art of writing organization, secondary teachers might insist that the child continue to follow a rigid five-paragraph essay template taught in the school's writing textbooks. A school system that adopts literature textbooks with abridged versions of novels and other writings might frustrate gifted children who crave entire works.

The key to meeting the language arts needs of gifted learners lies in departure from curricular constraints. The best teachers and schools recognize that gifted language arts learners need to explore the arts of language at their own learning levels and speeds. Gifted children should not be instructed on material they have already mastered. Gifted children should be offered language arts instruction with appropriately challenging and complex material that allows them to use their minds well.

The remainder of this entry includes language arts curriculum strategies for implementation with gifted children. Some of the strategies involve differentiation or replacement of the curriculum and other strategies involve incorporation of typically extracurricular language arts learning into the language arts classroom. The purpose of these strategies is to extend the language arts learning of gifted children who have already mastered basic language arts skills typically taught to children their age. The teaching of these strategies can involve multiple disciplines, offer children choices, and give children opportunities for reflection. The strategies, when carefully implemented, can satisfy complexity, depth, and expressive needs of gifted children.

Strategies

Reading

Many gifted children learn to read at early ages. Indeed, early reading is one of the chief characteristics of gifted children. Gifted children who read extensively through the elementary school years typically excel in other language arts areas because advanced reading expands children's vocabularies, writing skills, and thinking skills.

Differentiating a reading curriculum for advanced readers presents little challenge for teachers in schools with good libraries and willing librarians. Librarians are generally adept at finding books appropriate for readers of all levels and interests. Advanced readers in elementary school benefit from being released from reading group instruction time to find appropriate books in the school library. Advanced readers in middle school and high school can sometimes benefit from having teachers learn their interests and feed those interests with appropriate books.

Reading lists, including lists of Newbery award winners for elementary school students and lists of books recommended for high school students by the College Board and by the American Library Association can provide fertile ground for extending the literature curriculum for gifted readers. Opportunities to interact with well-read adults, those who are able to draw on a vast knowledge of classic and current literature to interest gifted learners in reading and discussing the works, also can benefit gifted children. With careful adult guidance, gifted readers can find and enjoy advanced books on topics appropriate for their maturity levels.

Writing

Some gifted learners learn writing intuitively; they don't need to be taught how to use transitions, how to employ good voice, or how to vary their sentence structures. Some gifted learners automatically write in the style of their favorite authors, and some exude logic almost directly from their minds to their papers.

The best teachers recognize that writing curricula such as writing traits systems should be used sparingly with advanced learners, who might lose their writing fluency if forced to dissect their written works into traits such as ideas, content, organization, vocabulary, sentences, and conventions. Yes, gifted children can benefit from using writing traits rubrics, but teachers should think twice before giving children who have mastered one or more writing traits additional instruction and assignments on those traits.

One strategy for differentiating a school's writing curriculum and instruction to meet the needs of gifted children involves actually sharing the school's curriculum with the students and asking them to use their powers of abstraction, conceptualization, and synthesis to comment on what parts of the curriculum apply and what parts do not apply to their own learning about writing. Such metacognitive exercises extend beyond writing into critical thinking and evaluation.

Another writing strategy for use with gifted children is to encourage them to establish and build their own writing portfolios, with samples of a wide variety of writing forms and styles. When the portfolio assignments are relevant to their interests, students are more likely to feel responsibility and pride about their writing skills. Teachers can give each student an individualized checklist of the forms and styles to include in the student's portfolio. The teacher can customize each checklist to match the interests and abilities of the child. The writing assignments on the checklist can be blended with learning in other language arts areas including reading, grammar, and vocabulary development.

Grammar

Many teachers are reluctant to delve into the mechanics of grammar, perhaps because they themselves do not know grammar on a deep level. Few elementary and secondary teachers have backgrounds in linguistics, or extensive experience diagramming sentences. Often, secondary language arts teachers leave the teaching of grammar concepts to the foreign language department.

Gifted learners fortunate enough to have language arts teachers with linguistics backgrounds or with advanced sentence diagramming skills often thrive when learning grammar on complex levels. Even teachers without appropriate grammar backgrounds can introduce gifted learners to the many good Web sites available for teaching Reed-Kellogg sentence diagramming and advanced principles of grammar. College writing center Web sites often contain advanced grammar information presented in interesting ways.

To combine grammar learning with critical thinking skills, teachers can interest gifted learners in analyzing language arts textbooks from various grade levels to analyze when and how those books present grammar concepts. Also, teachers can introduce advanced learners to grammar style guides used by professional writers, including style guides by the Modern Language Association, the American Psychological Association, and various journalism organizations. Students can then write reports and present their findings, thus blending skills in presenting, writing, using correct grammar, and critical thinking.

Vocabulary

Children learn vocabulary naturally at an astounding rate. By some estimates, average children learn 5,000 vocabulary words during 4 years in high school. Children who read extensively and take challenging courses learn even more words during their high school careers, sometimes 10,000 or more in 4 years. Vocabulary acquisition is rarely a problem for gifted children who read extensively.

One method for helping gifted children blend vocabulary development with thinking skills involves teaching word roots and word families. Inquisitive minds love learning stories behind word roots, such as the fact that the root "bell" as in *bellicose* and *belligerent* came from the goddess Bellona, the wife of Mars, the Roman god of war. The word *philosophy* includes "phil," which means love, and "osophy," which means knowledge; philosophers are lovers of knowledge. Gifted children often enjoy learning that most common English word roots are also common in Spanish and French. Teaching word roots gives gifted children critical thinking skills with which to unlock English as well as other languages.

In addition to enjoying word roots, gifted children may also enjoy categorizing new words into families and learning their etymology. Teachers with knowledge of the history of the English language can fascinate children by reciting the Middle English prologue to Chaucer's *Canterbury Tales* from 1300, by displaying the incomprehensible Old English of *Beowulf,* and by explaining the Norman Conquest and its effects upon the English language. Why do we use the Anglo-Saxon words *cow* and *pig* for the animals in the field, but the French-originated words *beef* and *pork* for the meat on our plates? Etymological mysteries abound, which can fascinate children sent on treasure hunts to discover the origins of words.

Research Skills

Because research skills serve as road maps for the natural curiosity of gifted children, these children benefit from the teaching of research skills at early ages. As soon as young children learn to use the library, they can learn the Dewey Decimal System and other cataloging systems adopted by the libraries they visit. As soon as children learn to use the Internet to find information, they can learn how to evaluate Internet sources for reliability. Because one of the characteristics of gifted children is an enhanced sense of justice, many love investigating the veracity of Internet sources and uncovering bias.

Some gifted children also enjoy learning to use computer programs for organizing their research findings, and some enjoy learning about the many citation formats used in research. Teachers need not understand the intricacies of computer programs; most gifted children enjoy figuring out computer programs themselves. Rather than teach just one citation format to gifted children, teachers can encourage gifted children to compare and contrast several citation formats and learn where and when those formats are used. The results of this compare-and-contrast work can be incorporated into a child's writing portfolio and can be presented to other students.

Challenges and Opportunities

The spiral nature of the language arts curriculum in most schools provides both challenges and opportunities for the teaching of gifted children. The challenges exist because gifted children often master language arts concepts after one or two repetitions, yet the same concepts are repeated in the curriculum year after year, from introduction, to reinforcement, to mastery in time sequences intended for average children. The opportunities exist because the characteristics of gifted children and the purposes of the language arts curriculum match well. Complexity, challenge, and creativity can be added easily to the language arts curriculum.

Wenda Sheard

See also Classical Languages Curriculum, Gifted; Classics/Great Books; Secondary School, Writing Curriculum

Further Readings

Cramond, B. (1993). Key components of a complete language arts program for the gifted. *Roeper Review, 16*(1), 44–48.

Fehrenbach, C. R. (1994). Cognitive style of gifted and average readers. *Roeper Review, 16*(4), 290–292.

Johnson, D. T., Boyce, L. N., & VanTassel-Baska, J. (1995). Science curriculum review: Evaluating materials for high-ability learners. *Gifted Child Quarterly, 39,* 36–43.

VanTassel-Baska, J. (2002). Assessment of gifted student learning in the language arts. *Journal of Secondary Gifted Education, 13*(2), 67–72.

VanTassel-Baska, J. (2003). Differentiating the language arts for high ability learners, K–8. *ERIC Digest* E474306 2003-01-00.

VanTassel-Baska, J., Zuo, L., Avery, L. D., & Little, C. A. (2002). A curriculum study of gifted student learning in the language arts. *Gifted Child Quarterly, 46*(1), 30–44.

Latin America/South America, Gifted Education

The quest to identify and serve gifted students in Latin America and South America was initiated in the early 1970s. The most comprehensive resource available in this area is *La educación de niños con talento en Iberoamérica (The Education of Gifted Children in Ibero-America).* This significant work was published in 2004 by the Regional Office of Education of UNESCO for Latin America and Caribbean Countries. The report concludes, as noted later, that Hispanic America has undergone a trajectory similar to that of the United States:

- Sharing a democratic philosophy, preference has been given to understanding and meeting the needs of students with disabilities, whereas there is reticence to accept that the gifted and talented, misconceived as a privileged elite, should be granted additional advantages.
- There is a tendency to believe that giftedness excludes the possibility of a concomitant disability.
- There is universal agreement that giftedness and talent must be identified through multiple means and developed throughout the school experience.
- The private institutions located in large, prosperous cities, rather than the public sector, have led the movement to consider this population.
- Certain countries, Spain in particular, have promulgated national legislation to meet the needs of the gifted and talented but little has occurred in practice largely because of lack of funding.
- A primary concern has been to find an appropriate curriculum design within the regular program or in self-contained magnet centers, schools, or academies.
- Some schools promote acceleration, others favor enrichment, but research is lacking to support either model.
- Research is needed to validate theoretical approaches.
- Finally, there is a paucity of teacher training to identify and develop the diverse aptitudes and talents among the gifted population.

In most gifted education programs in South America, talent or *talento* refers to extraordinary aptitude in a specific field such as music, theater, or athletics, whereas giftedness or *superdotación* refers to general intellectual ability. The consensus favors a multidimensional view of intelligence, an operational definition of talent and giftedness, the notion that intelligence assumes divergent thinking, and, finally, that giftedness includes intellectual prowess, personality attributes, and appropriate environmental opportunity to develop abilities. Thus, identification should be viewed as a process of discovery and continuous nurturance of talent and potential.

Argentina, Brazil, Chile, Colombia, Cuba, Mexico, Peru, Spain, and Venezuela each have legislation, programs and services, and documented research on gifted and talented. These are documented in Table 1.

Table 1 Gifted Education in Latin/South America[1]

Argentina	
Legislation	
1993	*Ley Federal de Educación,* Ministerio de Educación, Ciencia y Tecnología, Chpt VII, Article 33.
1991	*Asociación de Padres Apoyo a la Creatividad y el Talento (ACT)* nonprofit organization raises awareness and support for the gifted.
1992–2002	*Instituto Creatividad y Talento (ICT)* offers classes of 12 students using a flexible, interdisciplinary, spiral curriculum that increases in depth and complexity.
	Closes its doors due to lack of funding and support.
1993	*Ley Federal de Educación,* Ministerio de Educación, Ciencia y Tecnología, Chpt VII, Article 33.
1993	*Fundación Evaluación de Talento y Creatividad* partners with the *Universidad Centro de Altos Estudios de Ciencias Exactas (CAECE)* to identify gifted and provide programming, professional development, and parent support. First to offer graduate training in gifted education.
1993	Schools promote early university enrollment based on ability and interest: Colegio Norbridge, Colegio San Bernardo de Claraval en Mendoza, Colegio Vera Peñaloza, Colegio Everardo de Casa Tilly.
1998	Buenos Aires recognizes high-ability students and establishes the position *maestra integradora* or resource teacher to serve students with disabilities and the gifted.
2000	*Centro para el Desarrollo del Alto Potencial (CEDAP)* assists schools with identification, teacher training in enrichment and acceleration, distance learning, creativity development, and parent seminars.
Programs and Services	
Acceleration:	Early entry must be approved by the LEA
	By exam in high school
	Grade skipping if child is intellectually and emotionally ready
Enrichment:	In regular education through resource teacher
	With age peers in regular education
	Thematic curriculum at greater depth and complexity
Brazil	
Legislation	
1960s	Helena Antipoff establishes a humanities center for gifted rural children, *Hacienda del Rosario,* Minas Gerais.
1973	*Centro Nacional de Educación Especial (CENESP).*
1978	Founding of Brazilian Association for the Gifted (private).

(Continued)

Table 1 (Continued)

1971	Federal law mandates attention be given to students with disabilities and to those with superior abilities. Law calls for (a) proper identification, (b) an organized system of instruction, (c) professional development of teachers, and (d) an operational definition of giftedness.
1995	Brazilian government adopts definition: the gifted are those who perform at high levels or exhibit high potential in general intellectual ability or specific aptitude in an academic or artistic area. Many argue that to give more attention to those who are privileged with superior abilities is elitist.

Identification

Generally carried out by private psychologists who have little training dealing with the gifted; therefore, few are identified. Exclusive use of tests of intellectual ability yields to inclusion of creativity measures and parent or peer nomination.

Programs and Services

Generally consist of extracurricular enrichment programs.

1972	*Proyecto Objetivo de Incentivo al Talento* challenges 500 students to move at their own pace and extend their creativity in the humanities and technological fields.
1975	*Programa para la Atención del Alumno Superdotado de la Secretaría de Educación del distrito federal* offers fine arts, literature, math, science, computers and chess to 600+ children/adolescents from public and private schools.

Chile

Legislation

1990	Educators become aware that gifted/talented students need to be understood and supported.
1998	*Decreto de Educación 220 del Ministerio de Educación* mandates diversity in education, implying due attention must be given to students with superior abilities. No distinction is made between the intellectually gifted and those with specific talents.

Identification

Teachers identify the gifted/talented using the criteria established by *PENTA-UC, Programa Educacional para Niños con Talento Académico:*

1. Personality characteristics
2. High logical and mathematical reasoning
3. High oral and written communication skills
4. High competency in social studies

Achievement tests in content areas and the Ravens Progressive Matrices as well as history of special awards are considered.

Programs and Services

Renzulli's Enrichment Model[2] has been adopted.

1993 *Pontificia Universidad Católica de Chile* identifies low SES children 9–10 years of age for an accelerated program in mathematics through high school.

2001 *Programa Educacional para Niños con Talento Académico* offers an enriched, inter-disciplinary program in the sciences and humanities, along with professional development for teachers.

Colombia

Legislation

1994 *La Ley 115 dentro del Título III de la Ley General de Educación* explains how persons with limitations or exceptional intellectual abilities are to be identified and served.

1996 *Decreto 2082* mandates the establishment of programs and services to students in private or public schools with a planned curriculum and teacher training.

Talent defined as general academic ability or in specific areas: theoretical talent, ability to create objects and processes, aptitude in science and technology, and emotional intelligence. Based on two philosophical principles: (1) All human beings have talent but there are those with superior talent; (2) early identification is necessary to prevent serious maladjustment, underachievement and failure.

Identification

Use measures to predict academic achievement, task commitment and perseverance, and high creativity. Look for students with high competencies and sustained focus to create products of higher quality and originality than those of age peers.

Use psychometric instruments of aptitude and interest, interviews and autobiographies, and classroom performance. The process includes a period of observation and exploration to determine if there is potential in a specific field.

Programs and Services

1980 First institutes emerged: Alberto Merani en Santa Fe de Bogotá and Alejandro Von Humboldt in Barranquilla.

2000 Private *colegios* or academies emerged: Cristóbal Colón, Camilo Torres, Rafael Uribe, Nicolás Esguerra, Francisco José Caldas, La Merced, República de Colón, Jorge Eliécer Gaitán, Florentino González, San Bernardo.

There are few public institutions. Most schools are located in the capital district of Bogotá.

Programs focus on the development of four stages:

1. Early identification for high potential at the primary grades.
2. Exploration of areas of interest at intermediate grades.
3. Identification of strengths and weaknesses in specific talent during early adolescence.
4. Implementation of educational plan under supervision.

(Continued)

Table 1 (Continued)

Research

Instituto Alberto Merani studies how gifted (IQ 130–170) interact with families. Most important influence in the development of talent is parent level of education, suggesting giftedness is related to privileged socioeconomic classes.

A statewide project in Itagui promotes academic achievement to improve the education and socioeconomic development of communities.

In Soacha, teachers are being trained to identify talented children early and further their growth and development in collaboration with university networks.

In 2002, the Fourth Latin American Congress on Giftedness and Talent in Santa Fe de Bogota brought to light the paucity of knowledge in the field, and the lack of university programs to train teachers and psychologists to identify and support the gifted.

During the last few years, government policies and initiatives are allocating funds to support scholarships for low SES gifted students to access private schools.

Cuba

Legislation and Programs

1970	The Castro government decrees establishment of special schools for students talented in mathematics and science.
1998	Eileen Donoghue and Bruce Vogell[3] describe the Lenin school or the *Instituto Preuniversitario Vocacional Ciencias Exactas Vladimir I Lenin.* The central boarding school enrolls 2,700 gifted boys and girls and provides a curriculum in the fine arts, humanities, science, and mathematics. An additional 14 regional schools that focus on math and science enroll 5,000 boys and girls.
	Patterned after the Russian model, the curriculum requires 20 hours per week of mathematics instruction, compared with 8 in regular schools. These are residential facilities, so students participate in a variety of after-school academic clubs, computer courses, and special seminars that prepare them for national competitions. Classes are scheduled for 11-week periods, followed by 3-day weekends which 11 students are required to spend at home with family.
	Admission requires recommendations from teachers, outstanding academic records, and successful performance on an admissions exam in mathematics and Spanish. The teacher/student ratio is 57:1, but all are committed to maintaining high academic performance standards. Teaching positions in these schools are highly competitive.
	Graduates from the Lenin Schools unfortunately do not have access to challenging university programs. In the past, many enrolled in Eastern European universities with support from socialist governments. The change in political alignments has limited these opportunities.
	Because the Cuban economy cannot absorb the number of talented math and science graduates each year, other Latin American countries import these students as a valuable human commodity.

Mexico

Legislation

Declaración de Salamanca supports services for students with disabilities.

1982	Concern for the gifted is viewed under the special education initiative. The standardization of the Wechsler Intelligence Scale for Children (WISC) identified gifted elementary students but no results are published.

1985 Eleven states initiate the gifted education movement.

1989–1994 *Programa de Capacidades y Aptitudes Sobresalientes (CAS)* was initiated as part of educational reform. Talent, gifted, and superior intellectual ability are used synonymously. CAS proposes that every state will design a model to address the needs of gifted students.

Identification

CAS in 13 of 30 states employs the same methods: sociometric surveys, the Renzulli-Hartman Scale, school grades, family socioeconomic status, interest survey and self-referral. Scores are ranked from high to low for selection.

In Monterey, the *Asociación Mexicana para el apoyo a sobresalientes (AMEXPAS)* uses the interest-a-lyzer on Howard Gardner's eight intelligences and other questionnaires.

In Cuernavaca, Morelos, observation, the Stanford Binet, and the Wechsler Intelligence Scale for Children—Revised (WISC-R) are used. *AMEXPAS* proposes to standardize identification and intervention strategies.

La Universidad de Guadalajara, Jalisco, and the *Centro the Estudios e Investigación de Creatividad Aplicada (CEICREA)* use the following: (a) For pre-identification, child and parent interview, Raven Colored Progressive Matrices, creativity tests, peer nomination, teacher recommendation; (b) To determine eligibility, the Benton Visual Memory Test, WISC-R, interest survey a parent multiple intelligences questionnaire; (c) To determine emotional health, anxiety and depression surveys and self-evaluation instruments.

Programs and Services

Games are considered pivotal because these tend to:

- Develop imagination and nurture creativity, independence, and a personal view of the world.
- Build logical thinking, inferential learning, planning, and metacognition.
- Develop moral and social values, such as teamwork and consensus building for the common good.
- Encourage spontaneity to examine reality from different perspectives and enjoy the creative process.
- Activate latent ideas and feelings and permit students to look at home/school factors that help them internalize reality and thus develop their own personality.

1997 Program is established in Sinaloa, Monterrey, Chiapas, and the federal district. A summer program is included.

1998 *Proyecto Talentitos by Centro de Estudios e Investigacion de Creatividad Aplicada* by Dolores Valadez Sierra proposes to help parents and educators guide children to become actualized, confident adults who use their creativity to face a competitive world. Program has served 400 students ages 3 to 12 and trained more than 200 teachers in summer and enrichment classes during the year. A newsletter is published with children's work and parent essays on how to guide gifted children.

Research

2002 Valadez[5] et al. from the University of Guadalajara used WISC to identify a 3% gifted population from 519 fourth graders in seven schools in Guadalajara and evaluated identification measures:

- Teacher questionnaires miss gifted underachievers.
- The Renzulli SCRBSS (6) yields high numbers as children are keen observers of each other's talents and abilities.
- Raven Matrices is a good tool for initial pool, but not for final selection and should not be used to determine intellectual abilities.
- Creativity tests identify only 50% of the gifted. Creativity is not exclusive to the gifted.
- Recommend combined use of standardized tests and questionnaires.

(Continued)

Table 1 (Continued)

Peru

Legislation

1971	Special education legislation is instituted.
1983	Ley General de Educacion 23384, Art 68 mandates special attention to those with disabilities as well as the *niño talentoso* or *sobresaliente*. Up to now focus is on the masses rather than the individual.
2001	*La guía de organización y funcionamiento de los programas de intervención con niños con necesidades educativas especiales por superdotación y/o talento*. Peru provides a guide for instructional organization of gifted programs.
2002	*Jefatura de Educación Especial Ley 28044 Art 18* promotes programs for gifted/talented, provides scholarships for those with low SES to continue their education, and calls for provisions of challenging curriculum within regular education.

Identification

There is no single process.

First level criteria: academic achievement, perseverance, task commitment, and motivation to learn.

Second level criteria: WISC-R 130 IQ + Renzulli Scales for Rating the Behaviors of Superior Students (1997), high score on interest/motivation.

Spain

Legislation

1970	*Ley General de Educación y Financiamiento de la Reforma Educativa* first mentions that attention will be given to needs of the *superdotados* for their own welfare and the benefit of society. Later, Article 53 adds "they will be instructed in the regular classroom but will be given individual attention to actualize their potential."
1990	*Libro Blanco para la Reforma del Sistema Educativo* states, "utilize curriculum enrichment to meet their needs effectively . . . and necessary resources to enable them to reach their potencial."
1995	*Decreto 696* specifically mandates that the system identify and provide for the needs of the intellectually gifted. Counseling programs in secondary schools will have the services of "trained psychologists and educators to meet the needs of the gifted and their parents." This addresses the gifted underachievers who may also have low self-esteem.
2002	*La Ley Orgánica de la Calidad de la Enseñanza (LOCE)* stipulates the administration shall: (a) pay specific attention to the intellectually gifted; (b) promote the early identification of the needs of the intellectually gifted; (c) regulate a flexible attendance schedule in various grade levels, independent of age; (d) establish centers equipped to provide appropriate services to the intellectually gifted; (e) provide professional development for teachers and support services for parents. Despite this legislation, the current situation is disappointing because the needs of the intellectually gifted are still not part of teacher training programs. Andalucía has published a pamphlet and questionnaire for teachers and counselors delineating steps to support and follow-up the progress of these students.

In Galicia, departments and special teams have been created to monitor the progress of 300 students who are receiving enrichment services.

In Madrid, flexible scheduling allows the intellectually gifted to proceed at a pace commensurate with their abilities and increased student participation in extracurricular programs.

In the Basque country, laws have been created to regulate the identification and implementation of differentiated curriculum.

The *Comunidad Foral de Navarra,* follows the state norms for identification and service by specially trained teams to include the gifted in the regular program.

Identification

Practices include standard measures of intellectual ability, specific aptitude, achievement batteries, measures of creativity and divergent thinking, along with teacher/parent/peer and self-nomination questionnaires.

Yolanda Benito and colleagues propose a 3-month referral process: First, a thorough evaluation of student abilities, creativity, self-concept, learning styles, problem-solving approach, interests and favorite activities, task commitment, and goals; second, review the school characteristics, resources, and quality of relationships between students and teachers; third, consider family characteristics, cooperation, and expectations. Finally, the community environment is tapped for resources that further student growth and development. A protocol is available to track the process from identification to parent consent for evaluation and implementation of intervention plan.

Venezuela

Legislation

1950 Jesuit priest Carlos Guillermo Plaza founds the first school for children with high aptitude.

Psychologist Andres Bello, founder of the Universidad Católica de Caracas, advocates for the gifted with attention deficits.

1967 Emergence of first special education classrooms for the deaf and blind.

1970 CREÁTICA establishes movement for the study of intelligence and promotes a student-centered approach for educational reform.

1973 *Fundación CENAMEC Centro nacional para el mejoramiento de la enseñanza de la ciencia* seeks to train teachers to develop creative, investigatory, active attitudes and thus influence their students. Founds Scientific Olympics in math, chemistry, physics, biology and oil industry.

1975 *Conceptualización y Política de la educación especial en Venezuela.* Establishes basic principles:

- *Democratización:* All children have the right to equal opportunity to develop their abilities.
- *Modernización:* Early intervention will prevent deficiencies.
- *Normalización:* evaluation of abilities to promote strengths and provide service. Include families in process.

Integración: A dynamic process that opposes segregation into special schools or classrooms.

1986 *La Ley Orgánica de Educación, Art 30 & 32.* Promotes focus on talented children. Clarifies misconception that gifted students are frequently referred for counseling due to ADHD or behavior problems.

A UNESCO publication, *The Education of Gifted Children in Ibero-America,* offers an overview of the education situation of gifted students in seven Latin American countries and in Spain. The Ibero-American conference on gifted and talented provides an opportunity for edcators in Hispanic-speaking countries to come together to discuss research and training in gifted education.

Notes

1. Benavides, M., Maz, A., Castro, E., Blanco, R. (Eds.). (2004). *La educación de niños con talento en Iberoamérica.* Oficina Regional de Educación de la UNESCO para América Latina y el Caribe. Santiago, Chile: Editorial Trineo S.A.
2. Renzulli, J. S., Reis, S. M. Y., & Smith, L. M. (1981). *The revolving door identification model.* Mansfield Center, CT: Creative Learning Press.
3. Donoghue, E. F., & Vogeli, B. R. (1998). Cuba's Schools for the Mathematically and Scientifically Talented. *Gifted Child Today Magazine, 21*(3), 32–35.
4. Renzulli, J. S. (1986). The three-ring conception of giftedness: A developmental model for creative productivity. In R. J. Sternberg & J. E. Davidson (Eds.), *Conceptions of giftedness.* Cambridge, UK: Cambridge University Press.
5. Valadez, S. D.,Villegas, V., & Gutiérrez, S. (2002). Identificación de niños sobresalientes en escuelas públicas de la ciudad de Guadalajara. Ponencia presentada en el IV Congreso Iberoamericano de Superdotación y Talento, celebrado en Santa Fe de Bogotá, Colombia, del 9 al 11 de octubre.
6. Renzulli, J. S., et al. (1997). *Escalas de Renzulli (SCRBSS) para la valoración de las características de comportamiento de los estudiantes superiores.* Salamanca: Amarú Ediciones.

Rosina M. Gallagher

See also Cultural Conceptions of Giftedness; Giftedness, Definition

Further Readings

Alencar, E., & Blumen, S. (2001). Programs and practices for identifying and nurturing giftedness and talent in Central and South America. In K. A. Heller, F. J. Mönks, & A. H. Passow (Eds.), *International handbook of research and development of giftedness and talent* (pp. 817–828). Oxford, UK: Pergamon.

Benavides, M., Maz, A., Castro, E., & Blanco, R. (Eds.). (2004). *La educación de niños con talento en Iberoamérica* [The education of gifted children in Ibero-America]. Oficina Regional de Educación de la UNESCO para América Latina y el Caribe. Santiago, Chile: Editorial Trineo S.A.

Donoghue, E. F., & Vogeli, B. R. (1998). Cuba's schools for the mathematically and scientifically talented. *Gifted Child Today Magazine, 21*(3), 32–35.

Renzulli, J. S. (1986). The three-ring conception of giftedness: A developmental model for creative productivity. In R. J. Sternberg & J. E. Davidson (Eds.), *Conceptions of giftedness.* Cambridge, UK: Cambridge University Press.

Renzulli, J. S., Reis, S. M. Y., & Smith, L. M. (1981). *The revolving door identification model.* Mansfield Center, CT: Creative Learning Press.

Tourón, J., Tourón, M., & Silvero, M. (2005). The Center for Talented Youth Spain: An initiative to serve highly able students. *High Ability Studies, 16*(1), 121–135.

Leadership

More than 7,000 books and articles have been written on leadership. A great deal is known about leadership, although considerably less about early precursors of leadership, how leadership develops in youth, and the relationship of leadership ability and intellectual giftedness. Several youth organizations have played important roles in creating early leadership opportunities for children and adolescents. For example, one of the most widely recognized youth organizations, the Boy Scouts of America, celebrates its 100th anniversary in 2010. In the United States today, more than 3.9 million youth are members of the Boy Scouts and Girl Scouts. Scouting is hugely popular internationally; membership in Indonesia exceeds 8 million; there are almost 2.7 million scouts in India, and more than 1 million scouts in the Philippines and Thailand.

Other youth organizations that are value-based and that emphasize group activities, character development, and civic engagement include the American Youth Foundation and 4-H. Along with the scouting movement, these youth organizations have played a significant role in early leadership development opportunities for youth. This entry provides a brief discussion about what researchers know and don't know and likely future directions of youth leadership development.

What Is Leadership?

Leadership is persuasion; it involves influencing other people to pursue a common goal or mission that is considered important to the group. Leadership is *not* domination; leadership requires others to willingly adopt the goals or mission of the group as their own, even for a brief period of time. Leadership requires creating a shared vision, building trust and confidence, and enabling others to act toward a common goal. Fred Fiedler developed a contingency or situational theory of leadership. Fiedler proposed that three important situational dimensions influence the leader's effectiveness: leader-member relations, task complexity/structure, and the power inherent in the leadership position. Fiedler's contingency leadership model implied that leadership style is difficult to change. Paul Hersey and Kenneth Blanchard (coauthor of the *One Minute Manager*) extended and modified Fiedler's model and articulated a three-dimensional approach for assessing leadership effectiveness. Their situational leadership model suggested that successful leaders do adjust their styles. For Hersey and Blanchard, the key issue in making these leadership style adjustments is follower maturity; in other words, the group member's readiness to perform in a given situation. Hersey and Blanchard also recognize the importance of the leader's task and relationship behaviors, and how the individual's leadership style interfaces with the task situation. Hersey contends that successful leaders are those who can adapt their behavior to meet the demands of their own unique situations. Adaptability is central to this model; the leader must adapt a combination of directive behaviors and supportive behaviors appropriately to the readiness of others to perform specific tasks or functions.

It is beyond the scope of this entry to mention all of the leading theorists who have affected the leadership field. However, it would be remiss to not mention the significant work of Warren Bennis. Bennis is a popular guest speaker and regular presidential advisor whose writings and lectures introduced leadership to a mass audience. An early student of group dynamics in the 1950s, Bennis evolved into a futurist in the 1960s and 1970s. Bennis argues that leadership is not a rare skill or inborn trait; he posits that leaders are made rather than born, and that leaders need not be charismatic or brilliant individuals to be successful. He also contends that leadership is not about control, direction, or manipulation. Bennis believes that effective leaders create compelling visions; elicit trust, optimism, and hope in others; and translate their visions into actionable plans.

Characteristics of Effective Leaders

Several taxonomies of leadership behaviors have been proposed, both in the adult and youth leadership literatures. Hundreds of leader behaviors and characteristics have been written about in both the popular and academic leadership literatures. The following 10 categories of leader behaviors and characteristics have appeared most frequently:

1. Planning and organizing
2. Problem-solving and competence
3. Creative, innovative, and imaginative
4. Motivating and inspiring
5. Forward-looking
6. Supportive and caring
7. Managing conflict and team-building
8. Networking
9. Delegating
10. Courageous

A recent, large-scale, international study by James Kouzes and Barry Posner asked people what they lookfor and admire in their leaders. More than 75,000 people participated in the investigation. The top–four-ranked leadership characteristics were honesty, forward-looking, inspiring, and competent. These findings were corroborated in 10 countries. Honesty emerged as the single most important factor; leaders are expected to inspire trust, be principled, know right from wrong, and have integrity. The ability to look ahead and share a vision for the future was consistently recognized as a critical leadership skill. Leaders must also be enthusiastic, energetic, optimistic, and communicate a positive view for the future. Finally, leaders must bring relevant experience and sound judgment to the task—if they hope to inspire confidence they must have a track record of success and ability to get things done.

Recent breakthroughs in the study of the physiology of the brain provide intriguing insights into the neuroscience of leadership. Imaging technologies such as functional magnetic resonance imaging (fMRI) and positron emission tomography (PET), in conjunction with brain wave analysis technologies such as quantitative electroencephalography (QEEG), have helped identify, for the first time, important linkages between the brain and the mind (how we perceive, think, feel, and act). These fascinating findings have implications for leadership. For example, brain research confirms that change is unexpectedly difficult because it provokes sensations of physiological discomfort. Trying to change any hardwired behavior requires considerable effort and will be resisted by the basal ganglia, the habit-center part of the brain that operates largely without conscious thought. Messages from effective leaders must be able to shift our focus from experiencing fear (what Daniel Goleman, in his popular book *Emotional Intelligence*, poetically describes as preventing "amygdale hijack"), to drawing our attention and metabolic energy to the prefrontal region of our brain. Leaders have the best chance of encouraging others to take risks and entertain change if their message connects with the prefrontal region of the brain rather than the more primitive and older parts of our mammalian brain, remnants of our evolutionary history.

Leadership, Giftedness, and Youth

As mentioned earlier, researchers know a lot about adult leadership. They know considerably less about precursors of early leadership, or how best to encourage or develop leadership skills and competencies in youth. More than 25 years ago, federal definitions of giftedness included leadership ability as one type of giftedness. And many gifted authorities, particularly Frances Karnes, have long contended that youth leadership training is important and worthwhile. Some in the gifted field have argued that adult leadership models are not applicable to leadership among youth; others see important conceptual parallels and practical similarities between youth and adult leadership. Youth leadership remains undertheorized and marked by few empirical studies. For example, many gifted authorities suggest that youth leadership requires creative problem-solving ability and at least moderately high intellectual ability. This is a reasonable assumption. However, it has not yet been empirically tested.

Steven Pfeiffer has developed a 72-item teacher-completed gifted rating scale for children ages 6.0 to 13.11. The *Gifted Rating Scale-School Form* (*GRS-S*) is based on a multidimensional model of giftedness and includes six scales: Intellectual Ability, Academic Ability, Creativity, Artistic Talent, Leadership Ability, and Motivation. Each of the *GRS-S* items is rated on a nine-point scale divided into three ranges: 1–3 = below average; 4–6 = average; and 7–9 = above average. The *GRS-S* classification system indicates the *likelihood* that children are gifted in leadership or one of the other areas, based on their *T* scores.

The *GRS-S* leadership scale consists of 12 items that reflect the child's ability to motivate others toward a common or shared goal. The leadership scale was developed based on a review of the youth leadership literature, on focus groups with experts in the gifted and leadership fields, and careful review of psychological literature of leadership. Four illustrative *GRS-S* leadership items are: *demonstrates good social judgment, recognizes the feelings of others, earns the respect and trust of others,* and *makes things happen.* Studies show it to be a reliable and valid measure of the leadership construct.

The *GRS-S* leadership scale has been used in youth leadership development programs to measure growth and progress as a result of participation in the program. An article by Pfeiffer and his colleagues in the summer 2006 issue of *The School Psychologist* provides a simple methodology for educators to use to measure change in leadership skills.

Pfeiffer contends that not every youth (or adult) can develop into a *gifted* leader. Almost any child or adolescent—gifted or not gifted—if provided appropriate opportunities and adequately motivated, can learn new, and refine existing, skills, attitudes, and values that are associated with effective leadership. For example, even young children can learn to demonstrate more advanced social judgment and become more adept at recognizing the feelings of others (two leadership items on Pfeiffer's *GRS*). Some children, because of a combination of aptitude, personality, temperament, interest, and good fortune, will develop into gifted leaders. Participation in community-based programs such as 4-H and Scouts, church youth groups, extracurricular school activities, and youth leadership development programs all provide unique and valuable opportunities for early exposure to leadership roles and observing important skills associated with leadership.

Future Directions

The gifted field lacks even one large-scale, longitudinal study that has followed a large cohort of high-ability children and looked specifically at early precursors of evolving leadership competence. Researchers know a lot about leadership from the adult leadership literature. As mentioned earlier, for example, researchers know that almost all people, irrespective of which country they are from, consider honesty, forward-looking, inspiring, and competence as the four critical characteristics of effective adult leaders. Honesty emerges as the single most important factor; leaders are expected to inspire trust, demonstrate unwavering integrity, and know right from wrong. The ability to look ahead and create a shared vision for the future is also seen as a critical leadership skill. Effective leaders must be enthusiastic, energetic, and optimistic. Finally, effective leaders must bring relevant experience and have sound judgment. These are valuable insights to help guide those of us interested in understanding more about early precursors of leadership and the design of effective youth leadership development programs.

Much work remains to fill in the gaps in our understanding of precursors of leadership and how best to develop leadership skills and abilities for today's youth (and tomorrow's leaders). Recent breakthroughs in the neurosciences offer valuable insights to help researchers better understand the neural mechanisms underlying behavioral change and influence. New insights can be expected in the coming years as a growing number of researchers begin to investigate this fertile area.

Steven I. Pfeiffer

See also Academic Talent; Creative Leadership; Gifted Rating Scales; Group Dynamics; Neuroscience of Leadership

Further Readings

Bennis, W., & Biederman, P. W. (1997). *Organizing genius: The secrets of creative collaboration.* Cambridge, MA: Perseus Books.

Karnes, F. A., & Chauvin, J. C. (2000). *Leadership development program.* Scottsdale, AZ: Gifted Psychology Press.

Kouzes, J., & Posner, B. (2009). The leadership challenge. Retrieved January 24, 2009, from http://www.leadershipchallenge.com/WileyCDA

Matthews, M. S. (2004). Leadership education for gifted and talented youth: A review of the literature. *Journal for the Education of the Gifted, 28,* 77–113.

Pfeiffer, S. I. (Ed.). (2008). *Handbook of giftedness.* New York: Springer.

Pfeiffer, S. I., Kumtepe, A., & Rosado, J. (2006). Gifted identification: Measuring change in a student's profile of abilities using the *GRS. School Psychologist, 60,* 106–111.

World Scout Committee. (2008). *Triennial report 2005–2008.* Geneva: World Scout Bureau.

Learning

Learning is a broad term that refers to any response change as a result of experience (e.g., habituation or classic conditioning). When it comes to skill learning, such as learning to play an instrument, to solve mathematical problems, or to appreciate a Shakespearean play, the term *intentional learning* is typically used, rather than *incidental learning.* Learning in formal education settings can be best characterized as an active, motivated process of acquiring cognitive representations and structures (knowledge), skills (routines and procedures that serve specific functions), and dispositions (certain ways of thinking, modus operandi) relative to important aspects of the physical, social, and symbolic worlds. Historically, three broadly conceptualized metaphors have been used to guide learning theory and research: learning as forming stimulus-response associations (the behaviorist/empiricist view), as acquisition of cognitive structure and knowledge construction (the cognitive/rationalist view), and as becoming attuned to affordances and constraints through participation in a community of human practice (the situative/pragmatist-sociohistoric view). These general models are concerned with the underlying processes leading to learning and transfer. Sources of variations (individual differences) in learning may not be covered by the general process models. Ironically, none of the three models are intended to explain individual differences in learning. For example, possible genetic influences on learning differences are not even mentioned as a relevant aspect of learning, nor is the extent to which the organism-environment interaction may significantly account for differential trajectories of individuals' learning histories. An adequate learning theory ought to be capable of describing characteristics of gifted learners as well as explaining underlying processes of advanced learning.

In school settings, gifted learners are often identified through their advanced mastery of certain content, or more behaviorally, the ease of learning. Although both the rate of learning and asymptotic performance (where additional learning efforts no longer produce performance gains) are used as markers of giftedness, in reality, the rate of learning (e.g., the fan-spread effect of achievement over time) is more easily observed than is asymptotic performance. There are two competing explanations for manifestations of exceptional learning in childhood. One explains the ease of mastery as a *learning advantage;* that is, gifted learners pick up the right information and get into the heart of the matter at a much faster rate than do most of their peers under instructional conditions or through self-directed explorations. The alternative explanation is that the ease of learning represents a developmental precocity; that is, the early maturation affords a distinct advantage, which may or may not dissipate over time. This entry describes cognitive, social and situative, and integrative perspectives of learning.

Cognitive Perspectives

Cognitive Efficiency or Sophistication?

A cognitive model of learning would trace individual differences in learning to cognitive process differences. There are two main hypotheses regarding the cognitive advantage enjoyed by some students in learning: cognitive efficiency and cognitive sophistication. The cognitive efficiency models typically use basic processing mechanisms such as processing speed or working memory capacity as underlying individual differences in learning. Sometimes, the researchers even try to pinpoint neurophysiological underpinnings of cognitive efficiency. In contrast, the cognitive sophistication models resort to higher-order constructs for explaining the learning advantage. They include strategy use, cognitive and metacognitive insights, and executive control of learning processes. Researchers in this tradition typically use complex learning and problem-solving tasks to elicit more complex cognitive behavior or action. The two kinds of models reveal epistemological differences regarding the locus of superior cognition underlying learning. The cognitive efficiency models view giftedness as a mental capacity directly supported by neural infrastructure, and the cognitive sophistication models view giftedness as resourcefulness supported by a repertoire of mental skills and knowledge. The cognitive efficiency perspective lends itself to a more reductionistic explanation of gifted behavior, and the cognitive sophistication perspective implies a self-organized, self-directed pattern of behavior emergent in the person-task interaction. Both arguments may be valid to some extent.

Domain-Specific or Domain-General?

General cognitive models of learning imply an all-purpose information processing architecture. The domain-generality of learning mechanisms is increasingly contended in the learning literature. Children appear to have intuitive grasps of domain-specific principles (e.g., about numbers, physical objects, living things, and intentions of others), which guide their learning in both instructional and noninstructional settings. Dedicated mechanisms process a particular type or class of information, in encoding mode (e.g., verbal vs. visual-spatial), as well as content representation (social vs. physical). Similarly, individuals have their privileged domains in which information uptake and organization seem particularly easy and "natural" to them, and the topics involved affectively appeal to them. The most distinct example of the domain-specificity of advanced learning is child prodigies who demonstrate the unusual ease of learning in certain domains (e.g., mathematics, music, chess) but are otherwise similar to age peers in their developmental profiles, suggesting a strong perceptual and intuitive basis for learning and understanding their favorite subjects that otherwise need to be mastered in an analytic fashion. However, the basic structure of domain knowledge and skills, which are culturally created symbol systems and meaning structures, are unlikely to be somehow genetically encrypted or innately prescribed. In other words, learning in culturally created and defined domains still needs to be scaffolded through instruction and coaching, and domain-general learning abilities and skills are needed to construct domain-specific knowledge and skills.

A more eclectic scenario is that both domain-specific (i.e., dedicated mechanisms) and domain-relevant general processes are involved in learning, and the process of mastering a complex domain is less like acquiring fragmented pieces of knowledge and more like a developmental process that shows dynamic changes and phase transition to increasingly complex organization of cognitive landscapes and action schemes. Jerome Bruner identified sensitivity to constraints, organized persistence, and connectivity of ideas as three main tenets of successful buildup of knowledge. At a more practical level, David Lohman identified the initial fast rate of learning and achievement, coupled with the ability to reason specific symbol systems in the achievement domain, as evidence of exceptional or advanced learners. According to current understanding of intricate content-process relations, on the one hand, the reasoning ability cannot be completely dissociated from content knowledge; on the other hand, the underlying logic of content knowledge is not transparent and entails inference and abstraction based on rules not specified in the content knowledge. It is useful to evoke the Systems 1 and 2 classification of cognition to achieve a dialectic synthesis. According to this classification, System 1 processes are perceptual and intuitive in nature, characterized as effortless, fast, evocative (affective), rigid, impervious to conscious manipulation and voluntary control. System 2 processes are conceptual and analytic in nature, characterized as effortful, slow, enactive (conative), flexible, subject to conscious manipulation and voluntary control. Thus, System 1 processes tend to be dedicated to domain-specific information processing, and System 2 processes are more versatile and less specialized. David Yun Dai and Joseph S. Renzulli suggest a bottom-up and top-down iterative process whereby knowledge gain through System 1 processes are elevated or articulated to the System 2 level for reorganization and flexible use, and knowledge and skills constructed by System 2 intentional learning processes are relegated or mechanized to System 1 representations and routines to enhance the system's efficiency. Lannie Kanevsky's model of learning potential also contains both domain-general and domain-specific components.

Quantitatively or Qualitatively Different?

A question continually debated about the cognitive advantages of gifted learners is whether they differ quantitatively or qualitatively. In other words, is the advantage a matter of degree or kind? This is an important question because giftedness is seen as a condition of exceptionality, and thus implying a qualitative difference. When gifted students are compared with average students on major information processing parameters, the research findings typically do not support a strong argument for qualitative differences; that is, both groups use the same cognitive processes, but with different degrees. However, when intra-individual patterns or configurations of different abilities (i.e., strengths and weaknesses) are used to predict learning and developmental trajectories, qualitative differences even among gifted learners themselves emerge. Some theoretical speculations can be made based on the categories discussed earlier. First, when cognitive efficiency is concerned, the differences can be best described as quantitative (e.g., faster speed, quicker automatization of new learning, or more pieces of information held, processed, and manipulated per unit of time). When cognitive sophistication (e.g., use of different strategies and styles; metacognition and transfer) is concerned, qualitative differences are more likely to be observed; this may be true even among the identified "gifted." Second, when learning mechanisms are domain-general, one is more likely to observe quantitative differences; for example, correlations between general intelligence and targeted task performance tend to be higher when more complex cognitive tasks are involved. In contrast, when unique, domain-specific learning mechanisms are involved, we might observe qualitative differences because these mechanisms may be manifested in an all-or-none fashion (e.g., a domain-specific modular device is either present or absent; the notion of possessing a certain degree of a functional module does not make sense). Finally, we might consider learning processes (e.g., thinking and reasoning) to show quantitative differences, but long-term developmental and learning outcomes (cognitive structure or knowledge organization) can be qualitatively different.

Social and Situative Perspectives

Learning is situated in a specific functional context, involving other people, with expertise, resources, and tools distributed in that environment. Therefore, it is limiting to think of learning as a solo act of the learner, as if the learning process resides in the learner's head. From a situative perspective, learning means participating in specific kinds of culturally sanctioned human activity, and gradually moving from the periphery to the center. With experts serving as mentors and coaches, the learning process can be described as cognitive apprenticeship during which significant amounts of observational learning (vicarious experiencing, modeling, etc.) occur. This perspective emphasizes the important function of communities of learners, scholars, artists, and other professionals who are committed to perfecting their trades and who mutually stimulate one another to excel at a level humanly possible. Social and technical facilitation of advanced learning at an elite caliber is supported by evidence that some musical pieces deemed impossible to play a century ago are now part of the repertoire of student performance in music conservatories. However, the expertise research suggests the extent to which one can sustain this kind of participation is constrained by individuals' fit for extended deliberate practice, a form of practice that is focused and intensive, and is by nature not enjoyable. From this situative perspective, learning is not confined to any specific settings such as school, and it is often a by-product of pragmatic efforts to solve a problem or overcome an obstacle. Indeed, learning is more authentic and effective in work settings than in classrooms, according to this school of thought. Sustained efforts to understand and problem solve in a domain led to highly sophisticated knowledge and practical skills (i.e., expertise). Exceptionally advanced learning, from the cases of child prodigies to those of to-be Nobel Laureates, does not violate this social and situative principle of learning; substantial domain experience and efforts are invested to develop high-level expertise and creativity.

Integrative Perspectives

Reckoning with the complexity of skill learning and knowledge building naturally leads to the conclusion that learning should be best seen as fundamentally context-bound, involving purposes and structures of the learning activity, social contexts that support learning, and individuals' strengths and weaknesses relative to the learning task at hand (i.e., aptitudes and inaptitudes as Richard Snow defined them). Although cognitive strengths are clearly important in accounting for learning differences, motivational and emotional factors also play an important role. For example, when presented with a cognitively demanding task, gifted students reported feeling more challenged than did regular students, which is counterintuitive. However, the feeling of being challenged indicates a level of alertness conducive to achievement motivation. Gifted children also display a tendency to turn inward, presumably to think through a problem before taking specific steps, rather than relying on external helps or expertise. Gifted students have also been found to have a better calibration (i.e., more accurate estimate) of their ability to solve a given problem, a skill important for monitoring progress, setting up proper, realistic levels of self-efficacy, and allocating proper resources for learning.

The ability to learn and fashion complex thoughts about the world and self is an essential ingredient of human intelligence. David Perkins identifies three sources of intelligent cognition and behavior, hence individual differences in learning: neural, experiential, and reflective. *Neural intelligence* refers to the contribution of biological variations in neural efficiency, either globally or in modular forms, that supports cognitive functions. *Experiential intelligence* refers to the contribution of experience and knowledge to crystallized and fluid abilities, particularly domain-specific knowledge and skills that are highly tuned to particular types of information or environment. *Reflective intelligence* refers to the contribution of metacognition and reflective self-guidance to intelligent behavior. Although neural efficiency has been long argued as a biological advantage that distinguishes gifted children from their age peers, experiential and reflective aspects of intelligence have been increasingly recognized as bases for exceptional learning advantages. A learning theory that accounts for both individual differences (including the highly advanced learning and achievement) and underlying processes needs to integrate all three sources of intelligence in conjunction with contextual and motivational factors.

David Yun Dai

See also Aptitudes; Cognition; Expertise; Intelligence; Intelligence Theories

Further Readings

Barab, S. A., & Plucker, J. A. (2002). Smart people or smart context? Cognition, ability, and talent development in an age of situated approaches to knowing and learning. *Educational Psychologist, 37,* 165–182.

Bruner, J. S. (1962). *On knowing.* Cambridge, UK: Belknap Press.

Dai, D. Y., & Renzulli, J. S. (2008). Snowflakes, living systems, and the mystery of giftedness. *Gifted Child Quarterly, 52,* 114–130.

Dai, D. Y., & Sternberg, R. J. (2004). Beyond cognitivism: Toward an integrated understanding of intellectual functioning and development. In D. Y. Dai & R. J. Sternberg (Eds.), *Motivation, emotion, and cognition: Integrative perspectives on intellectual functioning and development* (pp. 3–38). Mahwah, NJ: Lawrence Erlbaum.

Kanevsky, L. (1995). Learning potentials of gifted students. *Roeper Review, 17,* 157–163.

Lohman, D. F. (2005). An aptitude perspective on talent identification: Implications for identification of academically gifted minority students. *Journal for the Education of the Gifted, 28,* 333–360.

Perkins, D. N. (1995). *Outsmarting IQ: The emerging science of learnable intelligence.* New York: Free Press.

Snow, R. E. (1992). Aptitude theory: Yesterday, today, and tomorrow. *Educational Psychologist, 27,* 5–32.

Learning Disabilities

Growing numbers of gifted students are challenged by a variety of learning disabilities that compromise their academic and social development. These disabilities may take the form of difficulties learning to read, write, or understand mathematics. Gifted students may experience cognitive processing issues such as remembering details, following directions, and organizing tasks. Other students may have difficulty focusing and sustaining attention or completing assignments. Finally, the deficits may involve understanding and coping with social and emotional demands placed on the students. Often these talented but challenged youngsters have difficulties in all three realms. Because of the duality of their characteristics—gifts and challenges—this special population of gifted students is often referred to as *twice exceptional.* This designation draws attention to the duality of their needs to accommodate the gift while addressing the learning challenge. This entry first presents samples of students who are gifted and learning disabled. A description of traits follows. The entry concludes with suggestions for meeting their needs.

Examples

Alan is a curious young man whose intense and adultlike interests often set him aside from his age-mates. His natural curiosity and passion for particular topics feed his desire for knowledge and inquiry. Indeed, his parents report, "Alan is never bored." Alan reads above grade level and comprehends information in the realm of nonfiction. His math skills far outweigh those of his peers, and his ability to remember both verbal and spatial information are extraordinary. These are the characteristics associated with students who are gifted and talented. But Alan has great difficulty completing his work and sitting still for long periods. He often has difficulty getting along with his peers and is often excluded from the group because of his impulsivity and emotional outbursts. Alan is a gifted child with attention deficits. His particular learning profile dictates that he needs intellectual challenge but environmental modifications that will help him complete assignments and develop appropriate coping behaviors.

Susan is a poet whose use of imagery in her writing is outstanding. Her sensitivity and understanding of the human condition shows her high levels of interpersonal intelligence. Susan has a severe disability in mathematics. She has no concept of time, money, or distance. She has severe anxiety attacks during math class and often becomes physically ill. Susan needs a dual placement—advanced writing opportunities and remedial math. She will also need counseling to help her cope with

Table 1 Deficit Behaviors

	Attention Deficit Disorder (ADHD)	*Specific Learning Disabilities (SLD)*
Academic difficulties	May have difficulty beginning or completing tasks	Speaks well but reads poorly Confuses similar letters and words
	May have difficulty with listening tasks	Dysgraphic Dyslexic Discalculia
	May have difficulty expressing ideas in writing	Problems with short-term memory
	Strengths in critical and creative thinking	Very knowledgeable in specific areas
	May prefer spatial tasks	May prefer spatial tasks
Attention issues	Fidgets; squirms; is restless	Short attention span
	Difficulty remaining seated	Is overactive or inactive, listless
	Easily distracted	Easily distracted
Organizational issues	Has difficulty following directions and finishing tasks	Has difficulty understanding or following directions Has difficulty in expressing or organizing thoughts verbally or in writing Has difficulty functioning when there is no structure or predictability (nonverbal learning disability)
Social issues	Cannot read the social context well	May have problems reading the social context (nonverbal learning disability)
Behavioral issues	Often interrupts or intrudes on others	Will become disruptive to avoid difficult tasks
Impulsivity	Often engages in physically dangerous activities without considering possible consequences	Is impulsive; cannot foresee consequences
	Blurts out answers to questions	

her depression resulting from the discrepancy between what she can and cannot do.

Christian can build anything with Lego® bricks. He excels in tasks that require engineering and design. His skills in science and math are also superior. But Christian experiences great difficulty listening in class and taking notes. He cannot express his ideas in writing and has difficulty reading. His poor skills in both organization and attention provide evidence that Christian has attention deficits and dyslexia. To achieve to his potential, Christian will need opportunities to participate in engineering and design as well as be afforded specific accommodations that will allow him to access information other than by reading, unlimited use of technology for writing and researching, and perhaps more time on task completion.

Traits

All these students would be considered twice exceptional. They exhibit remarkable gifts and talents in specific areas. They may have outstanding vocabularies, in-depth interests, creative abilities, and extensive knowledge in one or more areas. These same youngsters simultaneously experience difficulties in learning, attending, or meeting social and emotional expectations. These learning challenges result in students being identified with learning and attention challenges. Table 1 outlines characteristics associated with these difficulties.

Effective Strategies

A comprehensive educational plan for these students should address both talent development and accommodations. Most individual educational plans focus on student deficits. Even parents may be reluctant to push talent development when students struggle with core subjects. However, selective attention to only one set of needs may compromise the effectiveness of programs designed to nurture individual development of twice-exceptional students.

Effective plans would consider creating the optimal learning environments (intellectual, emotional, and physical). Such environments offer students appropriate talent development opportunities and intellectual challenge such as acceleration in areas of strength, mentorships, and independent studies. To accommodate problematic weaknesses, classrooms should provide academic support. For example, students may be provided with books on tape, a quiet place to complete assignments, a choice of resources and projects, use of technology to learn and produce, more time to complete tasks, and a note taker. Finally, schools should provide counseling opportunities to assist students to advocate for themselves, develop strategies for coping with their challenges, and become aware of their gifts, talents, and career goals. Plans should be devised using a team approach consisting of the classroom teacher, learning support specialist, teacher of the gifted and talented, parents, and the student.

Susan Marcia Baum

See also Asperger's Syndrome; Attention Deficit Hyperactivity Disorder; Differentiation; Multiple Intelligences; Twice Exceptional

Further Readings

Baum, S. M., & Owen, S. V. (2004). *To be gifted and learning disabled: Strategies for helping bright students with LD, ADHD, and more.* Mansfield Center, CT: Creative Learning Press.

Levine, M. (2002). *A mind at a time.* New York: Simon & Schuster.

Learning Styles

Learning styles describe how students prefer to learn. Despite their intellectual gifts, not all highly able students are challenged and engaged in their classrooms. Creativity, for instance, may not be encouraged, accommodated, or commended by some teachers at any grade level, and yet creative expression may be needed in some individuals, as well as natural and instinctual. Expression through visual arts, music, poetry, and hands-on construction may be much more comfortable for some than is expression through traditional homework assignments and tests. Learning disabilities may also interfere with learning. Behavior may be a problem as well. Both problematic behavior and underachievement may reflect problems related to the fit of learning style in the classroom.

This entry first describes types of learning styles. Next, this entry discusses the Learning Styles Inventory as an assessment tool and Anthony Gregorc's categorization of learning styles. Last, the implications of identifying an individual's learning style(s) are considered.

Types

Visual learners probably have the easiest fit in typical classrooms and are the most common. They respond positively to written information, notes, diagrams, pictures, and written tests, for example, and their learning preference matches typical teachers' visual teaching style, as well as the format of commonly used standardized tests for measuring individual and school progress. Visual learners can translate written words into mental images and then into test answers. If they are motivated to perform in the classroom and in large-group testing situations, their academic performance is likely to match their measured intellectual ability. These learners, and their parents and teachers as well, may find it difficult to understand why other learners with high capability struggle in the classroom. Even the class binders and assignments of visual learners are likely to be orderly. They can perhaps stay focused on what the teacher is doing and may also have no trouble turning in assignments on time and planning ahead.

In contrast, about half as many students are likely to prefer to learn through their ears. Reading aloud may enhance their learning, and they are likely to be comfortable receiving information orally from teachers. Their inclination and preferences may lead them to choose seating so that they can hear the teacher easily. Their learning style probably has a fairly good fit with academic work in schools, though not as good as those with a visual preference. A third learning style is found in a small percentage of the general population. Students with a kinesthetic preference prefer hands-on experiences, learning through touch, movement, role plays, and project construction, for instance. These students may struggle academically in classrooms geared only to visual and auditory teaching styles.

These learning preferences should be viewed on a continuum. Some gifted students may have equal preferences among the three styles just described, or equal visual and auditory preferences, for example.

Learning Style Inventory

In the late 1970s, Joseph Renzulli developed the first learning-styles assessment for gifted and talented students, called the Learning Styles Inventory, to investigate the preferred learning modes of students. Students complete the inventory to identify the ways that they prefer to learn, for example, through learning modes such as independent study, programmed instruction, drill, discussion, or lecture. Renzulli conducted a number of research studies with this inventory, finding that gifted and talented students more often preferred independent study and simulations.

Gregorc's Categorization

In the 1980s, Gregorc introduced another conceptualization of learning styles, categorizing them as concrete, abstract, sequential, and random and offering explanations of various combinations of these. His categorization goes further than do categories commonly recognized by educators, who, for example, divide learners into global learners, who first develop a general framework and then fit specific information into it, and sequential or analytical learners, who focus first on details to gain overall understanding. Gregorc added the preferences of concrete (literal, actual, hands-on) or abstract (theoretical, conceptual, symbolic) content, leading to four combinations of preferred styles. Abstract (using reason and intuition) and concrete (using the senses) are *perceptional* preferences. Sequential (linear) and random (nonlinear) are *ordering* preferences.

The combinations of Gregorc's conceptualizations of preferences are explained as follows. *Concrete-sequential* learners like organized, sequential lessons, concrete materials, step-by-step instructions, experiential learning, demonstrations, computer-assisted instruction, and concrete examples. *Concrete-random* learners like trial and error, make intuitive leaps, and prefer independent study projects, discovery learning, constructivist teaching, and problem-solving activities. *Abstract-sequential* learners think in conceptual pictures, grasp ideas easily through reading and listening, and like reading, lectures, essay-writing, and concept mapping. *Abstract-random* learners prefer unstructured delivery of information, tend to enjoy group discussion and cooperative learning, and multisensory experiences. Although little research has been conducted on Gregorc's work on learning styles, his work has been popular with teachers of gifted and high-potential learners.

Gregorc also discussed receptivity in abstract- and concrete-random learners to information coming from multiple sources simultaneously and without an obvious goal, in contrast to strong preferences in sequential learners for information from one source at a time and in successive, connected parts. Such differences are important to consider when matching learning and teaching styles. Environmental stimulation is related to this concern. Highly stimulating, colorful posters, and other eye-catching products on classroom walls may actually interfere with learning for some students, much to the puzzlement of teachers who assume that all students appreciate such color and texture. Other students may prefer and even need that visual stimulation to feel comfortable.

Implications

Information about learning styles can be helpful for gifted students who wonder why they do not have as comfortable a fit academically as do others who are identified as gifted—or who simply are curious about individual teaching and learning differences. When gifted students successfully seek, perhaps on the Internet, or are given information by counselors and teachers about learning differences and preferences, these students can perhaps make adjustments when teachers' teaching styles do not match learning preferences. Such information can also provoke helpful self-reflection related to identity development, personality, personal strengths and limitations, level of comfort in various classrooms, preferences for teachers, and even future career options. Even young gifted students can benefit from information about learning styles, helping them make sense of their behaviors, struggles, and differential responses to various academic areas and teachers. Through their own insight about preferences or through assistance from school personnel, they may be able to figure out how to compensate for lack of fit with visual instruction, for instance. Special-education teachers with expertise in learning styles and disabilities may be appropriate consultants when learning is compromised and frustrating or a diagnosable learning disability is suspected.

When teachers take the time to identify students' learning-style preferences, they should make every effort to avoid stamping a child with a learning style in the manner that some children are labeled according to intelligence level or disability. In rare cases, certain students may prefer to pursue most of their studies through a single method such as independent study, but most learners vary their preferences for different instructional techniques based on their age and the subject matter. When teachers intentionally use a variety of teaching methods, not just one that reflects their own learning and teaching preference, they are likely to be more effective with a classroom of students with widely varying learning-style preferences, including those whose preferences are fairly balanced.

Jean Sunde Peterson

See also Academic Self-Concept; Disabilities, Gifted; Dropouts, Gifted; Learning Disabilities; Underachievement

Further Readings

Renzulli, J. S., Rizza, M. G., & Smith L. H. (2002). *Learning styles inventory—Version III: A measure of student preferences for instructional techniques.* Mansfield Center, CT: Creative Learning Press.

Renzulli, J. S., & Smith, L. H. (1978). *The learning styles inventory.* Mansfield Center, CT: Creative Learning Press.

Renzulli, J. S., & Smith, L. H. (1984). Learning style preferences: A practical approach for classroom teachers. *Theory Into Practice, 18,* 44–50.

Legal Issues for Gifted

Unlike students with disabilities, gifted students are not protected under federal law. As such, the methods by which gifted students are identified and served vary across states and depend on state legislation or state board of education rules and regulations. With many states having permissive legislation and others having no legislation, dispute resolution strategies are needed to help parents ensure their gifted child receives an appropriate education. However, with limited protection under the law, school systems often prevail when disputed issues reach the courts. This entry describes dispute resolution strategies, seminal cases, the Office for Civil Rights, and implications of legal issues for gifted students.

Dispute Resolution Strategies

When issues regarding the education of a child cannot be resolved by parents and schools, dispute resolution strategies should be used. These strategies must begin at the lowest level. Negotiation, mediation, and due process are alternative avenues to litigation in resolving disputes.

Negotiation is an informed process by which both parties can discuss a problem to reach a compromise. Everyone involved should know the state laws and rules and regulations as well as local policies regarding gifted education. The process should begin at the level at which the dispute arose, which is usually with the classroom teacher. If negotiations are not successful at this level, then parents should meet with others up the administrative ladder—the principal, superintendent, and school board. Detailed notes should be kept of all correspondence and meetings. Mediation is the next step, if the issue(s) cannot be negotiated.

Mediation is a nonadversarial, voluntary process in which disputing parties can meet with an impartial, third-party facilitator. There are a number of advantages to mediation, which include reduced cost, expeditious processes, improved relationships, collaborative resolutions, confidentiality, empowerment of participants, and allowances for flexibility. A written mediation argument should be signed by both parties. If the issues can not be resolved through mediation, the next step is due process.

An aggrieved party has the opportunity to be heard by an impartial hearing officer during due process. There are several common requirements across the 16 states offering due process for the gifted:

- A notice to all parties that a hearing has been scheduled.
- Both parties can present evidence, have witnesses, and have oral arguments.
- Counsel may be present.
- Written and oral records of the proceedings are kept.
- The hearing officer writes a decision based on the arguments and evidence presented.

The last resort in dispute resolution is litigation, which is costly in time and money. Tuition reimbursement, early entrance, appropriate programming, twice exceptional, admissions, and personnel issues have all been addressed in court cases.

Seminal Cases

The federal courts become involved when issues pertaining to gifted education involve constitutional or statutory challenges. In *Student Doe v. Commonwealth of Pennsylvania* (1984) and *Student Roe v. Commonwealth of Pennsylvania* (1987), the use of minimum cutoff scores for admission into gifted programs was challenged. The courts in both cases found that minimum cutoff scores could be reasonably used for such purposes and did not violate the equal protection or due process clauses of the Fourteenth Amendment.

Broadley v. Board of Education of the City of New Meridian (1994) and *Centennial School District v. Department of Education* (1988) are two seminal cases regarding gifted students with contradictory outcomes that reached the state high courts of Connecticut and Pennsylvania, respectively. Subsequent courts have relied on the rulings from these two cases in reaching decisions.

In *Centennial,* the court found that regardless of an existing enrichment program, a school district was not relieved of the responsibility of providing a student with an appropriate academic education. In contrast, the *Broadley* court ruled that the state's guarantee of a constitutional right to a free public education does not afford gifted students the right to special education.

According to Perry A. Zirkel, a distinction should be made between "gifted alone" and "gifted plus" cases when reviewing case law. "Gifted alone" are those students eligible for gifted education without any other special legal protection, and "gifted plus" are those students who are gifted, but are also eligible for other federal, legal protections (e.g., students with disabilities under the Individuals with Disabilities Education Act, and minority gifted students under Title IV of Civil Rights Act). Because of lack of federal protection, there are far fewer gifted alone than gifted plus cases.

The Office for Civil Rights

In the U.S. Department of Education, the Office for Civil Rights (OCR) is charged with enforcing five federal civil-rights laws prohibiting discrimination on the basis of color, national origin, race, gender, and disability in activities and programs receiving federal funds. Investigating complaints, compliance reviews, and providing technical assistance to institutions to achieve voluntary compliance with OCR standards are the major responsibilities.

School districts must prove that their policies do not discriminate against gifted students. School districts should appoint a biracial committee to write guidelines for screening and identification that do not discriminate and inform parents, teachers, students, and the community. In-service training about gifted characteristics should be given on an annual basis to all school personnel. Validated instruments must be used with respect to the population for whom they are being used. Districts should monitor for discrimination and make changes when necessary.

Implications

The absence of a federal mandate; the lack of legal precedence; and permissive, if any, state legislation regarding the educational rights of gifted students have all hampered parents through the litigation process and have resulted in decisions that have mainly favored school districts. A review of national interest in gifted education indicates a reactive rather than proactive stance regarding policy development in gifted education.

Frances A. Karnes and Kristen R. Stephens

See also History of Gifted Education in the United States; Javits Program; No Child Left Behind; Parenting

Further Readings

Karnes, F. A., & Marquardt, R. G. (1991). *Gifted children and legal issues in education: Parents' stories of hope.* Scottsdale, AZ: Great Potential Press.

Karnes, F. A., & Marquardt, R. G. (1991). *Gifted children and the law: Meditation, due process, and court cases.* Scottsdale, AZ: Great Potential Press.

Karnes, F. A., & Marquardt, R. G. (2000). *Gifted children and legal issues: An update.* Scottsdale, AZ: Great Potential Press.

Karnes, F. A., Stephens, K. R., & McCard, E. (2008). Legal issues in gifted education. In F. A. Karnes & K. R. Stephens (Eds.), *Achieving excellence: Teaching the gifted and talented.* Columbus, OH: Pearson Merrill/Prentice Hall.

Levels of Gifted

Giftedness—high intellectual ability—is part of the overall continuum of intelligence within the human population. Just as there are degrees of slow learning—lower learning abilities—the range of abilities within the gifted population is considerable. Inborn abilities drive interests and are especially evident in young children whose environment is flexible and responsive to their needs. When one examines the early interests and behaviors of a child, insight is gained into both the level and the profile of intellectual gifts. This entry describes the levels of giftedness theory and implications for bright students.

Deborah L. Ruf developed *levels of giftedness theory* to explain the differences that she observed in children at different ability levels. Although research remains to be done to confirm the characteristics at each level, evidence from studies of prodigies, of talent search participants, of high achievers and perfect scorers on achievement tests, and of the general gifted population supports differences in characteristics and needs.

For ease of description, the range of giftedness can be divided into five levels and identified by early behaviors before intelligence testing. Level One is basically bright to moderately gifted, Level Two is highly gifted, Levels Three and Four are exceptionally gifted overall or profoundly gifted in one domain, and Level Five is profoundly gifted in all or almost all areas. What the students at different levels need for good friendships and adequate academic support varies greatly, and these early childhood milestones are easily observed before children start school.

Table 1 provides data for three of the five levels during five preschool-years age periods. All the behaviors listed in Table 1 are advanced compared

Table 1 Early Childhood Milestones by Level of Giftedness

Age Range	*LEVEL ONE*	*LEVEL THREE*	*LEVEL FIVE*
4 to 12 months		Almost all know what someone is talking about by 6 months; most look at and turn pages of books alone by 10 months, make their families know what they want, books, a favorite interest; some play with shape sorters by 11 months; many recognize some colors, shapes, numbers, and letters.	Half speak well by age 1; most independently look at and turn pages of books before 6 months, know and say some words by 5½ to 9 months, play with shape sorters before 11 months; all have large receptive vocabularies by 8 to 9 months, have favorite TV or videos by 6 to 8 months; many recognize and pick out specific numbers and letters by 10 to 14 months.
12 to 18 months	Most know and say many words before 18 months.	Many recognize and pick out specific numbers and letters by 12 to 15 months; most have large vocabularies, receptive and expressive, by 16 months, know many colors by 15 to 18 months; many "read" many sight words between 15 and 20 months.	Many read numerous sight words by 15 months, rote count to 10, many higher, by 13 to 20 months; most are good at puzzles before 12 months, 35+ piece puzzles by 15 months; all know colors, numbers, alphabet, and shapes by about 15 months, show musical aptitude before 18 months.
24 to 30 months	Most sit still and attend to TV-type activities by 18 to 30 months.	Many start to "read" words on stores and signs by 20 months, show interest in letter sounds and sound out short words.	
3 to 4 years	Recognize simple signs, own written name, and know alphabet and simple addition and subtraction.	Many question the reality of Santa Claus or Tooth Fairy–type figures at 3 to 5 years, have high interest in factual information, how things work, science; keyboard or type by 3 to 4½ years; memorize or read simple books by 3½ years; most "read" words on signs and stores, print letters, numbers, words, and their names, know many sight words by 3 to 3½ years; most grasp skip counting, backward, basic addition and subtraction by age 4 years.	All question the reality of Santa Claus or Tooth Fairy–type figure by 3 or 4 years, show interest in pure facts, almanacs, dictionaries, etc, by age 3½, play adult level games—ages 12 and up—by 3½ to 4 years, read children's chapter books by age 3½ to 4½ years, understand abstract math concepts and basic math functions by age 4.
5 to 6 years	All read simple signs; most read beginner books, are independent on computer and keyboard, grasp counting and basic number facts.	Many understand some multiplication, division, and some fractions by 5½ years; most read children's-level chapter books by 4½ to 5½ years and read for pleasure and information; all read 2 to 5 years beyond grade level.	All read 6 or more years beyond grade level by age 6.

Age Range	*LEVEL ONE*	*LEVEL THREE*	*LEVEL FIVE*
Other milestones	All read chapter books by age 7 to 7½ years; 2 to 3 years beyond grade level by age 7.	Most read for pleasure and information by 6 years; all read 2 to 5 years beyond grade level by age 6; all read youth and young adult chapter books independently by age 7 to 7½.	

Source: Ruf, D. L. (2005). *Losing our minds: Gifted children left behind.* Scottsdale, AZ: Great Potential Press.

with those of average young children. The earlier any of the behaviors occur, the more likely the child is highly to exceptionally gifted. Whatever the early learning trajectory, acquisition of skills can be expected to continue at a similar pace throughout the individual's life if the learning environment continues to respond in a timely manner to the individual's talents.

Deborah L. Ruf

See also Davidson Institute for Talent Development; Early Identification; Gifted Rating Scales; Highly Gifted; Very Young Gifted

Further Readings

Gottfried, A. W., Gottfried, A. E., Bathurst, K., & Guerin, D. W. (1994). *Gifted IQ: Early developmental aspects: The Fullerton longitudinal study.* New York: Plenum Press.

Gross, M. U. M. (1993). *Exceptionally gifted children.* New York: Routledge.

Hollingworth, L. S. (1942). *Children above 180 IQ Stanford-Binet.* Yonkers-on-Hudson, NY: World Book.

Osborne, J. B. (February, 2000). *Gifted children: Are their gifts being identified, encouraged, or ignored?* Retrieved August 23, 2008, from http://www.aboutourkids.com

Ruf, D. L. (2005). *Losing our minds: Gifted children left behind.* Scottsdale, AZ: Great Potential Press.

Life Satisfaction

Life satisfaction, subjective well-being, and happiness are psychological and everyday expressions of living the good life. The broad psychological category for these ideas is quality of life, which includes successful performance throughout the life, personal accomplishments and expectations, emotions, life experiences, physical activity and health, and the individual's reactions to these. Life satisfaction is stable over time, but does undergo some change with the changing circumstances of a person's life. The study of life satisfaction and the other expressions of quality of life for the gifted are undertaken to better understand and encourage the development of the gifted individual's strengths, development of friendships and relationships, positive responses to adversity, and social and emotional health for the person across his or her life time. This entry describes various approaches to understanding life satisfaction, and how appropriate gifted education enhances life satisfaction of gifted students.

Dimensions of well-being or satisfaction include finding one's meaning or purpose in life, the development of personal growth in talents though challenge and the overcoming of obstacles, creating and sustaining environments that facilitate personal thriving, learning to be autonomous (at least in Western cultures), and finding and maintaining positive relationships and friendships, which may be the most important dimension for well-being. Intelligence is a "protective factor" in that high intelligence can help a person cope with a variety of life stressors as well as provide the capacity to attain greater life satisfaction. Nevertheless, if gifted children are denied stimulation, challenge, and opportunities for positive peer relationships, caring guidance, the pursuit of a meaningful life, the benefits of intelligence may be neutralized.

A person's success in accomplishing and integrating his or her life in these areas results in more productivity and enjoyment of the activities in which the person is involved. A person's overall outlook on life, with its periodic aggravations and pleasures, enhances or reduces an individual's life satisfaction. Positive and negative emotions also speed up or slow down the development of constructive outcomes in an individual's life. The work in which an individual engages must challenge the individual, or the activity will not develop into a lifelong passion. Human beings find satisfaction in developing their innate capacities into realized performances. The more an individual's capacity is realized or the greater the complexity of the task undertaken, the greater the satisfaction or enjoyment. Gifted individuals need intellectual, creative, emotional, and physical challenges to thrive and become passionate about their lives.

Gifted children often find tasks required at school to be too easy and success in them to be attainable with minimal effort. Although their efforts are minimal, their answers and work are often met with high praise, good grades, and rewards. Appearing to do well, but without sufficient challenge will not lead to life satisfaction as children or later as adults. In most classrooms, the gifted receive the same materials, instruction, questions, and homework as everyone else. Programs for the gifted are often short and may not have the time or permission of other teachers to delve deeply into specific content. These limited interventions tend not to produce the high levels of achievement or satisfaction in the gifted. Accelerative options often allow a closer match between the gifted child or adolescent's ability and his or her learning. This better matching facilitates talent development and satisfaction. Special programs for the gifted also provide a venue for the development of friendships and coming to understand more clearly personal goals and visions for life.

Parents, teachers, friends, mentors, coaches, and even strangers demand or provide direction in developing lifetime dispositions, habits, and behaviors. These ways of behaving or living, whether observed in others by the gifted or imposed on the gifted by others such as parents, teachers, or mentors can have a positive or negative effect on personal well-being, life satisfaction, and happiness during adolescence and their adult lives. Consistently lived habits define the individual's character. These habits or virtues are basic to the gifted individual's progress in finding personal individual satisfaction and happiness across the individual's life time.

Appropriate curricular differentiation for the gifted increases and enhances their life satisfaction, partly because it exposes them to advanced content and processes. This exposure allows the gifted to learn and do things earlier than other children do or to access opportunities usually available only to adults. The enthusiasm and fun a gifted child or adolescent enjoys while engaged in a challenging activity demonstrates satisfaction. Even when the individuals return to more mundane or less stimulating activities, they retain some of the motivation, the fondness for the content, materials, and the people involved in the experience, and they seek to return to similar kinds of experiences.

Appropriate education for the gifted must include both the development of talent and the development of relationships. Too much focus on one to the exclusion of the other leaves the person unidimensional in development, which ultimately leads toward unhappiness and dissatisfaction. A third dimension for developing life satisfaction is spirituality. Development in this area provides purpose, perspective, and understanding of their lives. It also guides and strengthens their autonomy and their resolve in dealing with difficult issues. When a gifted individual develops his or her talent, relationships, and spirituality, and this development is accentuated with the good flavors of other dimensions of development such as learning to be physically active, he or she finds greater happiness, better health, and deeper satisfaction with life.

Michael F. Sayler

See also Aspiration Development and Self-Fulfillment; Character and Moral Development; Differentiation; Emotional Development; Friendships; Meaning of Life; Resilience; Self-Actualization; Self-Efficacy/Self-Esteem

Further Readings

Adams-Byers, J., Moon, S. M., & Whitsell, S. S. (2004). Gifted students' perceptions of the academic and social/emotional effects of homogeneous and heterogeneous grouping. *Gifted Child Quarterly, 48,* 5–20.

Diener, E. (1984). Subjective well-being. *Psychological Bulletin, 95*, 542–575.

Fredrickson, B. L., & Losada, M. F. (2005). Positive affect and the complex dynamics of human flourishing. *American Psychologist, 60*, 678–686.

Gross, M. U. M., & van Vliet, H. (2005). Radical acceleration and early entry to college: A review of the research. *Gifted Child Quarterly, 49*, 154–171.

Peterson, C. (2006). *A primer in positive psychology.* New York: Oxford University Press.

Ryff, C. D., & Singer, B. (2003). Ironies of the human condition: Well-being and health on the way to mortality. In L. G. Aspinwall & U. M. Staudinger (Eds.), *A psychology of human strengths: Fundamental questions and future directions for a positive psychology* (pp. 271–287). Washington, DC: American Psychological Association.

Sayler, M. F. (2008). Gifted and thriving: A deeper understanding of the meaning of GT. In L. Shavinina (Ed.), *The handbook on giftedness.* New York: Springer Science.

Seligman, M. E. P. (2002). *Authentic happiness.* New York: Free Press.

Zaff, J., Smith, D., Rogers, M. F., Leavitt, C. H., Halle, T. G., & Bornstein, M. H. (2003). Holistic well-being and the developing child. In M. Bornstein, L. Davidson, C. Keys, & K. Moore (Eds.), *Well-being: Positive development across the life course* (pp. 23–34). Mahwah, NJ: Lawrence Erlbaum.

Literary Creativity

Literary creativity is the application of creative thought or action to the domain of written expression. Literature is one of the major domains where creativity can be observed and includes poetry, dramas and plays, prose such as fiction and essays, and oral literature, such as folktales or ballads. Literature is an important domain to consider in light of creative poets, playwrights, and novelists, and it is important to understand in terms of Howard Gardner's theory of multiple intelligences because linguistic intelligence is also concerned with the written word. This entry covers some of the theories about literary creativity, the characteristics of persons creative in the literary arts, and some of the challenges that individuals in the domain of literature face.

Theories of Literary Creativity

The theories and ideas about literary creativity center on why writers create literature, why literature is enjoyable and valued by readers, and how those writers function creatively within their domain. Sigmund Freud theorized about creative literature by drawing on his own theories of the ego, dreams, and neurosis and considered himself a writer as well. Frank Barron, in his study of creative writers at the Institute for Personality Assessment and Research, administered a wide variety of personality tests to assess the characteristics of writers. Mihaly Csikszentmihalyi, conversely, draws together his observations about creative individuals within the domain of literature by tying together several key concepts that seem to be shared among prominent writers. Both theories are concerned with intuition and the unconscious, with Freud and Barron focusing more on the psychological mechanisms that literary creativity serves and Csikszentmihalyi focusing more on how creative writers develop.

Freud's Theory

Freud theorized about literary creativity, drawing upon his own ideas about neuroses, dreams, and therapy. He postulated that literature was inherently autobiographical in nature. That is, writers egotistically portray themselves as the hero. Freud also thought writers are halfway between normal, psychologically healthy adults and neurotics. Although normally healthy adults are ashamed of their fantasies and suppress them, either because they are seen as childish or they are improper, immoral, or outside of societal norms, writers feel compelled to communicate these fantasies. Neurotics are compelled to confess their fantasies to their therapist to remove their symptoms, but writers do not exhibit neurotic symptoms. Freud saw writing as a defense mechanism that manifested itself through creativity, rather than through neurotic symptoms and pathologies. Writing, Freud thought, was a form of confession as seen in therapy, which is why he thought that writers could be thought of as borderline neurotics.

In addition, Freud speculated about why literature is so pleasurable for both the reader and the writer. He wondered why people enjoy the fantasies that writers give them, but not the fantasies that they hear from other people. Freud thought that autobiographical character of literature is softened by the writers, which appeases the initial revulsion that people feel from hearing about the intimacies of others. This is similar to Freud's concept of the structure of dreams, where distortion suppresses our tendency to censor ourselves. Also like dreams, the hero of the stories is our own Ego, although the Ego may also be split into several different characters.

Freud believed that literature drew people in with its aesthetic form. Furthermore, Freud thought that writing was pleasurable to the writer and the reader because it was therapeutic. Through writing, we can live out wishes and ambitions without self-reproach or feeling ashamed. Moreover, we can live out dangerous situations through writing or reading without any actual threat. Whereas these situations would normally not be pleasurable in reality, they become pleasurable through literature because they hold no threat of harm. The situations that literature creates promote emotional release, which is why Freud felt that they were therapeutic.

Freud's theory of literary creativity is rooted deeply in his own ideas about psychology. Although creative writing functions as a form of therapy for both the writer and the reader, the fantasies themselves and the compulsion to communicate those fantasies are assumed to be neurotic in nature. His theory paints an almost romanticized view of writers, believing them to be borderline neurotics, a view that sets creative writing as both a blessing and a curse.

Barron's Theory

Barron extensively tested 66 professional creative writers on intelligence tests, projective tests, and objective personality tests. He found writers to be highly intelligent—scoring in the highest percentiles on the already extremely difficult Terman Concept Mastery test; to be fairly "unsocialized" in that they were nonconforming and had little interest in others' opinions of them; and to be highly intuitive, open to new experiences, and introverted. Barron found that the most extreme difference between creative writers and ordinary people was in their vivid fantasy life and original imagination. Like Freud, he discovered great inner conflict in his writer subjects. They had often suffered great hardship to pursue their work and had great internal struggles as well as external difficulties in life. Barron believed that writers wrote to create their own cosmology: to create a different, richer, more meaningful universe than the one in which they found themselves.

Csikszentmihalyi and Literary Creativity

Csikszentmihalyi drew his conclusions about literary creativity not from theory, but from observing eminent writers and poets within the field of literature. He observed that writers allow people to recognize their feelings and emotions and to analyze those emotions carefully. Although people may not be able to carefully think about their emotions in their daily lives, they are allowed the chance to slowly consider and evaluate those emotions at leisure while reading. Within this vein of thought, we are furthermore able to recognize the shared and enduring qualities of humankind. In this sense, Csikszentmihalyi's observations about literary creativity are similar to that of Freud's own theories—literature can foster insight, lead to a deeper understanding of ourselves, and serve as experiences that are almost therapeutic.

The concept of balancing intuition with reason and logic with illogical ideas is central to Csikszentmihalyi's thoughts about literary creativity. Listening to ideas that come suddenly, seemingly from nowhere, is only one aspect of creating literature. The other half is the ability to scrutinize these thoughts and ideas with reason and logic. An idea will go to waste if there is no way to understand how to reasonably implement it into the writing. It is important, he states, to balance passion with discipline and in this way, writers can produce creative pieces of literature. When examined carefully, an intuitive or irrational thought or feeling can be described and connected to other thoughts and feelings, thus making the act of writing a meaningful expression.

Characteristics of People Within the Literary Arts

Csikszentmihalyi found several common factors by observing prominent creative writers in the field of literature. First is that creative writers become immersed in the domain of literature. They do this by becoming avid readers and memorizing the work of writers that they admire. Through memorization, they internalize the work of those they respect and integrate it into their own writing style. In addition, creative writers take the sides of other writers within the writing community. In these ways, the writers completely immerse themselves in their domain.

Creative writers typically have a domain they are knowledgeable about outside of literature itself. This could be knowledge of physics or biology, for instance. This domain-specific knowledge is integrated into the creative writer's work. Thus, having knowledge outside of the realm of literature gives writers the opportunity to blend their knowledge with writing to enhance their work.

For instance, Madeline L'Engle, a novelist of children's fantasy stories, used her knowledge of microbiology and quantum physics within her books. Anthony Hecht, a poet, used his knowledge of music and geometry in his work. This extra domain knowledge enhanced their writing, and the ability to weave dissimilar ideas together is in of itself a creative act and is another outlet for expression.

Another characteristic of creative writers prominent within literature is their integration within the field of literature. Writers work with other younger writers and become friends with older writers. They establish relationships and connections, thereby becoming enmeshed within the social network of that field. Creative writers also become attracted to innovative schools and journals, which helps further enmesh them into the social network of their field while allowing the opportunity for transmitting knowledge among their peers.

It seems important then, at least among writers who are eminent within their fields, to become totally immersed in their domains to improve and evolve their own writing, to have interests outside of literature that they can integrate into their writing, and to become involved with their peers and colleagues.

Literary Creativity and Mental Disorders

Some evidence shows that those who are creative within the domain of literature may be more sensitive to affect disorders, such as bipolar mood disorder. Bipolar consists of episodes of elevated mood—specifically mania—and sometimes, but not always, depressed mood. These moods are on a continuum from severely depressed, moderately depressed, normal mood, and hypomania (just below a manic state), to mania. The depressive states can cause fatigue, hopelessness, physical and mental sluggishness, and suicidal ideation, and the manic states can lead to an excessive amount of energy, sleeplessness, illusions of grandeur, and hallucinations or delusions. In bipolar disorder, moods can shift rapidly between two extremes, making it a particularly dangerous state to be in. However, the less severe mood states, particularly hypomania, do not produce delusions or hallucinations and may be characterized as an unusually good mood.

Specifically for literary creativity, Nancy Andreasen found high incidences of affect disorders among eminent writers, and Kay Redfield Jamison discovered that approximately 20 percent of the poets that appeared in the *New Oxford Book of American Verse* had symptoms of bipolar mood disorder. Among the writers that Jamison studied, a significant proportion of them experienced brief episodes of hypomania, which is a symptom of bipolar mood disorder. Eugene Fodor and Bobbi Laird established a connection between creative writing and bipolar symptoms. Children with inclinations toward bipolar disorder who experienced a significantly enhanced mood during play therapy wrote more creative poems than did children who did not experience an elevated mood.

These mood states might be conducive to the act of creative writing. Hypomania may contribute to an original and flexible way of thinking, while giving ample reserves of energy in which to be productive. Conversely, a mildly depressed state may be conducive to helping the writer become a good editor of his or her work. Therefore, sensitivity toward more elevated and more depressed mood states might contribute to the creative writer's ability to produce emotionally evocative pieces of literature.

The increased ability to experience a wide array of emotions might also help creative writers specifically with their abilities to stimulate emotion to their readers, as well as their complex abilities to tie emotions to other states of being. So, even though bipolar mood disorder may be a debilitating mental disease, some of its features may be met with resiliency from the creative writers who become prominent and harnessed in ways that fuel their creativity.

Moreover, some evidence suggests that some writing may actually be therapeutic. When looking at writers separately rather than all together—that is, separating fiction writers, nonfiction writers, playwrights, and poets—writers of fiction and nonfiction and playwrights have lower incidences of mental illness than do poets. Specifically, poets have been shown to have the most risk factors throughout their lives, being at greater risk for mental illness, suicide, and early death. Looking even more closely at poets, we can see that suicidal poets are more likely to use more first-person singular pronouns, such as *I,* than plural pronouns, such as *us* or *we.* However, there is no evidence suggesting that the greater usage of positive or negative words affects the likelihood that a poet is suicidal. This suggests that poets who are more socially connected may be at a lower risk for committing suicide.

Despite the connections between literary creativity and mental illness, evidence suggests that creative writing produces positive effects. For example, expressive writing can help survivors of trauma, as well as providing general benefits to physical and mental health. Therefore, a narrative form of writing that encourages expression can have several positive benefits. This serves as an important point when considering the mental health of poets because poetry may not as easily carry the same narrative structure as other writing does.

There is a relationship between literary creativity and mental health; however, it is important to look at this within the context of specific writing structures. Creative writing holds many benefits, as long as the writer is using talents to structure narrative pieces that are also emotionally evocative and that establish social connections with others.

Amber Larson

See also Creativity, Definition; Creativity Theories; Multiple Intelligences; Optimal Development; Playwrights; Poets Laureate; Talented Readers; Writers

Further Readings

Andreasen, N. C., & Canter, A. (1974). The creative writer: Psychiatric symptoms and family history. *Comprehensive psychiatry, 15,* 123–131.

Barron, F. X. (1992). Creative writers. In R. S. Albert (Ed), *Genius and eminence.* London: Pergamon.

Csikszentmihalyi, M. (1996). *Creativity: Flow and the psychology of discovery and invention.* New York: Harper Perennial.

Fodor, E. M., & Laird, B. A. (2004). Therapeutic intervention, bipolar inclination, and literary creativity. *Creativity Research Journal, 16,* 149–146.

Freud, S. (1908). Creative writers and day-dreaming. In J. Strachey (Ed.), *The standard edition of the complete psychological works of Sigmund Freud* (pp. 143–153). London: Hogarth Press.

Jamison, K. R. (1989). Mood disorders and patterns of creativity in British writers and artists. *Psychiatry, 52,* 125–134.

Kaufman, J. C., & Sexton, J. D. (2006). Why doesn't the writing cure help poets? *Review of General Psychology, 10,* 268–282.

Locus of Control

Locus of control is a person's interpretation of what causes and controls the events in his or her life. Julian Rotter proposed the construct of locus of control in the 1960s as *locus of control of reinforcement* combining elements of cognitive and behavioral psychology. This is the belief that either the person or something outside of the person is in control of his or her life. In normal development, an individual progresses from an external orientation as an infant to a more internal orientation as an adult. This developmental shift occurs as the child grows and feels increasingly competent and independent in responding and controlling the various circumstances and events of his or her life. The belief that one is in control of the controllable aspects of one's life is psychologically and developmentally healthy. Locus of control is an important aspect of personal attributions of success and failure. Attributions profoundly affect success of the gifted in school and life. The gifted can be helped in developing a positive and internal locus of control that will facilitate their success and happiness, as discussed in this entry.

Internal locus of control and external locus of control are two ends of a continuum rather than an either-or dichotomy. A person is not entirely internal or external in his or her beliefs, but falls somewhere along a continuum between these two extremes. The specific position on the continuum is somewhat context specific and amenable to interventions and change. Although locus of control is often discussed as though it were a stable personality construct, the theory and research suggest that it is a learned and changeable disposition.

Locus of control is closely linked to personal attributions of success and failure. Bernard Weiner's attribution theory has three dimensions: the person's locus of control, the stability of the causal element (e.g., personal ability, task difficulty), and whether the causal element is controllable (e.g., personal effort, luck). Gifted students may develop dysfunctional explanations of their success when school tasks are too easy. These explanations include a belief they will always learn things quickly and easily, get all questions correct, and never make mistakes. Success in challenging academic tasks is more likely to develop appropriate attributions and increased internal orientations. Internality of control increases in gifted children or adolescents when they perceive their success in a challenging activity as dependent on their effort, that their abilities are sufficient to be successful, and that the task though difficult is doable. In challenging accelerated educational programs, the gifted have to work hard and struggle more to be successful and competitive with the others in the program. An internal orientation supports the efforts this takes better than does an external one.

Gifted children with an internal locus of control are more likely to take responsibility for their actions and inactions. They are not easily swayed by the negative or overly positive opinions of others. They do better at tasks when they can work at their own paces. The gifted generally develop a healthy internal locus of control, and those gifted who are deeply challenged academically such as those experiencing grade acceleration even more likely to have an internal control orientation.

Developing an internal locus of control among the gifted is encouraged when they are helped to identify those areas in life and in school where they can exercise control. Internality is also enhanced when the gifted are helped to know which areas of their lives are not within their control and therefore may not be worth struggling to change. Assuming control over the various important things in their lives facilitates academic achievement and encourages healthy psychological development among the gifted in related areas such as self-efficacy, resilience, personal goal setting, and decision making. A healthy locus of control helps avoid dysfunctional perfectionism, hiding or denying their giftedness, and underachievement.

Not all gifted have or maintain an internal orientation. An overly external orientation is associated with dysfunctional perfectionism. Providing external rewards for tasks that gifted children already like to do reduces their enjoyment of the activity; in this case, the locus of control shifts from internal to the child to external and with the teacher. Gifted children with an external locus may feel helpless without the concrete direction of others. They may also blame their teachers, parents, other students, or events and circumstances outside of themselves for their poor performances. Externally oriented gifted students attribute success to luck, good teaching, or chance factors rather than to their own efforts.

A related effect is the relationship between a gifted child's locus of control and his or her delay of gratification (to put off a pleasant, but less important effect to accomplish a substantial goal that may take more time and effort right now). Willingness to accept and embrace this delay is supported by an internal locus of control. An internal orientation facilitates the development of self-efficacy, hopefulness about future successes, and a more self-ordered and disciplined task orientation.

Michael F. Sayler

See also Emotional Development; Intrinsic Versus Extrinsic Motivation; Perfectionism; Resilience; School Attitudes; Self-Efficacy/Self-Esteem

Further Readings

Ford, D. Y., & Harris, J. J. (1992). The American achievement ideology and achievement differentials among preadolescent gifted and nongifted African American males and females. *Journal of Negro Education, 61,* 45–64.

Fournier, G., & Jeanrie, C. (2003). Locus of control: Back to basics. In S. J. Lopez & C. R. Snyder (Eds.), *Positive psychological assessment: A handbook of models and measures* (pp. 139–154). Washington, DC: American Psychological Association.

Heller, K. A., & Ziegler, A. (1996). Gender differences in mathematics and the sciences: Can attributional retraining improve the performance of gifted females? *Gifted Child Quarterly, 40,* 200–210.

Hoekman, K., McCormick, J., & Gross, M. U. M. (1999). The optimal context for gifted students: A preliminary exploration of motivational and affective considerations. *Gifted Child Quarterly, 43,* 170–193.

Rotter, J. B. (1990). Internal versus external control of reinforcement: A case history of a variable. *American Psychologist, 45,* 489–493.

Sayler, M. F., & Brookshire, W. K. (1993). Social, emotional, and behavioral adjustment of accelerated students, students in gifted classes, and regular students in eighth grade. *Gifted Child Quarterly, 37*(4), 150–154.

Schunk, D. H. (1987). Peer models and children's behavioral change. *Review of Educational Research, 57,* 149–174.

Siegle, D., & Reis, S. M. (1995, Winter). Gender differences between student and teacher perceptions of ability and effort. *National Research Center on the Gifted and Talented Newsletter,* 6–7.

Weiner, B. (1986). *An attributional theory of motivation and emotion.* New York: Springer.

Mathematical Creativity

Mathematics is often viewed as a field where the ability to apply theorems and algorithms is essential to the development of a deep conceptual understanding. Overlooked is the fact that the theorems and algorithms taught are the creative products of the application of mathematics. All students need insight into the creative process as well as the product of mathematics, but for gifted students, neglecting the creative side of mathematics often results in boredom and loss of interest. A conceptual understanding of mathematical creativity, the difference between academic and creative talent, and ways to develop creativity are all necessary to meet the needs of the gifted.

Defining Mathematical Creativity

Attempts to define mathematical creativity have yielded a multitude of definitions. Some apply the concepts of fluency, flexibility, and creativity to the way students approach problem solving. Others consider the manner in which students formulate problems, or find new relationships, and test their theories. Mathematical creativity can also be viewed in terms of an individual's ability to elaborate on what is known by extending or improving problem-solving methods. An aspect of sensitivity is involved as well; the ability to see beauty or efficiency in the mathematics employed, a level of conceptual understanding necessary to assess cause and effect within a mathematical context, and the ability to offer constructive criticism of standard mathematical problem-solving methods. Regardless of the definition accepted, creativity in mathematics is essential for the advancement of the discipline and in solving problems encountered in the real world.

Academic Ability and Creativity

Although debate exists concerning whether the elements of mathematical creativity are general in nature, domain specific, or some combination, scholars agree that some mathematical knowledge is required for mathematical creativity to emerge. Yet, simply possessing mathematical knowledge does not imply creativity. Students may be able to apply a variety of problem-solving strategies to converge on the same solution, yet never evaluate the appropriateness of these strategies or explore alternate methods. An unwillingness to take risks or the attitude that there is one right way to solve a problem often causes students to fixate on rules and procedures rather than the nature of the problem. When mathematics is approached in this way, creativity is limited; students develop fixed dispositions in their responses to and interpretations of problems.

Henri Poincaré described the work of mathematicians not as the simple application of rules, but rather as the selective choice of ideas to create useful new ways to solve problems. He viewed the process as a period of hard work followed by a period of rest in which the idea incubates within the subconscious. The incubation period is followed by illumination during which the mathematician solves the problem and confirmatory work in which he or she seeks to extend the methods developed to a wider set of problems. The use of standardized test scores as the only means to identify mathematical giftedness runs counter to Poincaré's process, reducing the concept of mathematical ability to simply accuracy of computation and speed of response. Such tests neglect the value of sustained effort and time needed for reflection that provides the fertile environment necessary for creativity to flourish.

Poincaré's process of mathematical creativity can be found in contemporary writings. Edward Silver suggested that creativity is closely related to deep, flexible knowledge in the domain; associated with long periods of work and reflection rather than rapid, exceptional insight; and influenced by experience. In a comparative study of academically and creatively gifted high school mathematics students, Eunsook Hong and Yvette Aqui found the creatively gifted group to be significantly more resourceful cognitively. Robert Sternberg believes that creative mathematical thinking is essential for an individual to extend the learned mathematics to problems encountered outside the classroom. Although strong analytical skills are often sufficient for high levels of academic performance through lower-level graduate courses, he concluded that creativity is the better predictor of success as a mathematician.

Developing Mathematical Creativity

Creativity needs time to develop and thrives on experience. Too often mathematics is taught as if it is simply a manner of recognizing the correct path for solving a problem and assessed by the correctness of the solution. A meaningful and accurate solution remains the objective; however, students need to learn and value the cognitive processes as well. Inquiry, inference, and reflection are essential skills in the development of creative mathematical thinking. Teaching mathematics for creativity involves making explicit the implicit actions used to solve problems. Students need to struggle with ill-formed problems, as well as explore and experiment with their ideas on how to solve problems. They need opportunities to refine and generalize their methodologies and solutions. In the 1965 film, *Let Us Teach Guessing*, George Pólya presented a class of undergraduate students a deceptively simple problem statement. He guided his students in reformulating the problem into more manageable elements, tailored his instruction to focus his students' guesses on possible solutions, sought to generate and test rules for the patterns observed, and then challenged his students to extend the rules they developed to other cases. Using a holistic approach to problem solving, he modeled the processes mathematicians undertake in the context of new content knowledge for his students. In this way, his students constructed their own understanding of mathematics and began to build the habits of the mind necessary for creative mathematical work.

Eric L. Mann

See also Academic Talent; Creativity, Definition; Mathematical Intelligence; Mathematical Talent; Study of Mathematically Precocious Youth

Further Readings

Hadamard, J. (1945). *The psychology of invention in the mathematical field.* Mineola, NY: Dover Publications.

Hong, E., & Aqui, Y. (2004). Cognitive and motivational characteristics of adolescents gifted in mathematics: Comparisons among students with different types of giftedness. *Gifted Child Quarterly, 48*(3) 191–201.

König, G. (Ed.). (1997). Fostering of mathematical creativity [Special Issue]. *Zentralblatt für Didaktik der Mathematik* [International Reviews on Mathematical Education], *29*(3). Retrieved September 11, 2007, from http://www.emis.de/journals/ZDM/zdm973i.html

Sternberg, R. J., & Ben-Zeev, T. (Eds.). (1996). *The nature of mathematical thinking.* Mahwah, NJ: Lawrence Erlbaum.

Mathematical Intelligence

Mathematical intelligence is considered a strong indicator of general intelligence, and items requiring numerical and spatial reasoning have historically been a component of what constitutes an IQ or "*g*" score. The traditional view of mathematical intelligence as a construct measurable by a standardized battery leaves little room for the role of imaginative thinking and does not take into consideration the extracognitive and sociocultural factors that influence a person's mathematical creativity. Because mathematical intelligence is often associated with mathematical giftedness and mathematical creativity, a differentiation of the various terms is necessary and explained in this entry. Mathematical intelligence is described from the point of view of extant research findings in the domains of mathematical cognition, psychology, sociocultural research, and gifted education.

Mathematical Giftedness

The construct of intelligence in general and mathematical intelligence in particular have been topics of great controversy since the advent of psychometric testing. For example, most modern-day intelligence tests, which have evolved out of the original Binet-Simon test and the Stanford-Binet test developed by Lewis Terman, consist of subtests that measure numerical reasoning, digit memory, letter–number sequencing, digit symbol-coding, picture completion, block design, matrix reasoning, symbols, and object assembly. In other words, logical, quantitative, and visual-spatial reasoning play a significant role in IQ tests. This view of intelligence has been criticized as being problematic, however, because the items do not take into consideration sociocultural and environmental variables that can influence performance, particularly among minorities and non-native English speakers. High scores on the Stanford-Binet have been traditionally used as an indicator of giftedness and a predictor of academic success in school and beyond. Similarly, psychometric batteries such as the SAT, ACT, and GRE (Graduate Record Examination) consist of a mathematics portion that claims to predict academic success in college.

In the studies conducted in the domain of cognition, mathematical intelligence in an individual can be defined in terms of the following: (a) the ability to abstract, generalize, and discern mathematical structures; (b) the ability to employ data management techniques; (c) the ability to master principles of logical thinking and inference; (d) analogical, heuristic thinking and posing related problems; (e) flexibility and reversibility of mathematical operations; (f) an intuitive awareness of mathematical proof; (g) the ability to independently discover mathematical principles; (h) the ability to apply decision-making abilities in problem-solving situations; (i) the ability to visualize problems and/or relations; and (j) the ability to distinguish between empirical and theoretical principles.

Mathematical intelligence in the general population has been classified by numerous theorists using a hierarchical model. For instance, Zalman Usiskin, a mathematics educator at the University of Chicago, proposed an eight-tiered hierarchy to classify mathematical talent, which he ranges from Level 0 to Level 7. In this hierarchy Level 0 (No Talent) represents adults who know very little mathematics; Level 1 (Culture level) represents adults who have rudimentary number sense as a function of cultural usage, and their mathematical knowledge is comparable to those of students in Grades 6–9. It is obvious that a very large proportion of the general population would fall into the first two levels. The remaining population is thinly spread out into Levels 2 through 7 on the basis of mathematical talent. Level 2 represents honors high school students who are capable of majoring in mathematics as well as those who eventually become secondary math teachers. Level 3 (the "terrific" student) represents students who score in the 750–800 range on the SATs or 4 or 5 in the Calculus AP exams. These students have the potential to do beginning graduate-level work in mathematics. Level 4 (the "exceptional" student) represents students who excel in math competitions and receive admission into math/science summer camps and/or academies because of their talent. These students are capable of constructing mathematical proofs and able to "converse" with mathematicians about mathematics. Level 5 represents the productive mathematician. This level represents students who have successfully completed a Ph.D. in mathematics or a related mathematical science and are capable of publishing in the field. Level 6 is the rarified territory of the exceptional mathematician; it represents mathematicians who have made significant contributions to their particular domains and been conferred recognition for their work. Finally, at Level 7 are the all-time greats, including the Fields Medal winners in mathematics. The Fields Medal was established by John Charles Fields (1863–1932) and is the equivalent of the Nobel Prize for the field of mathematics. This level is the exclusive territory of giants or exemplary geniuses like Leonard Euler, Karl Friedrich Gauss, Bernhard Riemmann, Srinivasa Ramanujan, David Hilbert, and Henri Poincaré, among others. The hierarchical model of Usiskin has been extended by Bharath Sriraman by taking into consideration the need to differentiate between the constructs of mathematical giftedness and mathematical creativity implicitly assumed in the model.

In the former Soviet Union in the time period from 1950 to 1970, numerous experiments were conducted with mathematically capable students in order to discern their specific mathematical abilities. This research characterized the mathematical abilities of gifted children holistically as comprising analytic, geometric, and harmonic components and argued that gifted children usually have a preference for one component over the others. The analytic type has a mathematically abstract cast of mind, the geometric type has a mathematically pictorial cast of mind, and a harmonic type is a combination of analytic and geometric types. For instance, given the same problem, one gifted child might pursue an analytic approach, whereas another would pursue a geometric approach. Another classification of styles of mathematical giftedness suggests the empirical type and the conceptual type. In this classification the empirical type would have a preference for applied situations, immediately observable relations, and induction, whereas the conceptual type would have a preference for theoretical situations and deduction. The Soviet psychologist V. A. Krutetskii observed that one of the attributes of mathematically gifted students was the ability to switch from a direct to a reverse train of thought (reversibility), which gifted students performed with relative ease. The mathematical context in which this reversibility was observed was in transitions from usual proof to proof via contradiction (*reductio ad absurdum*), or when moving from a theorem to its converse.

Mathematical Creativity

Another aspect of mathematical intelligence is that of mathematical creativity. Most extant definitions of mathematical creativity found in the mathematics and mathematics education literature is vague or elusive. This may be because of the difficulty of describing this complex construct. For instance, mathematical creativity has been defined by mathematicians like Poincaré via the use of various metaphors such as the ability to discern, choose; to distinguish between acceptable and unacceptable patterns; and nonalgorithmic decision making. The literature on students who are mathematically creative at the pre-university level (K–12) is also vague. Exceptional mathematical ability has been associated with the Einstein syndrome and Asperger's syndrome. The Einstein syndrome is characterized by exceptional mathematical ability but delayed speech development, whereas Asperger's syndrome is a mild form of autism. At the K–12 level, one normally does not expect works of extraordinary creativity; however, it is certainly feasible for students to offer new insights into a math problem or a new interpretation or commentary on a literary or historical work. The psychologist Robert Sternberg defines creativity as the ability to produce unexpected original work that is useful and adaptive. Other definitions, such as those formulated by Paul Torrance, usually impose the requirement of novelty, innovation, or unusualness of a response to a given problem. Confluence theories of creativity define creativity as a convergence of knowledge, ability, thinking style, motivational, and environmental variables. A synthesis of the numerous definitions of creativity leads to a generally accepted definition of mathematical creativity as the ability to produce original work that significantly extends the body of knowledge, and/or opens up avenues of new questions for others.

The existing research also indicates that mathematically creative individuals are prone to reformulating the problem or finding analogous problems. They are also different from their peers in that they are fiercely independent thinkers, tend to persevere, and tend to reflect a great deal. Although some of the cognitive and affective aspects of mathematical creativity are now known, some theorists claim that numerous extracognitive factors play an important role in the manifestation of mathematical intelligence in creative acts. These factors include beliefs, aesthetics, intuitions, intellectual values, self-imposed subjective norms and standards, and chance as contributing to astonishing acts and products of creative endeavors.

Some theorists contend that although the field of psychology has an established body of research that has examined factors such as the influence of personality and sociocultural influences contributing to creative behavior, the study of beliefs, aesthetics, intuitions, values, and chance is necessary to complement and convey a complete picture of creativity. In sociocultural frameworks for mathematics such as that proposed by Alan Bishop, mathematical intelligence is viewed as being engaged in and aware of the six pancultural human activities, which are (1) playing, (2) designing, (3) locating, (4) explaining, (5) counting, and (6) measuring.

Implications

One important implication for teachers of mathematics is that many of the traits of highly able individuals are in fact cultivatable in the classroom. For instance, the role of analogical reasoning is highlighted as a trait of exceptional creativity, yet the use of analogies and metaphors vanishes in the school curricula as imagination is replaced by conformity as students progress through Grades K–12, particularly in science and mathematics. Research in the 1980s on problem solving focused partly on analogical behaviors engaged in by expert and novice problem solvers. This research revealed that expert problem solvers in mathematics and science engaged in metaphorical processes as they constructed problem representations, and they looked for analogies between the problem at hand and other familiar situations. A recent longitudinal cross-cultural study conducted with young children in Australia and the United States reported that spontaneous analogies employed by children in everyday language in natural settings were by and large absent when children employed the language of mathematics, that is, engaged in mathematical reasoning, which suggests that practitioners need to encourage this natural facility in mathematics classrooms.

Real-world problems are full of uncertainty and ambiguity. Creating, as opposed to learning, requires that students be exposed to the uncertainty as well as the difficulty of creating original ideas in mathematics, science, and other disciplines. This ability requires the teacher to provide affective support to students who experience frustration over being unable to solve a difficult problem. Students should periodically be exposed to ideas from the history of mathematics and science that evolved over centuries and took the efforts of generations of mathematicians to finally solve. Cultivating this trait will ultimately serve mathematically gifted students to make the transition to the professional realm. The Hamburg Model in Germany, which is focused on allowing gifted students to engage in problem-posing activities, followed by time for exploring viable and nonviable strategies to solve the posed problems, captures an essence of the nature of professional mathematics, where the most difficult task is often to formulate the problem (theorem) correctly.

Bharath Sriraman

See also Cognition; Intelligence Testing; Mathematical Creativity; Mathematically Precocious; Mathematics, Curriculum

Further Readings

Bishop, A. J. (1988). *Mathematical enculturation: A cultural perspective on mathematics education.* Dordrecht, the Netherlands: Kluwer Academic.

Bredo, R. (2006). Conceptual confusion and educational psychology. In P. Alexander & P. Winne (Eds.), *Handbook of educational psychology* (2nd ed., pp. 43–58). Mahwah, NJ: Lawrence Erlbaum.

English, L. (Ed.). (2004). *Mathematical and analogical reasoning of young learners.* Mahwah, NJ: Lawrence Erlbaum.

Shavinina, L. V., & Ferrari, M. (Eds.). (2004). *Beyond knowledge: Extra cognitive aspects of developing high ability.* Mahwah, NJ: Lawrence Erlbaum.

Sriraman, B. (2005). Are mathematical giftedness and mathematical creativity synonyms? A theoretical analysis of constructs. *Journal of Secondary Gifted Education, 17*(1), 20–36.

Sriraman, B., & Dahl, B. (2007). On bringing interdisciplinary ideas to gifted education. In L. V. Shavinina (Ed.), *The international handbook of giftedness.* New York: Springer Science.

Sternberg, R., & Ben-Zeev, T. (Eds.). (1996). *The nature of mathematical thinking.* Mahwah, NJ: Lawrence Erlbaum.

Mathematically Precocious

Precocity in mathematical ability is a well-documented phenomenon in the history of science and mathematics. The history of mathematics and the literature in gifted education indicates that mathematical precocity is a relatively rare trait in the general population and one that typically manifests at a young age. Fortunately, it can be identified via above-level testing. Such individuals' abilities develop and thrive when they are mentored early in their lives and provided affective support in addition to curricular programming appropriate for their abilities.

Mathematically Precocious Individuals

Mathematical precocity is typically found in anecdotes of child prodigies such as Blaise Pascal (1623–1666), Carl Friedrich Gauss (1777–1855), Rowan Hamilton (1805–1865), Srinivasa Ramanujan (1887–1920), Shakuntala Devi (1939–), and Terrence Tao (1975–), among others. Many of these prodigies were known for their phenomenal computing abilities that involve complex arithmetic and number theoretic operations on large numbers.

Some well-documented and historically accurate anecdotes indicate the profound nature of such an individual's precocity. At the age of 11, Pascal had composed a treatise on the sounds of vibrating bodies in spite of his father forbidding him to study mathematics lest it interfere with Pascal's schooling in the classical languages. At the age of 12, Pascal constructed an independent proof that the sums of the angles of a Euclidean triangle are invariant and equal two right angles, with a piece of coal on a wall. Pascal was then allowed the luxury of sitting in on meetings held in the monastery housing Marin Mersenne, where mathematical geniuses like Descartes, Desargues, and Gassendi often gathered.

Hamilton displayed unusual precocity in the realm of languages and by the age of 13, under the tutelage of his uncle, learned most classical and modern European languages in addition to Hindustani, Persian, Sanskrit, and Arabic. His genius in mathematics manifested only after his entry into Trinity College in Dublin, culminating in his discovery of the mathematical structure of quaternions in 1843.

Ramanujan, called one of the greatest mathematical geniuses of the 20th century, was self-taught and found his love and astonishing ability for mathematics at the age of 13 by mastering an advanced trigonometry book by S. L. Loney, and the nearly 5,000 theorems found in *A Synopsis of Elementary Results in Pure and Applied Mathematics,* by George S. Carr. Later, with the help of G. H. Hardy at Cambridge, who recognized his brilliance, Ramanujan made profound contributions to analytic number theory, analysis, series, and continued fractions. During his lifetime, Ramanujan is said to have discovered nearly 4,000 mathematical theorems in the forms of identities and equations.

Devi, the daughter of a trapeze artist, was a calculating prodigy who demonstrated her unusual counting talents in card games at the age of 3. She had the ability to perform mathematical computations faster than computers, an ability that did not wane in adulthood. She mentally extracted the 23rd root of a 201 digit number in 1977, and in 1980 demonstrated her abilities to the computer science department at Imperial College in London by correctly multiplying two randomly selected 13-digit numbers in 28 seconds.

Finally, Tao, whose early mathematical precocity is well documented in the current gifted education literature, was already attending high school–level courses at the age of 8, and scored a 760 on the SAT—Mathematics. He was awarded the Fields Medal in Mathematics, the highest honor given to mathematicians under the age of 40 who have made seminal contributions to the development of the field.

Even though mathematical precocity is most frequently found among child prodigies, the literature contains eminent examples of precocious individuals who were relatively late bloomers in their seminal contributions to mathematics, such as Abraham DeMoivre (1667–1754), Karl Weierstrass (1815–1857), Emmy Noether (1882–1935), and Abraham Robinson (1918–1974).

Testing and Programming

Julian Stanley's landmark Study of Mathematically Precocious Youth (SMPY), started at Johns Hopkins University in 1971, introduced the idea of above-level testing for the identification of highly gifted youth. From 1980 to 1983, in SMPY, 292 mathematically precocious youth were identified on the basis of the SAT. These students scored at least 700 on SAT—Mathematics before the age of 13. SMPY also generated a vast amount of empirical data gathered over the past 30 years, and resulted in many findings about the types of curricular and affective interventions that foster the pursuit of advanced coursework in mathematics.

Given the profound abilities of mathematically precocious students, programming can be delivered for these students via acceleration, curriculum compacting, and differentiation. There exists compelling evidence from longitudinal studies conducted in the former Soviet Union by V. A. Krutetskii that highly mathematically gifted students are able to abstract and generalize mathematical concepts at higher levels of complexity and more easily than their peers in the context of arithmetic and algebra. These results were recently extended for the domains of problem solving, combinatorics, and number theory by Bharath Sriraman. The literature indicates that acceleration is perhaps the most effective way of meeting precociously gifted student programming needs. Mathematics, unlike any other discipline, lends itself to acceleration because of the sequential developmental nature of many elementary concepts. The very nature of acceleration suggests that the principles of curriculum compacting are applied to trim out an excessive amount of repetitive tasks. In addition, the effectiveness of radical acceleration and exclusive ability grouping, as extensively reported by Miraca Gross in her longitudinal study of exceptionally and profoundly gifted students in Australia, indicates that the benefits far outweigh the risks of such an approach. Most of the students in Gross's studies reported high levels of academic success in addition to normal social lives. Simply put, the purpose of curricular modifications such as acceleration, compacting, and differentiation for mathematically precocious students is to tailor materials that introduce new topics at a faster pace that allows for high-level thinking and independence reminiscent of research in the field of mathematics.

Besides the use of curriculum compacting, differentiating, and acceleration techniques, many school programs offer *all* students opportunities to participate in math clubs and in local, regional, and statewide math contests. Typically, the exceptionally talented students benefit the most from such opportunities. In many countries (such as Hungary, Romania, Russia, and the United States), the objective of such contests is typically to select the best students to eventually move on to the national and international rounds of such competitions. The pinnacle of math contests is the prestigious International Math Olympiads (IMO), where teams of students from different countries work together to solve challenging math problems. At the local and regional levels, problems typically require mastery of concepts covered by a traditional high school curriculum with the ability to employ or connect methods and concepts flexibly. At the Olympiad levels, however, students in many countries are trained in the use of undergraduate-level algebraic, analytic, combinatorial, graph theoretic, number theoretic, and geometric principles.

Models for Indentifying and Developing Mathematical Precocity

Whereas most extant models within the United States, such as those used in the Center for Talented Youth (CTY) at Johns Hopkins University, tend to focus on accelerating the learning of concepts and processes from the regular curriculum, thus preparing students for advanced coursework within mathematics, other models such as the Hamburg Model in Germany, are more focused on allowing gifted students to engage in problem-posing activities, followed by time for exploring viable and nonviable strategies to solve the posed problems. This approach in a sense captures an essence of the nature of professional mathematics, where the most difficult task is often to formulate the problem correctly and to pose related problems.

Another successful model for identifying and developing mathematical precocity is found in historical case studies of mathematics gifted education in the former USSR. The Russian mathematician and pedagogue B. V. Gnedenko claimed that personal traits of creativity can appear in different ways in different people. One person could be interested in generalizing and in a more profound examination of already obtained results. Others show the ability to find new objects for study and to look for new methods in order to discover their unknown properties. The third type of person can focus on logical development of theories, demonstrating an extraordinary sense of awareness of logical fallacies and flaws. A fourth group of gifted individuals would be attracted to hidden links between seemingly unrelated branches of mathematics. The fifth would study historical processes of the growth of mathematical knowledge. The sixth would focus on the study of philosophical aspects of mathematics. The seventh would search for ingenious solutions to practical problems and look for new applications of mathematics. Finally, someone could be extremely creative in the popularization of science and in teaching.

The history of Soviet mathematics provides an example of the coexistence of two different approaches to mathematics education, one embedded into the general lay public educational system implementing the blueprint based on the European concepts of the late 19th century, and the other focusing mainly on gifted children and having flourished starting from the 1950s onward. The latter took the form of a complex network of activities, including mathematics clubs for advanced children (Russian "кружки" [*kruzhki*], literally "circles" or "rings," usually affiliated with schools and universities but some were also home based), Olympiads, team mathematics competitions (*matboi,* literally "mathematical fight"), extracurricular winter or summer schools for gifted children, publication of magazines on physics and mathematics for children (the most famous being *Kvant,* literally "Quantum"), among others. All these activities were free for all participating children and were based solely on the enthusiasm of mathematics teachers or university professors. This process led to the creation of a system of formation of mathematical elite in the former USSR focused first and foremost on extremely gifted children, which was in sharp contrast to the egalitarian, regular state-run schools targeting average students. The young Andrey Kolmogorov (1903–1987), a highly precocious child who went on to become one of the most eminent mathematicians of the 20th century, was able to benefit from the unique extracurricular pedagogical environment provided by this system.

Research Findings

Recently, David Lubinski and Camilla Benbow compiled a comprehensive account of 35 years of longitudinal data obtained from the Study of Mathematically Precocious Youth (SMPY). They reported the findings from 20-year follow-ups on various cohort groups that participated in SMPY. These researchers found that the success of SMPY in uncovering antecedents such as spatial ability, tendency to independently investigate, and research oriented values, were indicative of potential for pursuing lifelong careers related to mathematics and science. The special programming opportunities provided to the cohort groups played a major role in shaping their interest and potential in mathematics, and ultimately resulted in "happy" choices and satisfaction with the career paths chosen. Another finding was that significantly more mathematically precocious males entered into math-oriented careers as opposed to females, which Lubinski and Benbow argue is not a loss of talent per se, since the females did obtain advanced degrees and chose careers more oriented to their multidimensional interests, such as administration, law, medicine, and the social sciences. Programs such as SMPY serve as a beacon for other gifted and talented programs around the world, and provide ample evidence of the benefits of early identification and nurturing the interests of mathematically precocious individuals.

Bharath Sriraman

See also Eminence; Genius; Mathematical Creativity; Mathematical Talent; Prodigies; Study of Mathematically Precocious Youth; Very Young Gifted

Further Readings

Benbow, C. P., Lubinski, D., & Sushy, B. (1996). The impact of SMPY's educational programs from the perspective of the participant. In C. P. Benbow & D. Lubinski (Eds.), *Intellectual talent* (pp. 266–300). Baltimore: Johns Hopkins University Press.

Davidson, H. M. (1983). *Blaise Pascal.* Boston: Twayne Publishers.

Feldman, D. H. (1993). Child prodigies: A distinctive form of giftedness. *Gifted Children Quarterly, 37*(4), 188–193.

Freiman, V., & Volkov, A. (2004). Early mathematical giftedness and its social context: The cases of Imperial China and Soviet Russia. *Journal of Korea Society of Mathematical Education Series D: Research in Mathematical Education, 8*(3), 157–173.

Genkin, S., Fomin, D., & Itenberg, I. (1996). *Mathematical circles: Russian experience.* Providence, RI: American Mathematical Society.

Gnedenko, B. V. (1991). *Введение в специальность: математика* [Introduction in specialization: Mathematics]. Moscow: Nauka.

Gross, M. U. M. (1986). Radical acceleration in Australia: Terence Tao. *Gifted Child Today.* Retrieved December 17, 2008, from http://www.gt-cybersource.org/Record.aspx?NavID=2_0&rid=11273

Gross, M. U. M. (1993). Nurturing the talents of exceptionally gifted children. In K. A. Heller, F. J. Monks, & A. H. Passow (Eds.), *International handbook of research and development of giftedness and talent* (pp. 473–490). Oxford, UK: Pergamon.

Kiesswetter, K. (1992). Mathematische Begabung. Über die Komplexität der Phänomene und die Unzulänglichkeiten von Punktbewertungen. *Mathematik-Unterricht, 38,* 5–18.

Krutetskii, V. A. (1976). *The psychology of mathematical abilities in school children* (J. Teller, Trans., J. Kilpatrick & I. Wirszup, Eds.). Chicago: University of Chicago Press.

Lubinski, D., & Benbow, C. P. (2006). Study of mathematically precocious youth after 35 years: Uncovering antecedents for the development of math-science expertise. *Perspectives on Psychological Science, 1,* 316–345.

Sriraman, B. (2002). How do mathematically gifted students abstract and generalize mathematical concepts. *NAGC 2002 Research Briefs, 16,* 83–87.

Sriraman, B. (2004). Gifted ninth graders' notions of proof. Investigating parallels in approaches of mathematically gifted students and professional mathematicians. *Journal for the Education of the Gifted,* 27(4), 267–292.

Mathematical Talent

Mathematical talent is a resource much in demand in our increasingly technological world. In many ways, however, it is elusive—hard to define in a single sentence. Because it is inextricably connected to human beings, it is as complicated as the human experience itself. In this entry, the definition of mathematical talent is discussed, and then links from this definition to the identification process and programming for talented math students are explored.

An introduction to the definition of mathematical talent is probably best done by stating what it is not. It is not a single construct nor is this talent the same for every student. Thus, it follows that it cannot be measured by a single instrument. Rather, mathematical talent is multidimensional, just as the discipline of mathematics itself is multidimensional.

Definition

In our society, the definition of mathematical talent is confounded because of students' different levels of experience with mathematics due to their varying backgrounds and schooling. For example, just because a student has never had exposure to prime numbers does not mean that he or she cannot understand them or solve interesting, complex problems with prime numbers. This student might have difficulty in a testing situation, however, until the initial exposure has taken place. The National Council of Teachers of Mathematics (NCTM) established a task force in 1994 to look at issues surrounding mathematically talented students and to make recommendations regarding identification and programming. The definition of the task force talks about mathematical promise as comprised of ability, motivation, belief, and experience or opportunity. The task force emphasized that students who are mathematically promising have a wide range of abilities and a whole continuum of needs based on those abilities.

Characteristics

As noted above, there are different types of mathematical talent. Some students are abstract thinkers. They tend to be very strong algebraically in looking for patterns and making generalizations. Others have talents that are more spatial and can visualize problems pictorially. They can move objects around in their mind to view them from different angles and positions. Still others have a combination of both skills. Speed in doing problems, computational facility, and ease of memorizing number facts and formulas are often associated with mathematical talent. In fact, sometimes these are the criteria by which students are identified as having talent. However, researchers have found these characteristics are not a requirement for someone to have mathematical talent. Talented students may possess some or all of these characteristics, but they are not evident in all talented students.

Rather, characteristics that define mathematical talent are more related to posing and solving complex mathematical problems. These characteristics include eagerness to solve challenging math problems, using creative and unusual ways to solve math problems, persistence in problem solving, looking at the world from a mathematical perspective, switching strategies easily when solving problems, solving problems abstractly without the need for concrete materials, organizing data and information to discover mathematical patterns, and enjoying challenging math puzzles and logic problems. This is not an exhaustive list of characteristics nor does every student with mathematical talent display all of these characteristics. However, students who are curious about mathematics and have a talent for solving interesting, complex problems and creating new problems are students who deserve special nurturing in the area of mathematics.

Identification

Because mathematical talent is varied and displayed in different ways and at different times, identification needs to include a variety of measures. It should be a process that is flexible and ongoing. This is especially true in identifying students who lack mathematical experiences, yet have talent potential. Because standardized tests such as IQ tests and achievement tests have statistical backing, they are often used to identify students for programming. However, these tests usually concentrate on low-level tasks that do not require the unique problem-solving skills of talented students. Students with language differences and other learning differences are often missed as well. NCTM cautions against using these tests as the *sole* means of identification. If using standardized tests that are not specifically designed for talented students, out-of-level testing should be used to prevent a ceiling effect. This technique, pioneered at Johns Hopkins University by Julian Stanley and studied through the present by Camilla Benbow and David Lubinski's Study of Mathematically Precocious Youth (SMPY), has been found to identify even the most extraordinarily gifted students.

Rating scales that ask teachers to comment on student behaviors can also help with the identification process. Research-based scales rather than teacher-invented checklists are more valid and reliable. These scales often help teachers look at students from a different perspective, focusing on creative and critical thinking rather than computational speed and accuracy. Performance-based tasks in which students are involved in problem solving can provide additional insight. Teacher observation during tasks and/or student written work can provide new information about student thinking. Student grades, interviews, and parent- and self-nomination are other ways to uncover mathematical talent. In conclusion, researchers and NCTM recommend using multiple measures of identification to ensure a more inclusive talent pool of students.

It is also important to recognize that students who are talented in mathematics may not be talented in other areas and vice versa. Gardner's *theory of multiple intelligences* speaks to this. When part of the brain is damaged, as in people who experience strokes, people may lose their mathematical abilities but still speak, and some people who lose their linguistic abilities are still able to do mathematics. It is possible, according to this theory, for students to have mathematical giftedness in relative isolation from other abilities. This has implications for gifted mathematics education. Some teachers have been surprised to learn that a student who has reading and writing difficulties may have very strong mathematical reasoning ability.

Programming

The primary goal in determining programming is finding an optimal match between student ability and curriculum instruction. Options include acceleration, enrichment activities, and a combination of both. Within these options there are a variety of instructional approaches such as pull-out programs, ability grouping, cluster grouping, curriculum compacting, differentiation, special programs and schools for mathematically talented students, and individual mentoring. Selecting the appropriate curriculum is critical. Because of the linear nature of mathematics, Stanley and his colleagues have argued that mathematics is the best candidate for an accelerated curriculum, and results of accelerated instruction for mathematically talented students have produced impressive gains in achievement in short periods of time. Whether enrichment, differentiation, or acceleration is used, it must be a rigorous curriculum that is able to challenge and engage students. A good goal to keep in mind is a very simple one: Every student should learn something new and meaningful in mathematics every day.

M. Katherine Gavin

See also Mathematical Creativity; Mathematical Intelligence; Mathematically Precocious; Talented Girls, Mathematics

Further Readings

Assouline, S., & Lupkowski-Shoplik, A. (2005). *Developing math talent: A guide for educating gifted and advanced learners in math.* Waco, TX: Prufrock Press.

Gardner, H. (1983). *Frames of mind: The theory of multiple intelligences.* New York: Basic Books.

Gavin, M. K. (2005). Are we missing anyone? Identifying mathematically promising students. *Gifted Education Communicator, 36*(3 & 4), 24–29.

Sheffield, L. J. (Ed.). (1999). *Developing mathematically promising students.* Reston, VA: National Council of Teachers of Mathematics.

MATHEMATICS, CURRICULUM

Mathematics curriculum has been the center of continued debate in the public arena since the launch of *Sputnik* more than 50 years ago. There is ongoing controversy about what mathematics content should be included in the school curricula, as evidenced in the so-called Math Wars (in the United States) and similar differences of curricular opinion elsewhere. There are major differences in the mathematical abilities between the mathematically gifted and talented students and their age-mates, and these differences can be addressed both in the mixed ability and exclusive ability classroom via the use of appropriate programming techniques such as curriculum acceleration, compacting, and differentiating. In certain instances, radical acceleration offers the best intellectual opportunities for the profoundly gifted students. The curriculum at the secondary level is typically enriched with Honors and/or Advanced Placement (AP) courses. However, many believe this one-size-fits-all approach leaves much to be desired in terms of meeting the needs of mathematically gifted students with cognitive and affective traits different from the general group.

Curriculum Terms and Techniques

Some terms used within the existing research literature on curriculum relevant for this entry are (1) contest problem training, (2) curriculum compacting, (3) curriculum differentiation, (4) heterogeneous and/or homogeneous grouping, (5) radical acceleration, and (6) summer programs.

1. *Contest problem training* is used to refer to specific mathematical techniques from the areas of algebra, analysis, combinatorics, geometry, number theory, and so on, which are useful to solve a wide variety of contest problems.

2. *Curriculum compacting* simply means eliminating previously mastered work (typically involving routine computations and procedures) to condense the regular curriculum for gifted learners.

3. *Curriculum differentiation,* as defined by various theorists, means tailoring the curriculum to meet the specific needs of learners of varied abilities. Although this term was initially used to refer to the varied needs of gifted learners, it has mutated into meaning tailoring the curriculum and the classroom environment to create different learning experiences for all students.

4. *Homogeneous grouping* refers to the grouping of learners at the same ability level; whereas *heterogeneous grouping* allows for learners of mixed ability levels to work together on ongoing class activities, projects, and the like. Sometimes the term *exclusive grouping* is used to refer to homogeneous or same-ability grouping.

5. *Radical acceleration* refers to the practice of grade skipping and early university entrance for profoundly gifted learners. These learners typically have IQs over 180.

6. *Summer programs* are typically 1- to 4-week courses held on university campuses in which mathematically gifted students are exposed to new topics in mathematics as well as mathematics' far-reaching applicability and relevance to the everyday world.

Given the differences in mathematical abilities between mathematically gifted students and their peers, curriculum compacting, differentiation, and acceleration can be applied effectively to the mathematics curriculum to meet the needs of mathematically gifted students. Numerous studies have shown that acceleration is perhaps the most effective way of meeting gifted student programming needs. Mathematics, unlike any other discipline, lends itself to acceleration because of the sequential developmental nature of many elementary concepts. The very nature of acceleration suggests that the principles of curriculum compacting are applied to trim out the excessive amount of repetitive tasks. Differentiation occurs naturally because acceleration allows gifted students with the opportunity to get through the "typical" traditional high school curriculum of geometry–algebra2–precalculus–calculus much faster than the norm of 4 years.

Julian Stanley's landmark Study of Mathematically Precocious Youth (SMPY) and the more than 250 papers produced in its wake provide excellent empirical support for the effectiveness of curriculum acceleration and compaction in mathematics. This study, started by Julian Stanley at Johns Hopkins University in 1971, generated a vast amount of empirical data gathered over the past 30 years, and has resulted in many findings about the types of curricular (acceleration, compacting, etc.) and affective interventions that foster the pursuit of advanced coursework in mathematics. Simply put, the purpose of curricular modifications such as acceleration, compacting, and differentiation for mathematically gifted students is to tailor materials that introduce new topics at a faster pace that allows for high-level thinking and independence reminiscent of research in the field of mathematics.

Besides in-school modifications, many schools offer students opportunities to participate in math clubs and math contests. Many countries have national contests that allow the most talented students to progress to international math contests. The International Math Olympiads (IMO), where teams of students from different countries work together to solve challenging math problems, are the contests in which the brightest math students in the world have an opportunity to display their talents. Local contests require the expert use of high school mathematics; at national and international levels, however, students are expected to master undergraduate level algebraic, analytic, combinatorial, graph theoretic, number theoretic, and geometric principles. The rationale for the increasing use of discrete mathematics in contest problems is that discrete mathematics, unlike continuous mathematics, is accessible to students, starting at the elementary levels, because it builds from simple enumerative techniques. In an often-quoted survey article in the literature, arguments for the inclusion of combinatorial mathematics in the school curriculum are based on the following reasons: (a) its independence from calculus; (b) its usefulness to teach concepts of enumeration, making conjectures and generalizations; (c) numerous applications to the physical, natural, and computing sciences, probability, number theory, and topology; (d) the opportunities created for using computing tools, but also illustrating the limitations of such tools. Last but not least, discrete mathematics and their applications illustrate recent developments in mathematics, thereby allowing students to develop a feeling for how mathematics grows. A synthesis of the body of studies on combinatorial thinking and discrete mathematics in general supports the successful use of such problems within the mathematics curriculum, with significant benefits for the abstraction and generalization capabilities of mathematically gifted students.

Integrated Curricula

In fact, *all* of the NSF-funded reform-based mathematics curriculum projects in the 1990s that resulted in the writing of integrated mathematics curricula include a heavy dose of discrete mathematics. High school curricula such as the Core Plus Mathematics Project (CPMP) developed at Western Michigan University and the Systemic Initiative for Montana Mathematics and Science (SIMMS) developed at the University of Montana are based on the premise of situating mathematics in authentic real-world contexts that require the modeling of a given situation, which in turn motivates or creates the need for the use of mathematical techniques and concepts. Unlike the traditional high school curricula with calculus at its pinnacle, these two authentic integrated mathematics curricula introduce students to discrete mathematics, combinatorics, transformational geometry, matrix algebra, statistics, modeling techniques, and informatics.

Secondary mathematics is usually the gateway to an exposure to both breadth and depth of mathematical topics. However, most traditional mathematics curricula are still anchored in the traditional treatment of mathematics, as opposed to an interdisciplinary and modeling based approach of mathematics used in the real world. Barbara Kerr points out that high school mathematics also serves as the gatekeeper for many areas of advanced study, and the traditional treatment of mathematics with little or no emphasis on modeling based activities that require team work and communication have historically discouraged gifted girls from pursuing 4 years of high school mathematics. This deficit is difficult to remediate at the undergraduate level and results in the effect of low numbers of students capable of graduate-level work in emerging interdisciplinary fields. This suggests curricular initiatives that involve the study of the modeling of complex systems that occur in real-life situations from the very early grades.

Advanced Placement and the International Baccalaureate Program

AP mathematics courses were never explicitly designated as courses for mathematically gifted students, with adequate programming considerations for the needs of gifted students. Instead they were historically meant to be college courses offered at the high school level available to seniors motivated to take such courses. The International Baccalaureate Program (IBP), on the other hand, was specifically designed as a pre-university preparatory program for academically gifted students; it includes six areas of study (including mathematics), a capstone course on epistemology, and a senior thesis (essay). As previously stated, AP courses have unfortunately become a convenient one-size-fits-all approach to meeting the needs of mathematically gifted students without any attention to research on programming techniques for these students. The same is unfortunately true for IBPs. There is a lack of research on the long-term effectiveness of AP/IBPs for the curricular needs of mathematically gifted students. The National Research Council report of 2002 assessed the effectiveness of AP/IBPs currently in place in the United States and found the following: (a) Conceptual understanding is often not emphasized; (b) Collaborative projects are not emphasized; (c) There were contextual shortcomings; and (d) There were questions surrounding the validity of assessment instruments.

Changing Nature of Mathematics

The literature also shows that the nature of mathematics itself has changed over time. The experiential world of the 21st-century student and teacher is characterized by complex systems such as the Internet, various multimedia, sophisticated computing tools, global markets, virtual realities, access to online educational environments, and more, and emerging fields such as bioinformatics and mathematical genetics, cryptography, mathematical biology, and others that call for different mathematical skills such as the ability to model complex systems and problem solving. Authentic integrated mathematics curricula such as those reported in this entry offer all students opportunities to experience the relevance and applicability of mathematics to the world around them. Contests offer the more able students opportunities to learn and apply mathematical principles to both pure and applied math problems and create a sound foundational base for advanced coursework in mathematics at the university level. The free availability of resources and access to researchers via the Internet offers a multitude of possibilities for the classroom practitioner both to enrich and to adapt traditional mathematics curricula to make them relevant for today's world. It is hoped that practitioners, with the help of researchers, can effectively transform the extant research into effective classroom and curricular practice, with students ultimately benefiting from such a symbiosis.

Future Research

One of the underaddressed areas of gifted and talented education is empirical studies that examine the effectiveness of reform-based mathematics curricula, particularly with mathematically gifted students. Although numerous claims are made for the benefits of modeling-based mathematics curricula for increasing achievement, there is scant empirical evidence presented on the changes of achievement levels of mathematically gifted students. Another fruitful area of research would be to follow the career trajectories of mathematically gifted students through college and qualitatively investigate the impact of mathematics school curricula on their choices of and success in majors involving a heavy use of mathematics.

Bharath Sriraman

See also Mathematical Creativity; Mathematical Intelligence; Mathematically Precocious; Mathematical Talent

Further Readings

Benbow, C. P., Lubinski, D., & Sushy, B. (1996). The impact of SMPY's educational programs from the perspective of the participant. In C. P. Benbow & D. Lubinski (Eds.), *Intellectual talent* (pp. 266–300). Baltimore: Johns Hopkins University Press.

Kerr, B. A. (1997). Developing talents in girls and young women. In N. Colangelo & G. A. Davis (Eds.), *Handbook of gifted education* (2nd ed., pp. 483–497). Boston: Allyn & Bacon.

Lesh, R., & Sriraman, B. (2005). John Dewey revisited—Pragmatism and the models-modeling perspective on mathematical learning. In A. Beckmann, C. Michelsen, & B. Sriraman (Eds.), *Proceedings of the 1st International Symposium on Mathematics and Its Connections to the Arts and Sciences* (pp. 32–51). Berlin: Franzbecker Verlag.

Sriraman, B. (2002). How do mathematically gifted students abstract and generalize mathematical concepts. *NAGC 2002 Research Briefs, 16,* 83–87.

Sriraman, B. (2005). Are mathematical giftedness and mathematical creativity synonyms? A theoretical analysis of constructs. *Journal of Secondary Gifted Education, 17*(1), 20–36.

Sriraman, B., & Dahl, B. (2008). On bringing interdisciplinary ideas to gifted education. In L. V. Shavinina (Ed.), *The international handbook on giftedness.* London: Springer.

Sriraman, B., & Steinthorsdottir, O. (2007). Secondary mathematics. In J. Plucker & C. Callahan (Eds.), *Critical issues and practices in gifted education: What the research says* (pp. 355–367). Waco, TX: Prufrock Press.

Meaning of Life

What is the meaning of life? This question has been asked by billions of people for thousands of years. The question is usually first asked by individuals during their teenage years. Because of their advanced knowledge and intense curiosity, gifted individuals may begin to ask these questions as children. The question tends to resurface at many times—often during times of crisis and often around the issue of death.

People are interested in the meaning of life, in part, because human beings are aware of their mortality and the shortness of life. Many people care whether their lives matter beyond their small circles of life and after their deaths. These feelings prompt individuals to seek a transcendent meaning for their lives. Religion and psychotherapy offer two different approaches for finding meaning. Generally, religion offers guidance through scripture and the reliance on faith, whereas psychotherapy encourages individuals to ask themselves the difficult questions and to seek truths about what matters most to them. Meanwhile, social scientists continue to employ the scientific method in order to develop more precise conceptual frameworks and to learn more about processes, correlates, and outcomes of the search for the meaning of life.

In this discussion is an overview of the speculations about the meaning of life from the various spheres of inquiry. First, the entry discusses a view from the religious sphere, then from the secular spheres of philosophy and psychotherapy. Finally, the entry summarizes how the scientific method has been used to study the topic and what has been learned thus far and the implications for gifted and creative students.

A Religious View

Irving Yalom distinguished between the "cosmic" and "terrestrial" meaning of life. Cosmic meaning refers to the existence of a grand design or an all-encompassing interconnectedness of life. Cosmic meaning usually implies the existence of God and spirituality. Terrestrial meaning refers to whatever is deemed by an individual to be meaningful in his or her life. Religions tend to embrace the cosmic view. Judeo-Christian doctrine, for example, teaches that God has a plan for humanity but that humans are incapable of understanding the complexity of the plan. As such, the ultimate meaning of life remains an incomprehensible mystery to humans. Religious doctrine offers guidance for how to live and prescribes faith in God's will in response to perplexing and troubling questions like: Why does God allow humans to suffer and allow horrific injustices to occur?

Views From Philosophy and Psychotherapy

Secular scholars and philosophers formulate their views of the meaning of life from their personal observations of life and subsequent contemplation. Ever since the European Enlightenment, some of the greatest minds have thoughtfully considered the question and then categorically rejected the idea of a cosmic meaning. As an atheist, Sigmund Freud viewed faith and trust in God as a sort of regression in which people childishly cling to a wish for a supreme parent in God. Arthur Schopenhauer, generally considered the most pessimistic of philosophers, not only argued that life was meaningless, but extolled the act of suicide and cursed romantic love because it was responsible for the continuance of "the pitiful human race."

Albert Camus, the French existentialist, put forth a perspective on the meaning of life in his retelling of "The Myth of Sisyphus." The myth describes a man who is condemned in Hades to roll a boulder up a hill repeatedly, only to see it roll down again. Camus suggested that our efforts in life may be similarly futile and meaningless. And yet, in Camus's version of the myth, Sisyphus has a joyful demeanor, suggesting that he has found meaning in his task by maintaining an inner dignity and defiance.

In the field of psychotherapy, Viktor Frankl has had a considerable impact in regard to the topic of the meaning of life. Inspired by his experience in a concentration camp during the Second World War, he concluded that even in the most dire circumstances, individuals are free to choose and are responsible for their choices. For him, the meaning of life can be found in one's actions in and appreciations of the world and, if those possibilities are unavailable in the circumstances, in the free acceptance of one's fate. Frankl created a therapy called *logotherapy,* the focus of which is to facilitate one's search for meaning in life.

Empirical Research

Only recently has the scientific method been applied to the topic of the meaning of life. Researchers do not directly ask what the cosmic meaning of life may be, because that is not an empirical question. Rather they ask questions such as, Is the search for meaning a universal characteristic of human beings? What do individuals believe regarding the meaning of life and how are those beliefs related to other psychological variables? The theoretical underpinnings of most of this research include existentialism, constructivism, and phenomenology. Both qualitative and quantitative methodologies are used. Among some of the major findings are the following: The need for meaning seems to be virtually universal, and many people struggle with the specter of meaninglessness in their lives. Meaninglessness is associated with psychological symptoms like low self-esteem, substance abuse, and depression. Individuals most often find meaning in love, work, self-actualization, service to others, and in God or spirituality.

Implications for Gifted and Creative Students

Because gifted students are often advanced in reading abilities, they may grapple with meaning of life issues at an earlier age. Teachers and counselors of gifted students need to be prepared to discuss these issues in developmentally appropriate ways. In addition, the research on meaning of life shows that meaning does not simply arise out of one aspect of life, but from many paths, and guidance must include exploration ranging from relationships, work, existential and spiritual issues, and service to others and the world. In addition, creative students, being more open to experience, may investigate meaning of life from unorthodox sources, from far-ranging literature such as science fiction to unusual psychological and social experiences, such as altered states of consciousness and experimental social and religious groups. Although these attempts to find meaning may be disturbing to parents and community, mentors of gifted students need to be prepared to discuss and provide wise guidance to the young person in search of his or her truth.

Richard T. Kinnier, Tyler M. Barratt, and Sarah K. Dixon

See also Life Satisfaction; Optimal Development; Spiritual Intelligence; Spirituality

Further Readings

Camus, A. (1955). *The myth of Sisyphus.* New York: Knopf.

Durant, W. (1932). *On the meaning of life.* New York: Ray Long & Richard R. Smith.

Frankl, V. (2000). *Man's ultimate search for meaning* (4th ed.). Cambridge, MA: Perseus Press.

Kinnier, R. T., Kernes, J. L., Tribbensee, N., & VanPuymbroeck, T. (2006). *The meaning of life according to the great and the good.* Bath, UK: Palazzo Editions.

Men, Gifted

Although research studies of gifted boys are limited in number, studies of gifted men are even more scarce. Since the 1920s, when Lewis Terman sought to change the lens through which society viewed giftedness, few researchers have examined the life experiences of gifted males beyond their secondary school and collegiate years. This group deserves greater attention in order to better understand the intellectual and emotional needs of this population. A review of literature uncovered only two recent studies, described below.

A 2001 study examined the adult experiences of 13 men who were enrolled in a gifted program in the early 1960s. They were selected for the program in the fourth grade because their scores on a variety of instruments indicated very high academic potential. At the time of the study, the men were approaching 50 years old. Among the 13 interviewed were four businessmen, two accountants, two engineers, one freelance archaeological consultant, two lawyers, one physician, and one social activist. Following a structured interview protocol, the researchers conducted telephone interviews lasting approximately one hour. The interviews incorporated questions about childhood, adolescence, marital and family life, career history, and life satisfaction.

The participants reported feeling socially isolated from their peers as young children. This social isolation, combined with guilt resulting from the preferential treatment they received as gifted students in an exclusive program, contributed to a strong desire to act and be viewed by others as normal. They struggled with whether to accept the label of giftedness and appear "intellectual" or reject it in order to prove they were "just one of the guys." Many of the men had a strong need to fulfill the expectations of parents and teachers; they intuitively understood parental expectations and in an effort to gain their parents' approval, used their gifts and talents to meet or exceed those expectations. The researchers found that although these men grew up in the context of rebellion and the social movement of the 1960s and 1970s, they did not see this significant social upheaval as relevant to their lives. Instead, they conducted themselves in accordance with the more traditional cultural expectations and tried to fulfill the expectations of the adults in their lives.

The participants who had skipped a grade during their schooling highlighted how intellectual differences from their age-mates often led to social difficulties. At the same time, age differences with their older classmates often led to embarrassment or social awkwardness, and they were left to figure out for themselves how to mange social relationships appropriately. These men were ambivalent about their giftedness and determined to preserve a masculine identity. The most critical concern about masculinity revolved around difficulties with emotional expressivity and relationships with women. Several of them believed that their quiet stoicism had removed them emotionally from the women they cared for the most.

Despite their preparation for leadership, the outstanding education these men received as boys, and the high expectations of their teachers and parents, these men were not at all concerned about achieving eminence. They focused on pursuing contentment rather than high achievement or recognition. Furthermore, the researchers maintained that these men lacked a sense of vocation or calling. Multipotentiality and professional disappointments led to indecision and career compromise for the gifted men, while passion for their work or a sense of vocation seemed largely lacking.

The life stories of these men were characterized by one of two significant relationship patterns. Four of the men married their first serious partner and enjoyed long-term stable marriages. The others appeared to have troubled relationships with women, with more than half having divorced at least once. Acknowledging their marital failures as their greatest, and sometimes only, failure, most of the men attributed their marital problems to their difficulty with emotional expression.

The researchers noted that these men lived according to the values and standards of their communities. They were all hard-working providers who expressed satisfaction with the financial security they had acquired, and even greater happiness if their profession provided an intellectually stimulating environment. They appeared to be successful, yet few found the courage to pursue their dreams and several spoke of unfulfilled dreams of service or creative work. Many hoped to make greater social contributions later in their careers or in retirement.

A second study examined paternal influences on prominent, gifted American men. A team of researchers conducted a comprehensive analysis of biographical materials to identify factors in the father–son relationships that influenced talent development in high-achieving gifted males. The 10 subjects included in the study represented the baby boom generation and included prominent gifted men from a variety of talent domains.

Each participant benefited from a father–son relationship characterized by his father's unconditional belief in him. The strong encouragement and helpful guidance these fathers provided throughout their sons' lives were evident in a variety of ways. Several of the fathers were attentive listeners, while others offered helpful advice. Some fathers taught their sons skills necessary to achieve within their chosen profession, while others contributed to their sons' success through coaching or other forms of support.

The researchers found that these fathers maintained high expectations for their sons but did not pressure them to follow a particular path in life. They did not insist that their sons follow in their footsteps, nor did they impose any particular goals or aspirations. Rather, they simply expected their sons to strive always to do their best in whatever domain they chose. These high expectations, which included doing well in school, were conveyed to their sons throughout childhood and adolescence and were reinforced during their early career years.

These fathers were industrious men with a strong work ethic. Though several were not well educated, all worked very hard to provide for their families, instilling in their sons their philosophical view of hard work. This strong belief in the value of hard work provided a model of inspiration for their sons.

The researchers also found evidence that these men expressed pride in their sons' accomplishments, which naturally encouraged their sons to continue their pattern of achievement. Though the fathers took great pride in their sons' achievements, both fathers and sons held each other in high esteem and respected each other as men. These fathers appreciated and respected their sons for becoming the industrious, high-achieving men they were. The sons, in turn, expressed admiration for their fathers' approach to life in general: their resilience, their dedication to their families, and the ways in which they supported their children's development. These gifted men looked to their fathers as models of success, followed their example, and listened to their encouragement and advice.

Thomas P. Hébert

See also Boys, Gifted; Eminence; Sex Differences in Creativity

Further Readings

Hébert, T. P., Pagnani, A. R., & Hammond, D. R. (in press). Paternal influence on high achieving gifted males. *Journal for the Education of the Gifted.*

Kerr, B. A., & Cohn, S. J. (2001). *Smart boys: Talent, manhood, and the search for meaning.* Scottsdale, AZ: Great Potential Press.

Mensa

Mensa International is an organization whose published goals are "to identify and foster human intelligence for the benefit of humanity, to encourage research in the nature, characteristics and uses of intelligence, and to promote intellectual and social opportunities for its members." Founded in England in 1946 by attorney Roland Berrill and scientist Lance Ware, the name Mensa, from the Latin meaning "mind, table, or month," was chosen to suggest the regular meeting of great minds to discuss topics of interest around a table. Mensa invites membership from individuals worldwide, children, youth, and adults alike, who have been identified as possessing superior intellectual ability.

Mensa members come from a diverse group of people who have intense, varied interests and like to voice their opinion. They generally range between 20 and 60 years of age, and in education from high school dropouts to those holding multiple graduate degrees. Some are on welfare and others have acquired great wealth. Their occupations vary from professionals, educators, scientists, computer programmers, artists, musicians, athletes, clergy, police officers, firefighters, and members of the armed forces, to homemakers, farmers, clerks, laborers, truck drivers, and entrepreneurs. Some are well-known, award-winning personalities, many are ordinary citizens who lead interesting private lives. To become a Mensan, the only qualification is to formally report a score at the 98th percentile (meaning a score that is greater than or equal to that achieved by 98 percent of the general population taking the test) on an approved intelligence test that has been administered and supervised by a qualified examiner. High intellectual ability should not be equated with "genius," an elusive category that most researchers agree cannot be defined solely through psychological testing.

The benefits of membership include opportunities to participate in discussion groups, social events, and annual meetings, and to subscribe to several publications. International Mensa offers more than 200 Special Interest Groups (SIG) to address passions in popular fields such as economics, astronomy, biochemistry, criminology, or space science. But there are also groups interested in chess, poker, scuba diving, UFOs, and witchcraft. Sports include the classics and others such as ballooning, skydiving, motorcycling, and skeet shooting. And members are free to start a SIG of their choice. Mensa chapters organize local and regional workshops and special events, publish national newsletters and magazines, and conduct annual conferences that feature notable international speakers.

American Mensa was founded in 1960 by Peter and Ines Sturgeon. As of March 2007, it serves 54,000 members at 134 local chapters throughout the nation, the District of Columbia, and all the U.S. protectorates; its national office is in Arlington, Texas. The largest chapters are in greater New York and Chicago. About 41 percent of its members are between ages 44 and 61, but many new members are under 18. American SIGs include popular fields such as philosophy, astronomy, computers and sci-fi movies, arts and crafts, games and sports like chess, golf, motorcycling, and scuba diving, and special groups for teens and military members and veterans. More than half its members have a college degree, and many speak at least two languages besides English. Local chapters are recognized for community service efforts to raise money for scholarships and charitable causes, and for educational activities such as judging and granting awards at science fairs.

Persons interested in applying for membership have several options. They may take any of 200+ approved standardized aptitude tests administered and supervised by a certified examiner, or they may apply to take the standard Mensa Admission or Culture Fair test batteries. To qualify, scores must be at the 98th percentile. A previous test score administered by a school or private psychologist or agency can also be used if prepared according to Mensa guidelines. American Mensa offers a sample mini quiz online with answers and scoring directions for individuals who wish to practice their reasoning skills.

The Mensa Education & Research Foundation (MERF) was established to promote Mensa's mission: the nurturing of human intelligence, the world's most important resource. MERF is a philanthropic, nonprofit organization, governed by a volunteer Board of Trustees and the American Mensa Executive Committee. As noted in its annual report, the foundation sponsors several major activities with assets that exceeded $2 million in 2006. An annual *Colloquium* examines contemporary issues and new directions with international authorities. The *Mensa Research Journal* publishes scholarly articles that expand learning, research, and intelligence. Subscription is open to the general public. *Mensa for Kids* is a Web site that provides challenging activities for children and youth, as well as resources for parents and teachers of the gifted.

The foundation also grants awards and scholarships. MERF recognizes individual creativity, exceptional teaching, excellence in writing and research, and lifetime achievement. Scholarships for students are based totally on written essays. Grades, academic programs, or financial need are not considered.

Rosina M. Gallagher

See also Genius; Intelligence; Intelligence Testing

Further Readings

American Mensa Web Site: http://www.mensa.org; email address, info@americanmensa.org

Mensa CultureQuest®-ion of the Day: http://www.us.mensa.org/culturequestion

Mensa for Kids Web Site: http://www.mensaforkids.org

Mensa International Web Site: http://www.mensa.org

Mentoring Gifted and Talented Individuals

Eminent individuals tend to attribute their success to expert mentoring. For example, 48 of the 92 American Nobel Laureates cited previous Nobel Laureates as their mentors. A distinguishing feature of a mentoring relationship as compared to a teacher–student relationship is the expectation that the relationship will extend beyond specific learning goals or courses. For example, expert mentors not only share content and skills with their mentees, but also provide tacit or insider knowledge about finding a professional niche, making connections, and enhancing both creative potential and self-confidence.

Mentor–Student Matching

Although talented students and their families may choose mentors based on a mentor's ability to set challenging standards and high expectations, they must also keep in mind that effective mentoring relationships can involve emotional bonds between students and their mentors. Mentors may have to guide their mentees through setbacks and discouragement, and like most significant human relations, mentor–mentee relationships may involve conflicts and compromises. Healthy bonds are more likely to develop when mentors and mentees share similar attitudes, values, and lifestyles.

Role Models

Effective mentorships look different at different stages in the talent development process. In the more advanced stages mentors generally serve as role models, leading as much by example as by instruction. Interviews with young scientists (who became future laureates) indicated that higher standards put forth by their mentors were internalized through (a) the mentors' own exemplary behavior and work, thus providing a model to be emulated; (b) the insistence that high standards be met by the mentees; and (c) the mentors' critical evaluation of their mentee's work.

Socialization of Mentors' Students

Mentors provide their mentees with the knowledge needed to actively engage in and excel in the chosen domain, demonstrating how to deal gracefully with both success and failure. In essence, mentors prepare protégées for a position at the top of their field. Mentees not only further their exploration and interest in a field, but also learn about the lifestyles, values, roles, and activities associated with the elite experts in their specific careers. They also learn the criteria for determining a good research or artistic question, and the appropriate times and ways in which to take creative risks. Thus, through the mentor's behavior, the student learns how to develop a reputation in his or her field as an elite professional. A mentee benefits from his or her relationship with the mentor not just by acquiring specific knowledge but also by learning work methodologies and styles of thought.

In order to socialize their students into a domain or field, mentors may also suggest that their mentees have a variety of experiences outside of formal instruction. For example, participation in competitions can serve as a stimulus for further interest and exploration of the field as well as introducing mentees to other interested young people who can provide peer stimulation. In addition, having a leading expert in the field as a mentor helps the mentee gain individual recognition in the field.

Mentoring Across Stages of Talent Development

At each stage of the talent development process, the goals of mentoring are different, the relationship is more or less intense, and the method by which mentors are selected changes. The process can be described in a number of ways. In terms of content and skills, mentors develop their mentees' abilities into competencies. These competencies are then transformed into expertise through a series of challenges involving high-level knowledge and skills. Through this experience, mentors encourage seizing rather than dreading difficult challenges, such as overcoming disenchantment and failure.

The relationship between the mentee and the mentor grows and develops through many different stages: (a) introduction—the recognition of exceptional talent in a mentee; (b) initiation—whereupon both mentee and mentor build a trustful relationship; (c) cultivation—sharing professional skills, setting performance and behavior standards, and encouraging risk taking; (d) separation—when mentors urge their mentees to explore their own unique direction; and (e) redefinition—the establishment of an increasingly collegial and equal-status relationship.

The initial mentors of young, talented students should serve as guides and sources of encouragement, making the exploration of the field playful and engaging. Once the talented individual is committed to the field, mentors (often different from the initial mentor) need to target the skills, knowledge, and attitudes to be mastered by the mentee. Once the talented individual has developed sufficient expertise in a domain, mentors are less likely to be selected by the mentee himself or herself. Instead, at this third stage, the protégée is sought out by mentors seeking a particular type of protégée who can help express and implement the mentor's ideas. Thus, a gifted individual may have different mentors, each mentor possessing distinctive resources that can meet the cognitive, psychosocial, and instructional needs of the mentee at different stages of talent development.

Rena F. Subotnik and Maya M. Bassford

See also Aspiration Development and Self-Fulfillment; Eminence; Guidance

Further Readings

Bloom, B. S. (1985). *Developing talent in young people.* New York: Ballantine Books.

Subotnik, R., & Jarvin, L. (2005). Beyond expertise: Conceptions of giftedness as great performance. In R. J. Sternberg & J. E. Davidson (Eds.), *Conceptions of giftedness* (pp. 343–357). New York: Cambridge University Press.

Zorman, R. (1993). Mentoring and role modeling programs for the gifted. In K. A. Heller, F. J. Mönks, & A. H. Passow (Eds.), *International handbook of research and development of giftedness and talent* (pp. 727–741). New York: Pergamon.

Zuckerman, H. (1996). *Scientific elite.* New Brunswick, NJ: Transaction Publishers.

Meta-Analyses of Gifted Education

Meta-analysis is a quantitative method of summarizing research results on a given topic. General steps in a meta-analysis include stipulating methodological criteria that studies must meet to be included; using replicable criteria to locate as many qualifying studies of the topic as possible; and quantifying the results of the studies, using a common metric so that the direction and magnitude of findings across studies can be statistically determined. This metric is an *effect size,* which expresses differences between groups in standard deviation units. The range of possible values is approximately +3.00 to –3.00. Commonly used guidelines indicate that effect sizes are negligible below 0.2, small from 0.2 to 0.5, medium from 0.5 to 0.8, and large at or above 0.8. Meta-analyses have been used in an effort to better understand various approaches to educating gifted students, including ability grouping, acceleration, and cooperative learning. By far the most common focus of meta-analytic research has been ability grouping.

Ability Grouping

The practice of ability grouping, in which students are placed in learning groups with others of similar aptitude, has generated extensive controversy in the field of education. Arguments in favor of the practice include statements that such grouping helps teachers more effectively meet students' needs by narrowing the focus necessary in delivering material, and that it helps facilitate curricular modifications appropriate to the type of student being taught. Arguments against the practice include concerns that grouping reduces the performance of students in lower-ability groups by reducing the expectations their teachers have of them, that it discriminates against minority students by disproportionately placing them in lower-ability groups, and that it promotes inequity through unfair allocation of resources (e.g., assigning the best teachers to the highest-ability groups).

Part of the reason why controversy persists is that research results vary across studies. Meta-analyses have been used in an attempt to zero in on well-designed studies and then quantify their results to seek a scientific answer to questions about ability grouping. Typically, these meta-analyses focus on studies that measure outcomes using scores on standardized achievement tests. Some also include studies of social and emotional outcomes, such as general self-concept or self-esteem, attitudes toward the specific subject matter taught, or attitudes toward school in general. Unfortunately, even the results of meta-analyses have been controversial, with some authors concluding that ability grouping is ill advised, and others concluding that it is a well-supported educational strategy.

To some extent, differences in conclusions are related to differences in the criteria used to qualify studies for inclusion in a meta-analysis. For instance, some researchers prioritize or even restrict studies to those that use random assignment of students to grouped versus ungrouped classes. Random assignment of participants to research conditions is a basic requirement of experimental design, and is a key element in allowing conclusions about cause and effect. For some types of ability grouping, however, random assignment does not accurately reflect the way in which students are selected for participation in groups. For example, some meta-analyses include studies of accelerative groups for gifted learners. In practice, students selected for acceleration are identified by more than just their ability level. Factors such as personality style, motivation, friendship patterns, and age (to name just a few) often are considered as well. Therefore, randomly assigning high-ability students to accelerated versus unaccelerated classes for the purpose of research may not reflect the reality of the practice as it is used in school settings.

In some meta-analyses, findings favoring grouping are discounted if the conditions using grouping also modify the curriculum for the various groups. The logic is that research must isolate the practice of grouping from other potential influences on student learning to truly study the effectiveness of grouping itself. Again, this criticism is based on basic research principles. When more than one factor varies at the same time, a *confound* is created. Confounds obscure the results of research because outcomes cannot be attributed clearly to any one factor. In the case of ability grouping, however, one of the key arguments supporting the practice rests on its facilitation of curricular modifications that better meet the needs of students at particular ability levels.

Despite the points of contention described above, a review of some of the key meta-analyses of ability grouping yields several common conclusions.

Ability Grouping Is More Effective Than Tracking

Although some authors have used the terms *ability grouping* and *tracking* synonymously, their meanings are different. Tracking typically involves assignment of students to one group for all academic subjects, based on a measure of general ability, such as IQ. In contrast, ability grouping often is implemented for one academic subject at a time, using performance in that subject area to determine placement. In some cases, ability grouping also facilitates student movement among groups to a greater extent than does tracking, which tends to involve long-term student placement. Meta-analytic studies have indicated that tracking has little to no effect on academic performance, but ability grouping has been associated with increased academic performance.

Curriculum Modification Is Necessary to Effective Ability Grouping

In some cases, students are grouped according to ability but all groups are presented with the same curriculum. In other cases, the curriculum is adjusted to suit the ability level of the students being taught. Meta-analyses that consider this aspect of grouping practices indicate that the effectiveness of ability grouping corresponds to the extent to which the curriculum is modified to meet the needs of the group.

Gifted Students Benefit From Ability Grouping

Many meta-analytic studies of ability grouping calculate results separately for high-, average-, and low-ability students. Those studies that do so find that gifted/high-ability students achieve better when they are placed in ability groups and presented with appropriately modified curricula than when they are placed in mixed-ability settings.

Low-Ability Students Do Not Suffer From Ability Grouping

A common argument against ability grouping is that it is harmful to lower-ability students. Meta-analyses have not supported this argument. When ability levels are considered separately, meta-analyses find that low-ability students' academic achievement in ability-grouped settings is equal to or better than their achievement in heterogeneous settings. Where average effect sizes across studies are provided, they range from −0.02 to 0.29. Further, as noted below, low-ability students may tend to have higher self-esteem when they are ability grouped than when they are educated in heterogeneous settings.

Ability Grouping Has Few Clear Effects on Social/Emotional Adjustment

Some of the studies on which meta-analyses of gifted education are based consider only academic outcomes. Those that consider social/emotional variables are not consistent in which variables they include or how those variables are measured. Because of the relatively small amount of data available in this area, they sometimes cannot be subjected to meta-analytic procedures. Meta-analyses that do attempt to explore social/emotional variables typically find negligible effects of ability grouping, but some exceptions exist. One meta-analysis reported that students in general (not only gifted students) reported more positive attitudes toward the subject being taught when it was taught with ability grouping (effect size [ES] = 0.37). One reported that gifted students taught in heterogeneous settings had better attitudes toward their peers than those taught in ability groups (ES = −0.456). Two meta-analyses reported small effects of grouping on self-esteem that were consistent with social comparison theory—that is, low-ability students had slightly higher self-esteem in ability groups than in heterogeneous settings, and high-ability students had slightly lower self-esteem in ability groups than in heterogeneous settings. All effect sizes were less than 0.20, however, except for one finding that low-ability students had higher self-esteem in remedial than in heterogeneous classes (ES = approximately 0.35, based on three studies).

Other Topics

Acceleration

A meta-analysis of 26 studies investigating the effects of whole-grade academic acceleration considered two main types of studies: those comparing students who accelerated with students of the same age and ability who did not, and those comparing students who accelerated with IQ-matched students in their new class, who are one year older than they (13 studies each). Results indicated that gifted students achieve more in accelerated than unaccelerated classes, with an effect size of 0.88. Also, gifted students who accelerate achieve at levels comparable to those of equally intelligent, older students in their new classes; the average effect size in such studies was 0.05, indicating no difference between accelerated students and their older, unaccelerated classmates. No consistent effects were found for nonacademic outcome variables, such as attitudes toward school, participation in school activities, or popularity with peers.

Cooperative Learning

A meta-analysis of eight studies considered the effectiveness of teaching high-achieving (not necessarily gifted) students along with lower-achieving students using cooperative learning versus individual learning. The eight studies focused only on short-term mathematics and science interventions requiring the acquisition of elementary knowledge, and only at grade levels prior to high school. Also, the classes used different cooperative learning strategies across studies, and the cooperative nature of student interaction was not confirmed. Results indicated that the high-achieving students achieved more with heterogeneous cooperative grouping than with individual learning, with an effect size of 0.26. Further, five studies considered the learning of high-achieving students in homogeneous versus heterogeneous cooperative groups; these studies showed an advantage for homogeneous groups, with an average effect size of 0.22.

Pull-Out Programs

A meta-analysis of studies focusing on pull-out programs for gifted students supported the effectiveness of such programs. Nine studies included measures of achievement, creativity, and/or critical thinking as outcome variables, with specific choices depending on the type of pull-out program studied. Positive effects of pull-out programs were found in all three of these areas (0.65 for achievement, 0.44 for critical thinking, and 0.32 for creative thinking measures).

Four studies included self-concept as an outcome variable, but one was excluded from the meta-analysis because it produced an effect size significantly different from those in the other three studies, showed pre-intervention differences in self-concept between groups, and suffered from attrition of participants. It should be noted, however, that this study produced an effect size of –0.76, indicating that students who participated in a pull-out program had lower self-concepts than those who did not. The other three studies, analyzed together, showed no significant relationship between pull-out program participation and self-concept.

Common Results

The technique of meta-analysis has been applied to several aspects of gifted education, but none more so than ability grouping. Despite some disagreement among authors regarding the overall implications of these meta-analyses, common results can be identified. These findings indicate that relatively flexible ability groups are more effective than rigid tracks, but that ability grouping does not significantly benefit either high- or low-ability learners unless curricula are modified according to the needs of the group. With appropriate curricular modifications, gifted students achieve more with ability grouping than without it, and low-ability students achieve at least as well as they do in heterogeneous settings. Meta-analytic research on ability grouping and social/emotional adjustment has found no consistent effects, but such work is difficult because relatively few studies consider such outcomes, and those that do involve many different dependent variables. Meta-analyses of other forms of gifted education suggest that both acceleration and pull-out programs are effective for gifted students. Also, cooperative learning has been found to be more effective than individual learning, especially when the cooperative groups are homogeneous. Overall, most types of special educational interventions for gifted students have been found to be at least somewhat effective, but the greatest effects tend to be found for approaches that group gifted students homogeneously and then modify the curriculum to fit their needs.

Mary Ann Swiatek

See also Controversies in Gifted Education; Instructional Management; Self-Contained Classroom; Specialized Secondary Schools

Further Readings

Goldring, E. B. (1990). Assessing the status of information on classroom organizational frameworks for gifted students. *Journal of Educational Research, 83*(6), 313–326.

Hoge, R. D., & Renzulli, J. S. (1993). Exploring the link between giftedness and self-concept. *Review of Educational Research, 63*(4), 449–465.

Kulik, C.-L. C. (1985, August). *Effects of inter-class ability grouping on achievement and self-esteem.* Paper presented at the annual meeting of the American Psychological Association, Los Angeles, CA. (ERIC Document Reproduction Service No. ED 263492)

Kulik, C.-L. C., & Kulik, J. A. (1982). Effects of ability grouping on secondary school students: A meta-analysis of evaluation findings. *American Educational Research Journal, 19*(3), 415–428.

Kulik, C.-L. C., & Kulik, J. A. (1984, August). *Effects of ability grouping on elementary school pupils: A meta-analysis.* Paper presented at the annual meeting of the American Psychological Association, Toronto, Ontario, Canada. (ERIC Document Reproduction Service No. ED 255329)

Kulik, J. A. (2003). Grouping and tracking. In N. Colangelo & G. A. Davis (Eds.), *Handbook of gifted education* (3rd ed., pp. 268–281). Boston: Allyn & Bacon.

Kulik, J. A., & Kulik, C.-L. C. (1984). Effects of accelerated instruction on students. *Review of Educational Research, 54*(3), 409–425.

Neber, H., Finsterwald, M., & Urban, N. (2001). Cooperative learning with gifted and high-achieving students: A review and meta-analyses of 12 studies. *High Ability Studies, 12*(2), 199–214.

Slavin, R. E. (1987). Ability grouping and student achievement in elementary schools: A best-evidence synthesis. *Review of Educational Research, 57*(3), 293–336.

Slavin, R. E. (1990). Achievement effects of ability grouping in secondary schools: A best-evidence synthesis. *Review of Educational Research, 60*(3), 471–499.

Vaughn, V. L. (1991). Meta-analyses and review of research on pull-out programs in gifted education. *Gifted Child Quarterly, 35*(2), 92–98.

MIDDLE SCHOOL, LITERATURE CURRICULUM

Middle school literature curriculum refers to the content, organization, and materials that comprise the course of study in Grades 6–8 English, language arts, or reading classes. Specific to gifted education, it describes the attributes and types of curricula that can develop advanced literary skills and understanding for talented readers, both in programs or courses for students with formally identified verbal talents, and in the general education setting.

Literature Curriculum Content

A number of characteristics define high-quality middle school literature curriculum for all readers, including those who are talented. In general, curriculum should be rooted in concepts, principles, ideas, and skills most essential to the disciplines related to literature (e.g., literary criticism, journalism, history); be relevant to the experience of young adolescents; facilitate the development of students' identities as readers; and move students toward greater expertise as critical readers and thinkers in ways and at a pace commensurate with their readiness needs.

Middle school literature curriculum also supports the development of advanced literary skills. According to the National Assessment of Educational Progress 2007 Reading Report Card, eighth graders who respond to selected texts at an advanced level are able to explain abstract themes and ideas in the text, make and support analytical interpretations, make self-to-text connections and text-to-world-event connections, and respond to what they read thoroughly and thoughtfully. Specific to fiction texts, students performing at an advanced level can use their understanding of characters to interpret an author's purpose, explain the importance of setting to plot using textual support, retrieve explanatory text from dense text, and explain how narrative devices function in a story. High-quality middle school literature curriculum equips talented readers with these and other processes indicative of a progressively expanding capacity as a reader such as comparatively analyzing texts, synthesizing texts at a conceptual level, and forming unique literary interpretations.

Literature Curriculum Organization

Approaches for organizing middle school literature curriculum content include conceptual or thematic organization, genre study, and integration with other subjects, such as social studies. In recent years, middle school education has emphasized personal connections to text through methods such as reader response, student-led discussions (e.g., literature circles, book clubs), and journaling. Critics of this approach suggest that it may encourage the idea that reading is an individual and isolated event. Still, most experts agree that middle school literature curriculum should provide numerous opportunities for students to self-select reading material in both structured and unstructured ways.

The *schoolwide enrichment model—reading* (SEM—R), recently developed by Sally Reis and her colleagues, is one framework for organizing literature curriculum. The model employs three phases designed to increase student exposure to and interest in high-quality texts, strengthen students' reading and thinking skills, engage in independent reading with appropriately challenging texts, and respond to texts in authentic ways. Although it has been implemented primarily at the elementary school level, some research on the model has included sixth-grade classrooms. Results document the model's positive impact on students' reading enjoyment, habits, and achievement.

The *integrated curriculum model* (ICM) is another framework for literature curriculum. The Center for Gifted Education at The College of William and Mary has designed language arts and novel units according to the model, primarily with high-ability learners in mind. Above-grade-level literature representing various genres, cultures, and time periods—and connected to the concept of change—forms the core of the units. Unit activities are focused on literary analysis and interpretation through discussion, persuasive writing, research, and personal connections. Research on the effectiveness of the language arts units—some of which include some sixth-grade classrooms—reports gains in literary interpretations and analysis skills for students in treatment classrooms.

Selecting Reading Materials for Literature Curriculum

Selecting books and other reading material for middle school literature curriculum involves several considerations. Collectively, readings should be increasingly complex, represent a range of viewpoints and cultures, and push readers to expand and hone their reading repertoire and skills. By definition, talented readers in the middle grades can read and understand above-grade-level texts, typically two grade levels or higher. Because these readers might be able to decode and comprehend a novel (for example) written for a more mature audience but lack the context or experience to integrate the novel's themes or implications, selections must be challenging to ensure growth as well as be developmentally appropriate. This highlights a potential dilemma in selecting literature for talented readers: how and whether to balance young adult fiction, adult fiction, and "classic" literary selections, as well as what form the sources for these genres should take (e.g., trade book, basal series). One program often cited as a high-quality approach to exposing students to challenging, influential literature is the Junior Great Books program. The program emphasizes multiple literary interpretations through a process called *shared inquiry* and offers unabridged and abridged materials in anthology form.

The rich and varied interests and experiences of middle school readers is another criterion to consider in selecting literature. There is no research that indicates that talented readers have reading interests that are qualitatively different from those of their grade-level peers. The talented reader may have a wide range of reading interests, or have interests more intensely focused on certain genres, authors, and text types. In general, early adolescents are interested in reading texts to which they can relate. This might include reading stories in which young adults play prominent roles that are set in school, extracurricular, or family contexts, or that address issues common to early adolescent experiences, such as relationships, or identity development. Serial fiction, science fiction, mystery, and fantasy are genres that appeal to many readers in the middle grades.

Equally important in choosing texts for middle school literature curriculum is the use of texts in which students might *not* be interested independent of a teacher's encouragement. This includes selections that give readers access to a wide range of diverse experiences, cultures, and views; promote self-discovery; facilitate the development of deficient skills; and allow students to explore unfamiliar ideas.

Clearly a key goal of reading and literature in the middle grades is to encourage young readers to find increasing satisfaction in reading. Because middle-grade students read at varying levels of sophistication, in pursuit of different interests, and exhibiting different reading patterns, instruction in reading and literature during these grades will necessarily be responsive to these differences in order to ensure that each learner becomes a more skilled and enthusiastic reader.

Carol Ann Tomlinson and Jessica Hockett

See also Classics/Great Books; Curriculum Models; Gifted Readers; Middle School, Writing Curriculum; Secondary School, Literature Curriculum

Further Readings

Beane, J. (1997). *Curriculum integration: Designing the core of democratic education.* New York: Teachers College Press.

Reis, S. M., Eckert, R. D., Schrieber, F. J., Jacobs, J. K., Briggs, C., Gubbins, et al. (2005). *The schoolwide enrichment reading mode: Technical report* [RM05214]. Storrs, CT: National Research Center on the Gifted and Talented.

VanTassel-Baska, J., & Little, C. (2003). *Content-based curriculum for high-ability learners.* Waco, TX: Prufrock Press.

Middle School, Mathematics Curriculum

Mathematics is an intellectually demanding, challenging, and exciting content area and, for some students, a content area upon which a future career can be built. The child's informal mathematical future begins with the parent but formally begins the moment she or he walks through the schoolhouse door. Teachers of mathematics at every grade level, starting at kindergarten, must understand mathematics conceptually in addition to the algorithms that they learned in their formal schooling. This conceptual understanding is developed through multiple representations, such as physical objects, drawings, charts, graphs, and symbols. At the middle school level, the primary challenge is to continue the conceptual understanding through multiple representations when offering advanced content to the mathematically talented student. A secondary challenge is to allow that student the opportunity to explore mathematical concepts and ideas beyond the standard curriculum and textbook through differentiation.

Curriculum Implementation

Teachers of mathematically talented students need to have confidence in their own mathematical knowledge and teaching abilities in order to understand and accept the divergent and sometimes creative thinking abilities of their gifted students. More often than not, untrained or inexperienced teachers provide the mathematically gifted and talented students with what is available, such as enrichment worksheets, but it is important to realize that extra quantity does not indicate mathematical quality.

For many mathematics teachers, the textbook is a primary guide to implementing the curriculum. Late in 1997, the Carnegie Corporation of New York agreed to fund the first of a series of evaluations of textbooks in mathematics and science, and work began in early 1998 on middle school math curriculum materials. Project 2061, as it was named, found that most of the textbooks are inconsistent and weak in coverage of conceptual benchmarks in mathematics, weak in their instructional support for students and teachers, and provide little development in sophistication of mathematical ideas from Grades 6 to 8. The evaluation also found that a majority of textbooks are particularly unsatisfactory in providing a purpose for learning mathematics, taking account of student ideas, and promoting student thinking. This research highlights the finding that middle school students experience repetitious and nonchallenging mathematics programs. As a result, their achievement and interest in mathematics stalls, and they may not be able to take advantage of the full range of academic and career options in the future. Mathematically talented middle school students need a curriculum that can be differentiated by level, complexity, depth, and breadth. This type of curriculum, however, cannot be supported by the textbooks being used in the typical mathematics classroom.

Since most researchers would agree that talented young mathematicians would benefit from appropriate levels of challenge, it is unfortunate that current research indicates they seldom receive it. In research conducted on differentiated instruction, most middle school teachers struggle with how to differentiate math instruction effectively for their most talented math students. In one in-depth observation study of 46 American classrooms by researchers at the National Research Center on the Gifted and Talented, little differentiation in instructional and curricular practices was implemented by classroom teachers for gifted and talented students in the regular classroom. Karen Westberg found that across five subject areas and 92 observation days, gifted and talented or high-ability students experienced no instructional or curricular differentiation in 84 percent of the instructional activities in which they participated, including mathematics.

Instructional Strategies

Many talented middle school students do not profit from conventional instruction in mathematics, so their teachers need to seek alternative methods to motivate these students to become internally driven learners by teaching them to self-analyze, self-reference, self-evaluate, and self-correct. Mathematically talented students need the opportunity to pursue open-ended investigations of increasing complexity to develop their mathematical skills and reasoning techniques. These students need a differentiated and compacted curriculum, as well as enrichment activities that involve "self-selected" mathematical areas for advanced content learning, self-paced instruction supplemented with enrichment activities, and acceleration combined with enrichment. Each of these strategies is supported by research.

Methods for differentiating curriculum and instruction for talented young adolescent mathematicians do exist, and some research supports the effectiveness of specific instructional and curricular strategies for use with these students. For example, the use of instructional level grouping has been successful with talented math students, resulting in increased understanding in mathematics. In general, grouping academically talented students together for instruction has been found to produce positive achievement outcomes when the curriculum provided to students in different groups is appropriately differentiated. In other words, it is the instruction that occurs within groups that makes grouping an appropriate instructional strategy.

Another strategy that can be successful with talented middle school math students is curriculum compacting. In this process, assessment procedures are used to learn what students already know, documenting that knowledge and replacing what is known with more challenging material, some of which is based on students' interests.

For teachers who can compact curriculum, differentiation in mathematics instruction can provide less tedious review work and more challenging mathematics problem-based work that reflects the students' ability level in math rather than their age. This type of differentiated instruction should gear instruction toward the students' strengths and interests, provide the students with advanced content that enables them to interact with depth and complexity, and focus on developing higher-level and more concept-based skills. Acceleration, another research-based strategy, also challenges and engages mathematically talented middle school students, resulting in higher levels of achievement. Because mathematics is one of the most linear of domains, with clear benchmarks and progression, it is as an area well suited to acceleration approaches. Any approach that allows mathematically talented students to learn at their own rate and with appropriate complexity will prepare them for one milestone in the lives of many gifted students: the early administration of the SAT for the Talent Search Programs. Seventh graders may sit for this college entrance examination, and those who perform well on these out-of-level tests will be invited to special out-of-school and summer programs that will further extend their education in mathematics and related fields.

What also makes a difference in more challenging mathematics instruction at the middle school level, according to Kristie Jones and James Byrnes, is conceptual thinking, learning, and understanding; active participation; and authentic and meaningful tasks. The use of higher-level questioning and opportunities to incorporate prior knowledge into mathematical experiences also enables talented readers to build upon previous strengths. Discussing conceptual math problems in groups, for example, gives talented math students in middle school the opportunity to interact with intellectual peers and discuss their ideas and solutions in greater depth when a teacher facilitates these discussions. Teachers should focus on themes and ideas, rather than on simple math facts. A one-size-fits-all approach will not enable teachers to meet the needs of mathematically gifted students at all grade levels. Having talented students understand conceptual mathematics is more powerful for developing problem-solving skills rather than just applying algorithms. This applies for both the teacher and the students. It is important to remember that speed in mathematics is secondary to insight, so simply giving more work in a class period will not make a difference.

Encouraging mathematically talented students to maintain a math portfolio is another way to motivate learners to be self-directed. The portfolio should include a collection of work that illustrates the learner's accomplishments and growth in mathematical thinking over a given length of time. In addition, the portfolio offers insights into the student's understanding, attitude, writing, and problem-solving skills, and presents a picture of the student's progress in mathematics. In conjunction with the portfolio, applying the *enrichment triad model* developed by Joseph Renzulli can ensure that mathematically talented students become accountable for their own learning. Using the Type III phase of the triad model can encourage students to view themselves as mathematicians while progress in the portfolio can be observed and assessed by the student, teacher, parent, college admissions officer, and eventually a future employer.

Rachel R. McAnallen

See also Adolescent, Gifted; Elementary School, Mathematics Curriculum; Mathematical Creativity; Mathematically Precocious; Mathematical Talent

Further Readings

Assouline, S., & Lupkowski-Shoplik, A. (2006). *Developing mathematical talent.* Waco, TX: Prufrock Press.

Johnsen, S. K., & Kendrick, J. (2005). *Math education for gifted students.* Waco, TX: Prufrock Press.

National Council of Teachers of Mathematics (NCTM). (2000). *Principles and standards for school mathematics.* Reston, VA: National Council of Teachers of Mathematics.

Renzulli, J. S. (1977). *The enrichment triad model.* Wethersfield, CT: Creative Learning Press.

Stigler, J., & Hiebert, J. (1999). *The teaching gap.* New York: Free Press.

Westberg, K. L., Archambault, F. X., Jr., Dobyns, S. M., & Salvin, T. J. (1993). *An observational study of instructional and curricular practices used with gifted and talented students in regular classrooms* (RM93104). Storrs, CT: University of Connecticut, National Research Center on the Gifted and Talented.

Middle School, Science Curriculum

It is during the middle school years that young adolescents form attitudes about education, particularly a subject like science, and its relevance to their future. Middle school (usually Grades 6–8) is a school between elementary school (usually Grades 1–5) and high school (usually Grades 9–12); the local school district determines what grades are in a given middle school.

In most middle schools, students change teachers after each period, which can range from 50 to 90 minutes. Students usually enroll in five or six courses, including science, that are taught by different teachers. Students often have the opportunity to take elective courses, including advanced courses in science. Middle school can be thought of as a transitional time between elementary school and high school.

Every middle school classroom represents a wide array of abilities. Given the typical variation in middle school populations of students, it is important that all students' needs be met, ranging from those who are struggling to those who have high abilities—the gifted, talented, and creative students. High-ability students may differ from other students in cognitive abilities, motivation, and styles of learning. As a result, high-ability students may also differ from other students in terms of their educational needs in a content area such as science.

Nature of the Middle School Student

Early adolescence, between ages 10 and 15, is a time of great change. The changes in students can be fast and unpredictable. The students are experiencing changes associated with moving from elementary schools to middle schools. The students are also experiencing rapid physical, cognitive, social, and personality changes associated with moving from childhood into adolescence.

Due to a variety of social transformations, such as changes in the family structure and a world dominated by the media, the sociocultural context young adolescents are growing up in today is significantly different from that of only a few years ago. There is great diversity among students in terms of their interests, prior experiences, and home environments.

Gifted, Talented, and Creative Middle School Students

With respect to high-ability students, the joint position advocated by the National Association for Gifted Children and the National Middle School Association is that middle school teachers should "develop increasing awareness of and skills necessary to address the full range of learner needs—including needs of those who already demonstrate advanced academic abilities and those who have the potential to work at advanced levels." The implication is that middle school teachers should attend to both equity and excellence when working with their students in science and other content areas. Historically, that has been easier said than done.

There have always been controversies over how the middle school curriculum should meet the needs of high-ability students in science, as well as other areas. One controversy is over equity: For some teachers, equity implies that all students should have an equal opportunity to achieve in areas such as science, whereas for other teachers, equity implies that all students should have an opportunity to reach their potential, and some students may have a higher potential than others. A second controversy has been over ability grouping: A heterogeneous grouping of students may be consistent with democratic values, but a homogeneous grouping may increase the likelihood that high-ability students will achieve their potential. A third controversy is labeling: Identifying some students as gifted, creative, or talented benefits them, but may hinder others by creating a feeling of elitism. A fourth controversy is over cooperative learning in heterogeneous ability groups: High-ability students may not benefit as much as the other students in the groups.

These controversial issues must be resolved in each middle school, according to Susan Rakow, author of the book *Educating Gifted Students in Middle School.* Teachers, administrators, and parents should resolve the issues, she says, by defining the role of teachers of high-ability students, developing and implementing effective programs, and applying curriculum practices that have been validated through research and classroom practice.

Middle School Science Curriculum

In the National Science Education Standards developed by the National Research Council, there are four fundamental principles that underlie effective middle school science curricula: (1) All students can learn science, and all students should have the opportunity to become scientifically literate; (2) Learning science is an active process; (3) School science reflects the intellectual and cultural traditions that characterize the practice of contemporary science; and (4) Improving science education is part of systemic education reform. These principles are intended to help students learn science as inquiry and to master concepts in physical science, life science, earth and space science, science and technology, science in personal and social perspectives, and the history and nature of science. However, the National Science Education Standards do not address the National Middle School Association and the National Association for Gifted Children joint recommendation to address the needs of students "who already demonstrate advanced academic abilities and those who have the potential to work at advanced levels."

Middle school science curricula may let not only high-ability students down in science, but all students as well. Based on reports over recent years, it is clear that students have not been achieving well in science. Advanced courses—when they exist at all—have had relatively low enrollment, and girls and minority students continue to be underrepresented in such courses. Often, middle school teachers are inadequately prepared to teach science, even when they have a certification in science, and the curriculum time allocated to science has been cut relative to the time allotted to other content areas. Economics also play a role in the problem with tight school budgets because science is more equipment-intensive than mathematics or social studies. As a result, science learning is often passive, relying mainly on a textbook, rather than active, emphasizing activities and experiments.

Project 2061 of the American Association for the Advancement of Science has published benchmarks of scientific literacy goals that concentrate on a common core of learning in science. Recently, Project 2061 conducted a curriculum review—"How Well Do Middle School Science Programs Measure Up?"—to see how well middle school programs attained the key scientific goals specified in national science standards. Using research-based criteria, nine widely used programs were examined by teams of curriculum experts who found that key ideas were generally present in the programs but were typically buried in layers of detailed or unrelated ideas. The findings of the Project 2061 curriculum review suggest that middle school science curricula merit immediate revision in order to better serve the needs of students at all levels of ability.

In the present climate of science education reform, the middle school science curriculum has taken center stage. What role the instruction of high-ability students plays in this curriculum is controversial and continues to be debated by all stakeholders—students, parents, teachers, counselors, administrators, and educational policymakers.

High-Ability Students and the Science Curriculum

It is essential that middle school science curricula support the learning of all students, including high-ability students. This goal is consistent with current calls for national scientific excellence by organizations such as the National Science Foundation, the National Academy of Sciences, and the American Association for the Advancement of Science. The continued economic prosperity of the United States, which depends heavily on scientific innovation, requires at a minimum that all students be scientifically literate. In addition, it requires that a significant number of students excel at the highest levels in science.

A common complaint of high-ability students (and their parents) is that the students are being held back by an educational system that teaches at an average pace and promotes average content of science courses. There is a need to offer more advanced science courses in the middle school, as well as the opportunity for students to take high-school science courses when that can be arranged. But a successful middle school science curriculum for high-ability students depends upon more than courses with advanced content in physical science, life science, earth and space science, and science and technology. It depends upon steps carried out by all stakeholders working together as partners, to ensure that the curriculum is successful.

Successful Science Curricula for High-Ability Students

The joint position statement of the National Association for Gifted Children and the National Middle School Association implies the following steps should be taken when designing a science curriculum for high-ability students. First, students with high ability should be identified to provide them with the science-learning experiences they need. Teachers should regularly use formal and informal assessment strategies to identify students' strengths and needs in science. When doing this, teachers should be guided by a specific plan that emphasizes the use of multiple approaches to identify high potential in students from minority and low economic groups. Students, parents, teachers, counselors, and administrators are stakeholders in this plan: All should have input into it and work to make it successful.

Second, in addition to identifying high-ability students, ongoing assessment should inform teachers' classroom practice in the area of science. Teachers should use pre-assessments, in-process assessments, and postassessments to give students continuous opportunities to demonstrate both their current level and their potential level of knowledge and skill in science. In addition to knowledge and skill, the emerging interests and learning styles of high-ability students should be assessed. The outcomes of these assessments should be used by teachers to adapt curricula to ensure that high-ability students have opportunities to realize their potential.

Third, teachers should ensure that the science curriculum genuinely challenges high-ability students.

The science curriculum should be restructured to help high-ability students learn at deeper levels the ideas that are essential to doing science in the real world. High-ability students, in particular, require regular opportunities to work at advanced levels that challenge them to make significant gains in their science knowledge and skills. Problem-based learning in teaching science is particularly advantageous to high-ability students, in terms of both motivation and achievement. Emphasis on a differentiated curriculum allows advanced students to develop independent and self-directed study skills. High-ability students should have the opportunity to pursue interests, design their own projects and experiments, and compete in science fairs at local, state, national, and international levels.

Fourth, technology should play an important role in science curricula for high-ability students. For example, by means of the Internet, high-ability students can access scientific journals and databases to extend their learning in science. High-ability students can also take advantage of sophisticated demonstrations, simulations, and interactive experiments on the Internet. By means of e-mail, collaboration with scientists, science teachers, and students anywhere in the world can occur.

Fifth, high-ability students will benefit from middle school science curricula when partnerships are formed among the students, their parents, teachers, counselors, and school administrators—all of whom will serve as advocates for high-ability students. These partnerships will help ensure equity and excellence for the students in learning science. Teachers and administrators should help parents to identify, understand, and support the science learning of their high-ability students. Constant communication among members of the partnership is essential for high-ability students to reach their potential in the area of science. These partnerships can help create a middle school climate that supports excellence in science.

Sixth, a successful middle school science curriculum for high-ability students takes advantage of community resources for contextual learning. Scientists working in area industries, hospitals, and colleges can participate in mentoring programs that provide science enrichment experiences beyond those normally available in courses or school lab experiences. These investigations help high-ability students to understand the connections between science and society and facilitate their thinking critically and creatively about important problems.

A curriculum model for problem-based learning in science that meets many of these criteria has been developed by the Center for Gifted Education at William and Mary. The *Guide to Teaching a Problem-Based Science Curriculum* is an implementation supplement to the College of William and Mary's seven problem-based science curricular units. It describes this curriculum and problem-based learning, discusses teachers' education through the William and Mary professional development workshops, and includes research evidence for the effectiveness of the curriculum based on a quantitative nationwide evaluation of one of its units (Acid, Acid Everywhere). There is a table that compares the William and Mary units to both the National Science Education Standards and Project 2061's Benchmarks for Science Literacy. Although these units are modeled on national education standards, they introduce higher-level concepts earlier, and cover fewer topics with more depth.

Future Directions

The middle school science curriculum—and its implications for high-ability students—will likely continue to evolve as a result of ongoing reform initiatives by concerned organizations such as the National Association for Gifted Children and the National Middle School Association. In these reform initiatives, it is important to ensure that both equity and excellence are achieved. These are not mutually exclusive goals. On the contrary, they are inextricably linked. A middle school science curriculum that achieves these goals is one that addresses the full range of students' needs—including the needs of those who have already demonstrated advanced academic abilities and those who have the potential to work at advanced levels.

Shawn M. Glynn, K. Denise Muth, and Patricia Doney

See also Children, Middle School; National Association for Gifted Children; Science, Curriculum

Further Readings

Kesidou, S., & Roseman, J. E. (2002). How well do middle school science programs measure up? Findings from Project 2061's curriculum review. *Journal of Research in Science Teaching, 39*(6), 522–549.

Meeting the needs of high-ability and high-potential learners in the middle grades: A joint position statement of the National Middle School Association and the National Association for Gifted Children (2005). Available from http://www.nmsa.org/AboutNMSA/PositionStatements/GiftedChildren/tabid/119/Default.aspx

Rakow, S. (2005). *Educating gifted students in middle school.* Waco, TX: Prufrock Press.

Rakow, S. (Ed.). (2000). *NSTA pathways to the science standards: Guidelines for moving the vision into practice, middle school edition* (2nd ed.). Arlington, VA: National Science Teachers Association.

VanTassel-Baska, J., & Little, C. A. (Eds.). (2003). *Content-based curriculum for high-ability learners.* Waco, TX: Prufrock Press.

Middle School, Social Studies Curriculum

Thomas Jefferson suggested that the American education system should prepare students to become knowledgeable U.S. citizens who could actively participate in a democratic form of government. Toward a similar end, the National Council for the Social Studies suggests that students participate in an integrated study of the social sciences and humanities to promote civic competence, drawing upon such disciplines as anthropology, archaeology, economics, geography, history, law, philosophy, political science, psychology, religion, and sociology, as well as appropriate content from the humanities, mathematics, and natural sciences. Such experiences should be designed to help young people develop the ability to make informed and reasoned decisions for the public good as citizens of a culturally diverse, democratic society in an interdependent world. It is particularly critical that, as potential leaders, gifted, talented, and creative students be guided to an understanding of their place in society and the world.

In order to adequately address such goals for social studies education in middle school classrooms, it is imperative that teachers use high-quality social studies curriculum and teach it in a way that engages students with the essential ideas of history, government, economics, and geography—allowing middle school learners to see themselves as contributors to their own world and to the broader world they will increasingly impact over time. Following is an examination of what constitutes sound curriculum for the middle grades, for social studies classrooms, and for middle school social studies classrooms.

Quality Curriculum for Middle Grades

Turning Points 2000: A Design for Improving Middle Grades Education, a seminal reform document for middle-level education, makes several recommendations for developing and implementing curriculum for middle school students. Five key assertions made by this report are that curriculum must (1) be grounded in academic standards for what students should know and be able to do, (2) be made relevant to the issues that adolescents deal with, (3) be based on how middle school students best learn, (4) incorporate various assessments to allow students to best demonstrate their knowledge of the content, and (5) use a backward design process in developing curriculum—that is, identification of content standards, planning assessment tightly aligned with the designated content standards, and then determining how best to prepare students to succeed with the assessments that reflect an understanding of the content standards.

Content Standards

Currently, content standards for social studies are designated at the state level for public schools in most states. In some cases, the standards are presented in ways that guide teachers in helping students see important aspects of social studies and in ensuring that students can apply and transfer what they learn. In other instances, standards are presented as a sort of grocery list of information and skills that lacks coherence and often lacks meaning as well. In the latter instances, it is important for teachers—perhaps working with content specialists—to craft the lists of standards into a curriculum that helps students understand the concepts and principles that provide structure and meaning for social studies; connect the various aspects of social studies; connect the events, the people, and link ideas from social studies to their own experiences; and develop the habits of thought and mind that will ultimately allow them to be informed and contributing citizens. The National Council for the Social Studies suggests that standards-based social studies curriculum K–12 be developed around the following concepts, which they call thematic strands: Culture; Time, Continuity, and Change; People, Places, and Environment; Individual Development and Identity; Individuals, Groups, and Institutions; Power, Authority, and Governance; Production, Distribution, and Consumption; Science, Technology, and Society; Global Connections; and Civic Ideals and Practices. A brief examination of these concepts or thematic strands suggests that they are particularly applicable for middle grades social studies during a developmental period when young adolescents are eager to understand their world better and to develop a clearer sense of their possible roles in that world.

Strand I: Culture

The study of cultures should include diverse societies so that students are exposed to multiple perspectives. Not only will this widen their view of the world, but it can also help students to gain a greater understanding of themselves in relation to their own culture(s).

Strand II: Time, Continuity, and Change

The world is constantly changing, and students should be given opportunities to explore questions that deal with these changes. For instance, students might investigate how the world has changed in the past decade and what this might mean for the future. Providing students with expertlike learning activities through which they take on the role of historian to explore continuity and change over time will help them make connections with the present and future, both in their own society and across various cultures. Again, students should have opportunities to envision how past events have shaped their own lives.

Strand III: People, Places, and Environments

Students should also investigate how environments both shape and are shaped by the people who inhabit them. For instance, why did certain cultures settle in particular areas? What impact have these groups had on the areas where they settled? Students should come to understand interdependent relationships between the people and the places and environments where they live. Exploring this reciprocal association can help students think more critically about their surroundings.

Strand IV: Individual Development and Identity

The big question explored in this strand is how culture and elements of culture shape individual experiences, beliefs, values, and more—asking how a person's identity is influenced by his or her culture. As students progress from youth to adulthood, the perspectives they have on this strand will change, moving from a more concrete focus, for instance, on older family members, role models, and the like, to a better understanding of their own identity and development.

Strand V: Individuals, Groups, and Institutions

Governmental and societal organizations such as churches and schools have a profound impact on people's lives. Students should be permitted to explore how these organizations both create and reflect societal values, as well as how they are formed and change over time, including the impacts of these institutions on their own lives.

Strand VI: Power, Authority, and Governance

The middle school years are a time of great exploration for students. One of the issues with which young adolescents grapple is the role of authority and governance in their lives, and the power that institutions have over them. Further, these students need to develop an increasing sense of civic understanding and responsibility, and how individual rights and responsibilities relate to and affect them. Middle school students should build on the more concrete understandings developed in elementary school and apply them to increasingly more complex issues.

Strand VII: Production, Distribution, and Consumption

From an economics perspective, it is important for middle school students to explore the concept of how limited resources are distributed, including the geographic distribution and consumption of resources. Again, increasing levels of depth and complexity in examination of issues and application of understandings are necessary for student growth.

Strand VIII: Science, Technology, and Society

Middle school students are ready to examine the role science and technology play in society, how lives are affected by technological changes, and the conditions under which such changes work for the betterment or detriment of society.

Strand IX: Global Connections

As the world becomes more and more interconnected, it is imperative that students learn about topics that relate to their increasingly globalized society. Issues might include the following: military operations, economic resources, humanitarian responsibilities, energy consumption, and world religions. In middle school, students are increasingly capable of postulating and investigating solutions to these issues, as well as thoroughly analyzing the issues surrounding these topics.

Strand X: Civic Ideals and Practices

In order to participate fully in any society, it is essential that students are prepared to assume this role. Learning the roles and responsibilities of citizens is an excellent place to start. Students can also examine their lives and how they might be able to make a difference in society. Middle school students benefit from looking at their own ideals and the actual practice of citizenship.

Relevant Curriculum

Not only does concept- and principle-based curriculum make standards more meaningful, but it also provides a framework for students to relate the curriculum to the world outside of school as well as their own lives. Middle schoolers have a storehouse of knowledge when they enter the middle grades, with much of the knowledge framed by their social and personal concerns. Thus, finding ways to connect curriculum to students' current mental schema can lead to more meaningful and lasting learning. Further, given the increasing academic diversity among school populations, personal and cultural relevance is a vehicle for optimizing learning. Social studies curriculum that is relevant to middle-grade learners will likely help them sustain interest and concentration while it helps them answer questions they find compelling.

Addressing a Diversity of Talents and Interests

Social studies curriculum and instruction can be designed as though all middle school students were essentially alike, but academic outcomes are improved when teachers address the very wide array of developmental needs that are a hallmark of the middle grades. The National Middle School Association (NMSA) notes the need for teaching approaches to accommodate the varying skills, knowledge levels, abilities, cultures, interests, and learning preferences of middle school students. Effective teaching for young adolescents, NMSA advises, will involve some direct instruction, but will be characterized by more student-centered strategies such as experiments, demonstrations, surveys, opinion polls, simulations, inquiry-based tasks, group projects, and independent studies. Student choice is an important element for middle schoolers as they move toward increasing autonomy as learners. Using a variety of strategies helps to ensure that gifted and talented students will have many ways of challenging themselves and expressing their growing interests.

Assessing to Support Student Growth

In order to understand the varied needs of middle schoolers and to address them effectively in the social studies classroom, it is essential for teachers to utilize ongoing and varied assessments of students' knowledge, understanding, skills, interests, and learning preferences. Assessment should include pre-assessment or diagnostic assessment, ongoing or formative assessment, and final or summative assessment. Pre-assessments may include checklists, surveys, inventories, and the like. Formative assessments may include teacher questioning, teacher observations, journal entries, homework, exit cards, and more. Summative assessments may include traditional tests and quizzes, projects, and other authentic applications of student knowledge, understanding, and skill. Effective assessment will assist teachers both in charting student growth and in modifying instructional plans to ensure consistent student growth. Effective assessments are also responsive to students' varying needs for level of challenge and mode of expressing learning.

Backward Design of Curriculum

When designing curriculum "backward," teachers start with the learning goals clearly in mind and work backward from those goals to ensure alignment of outcomes, assessments, and curriculum. That is, instead of planning instruction around topics first and later creating assessments, teachers first identify content goals based on what students should know, understand, and be able to do. They then decide on effective means of assessing those outcomes. From that point, they then develop instruction designed to ensure that students achieve the learning goals and have maximum opportunity for success on assessments used to determine student proficiencies.

Elements of Effective Curriculum

Effective middle-grades social studies curriculum is responsive to the needs of young adolescents to understand themselves and their potential roles in the world. It supports their increasing ability to think critically and abstractly, and it enables them to become increasingly autonomous as learners. It responds to their varied backgrounds, readiness levels, interests, and modes of learning. To that end, effective middle-level social studies curriculum helps students develop conceptual frameworks of understanding, acquire essential knowledge and skill, attach what they learn to their own experiences, apply what they learn to issues in the world around them, develop habits of mind and work that support academic success, and develop personal interests and strengths.

Carol Ann Tomlinson and Eric M. Carbaugh

See also Middle School, Literature Curriculum; Middle School, Science Curriculum; Middle School, Writing Curriculum; Middle School Movement

Further Readings

Manning, M. (1993). *Developmentally appropriate middle level schools.* Wheaton, MD: Association for Childhood Education International.

National Council for the Social Studies. (1994). *Curriculum standards for social studies: Expectations for Excellence.* Silver Spring, MD: Author.

National Middle School Association. (1995). *This we believe: Developmentally responsive middle level schools.* Columbus, OH: Author.

Middle School, Writing Curriculum

The development of effective skills of written communication is a core academic enterprise in the middle school. Writing is generally not, however, considered an academic discipline or subject area in itself, but rather a set of skills developed and applied across all disciplines in the service of multiple purposes. Although writing is essential to all subject areas, the teaching of writing in middle school is most explicitly incorporated into an English or language arts curriculum.

Several levels of opportunity exist for developing writing talent in the context of the middle school curriculum. These range from differentiated instruction in the core curriculum, to the exploration of potential interests and talents related to writing through short-term elective and enrichment opportunities, to more intensive, individualized learning options. Though potential in the area of writing is related to an individual's general and specific linguistic skills, the development of accomplished writing is a function of the dynamic interplay between—at the very least—linguistic skills, other cognitive skills, interests, motivation, habits of mind, and learning experiences.

Gifted and Talented Writers in the Middle School

Young adolescent writers vary greatly in their facility with both the basic building blocks and the more complex components of narrative, expository, and other forms of writing. Even in exceptional students in this age range, the process and products of writing typically represent a combination of elements characteristic of both novice and more expert writers. The broad goal of curriculum and instruction is to advance each student as far as practicable toward more expert writing.

In considering exceptional writing in young adolescents, it is necessary to distinguish between the advanced use of language, and the sophisticated understanding and application of structural elements and narrative structures in writing. The relatively limited research into the work of exceptional writers in the middle school years suggests that linguistic skills, such as appropriate use of figurative language; use of unusual and mature vocabulary in writing; poetic rhythm; and sophisticated syntax, phrase structure, and/or punctuation, can distinguish work that is identified as exceptional from that considered more typical or "average." In their levels of mastery in these areas, similar to those described by Jane Piirto in her studies of younger prodigious writers, some students may be significantly advanced compared to age peers. Yet even students who demonstrate advanced use of language and content in writing do not necessarily exhibit corresponding advancement in conceptual understanding and application of components such as complex narrative forms, goals for writing, genre, and an appreciation of the intended audience. In addition, even students with highly advanced language might not have highly developed skills of planning, accessing, and evaluating relevant information, revising, and editing, which are characteristic of more developed writers.

Although students with advanced knowledge and skills in language might show potential for exceptional writing, others with exceptional talent arrive in middle school without prerequisite language skills for more advanced levels of written accomplishment. Still others present with specific learning disabilities, such as dyslexia, that affect the acquisition of some language-related skills (e.g., spelling) but leave intact the capacity to comprehend, manipulate, and generate complex, abstract ideas. As is the case with any curricular area and any group of students, teachers must be simultaneously conscious of both group and individual differences in planning opportunities for talent development.

Differentiation of the Core Writing Curriculum

A joint statement issued by the National Association for Gifted Children (NAGC) and the National Middle School Association (NMSA) on meeting the needs of high-ability and high-potential learners in the middle grades emphasizes the need for curriculum responsive to differences in cognitive skills, interests, motivation, and preferred modes of learning potentially occurring in gifted individuals. For all middle school students, effective curriculum enables the acquisition of essential disciplinary knowledge; the development of key skills; the nurturance of understanding of meaningful concepts, principles, and ideas within and across disciplines; the opportunity to learn about oneself and others through curriculum; and the opportunity to frame and address authentic, real-world problems.

It is within this framework of quality curriculum for all students that the development of writing talent can be optimized through modifications that address student differences, regardless of whether students are served within the general education classroom or through distinct classes for identified gifted students. Students' current and developing levels of readiness for advanced writing can be addressed through modifications that seek to: (a) challenge students with advanced language knowledge and skills to develop further in this area through access to advanced resources (e.g., advanced vocabulary lists) and learning activities; (b) bolster the language knowledge and skills of students with potential who lack prerequisites for advanced writing; (c) expose students to increasingly complex texts (i.e., those with more sophisticated narrative structures and use of literary devices) that might serve as models for their own efforts; and (d) guide students explicitly through the process of establishing a purpose for writing, developing ideas for writing, developing drafts, revising, and editing, at a level of complexity commensurate with students' readiness.

Curriculum can be differentiated in response to student interest to support the development of writing talent by (a) encouraging students to experiment with different writing styles and genres; (b) allowing students to pursue an interest in the work of particular authors, and to investigate those authors' work habits, inspirations, and writing processes; (c) allowing students to mimic the style of favorite authors as they come to understand how elements interact to produce style; (d) allowing opportunities for student choice of topics for writing, including topics drawn from multiple disciplines; (e) providing opportunities for students to explore their own lives and emerging identities through writing (e.g., through reflective journal writing, or by explicitly linking literary concepts, such as writer's voice, to students' own experience, such as their own emerging "voice"); and (f) providing opportunities for prolonged, independent or group writing projects in areas of interest.

Differentiation in response to student learning profiles can support talent development in writing by (a) providing options for students' expression of understanding of a particular concept or text (e.g., analytical criticism vs. creative writing); (b) encouraging different ways of working through the prewriting process (e.g., enabling students to use audiovisual recordings, sketches, mind-maps, or diagrams to record and develop ideas for writing); (c) assisting students to use comfortable modes of expression to support writing (e.g., helping students incorporate visual metaphors into their written work, develop photographic essays supported by poetry or prose, or create audiovisual presentations of ideas also expressed in more formal writing).

Effectively differentiated middle school writing curriculum both challenges students whose writing is already advanced beyond grade-level expectations and alerts teachers to writing potential in students who have yet to demonstrate advanced performance. Ongoing assessment of students' current levels of readiness, developing interests, and learning preferences is essential in determining ongoing instructional needs in various aspects of writing. Curriculum that is differentiated to meet the needs of high-potential and high-ability students is supported by several components of the middle school philosophy, including flexible grouping and use of time, attendance to affective development, a focus on developing interests through exploration, and collaboration between interdisciplinary teams of teachers and specialists.

Opportunities for Exploration Through Elective Study

Middle-level education values young adolescence as a period of great exploration and developing awareness. All middle school students benefit from exploring areas of interest that have the potential to become passions, and from developing their emerging talents. For those with advanced writing skills or significant potential as writers, exposure to and experimentation with different forms, genres, and outlets for writing; writing for different audiences; and reflecting on the match between their own work preferences and those of practicing writers are important components of talent development.

Some enrichment opportunities in writing are suitable for all students. For example, seeing practicing writers talk about and share their work or taking field trips to see poetry readings, drama performances, or museum exhibits pertaining to writers and writing are likely to engage most students. Other opportunities require greater investment of interest and time, such as short-term elective courses offered in many middle schools and designed to expose students to areas of potential interest in a more concentrated way. In writing, electives might be offered in scriptwriting, poetry, scientific writing, or speechwriting. Many schools also offer "clubs" that bring together students with similar interests, and writing talent might be developed in this context. The goal of these enrichment opportunities is for students to "try on" potential long-term interests, including those that might intersect with domains of particular talent.

Individualized Opportunities for Development of Writing Talent

At a more intensive level, students may be guided individually to develop specific writing abilities. Personalized curriculum plans can take a variety of forms, and can occur outside both the core and exploratory layers of curriculum. At this level, a student's motivation and interest are central, because more independent curriculum requires sustained effort and commitment on the part of the student. Opportunities at this level are negotiated between teachers and individual students, and are designed to foster knowledge and skills in specialized areas of interest and/or talent not ordinarily targeted in middle school curriculum.

In writing, individualized or personalized plans can be designed to develop advanced and increasingly professional written products. For example, a student with advanced expository writing skills might be guided to write an essay exploring a topic of interest, such as the ethics of stem cell research, for entry in a national or international essay competition. Another student might create an extended anthology of original poetry, organized around a central theme, with the long-term goal of submitting the work for publication. These representative cases, reminiscent of Type III enrichment opportunities described in Renzulli's schoolwide enrichment model, exemplify the significant time commitment and skill level that can be involved in extended individual projects for talent development; a commitment that not all students would elect to undertake. In many cases, the teacher negotiating the parameters of the project with a student will not possess the specialized knowledge necessary to guide the project to its conclusion, and will therefore arrange for the student to work with another teacher, or arrange a suitable mentor (e.g., through a high school, university, or professional association) to work with the student.

Talented writers might also be supported in accessing extended out-of-school opportunities in order to meet their need for challenge. For example, a particularly talented middle school writer might benefit from participation in a high school or college credit course in writing, one of many online writing courses taught by professional writers, or a summer program designed to develop the talents of young writers. As with all curricular options, these courses are selected to meet the individual's specific needs at a particular stage of talent development.

Carol Ann Tomlinson and Jane Jarvis

See also Elementary School, Writing Curriculum; Mentoring Gifted and Talented Individuals; Middle School, Literature Curriculum; Middle School Enrichment; Secondary School, Writing Curriculum

Further Readings

Council for Exceptional Children. (1996). *Gifted education and middle schools.* Reston, VA: Author.

McKeough, A., Generaux, R., & Jeary, J. (2006). Structure, content, and language usage: How do exceptional and average storywriters differ? *High Ability Studies, 17*(2), 203–223.

Piirto, J. (1989). Does writing prodigy exist? *Creativity Research Journal, 2,* 134–135.

Tomlinson, C. A. (2003). *Fulfilling the promise of the differentiated classroom: Strategies and tools for responsive teaching.* Alexandria, VA: Association for Supervision and Curriculum Development.

Tomlinson, C. A., & Eidson, C. C. (2003). *Differentiation in practice: A resource guide for differentiating curriculum, grades 5–9.* Alexandria, VA: Association for Supervision and Curriculum Development.

VanTassel-Baska, J., Johnson, D., & Boyce, L. N. (Eds.). (1996). *Developing verbal talent: Ideas and strategies for teachers of elementary and middle school students.* Boston: Allyn & Bacon.

VanTassel-Baska, J., Zuo, L., & Avery, L. D. (2002). A curriculum study of gifted-student learning in the language arts. *Gifted Child Quarterly, 46*(1), 30–44.

Middle School Enrichment

Enrichment is the most commonly reported school provision for students identified as gifted. Despite this, enrichment remains a concept that is hard to define clearly. The term *enrichment* has been used to refer to curriculum as well as program delivery services. In the middle grades, enrichment is also defined and implemented in many ways. For some middle school settings, enrichment can take the form of extracurricular activities or school clubs; for other settings, enrichment might take the form of a pull-out class in which students work on individual projects; in still others, enrichment may inappropriately mean expanded assignments when a student demonstrates proficiency with designated goals or when the student completes assigned work. For purposes of this entry, middle school enrichment is defined as in-class, cocurricular, or extracurricular options designed to meet the academic and developmental needs of young adolescents through a variety of approaches.

Meeting the Learning Needs of High-Ability and High-Potential Learners

In 2005, the National Middle School Association (NMSA) and the National Association for Gifted Children (NAGC) crafted a joint position statement describing their shared commitment to developing schools and classrooms in which both equity and excellence are persistent goals for each learner. The statement includes specific calls to action for middle school leaders and educators, including the following:

- Ensure that teachers have meaningful knowledge and understanding about the needs of gifted adolescents, including training in differentiated instruction so that the needs of all students—including those with advanced performance or potential—are appropriately addressed.
- Ensure a continuum of services including options such as differentiation, advanced classes, acceleration, short-term seminars, independent studies, mentorships and other learning opportunities matched to the varied needs of high-potential and high-ability learners.
- Use a variety of developmentally appropriate instructional practices to enable each student to experience a high degree of personal excellence. (National Middle School Association & National Association for Gifted Children, 2005)

These guidelines provide a foundation for effective curriculum for high-ability and high-potential middle school students and indicate the need to develop curriculum and instruction that is responsive to the needs of high-ability and high-potential young adolescents.

Neuroscience research has suggested that the young adolescent brain is in a promising state of flux, signaling the most transformational period of development in a young person's life other than infancy. This span of development is a use-it-or-lose-it time for the brain. Brain synapses are developing rapidly and those pathways that are rarely used are being "pruned" in order to strengthen the developing paths. With this in mind, teachers of young adolescents should persistently call upon students to reason, think abstractly, and exercise critical analysis in their learning experiences. Effective enrichment can provide an opportunity to infuse these critical attributes into the middle school environment. An examination of enrichment in the middle school context illustrates ways in which enrichment can be part of a continuum of services designed to meet the needs of middle schoolers, including those with advanced performance or potential.

The concept of enrichment in gifted education is perhaps most closely connected with the work of Joseph Renzulli and his colleagues. Renzulli's *schoolwide enrichment model* explicitly defines enrichment as those activities that respond to student interest and learning style and that are geared toward providing advanced-level activities and is well aligned with the NMSA/NAGC guidelines for teaching highly able middle school students—including the belief that enrichment is valuable for all students, not just high-ability and high-potential learners, as long as it addresses the needs of the particular learner, is an extension of high-quality curriculum, and is supported in ways that strengthen the student intellectually and affectively. Ideally, all students will be challenged, and even the brightest students will have special opportunities to reach for greater knowledge and skills.

Enrichment Options

Enrichment can be an integral part of the school within a classroom or within cocurricular or extracurricular settings. The following explanations delineate enrichment options that can be found in a variety of middle school settings.

Exploratory Programs

Enrichment in the middle grades is often found in the form of exploratory programs such as short-term classes or workshops in which students can try out career, recreational, life-skill, or arts-related activities. Exploratory classes and workshops that use integrated curricular studies culminating in student-produced, real-world projects can also provide sources of high-quality enrichment that increase student motivation and extend challenge in school.

Exploratory curriculum allows students with wide-ranging interests and academic needs more opportunity for personal development. Because the middle years are a time in which students actively formulate their identities, middle school learners are inevitably interested in investigating a broad range of topics and ideas. Having the opportunity to do so is critical in establishing new passions and extending existing ones, as well as supporting a positive attitude toward self and achievement during adolescence. Learning opportunities that support middle school students in reaching beyond their academic comfort levels can add depth and breadth to the learning experiences of young adolescents.

Middle schools can provide content-oriented enrichment opportunities through short, exploratory courses such as foreign language, technology, art, music, broadcasting, and the like. Exploratory options such as these may be a part of the class time (curricular), outside of class time but within the school day (cocurricular), or provided outside of regular classroom hours (extracurricular).

During class time, teachers can provide exploratory, interest-based short courses that are related to classroom content as well as providing interest-based options in the form of independent studies, enrichment centers, interest groups, and so on. Further, middle schools may offer a range of cocurricular enrichment options that extend course content, such as Mathletics or MATHCOUNTS that extend the middle school math curriculum. Finally, extracurricular exploratory activities, such as computer, genealogy, gaming, or photography clubs, may introduce students to new interests or extend existing ones. Whatever the format, enrichment offered through exploratory options should be rooted in principles of high-quality curriculum and instruction.

Mentoring

Another option for middle school enrichment is mentoring—or a structured, ongoing relationship in which someone more skilled in a domain supports the development and growth of someone less skilled in that domain. Middle school students are curious about questions and topics of importance to them. They also often feel both pulled and repelled by key adults in their lives. Adult mentors who can help students develop new competencies or extend existing interests can thus meet the dual need of young adolescents to extend their horizons and have positive adult relationships.

Middle schools can support mentoring in a variety of settings. After-school and weekend mentoring opportunities can benefit a wide variety of students. Such extracurricular settings are ideal for mentors who may be unable to meet students during regular school hours and for settings that are not available to students and mentors during the school day. Some schools use mentors in classroom and cocurricular contexts to enhance or extend a topic of study. Technology offers one vehicle for classroom and cocurricular mentorships. For instance, middle school science students might regularly contact university science students by e-mail to discuss experiments they are designing and carrying out. When planning mentoring programs, it is prudent to consider the following:

- *Developmental needs of the students.* At a given time, some middle school students are ready for mentor relationships, whereas others may not be.
- *Clear expectations for students and mentors.* Carefully designed mentorships with guidelines for mentors provided by the school are critical. Clear school and parental expectations for students are also essential to success.
- *Support systems within the school.* It is important to recognize that although the mentors may be experts in their fields, they may not have a clear understanding of the developmental needs of adolescents. It is important to provide training and guidance to support new and evolving mentor–mentee relationships.

In-Class Extension Activities

Middle schools can also use in-class extension activities as an important source of meaningful enrichment for young adolescents. Teachers can develop or provide extension activities to ensure that students have the following: (a) meaningful work to do when they finish required tasks, (b) appropriately challenging work to do in lieu of required work on which they demonstrate mastery, or (c) opportunities to engage in extended learning about topics, ideas, or events they are studying in class. In a middle school language arts class, for example, a teacher might provide an extension opportunity during a novel study of Lois Lowry's *The Giver* by developing interest centers on eugenics and future studies, both of which are topics related to this science fiction novel about a "perfect society."

Extension activities, as in all enrichment opportunities, need to be (a) carefully planned; (b) based on explicit expectations for student knowledge, understanding, skill, and working arrangements; (c) guided by ongoing assessments to address student interests, learning profiles, and readiness needs; and (d) actively supported by teachers who ensure that students develop the knowledge, understanding, skills, and habits of mind necessary to function as increasingly independent inquirers.

Promoting Equity and Excellence in Enrichment

Enrichment can provide high-ability and high-potential middle school students with opportunities for challenge and motivation. When planned with student needs in mind, enrichment can raise ceilings of expectation and performance for highly able students, thus contributing to personal excellence for these students and lifting ceilings of excellence in the middle grades. Yet, enrichment should not be limited to students identified as gifted. It is likely to be beneficial for all students at some times and in some subjects in the middle school years. It is also likely that enrichment will be inappropriate for many advanced learners at some times and in some subjects during the middle grades. Opening up enrichment opportunities for a broad range of students ensures equity of access to rich learning opportunities and can also serve as a catalyst for talent identification and nurturance in students whose abilities might otherwise be overlooked and underdeveloped.

Carol Ann Tomlinson and Jennifer G. Beasley

See also Middle School, Literature Curriculum; Middle School, Social Studies Curriculum; Middle School, Writing Curriculum; Middle School Movement

Further Readings

Clark, B. (1983). *Growing up gifted: Developing the potential of children at home and at school* (2nd ed.). Columbus, OH: Merrill.

Csikszentmihalyi, M., Rathunde, K., & Whalen, S. (1993). *Talented teenagers: The roots of success and failure.* Cambridge, UK: Cambridge University Press.

Erb, T. O. (Ed.). (1997). *Dilemmas in talent development in the middle grades: Two views.* Columbus, OH: National Middle School Association.

Renzulli, J. S. (1977). *The enrichment triad model: A guide for developing defensible programs for the gifted and talented.* Mansfield Center, CT: Creative Learning Press.

Tomlinson, C. A., & Doubet, K. J. (2006). *Smart in the middle grades: Classrooms that work for bright middle schoolers.* Westerville, OH: National Middle School Association.

Middle School Movement

The middle school movement began in the 1960s and gained impetus in the 1970s as a reaction to junior high schools that were typically, as the name suggests, junior versions of a high school. Operating in a highly teacher-centered and often factorylike manner, junior high schools gave ample evidence of being poorly suited to address the needs of young adolescents.

Founders and proponents of what came to be known as middle schools emphasized the need to establish a kind of school centered on and responsive to the needs of students from approximately 10 to 14 years of age. Students in this age group are highly variable in physical, emotional, intellectual, social, and moral development. Students in this age span may go through periods of time where they are self-absorbed, focused on friends, moody, argumentative, impulsive, and/or volatile. They also are increasingly able to deal with abstractions, developing good logic and problem-solving skills, increasingly able to work independently, passionate about issues such as fairness and justice, and able to examine ideas from varied perspectives. These students, suggest proponents of middle schools, need settings in which they are understood, feel safe, can actively grapple with ideas, work in a variety of social contexts, find reason to believe in themselves and their current and future prospects, have freedom to move about, and engage in work that they see as important and relevant. This entry discusses the fit of gifted education within the middle school movement and the differing perspectives of advocates for the middle school movement and advocates for gifted education.

Early Divides

During the 1990s, there was overt tension between advocates for gifted education and advocates for the middle school movement. Certainly some of the divide between the two groups stemmed from an equity emphasis in the middle school movement and an excellence emphasis in gifted education. That is, many middle school leaders stressed the importance of middle schools as the last, best opportunity for students from low-income backgrounds and students of color to be supported in achieving underpinnings necessary for continued academic success. To that end, middle school proponents emphasized the inherent dangers of tracking and ability grouping, which, when done without concern for equity and diversity, can be disadvantageous for students who struggle in school for a variety of reasons. By contrast, many proponents of gifted education supported ability grouping based on research suggesting it was a viable means of increasing academic challenge—or academic excellence—for highly able learners. Related to the different perspectives regarding ability grouping were the two groups' perspectives on cooperative learning. Middle school advocates strongly supported cooperative learning as a means of ensuring educational equity, and advocates of gifted education decried the approach as ineffective in providing academic challenge for advanced learners. A third source of tension likely stemmed from an early failure of middle school advocates to delineate what constitutes an appropriate middle level curriculum, leaving proponents of gifted education to perceive middle schools as institutions largely devoid of an academic emphasis.

More Recent Perspectives

Beginning in the 1980s and moving forward, proponents of middle level education and gifted education have worked to find common ground in their perspectives. In addition to shared initiatives and joint position statements by the National Middle School Association and the National Association for Gifted Children, an examination of current literature on the middle school movement is more specific in its statements about addressing the needs of advanced learners in the middle grades as well as in its statements about the nature of effective middle grades curriculum. The latter descriptions support development of personal excellence and align easily with much of the literature in gifted education about what constitutes effective curriculum and instruction for highly able learners. In addition, many in the field of gifted education have increasingly emphasized the need for that field to play a leadership role in identifying and developing abilities in students from low-income and culturally/economically diverse backgrounds, which suggests a commitment to equity and implies a willingness to play a role in talent development in more heterogeneous settings as a way to identify and extend capacity in groups traditionally underserved in programs for gifted learners. Thus, in recent years, both groups share, at least to some degree, a stated intent to support both equity and excellence in the middle grades.

Common Ground

Although there are lingering tensions between some advocates for gifted education and some advocates of the middle school movement based largely on different preferences regarding instructional grouping of young adolescents, there are many aspects of current middle school language that provide ample ground for collaboration between middle school advocates and advocates for students identified as gifted. Contemporary middle level writing suggests many areas of shared belief, including goals of responding to individual differences; having adult advocates for every student to support each student's intellectual and personal development; ensuring continuous progress for each student; establishing high expectations in the classroom; creating a climate of intellectual development; developing curriculum that is grounded in rigorous, public academic standards; fostering critical thinking; using a variety of instructional practices to address varied student needs; employing organizational flexibility; and using assessment that promotes learning for each student.

It is likely that current lack of middle school fit for gifted learners exists not because of a vision of middle level education that is inappropriate for the needs of highly able middle schoolers, but rather because of the difficulty in implementing an appropriate vision. That difficulty is pervasive in the history of reform initiatives in American education. The challenge of translating the vision into reality, however, leaves ample room for contributions by those in the field of gifted education who also advocate many aspects of the vision as necessary for effective public education.

Carol Ann Tomlinson

See also Middle School, Literature Curriculum; Middle School, Science Curriculum; Middle School, Social Studies Curriculum; Middle School, Writing Curriculum; Middle School Enrichment

Further Readings

Jackson, A., & Davis, G. (2000). *Turning points 2000: Educating adolescents in the 21st century.* New York: Teachers College Press.

National Middle School Association. (1995). *This we believe: Developmentally responsive middle level schools.* Columbus, OH: Author.

National Middle School Association. (2003). *This we believe: Successful schools for young adolescents.* Westerville, OH: Author.

National Middle School Association & National Association for Gifted Children. (2005, January). *Meeting the needs of high-ability and high-potential learners in the middle grades: A joint position statement.* Retrieved December 22, 2005, from http://www.nmsa.org/AboutNMSA/PositionStatement/GiftedChildren/tabid/119/Default.aspx

Stevenson, C. (1998). *Teaching ten to fourteen year olds* (3rd ed.). Boston: Allyn & Bacon.

Tomlinson, C., & Doubet, K. (2006). *Smart in the middle grades: Classrooms that work for bright middle schoolers.* Westerville, OH: National Middle School Association.

Midwest Academic Talent Search

The Midwest Academic Talent Search (MATS) is one of several talent search programs in the United States that uses off-level testing to assess the abilities of academically gifted children. Talent search programs like MATS have a history of 25 years or more and have become a prominent service delivery model in the United States for both assessment and educational programming for gifted children.

MATS is conducted by the Center for Talent Development of the School of Education and Social Policy of Northwestern University in Evanston, Illinois. MATS is an annual program that involves assessment of children in Grades 4 through 9 via above-grade-level tests, including the Explore test, the ACT (American College Test), and the SAT (Scholastic Aptitude Test).

Underlying Rationale

Underlying the MATS program is the belief that the typical tests used to assess achievement within schools are not appropriate for gifted children. Because these tests are designed for heterogeneous groups of students, they suffer from ceiling effects due to the lack of sufficiently difficult items. As a result, on-grade-level tests are too easy for gifted learners and do not provide adequate measurement of their abilities. The use of on-grade-level tests to assess the abilities of gifted learners is akin to using a yardstick to measure height. The measuring instrument cannot discern differences in height beyond that of 3 feet. Similarly, on-grade-level tests can determine students' mastery only of grade-level material but not what students know and understand beyond that. Many gifted students can reason and think beyond what is expected on the basis of their age or grade. MATS uses tests designed for older students with younger students, thereby providing more accurate measurement of their abilities in key areas. Through the use of tests such as the ACT, SAT, and Explore, gifted students' level of ability (e.g., moderately gifted, highly gifted) in several key domains (math, verbal, science reasoning, and English) can be determined. Use of these tests with children of these ages is also appropriate because differentiation of cognitive abilities (e.g., relative strengths and weaknesses in different areas) is known to occur in early adolescence. The MATS program assists students in Grades 3 through 9 who are already scoring well on on-grade-level tests (e.g., at the 95th percentile or higher) to register for and take an appropriate above-grade-level test.

Students in Grades 3 through 6 take the Explore tests, typically given to eighth graders. Students in Grades 6 through 9 take the SAT or ACT, typically given to high school juniors and seniors. MATS participants take these tests on Saturdays at national test centers located near their homes.

Services to Families and Schools

The MATS program is more than just testing. Subsequent to testing, MATS participants receive information that helps them to interpret and understand their scores on the above-grade-level tests. For example, in the MATS program, they receive percentile rankings for their scores based on students their own age who took the test, that is, other gifted students. They are given recommendations for out-of-school programs such as contests and competitions, summer programs, and distance learning programs that they are eligible for based on their scores and that will further develop their abilities. They receive information directly from the Center for Talent Development on its educational offerings for gifted students as well as brochures and information from other gifted centers and institutions that offer special programs for gifted learners. Students and families receive academic advising regarding sequences of courses to take in Grades 4 through 12, depending on a student's abilities and areas of strength. Families of MATS participants also receive information about giftedness, talent development, and parenting via print materials including magazines, newsletters, and the like, as well as access to experts in gifted education through conferences and seminars. Students who participate in MATS continue to receive information about special programs until the end of high school.

In addition to serving students and families, MATS reports students' scores back to their school so that their school administrators can make appropriate adjustments and accommodations for them based on their tested abilities. MATS also provides information to school officials that enables them to do this, such as recommendations for in-school programs that are matched to different scoring levels. For example, some students need enrichment and acceleration of 1 year only and others need acceleration of 2 or more years in an area of strength. Thus, participation in MATS opens up many opportunities for growth and talent development to gifted students.

Research Support

The model of above-grade-level testing that underlies the MATS program was begun by Julian Stanley at Johns Hopkins University. Currently, more than 30,000 students, primarily from the Midwest, participate annually in MATS, and more than 150,000 students participate annually in testing nationwide through other similar programs at Duke University, Johns Hopkins University, and the University of Denver. Many of the components of the Midwest Academic Talent Search, including the efficacy of criteria to participate, the scoring levels of students compared to older students who typically take the tests, and the predictive validity of scores for later educational achievement, have been well researched by researchers at Northwestern University and the other talent search centers. On average, students who take these tests score as well or better than the older students who typically take them. SAT scores can predict students' college majors and career choices. Further, students' SAT, ACT, and Explore scores can be used to place students in educational programs that are appropriate for them in pacing and level, and specifically, can be used to determine which students can profit from and succeed in accelerated learning experiences. Students who participate in talent search in middle school are much more likely to pursue rigorous courses of study in high school and college.

Paula Olszewski-Kubilius

See also Identification; Mathematically Precocious; Middle School, Literature Curriculum; Middle School, Mathematics Curriculum; Talent Searches; Verbal Ability

Further Readings

Olszewski-Kubilius, P. (1998, Spring). Research evidence regarding the validity and effects of talent search educational programs. *Journal of Secondary Gifted Education,* 9(3), 134–138.

Olszewski-Kubilius, P. (1998, Spring). Talent search: Purposes, rationale and role in gifted education. *Journal of Secondary Gifted Education,* 9(3), 106–114.

Montessori Schools

In the current educational era, with the advent of the No Child Left Behind act and its emphasis on educational standards, funding for gifted children often runs dry. It may therefore be important for parents to examine alternative educational options for their gifted children, who tend to be independent learners, who often struggle in classrooms where repetition and conformity are stressed and individual expression is shunned. Montessori schools were founded on the basis that children have the innate capacity to teach themselves, and that schools should allow students to direct their own learning. For this reason, Montessori schools may be an excellent alternative for gifted students.

Montessori Education

Montessori schools were founded and developed by the Italian educator Maria Montessori in the early 20th century and are based on the philosophy that children have an innate tendency and ability to learn culturally appropriate tasks. In her book *The Absorbent Mind,* Montessori describes with fascination the incredible cognitive development in the first 3 years of a child's life: "The child grows up speaking his parents' tongue yet to grown-ups the learning of a language is a very great intellectual achievement. No one teaches the child, yet he comes to use nouns, verbs and adjectives to perfection" (p. 6).

One of Montessori's core beliefs was that all children have a natural desire and ability to learn, and therefore that the basic task of teachers should not be to impart knowledge but rather to provide students with stimulating environments in which to explore and learn. The onus of learning is thus put on the child, and instead of directly instructing, the teacher's primary job is to expose the child to a wide array of subjects that are chosen to be optimally challenging to each student. Unlike traditional public schools where schedules are rigid, students in Montessori schools can choose to work on an activity for as long as they like.

Montessori schools also foster a democratic system for creating order in the classroom; students have direct input into creating and enforcing school rules, and teachers try to encourage students to resolve conflicts on their own, and intervene only when necessary.

Gifted Students and the Montessori Method

Gifted students have a number of characteristics that make Montessori schools particularly amenable to their needs. First, they tend to enjoy independent work, which is the essence of the Montessori method. In order to supplement their students' independent work, Montessori teachers work to match the challenge of a given activity to each individual student's skill level. This allows gifted students, who are often bored by the slow pace in a traditional public school setting, not only to progress at their own pace, but also to work on material that is both stimulating and challenging.

Gifted students also tend to become intensely immersed in activities that they find interesting, challenging, and rewarding. Montessori schools, unlike traditional schools, which often employ rigid scheduling, encourage students to engage in activities for as long as they like, and therefore allow them to maximize learning during these highly creative interludes. Montessori felt that children were, in fact, the best judges of their own educational needs, and that just as an infant attends to the stimuli needed to learn language, older children too have an innate capacity to choose exactly what they need in order to learn.

Gifted students often seek the opportunity to integrate knowledge from a variety of disciplines. They are interested in cause-and-effect relationships, and in transferring concepts outside a particular discipline. Montessori schools are particularly effective in this area, constantly striving to relate a student's work in one area to projects in other disciplines. The Montessori method will therefore allow gifted students to make connections between what they learn and the world in which they live, and to alleviate the frustration caused by the strict segregation of subject matter that takes place in traditional public school settings.

Gifted students also often struggle socially in mainstream public schools, likely because their advanced cognitive capacities make it difficult for them to relate to less gifted students their own age. Moreover, gifted students often possess a capacity for moral reasoning, or a sense of justice and fairness, that is more advanced than that of their peers. This often makes it hard for them to understand the behavior of children their own age and can lead to social isolation that in turn may contribute to high levels of depression, anxiety, and suicidal ideation among the gifted.

Another area in which Montessori schools serve the interests of the gifted is in their adoption of an egalitarian system of class management. Students not only play a role in designing class rules, they also help to maintain and enforce those rules. Classrooms are multi-age, which allows older students to take on leadership roles and younger ones to learn by example. Montessori teachers encourage students to sort out their own problems before intervening. Within this system, students are encouraged to perform routine classroom tasks such as watering the plants and sweeping the floors, and are encouraged to help their teacher whenever help is needed. Students also have more freedom within the school day. They are allowed to take bathroom breaks or eat snacks at their leisure and to talk quietly to friends and move around the classroom as they please. This loose egalitarian system suits the needs of the self-motivated, cognitively gifted student, who may feel bogged down by traditional, rule-driven classrooms.

Montessori schools, with their emphasis on independence, individuality, integrative interdisciplinary curriculum, and a democratic system of class management, would seem to be the perfect setting for the gifted to excel, providing a welcoming place for students who often feel strange in a public school setting and who may even go so far as masking their talents in order to fit in with their classmates.

The benefits of Montessori education for the gifted is merely speculative, at this point, as there is not yet empirical evidence to support it, but based on the school's theory and the specific needs of gifted students, there seems to be a logical connection. Because of the diversity of their gifts, there may not be one perfect educational setting for all talented students, and parents should be encouraged to explore all academic options.

David Martin

See also Boys, Gifted; Giftedness, Definition; Girls, Gifted; Highly Gifted; Very Young Gifted

Further Readings

Gitter, L. L. 1970). *The Montessori way.* Seattle, WA: Special Child Publications.

Lillard, P. P. (1996). *Montessori today: A comprehensive approach to education from birth to adulthood.* New York: Schocken Books.

Loeffler, M. H. (1992). *Montessori in contemporary American culture.* Portsmouth, NH: Heinemann Educational.

Montessori, M. (1912). *The Montessori method.* New York: Frederick A. Stokes.

Montessori, M. (1948). *The discovery of the child.* Adyar, Madras 20, India: Theosophical Society.

Montessori, M. (1964). *The absorbent mind.* Wheaton, IL: Theosophical Publishing House.

Montessori, M. (1965). *The advanced Montessori method: Spontaneous activity in education.* Cambridge, MA: Robert Bentley.

Montessori, M. (1966). *The secret of childhood.* Notre Dame, IN: Fides Publishers.

Tittle, B. M. (1984). Why Montessori for the gifted? *Gifted Child Today, 33,* 3–7.

Moral Development

Moral development and moral education are increasingly being discussed by educators, psychologists, counselors, and parents. Incidents of school violence in public and private schools have focused awareness on these issues. In addition, the lack of high levels of moral development is reflected in headlines concerning fraud and dishonesty in corporate settings, legal proceedings, politics, sports, and entertainment. The role that schools could and should play in moral development is still a subject of controversy; yet, systematic research has been conducted throughout the 20th century by educational scholars, notably by Jean Piaget, Lawrence Kohlberg, Carol Gilligan, Kazimierz Dabrowski, John Coles, Rushworth Kidder, and E. Paul Torrance and Dorothy Sisk.

Jean Piaget

According to Piaget, all development emerges from action, and children construct and reconstruct their knowledge of the world as they interact with the environment. Piaget observed children at play, and noted that their adherence or nonadherence to rules in games indicated a developmental process of morality. He concluded that all children begin in a *heteronomous* stage of moral reasoning characterized by strict adherence to rules, duties, and obedience to authority. The powerlessness of children and their egocentrism reinforce their heteronomous moral orientation. Later, in interaction with other children, the child develops toward an *autonomous* stage of moral reasoning. Piaget concluded from his work that schools should concentrate on cooperative decision making and problem solving to nurture moral development.

Lawrence Kohlberg

Kohlberg modified and elaborated on Piaget's work, and he proposed that children form ways of thinking through experiences that include understandings of moral concepts, such as justice, rights, equality, and human welfare. Kohlberg identified six stages of reasoning grouped into three major levels. At the first level, the Pre-Conventional level, moral judgment is characterized by a concrete, individual perspective. Within this level, Stage 1 consists of a heteronomous orientation in which the child avoids breaking rules to avoid physical consequences. Similar to Piaget's framework, the reasoning in Stage 1 is egocentric. In Stage 2, there is an emergence of moral reciprocity, and the child follows rules only when it is in someone's immediate interest. At the Conventional level, in Stage 3, the individual is aware of shared feelings, agreements, and expectations, and defines what is right in terms of what is expected by people close to the child. Being good involves trust, loyalty, respect, and gratitude in maintaining mutual relationships. In Stage 4, the individual is moving away from local norms and role expectations and defining what is right in terms of the laws and norms of the larger social system. At the Post-Conventional level, in Stage 5, the individual reasons using ethical fairness principles and understands that elements of morality such as regard for life and human welfare transcend particular cultures and societies. Stage 6 remains a theoretical endpoint following the five stages of creation of personal moral principles based on transcendence of cultures.

The goal of moral education according to Kohlberg is to encourage individuals to move to the next stage of moral development. Kohlberg's theory is grounded in Piagetian assumptions of cognitive development in that individuals interacting with the environment and with others will experience information and ideas that are different from their view, and through the process of equilibration, development to the next stage occurs. Kohlberg used moral dilemmas in which individuals discuss contradictions presented in scenarios and consider a course of actions. Kohlberg demonstrated his concept of moral education in schools-within-schools in which students participated as community members and sought consensual rather than majority rules. The role of teachers is crucial in the "just community" schools in that they promote rules and norms that reflect a concern for justice and rights in the community, and ultimately enforce the rules.

Carol Gilligan

Gilligan questioned Kohlberg's exclusive use of males in his work, and suggested that a morality of care could serve in the place of the morality of justice and rights suggested by Kohlberg. Gilligan said a morality of caring and responsibility is premised in nonviolence, whereas a morality of justice and rights is based on equality. In the five Kohlberg stages, one does not treat others unfairly (justice); and in the work of Gilligan, one does not turn away from someone in need of care. The morality of care emphasizes interconnectedness, and according to Gilligan emerges to a greater degree in girls owing to their early connection in identifying with their mothers. This gender debate is unsettled, but Gilligan's work has contributed to an increased awareness that care is an important component of moral reasoning and moral development.

Kazimierz Dabrowski

The Dabrowski *theory of positive disintegration* can be considered a theory of moral development. It consists of five levels ranging from total self-interest to a primary concern for others. In Level I, Primary Integration, the individual is egocentric and competitive, and there is no empathy for others, and when things go wrong it is the fault of someone else. In Level II, Unilevel Disintegration, individuals are motivated by what others think, a need for approval, and fear of punishment. In this level, conflicts may occur between the values of the family and the social group. In Level III, Spontaneous Multilevel Disintegration, individuals begin to develop an inner core of values, and intense inner conflicts occur when they become dissatisfied with how they are measuring up to their ideal, or personal standards. Dabrowski considered Level III a level of positive maladjustment in that individuals are reaching toward a higher level of development. In Level IV, Organized Multilevel Disintegration, individuals have learned to adjust to their ideal and are able to accept themselves and others with a strong sense of responsibility, and are becoming committed to serving others. They demonstrate empathy, compassion, and self-awareness. In Level V, Secondary Integration, individuals' lives are characterized by service to humanity, and they live according to the highest universal principles and values.

Rushworth Kidder

Kidder defined moral courage as being driven by principle, and he identified three strands in moral courage: (1) a commitment to moral principles, (2) an awareness of the danger involved in supporting these principles, and (3) a willingness to endure the danger and its consequences. He stressed that acts of moral courage have risks of humiliation, ridicule, and contempt, which is similar to the disintegration that Dabrowski described when an individual in Level III breaks from the group to reach toward a higher level of development. Kidder and Mikhail Gorbachev convened a meeting in San Francisco to engage 272 global thinkers to identify core values; they identified compassion, honesty, fairness, responsibility, and respect. The group concluded that these values were at the heart of humanity's search for shared values.

Robert Coles

Coles stated that children's moral character is greatly influenced by their social environment, upbringing, and examples from their parents. He said that the moral character of a child is often developed in the early years, sometimes as young as one year of age. He stressed the internal struggle in the adolescent years as individuals are involved in testing and challenging the value system that they were brought up with, and the formation of their own personal moral system. He defined moral intelligence as learning how to be with others, and how to behave in the world. Coles stressed that children look to parents and teachers for clues on how to behave, as they go about their lives demonstrating in action their assumptions, desires, and values.

E. Paul Torrance and Dorothy Sisk

Torrance and Sisk noted that many great teachers and leaders speak and act in accordance with perceptions and values reflecting a larger perspective, and as a result their words and actions awaken within others the recognition of universal truths. Through lives of service and inquiry, these individuals employ what Torrance and Sisk called spiritual intelligence, living at a level of moral development that includes a sense of purpose and a kind of otherworldliness, being in the world but not of it. Their theory of spiritual intelligence is based on an examination of psychology, science, the ancient wisdom and traditions of Eastern mysticism, the wisdom of Native American traditions, and indigenous peoples. They defined the core capacities of spiritual intelligence as concern with cosmic/existential issues and the skills of meditation, intuition, and visualization. The core values are connectedness, unity of all, compassion, and a sense of balance, responsibility, and service. The core experiences are awareness of ultimate values and their meaning, peak experiences, feelings of transcendence, and heightened awareness. The key virtues of spiritual intelligence are truth, justice, compassion, and caring. The symbolic systems include poetry, music, dance, metaphor, and stories. The brain state of spiritual intelligence is rapture as described by Michael Persinger and V. S. Ramachandran. Taking just the theme of connectedness, the disciplines of history, physics, psychology, and literature can be taught using connectedness as an organizing theme.

Unique Perception of Gifted Children

Gifted children and adults seem to have a unique perception of themselves and the world that includes heightened idealism and a sense of justice that appear at an early age. They have emotional intensity and advanced levels of moral judgment, and these two characteristics coupled with their advanced cognitive ability enables them to understand social and moral issues. However, they lack the ability to cope with the issues emotionally, and they may feel frustration over not being able to address them. In addition, their advanced level of moral judgment makes them highly critical of injustice and the lack of integrity in individuals and society, which can cause them to become overwhelmed by their knowledge of societal issues and problems, and their inability because of their youth to address them in a meaningful manner.

The suggestions of Piaget to involve children in cooperative decision making and problem solving to nurture their moral development; and the exploration of moral dilemmas advocated by Kohlberg focusing on *justice and right;* and on *care* as suggested by Gilligan, can help foster the moral development of gifted students. Kidder said moral courage can be developed using his three principles: being committed to moral principles, being aware of the danger involved in supporting these principles, and being willing to endure the danger. Sisk and Torrance advocated helping gifted students to develop a sense of responsibility and awareness of their gifts, and ways to give those gifts back to society to live at a level of moral development that includes a sense of purpose. Educating for moral development has within it the hope of developing the capacity of gifted students to discover what is essential in life; particularly, in their own lives, and in the words of E. Paul Torrance, "to nourish the world."

Dorothy Sisk

See also Character and Moral Development; Cognitive Development; Emotional Development; Social Development; Spiritual Intelligence; Spirituality

Further Readings

Coles, R. (1997). *The moral intelligence of children.* Singapore: Bloomsbury Press.

Dabrowski, K., & Piechowski, M. (1977). *Theory of levels of emotional development* (Vols. 1 & 2). Oceanside, NY: Dabor Science.

Gilligan, C. (1982). *In a different voice: Psychological theory and women's development.* Cambridge, MA: Harvard University Press.

Kidder, R. (2001). *Moral courage.* New York: HarperCollins.

Kohlberg, L., & Turiel, E. (1971). Moral development and moral education. In G. Lesser (Ed.), *Psychology and educational practice.* New York: Scott, Foresman.

Piaget, J. (1965). *The moral judgment of the child.* New York: Free Press.

Sisk, D., & Torrance, E. P. (2001). *Spiritual intelligence: Developing higher consciousness.* Buffalo, NY: Creative Education Foundation Press.

Motivating Gifted Students

Understanding achievement motivation is relevant to giftedness because it plays an essential role in enabling intellectually gifted students to fulfill the promise of their exceptional abilities and in preventing their underachievement. Achievement motivation may be defined as the initiation, persistence, and direction of personal effort toward achievement goals. Contrary to popular opinion, not all gifted students are motivated to achieve in school. There is wide variation in the achievement motivation of gifted students. Furthermore, it is often taken for granted that gifted students will automatically do well in school because they learn quickly. Hence, lack of achievement motivation may go undetected because their academic work is acceptable, but closer inspection reveals they are underachieving for motivational reasons. Gifted underachievers may include those who are merely "coasting" through academic subjects because they are preoccupied with achieving in areas more meaningful to them; those who avoid rigorous courses because they fear failing to make "A" grades and blemishing a perfect grade-point average; and those who drop out of a gifted program because they do not perceive the personal or cultural relevance of school learning. All are gifted but underachieving because they lack the achievement motivation necessary for academic success matching their abilities.

The next two sections explain, illustrate, and provide educational recommendations for two complementary motivational beliefs that promote the achievement of gifted students: self-efficacy beliefs that influence achievement challenges, and value beliefs that influence achievement choices. The final section summarizes how these motivational beliefs may work together to promote optimal achievement motivation for gifted students.

Self-Efficacy Beliefs

Self-efficacy is one's self-confidence to perform a specific achievement task based on a personal evaluation of past performance. For example, a student may have developed low self-efficacy for solving acceleration problems in physics because she or he struggled and performed poorly when first attempting them. A frustrating history of poor performances will likely deflate confidence and make students reluctant to continue working on these problems unless they are taught to reevaluate initial mistakes as an opportunity to learn and try again. In general, students with low self-efficacy may experience anxiety, select easier assignments or courses, stop trying, or perform poorly, not because they lack capacity but because they lack confidence in their capacity.

The research on gifted students' self-efficacy is limited but revealing. Their beliefs about math skills are both higher and more accurate than regular students. Gender differences in self-efficacy for gifted students mirror the pattern of regular students; gifted girls perform math as well as gifted boys, but beginning in high school their self-efficacy drops. Cultural expectations during middle and high school appear to play a detrimental role by socializing girls' lower self-efficacy beliefs for math. The development of gifted boys' higher self-efficacy for math during high school appears to give them a significant motivational advantage; they exhibit greater confidence for solving difficult math problems, learning from mistakes, selecting advanced math courses, and preparing for math-related careers.

Fortunately, external influences such as cultural expectations and past performances do not completely determine self-efficacy beliefs. Applying the following recommendations, educators can help gifted students to reevaluate negative external influences and strengthen their intellectual confidence: Use an authoritative teaching style to encourage and support students' challenging achievement goals; provide mastery-related feedback to assist students to achieve their goals; model effective learning strategies that demonstrate how students can achieve their goals; and offer verbal encouragement when needed. An authoritative teacher could provide both high intellectual challenge and high instructional and emotional support, especially for gifted students who lack confidence. Initially, for the class, the teacher could model and verbally highlight how to make complex acceleration problems more manageable by breaking them into smaller parts and prioritizing steps. Next, the teacher could teach students to use an effective strategy such as visually representing the key parts of the problems with a diagram. After modeling how to apply the steps and diagram, the teacher could provide individual guided practice by circulating around the room, observing students, and giving individual feedback as students work on sample problems. If the teacher observes a student making mistakes, it is possible to reassuringly attribute the student's mistakes to the need for more effort and effective strategies over which the student has internal control: "Please redo this problem again and remember to use the diagram to identify the key parts." When the teacher observes the student correctly solving a problem, it then becomes possible to attribute this success to effort and effective strategies to build confidence: "Excellent work; I see that you correctly reworked this problem by diagramming the key parts." If the student needs additional support, the teacher may pair him or her with another student at a slightly higher level of confidence and competence who can share personal self-efficacy stories of overcoming mistakes and using effective strategies.

In contrast to an authoritative approach, an authoritarian teacher or parent who demands high challenge without adequate support will likely compound students' frustration and further weaken their self-efficacy. This demanding style causes students to become superficially preoccupied with avoiding mistakes instead of learning from them. Conversely, the permissive teacher or parent who provides high support but inadequate challenge may make students feel comfortable but will not press them to take the necessary risks to develop intellectual confidence. Least helpful, the neglectful teacher or parent fails to provide adequate challenge and support necessary for the development of intellectual confidence.

Merely providing opportunities for successful learning is not sufficient to build self-efficacy, especially for gifted students who are so bored with easy academic courses that they turn to advanced computer games, reading extracurricular material, or engaging in self-directed creative projects to provide genuine challenge. If gifted students think success is due merely to simple routine assignments, they will not attribute it to their advanced thinking skills but to easy tasks. They will not have an opportunity to develop confidence in their advanced skills unless genuinely challenged to use them. Some teachers and parents equate successful challenges with memorizing massive amounts of factual information for tests and making high grades, but this is not the kind of meaningful challenge necessary to build gifted students' confidence in their advanced thinking skills. To be meaningfully challenged, they need opportunities to explore topics in depth by doing creative assignments, conducting independent studies, performing original research, working with professional mentors, and taking university classes. They also need opportunities to accelerate learning by working at their own pace, studying with students grouped by skill level, using compacted curricula to eliminate redundancy and routine work, and skipping grade levels when needed.

Value Beliefs

Self-efficacy beliefs are one's confidence to take on and attain challenging achievement goals. Complementing self-efficacy, value beliefs are the subjective reasons and benefits for choosing and continuing to achieve. Researchers have identified different values, including interest, usefulness, and importance. Interest is the personal enjoyment of an achievement task. Usefulness is the practical benefit of an achievement task. Importance is the personal significance of doing well on an achievement task.

In general, research shows that students with high value for learning a subject tend to pay attention more, persist longer, use deeper learning strategies, and elect to continue learning. Although students with high self-efficacy are more able to take on and complete challenging achievement tasks, students with high values are more willing to choose and to continue pursuing achievement tasks in the future.

Consistent research findings show that gifted students of all ages are more intrinsically interested in academic achievement than regular students. Yet, gifted students who are interested in academics may also have conflicting interests in social areas such as peer relations and nonacademic subjects such as music and sports. Gifted girls may experience value conflicts between academics and social needs that cause them to hide their achievements or minimize them by using self-handicapping strategies. Also, minority students may experience value conflicts between academics and cultural values that cause them to minimize or reject academic achievement values.

Gifted students who are the most committed to their talent development generally perceive talent-related academics as both highly interesting in the present and highly important for career goals. Students who perceive their talent as merely a momentary interest that lacks future importance are not likely to stay committed. Conversely, students who perceive their talent as important for the future but not interesting in the present are also not likely to remain committed.

Teachers and parents can motivate gifted students by using a value-based learning approach: Determine students' learning values, create learning activities related to their values, and allow students' choice in what and how they learn and how they are evaluated. To determine students' learning values ask, listen, observe, and survey to discover their interests, what is important to them, and what is useful to them. Find out about their heroes, hobbies, use of leisure time, and extracurricular activities. To create learning activities related to their values, teachers might include opportunities for exploratory classes, interest groups, minicourses, science or social studies projects, clubs, or internships. To allow choice, teachers might offer options to study a variety of subtopics within a general topic; allow students to learn by using different learning styles and multiple intelligences; and allow students to demonstrate and share what they have learned using multiple methods such as essays, oral reports, exhibits, PowerPoint presentations, or creative performances.

Complementary Influences

Self-efficacy and value beliefs are complementary motivational influences on academic achievement. They compensate and mutually reinforce each other. Consider gifted students who are intellectually confident about a particular subject but do not value it. This lack of value will lessen their achievement motivation unless compensated by high confidence. On the other hand, consider gifted students who highly value a subject but lack intellectual confidence. This lack of confidence will lessen their achievement motivation unless compensated by high value. As self-efficacy and value increase, they begin to mutually reinforce each other. Teachers and parents may optimize achievement motivation by enhancing both students' self-efficacy for and value of academic learning.

Dan Rea

See also Dropouts, Gifted; Locus of Control; Perfectionism; Underachievement

Further Readings

Csikszentmihalyi, M., Rathunde, R., & Whalen, S. (1993). *Talented teenagers: The roots of success and failure.* New York: Cambridge University Press.

Ford, D., Alber, S., & Heward, W. (1998). Setting "motivational traps" for underachieving gifted students. *Gifted Child Today, 21*(2), 28–33.

Parke, B. (1992). *Challenging gifted students in the regular classroom.* Reston, VA: Clearinghouse on Handicapped and Gifted Children. (ERIC Digest No. E513)

Patrick, H., Gentry, M., & Owen, S. V. (2006). Motivation and gifted adolescents. In F. Dixon & S. M. Moon (Eds.), *The handbook of secondary gifted education.* Waco, TX: Prufrock Press.

Phillips, N., & Lindsay, G. (2006). Motivation in gifted students. *High Ability Studies, 17*(1) 57–73.

MULTICULTURAL ASSESSMENT

The purpose of gifted education is to select able learners and educate those children appropriately, with the view of producing gifted young adults who actually make creative contributions to a profession or recognized field of endeavor, be it music or math, physics or painting, computer science or costume design, or devising winning strategies tailored to the talents of a particular basketball team. Traditional definitions of giftedness are norm referenced, usually with some combination of tests, but with IQ being the key factor in admissions identification. The result has been that too many children selected on IQ alone have been (or should have been) furloughed from the program for lack of achievement. Yet a very high IQ is, according to the traditional model, the essence of giftedness. School, however, relies on achievement.

Most programs for the gifted admit a few children who are marginally qualified in order to "round out" a public school's minimal enrollment requirements or to meet a private school's financial obligations. To change this condition and achieve greater diversity and equity of students at the same time, Ernesto Bernal has developed a selection procedure that admits only the qualified but does so in a way that disaggregates the data before making the admissions decision, thereby giving a new meaning to the term *qualified.*

Generalists and Specialists

Although most adult gifted learners have become specialists, early specialization is especially true of children who live in poverty, who have neither the resources nor, frankly, the time or the interest to cultivate general academic achievement. Disaggregated achievement data will show each applicant's strong points, and these speak directly to his or her academic abilities. High achievement in any core area, after all, involves both motivation and ability.

The "generalist" model is the one that gifted programs in public education have been using generally. Gifted and talented programs believe that generalists have learned to succeed in all aspects of schooling and that school usually produces generalists, even if these students were specialists at the start.

In one study of two middle school magnet programs and one high school magnet, 10 percent of the children who applied for admission were specialists. Everyone with an interest in attending a magnet was told that they might qualify by making "commended" passing scores (a cutoff above the passing score) on the state-mandated examinations and by getting good teachers' recommendations. A number of these students made only passing marks on one or two tests, yet had very high scores on some of the other tests. These students, however, were not often selected in order to "make" the classes in the enrollment sense, but the weaker generalists were. The application of the generalist model leads to the use of composite scores on IQ and achievement tests. It not only misses many able learners in particular fields but also frequently relegates the institution to having to select the least qualified of the generalists in order to fill out their classes.

By selecting specialists as well as generalists in the prescribed way and by selecting from each disaggregated list of variables or tests, the schools could get the very best or at least the very highest scoring. The down side is that some of the specialists would probably not initially be motivated to do well in courses in which they had little interest, preferring to devote more time to activities of their own choosing, much as gifted adults do. Teachers may really have to *teach* to them.

No one would deny that the brightest mathematician needs exposure to the best teachers of social studies or literature. Schools might even come to allow that it is acceptable for some students *not* to pursue an A in every subject, much like the universities that appeal to specialized students do. In fact, many middle school and high school teachers who teach advanced classes were themselves specialists in school and "got by" in college studies with Cs and Bs while making most of their As in their major and minor subjects.

Gifted generalists often need more advanced vocational counseling than gifted specialists, else they may make repeated false starts in their choice of majors and take too many years to complete a bachelor's degree. Specialists, on the other hand, need to be certain that their chosen fields are in line with their personalities and need to sample related life experiences before finally committing to a career choice. In both cases, counselors and mentors who work with the gifted can help.

Identification Process

One method of increasing diversity and fairness is out-of-level testing by one grade level to ensure that the resultant scores are more accurate, since many of the students will score at the upper ranges in their areas of strength, where it is difficult to tell the differences among applicants.

IQ tests are not the only ways to measure intelligence, and IQ tests should not be regarded as the sole predictors of children's futures in professional or artistic endeavors.

The basic psychometric quality for the tests and other instruments used in admissions for gifted and talented programs has to do with their predictive validity. These tests should be indicators of whether a child has the potential for achieving giftedness by high school graduation or eminence by mature adulthood. In any case, predictive validity studies typically require an extensive follow-up of students, a feature that public gifted education needs to develop. Adjustments in the criterion scores on tests used for initial screening can then be made empirically according to such characteristics of the student as type of giftedness, age/grade when the student was tested, ethnicity, gender, and socioeconomic status.

Documentation of results is important, but is only rarely done. For example, it is important to document the results of the children who qualify only on the basis of IQ, to see how these children compare (a) to those who qualified for the program on only one or two scales of an achievement test; (b) to those who qualified on three or more achievement scales; and (c) to those who qualified under both achievement and ability criteria. Outcomes should include a number of exclusively gifted criteria: furloughs from the gifted and talented program, achievement in college and later in life, "false starts" in college, and, for those still in high school who need more proximal measures, scores on Advanced Placement (AP) tests and ACTs or SATs, grades on Advanced Level Products, number and extensiveness (years) of scholarships earned, and actual college placements (not just admissions). The ultimate fates of generalists and specialists, both, can be specified empirically, not as a matter of personal belief. Educators might be surprised at the results of such follow-ups.

Teacher Nomination

Furthermore, reliance on teachers to initiate the assessment-selection cycle actually makes their power to nominate the most important factor in the identification process, what is called a threshold variable, because it can block any further consideration of a child's qualifications. Considerable bias enters at this crucial point unless the teachers are well trained in both gifted and talented identification strategies *and* multicultural education. In the case of students who are English language learners (ELLs), the teacher must know the child's native language and culture well enough to detect a high level of linguistic sophistication, for example, or appreciate the role reversal and linguistic-cognitive facility necessary for a child to serve as an interpreter for her or his newcomer family. Also, Max Plata has shown that teachers tend to nominate and rate highly those Hispanic students who are most acculturated, not those who maintain strong ethnic bonds and exhibit traditional behaviors.

Talent Pools

These issues make a compelling case for selecting students for the gifted and talented program only after they have been tried out in a talent pool under the mentorship of a gifted and talented teacher who can provide an advanced opportunity to learn. Teachers can certainly contribute knowledge about a child's learning characteristics and motivation, for instance. A talent pool in the early elementary years may eliminate the need for premature labeling of a child as gifted yet still allow different children to slip in and out of the gifted and talented learning and creating mode as needed (somewhat like Renzulli's *revolving door identification model*).

Talent pools take the guesswork out of selection to a great extent, precisely because they reveal actual performance and achievement. Talent pools can offer a practical definition of giftedness by focusing on pupil products, which are essential to identification.

The Able Learner

First, there are few truly gifted children who, as children, make independent, creative contributions to a field. Second, the task of gifted education is to select able learners and cultivate them to become gifted and talented young adults. The selection process is only a way to pick the ones who, with the right development, will turn out to be the gifted young adults and the leaders or disciplinary experts of tomorrow. Giftedness is thus left as the goal of gifted education, not as the starting point.

The "best and brightest" children require the best teachers in every discipline, teachers who want to work with bright kids and meet their needs, even if this means getting some of the children motivated and interested in learning.

Implications for Education Professionals

The selection of gifted and talented students for the program has implications for the professional development of teachers, counselors, and administrators.

- Education professionals can open many avenues for nominating students. They can encourage peer, parental, and self-nominations. Gifted and talented students in the third grade and above who are already in the gifted and talented program often know other capable children who have not yet been selected.

- In order to avoid the problems caused for culturally or linguistically different students by late nomination to the gifted and talented program, educators can provide such programmatic options as dual-language gifted and talented or highly differentiated instruction in ESL classes, and ensure that all schools in the district can accept students beyond, say, Grade 2. If one's district has bilingual teachers, one can train the teachers in bilingual education and design a dual-language option for gifted and talented students in selected schools, programs where the parents of native speakers of English and ELLs empower the school to bring their gifted children together to receive their academic instruction in all core areas in both languages, develop high levels of proficiency in two languages, and secure thereby the cognitive advantages of bilingualism to children's development.

- The incorporation of matrices summarizes—and weights—the results of previous assessments and performance, such as scores, grades, and behavioral factors. As a result, these matrices can bias the selection-identification process if these instruments have not been empirically validated for the district. It does not matter that the matrix in question is commercially available or "looks" to be valid; wrong weights can turn an otherwise good summary into an invalid one.

It is important that all rating scales be validated against the critical indicators of performance of gifted and talented students. A representative from the R & D office in the district can help design the study, or an independent consultant who can work with the Gifted and Talented Coordinator can be contracted to get this done. Gifted and Talented Project Coordinators should remember that evaluation research is an important tool for improving the selection process itself. An objective evaluation might find that major parts of the process are flawed and need to be reconceptualized.

- The use of multiple criteria should be promulgated in a multiple regression manner so that all the gifted and talented students can be selected and educated, and the gifted and talented program can have a validated system of selection. Multiple criteria also permit some criteria to compensate for others and to identify content specialists, thereby promoting diversity in the selection of students.

- Including portfolio assessments in the selection battery as an avenue for certain children to qualify for the gifted and talented program allows children's actual intellectual performances, not just test scores, to be included prior to selection. Linda Silverman warns that the use of tests that rely almost exclusively on sequential cognitive processing will screen out children with a strong visual-spatial learning style. Different avenues to selection, including leadership and musical skills, should be available.

- Although there are a few economically disadvantaged gifted children who can compete on the composite score, many poor and minority students who do well on only one or two subtests of a larger achievement battery will nevertheless make outstanding gifted and talented students and often do better than some of their advantaged peers in the long run.

- Consequently, a sole high score on a subtest on either reading or mathematics or science or social studies should suffice for the diagnosis of "capable learner." The final step is to review children's products for advanced content and creativity.

Additional Considerations for Equitable Assessment

Teachers and diagnosticians should be trained in how assessment can be made helpful to students. Assessment criteria for admission, for example, should be diagnostic as well as selective, so that students may find their results useful in designing their courses of study and providing vocational guidance.

An updated, multicultural review of the notion of giftedness is appropriate in order to improve the contributions made by teachers to the selection of children of poverty and culturally and linguistically different backgrounds. Too often the children's beliefs and social practices mask their giftedness from the eyes of teachers who are not used to noting intelligent behaviors among them.

Ernesto M. Bernal

See also Identification; Intelligence; Multicultural Curriculum; Underrepresentation

Further Readings

Alamprese, J. A., & Erlanger, W. J. (1989, March). *No gift wasted: Effective strategies for educating highly able, disadvantaged students in mathematics and science: Vol. 1. Findings* (Report prepared under contract No. 300–87–0152, U.S. Department Education, OPBE). Washington, DC: Cosmos Corporation.

Bernal, E. M. (2003). Delivering two-way bilingual immersion programs to the gifted and talented: A classic yet progressive option for the new millennium. In J. F. Smutny (Ed.), *Underserved gifted populations: Responding to their needs and abilities.* Cresskill, NJ: Hampton Press.

Dai, D. Y., & Renzulli, J. S. (2000). Dissociation and integration of talent development and personal growth: Comments and suggestions. *Gifted Child Quarterly, 44*(4), 247–251.

Howard, E. R., & Sugarman, J. (2001, March). *Two-way immersion programs: Features and statistics.* Washington, DC: ERIC Clearinghouse on Languages and Linguistics, Center for Applied Linguistics. (ERIC Document Reproduction Service No. EDO-FL-01–01)

Masten, W. G., & Plata, M. (2000). Acculturation and teacher ratings of Hispanic and Anglo-American students. *Roeper Review, 23*(1), 45–46.

Passow, A. H. (1985). The gifted child as exceptional. In J. Freeman (Ed.), *The psychology of gifted children* (pp. 23–34). New York: Wiley.

Silverman, L. K. (2003). The power of images: Visual-spatial learners. *Gifted Education Communicator, 34*(1), 14–17, 38–40.

Sternberg, R. J. (1984). Testing intelligence without IQ tests. *Phi Delta Kappan, 65*(10), 694–698.

Sternberg, R. J. (2000). Patterns of giftedness: A triarchic analysis. *Roeper Review, 22*(4), 231–235.

Valdés, G. (2003). *Expanding definitions of giftedness: The case of young interpreters from immigrant communities.* Mahwah, NJ: Lawrence Erlbaum.

Multicultural Creativity

Culture determines what parents and schools will teach their children based on the needs of the community. Multicultural creativity is based on an expanded concept of giftedness in which unrecognized multiculturally creative students have shown exceptional abilities that have not been valued due to the difficulty of identifying their talents. The concept of multicultural people refers to individuals who belong to or are very comfortable in living and interacting in more than one culture and who, because of it, have the potential to produce unique strengths such as bilingualism, cognitive development, and multiculturalism.

Demographic changes in the United States have brought a significant number of culturally diverse populations. Continuous mass immigration had been a feature of economy and society since the first half of the 19th century. The absorption of the stream of immigrants became, in itself, a prominent feature of the United States. About 25 percent of the total U.S. population report that they belong to a race other than European American; this group consists of Black or African Americans, Asian Americans, American Indian or Alaska Natives, Native Hawaiian or other Pacific Islanders, Hispanics or Latinos, and also by people who belong to more than one race or a race different from the ones mentioned above. Cities like New York, Los Angeles, and Miami are characterized by their diverse population, in which Latinos and Asians are the main growing groups. Immigrant cultures in the United States are mixed and amalgamated, developing new subcultures within a given ethnic group. In 1992, the U.S. Census Bureau reported that the number of biracial children was increasing faster than the number of monoracial babies; more than 100,000 biracial children have been born every year since 1989; and since that time, more than 1 million first-generation biracial babies have been born.

Diverse students in the United States are predominantly Latino or Hispanic, Asian, African American or Black, and Native American. Latinos in the United States are well known for the rapid growth of their numbers. According to the Surgeon General's report in 1999, census projections reported that by 2050 the number of Latinos will increase to 97 million, becoming nearly one-fourth of the U.S. population. This dynamic group is a community of first-, second-, and third-generation immigrants who have uprooted their families and left homes, friends, and relatives for economic, political, professional, ideological, and educational reasons. Asians comprise people who come from more than two dozen Asian nations such as Cambodia, China, Korea, Japan, India, Vietnam, and Thailand, to mention a few. This group is expected to continue to grow, reaching close to 41 million by 2050. Native Americans are those whose origins are found in any of the original peoples of North America and who maintain cultural identification through tribal affiliation or community recognition. Although not as fast-growing as the previous groups mentioned, projections on Native Americans indicate an increase in their population.

The focus of this entry is on the United States, but it is clear from international trends that the world is becoming a multicultural society; immigration and emigration are powerful forces on every inhabited continent and in every industrialized country. In the future, most societies will benefit from the meeting of many cultures, producing creative work across domains of human endeavor.

Education and Multicultural Creativity

The term *multiculturalism* refers to both a state of cultural and of ethnic diversity within the demographics of a particular social space. A multicultural individual is one who experiences two or more cultures at the same time, learns the languages spoken, believes in the values established, lives important traditions, and possesses a great sense of belongingness in the cultures the person belongs to.

It has been said that children who belong to more than one culture enrich the U.S. educational system but also represent challenges to educators, policymakers, and parents due to their unique educational characteristics. Today's monocultural and monolingual education does not offer the tools and resources needed by multicultural students to capitalize on their unique strengths. On the other hand, when students who are culturally and linguistically diverse are properly guided and instructed, they have the potential to produce unique strengths.

Following are some of the strengths that multiculturally creative students bring to the education system:

Skills in their first (native) language, which includes listening, speaking, reading, and writing. Concepts already learned by bilingual learners can be easily transferred into English and developed as students apply them to many second-language activities. Bilingualism enhances cognitive and social growth, competitiveness in a global marketplace, national security, and understanding of diverse peoples and cultures.

Bicultural cognitive and affective experiences that enable them to survive successfully in two worlds. By growing up in two or more cultures they possess the information concerning customs, languages, and perceptions of the world from each culture they belong to. This background knowledge will affect their conceptualization of the world and their personal insights. In addition, the use of more than one language increases their fluency, originality, flexibility, and elaboration in thinking. Bilingual learners may have two or more words for a single object or idea, they may enjoy more advanced processing of verbal material, more discriminating perceptual distinctions, more propensity to search for structure in perceptual situations, and more capacity to reorganize their perceptions.

Personal psychological insights and the capacity for empathy. This unique social intelligence allows multicultural students to gather valuable conceptualizations of the world around them in their first language. Proficiency in two or more cultures creates multiple systems for perceiving, evaluating, believing, and acting. It has been suggested that multicultural individuals are more likely to respect other people and other cultures that are different from their own; they develop an appreciation for the range of cultural competencies available to all human beings. Music, art, science, and social systems are likely to be transformed by the challenge of synthesizing new ideas from the many cultures of the world.

Victoria Elena Frebe

See also Bilingualism and Creativity; Cultural Conceptions of Giftedness; Literary Creativity; Multilingualism; Verbal Ability

Further Readings

Esquivel, G. B., & Houtz, J. (Eds.). (2000). *Creativity and giftedness in culturally diverse students.* Cresskill, NJ: Hampton Press.

Sogunro, O. (2001). Toward multiculturalism: Implications of multicultural education for schools. *Multicultural Perspectives, 3*(3), 19–33.

Wardle, F. (2000). Multiracial and multiethnic students: How they must belong. *Multicultural Perspectives, 2*(4), 11–16.

Multicultural Curriculum

The curriculum in American public and private schools is a curriculum that tends to support the lifestyle of the White upper-middle and upper classes, the groups that determine both the ethos and the directionality of American society. Yet American educators must ask why the power structure overlooks the moral/ethical, intellectual, historical, and cultural traditions of nondominant ethnic groups. Some educators believe that gifted education programs exclude the brightest children who are from nondominant ethnic groups, segregating the children of parents with social capital from those whose parents do not have it. Students traveling to Europe can be excused for missing school for a week, whereas the travel that migrant students do for the purpose of learning by earning, doing manual farm labor, is not recognized as being educational.

Also, many school systems fail to offer placement in the gifted and talented program to qualified poor and culturally and linguistically different students. Researchers have known for years that certain White students who do not qualify are sometimes admitted to the gifted and talented program, and some culturally and linguistically different students who do qualify are not.

Similarly, there are numerous examples of monocultural gifted and talented programs that deracinate bright culturally and linguistically different children; encourage the victims of poverty to blame themselves; never incorporate ethnic social issues into their social studies curriculum; do not debate sexism in educational, political, and economic institutions; rarely read literature authored by a person from a nondominant ethnic group; do not bring diverse American cultures' music to the concert stage or recital hall; or seek other countries' perspectives on world events.

Programs

The U.S. Department of Education's Javits Program and the Advanced Placement (AP) Incentive Program have funded a number of public school projects that hold great promise for extensive institutional change in how schools meet the needs of gifted English language learners (ELLs) and gifted students who are not native speakers of English. The Connecting Worlds/*Mundos Unidos* project was funded by the Javits Program in the El Paso (Texas) Independent School District (ISD) to nurture the dual-language gifted and talented program that previously received magnet school status from the district. Here gifted and talented students receive all core-area instruction in English and Spanish, each represented 50 percent of the time, without translation. The project had its first high school graduates in 2007.

A second project, Supporting Optimal Scholarship, was funded by the AP Initiative to effect change in the AP offerings in five of Austin ISD's high schools and in the pre-AP courses in seven of its middle schools—the campuses with the highest number of low-socioeconomic students that serve as feeders to the five target high schools. Once again, this effort to increase the proportion of low-socioeconomic students in these classes means that more than superficial adaptation would be necessary. Low-socioeconomic students in these schools were surveyed to determine what constraints keep them from signing up for the pre-AP or AP classes and what modifications would be necessary to make the courses more attractive and accessible to them. This feedback alerted the AP teachers to the skills that some students still have to develop in order to succeed in the rigorous AP classes or in college. The teachers were given extensive instruction in how to "multiculturize" and attune their classes in content and method to the needs of children from poverty backgrounds.

Equity

Gifted and talented education can be made more effective for *all* gifted students at the same time. Multicultural content can introduce perspectives that are not possible from a monocultural position. The prescription for professional development is on multicultural content and on teacher sensitivities about ethnicity, gender, class, and competition versus cooperation. There are several areas of cultural competence that teachers of multicultural curriculum must exhibit: awareness and acceptance of differences, awareness of own culture, the dynamics of cultures in contact, knowledge of the different cultures represented in the classroom, and adaptation of teaching skills to new cultural contexts.

The notion that children from nondominant ethnic groups and from the poorer socioeconomic classes are just as valuable as children from the Anglo upper–middle class and need the same respect and deference should be discussed and debated outright among participants during professional training sessions. These discussions can then serve as a basis for the repartee these teachers can expect to have in class with their own students, who in turn must come to terms with their own ethnicities and biases. The immediate outcomes of these debates do not matter, for the debate itself opens options that will be reevaluated throughout the lives of the teachers—and of the students.

Over a few years, minority gifted and talented teachers can be trained in multicultural education for the gifted and talented program. This can help to ensure an equal opportunity to learn and to promote the development of multiculturally competent future leaders among the students. Gender, cultural, and class issues are potent ways educators can promote critical thought and apply creative solutions to social problems.

As a matter of practice, if not of policy, more gifted and talented teachers of color should be placed in predominantly White gifted and talented programs. If this does not happen, it is likely that change will be so slow that it may seem imperceptible. Once a critical mass of teachers of color enter the gifted and talented program, however, many of the seemingly insurmountable difficulties of achieving equity will likely disappear, for the minority teachers can help their colleagues get a perspective on the issues and resolve the problems they perceive.

The integrated gifted and talented teachers should be engaged in cooperative curriculum development, selecting and designing educational materials, and expanding the effective methodologies employed in the education of gifted and talented children, for example, by adopting the use of Advanced Academic Products and their rubric-guided assessments.

It is important not to accelerate ELLs out of their ESL or bilingual programs just because they have been selected for the gifted and talented program. Instead, educators should make certain that these ELL gifted and talented students are receiving appropriately paced instruction in their content areas from ESL or bilingual teachers who have learned how to doubly differentiate instruction for gifted and talented students. In fact, educators should treat any effort to teach English to linguistically different gifted and talented students as enrichment. This way, the message that any language other than English is not of any value will not be communicated (at least not in class), and these ELL gifted and talented students may grow up to be both bilingual and bicultural, with all the associated cognitive and vocational benefits that such traits accrue.

The focus should continue to be on multidimensional and cross-cultural ways of finding the qualities of intellectual and creative potential of children, not just on the scores they earn, or else gifted and talented students from culturally and linguistically different groups may forever be excluded in greater proportions than Whites and not have an equitable opportunity to enter gifted and talented programs and, later, to be admitted to selective colleges or graduate or professional programs, either. That they may not take to the gifted and talented program in a completely conforming and "grateful" manner just has to be chalked up to the cultural diversity in the gifted and talented pool.

Multicultural Education

Though some schools may attempt to change the selection process, the gifted and talented curriculum and support services are not changed by these efforts. There is also the question of curriculum that fails to reflect the cultures of the students and the issues that count with them. A monocultural curriculum accounts for much of the variance in why some students from nondominant ethnic groups either eschew the gifted and talented program in the first place or elect to leave it soon after they are admitted—factors that contribute to their alienation and to underrepresentation as well. If the gifted and talented program had a reputation of responding to children from nondominant ethnic groups in a positive manner, then "acting White" could become a thing of the past.

Multicultural education requires educators not only to learn new attitudes, new pedagogy, and new content, but also how to integrate these into their everyday work with all gifted and talented students. Multicultural education helps White students discover whiteness; examines male privilege cross-culturally; and raises awareness of the dominant economic, political, and educational institutions. Multicultural education, in short, honors diverse cultural traditions and moral values; reflects the artistic, literary, and scientific accomplishments of the different groups; recognizes the intellectual and philosophical contributions made to the world by various cultures; utilizes pedagogy that capitalizes upon the repertoire and learning styles of each group; and purchases educational materials that reflect their social realities. Multicultural education, then, legitimizes individual choice, so that "majority" and "minority" students alike can acculturate without shame, maintain their cultural identities, or become multiculturally and bilingually competent.

Multicultural education must deal with current issues and leaders, and use the differences among groups to explore the underlying realities that are at the core of what society has constructed. What is more, the underlying motive for engaging these activities is to empower students to act responsibly, better control their own destinies, and make a difference in society as well.

Ernesto M. Bernal

See also Multicultural Assessment; Underrepresentation

Further Readings

Banks, J. A. (1993). Multicultural education: Development, dimensions, and challenges. *Phi Delta Kappan, 75*(1), 22–28.

Bernal, E. M. (2007). The plight of the culturally diverse student from poverty. In J. VanTassel-Baska & T. Stambaugh (Eds.), *Overlooked gems: A national perspective on low-income promising learners* (pp. 27–30). Washington, DC, and Williamsburg, VA: National Association for Gifted Children, and College of William and Mary, Center for Gifted Education.

Bourdieu, P. (1984). *Distinction: A social critique of the judgment of taste.* Cambridge, MA: Harvard University Press.

Harris, C. I. (1993). Whiteness as property. *Harvard Law Review, 106*(8), 1709–1791.

Nieto, S. (2000). *Affirming diversity* (3rd ed.). New York: Longman.

Ogbu, J. U. (2003). *Black American students in an affluent suburb: A study of academic disengagement.* Mahwah, NJ: Lawrence Erlbaum.

Philips, S. U. (1976). Commentary: Access to power and maintenance of ethnic identity as goals of multicultural education. *Anthropology and Education Quarterly, 7*(4), 30–32.

Valdés, G. (2003). *Expanding definitions of giftedness: The case of young interpreters from immigrant communities.* Mahwah, NJ: Lawrence Erlbaum.

Multilingualism

Multilingualism, and also bilingualism, refers to a person's ability to speak more than one language. Although there are many ways to become bi- or multilingual, the capability of becoming multilingual is universal to all humans, barring severe mental and/or language impairment. Verbal aptitude as well as verbal giftedness may play a part in becoming multilingual, but they are not necessary preconditions for successful language learning. Finally, bi- and multilinguals who are also gifted are frequently overlooked in schools, as these children may be in the process of learning the language of the classroom and are assessed by instruments that have been normed on monolingual children.

Bilingualism and multilingualism are technically not synonyms, because bilingualism refers to the ability to speak two languages and multilingualism refers to the ability to speak multiple languages, though the terms will be used interchangeably here. Also, a distinction is drawn between minority and majority languages, where the majority language is the language spoken by the most socially powerful community and the minority language is the language spoken by a smaller, less powerful group, such as an immigrant or indigenous community.

Becoming Multilingual

Many factors can influence the development of bilingualism, including the age of acquisition, which will be discussed here. Other factors include the manner of acquisition, identity, motivation, and language community. Children who are raised in a bilingual environment from birth, where each parent speaks a different language, for instance, are referred to as simultaneous bilinguals. The cognitive processes of becoming bilingual at this age mirror the processes of a monolingual child acquiring one language and fall under the scope of *first language acquisition.* For this reason, simultaneous bilinguals are traditionally assumed to be equally proficient in both languages. Sequential bilinguals, on the other hand, learn a second or subsequent language after learning their first language. The cognitive processes involved are different to some extent from first language acquisition, and the process is referred to as *second language acquisition.* There are also associated age-of-acquisition effects in second language acquisition, such that few sequential bilinguals become as proficient as simultaneous bilinguals or native speakers.

Verbal Giftedness and Multilingualism

Howard Gardner was one of the first researchers to suggest that linguistic intelligence is separate from general intelligence, and he has shown that linguistic intelligence can exist independently of other forms of intelligence. However, all normally developing children acquire their first language(s) as a result of a process innate to humans. In addition, linguistic intelligence and verbal giftedness may facilitate success in learning a second language, but they do not guarantee multilingualism nor do they indicate that all bilinguals, particularly sequential bilinguals, are gifted. Yet the variable degrees of success in second language acquisition indicate that there are many factors involved in becoming bilingual, and verbal giftedness may well play a part in the most successful cases.

Bi- and Multilingual Children and Giftedness

Bilingual children, especially minority language children, are frequently overlooked in assessing giftedness for a number of reasons. First and foremost, children who are still in the process of learning the language of the classroom may not be able to demonstrate their full intellectual potential, especially in monolingual environments. Moreover, many of the assessment instruments used to determine giftedness have been normed on monolingual children, and research has shown that bilingual children perform differently on standardized measures as compared to monolingual children. In addition, these measures, such as the WISC (Wechsler Intelligence Scale for Children) or the SAT—V (Scholastic Aptitude Test—Verbal), focus on academic skills, which may not reflect the abilities of gifted bilingual children, especially on verbal tasks. Last, the educational policies and attitudes concerning minority language students may affect the identification of gifted bilingual children, especially if monolingualism in the majority language is seen as the norm. In this case, children who do not speak the majority language are seen as deficient, and the rapid acquisition of the majority language is considered normal rather than valued as a talent.

There is a small, growing body of research concerning gifted bilingual children. Ernesto Bernal, for instance, has focused on identifying and supporting gifted bilingual children, especially those who may not be verbally gifted. In particular, he has advocated for the early identification of gifted bilingual children, even before they have become fully proficient in the classroom language. He argues that these children benefit from early identification and the subsequent access to gifted programs, especially if those programs are bilingual. Alternatively, Guadalupe Valdés has looked at the special case of children, referred to as *language brokers,* who interpret for their families and community members. Language brokers utilize a wide range of skills in interpreting (i.e., sensitivity to social roles); draw on cognitive resources such as memory and comprehension speed; and must interpret in a wide variety of situations, which requires both an understanding of the language involved as well as knowledge of the underlying themes and topics. For instance, a child who interprets in a medical situation must understand doctor–patient relations, understand and convey the topic being discussed, and be able to temporarily assume the roles of doctor and patient, such that misunderstandings are anticipated and prevented. Consequently, Valdés has suggested that these children also demonstrate characteristics typical of giftedness.

Kara T. McAlister

See also Bilingualism and Creativity; Multiple Intelligences; SAT; Verbal Ability; Wechsler Intelligence Scale for Children–Fourth Edition

Further Readings

Baker, C., & Prys Jones, S. (Eds.). (1998). *Encyclopedia of bilingualism and bilingual education.* Clevendon, UK: Multilingual Matters.

Bernal, E. (1994, April). *Finding and cultivating minority gifted/talented students.* Paper presented at the National Conference on Alternative Teacher Certification, Washington, DC.

Garcia, E. E., & Flores, B. (Eds.). (1986). *Language and literacy research in bilingual education.* Tempe, AZ: Arizona State University, Center for Bilingual Education.

Gardner, H. (1983). *Frames of mind: The theory of multiple intelligences.* New York: Basic Books.

Valdés, G. (2003). *Expanding definitions of giftedness: The case of young interpreters from immigrant communities.* Mahwah, NJ: Lawrence Erlbaum.

Multiple Intelligences

The theory of multiple intelligences was developed by Howard Gardner in the early 1980s. According to Gardner, individuals possess eight or more relatively autonomous intelligences that they use to create products and solve problems. The eight intelligences identified by Gardner are linguistic, logical-mathematical, spatial, musical, bodily-kinesthetic, naturalistic, interpersonal, and intrapersonal.

Multiple intelligences theory is a departure from the traditional conception of intelligence that stretches back to the start of the 20th century. In the early 1900s, French psychologist Alfred Binet designed a 30-item intelligence test for identifying schoolchildren in need of special education. Binet's test gained a wider audience after American psychologist Lewis Terman developed a commercial version for use in schools and the workplace. Around the same time as Binet's pioneering work, English psychologist Charles Spearman published a paper on "general intelligence" (g) in which he argued that all forms of intellectual activity stem from a unitary or general ability for problem solving. Although Binet and Terman had developed their scales with the goal of predicting particular types of performance and *not* as a general measure of intelligence, their work was taken as support of Spearman's theory. And, in fact, Spearman's unitary conception of intelligence went relatively unchallenged for much of the 20th century.

Development of Multiple Intelligences Theory

In 1983, Howard Gardner published a book titled *Frames of Mind* that was inspired by several simple but powerful questions; Gardner wondered whether talented chess players, musicians, and athletes could be considered intelligent in their respective fields and, if so, why these abilities were not considered in traditional conceptions of intelligence. Out of these initial questions came Gardner's assertion that intelligence is better conceived of as multiple rather than unitary in nature. Though proponents of general intelligence believe a high IQ score to indicate an individual's potential for high achievement across a wide spectrum of intellectual activities, multiple intelligences theory conceives of its eight intelligences as relatively autonomous from one another. In other words, an individual who demonstrates a particular aptitude in one intelligence does not necessarily demonstrate comparable aptitude in another intelligence. Rather, individuals can be thought of as possessing profiles of intelligence in which they demonstrate varying levels of strength and weakness for each of the eight intelligences. Thus, it is a misunderstanding of multiple intelligences theory to claim, for example, that a particular individual possesses "no" logical-mathematical intelligence. It is certainly possible for an individual to demonstrate a low skill level in logical-mathematical intelligence, but, excluding cases of severe brain damage, all individuals possess the full range of intelligences.

Most proponents of general intelligence conceive of intelligence as an innate trait with which one is born and can do little to change. In contrast, multiple intelligences theory regards intelligence as a combination of heritable potentials and of skills that can be deepened through relevant experiences. For example, one individual might be born with a strong potential for spatial intelligence that allows him or her to read maps quickly and easily while another individual needs to study and practice diligently in order to acquire a similar level of expertise. Both individuals achieve strong levels of performance in spatial intelligence, though their pathways to acquiring this skill differ.

Identifying the Intelligences

Multiple intelligences theory remains controversial in psychology due, in large part, to the evidence upon which the theory is based. Most other theories of intelligence are based upon empirical data collected from psychometric instruments or experimental studies in which subjects are presented with test items believed to assess intellectual capability. The theory of multiple intelligences, in contrast, draws from a wider and more varied body of data. Specifically, Gardner developed multiple intelligences theory by synthesizing research from evolutionary biology, neuroscience, anthropology, psychometrics, and psychological studies of prodigies and savants. From these varied sources, Gardner developed several criteria for identifying an intelligence. These criteria are described by Mindy Kornhaber, Edward Fierros, and Shirley Veneema in their 2004 book, *Multiple Intelligences: Best Ideas From Research and Practice:*

- It should be seen in relative isolation in prodigies, autistic savants, stroke victims, or other exceptional populations. In other words, certain individuals should demonstrate particularly high or low levels of a particular capacity in contrast to other capacities.
- It should have a distinct developmental trajectory. That is, different intelligences should develop at different rates and along paths that are distinctive.
- It should have some basis in evolutionary biology. In other words, an intelligence ought to have a previous instantiation in primates or other species and putative survival value.
- It should be susceptible to capture in symbol systems.
- It should be supported by evidence from psychometric tests of intelligence.
- It should be distinguishable from other intelligences through experimental psychological tasks.
- It should demonstrate a core information-processing system. That is, there should be specifiable mental processes that handle information related to each intelligence.

Shortly after issuing the original theory, Gardner pointed out an important distinction. An *intelligence* is a raw intellectual potential to process certain kinds of information in certain kinds of ways. In contrast, a *domain* or *discipline* is an organized body of skill and knowledge in a culture. Observers cannot directly measure intelligences; they can only infer an intellectual strength from the ease with which an individual improves his or her performance in a domain. Thus, for example, high performance in the domain of surgery or of aviation suggests high spatial intelligence; and an individual with high bodily- kinesthetic intelligence is likely to achieve success in the domains of athletics, dance, or crafts.

From the aforementioned criteria, Gardner conceived of eight distinct intelligences. These intelligences are best described in terms of the domains in which individuals with high intellectual potentials are likely to be found. Thus, for example, individuals with high *linguistic intelligence* are able to analyze information and create products involving oral and written language such as speeches, books, and letters. Politicians, poets, and trial attorneys typically possess profiles of intelligence high in linguistic intelligence. *Logical-mathematical intelligence* allows individuals to create proofs, solve equations, and carry out complex calculations. Engineers, scientists, and analytic philosophers are likely to be highly skilled in this intelligence. *Spatial intelligence* allows individuals to understand maps and other types of graphical information. Architects and graphic designers typically demonstrate high levels of aptitude for spatial intelligence. *Musical intelligence* enables individuals to create and make meaning of different patterns of sound. Violinists, DJs, and scientists specializing in bird calls or whale songs are all likely to possess profiles of intelligence high in musical intelligence. *Bodily-kinesthetic intelligence* entails using one's own body to create products or solve problems. Surgeons, athletes, and dancers typically demonstrate high levels of aptitude in bodily-kinesthetic intelligence. *Interpersonal intelligence* reflects an individual's ability to recognize and understand other people's moods, desires, motivations, and intentions, while *intrapersonal intelligence* reflects an individual's ability to recognize and assess these characteristics within him- or herself.

Gardner's original theory of multiple intelligences identified the seven intelligences described above. However, in the mid-1990s, Gardner determined that naturalistic intelligence also met the criteria for identification as an intelligence. *Naturalistic intelligence* enables individuals to identify and distinguish among various types of plants, animals, weather formations, and other products of the natural world. Individuals with high levels of naturalistic intelligence might be suited for careers in zoology, meteorology, and botany.

Existential intelligence has been described as the intelligence of big questions—the ability to consider issues of life, death, love, being, and the like. Individuals with a high aptitude for existential intelligence might be drawn to careers in philosophy, poetry, or theology. Gardner has jokingly referred to existential intelligence as a "half-intelligence" because, thus far, it has been found to meet a substantial number of the criteria for identification as an intelligence, but not all of them. For now,

Gardner has held off on classifying existential intelligence as a full-fledged ninth intelligence.

Other researchers have suggested the existence of additional intelligences: moral intelligence, humor intelligence, cooking intelligence, and so on. To date, however, Gardner has found none of these proposed intelligences to meet a substantial number of the criteria for identification as a unique intelligence. That said, Gardner leaves open the possibility of advances in fields such as genetics or neuroscience leading to the identification of additional intelligences in the future or, even, the reconstitution of existing intelligences. For example, it is possible that the intelligence currently identified as logical-mathematical intelligence will be found to be composed of several subintelligences: a subintelligence for processing small numbers, a subintelligence for estimation, and so on. Such adjustments to the current theory of multiple intelligences are virtually inevitable. Determining the precise number of intelligences, however, is far less important than multiple intelligences theory's overarching premise that intelligence is better understood as multiple rather than general.

Multiple intelligences theory is a departure from the traditional conception of general intelligence and has been the target of substantial critique from the scientific community since its emergence in the 1990s. One criticism is that a theory such as multiple intelligences theory that was developed through a synthesis of existing research requires empirical validation that neither Gardner nor anyone else has provided. A second criticism of multiple intelligences theory focuses on Gardner's claim that "g" (or general intelligence) has little explanatory power beyond predicting success in school. Researchers such as Daniel Willingham and Linda Gottfredson have reported that an individual's performance across a variety of intellectual tasks tends to be highly correlated and that traditional IQ tests are, in fact, strong predictors of a variety of outcomes, including future job performance. Other researchers have added that tests measuring Gardner's individual intelligences highly correlate with traditional IQ tests as well.

Applications of Multiple Intelligences Theory

Educators from a diverse range of schools in dozens of different countries have embraced the theory with tremendous enthusiasm. Nevertheless, it is important to bear in mind that multiple intelligences theory offers neither an established curriculum nor an educational goal for either students or educators to pursue. Rather, the theory of multiple intelligences is an *idea* about the concept of intelligence. Thousands of different teachers, schools, and researchers have applied this idea to education in many different ways. Some schools have utilized the vocabulary of multiple intelligences theory among their faculty to discuss the strengths and weaknesses of their students. Other educators have explicitly sought to develop curricula and lesson plans that allow students to draw upon several different intelligences. The most effective uses of multiple intelligences theory have been those that recognize multiple intelligences theory to be a tool for achieving a particular educational goal rather than an end in itself.

One school that has effectively utilized multiple intelligences theory to support teaching and learning is the New City School in St. Louis, Missouri. The New City School is an urban elementary school that began in 1988 to design and implement curriculum that allows students to draw upon all eight of their intelligences. Rather than shifting the school's goals to adapt to multiple intelligences theory, however, the New City faculty recognized that multiple intelligences theory held the potential to support their existing beliefs that all children are talented in different ways, that the arts are a critical piece of the elementary school curriculum, and that children need to learn interpersonal skills in the same ways that they learn their academic subjects. In short, educators at the New City School believe that schools should be places where students learn to solve problems in a variety of ways. They have found multiple intelligences theory to provide a useful framework for achieving this educational goal.

A very different application of multiple intelligences theory can be found at Danfoss Universe. Danfoss Universe is a 10-acre science experience park that opened in 2005 near Sønderborg, Denmark. The park includes a museum-sized building called the Explorama that contains dozens of hands-on exhibits through which visitors learn about their various intelligences. For example, an exhibit on musical intelligence allows visitors to create their own melodies on a theremin—an electronic instrument that responds to movement rather than touch. By moving their hands in different directions and in different patterns within the vicinity of two antennae, visitors are able to produce and learn about different melodies. Another exhibit called Teambot is designed to highlight interpersonal intelligence. In this exhibit, museum visitors must work cooperatively to design a robot arm capable of moving an object from one location to another. Through these and many other exhibits, Danfoss Universe encourages visitors to reflect upon their own profiles of intelligence—their own intellectual strengths and weaknesses. Visiting can be a powerful learning experience.

Future Outlook

For more than 25 years, educators at every level, from every type of school, and from virtually every corner of the world have drawn upon multiple intelligences theory to support teaching and learning. The idea that individuals possess profiles of intelligence with varying strengths and weaknesses aligns with educators' daily experiences in working with diverse groups of students. It is likely for this reason that, even as high-stakes testing seeks to prioritize students' linguistic and logical-mathematical intelligences, there remain numerous schools such as the New City School committed to developing all eight of their students' intelligences. The next decade promises to be an exciting one for multiple intelligences theory as advances in neuroscience and genetics will undoubtedly shed further light on the pluralistic nature of intelligence and lead to further refinements of the theory.

Scott Seider

See also Emotional Intelligence; Intelligence; Intelligence Testing; Intelligence Theories; IQ; SAT

Further Readings

Chen, J., & Gardner, H. (2005). Multiple intelligences: Assessment based on multiple intelligence theory. In D. Flanagan & P. Harrison (Eds.), *Contemporary intellectual assessment: Theories, tests and issues.* New York: Guilford Press.

Gardner, H. (1983). *Frames of mind: The theory of multiple intelligences.* New York: Basic Books.

Gardner, H. (2006). *Multiple intelligences: New horizons.* New York: Basic Books.

Gottfredson, L. (2002). g: Highly general and highly practical. In R. Sternberg & E. Grigorenko (Eds.), *The general factor of intelligence: How general is it?* (pp. 331–380). Mahwah, NJ: Lawrence Erlbaum.

Jensen, A. (1998). *The g factor: The science of mental ability.* Westport, CT: Praeger.

Kornhaber, M., Fierros, E., & Veenema, S. (2004). *Multiple intelligences: Best ideas from research and practice.* Boston: Pearson Education.

Olson, L. (1988, January 27). Children flourish here: Eight teachers and a theory changed a school world. *Education Week,* 7(8), 18–19.

Willingham, D. (2004, Summer). Reframing the mind. *Education Next,* pp. 19–24.

Multipotentiality

Multipotentiality was defined by Ronald Fredrickson as "any individual who when provided with appropriate environments, can select and develop any number of competencies at a high level" (p. 268). Multipotentiality is readily seen among gifted individuals, as many have the ability to develop the necessary, specific skills to perform well in a variety of situations and possess a large number of interests. Multipotential individuals are more prevalent among the gifted population than "early-emergers," who possess intense and early interest and talent in a particular area. Multipotential students often show a pattern of high achievement in schoolwork and regular involvement in a variety of social, athletic, community, and solitary activities.

Multipotentiality has been a major concern for gifted individuals, especially when attempting to make a career decision. They often receive high-flat profiles when taking vocational or interests assessments. This indicates that they possess a large number of interests and skills; therefore, having a clear focus is difficult because a vast amount of opportunities exist. Hence, multipotential individuals often have trouble choosing a career, which can result in distress. Further, multipotential individuals may have difficulty developing a sense of purpose because they cannot easily integrate or prioritize their abilities and talents.

It is incorrect to assume that although intellectually gifted, multipotential students will be able to be successful on their own, without any guidance. Indeed, many gifted individuals report pressure to commit prematurely to the wrong career choice. Without a clear focus, multipotential individuals often prolong a career decision or resort to choosing a career haphazardly. They may choose an occupation quickly to reduce dissonance caused by competing career options or choose based on the influence of peers or family. Further, they may not become aware of other options if they focus on one strength.

To address these concerns, Barbara Kerr and her colleagues have recommended using value-based counseling, as it can be more effective for multipotential individuals than traditional vocational assessments and career counseling, which match students' abilities and interests to a particular occupation. The purpose of value-based counseling is to promote making career decisions based upon values, rather than on the more traditional focus of abilities, interests, the job market, or others' expectations. Value-based interventions include life-planning workshops, vocational and value assessments, and individual counseling. Value-based counseling can lead to a better sense of identity and purpose as well as a defined career path.

In addition, various techniques have been suggested to address the specific needs of multipotential individuals. Helping to facilitate contacts with other multipotential individuals such as peers, role models, or mentors can help validate career indecision and reinforce the idea that vocational choices are ongoing, and not a one-time decision. Contacts may also help multipotential individuals to make new discoveries about their interests through opportunities they provide. Assisting multipotential students to locate hands-on experiences, such as internships in fields related to the student's interests, are beneficial as well. Identifying or creating careers that integrate a large number of the student's interests and abilities is another way to address multipotentiality. In addition, individual counseling during the career search process can be useful to address the specific needs of the individual.

Another perspective to address vocational concerns for multipotential individuals is to embrace the magnitude of skills and interests they possess rather than focus on finding one occupation that will be suitable. Multipotential individuals who can be flexible and view themselves as being qualified for a large number of positions may find some relief for their vocational distress. Further, helping multipotential individuals recognize that they may be just as happy in one occupation as another, or that their ability to adapt to a large number of situations, may also be constructive. This perspective may help multipotential individuals feel a better sense of control and direction in their career path.

Some researchers argue that there is little empirical evidence for the existence of multipotentiality as a concept. Kerr has argued, however, that the populations showing little multipotentiality have been with Talent Search students, whose high performance on specific tests of aptitude suggests early emergent, focused career interests. Regardless of one's stance on multipotentiality, recognizing the specific needs of gifted individuals is crucial, especially when individuals lack guidance and display distress over the lack of differentiation in their interests and talents.

Rhea L. Owens

See also Adolescent, Gifted; Career Counseling; College, Gifted; Giftedness, Definition

Further Readings

Achter, J. A., Benbow, C. P., & Lubinski, D. (1997). Rethinking multipotentiality among the intellectually gifted: A critical review and recommendations. *Gifted Child Quarterly, 41*(1), 5–15.

Colangelo, N., & Zaffrann, R. T. (Eds.). (1979). *New voices in counseling gifted.* Dubuque, IA: Kendall/Hunt.

Fredrickson, R. H., & Rothney, J. W. M. (Eds.). (1972). *Recognizing and assisting multipotential youth.* Columbus, OH: Charles E. Merrill.

Kerr, B. A. (1981). *Career education for the gifted and talented.* Columbus, OH: Educational Resources Information Center Clearinghouse on Adult, Career, and Vocational Education.

Kerr, B. A., & Sodano, S. (2003). Career assessment for gifted students. *Journal of Career Assessment, 11*(2), 168–176.

Musical Creativity

Musical creativity is the ability through which subjects can express their own, personal relationship with the domain of sound, employing skills of the mind, body, and spirit. It can be found in every act related to music making, such as listening, performing, improvising, conducting, arranging, composing, and more. Musically gifted and talented people possess to a high degree what Howard Gardner defines as musical intelligence; one aspect of this type of intelligence is musical creativity. Although most humans possess the capacity to make music, musical ability is one of the earliest developing abilities, and research has shown that it must be nurtured and trained from an early age in order for the capacities to grow rather than atrophy.

In fact, most researchers consider creative thinking and acting in music as a mostly acquired behavior, claiming that musical creativity can be nurtured. They believe that everybody has the potential to produce music; most musical abilities, such as the ability to perform or compose a piece, or to make a musical improvisation, are linked more with the chances offered by the environment (exposure, learning opportunities, etc.) than to talent. This can be demonstrated by tests focused on creative thinking in music: Students who had music lessons and experienced through those lessons products and processes of musical creativity, scored higher than those who had had no music lessons.

For these reasons, a creativity-promoting music education should be given to all children and adults in order to enhance their musical knowledge and skills and promote their experience of the self and others. Moreover, because people can express with music their thoughts, feelings, memories, and fancies in a socially acceptable way, fostering musical creativity is one of the most important and widespread aims of music education.

Promoting Creativity

Different teaching styles have been studied with the aim of recognizing their effects on the development of creative thinking in music. The teacher-controlled style can undoubtedly promote positive outcomes in the student's musical development, but only the learner-centered teaching style can support and enhance learners' creative improvement, not to mention their psychological and social development. Creative teaching has therefore been proved to be essential for creative learning.

A creativity-promoting music education can be based on many different, not alternative but complementary methods. The main ones are as follows:

- Cultivating students' music awareness
- Showing students the products of musical creation and analyzing the creative processes that led to these products
- Contributing to students' active involvement in the learning process
- Giving students opportunities to experience music as their own
- Encouraging analysis of musical products
- Enhancing students' ability to think critically
- Stimulating students' imagination
- Encouraging students to find analogies and differences between basic elements in music and the arts (e.g., such as dot, line, color, form, texture, rhythm, balance, repeated modules, ornamental elements, etc.)
- Allowing students to seek analogies and differences between musical motifs and body movements (e.g., walking, jumping in place, jumping from A to B, slithering)
- Establishing comparisons between music pieces and paintings, sculptures, architectures, poems, dances, and the like
- Appraising and encouraging students' self-expression through musical products

In the past, it was thought that musical creativity could be expressed mainly through composition and improvisation. Nowadays, music pedagogues claim that creativity is central to all musical activities and takes place in different kinds of tasks: listening, analyzing, and evaluating music, performance, improvisation, and composition.

In creative listening to, analyzing, and evaluating music, subjects are actively involved in identifying, comparing, and appraising melodic, harmonic, and rhythmic elements, musical structures, styles, and so on.

In performing, subjects can express their creativity by making personal choices in many fields:

for instance, in dynamics (selecting which sounds shall be performed louder, and which softer), in timing (selecting the tempo of a piece), in agogics (selecting which sections shall be performed faster and which slower), in timbre (selecting an appropriate touch or sound for each musical phrase), in the use of embellishments (selecting if and how a phrase could be decorated through embellishments such as trills, mordents, etc.).

In improvisation and composition, subjects reveal their creativity by selecting elements belonging to their own theoretical knowledge and practical experience and bringing them together in new ways: musical form and style, melodic and rhythmic patterns, repetitions and variations, tonal stability/instability, and so on. In using these elements, a creative subject will maintain some characteristics given by tradition, and change other characteristics in order to realize a musical product that reflects his or her thoughts, feelings, and preferences.

A subject will obviously choose something he or she likes, and a subject generally likes something he or she knows well and considers familiar. Indeed, behavioral experiments have shown a significant connection between how well one knows something and how much one likes it.

Therefore music educators should allow their students to know and practice as many musical variables as possible: styles (Western art music, ethnic, commercial popular, rock, etc.), genres based on different mediums (acoustic, electronic, etc.), instruments and nontraditional sound sources, forms, works of composers, performances of interpreters, and so forth. In fact, the more learners understand and practice the musical language, the more they enlarge their musical background. Thus they will have more musical elements at their disposal and be able to improve their musical creativity.

Tools and Strategies

Information technology is present in our everyday lives as well as in our cultural lives; it follows that in music education the relationship between new technology and learning is gaining more and more significance.

The use of digital tools is very effective in enhancing the user's musical creativity, because it promotes indirect acquirement of powerful, complex musical processes. This strategy puts into practice the Pragmatists' famous principle of "learning by doing." The core concept of this approach is to place the user in a situation where specific musical processes can be acquired in an almost intuitive way. In fact, they are practiced and developed without initial, specific theoretical input, in the interaction that results between the user and the system.

For example, there are systems based on a question/answer scheme that can promote creativity in improvisation. Each phrase played by a user is continued or answered by the system in the same style. As the musical phrases produced by the system are similar but not identical to those proposed by the user, the interaction is structured on ever-changing musical phrases. In this way these devices can enhance musical invention and exploration.

Moreover, synthesizer and specific computer programs can be used with the aim of promoting musical creativity in composing. These devices can make many musical elements available to the user, who can compose pieces by putting them together in a personal way. Among these elements are vocal and instrumental timbres, melodic and rhythmic patterns, specific sound combinations such as chords and clusters, and accompaniments in different styles.

Alessandra Padula

See also Creativity Training; Musical Intelligence; Music Education; Technology

Further Readings

Parncutt, R., & McPherson G. E. (Eds.). (2002). *The science and psychology of music performance: Creative strategies for music teaching and learning.* New York: Oxford University Press.

Rowe, R. (2001). *Machine musicianship.* Cambridge: MIT Press.

Sloboda, J. A. (Ed.). (1988). *Generative processes in music.* Oxford, UK: Oxford University Press.

Musical Intelligence

From the classical compositions of Mozart to the reggae rhythms of Bob Marley, the works of many singers and musicians are respected as valuable cultural contributions, and it is likely that this has generally been the case throughout human history. Archeological and anthropological evidence suggest that music has been performed and appreciated across eras and cultures. Given the ubiquity of music, the claim made by Howard Gardner for the importance of a musical intelligence seems plausible, in that it is clear that there are large individual differences in musical ability and skill.

Gardner indicated that musical intelligence involves the composition, performance, and appreciation of music, with pitch and rhythm as the core elements of music. Individuals who are described as musically intelligent would possess greater sensitivity to these elements than would those who are considered to be less musically intelligent. However, some authors such as John Sloboda have suggested that the notion of musical intelligence is derived from the relatively modern and Western idea that music performance must be relegated to the domain of the expert—presumably, the highly musically intelligent.

Development of Musical Intelligence

It seems clear that infants are predisposed to enjoy and to generate music. The universality of rocking and singing to babies would seem to indicate a very early receptivity to music. At 2 months, babies can match the pitch, intensity, and contour (the pattern of pitch within a melody) of songs. Babies recognize pitch and tempo differences, and they prefer songs they heard when still in the womb to unfamiliar songs. That babies show some level of musicality is clear. What is less clear is the nature and origin of individual differences in musical intelligence, and when these differences become noticeable.

Gardner cited the very early accomplishments of child prodigies as evidence that some individuals are biologically predisposed to high musical achievement. Other authors have noted the unreliability of accounts of very early achievement, and have pointed to intensive instruction and practice as key components in the early development of these prodigies.

There is a widely held belief among students and music educators that without innate musical talent, a child is unlikely to ever achieve musical excellence. On the other hand, some recent research evidence has suggested that, in general, accomplished musicians differ from less accomplished musicians not in early indicators of exceptionality but, rather, in opportunities and in hours of practice. Some have argued that such research indicates only that instruction and practice are necessary but not sufficient requirements for excellence in musical performance—that is, without some requisite level of musical ability, opportunity and hard work are unlikely to yield excellent levels of musical achievement.

Given the substantial heritability of other cognitive abilities (e.g., about 50 percent for general cognitive ability), it seems likely that there would be at least some genetic influence on musical ability. Behavioral genetic studies of musical ability and/or achievement are few and limited by available criterion measures, but seem to suggest a heritable component to musical abilities. For example, a study of identical and fraternal twins suggested that genetic variation accounted for at least 70 percent of the differences between people in musical pitch recognition ability; in contrast, the effect of the family or household was zero. Studies of musical *achievement,* however, have suggested substantial influence of the shared family environment. It is likely that musical achievement is more influenced by upbringing than are many other cognitive abilities, partly due to the relatively unequal exposure to musical training across families. At this point, it seems reasonable to assume that both genetic and environmental influences are involved in the development of individual differences in components of musical intelligence.

Music and Other Abilities

There have been suggestions that musical ability is related to mathematical ability. Gardner himself suggested that the relationship between math and music was likely one of interest, in that mathematicians tend to enjoy the patterns of music, but that musicians are probably not unusually interested in mathematics. He has also hypothesized that there are families and ethnic groups that emphasize both scholastic and musical achievement, resulting in children who tend to show high achievement in both mathematics and musical performance.

Musical ability has shown small but consistent positive correlations with general cognitive ability as well as with some narrower abilities. In studies comparing musicians with nonmusicians, however, there are generally few or no differences in measured cognitive abilities, broad or narrow. It seems likely that the correlations between musical ability and general cognitive ability would be greatest when the sample is of diverse intellectual ability and musically untrained. Research has suggested that musical training in childhood might lead to small but lasting gains in psychometric intelligence and academic performance, and that these gains are not specific to any particular narrow cognitive ability.

Music and the Brain

Efforts have been made to localize areas of the brain that are responsible for musical ability. It was once thought that music was a "right brain" activity, along with visual art, but the evidence now indicates that neural networks related to music run through both hemispheres. Listening to music, composing music, and performing music would seem to engage nearly every area of the brain. The auditory cortex processes the sounds of music, and frontal regions process the musical structure. Pleasurable arousal from music involves the mesolimbic system, and the foot-tapping and rhythmic movements associated with music involve the motor cortex. The cerebellum and basal ganglia are active in processing the rhythm and meter of music, with the cerebellum likely also involved in the emotional reactions to music.

Gardner stated that although musical ability was not as clearly localized in the brain as some other aspects of mental ability, the existence of amusia, a selective loss of musical ability due to brain damage, was evidence of some brain specificity for music. Studies involving patients with brain lesions have indicated that damage to the left hemisphere can result in the loss of abilities related to rhythm. Lesions on the right temporal lobe, on the other hand, have been associated with the loss of ability to perceive melody. Case studies highlight the autonomy of musical and linguistic abilities. There are brain damaged patients who have retained the ability to read music but not conventional text, and individuals who cannot recognize melodies but can recognize lyrics. There are patients who cannot recognize speech but can recognize music, and patients who cannot sing songs despite being able to speak the lyrics.

Brain studies of individuals with absolute or perfect pitch—the ability to identify and reproduce various pitches without being provided with a relative pitch—show relative enlargement of the left planum temporale, a portion of the auditory cortex. Other studies have focused on the estimated 4 percent of the population that has tone deafness, otherwise known as congenital amusia. These individuals have otherwise normal auditory, memory, language, and intelligence, but are unable to recognize melodies or detect pitch changes, perhaps as a result of malformations in the right auditory cortex.

The cerebellum seems to be involved in the processing of rhythm and meter, and perhaps also in the emotional experience of music. The cerebellum has been found to be strongly activated when individuals listen to music, but not when they listen to noise. Similarly, the cerebellum shows greater activation when people listen to music they enjoy versus music they do not enjoy and to familiar versus unfamiliar music. Interestingly, the neocerebellums are enlarged in individuals with Williams syndrome, a genetic disorder characterized by intellectual impairment, musicality, and extreme sociability. The neocerebellum tends to be smaller than normal in individuals with autism, who may also have intellectual impairments, but are also characterized by emotional detachment and a failure to enjoy or understand the emotional qualities of music.

Evolutionary Basis

Many evolutionary theorists, including Darwin, have speculated that musical intelligence was evolutionarily adaptive. In *The Descent of Man,* Darwin proposed that music played a role in sexual selection, and that musical tones and rhythms might have been first used by men or women to attract mates, and came to be used instinctively for that purpose. There would seem to be a nonhuman parallel in songbirds, in that some male songbirds attract mates with their extensive repertoires of songs.

Similarly, singing and dancing might have been used to demonstrate one's physical and mental health to prospective mates, by advertising one's stamina and creativity. Musical competence, like clever conversation, might have evolved to advertise one's intelligence to potential sexual partners. Another theory would suggest that one who exhibits well-developed musical ability would demonstrate to prospective mates that one has resources to spare, and can thus afford to spend time refining an unnecessary skill. Like the peacock's tail, musical intelligence could exist to advertise one's health and resources. The fact that interest in music seems to peak in adolescence reinforces theories that suggest a role of music in mate selection. Alternatively, music might have served an important role in the functioning of a society, in promoting group unity and reinforcing social bonds.

Another proposed evolutionary role for music is in the preparation of the brain for the development of language and other complex cognitive activity. Babies seem particularly sensitive to musical contour, which may be related to the contour of spoken language. Gardner noted that the structure of music was, in many ways, parallel to that of linguistic intelligence. Caregivers tend to speak to infants in a rhythmically slower fashion in a higher pitch, and with exaggerated pitch differences. By the age of 2 years, children show a preference for the music of their own culture, which perhaps not coincidentally is around the same time that children show specificity in language processing.

Assessment

At this point, there is no single widely accepted measure of musical intelligence that is dominant in research and applied fields, nor has the assessment of musical intelligence sparked the intense research interest that has produced increasingly sophisticated batteries to assess other cognitive abilities. Gardner suggested that to test musical intelligence, individuals could be exposed to a new melody and be evaluated on how well they recognized, sang, and transformed it. One shortcoming of this strategy would seem to be that people will have had very different levels of exposure to musical training and practice; thus, this musical testing method would be likely to assess taught skills as much as aptitude.

Some well-known tests of musical ability include those of Carl Seashore of the University of Iowa, who published the first version of his *Seashore Measures of Musical Ability* in 1919. Seashore's tests were based on the premise that sensory capacities were the foundation of all musical abilities. Test-takers were required to discriminate pitch, loudness, tempo, timbre, and rhythm. Versions of the Seashore tests are still in use, but the tests of Edwin E. Gordon are more widely used in North America today. In 1965, Gordon introduced the *Musical Aptitude Profile* and then in 1979, he introduced tests of what he referred to as *audiation,* or the multistage cognitive process through which we give meaning to music. Although audiation is relevant to all aspects of music, Gordon's tests focus on the audiation of the core elements of tone and rhythm. An advantage to Gordon's tests is the availability of large-sample age norms.

Future research might benefit from a focus on the continued refinement of tests of musical ability and, in particular, tests that incorporate recent research findings related to cognitive, neurological, and emotional aspects of musical intelligence.

Beth A. Visser

See also Musical Creativity; Musical Talent Assessment; Music Education

Further Readings

Gardner, H. (1983). *Frames of mind.* New York: Basic Books.

Howe, M. J., Davidson, J. W., & Sloboda, J. A. (1998). Innate talents: Reality or myth? *Behavioral and Brain Sciences, 21,* 399–442.

Levitin, D. J. (2007). *This is your brain on music: The science of a human obsession.* New York: Plume.

Sloboda, J. (2005). *Exploring the musical mind.* Oxford, UK: Oxford University Press.

Musical Talent Assessment

In simple terms, musical talent is the ability to be keenly aware of sounds, to inwardly sense and manipulate these sounds, and to communicate these sounds to others with personal interpretation. The assessment of musical talent has drawn interest and controversy of opinion since the turn of the 20th century, with different viewpoints debated across different musical fields of study. A comprehensive approach to assessment recognizes the multifaceted nature of musical talent, which includes fine-tuned discrimination of sound (music aptitude), an adept cognitive-developmental process of learning through music (musical intelligence), the physical ability to perform well, and the creative/interpretive process of communicating ideas and emotions through sound.

Music Aptitude

The capacity to discriminate sound is detectable prior to birth and observable from infancy. Music psychologists define this capacity of aural discrimination as music aptitude. According to leading music psychologists Carl Seashore and Edwin Gordon, music aptitude is displayed in children from an early age prior to musical training, does not vary with intelligence, and is measurable reliably by the age of 10.

Gordon's battery of music aptitude tests assesses music aptitude from kindergarten to adulthood, all based on the concept of audiation. Audiation is internal realization of sound through recall or creation with the sound not physically present. Tests measure aural discrimination of pitch, rhythm, dynamics, and instrumental timbre. Gordon recommends the use of the *Intermediate Measures of Music Audiation* to measure high music aptitude in young children because its test ceiling is higher than the *Primary Measures of Music Audiation,* which measures normal music aptitude in Grades K–3.

Debate on the use of music aptitude testing as an assessment measure of musical talent encompasses the nurture–nature argument of musical talent being a product of skill development and achievement rather than inherent from birth. The use of music aptitude testing as one component of a talent assessment procedure provides an objective measurement of aural discrimination or fine-tuned listening ability.

Musical Intelligence

Musical intelligence describes the cognitive-developmental process of learning through music, with the assessment of musical talent reliant on how a student demonstrates conceptual understanding while problem solving in musical tasks. The concept of musical intelligence stems back to early Chinese and Greek theories of music and is included in the texts of Carl Seashore. More recently, Howard Gardner's theory of multiple intelligences was instrumental in extending the term to an audience beyond specialized musical fields.

Musical intelligence studies by Jeanne Bamberger, Lyle Davidson, and Larry Scripp show that talented students are adept at shifting between different representations of a musical task (performing, reading a score, listening) and are more inventive in the way they solve musical problems. Curricular-based assessment of musical intelligence includes portfolio development and domain projects that broaden musical performance to include production, perception, and reflection. Musical intelligence assessment emphasizes the student's creative functioning while engaged in musical tasks.

Musical Performance Ability

The audition is the traditional mainstay for recognition and assessment of musical talent in the fields of music performance and music education. Musical performance is inextricably meshed with commitment and achievement, with early detection of talent reliant on rapid skill development of performance abilities. John Sloboda and K. Anders Ericcson, researchers in the field of expertise of performance, argue that the element of deliberate practice over time is the deciding factor of musical talent rather than any innately determined superiority of musical capacities from birth.

The assessment of musical talent through an audition is problematic because of the inherent interpretive/subjective nature of its adjudication. Joanne Haroutounian, J. David Boyle and Rudolf Radocy, and Gene Wenner recommend development of a balanced dualistic form for performance assessment that includes rating specific elements of performance (technique, interpretation, performance skills) as well as qualitative comments (see Figure 1).

Musical Creativity—Creative Interpretation

The musical creative process involves internally realizing and interpretively manipulating sounds and communicating to others in a unique way.

Indicators of Potential Talent
Music Performance Assessment Form

Date__________ School__________

Student__________ Grade__________ Age__________

Instrument/Voice__________

Performance Information:

Title__________ Composer__________

Title__________ Composer__________

Title__________ Composer__________

Please assess each performance with a written critique in the open space on the front and back of the assessment form. Please assign ratings on the lines for each category.

1	2	3	4	5
FAIR	GOOD	VERY GOOD	EXCELLENT	OUTSTANDING

Performance Skill __________
- Accuracy
- Notes
  - Rhythm
  - Rests
  - Fingering
  - Slurs, articulation
- Memory
- Performs with ease, poise

Technique __________
- Dexterity and facility
- Clarity
- Tone quality
- Bowing, breath control

Interpretation __________
- Stylistically appropriate
- Phrasing
- Tempo
- Mood

Artistry __________
- Intensity & focus
- Creative involvement

TOTAL__________

Figure 1 Dualistic Performance Assessment: Critique and Quantified Musical Elements

Source: Haroutounian, J. (2007). Indicators of Potential Talent Music Performance Assessment Form.

Indicators of Potential Talent in Music
Observation Rating Scale

Student Name ______________________ Age __________ Grade ________________

School ______________________________________ Type of Class ________________

Person completing form ______________________________ Title ________________

You have known student ________ Years__________ Months Date: ________________

Please indicate how often the student listed above has shown the following behaviors by circling the appropriate number.

1	2	3	4
SELDOM OR NEVER	OCCASIONALLY	FREQUENTLY	ALMOST ALWAYS

Aptitude and Ability

I. Can remember and repeat melodies and rhythms.	1	2	3	4
2. Keeps steady pulse and responds to subtle changes in rhythm and tempo of music.	1	2	3	4
3. Can hear small differences in melodies, rhythm, and sounds.	1	2	3	4
4. Can differentiate individual sounds in context: identifies patterns, melodies, instruments in a musical composition, or specific environmental sounds.	1	2	3	4
5. Performs with accuracy and ease, learns quickly.	1	2	3	4

Creative Interpretation

6. Enjoys experimenting with sounds: making up songs and manipulating melodies and rhythms.	1	2	3	4
7. Is aware of slight changes in mood, loudness or softness, and sounds of different instruments in music.	1	2	3	4
8. Performs and reacts to music with personal expression, shows intensity and involvement with the music.	1	2	3	4

Commitment

9. Shows perseverance in musical activities: works with focused concentration, energy, and internal motivation.	1	2	3	4
10. Strives to refine musical ideas, sets high goals, constructively critiques musical work of others and self.	1	2	3	4

Please use the back of this form for further comments describing specific strengths or weaknesses of this student that would be helpful in determining the potential talent of this student in the area of music.

Figure 2 Indicators of Potential Talent in Music

Source: Haroutounian, J. (2002). *Kindling the spark: Recognizing and developing musical talent* (p. 182). New York: Oxford University Press. Reprinted by permission.

Musical creativity is observable at the earliest stages of musical learning through musical improvisation or play. As musical development advances, this creativity is realized generatively through musical improvisation and composition, interpretively through musical performance, extending to include creative listening and critique.

Haroutounian defines metaperception as the perceptive/cognitive functioning indicative of creative–interpretive decision making, parallel to metacognition in academic areas. Peter Webster offers an assessment tool using simple creative activities that measure extensiveness, flexibility, originality, and syntax in musical tasks, reflecting behaviors measured in general creative testing. Haroutounian, Sloboda, and Webster concur that creative interpretation in musical performance, listening, and critique are more complex to identify but are an integral part of the profile of musical talent.

Musical Giftedness and Talent

The field of gifted education has enlarged the parameters of intelligence to include artistic ways of knowing, which includes the recognition of musical talent. However, the comprehensive identification of musical talent has met challenges because of the lack of a cohesive identification procedure and the diminishing role of music programs in general in schools.

Both Haroutounian's and Barry Oreck's research recommends development of a simple talent identification tool usable at the classroom level to encourage arts talent identification. Haroutounian offers the *Indicators of Potential Talent in Music Observational Rating Scale* for initial identification of potential talent rating 10 musical characteristics categorized under aptitude and ability, creative interpretation, and commitment (see Figure 2).

Musical giftedness or exceptional talent in music is portrayed by the musical prodigy, who exhibits musical capabilities equal to those of a highly trained adult by the age of 10. David Feldman cautions that these extraordinary abilities often lie within the domain of music rather than extending to academic giftedness. Studies of the unique musical giftedness of the savant and individuals with Williams syndrome show isolated exceptional musical abilities in persons with low cognitive reasoning capabilities.

Requirements for Comprehensive Assessment

The multiple facets of musical talent provide assessment opportunities well beyond the traditional audition setting. Comprehensive assessment requires recognition of the inherent measurable components of music aptitude, keen observation of the behavior of students engaged in challenging musical tasks, and providing opportunities to assess the creative process of music making and interpretive musical performance.

Joanne Haroutounian

See also Artistic Ability; Creativity, Definition; Musicians; Prodigies; Talent Development

Further Readings

Bamberger, J. (1995). *The mind behind the musical ear: How children develop musical intelligence.* Cambridge, MA: Harvard University Press.

Haroutounian, J. (2002). *Kindling the spark: Recognizing and developing musical talent.* New York: Oxford University Press.

Haroutounian, J. (2007). Musical talent. In C. Callahan & J. Plucker (Eds.), *Critical issues and practices in gifted education* (pp. 409–427). Waco, TX: Prufrock Press.

Sloboda, J. (2005). *Exploring the musical mind: Cognition, emotion, ability, function.* Oxford, UK: Oxford University Press.

Music Education

Music education is a specific area of education that aims at the development of musical ability. According to Howard Gardner's theory of multiple intelligences, there is a specific musical intelligence that is probably a result of inborn characteristics and that can be developed by training. Musically gifted, creative, and talented people can probably profit best from high-quality music education, which includes the opportunity to have instrumental and vocal instruction. Nevertheless, as part of general education, music education should be given to all children and adults in order to enhance their knowledge and skills.

Effects of Music

The aims of music education are closely related to the effects of music. As a general rule, these pertain to the physical, cognitive, and psychological areas. With regard to physical health, listening to music can play a significant role in influencing fundamental physiological processes, for instance modifying heart and pulse rate, blood pressure, digestion, and activating certain regions of the brain. It can also enhance motor skills and acquisitions, such as relaxation, balance, joint mobility, and fluidity and economy of motion. As regards the cognitive area, several reports demonstrate that musical activity has positive effects on intelligence and achievement. With regard to psychological growth, listening to music can play an important part in influencing moods, feelings, and visualization; for example, activating reminiscences and fantasies.

Because music can have a wide range of effects, musical response can vary considerably. From time to time music education can promote some of these effects; as a consequence of this, the aims and goals of music education can change too. Historically, musical ability has been considered mainly in relation to aural abilities, but recently this conception has been modified. The fundamental aim of education is now considered to be the ability to transfer previously learned knowledge and skills to new domains. Therefore, research was done to see if the acquisition of the ability to identify different pitches, rhythms, chords, timbres, and the like, can be connected with the acquisition of other abilities outside the musical field. As a result of these studies, music education is now considered to have aims that pertain to the musical area itself (e.g., sound perception and comprehension, musical creativity), and to other, broader educational goals. For example, singing or playing music in ensembles unites the members of the group, and so it enhances social communication. Indeed, collective music making reinforces values; subjects who sing or play together are willing to identify themselves with the group values, and consequently to experience feelings of belonging to one another. These can in turn set up collective identities, in the cultural, national, or political field.

Musical training develops both musical ability and language, and enhances emotional intelligence, because it improves the ability to decode the emotions expressed in speech through prosody. Musical practice increases mathematical ability and extends the ability to perceive visual-spatial elements and understand their connections. The ability to memorize pitches has been shown to be related to a sequential way of processing information; this characteristic seems to be linked with logical thinking. Moreover, data from the National Center for Education Statistics show that students who attended music courses received better grades and more academic honors and awards than students who did not attend these courses.

It seems clear, therefore, that music competence can encourage physical and mental well-being, and can establish more neuronal connections, enhancing transfer of learning, promoting intelligence and creativity.

Goals

Among goals that pertain to the musical area in itself, there is the ability to listen to, read, and analyze music. This includes the knowledge of the language and grammar of music (identifying musical symbols and melodic structures) and the development of a sense of pulse (recognizing strong and weak beats), a sense of duration (imitating patterns of long and short sounds and silences), a sense of texture (differentiating single sounds from sound combinations), a sense of pitch (discriminating between high and low sounds), a sense of dynamics (distinguishing between loud and soft sounds), a sense of structure (recognizing musical forms), a sense of timbre (identifying the "voices" of different instruments), and a sense of style (recognizing different styles, such as Western art music and jazz).

Other important goals pertain to the following abilities: describing and evaluating music; arranging, composing, transposing, and adapting pieces; improvising and performing (singing or playing) expressively and technically accurately as a soloist. As music is one of the most important mediators of socialization, very significant goals concern improvising and performing in ensembles, with or without the leadership of a conductor, and conducting choral and/or instrumental ensembles.

Teaching Principles and Methods

The development of musical abilities can be improved with a holistic approach to musical experience, where listening, performing, composing, and appraising are linked together. Even the opportunity to have competent, regular, and frequent instruction is quite relevant. Teachers should describe music principles and show how to use them while trying to connect theory, facts, and skills, and allowing students to learn significantly. They should ensure that students have frequent opportunities to practice music and to participate successfully in appropriate music experiences. Moreover, students can derive great benefit from the opportunity to collaborate with music professionals within the school, and with artists, art organizations, and enterprises, which can support their musical development.

Among the most influential methods of music education are those of Zoltan Kodàly, Carl Orff, Emile Jacques-Dalcroze, and Kazuo Suzuki. The Kodàly method uses folk songs of the students' cultural heritage to involve them in reading and writing music, singing, playing instruments, and dancing. The Orff approach uses percussion instruments with the aim of developing students' creativity, and encouraging improvisation, composition, and movement. The Dalcroze method includes ear training, sight singing, performance, and improvisation. The Suzuki approach aims to teach small children to play an instrument from the age of 3; it is based on reading music notation, performing and memorizing pieces with the assistance of parents or other adults.

Musically Gifted Students

Musically gifted students can benefit from all of these approaches. The development of musical talent has been documented by Benjamin Bloom in his book on talent development. Musically gifted students need not only the highest quality musical training; they need mentors who can teach them the art of the audition, the establishment of a repertoire, and such fine-tuned skills as stage presence and interaction with audiences. Families of musically gifted students need to be willing to provide these specialized teachers and coaches, and may need to move to an area that would provide access to appropriate education. Musically gifted students often receive less recognition in school that academically gifted students, and may need out-of-school opportunities for recognition. Therefore, much of music education will continue to take place out of the school environment.

Alessandra Padula

See also Cognitive Development; Emotional Intelligence; Multiple Intelligences; Musical Creativity

Further Readings

Bloom, B. (1985). *Developing talent in young people.* New York: Ballantine Books.

Elliott, D. J. (1995). *Music matters: A new philosophy of music education.* New York: Oxford University Press.

Mark, M. L., & Gary, C. L. (1992). *A history of American music education.* New York: Schirmer Books.

Reimer, B. (1989). *A philosophy of music education.* Englewood Cliffs, NJ: Prentice Hall.

Musicians

The development and unique talents of a professional musician have intrigued psychologists, music researchers, and the general public for decades. Although the genres chosen may differ, from symphonic to jazz to pop/rock, musicians share similarities in factors that influence the development of these fine-tuned skills and talents. These factors include early perceptive capacities, environmental influences, the different stages of musical talent development, and the continuous unfolding of the specific properties of the musician's brain and "ear." In addition, the wonder of the prodigy and the mystery of the savant and those with Williams syndrome attest to the uniqueness of musical intelligence.

Early Perceptive Capacities

Children listen before they are born. Numerous prenatal studies have measured movements and startle reflexes to a mother's voice, music, and other environmental sounds. Studies have also indicated that infants can discriminate melodic contours, range, and tempo, and recognize songs heard while in the womb. Helmut Moog's 1970 studies indicated that 6-month-olds showed an attraction to "sensuously beautiful sound." Hanus Papoušek's studies have shown that intuitive parenting can echo an infant's vocal play, creating a preverbal musical conversation. Longitudinal studies of youngsters describe a growing awareness of the melodic contour scheme of pitches, with sliding pitch schemes and snatches of melodic ideas, leading to singing a song with stabilized pitch by the age of 6.

The discrimination of pitch and rhythm are the basic sensory attributes of music aptitude—inborn capacities that function from early childhood. Edwin Gordon and Carl Seashore's studies have shown that these capacities can be measured prior to training and that they basically stabilize by the age of 10. Environmental musical stimulation during the early years may contribute to the development of these capacities during the malleable years when the musically perceptive inner "ear" is still evolving.

Environmental Influences

The overall role of parental or family guidance and interest in music plays a pivotal role for youngsters who show musical talent. John Sloboda has found that children who receive high levels of exposure to and engagement in music through informal musical activities show a notable superiority in musical ability over their peers by the time they reach school age. Background studies of concert pianists, talented teenagers, and rock/pop musicians have indicated that parents need not have been musicians themselves to recognize that their children were drawn to music and to seek out instruction for them. Decades of studies showing the importance of early exposure to music have spawned a number of early childhood music curricula designed to enhance parent–child musical experiences from birth through age 5.

Nevaida Layton Lee Ries's study of children who sang spontaneously in homes where music was an important part of family life showed children singing with definite tonality by 2-1/2 years of age. Project Zero research found similar effects when parent–child interplay that included singing was a normal part of family life. There are numerous anecdotes of musical prodigies singing on pitch before they could speak. These talented youngsters often begin lessons as early as age 5, guided by parental interest.

Stages of Musical Development

Formal music instruction may begin as early as preschool, with Suzuki instrumental training beginning as early as age 3 and multiple piano methods available for preschool instruction. Lauren Sosniak's study of concert pianist talent development found that the earliest teachers worked well with young children and made lessons an enjoyable experience. Young children learn the basic techniques of playing and reading music in this first stage of musical talent development. Lessons emphasize "play and romance," with lots of encouragement, freedom to explore, and immediate rewards. Parents play an important role in monitoring consistency of practice at home.

The middle stage of development arrives at a point when the student musician reaches a level of technical proficiency and repertoire that requires more attention to precision in performance and discipline in practice. This stage may require a change of teaching studio to accommodate more rigorous training for the talented young musician.

Many professional musicians recall entering competitions and performance opportunities at this stage, experiences that provided a way to judge their progress and instill a sense of identity as a musician. Parental motivation and monitoring become less important at this stage, as the student acquires an internal motivation to achieve.

The role of practice is a significant factor in the development of musical talent. Studies of "deliberate practice," which involves intensive levels of concentration in solving musical problems, show that it takes 10 years of intensive preparation to achieve an expert level of performance. Some music psychologists believe that practice contributes much more than inherent talent to expert performance.

During the advanced stage of development, the musician acquires individuality and insight, generalizing previously learned concepts, and recognizing that music will play a significant role in his or her life. Talented students may receive instruction by a master teacher at this point, or seek multiple venues of musical experience through specialized programs or schooling, summer music camps, national competitions, or early entry into professional conservatories. Jenny Boyd has noted that students in the pop/rock and jazz fields may be performing professionally while still in their teens.

The Musician's Brain and "Ear"

Recent neurological research has discarded the notion that musicians are "right-brained," discovering that the process of music-making involves auditory, visual, cognitive, affective, and motor processing. Gottfried Schlaug and colleagues found that the musician's brain actually shows a pronounced left hemisphere dominance, with the planum temporale of musicians with absolute pitch enlarged on the left side; this is especially the case in those who began study before the age of 7. These studies suggest that the brain is "plastic" in the first decade of life, reinforcing the importance of active musical engagement in early childhood.

Absolute pitch has received increased attention in recent research. Absolute pitch is more common in musicians who began training at an early age. However, many talented musicians fail to develop absolute pitch, even after years of intensive training. Diana Deutsch and colleagues provided evidence of differences in absolute pitch between American and Chinese conservatory students who began training between the ages of 4 and 5, with 60 percent of the Chinese students having absolute pitch compared with 14 percent of the Americans. When musical training began between the ages of 8 and 9, 43 percent of the Chinese students had absolute pitch, compared with none of the Americans. (Of course, it must be noted that Chinese as a language employs pitch, whereas European languages do not.)

Special Gifts: Prodigy, Savant, and Williams Syndrome

A musical prodigy displays extraordinary talent at an early age and performs at a level of a highly trained adult in the field by the age of 10. Prodigies have an exceptional ear, with many (but not all) having absolute pitch at an early age. An extraordinary musical memory allows them to reproduce complicated music after hearing it a single time or briefly examining the score. Their retention of memorized repertoire far exceeds the norm. They persistently engage in deliberate practice, with stamina and the "rage to master" indicative of their personality.

Jeanne Bamberger describes the "midlife crisis" that faces many prodigies during adolescence following intensive early advancement. Immersion in learning and performance in childhood is confronted, in adolescence, with the need to pull ideas apart for reflection and analysis. Some prodigies have a difficult adjustment during this transition into the mature adult musician.

The musical savant is an individual of very low intelligence whose musical accomplishments resemble those of musical prodigies at a young age. Savants can replicate tunes after a single hearing and have an exceptional tonal memory. Musical savants are often visually as well as developmentally disabled. Their intense interest in music begins at a young age, they all have absolute pitch, and they are all pianists.

Persons with Williams syndrome, a chromosomal disorder, have mild to moderate developmental disability and an assortment of physical motor difficulties and heart problems. They also have exceptional tonal memory relative to absolute pitch, a strong rhythmic sense, and a passion for music. Neurological studies show that the brain of individuals with Williams syndrome is smaller than normal; however, part of the brain that is enlarged—the *planum temporale,* which is the same area enlarged in professional musicians with perfect pitch. Despite the rarity of this disorder, which occurs in 1 in 20,000 people, it has attracted many neurological studies to discover more about the uniqueness of musical intelligence.

Continuing Research

The development of a musician relies on a combination of musical talent capacities noticeable from early childhood with ongoing support and guidance by family members and teachers through the stages of talent development. Ongoing studies are providing new insights into the workings of the musician's brain and the intriguing capabilities of prodigious musicians, savants, and those with Williams syndrome. Professional musicians arrive on stage only through years of self-disciplined practice, motivation to succeed, and opportunities that provide an impetus to bring performance to a level of expertise.

Joanne Haroutounian

See also Musical Talent Assessment; Prodigies; Talent Development

Further Readings

Deliège, I., & Sloboda, J. (1996). *Musical beginnings: Origins and development of musical competence.* New York: Oxford University Press.

Haroutounian, J. (2002). *Kindling the spark: Recognizing and developing musical talent.* New York: Oxford University Press.

Kenneson, C. (1998). *Musical prodigies: Perilous journeys, remarkable lives.* Portland, OR: Amadeus Press.

Sloboda, J. (2005). *Exploring the musical mind.* Oxford, UK: Oxford University Press.

Sosniak, L. (1985). Learning to be a concert pianist. In B. Bloom (Ed.), *Developing talent in young people* (pp. 19–67). New York: Ballantine Books.

Naglieri Nonverbal Ability Test

The *Naglieri Nonverbal Ability Test–Second Edition* (NNAT2) is a nonverbal measure of general ability based on a testing method (see Figure 1) supported by nearly a century of research. NNAT2 items assess ability without requiring the student to read, write, or speak. Students must rely on reasoning using geometric designs, not on verbal skills. The NNAT2 has been developed with the goal of providing a means of testing intelligence that is a fair assessment across gender, race, and ethnicity. The NNAT2 is a revision of the *Naglieri Nonverbal Ability Test–Multilevel Form,* which was a revision of the *Matrix Analogies Test–Expanded Form* and the *Matrix Analogies Test–Short Form,* which were used extensively in educational settings.

Versions and Standardization

There are two versions of the NNAT2; one uses a traditional paper-and-pencil method and the other is presented and scored online. Both versions consist of seven separate sets of items organized into levels corresponding to different grades. Each set is made up of 48 items that are presented in the colors black, blue, white, and yellow (these colors are least influenced by color-impaired vision). Each level contains items shared from both the adjacent higher and lower levels, as well as exclusive items. The shared items were used to develop a continuous scaled score across the entire standardization sample. These items yield a total raw score that is converted to a Nonverbal Ability Index standard score set at a mean of 100 with a standard deviation of 16 through an intermediate value called a Scaled Score.

The NNAT was standardized on a large nationally representative sample of more than 33,000 students in Grades K through 12 (ages 5 through 18 years). The sample closely matches the U.S. population on the basis of geographic region, socioeconomic status, urbanicity, ethnicity, and school setting. The sample included children with special needs such as those with emotional disturbance, learning disabilities, hearing and visual impairment, and those who were mentally handicapped. Children with limited English proficiency were also included in the standardization sample. More details may be obtained from the *NNAT2 Technical Manual.*

Validity

The validity of the NNAT has been examined in a series of published research papers. Jack Naglieri and Margaret Ronning studied mean score differences and correlations to achievement for matched samples of White ($n = 2{,}306$) and African American ($n = 2{,}306$); White ($n = 1{,}176$) and Hispanic ($n = 1{,}176$); and White ($n = 466$) and Asian ($n = 466$) students in Grades K through 12. The three pairs of groups were carefully selected from a larger sample included in the NNAT standardization sample and matched on all demographic variables.

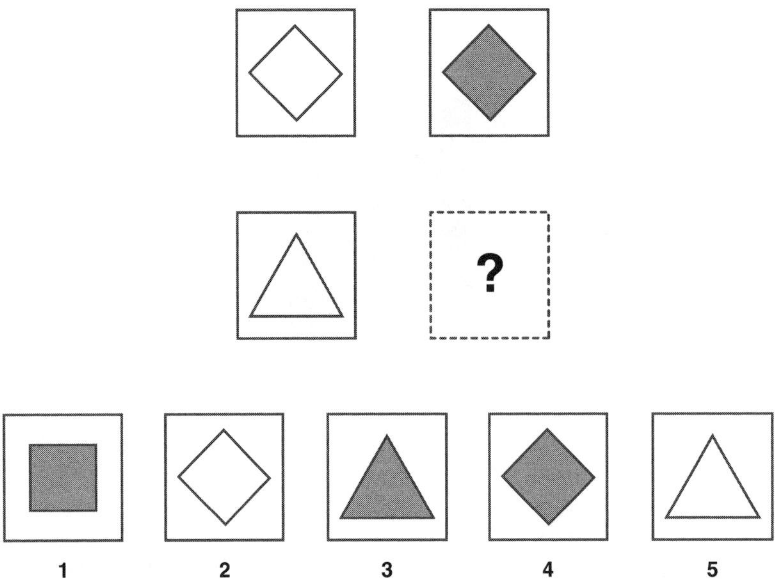

Figure 1 Illustrative Naglieri Nonverbal Ability Test–Second Edition item

Only small differences were found between the NNAT scores for the White and African American samples (Cohen's *d* ratio = .25), White and Hispanic (*d* ratio = .17), and White and Asian (*d* ratio = .02) groups. In addition, the correlations between NNAT and academic achievement were strong and consistent across Grades K through 12 and similar for each of the samples. The small mean score differences and the strong correlations strongly suggest that the NNAT has utility for fair assessment of minority children and that the scores the test yields are good for statistical prediction of achievement.

Jack Naglieri, Ashley Booth, and Adam Winsler examined the performance of Hispanic children with and without limited English proficiency (*N* = 296) who were administered the Naglieri Nonverbal Ability Test and the Stanford Achievement Test–Ninth Edition. The two groups of Hispanic children were matched on geographic region, gender, socioeconomic status, urbanicity, and ethnicity. The results showed that there was only a small difference (*d* ratio = .1) between the NNAT standard scores for the Hispanic children with limited English proficiency and those without limited English proficiency. In addition, the NNAT correlated similarly with achievement for the Hispanic children with and without limited English proficiency. The results suggested that the NNAT scores have use for assessment of Hispanic children with and without limited English proficiency and that these children earned scores that were close to average.

Jack Naglieri and Donna Ford studied the practical question: If the NNAT yields small mean score differences between minority and majority groups, would it identify similar percentages of White, Black, and Hispanic children as gifted? They used a sample of 20,270 children who were representative of the national school population according to socioeconomic status, urbanicity, and ethnicity. They found that 5.6 percent of the White (*n* = 14,141), 5.1 percent of the Black (*n* = 2,863), and 4.4 percent of the Hispanic (*n* = 1,991) children earned an NNAT standard score of 125 (95th percentile rank) or higher, and 2.5 percent of White, 2.6 percent of Black, and 2.3 percent of Hispanic children earned NNAT standard scores of 130 or higher (98th percentile). Their results suggested that the percentages of children earning high scores on the NNAT were similar across race and ethnic groups, suggesting that this instrument may help address the problem of the underrepresentation of minority students in gifted education.

Gender differences on the NNAT were examined by Johannes Rojahn and Jack Naglieri for the entire standardization sample. They found that the NNAT scores indicated that, on average, males and females earn the same scores on this nonverbal measure of ability.

The NNAT is an empirically validated nonverbal test of general ability that provides a method for equitably evaluating students who vary by culture, language, and gender.

Jack Naglieri

See also Identification; Intelligence; Nonverbal Tests

Further Readings

Naglieri, J. A. (1997). *Naglieri Nonverbal Ability Test Multilevel Form.* San Antonio, TX: Psychological Corporation.

Naglieri, J. A. (2003). *Naglieri Nonverbal Ability Test Individual Form.* San Antonio, TX: Psychological Corporation.

Naglieri, J. A. (2008). *NNAT2 manual.* San Antonio, TX: Pearson.

Naglieri, J., A. & Ford, D. Y. (2003). Addressing underrepresentation of gifted minority children using the Naglieri Nonverbal Ability Test (NNAT). *Gifted Child Quarterly, 47,* 155–160.

Naglieri, J. A., & Ronning, M. E. (2000). Comparison of White, African-American, Hispanic, and Asian children on the Naglieri Nonverbal Ability Test. *Psychological Assessment, 12,* 328–334.

Rojahn, J., & Naglieri, J. A. (2006). Developmental gender differences on the Naglieri Nonverbal Ability Test in a nationally normed sample of 5–17 year olds. *Intelligence, 34,* 253–260.

National Academies of Sciences

The National Academies of Sciences is an honorary society of scholars who are engaged in scientific and engineering research. Dedicated to the use of science and technology for the general welfare, the Academy was authorized initially as the National Academy of Sciences (NAS) by President Abraham Lincoln in 1863. In 1916, the National Research Council (NRC) was created to focus on public policy work, and incorporated under the umbrella of the NAS. The National Academy of Engineering was incorporated in 1964, and in 1970, the Institute of Medicine. Today, these three entities make up the National Academies.

The National Academy of Sciences was created to provide national leaders with independent scientific advice relating to public policy decisions. The membership of the NAS is elected from the United States' top scientists, engineers, and other experts—as many as 72 members and 18 foreign associates may be elected annually—based on their contributions to original research. All members operate as volunteers independent of any government framework while performing membership activities. Led by a council of 12 members and 5 officers elected from academy membership, the NAS currently boasts 2,100 members and 380 foreign associates. Of these, 200 have won Nobel Prizes. Outstanding members are recognized for their accomplishments in the field of science with awards and prizes ranging from $15,000 to $60,000. In 2008, 13 outstanding members were recognized for their achievements in the fields of biology, chemistry, solar physics, ecology, mathematics, oceanography, paleontology, social sciences, and psychology.

Publications and Funded Research

The NAS publishes a number of scientific papers, reviews, reports, and more. In 1914, the organization began publishing *Proceedings of the National Academies of Science,* a weekly multidisciplinary scientific serial focusing on colloquium papers, reviews, and actions taken by the organization. The National Academies Press publishes monthly research reports and more than 200 books each year issued by the NRC, the National Academy of Engineering, and the Institute of Medicine. The quarterly publication, *Issues in Science and Technology,* is a public policy forum for topics related to science and technology. *Women's Adventures in Science* is a biography series targeted to middle school girls and copublished by The Joseph Henry Press and Scholastic Library Publishing. It features trailblazing women in a variety of scientific fields from robotics to forensics. *Biographical Memoirs,* published since 1877, features the life memoirs and biographies of deceased Academy members.

More than 6,000 scientists from the National Academy of Sciences, the National Academy of Engineering, the Institute of Medicine, and the National Research Council volunteer to serve on committees to conduct and review cutting-edge scientific research. Funded primarily through federal and state agencies, as well as National Academies endowments, the studies produce between 200 and 300 reports on a wide range of scientific topics each year.

Activities and Resources

In addition to publications and funded research, the NAS promotes a number of science-related activities and resources. The Marian Koshland Science Museum in Washington, D.C., has been in operation since 2004. It features informative and entertaining exhibits on a variety of scientific topics, including the wonders of science, climate change, and DNA sequencing, as well as public events and educational programs.

Evolution Resources from the National Academies Press is a Web page designed to provide easy access to books, position statements, and additional resources on evolution education and research and to explore the links between scientific research and everyday life.

The Arthur M. Sackler Colloquia are organized four to six times a year by a committee of members from the Academy. Colloquia last 2 days, and typically feature presentations from leading scientists as well as a discussion among hundreds of other scientists on a broad range of interdisciplinary scientific topics.

The Kavli Frontiers of Science annual symposia have been organized by the NAS since 1989 for the purpose of bringing together talented young scientists to discuss their ideas and research. Approximately 25 scientists, all under the age of 45, are invited each year to present to a highly qualified trained group of researchers and writers, where they discuss research challenges and methodologies. The NAS has published the presentation proceedings from the years 1989, 1991, and 1992.

The National Academies Keck Futures Initiative is aimed at encouraging communication among researchers, funding organizations, universities, and the general public. Three core activities sustain the initiative, including conferences, grants, and communication awards. The Futures Initiative, which began its work in 2003 with a $40-million grant from the NAS and the Keck Foundation, is scheduled to run through 2018.

Cultural programs funded through the NAS include a number of rotating exhibitions and concerts that take place at the NAS building in Washington, D.C. Past exhibitions have included photography and painting exhibits as well as lectures related to a number of scientific topics. Concerts take place Sunday afternoons and often feature renowned, classically trained musicians and singers.

Distinctive Voices @ the Beckman Center is a popular series of lectures by scientists who speak about cutting-edge research that highlights innovation and discovery. The series takes place several times a month at the Beckman Center in Irvine, California, and is free of charge and open to the public.

Created in 1976, the Committee on Human Rights deals with the cases of 225 to 300 scientists who are unjustly imprisoned each year. The NAS works with the Institute of Medicine and the National Academy of Engineering under the guiding auspices of the Universal Declaration of Human Rights. Using the prestige of scientists from these three institutions, the Committee makes appeals to governments to encourage the release of these prisoners and provides moral support to detainees and their families.

Nancy Heilbronner

See also Nobel Prize; Scientifically Gifted; Scientists

Further Readings

National Academy of Sciences: http://www.nasonline.org/site/PageServer

National Academy of Arts, Sciences, and Engineering

The National Academy of Arts, Sciences, and Engineering (NAASE) program is an acceleration program for highly gifted students. The NAASE program was founded in 1999 to provide an academically challenging learning environment to assist gifted students in the development of their ability. This program is administered by the Belin-Blank Center for Gifted Education in affiliation with the University of Iowa, and provides an opportunity to enroll at the University of Iowa after the junior year of high school. Because this program does not include a transition stage for radical acceleration such as that provided by the University of Washington Early Entrance Program, the screening process is thorough to ensure the success of its students. To enter the NAASE program, students are expected to have completed their junior year in high school or the equivalent, to have a composite score on a standardized test such as the ACT or SAT at or above the national 95th percentile, and to have earned at least a 3.5 grade-point average (GPA) before applying to NAASE. Also, all qualified applicants are interviewed to determine each potential student's maturity, independence, and general readiness for the college environment.

Among many acceleration options, an early college entrance program such as the NAASE program is one of the radical acceleration programs for advanced high school students. Students enter college early to meet their intellectual needs. Although the early college entrance program is radical, college will provide valuable experience and motivation for learning if high-ability students are mature enough to adjust to college life. Also, advanced high school students may have experienced acceleration in any form by whole grade or by subjects.

If students are admitted to the university as NAASE students, they are automatically accepted as freshmen into the University of Iowa Honors Program. In these courses, unlike ones they may have experienced in high school, the NAASE students take challenging college-level classes and are eligible to undertake research with faculty members. When students decide to consider early college entrance, it can be a challenge to find suitable programs in prestigious universities because few early college entrance programs exist in the United States. The NAASE program offers high-quality courses and research along with support and guidance from the professional staff of the Belin-Blank Center. During the period from 1999 to 2006, 87 students from 15 states in the United States and 1 international student were enrolled on the NAASE program to meet their learning needs. Of these students, 82 percent were 17 years old at entry.

During the first year of the program, the NAASE students are required to live together in the honors residence hall. This residency provides students with the opportunity to socialize and to meet with professionals at the Belin-Blank Center for Gifted Education. Because research has indicated that homesickness is the primary difficulty for students during their first year at college, the program intends to help students develop a strong institutional connection. The Belin-Blank Center for Gifted Education offers a community for bright and motivated young scholars as well as a variety of specialized educational opportunities. In addition, the Belin-Blank Center leads the field in research and practice for talent development through its involvement in the development of curriculum resources for gifted students, the professional development of educators, the dissemination of information related to the education of gifted students, and its provision of an enhanced learning environment.

Although acceleration programs offer improved learning environments for gifted students, many parents and educators are cautious about acceleration programs like early college entrance because the success of these students in college is uncertain. However, a study performed by the Center for Talented Youth at Johns Hopkins University in 1994 found that 95 percent of the 175 youths in the study who had participated in acceleration programs perceived positive consequences, and less than 2 percent of the respondents reported negative effects. In their first year, NAASE students showed higher GPAs than the average GPA of regular freshmen in the college. Although some students have experienced negative consequences from acceleration, the majority have found acceleration to be a positive experience. Students enjoy in-depth learning in college, have the benefit of a peer group of similar ability, and are able to undertake research with faculty support during their college life. Furthermore, challenging courses both motivate students to learn more and promote self-esteem and a positive self-image.

Despite evidence that the majority of early entrance college students are academically successful, social and emotional issues cannot be overlooked. The NAASE program developers acknowledge that early college entrance programs should meet the individual's social as well as intellectual needs. The Belin-Blank Center provides a first-year weekly seminar with Belin-Blank Center staff members that deals with various topics, including study skills, learning styles, time management, communicating with teachers, and preparing for graduate school, to assist students' transition to college life. In addition, students in the NAASE program have opportunities to meet with a Belin-Blank Center graduate assistant to discuss any issues or questions they have as they begin their studies.

Research has shown that about half of the students who drop out of the NAASE program do so during the first year. This statistic suggests that students and parents should be well informed regarding the benefits and possible hardships of the first year of the transition. Because early college entrance has been considered a radical way of supporting gifted students, there must be full recognition of the academic, social, familial, and transition issues, and these issues must be balanced against the needs of students. To ensure the success of early college entrance, students, parents, and educators should acknowledge that many other options for acceleration, including advanced courses, mentorship programs, and precollegiate programs, are available. If students require greater academic challenge than other options can offer, then the NAASE program, which is an early entrance program to college, can provide valuable experiences for their growth. In addition to the need for academic challenge, emotional readiness and parental support will be necessary for the successful transition to college.

Mihyeon Kim

See also Acceleration Options; Belin-Blank Center; Early Admission, College

Further Readings

Muratori, M., Colangelo, N., & Assouline, S. (2003). Early-entrance students: Impressions of their first semester of college. *Gifted Child Quarterly, 47*(3), 219–238.

Noble, K. D., Vaughan, R. C., Chan, C., Sarah, C., Chow, B., Federow, A., et al. (2007). Love and work. *Gifted Child Quarterly, 51*(2), 152–166.

Olszewski-Kubilius, P. (1995). A summary of research regarding early entrance to college. *Roeper Review, 18*(2), 121–126.

National Association for Gifted Children

The National Association for Gifted Children (NAGC) is an organization of parents, teachers, educators, other professionals, and community leaders who collectively advocate for the unique needs of children and youth with demonstrated gifts and talents as well as those children who may be able to develop their talents and potential with appropriate educational experiences.

NAGC supports and develops policies, standards, and practices that encourage and respond to the diverse expressions of gifts and talents in children and youth from all cultures, racial and ethnic backgrounds, and socioeconomic groups. NAGC also supports research and development, staff development, advocacy, communication, and collaboration with other organizations and agencies to improve the quality of education for gifted and all students.

NAGC was founded more than 50 years ago by a group of educators and parents to serve an estimated 3 million academically gifted children in classrooms across the United States. For more than five decades, NAGC has worked to increase public awareness of the needs of gifted and high-potential children and to create positive changes in their classrooms. More than 8,000 teachers, parents, educators, and researchers belong to NAGC, an organization that invests its resources to train teachers, encourage parents, and educate administrators and policymakers on how to develop and support gifted children and to understand the loss to society if high-potential learners are not challenged and encouraged.

Many state gifted education associations are affiliates of NAGC, and they offer an array of services, education opportunities, and publications for their members. Many of these groups host state conferences and also provide speakers to local groups and advocate for gifted students in their state capitals. The NAGC publishes *Gifted Child*

Quarterly (GCQ), acknowledged to be the preeminent scholarly journal of the field of gifted education. Since 1957, *GCQ* has published manuscripts offering new information and creative insights about giftedness and talent development, including quantitative and qualitative research studies written by experts in gifted education and related fields as well as manuscripts reviewing policy and policy implications. *GCQ* also serves an archival function for NAGC, publishing position papers and other official documents of the organization.

NAGC also produces magazines for both teachers and parents. *Parenting for High Potential,* a quarterly magazine, is designed for parents and caregivers who want to help develop their children's gifts and talents. *Teaching for High Potential* is a journal for educators, offering practical guidance and classroom-based materials for educators striving to understand and challenge their high-potential learners.

NAGC believes that in order to ensure that highly able learners are adequately identified and nurtured in our schools, it is essential that teachers are educated in the relevant theory, research, curriculum strategies, and educational practices necessary for developing and sustaining classroom-based opportunities for advanced student learning. NAGC has addressed this issue through its many publications, annual conferences, and professional development programs, as well as its comprehensive Web site, which contains practical information and resources for parents and teachers. The Web site also includes PreK–12 professional standards to help educators identify the characteristics of exemplary gifted programming, nationally approved standards to accredit college and university teacher preparation programs in gifted education, position statements that are well researched, endorsed viewpoints of NAGC, advocacy guides, a listing of summer programs, and helpful links to articles and Web sites that provide information about gifted education.

Sally M. Reis

See also Council for Exceptional Children—The Association for the Gifted; Davidson Institute for Talent Development; *Gifted Child Quarterly;* Torrance Center for Creativity and Talent Development

Further Readings

National Association for Gifted Children: http://www.nagc.org

National Merit Scholarship Program

The National Merit Scholarship Corporation (NMSC) conducts two annual scholarship competitions based on student performance on the College Board's Preliminary SAT (PSAT/NMSQT), which is also known as the National Merit Scholarship Qualifying Test. Some gifted children perform sufficiently well on the PSAT/NMSQT to qualify for recognition, scholarships, and other benefits flowing from the program.

The National Merit Scholarship Program provides opportunities for gifted students to gain recognition, scholarships, and college acceptance. The participation rules and procedures are complex; students can find pertinent information on the program's Web site or from their high school counselors. Students typically begin the competition process in October of their junior year in high school. Special rules apply to students who intend to finish high school in fewer than 4 years.

This entry discusses the mission, procedures, and benefits of the National Merit Scholarship Program, and discusses special issues relating to the program.

Mission, Procedures, and Benefits

The NMSC is a nonprofit corporation founded in 1955. Its mission includes identifying and honoring academically talented students. The primary program of the corporation is the National Merit Scholarship Program, which recognizes approximately 50,000 students annually.

A new cycle of the National Merit Scholarship Program begins each October when high schools around the country administer the PSAT/NMSQT to approximately 1.4 million students, most of whom are high school juniors. In December, the students receive their scores. Each score report includes a selection index score, which is the total of the student's critical reading, math, and writing scores, each of which ranges from 20 to 80 points. A perfect selection index score is 240. In April, the NMSC uses a selection index cut point, usually near 200, to choose the top 50,000 scorers in the nation.

The following September, the NMSC names approximately 16,000 of those top students as semifinalists, and sends letters of commendation to the other 34,000 students. The selection index cut point varies by state, from near 200 to over 220. The NMSC varies the cut point in order to ensure that equal percentages of students are chosen from each state. Special rules determine cut points for boarding school students.

The NMSC invites each semifinalist to fill out an application form, write an essay, submit additional test scores, and send transcripts in order to advance in the scholarship competition. Of the 16,000 semifinalists, 15,000 advance to finalist status. Each year approximately 8,200 of the finalists win merit scholarships provided by the NMSC, corporations, and colleges. The total value of the National Merit scholarships awarded in 2007 exceeded 44.7 million dollars.

Some colleges and universities give full scholarships to students who advance to semifinalist status. The NMSC's 2007–2008 annual report shows which institutions attracted the largest numbers of National Merit awardees in 2008: Harvard University (285), the University of Texas at Austin (281), University of Southern California (254), Northwestern University (239), University of Chicago (222), Yale University (213), University of Oklahoma (178), Princeton University (175), Rice University (169), and the University of Florida (166). Carleton College has a high percentage of National Merit scholars in its student body; *The New York Times* reported that in 2006 Carleton admitted 99 National Merit scholars to its freshman class of 500.

Special Circumstances and Restrictions

Although the NMSC program is geared toward high school juniors, the official rules of the program invite students to participate in the program earlier if they intend to graduate early. Because NMSC will consider a student for scholarships during only one annual competition, students taking nontraditional paths through high school should choose with care which year they compete.

Lack of citizenship and poverty may pose barriers for some students who wish to participate in the program. The scholarship competition is restricted to students who are either U.S. citizens or permanent lawful residents (or applicants for permanent residence) who intend to become U.S. citizens as soon as possible. The College Board provides some fee waivers for low-income students.

Controversies and Research

Several controversies about the scholarship program have occurred. In 1994, the National Center for Fair and Open Testing filed a sex discrimination civil rights complaint against the College Board alleging that the PSAT was unfair to girls, who then made up 55 percent of the test-takers but only 39 percent of students winning National Merit scholarships. To settle the case, the College Board added a writing section to the PSAT. Because NMSC does not receive federal funds, it is not subject to the civil rights law involved in the case brought against the College Board.

More recently, a former College Board trustee raised claims that the test falsely defines merit and thus harms minority and poor students. Despite those claims, the College Board voted in 2005 to continue using the PSAT as the National Merit qualifying exam. In 2006, however, the University of California stopped giving scholarships to National Merit scholars, claiming that the scholar designation is unfairly based on just one test.

Results of the scholarship program occasionally have been used for research purposes. In one study, researchers found that a significant percentage of National Merit program scholars were judged as below the mastery level on standardized tests adopted by the state of Kentucky. The researchers assumed the validity of the National Merit scholar determinations and concluded that the Kentucky tests were highly suspect. In other studies, researchers have used National Merit scholar status as a proxy for gifted status.

Wenda Sheard

See also Academic Advising; Academic Talent; Guidance; Presidential Scholars; Scholarships

Further Readings

Closing the gender gap on the PSATs. (1996, October 14). *U.S. News & World Report.* Retrieved February 9, 2008, from Academic Search Premier.

Hoover, E. (2005, July 22). U. of California will stop financing National Merit Scholarships. *Chronicle of Higher Education, 51*(46), A25.

Lawton, M. (1996, October 9). PSAT to add writing test to settle bias case. *Education Week, 16*(6), 9.

National Merit Scholarship Corporation: http://www.nationalmerit.org

Noble, K. D., & Robinson, N. M. (1993). All rivers lead to the sea: A follow-up study of gifted young adults. *Roeper Review, 15*(3), 124–132.

Tutelian, L. (2007, April 22). At the top of the heap. *The New York Times*, pp. 4A, 14.

National Research Center on the Gifted and Talented

The National Research Center on the Gifted and Talented (NRC/GT) is a consortium of researchers dedicated to research on gifted and talented students. Directed by Joseph Renzulli, the NRC/GT was established in 1990 as the result of funding provided under the Elementary and Secondary Education Act of 1965 (ESEA; Title V, Part D, Subpart 6, Sec 5464(d); 20 U.S.C. 7253c(d)), otherwise known as the Jacob K. Javits Gifted and Talented Education Program. The statute charged the U.S. government with funding a national research center for education of gifted and talented youth to fund research activities on methods and techniques for identifying and teaching gifted and talented students and for using gifted and talented programming strategies and methods to serve all students. Hence, the mission of the NRC/GT from its inception has been to plan and conduct research on the psychology and education of high-potential youth from preschool through postsecondary levels and to investigate ways to integrate the practices of gifted education into regular classrooms and to develop ways to encourage the development of potential in students not ordinarily identified for gifted programs.

The NRC/GT has been committed to investigating practice-relevant questions and to creating consumer-oriented products. Accordingly, the NRC/GT has carried out a broad-based dissemination function. Very early in its existence, the directorate of the NRC/GT established a nationwide cooperative of researchers, practitioners, policymakers, and others with a stake in the education and psychological and social adjustment of gifted children and young people from all ethnic and cultural groups and from all socioeconomic strata.

Research Projects

In accord with the priorities of the federal legislation that established the Center, during the first year of the funding for the NRC/GT, the original consortium of universities (University of Connecticut, University of Georgia, University of Virginia, and Yale University) initiated research projects based on the agenda presented in response to the initial funding priorities focusing on identification, curriculum compacting, regular classroom practices in providing for needs of gifted students, learning outcomes related to grouping arrangements, program evaluation, curriculum modification based on Sternberg's triarchic theory of intelligence, and the identification of students from underserved populations from culturally diverse populations. In addition to the execution of these research projects, the NRC/GT carried out a national needs assessment to identify research priorities of the field, established relationships with more than 360 school districts as a Collaborative School District pool, and created a Consultant Bank with more than 175 members associated with nearly 100 universities. In the second year, studies of high-ability students in urban environments, staff development models, preservice teacher preparation, and the social and emotional adjustment of the gifted were added to the research agenda. In subsequent funding cycles, the U.S. Department of Education stipulated that there be increased emphasis on the importance of investigating the development of talent among students traditionally underserved in gifted programs. The research projects and principal collaborators from that time forward reflect that focus. As part of its contract with the U.S. Department of Education, the National Research Center on the Gifted and Talented was also commissioned by the U.S. Department of Education to carry out two national evaluations of the demonstration projects funded under the Javits Act and to sponsor annual conferences for the state directors of programs for the gifted.

With each funding cycle, the NRC/GT reformulated its research agenda according to the newly stipulated government priorities, the results of available research in gifted education, and education in general. The researchers at the University of Connecticut, the University of Virginia, and Yale remained the core of the NRC/GT through 2007 and were joined by researchers from several other universities at various points in its existence. The University of Connecticut and the University of Virginia have been funded to execute the current research project funded by the Department of Education.

The products produced as a consequence of the research of the NRC/GT have been designed to reach a wide spectrum of stakeholders. The audiences for NRC/GT products were identified as researchers, policymakers, administrators, teachers, counselors, and parents. Not only have the topics for research included areas of interest to these constituencies, but the types of products created as a result of the research and commissioned work by the NRC/GT represent a wide variety of outlets for communicating research findings. Hence, for each technical report produced, the authors were responsible for creating an executive summary that could be distributed independently of the full report. The researchers also wrote articles both for research journals in gifted education and in the general education field, and presented at local, regional, and national conferences. The Directorate of the NRC/GT has produced one-page bulleted summaries of the research findings, practitioner trifold brochures (some available in both English and Spanish), newsletters summarizing the research agenda and research carried out by the NRC/GT and other researchers, and videotapes with accompanying handout packets based on the Center's research. Through 2005, newsletters summarizing the NRC/GT research projects and other research being conducted in affiliated universities were distributed regularly. Nearly 3,500 presentations have been made to more than 1.5 million attendees by Center staff, and nearly 1,800 journal and magazine articles, books, and chapters have been published on NRC/GT work since 1990.

Products

In addition to the products related to the specific research studies of the Center, work was begun in 1990 to commission and publish work authored by members of the Consultant Bank on controversial topics identified by the National Research Center Advisory Board, representatives of the Consultant Bank, and later, on topics identified through the national needs assessment. The first of this series, the Research Based Decision-Making (RBDM) monographs, included reviews and meta-analyses of the literature on such topics as grouping practices, self-concept, cooperative learning, identification in the arts, and ability grouping authored by members of the Consultant Bank. RBDM monographs have been produced by NRC/GT collaborative researchers on additional topics ranging from attention deficient disorder and creativity, to counseling gifted African American students, to gifted students with behavioral problems. During the 2000–2005 funding cycle, the NRC/GT collaborated with the Great Cities' Universities (a coalition of 19 urban research universities dedicated to making a positive difference in urban environments) to commission four papers on strategies for producing high academic achievement among minorities and sponsored a symposium to respond to those papers. In addition, Senior Scholars were identified and invited to prepare monographs about the most defensible, research-based identification and programming practices. The authors were charged with providing a summary and analysis of a particular topic within the monographs as well as practical advice to practitioners and advice on what direction the field should be moving. Thirteen monographs were produced in the series. An NRC/GT Web site guides consumers to all the products of the NRC/GT as well as other Web sites in the field of gifted education. The available materials are organized by topic and author, and include the following: Acceleration, Affective Learning, Characteristics of Creative Students, Characteristics of Gifted Students, Curriculum Models, Definition of Giftedness, Elementary Program, Enrichment, Gifted Children With Disabilities, Grouping, History of Giftedness and Gifted Education, Identification Models, Middle School Programs, Parenting the Gifted Child, Primary Programs, Program Evaluation, SEM-R Study,

Secondary Programs, Self-Concept, Thinking Skills, and Underachievement. At the end of 2007, 113 monographs (NRG/GT research technical reports, Research Based Decision-Making Series, Senior Scholar Series, and research reports on other topics), 38 trifolds, four videotapes, and two CDs had been produced. The newsletter articles and all out-of-print monographs are available for free by downloading them from that Web site. Others may be obtained at cost from the NRC/GT.

Future Directions

The 5-year plan for research focus during 2006–2011 is an empirical study including quantitative and descriptive understandings of "what works in gifted education." The emphasis on identification, instructional/curricular models, and traditional and performance-based assessments is designed to demonstrate how to nurture and develop the talents and abilities of young people while promoting equity and excellence in the general education program.

Carolyn M. Callahan

See also Javits Program; Research, Qualitative; Research, Quantitative

Further Readings

Gubbins, E. J., St. Jean, D., Berube, B. N., & Renzulli, J. S. (1995). *Developing the gifts and talents of all America's students—1990–1995* (RM9522). Storrs: University of Connecticut, National Research Center on the Gifted and Talented.

Neag Center for Gifted Education and Talent Development: http://www.gifted.uconn.edu

Renzulli, J. S. (1991). The National Research Center on the Gifted and Talented: The dream, the design, and the destination. *Gifted Child Quarterly, 25,* 81–83.

Renzulli, J. S., & Reid, B. D., & Gubbins, E. J. (n.d.). *Setting an agenda: Research priorities for the gifted and talented through the year 2000.* Storrs: University of Connecticut, National Research Center on the Gifted and Talented.

University of Connecticut, University of Virginia, Yale University. (n.d.). *The National Research Center on the Gifted and Talented. 2000–2006 research studies: Abstracts and executive summaries.* Storrs: University of Connecticut, National Research Center on the Gifted and Talented.

Native American, Gifted

Native American gifted students, also called American Indian and First Nations students, may be the most underserved of all gifted populations in the United States. They have a history that is shared with many colonialized, indigenous people like the Aboriginals or Koorie of Australia, or the peoples of the Pacific Island nations. These include invasion of their lands, disruption or destruction of lifeways and spiritual traditions; violation of women and conscription of men into military, agricultural, or menial work of the conquerors; kidnapping and forced reeducation of children into the dominant culture's ways; and decimation or extinction of populations through disease, starvation, and murder. Native Americans also have their own unique history of many migrations, rise and fall of cities and nations, and a population that once ranged over two continents and diversified into hundreds of cultures and languages. The impact of history of subjugation, impoverishment, and the spread of disease and alcoholism is great upon this population of students; but so is the impact of the rich, compelling, complex world views of the tribes, nations, and communities that make up Native America. This entry first describes educational practices as they have evolved with Native American students, and early attempts by educators of gifted to develop identification and programming for Native Americans.

Indian Boarding Schools

Native American children, beginning in the 1870s, were subject to a national policy of "Americanization." The instrument of this process was the *Indian boarding school.* The original missionary-led schools on reservations were replaced by Bureau of Indian Affairs schools, and many Native American children were forcibly removed from their homes to attend boarding schools on the reservation or far from home in Indian Schools in cities and towns. These schools had as their goal the extinguishing of Indian languages (students were not allowed to speak their own languages); the replacement of Indian foods, clothing, and customs with European American ones; and the training of Indian children for vocational and agricultural work. Enrollment in these schools grew steadily, with the highest enrollment in the 1970s of 60,000 students out of a population of about 500,000 children and adults. Since that time, it has been documented that these students suffered psychological problems, abuse, and mismanaged and inferior education at most of these schools. The Indian Self-Determination and Education Assistance Act of 1975 encouraged community schools and community input into the educational process, resulting in many large Indian boarding schools being closed in the following decades. By 2007, only 9,500 American Indian children lived in Indian boarding schools, out of a rapidly growing population of 1.5 million.

Because the purpose of Indian boarding schools was complete assimilation, those students who adapted best to European American culture were recognized as the best and brightest. Students who obeyed the rules and passed courses with excellent grades might be recognized with awards, special tutoring, and occasionally scholarships to colleges. No efforts were made to identify or educate Native American students who did not assimilate or perform well in what was, for them, an alien culture. In each generation, a few extraordinarily resilient Native Americans not only succeeded in these schools, but have gone on to become leaders, educators, and policymakers.

Since the Indian Self-Determination and Educational Assistance Act, great changes have taken place in schooling of Native American children. Nevertheless, the legacy of the boarding schools remains in loss of languages and traditions; deracination of Native American students through adoptions to non-Indian families; displacement into urban centers; and disbursement as minority populations in urban, non-Indian schools.

Most Native American children now go to public schools, both on and off the reservation. A strong movement has begun among Native American people to reclaim language, culture, and religion, and many of the new community schools on reservations reflect this movement. Those Native American children who go to public schools with non-Indians off the reservation are likely to have only gifted education programs that are developed for white, English-speaking children.

Great Diversity and Profound Differences

Because there are 561 federally recognized tribes, nations, and communities of Native Americans, there is an extreme diversity of languages, history, traditions, and world views. Native American gifted children may speak only English; may have learned their tribal language as their first language, and speak English as a second language; may speak English, but have learned their tribal language in their home, often from grandparents; or may speak English, but are learning their tribal language in school. Many of these students are multilingual; for example, many Navajo students understand other Athabaskan languages such as Apache and use some of the Hopi language and the Spanish of their neighbors.

Each tribe has a history that may cover thousands of years of residence in the same place; of removal from homeland; or of having both land and customs devastated and families dispersed. For many Native American children, the grief resulting from the loss of culture is unresolved through generations. Many Native American scholars attribute the high rates of poverty, substance abuse, domestic abuse, and unemployment to the loss of cultural traditions, and see these risk factors as interrelated. The majority of scholars agree that the key to well-being for Native American youth is not assimilation into the dominant culture, but rather an education that embraces the tribal culture as well as providing skills that allow young people to succeed in the dominant culture. Given the great difficulties of providing sustenance and education in both cultures, biculturalism remains an ideal that is available to only a minority of students.

Although traditions include stories, songs, ceremonies, and ways of living and relating to others that are vastly different from one tribe to another, nearly all Native American people have a reverence for the knowledge and wisdom within these traditions. Because this knowledge has been passed down by their elders, and not from texts or school learning, elders' wisdom is cherished by most tribes. Finally, the world views of Native Americans are often profoundly different from those of non–Native Americans. Various scholars have attempted to describe common themes in Native American world views, and there is general consensus about a few of these. One difference is an emphasis upon a harmonious relationship with the Earth; all things, inanimate and animate, belonging to the Earth are regarded as sacred. Another is the belief that the life and interests of the community are more important than the life and interests of the individual. Within this context, individual achievement has little value apart from the good that results for the community. Competitiveness and self-promotion are seen as negative, selfish traits and cooperativeness and generosity are seen as critically important to good character. Despite this collectivist or communal orientation, great individuality in person tastes, interests, humor, friendships, and occupations is encouraged.

Harold Begay and C. June Maker, in "When Geniuses Fail: Na Dene' (Navajo) Conception of Giftedness in the Eyes of the Holy Deities," show how profoundly Native American views of giftedness and education can differ from European American conceptions. They show how, among the Navajo, giftedness is perceived as a special maturity, or *hoya,* that is a gift from the sacred deities. The gifts are described as follows:

> *Category 1: Ayoo Ba'iiliil*—Extraordinary transcendent power to cause effect
>
> *Category 2: Ayoo Ba'iideelni*—Skill to cause a consequence in concrete and immediate matters
>
> *Category 3: Ayoo t'aa doo le'i nizhonigo iil'I*—Exceptional ability to always do things or make things in the right way, exemplifying highly desired character values

These gifts may be manifested in childhood as a special capacity for healing, a role as caretaker of Earth and its beings, the symbols and ways of communication with the deities, and the ceremonies that bring health; for peacemaking through empathy; for leadership through consensus and self-discipline; for being a family provider; or for being skilled in traditional arts, cuisine, handling of livestock, making the home structure, storytelling, and teaching. The child's gifts are noticed and observed carefully by elders, who gradually introduce the child to adult knowledge and skills appropriate to the child's gifts. Begay shows the complexity and care that is taken in the teaching, for example, of the skill of a dry painting, with symbols represented by as many as 10,000 words, or of the memorization of many hours of oral chants and prayers. All of this intricate, highly emotional and spiritual teaching takes place with subtlety and quietness, so that gifted children learn to be humble and generous with regard to their talents.

Identification

Identification by intelligence tests, achievement tests, and current formulae are highly unlikely to select Native American students, except those who are most assimilated and therefore unaware of their own culture. Intelligence tests often contain items and tasks that are alien to Native American culture and world view. Achievement tests, in themselves, are antithetical to many Native American cultures that discourage intellectual competition. Most multiple choice tests begin with, "Choose the best answer," a concept that does not make sense to children whose word for "best" is not "the one that excels over others" but "the one that is most harmonious."

Stuart Tonemah was one of the earliest proponents of appropriate, multiple criteria assessment for Native American gifted students. He was active in the development of the American Indian Research and Development, Inc. (AIRD), project that examined assessment procedures to identify those that use the concept of multicriteria assessment. Only a few were found to be appropriate for use with American Indian and Alaska Native gifted. AIRD created the *American Indian gifted and talented assessment model* (AIGTAM), with multiple assessment techniques to predict future tribal leadership, individual fulfillment, and cultural understanding.

The multicriterion assessment approach allows students to be nominated by parents, school, community, tribe, peers, or themselves. Once a student is nominated, a case study approach using the Indian Student Biographical Data Questionnaire (ISBDQ) provides a variety of data regarding skills in leadership, creativity, visual arts, performing arts, and tribal/cultural understanding. A panel of Indian educators, gifted and talented educators, school administrators, and tribal representatives assists in making the decision.

Another approach to identification of Native American gifted was the DISCOVER Project (*D*iscovering *I*ntellectual *S*trengths and *C*apabilities while *O*bserving *V*aried *E*thnic *R*esponses), begun in 1987 under the direction of C. June Maker. Her theory of giftedness included the idea that the most important component of exceptional success was the superior ability to solve complex problems. The DISCOVER Projects were created to study, categorize, and measure a broad spectrum of "problem-solving strategies" used by various age groups of different ethnic, economic, and cultural backgrounds. Her research suggested that different intelligences could be measured effectively by observing the number and the choice of problem-solving strategies an individual uses.

Through a Javits grant, Maker was able to test the DISCOVER method with Navajo children, and found that the method was effective in identifying gifted children with advanced, specialized problem-solving abilities that would have been overlooked by conventional testing methods. Maker cautioned, however, that DISCOVER is not a curriculum, and that efforts need to be made to develop appropriate gifted education strategies for children identified with these techniques.

Native American Culturally Based Gifted Education

In studying gifted Native American students attending a summer program, AIRD found that Indian students preferred cooperative learning rather than conventional competitive classrooms. They learned that these students enjoyed being with their peers rather than spending all their time in regular classrooms. They incorporated these elements into program design. A holistic design that included physical, intellectual, social, emotional, and traditional components was used to enhance the greatest development of their potential. A cornerstone of the AIRD program design was the Individual Educational Plan that used the results of the assessment to create ways of teaching basic information, applying that information in real situations, and integrating that information into the rest of the student's knowledge and world view. The program made careful use of Native American role models and self-confidence-building exercises.

The Jacob Javits federal funding program for gifted education, with an emphasis on underserved populations, held great promise for the development of culturally appropriate gifted education programs for Native American gifted students. Funding for Native American gifted programs grew until 2006, when funding for the Javits program was cut. An example of a Javits program that integrated cultural identity into a gifted education program was the Dream Catchers Gifted and Talented Project for Arapahoe students. The Dream Catchers project had three interventions: Mastery Leaning, Creative/Artistic Expression, and Community Service/Social Responsibility. Programs like the Dream Catchers program have proliferated in tribal schools throughout the United States. In addition to these comprehensive programs are specific strategies that stress involvement with elders, learning traditional arts, and immersion in indigenous languages. Adopt-an-Elder programs provide stipends to elders to share history, language, and arts knowledge with students; Native American art galleries and museums provide programs for talented Native American art students; and community colleges located near reservations offer classes in Native American languages, available to advanced high school students.

Finally, the National Science Foundation (NSF) has funded programs designed to encourage talented Native American students in science. The Summer Science Camp for Native American Youth, developed by the Center for Native Peoples and the Environment (CNPE) at the State University of New York (SUNY) College of Environmental Science and Forestry (ESF) nurtures motivation and preparation for higher education in environmental sciences among Native American youth, through this summer science experience that combines scientific and traditional ecological knowledge. NSF also funded a guidance program for talented at-risk girls, serving Navajo, Pima, and Apache girls with math/science talent, at Arizona State University; the program was found to have built math/science self-efficacy, self-esteem, and hope for the future.

Final Thoughts

The above are rare examples of culturally appropriate gifted education. Most Native American gifted children are still identified in the usual ways and expected to succeed in gifted education programs that have little relevance to their own culture. Despite the many difficulties of attaining a culturally relevant education, maintaining self-esteem and self-efficacy, and finding a harmonious balance between achievement and giving back to the community, increasing numbers of Native American children are becoming successful as bicultural, bilingual members of American society.

Barbara Kerr

See also Cultural Conceptions of Giftedness; Underrepresentation

Further Readings

Begay, H., & Maker, C. J. (2007). When geniuses fail: Na Dene' (Navajo) conceptions of giftedness in the eyes of the Holy Deities. In S. N. Phillipson & M. McCann (Eds.), *Conceptions of giftedness: Sociocultural perspectives*. Mahwah, NJ: Lawrence Erlbaum.

Robbins, R. (1991). American Indian gifted and talented students: Their problems and proposed solutions. *Journal of American Indian Education, 31*(1), 56–63. Retrieved December 28, 2008, from http://jaie.asu.edu/v31/V31S1Ame.htm

Tonemah, S. A. (1991). Philosophical perspectives of gifted and talented American Indian education. *Journal of American Indian Education, 31*(1), 24–30. Retrieved December 28, 2008, from http://jaie.asu.edu/v31/V31S1phi.htm

Neuropsychology

Neuropsychology concerns itself with brain functioning in both healthy and pathological states, using tools such as functional imaging, specific cognitive or behavioral tasks, trained observation, and data gathering. A neuropsychologist is a licensed psychologist with expertise in how behavior and skills are related to brain structures and systems. This expertise is gained through special training during graduate school, as well as 2 years of formal training during internship and postgraduate years. Neuropsychologists often informally divide themselves into two groups, those who prefer engaging in research and those who focus on clinical work with patients. Clinical neuropsychology is the study of behavior and cognition as it is affected by neurodevelopmental anomalies and injuries and diseases that affect neurological functioning. Giftedness is rarely a topic of inquiry.

Neuropsychological Evaluations

Neuropsychological evaluations are typically requested specifically to help doctors and other professionals understand how the different areas and systems of the brain are working. Neuropsychological assessments are broader than traditional psychological or psychoeducational evaluations, and are often used to answer questions or resolve contradictions that remain after a more basic evaluation.

A neuropsychological evaluation typically assesses the following: general intellect; higher-level executive skills (e.g., sequencing, reasoning, problem solving); attention and concentration; learning and memory; language; visual-spatial skills (e.g., perception); motor and sensory skills; and mood and personality. Some abilities may be measured in more detail than others, depending on the specific situation.

The evaluation produces not only qualitative data about a person's neurological functioning, but it also provides objective benchmarks that allow comparisons to scores from people who are demographically similar. By using a database of scores from large groups of healthy people for comparison, a neuropsychologist can judge whether or not the scores are normal for the subject's age and educational background. The pattern of test scores can be reviewed to estimate whether or not there have been changes in certain abilities. How the subject goes about solving the various problems and answering questions during the examination will also be noted. These methods reveal a person's unique profile of strengths and weaknesses.

Neuropsychological assessment results can be used to understand an individual's situation in a number of ways:

- Testing can identify weaknesses in specific areas. It is very sensitive to mild memory and thinking problems that might not be obvious in other ways. When problems are very mild, testing may be the only way to detect them and formally identify them. Gifted individuals often perform at levels that require elevated skills, and subtle deficits and strengths can have a disproportionate effect when tasks are challenging.

• Testing can also help determine whether memory changes are normal age-related changes or if they reflect a neurological disorder. Testing might also be used to identify problems related to medical conditions that can affect memory and thinking, such as medication side effects, diabetes, metabolic or infectious diseases, or alcoholism.

• Test results can also be used to help differentiate among illnesses, which is important because appropriate treatment depends on accurate diagnosis. Different illnesses result in different patterns of strengths and weaknesses on testing. Therefore, the results can be helpful in determining which areas of the brain might be involved and what illness might be operating. For instance, testing can help to differentiate between Alzheimer's disease, stroke, or depression. Depression can profoundly undermine cognitive performance and a gifted, depressed child may be excluded from gifted programs in error.

• Sometimes testing is used to establish a baseline, or document a person's skills before there is any problem, such as before a medication trial. In this way, later changes can be measured very objectively. For example, a perfectionistic, inattentive child may respond well to a stimulant medication or it may heighten anxiety and worsen performance.

• Test results can be used to plan treatments that utilize strengths to compensate for weaknesses. The results help to identify what target problems to work on and which strategies to use. For example, the results can help to monitor and rehabilitate the recovery of skills after a neurological injury or to help an individual who is twice exceptional develop strategies for working around an attention deficit or tendency to become overloaded by sensory stimuli.

• Studies have shown how scores on specific tests relate to everyday functional skills, such as managing money, driving, or readiness to return to work. This applies to individuals with injury, but it can also be used to document competence of exceptional ability that exceeds that of a person's age peers.

A neuropsychological evaluation usually consists of an interview and testing. During the interview, a neuropsychologist may ask about symptoms; educational, work, and medical histories; medications; and other important factors. Testing involves taking pencil-and-paper or computerized tests and answering questions. The time required depends on the problem being assessed. In general, several hours would be needed to assess the many skills involved in processing information.

Pediatric Neuropsychology

Evaluating cognitive development in children is more challenging because their functional abilities are often described, accurately, as a moving target. Children's skills emerge on their own unique schedules, with some gross reference to the standard developmental trajectory. Injuries and deficits may not be apparent until children enter the middle and high school years; difficulty with abstract thinking appears as a problem only when children fail to master the reasoning abilities and self-regulation skills of normal development. If a 3-year-old throws a tantrum when a parent refuses to buy chewing gum, we call it normal (or maybe naptime). If a 17-year-old does it, we call it pathological.

Children are also part of larger systems, and any intervention requires working with parents, the schools, and medical practitioners. Speaking practically, there is no such thing as an individual intervention with a child. Children are usually referred to neuropsychologists for slightly different problems. These may include the following: difficulty in learning, attention, behavior, socialization, or emotional control; a disease or inborn developmental problem that affects the brain in some way; or a brain injury from an accident, birth trauma, or other physical stress. Testing can help detect the effects of developmental, neurological, and medical problems, such as epilepsy, autism, attention deficit hyperactivity disorder (ADHD), dyslexia, or a genetic disorder.

Different childhood disorders result in specific patterns of strengths and weaknesses. These profiles of abilities can help identify a child's disorder and the brain areas that are involved. For example, testing can help differentiate between an attention deficit and depression, or determine whether a language delay is due to a problem in producing speech, understanding or expressing language, social shyness, autism, or asynchronous development. A neuropsychologist may work with a physician to combine results from medical tests, brain imaging, or blood tests to sort through the effect of a child's difficulties. Testing provides a better understanding of the child's behavior and learning in school, at home, and in the community. The evaluation can guide teachers, therapists, and parents to help a child achieve better his or her potential.

Neuropsychological Evaluation of Gifted Individuals

Giftedness has not been a typical domain of study for neuropsychologists because the profession has historically been focused on pathological states. There have been no presentations at the national-level neuropsychology conferences nor have there been any articles in the primary journals addressing the issues of giftedness per se. Most neuropsychologists will not be familiar with the literature on giftedness, but they will have the advantage of being very familiar with the idea that an individual can have profound abilities and profound disabilities simultaneously. Neuropsychologists routinely see accomplished, brilliant individuals who have sustained strokes or mild traumatic brain injuries and now struggle to reconcile performing at the two end points of ability. Neuropsychologists are most helpful in evaluating twice-exceptional individuals, gifted individuals with complex medical or developmental histories, and individuals with perplexing or contradictory assessment findings.

Nadia E. Webb

See also Neuroscience of Creativity; Neuroscience of Intelligence; Neuroscience of Leadership; Twice Exceptional

Further Readings

Webb, J. T., Amend, E. R., Webb, N. E., Goerss, J., Beljan, P. F., & Olenchak, R. (2004). *Misdiagnosis and dual diagnoses of gifted children and adults: ADHD, bipolar, OCD, Asperger's, depression, and other disorders.* (2004). Scottsdale, AZ: Great Potential Press.

Neuroscience of Creativity

Creativity has been one of the single greatest influences on human civilization and culture. It allows individuals, cultures, and civilizations the ability to grow and to adapt to unique situations. Creativity allows people to create novel tools to make life easier, or create unique stories to describe the world, or come up with novel solutions to difficult problems. In short, creativity has allowed humankind to grow and thrive continuously and to adapt to any situation. Creativity plays a key role in problem solving, adaptation, and learning.

Creativity can be defined as a cognitive activity that results in a new or novel way of viewing a problem or a situation. Creativity is an indispensable tool, or potential, that we all share. It is associated with intelligence, imagination, insight, and innovation. It is not a single trait, ability, or skill, but rather a combination of several factors. Where creativity originates—more specifically, its location or origin in the brain—is a question that researchers have never previously been able to answer. The past 20 years, however, have seen the advent of new technologies that are allowing researchers to study the human brain as never before. Prior to brain imaging techniques, creativity was seen as a rather ambiguous topic, one that could not be easily defined or studied. Functional magnetic resonance imaging (fMRI) and positron emission tomography (PET) are two new tools that have allowed the study of the human brain in vivo, while it is working. Prior to this watershed period in research technology, scientists and researchers were forced to study creativity by indirect methods and simple guesswork. Now they are able to view the brain and which areas of it are actively working as individuals perform certain creative tasks, such as writing unique stories or thinking up images in their minds.

Theories and Research

Although the origins and seat of creativity have been studied repeatedly throughout the years, there has been no dominant theory in the last 20 years that has pulled together the contrasting and sometimes inconsistent studies of creativity.

What is known is that creativity is influenced by both genetics and the environment. It is a mixture of each individual's genes, combined with his or her unique environmental experiences and influences. It is novel, unique or unexpected, and appropriate, useful, and adaptive. It can be fostered and used by anyone, to differing extents and pursuits.

Initial studies of the neuroscience of creativity were actually done as far back as 1964, albeit by accident. Roger Sperry studied individuals who had received commissurotomies, which is the cutting of the corpus callosum. The corpus callosum serves as the bridge between the two hemispheres of the human brain; when it is cut, neither side can communicate with the other side. It is as if each hemisphere were alone in the human body. Sperry found that these "split-brain" individuals showed an astounding lack of creativity after the commissurotomy. He hypothesized that creativity was situated in the right hemisphere of the human brain. This belief has given way, however. The initial studies on this topic, published in 1964, were done with a small sample size and in a limited portion of the population (individuals with commissurotomies). Numerous studies since then have shown that both hemispheres contribute to creativity. Thus, there is no one seat of creativity in the human brain. Rather, creativity is derived from several different areas.

Arne Dietrich, currently working at the University of Beirut, Lebanon, is presently researching the neurocognitive mechanisms of creativity. Dietrich emphasizes the importance of using current cutting-edge knowledge in cognitive and neural processes as a stepping-stone for research into the neuroscience of creativity while eliminating the outdated beliefs that have plagued the field. Mark Jung Beeman has been studying how people think; specifically, high-level cognition in the neuroscience of insight and the "Aha!" experience.

Genetics and Environment

Genetics set a range in which the environment and experience have an effect on an individual. Genes provide the basis for the neuro-anatomical composition of the brain. Multiple research studies have looked at which specific receptors result in creativity. Several specific receptors have been found to manifest themselves in latent creativity. The higher the amount of dopamine, for example, that one has is related to increased goal-directed behavior. High dopamine levels in conjunction with temporal lobe function result in creative drive. Much research on the genetic basis of creativity has come from twin and adoption studies, as well as family genealogies.

Role of the Frontal Lobe

The human brain consists of several main structures and systems. The most frontal of these is the frontal lobe. This area is in charge of motor functions, executive functioning, planning, reasoning, judgment, impulse control, and memory. Behind this lobe is the parietal lobe, which deals with information processing, pain and touch sensation, spatial orientation, speech, and visual perception. Below this region is located the temporal lobe, which handles emotional responses, hearing, memory, and speech. The region of the brain farthest to the back is the occipital region. The occipital lobe controls vision and color recognition. In sum, the temporal-occipital-parietal region is devoted mainly to perception and long-term memory. The area in which to begin research into the neuroscience of creativity is the frontal lobe, specifically the prefrontal cortex.

The prefrontal cortex integrates highly processed information and complex cognitive behaviors, allowing cognitive functions such as self-construct, complex social function, willed action, planning, theory of mind, self-reflective consciousness, cognitive flexibility, and abstract thinking. It is believed to be involved with arousal, attention, consciousness, and personality expression. Because one of the keys to creativity is novelty, circuits in the prefrontal cortex are necessary to transform this novelty into creative behavior. These circuits make novelty fully conscious, evaluate its appropriateness, and implement its creative expression. Put another way, the prefrontal cortex allows highly integrative computations of conscious experiences, allowing novel combinations of information to be recognized and applied to works, such as science or art. It is necessary to store this information in order to compute the complex cognitive functioning necessary for creativity. Working memory, attention, and sustained and directed attention across time are the infrastructure that allows the mind to work creatively. The prefrontal cortex also inhibits inappropriate or maladaptive emotional and cognitive behaviors.

The prefrontal cortex can be further subdivided into the ventromedial prefrontal cortex (VMPFC) and the dorsolateral prefrontal cortex (DLPFC). Functional imaging studies have shown that the DLPFC is responsible for semantic memory retrieval, working memory, and sustained attention. The VMPFC is specialized for social function, abstract thought, and future planning. Working memory is the ability of the human brain to process information. It is a limited-capacity storage system that allows information to be kept online in order to be mentally manipulated and is responsible for our immediate conscious experience of the here and now. This is a requirement for abstract thinking, strategic planning, long-term memory access, cognitive flexibility, and sentience itself.

Types of Creativity

It is believed that novelty is inherent and inevitable due to the sheer volume of information processing that occurs in neural circuitry. Appropriateness, the second part of creativity, depends on the higher-order structures of the brain that assess the complex and variable rules that individuals come across in their culture. Thus, creativity is essentially Darwinian in that it uses a variation–selection process to determine which ideas are in fact creative.

There are believed to be four basic types of creativity. Novelty production occurs in either cognitive or emotional structures, combined with two types of processing, deliberate and spontaneous. All four types of creativity are assessed by the prefrontal cortex, allowing novel thought into consciousness; applying cognitive functions such as attention, working memory, and abstract thinking; and implementing of the results of the insight.

Controversies

There have been some controversies associated with creativity research. The first of these is the relationship between age and creativity; specifically, how creativity changes with age. Because creativity is reliant on the prefrontal cortex, it should be related to prefrontal cortex development across the life span. The prefrontal cortex is the last major brain structure to mature, around the early 20s. It is also the first to decline in old age. This explains the somewhat inappropriate and less-structured creativity of children and the declines in cognitive flexibility and working memory associated with old age. Despite the research discoveries, there is still disagreement over the exact relationship, with some arguing that increased age results in greater creativity, while still others argue that individuals are at their most creative as children. The simple answer, at this point, is somewhere in between. Between prefrontal cortex maturation and decline, individuals should be at their most creative.

Another controversy in the field is the relationship between creativity and knowledge. It is widely accepted that knowledge is essential for creative thinking; however, the nature of this relationship is not agreed upon. Some argue that too much knowledge restrains creativity, whereas others believe that increases in either are good for both. Still others believe that all problem solving is based on knowledge. It is important to note that knowledge is stored in the temporal-occipital-parietal regions of the brain and that creativity is made possible by the cognitive abilities of the prefrontal cortex.

Future Research and Current Knowledge

The neuroscience of creativity is a field that still holds much to be learned. Creativity tests and studies have given researchers a broad knowledge base to work from. The advent of brain-imaging techniques has allowed researchers to study this area as never before, but there is still much to be done. There is a lack of communication between neuroscience and creativity testing and research. It is important for both fields to come together more. None of the major measures of creativity has been used in combination with functional neuroimaging tools or other measures of the brain. In addition, the link between mental illness and creativity can and should be described more precisely than it has been to this point. Another topic of future research should be the influence of emotions on cognitive processes underlying creativity. Do altered moods, for example, result in greater or less creative ability? A final area of future research involves creating better and more accurate psychometric measures of creativity. Existing tests suffer from poor validity and inconsistent results. Instruments that better utilize working memory or sustained attention, for example, in tests of creativity, would provide better insight into the dependence of creativity on specific brain structures and regions.

The neuroscience of creativity is a complicated yet powerful field of research. Despite the initial difficulties in defining and studying creativity, more information is being discovered at a rapid rate. What is generally agreed is that creativity is both novel and appropriate to the given circumstances, and that it is a function of both genetics and the environment. It is evident that the prefrontal cortex enables cognition, which allows creative ability, the essence of cognitive flexibility. The prefrontal cortex allows cognitive abilities such as sustained attention, cognitive flexibility, judgment of propriety, and working memory required for creativity. Converging evidence from fMRI, PET, and EEG studies suggest that activation of the frontal lobes clearly differentiates creative from noncreative tasks, and that creative individuals have greater efficiency in frontal lobe functions. The temporal, occipital, and parietal regions of the brain allow perception and long-term memory storage, two other prerequisites for creativity. Though there is still much to be done in the field, researchers now know a great deal about the neuroscience of creativity.

Samuel Loren Deutch

See also Adolescent, Creative; Creative Process; Creativity, Definition; Creativity Assessment; Creativity in the Workplace; Creativity Theories; General Creativity; Genetics of Creativity; Psychotherapy; Relationship of Creativity to Intelligence

Further Readings

Damasio, A. R. (2001). Some notes on brain, imagination, and creativity. In K. H. Pfenninger & V. R. Shubik (Eds.), *The origins of creativity* (pp. 59–68). Oxford, UK: Oxford University Press.

Dietrich, A. (2004). The cognitive neuroscience of creativity. *Psychonomic Bulletin & Review, 11,* 1011–1026.

Kaufman, J. C., & Sternberg R. J. (Eds.). (2006). *The international handbook of creativity.* New York: Cambridge University Press.

Pfenninger, K. H., & Shubrik, V. R. (2001). Insights into the foundation of creativity: A synthesis. In K. H. Pfenninger & V. R. Shubrik (Eds.), *The origins of creativity* (pp. 213–236). Oxford, UK: Oxford University Press.

Runco, M. A. (2007). *Creativity theories and themes: Research, development, and practice.* New York: Elsevier Academic.

Solso, R. L., Maclin, M. K., & Maclin, O. H. (2005). *Cognitive psychology* (7th ed.). Boston: Pearson Education.

Neuroscience of Intelligence

Studies of twins show a strong genetic basis for differences in performance on psychometric measures of intelligence. Most estimates indicate 50 to 80 percent of the intelligence differences among people are due to heredity, with the highest heritability in older people. Since genes work through biology, there must be some biological basis to intelligence. Identifying the specific biological properties of the brain that are responsible for intelligence, however, has remained elusive. Once any brain property is found to be associated with intelligence, even if there is a strong genetic basis for the property, how that property develops and how it may be influenced by other biological and nonbiological factors are separate issues. An understanding of the neurobiological factors related to intelligence may have implications for optimizing brain development, learning, and cognitive performance. Treatments for the low intellectual ability that defines mental retardation might be possible in some cases. Concern about Alzheimer's disease has focused considerable interest on the potential for drugs to increase learning and memory, two critical aspects of intelligence. This raises a question as to whether any such drug could increase general intelligence (i.e., what is common among all cognitive tests, often called *g*) or specific cognitive abilities (e.g., mathematical reasoning). Creativity, which is related to intelligence, also may be related to specific brain characteristics amenable to change or enhancement.

With these motivations, neuroscience studies of intelligence are driven by increasingly sophisticated technology.

Studies to Locate Intelligence

Considerable research efforts have sought to identify whether single brain areas are related to intelligence. It has long been observed that significant brain damage to humans often does not result in a dramatic lowering of IQ scores. Even "psychosurgery" to sever the connections between the frontal lobes and the rest of the brain practiced in earlier decades (rarely used today) to treat schizophrenia and other mental conditions, produced little impairment in tests of general intelligence. Retrospective studies of humans after brain injury do not provide definitive maps of "intelligence areas," although specific areas for language and other cognitive abilities have been identified, and there is evidence that a network of these brain areas also underlies intelligence. Similarly, early lesion experiments in laboratory rats found that the severity of impaired performance during learning experiments was more related to the size rather than to the location of a brain injury, and more recent rat studies show discrete brain networks throughout the brain are related to general problem solving and that different networks are related to specific problems. The existence of a general cognitive factor underlying diverse problem solving in mice also is now well established. Together, both clinical lesion studies in humans and experimental lesion studies in animals indicate that intelligence may be represented throughout the brain rather than reside in a single specific center.

Brain Waves and Intelligence

The brain is constantly active as billions of neurons create and react to chemical and electrical interactions. One noninvasive technique to measure the electrical activity produced as neurons fire on and off is the electroencephalogram (EEG). Because the brain is always engaged in many simultaneous activities, all of which contribute to the overall EEG, spontaneous EEG is a noisy mixture. It is no surprise that attempts to correlate spontaneous EEG to measures of intelligence have been disappointing overall. However, there are a number of EEG techniques that separate specific brain responses to specific stimuli from the noise of the totality of all the brain's activity at any one moment. The most widely used technique is based simply on repeating the same stimulus many times and averaging a half-second block of the spontaneous EEG that occurs just after each stimulus presentation. With averaging, only the specific EEG response to the stimulus will be left because it is the same each time. This technique is called the average evoked potential (AEP), also referred to as the event-related potential (ERP). In general, modest correlations have been reported between some AEP parameters and intelligence measures. A number of detailed reviews of this literature are available.

One explanation for these correlations is that higher-IQ subjects process information more efficiently than lower-IQ subjects. Early studies suggested that brains that use fewer neurons to process sensory input save neural energy and function efficiently. Researchers found that shorter latencies or more complex wave forms were found in higher-IQ subjects. They argued that these results were a consequence of having a fast mind or an efficient brain. It was even hoped an AEP measure of efficient information processing would have practical screening uses to identify poor learners for early remedial attention. Subsequent attempts to replicate the relationship between AEP indexes and intelligence were inconsistent, however, and this work was critiqued on a number of technical grounds.

Recently, more advanced studies using AEP have focused on how high- and low-IQ individuals differ with respect to activation of different brain areas as various cognitive stimuli are processed. Using multiple electrodes across the entire scalp, researchers can create maps of brain activity as information flows among brain areas millisecond by millisecond. These EEG-based studies are powerful because they use sophisticated experimental designs. Overall, they suggest that high- and low-IQ subjects show differences in complex temporal sequences of activity (measured as various amplitudes and latencies) across multiple brain areas during performance on many cognitive tasks. The differences have been interpreted as consistent with the view that higher IQ is associated with more efficient brain processing. These data also encourage the idea that it may be possible to develop a reliable and valid EEG-based measure of IQ for widespread use, although this has not been achieved. There is a newer technology (magnetoencephalogram, MEG) that measures minute magnetic field changes generated from populations of neurons. MEG, which is more spatially accurate than EEG and considerably more expensive, is now being used to study temporal processing across brain areas and intelligence.

Search for Intelligence Centers

Starting in the 1980s, several neuroimaging technologies allowed researchers, for the first time, to visualize human brain structure and function in extraordinary detail, well beyond the relatively low spatial resolution of cortical EEG techniques. Positron emission tomography (PET), for example, uses low-level radioactive tracers to image regional increases or decreases in brain activity as a subject performs a cognitive task. The first modern neuroimaging study of intelligence used PET to determine specific brain areas active while subjects performed difficult nonverbal reasoning problems. The subjects who performed best on the nonverbal reasoning test, highly correlated with general intelligence, showed *less* brain activation in several areas distributed throughout the brain. This result was interpreted as evidence that intelligence was related to brain efficiency and that no one brain area was an intelligence center. Subsequent PET studies of learning, mental retardation, mathematical reasoning, and visual processing confirmed the importance of neuroimaging for identifying where individual differences in brain function across the entire brain were related to scores on psychometric tests. More recently, structural imaging studies using magnetic resonance imaging (MRI) have revealed that the amount of tissue (both gray matter and white matter) in specific brain areas is related to measures of intelligence. Moreover, these areas may differ for men and women, and for children and for young and older adults.

Most recent neuroimaging studies of intelligence use one of several MRI-based techniques. Fundamentally, MRI works by using strong magnetic fields to snap molecules alternately into and out of alignment rapidly. This produces information that is the basis for computing the spatial locations of where those molecules are located. Water molecules are especially amenable to MRI, and because the brain and blood are mostly water, brain tissue and blood flow can be imaged in great detail. Whereas PET is intrusive because it requires the injection of a radioactive tracer, MRI does not require any injection or radioactive tracer and is noninvasive. MRI can produce images of brain structure, function (fMRI), and chemistry (MRI spectroscopy). A recent review of the past 20 years of neuroimaging and intelligence research included 37 studies using PET and MRI techniques, including the newest studies using diffusion tensor imaging (DTI, another MRI technique well suited to image white-matter tracts). Overall, with few exceptions, the neuroimaging data support the hypothesis that intelligence is related to a network of areas distributed throughout the brain. Specifically, a frontal-parietal network, including both gray and white matter, appears to be a major backbone for intelligence. A similar network also appears to underlie basic cognitive functions, including attention and memory. This work suggests that a definition and a measure of intelligence could be based on how efficiently information flows through this network. The network includes areas where stimuli are first perceived and areas that integrate the sorting and interpretation of stimuli and their association to information in memory. Information processing efficiency may depend on having more gray matter or more white matter in specific areas, neurotransmitter levels or activity, or characteristics of individual neurons. These and many other possibilities remain to be determined by future neuroscience research.

The Genetic Irony

The role of genes in any of these brain parameters may be especially important. The idea that intelligence may be under strong genetic control usually is interpreted to mean that intelligence is relatively fixed because it is apparently not much influenced by environmental factors found within families. However, there already is evidence that genetic manipulation of specific receptors can lead to enhanced learning and memory in mice, and the mechanisms of this are under study in many laboratories. Moreover, the Human Genome Project has revealed a surprising finding that may cause a rethinking of simplistic genetic determinism. Prior to the completion of the entire mapping of the human genome, it was assumed that there must be at least 100,000 genes to account for all the known gene proteins. The biology assumption was that, generally, one gene made one product. However, the Human Genome Project has determined that there are fewer than 25,000 genes in a human, and it is now estimated that there may be more than 2,000,000 human gene products. This means that each gene can express itself in perhaps a thousand different ways. It could well be that unknown biological and environmental factors, called epigenetic factors, influence gene expression through mechanisms not previously known, and these influences may differ according to age and sex. Individual differences in intelligence, and perhaps creativity, may be based on these interactions that likely influence structural and functional brain characteristics. It may be possible to manipulate the genetic influence on intelligence by manipulating these other epigenetic factors once the neuroscience is better understood. As a consequence, it may be possible to increase intelligence and other cognitive abilities, including creativity, in ways not now imagined.

Richard J. Haier

See also Brain Imaging; Fluid and Crystallized Intelligence; Genetics of Creativity; Intelligence Testing; Intelligence Theories; Neuroscience of Creativity

Further Readings

Bouchard, T. J. (1999). IQ and human intelligence. *Science, 284*(5416), 922–923.

Haier, R. J., Jung R. E., Yeo R. A., Head, K., & Alkire, M. T. (2004). Structural brain variation and general intelligence. *NeuroImage, 23*(1), 425–433.

Haier, R. J., Jung R. E., Yeo R. A., Head, K., & Alkire, M. T. (2005). The neuroanatomy of general intelligence: Sex matters. *NeuroImage, 25*(1), 320–327.

Haier, R. J., Siegel, B. V., Nuechterlein, K. H., Hazlett, E., et al. (1988). Cortical glucose metabolic rate correlates of abstract reasoning and attention studied with positron emission tomography. *Intelligence, 12*(2), 199–217.

Jensen, A. R. (1998). *The* g *factor: The science of mental ability.* Westport, CT: Praeger.

Jung, R. E., & Haier, R. J. (2007). The parieto-frontal integration theory (P-FIT) of intelligence: Converging neuroimaging evidence. *Behavioral and Brain Sciences, 30*(2), 135–154.

Silverman, P. H. (2004). Rethinking genetic determinism. *Scientist, 18*(10), 32–33.

Tang, Y. P., Shimizu, E., Dube, G. R., Rampon, C., Kerchner, G. A., Zhuo, M., et al. (1999). Genetic enhancement of learning and memory in mice. *Nature, 401*(6748), 63–69.

Neuroscience of Leadership

For most of history the factors contributing to the development of leadership talent remained unclear. Recent advances in technology, however, have allowed researchers insight into the neurobiological underpinnings of leadership. New research suggests that certain brain structures are heavily involved in skills necessary for leadership and that a handful of neurochemicals play a powerful role in how and whether leadership is expressed.

Leadership

Currently, there is a lack of consensus about what leadership actually is. For example, cooperative leaders may lead by encouraging others to override self-interest in favor of group concerns. Other types of leaders, however, use social dominance to cement leadership status. Highly dominant leaders may be unpleasant, ambitious, and aggressive individuals who rule by force. This type of leadership is often seen in animal studies—the source of much of our current knowledge about leadership. Depending on species and social context, aggressive, forceful leaders may or may not lead effectively.

Although conceptions of leadership vary, many of the qualities and actions of leadership are readily recognizable. These may include personality factors such as charisma, dominance, flexibility, agreeability, and extraversion, and behaviors such as motivating, delegating, organizing, and planning. In today's complex world, leaders are also often intelligent, and capable of using their intelligence to predict outcomes and think critically. William Anderson and Cliff Summers suggest that leaders tend to react more quickly to social cues than do followers, and to terminate physiological and behavioral responses to social events more quickly as well.

Brain Structures and Leadership

Neural systems involved in social dominance are those related to emotion processing and social behavior. These include specific areas of the prefrontal cortex, sensory cortex, and limbic structures such as the amygdalae. R. Adolphs suggests a model for the roles these systems play in social behavior, beginning at the most basic level with the superior and inferior colliculi processing sensory information. More detailed processing occurs in the cortex, specifically the fusiform gyrus and superior temporal gyrus. The amygdalae and other limbic structures bind emotions to the information. Finally, higher-level cortical areas interpret the emotions and information by fitting the data into a representation of the social world and one's role in it. He notes that these processes are not linear, but rather interactive and multidirectional.

Neurochemistry of Leadership

Primate and human studies have linked a number of hormones and neurotransmitters to leadership and social dominance. Most often cited are serotonin, testosterone, cortisol, and dopamine, which work to modulate mood, motivation, and aggression. Serotonin is among the most studied modulators of social dominance. In mammals, including primates, higher levels of serotonin seem to lead to greater social dominance. In one well-known study by M. J. Raleigh, M. T. McGuire, G. L. Brammer, D. B. Pollack, and A. Yuwiler, researchers removed the naturally dominant males from groups of vervet monkeys, then manipulated the serotonin levels in the remaining males. In all cases, the males whose serotonin levels increased moved into the now vacant dominant positions in their groups, in part by using social skills and affiliation to enlist support from females. Males whose serotonin levels decreased showed increased aggression and lowered social status.

"More is better" is not necessarily the rule when it comes to serotonin and social dominance, however. Anderson and Summers note that socially dominant animals may actually have lower levels of baseline serotonin than do subordinate animals. They propose that faster than average response times in the activation of neurochemicals such as serotonin, testosterone, and dopamine may account for many of the advantages dominant animals have over subordinates, rather than higher chronic levels of these substances. This response time may account for dominant individuals' abilities to react quickly to social challenges, and just as quickly return to normal functioning.

Further complexity arises from the issue of where hormones and neurotransmitters are released. For example, a heightened release of mesocortical dopamine triggered by stressful events may decrease the ability of an organism to react effectively to stress, whereas prefrontal dopamine release may aid in overcoming fear in the face of stress, as noted by Dennis Charney. These seemingly contradictory findings suggest that caution should be used when attempting to interpret the role of neurochemicals in social dominance or leadership.

Nature and Nurture

A finding across the literature on the neurobiology of leadership and social dominance is that, although some predispositions may exist, nurture plays a strong role in the development of social dominance. Anderson and Summers note, for example, that the levels and relative availability of serotonin, testosterone, dopamine, and other neurochemicals that may contribute to social dominance are at least partially heritable, as is intelligence, another factor in social dominance. However, they also repeatedly stress that context impacts the ways that these factors are expressed. A good example of this phenomenon can be found in Raleigh and colleagues' study of social dominance in vervet monkeys with manipulated levels of serotonin. Although the monkeys with increased serotonin became socially dominant when the natural group leader was removed from the environment, the original dominant male regained dominance when returned to the group. This finding suggests that serotonin can increase male social status in unstable social situations, but not necessarily in situations in which social hierarchies are already established.

Moreover, the environment can directly influence levels of hormones or neurotransmitters, impacting leadership and social dominance. Testosterone, for example, tends to increase in environments where social challenges frequently occur. Thus, aggression, which is sometimes linked to testosterone and which may also be linked to lower social status, may or may not emerge in an individual or animal, depending on its environment. Further, while many environments punish aggression, others may select for it. These complexities demonstrate the difficulties of determining precisely how neurobiological and environmental factors interact to produce leadership traits.

Erin Sullivan

See also Brain Imaging; Neuroscience of Creativity

Further Readings

Adolphs, R. (2003). Cognitive neuroscience of human social behavior. *Neuroscience, 4,* 165–178.

Adolphs, R., Tranel, D., & Damasio, A. R. (1998). The human amygdala in social judgment. *Nature, 393,* 470–474.

Anderson, W. D., & Summers, C. H. (2007). Neuroendocrine mechanisms, stress coping strategies, and social dominance: Comparative lessons about leadership potential. *Annals of the American Academy of Political and Social Science, 614,* 102–130.

Charney, D. S. (2004). Psychobiological mechanisms of resilience and vulnerability: Implications for successful adaptation to extreme stress. *American Journal of Psychiatry, 16,* 195–216.

Raleigh, M. J., McGuire, M. T., Brammer, G. L., Pollack, D. B. & Yuwiler, A. (1991). Serotonergic mechanisms promote dominance acquisition in adult male vervet monkeys. *Brain Research, 559,* 181–190.

Nobel Prize

Alfred Nobel, in his will, established a fund to award an annual award for recent important discoveries, which became known as the Nobel Prize. Nobel was born in 1833 in Stockholm, Sweden, to a capitalist family known for its energy, ambition, creativity, and entrepreneurship. His creative successes in chemistry and business made him famous, though they were shadowed by his reclusive lifestyle. In this entry, the history of Nobel and the Nobel Prize is explored with respect to its creative visionary. The reader will also learn about the myriad ways that theoretical and practical creativity was employed to amass a fortune as well as the unique notoriety thrust onto prizewinners.

Background

It has been argued that Nobel Prizes are modeled after Nobel's family, who encouraged both creativity and literacy. Nobel's father could generate new ideas, a hallmark of creativity, but he could hardly read or write. He made and lost several fortunes, experiencing both fame and bankruptcy with his family in the munitions business. His creative successes allowed funds for his family to travel and to uniquely educate his children.

Alfred Nobel had only one year of public education. He was educated at home by his mother and by well-known scientists of the time such as Nikoli Zinin. He showed interests in chemistry and proficiency with languages, mastering, in addition to his native Swedish, German, English, French, and Russian. Still, his academic training was surpassed by his business acumen.

In the mid-1860s, before Nobel's brothers left munitions to make their oil fortunes in Baku, Azerbaijan, Nobel was asked to work on the problem of handling nitroglycerin safely. He eventually invented and patented a detonator that was hailed as the most important discovery ever made in the principle and practice of explosives. He took out patents in England, Switzerland, Belgium, France, and Finland. This detonation system was used by the Central Pacific Railroad to blast across the Sierra Nevada. The safe ignition of nitroglycerin saved millions of dollars for the corporation, but nitroglycerin remained unstable and dangerous and reports of mishandling mounted. Explosions and deaths were reported from all over the world. Nobel returned to the chemistry lab after the death of his younger brother in 1865 from a factory explosion.

In 1867, Nobel invented dynamite, the handling of which was nearly foolproof and therefore much less dangerous. It was a powerful explosive that, with precautions, was safe to handle. Nobel found that when nitroglycerin was absorbed in *kieselguhr,* or diatomaceous earth, it could be shaped into sticks that, when combined with his detonation system, proved highly stable. The demand for his "safe" explosives exploded and he built factories around the world, adding to his ever-increasing fortune. He held more than 350 industrial and scientific patents, founded over 75 companies in more than 15 countries, and was one of the richest men in Europe.

Establishment and Awarding of Prizes

Before he died, Nobel composed several complicated, lawyer-crafted wills to distribute his enormous holdings. Yet shortly before he died, he created a new will that was critically brief—consisting of a single paragraph—ambiguous, and legally imprecise. This will named no apparent heir; instead, the largest portion of his estate was given to establish an annual prize for recent important discoveries that benefited humankind. It was unclear how to determine what it meant for a discovery to be "important" or whether there was a difference between a "discovery" and an "invention." In his brevity, Nobel set the stage for countless court challenges between individuals and both academic and political institutions before even the first recipient could be vetted. The will indicated that one prize should go to the most important discovery in Physics, one to Chemistry, one to Physiology or Medicine, one to Literature, and one for the advancement of Peace. But the most vexing part of executing the will was that the estate was left to a foundation that had yet to be established.

Three Swedish academies and the Norwegian parliament took more than 2 years of vigorous debate to establish preliminary administrative foundations. A lot of money was at stake, and awarding the prizes would be time consuming and professionally daunting because the fields were extremely technical and specialized. Qualified nominators would have to be found from around the world as well as advisors, translators, and consultants. The will said nothing about compensating the adjudicators, although eventually it was decided that honorariums would be awarded at one-quarter the worth of the prize.

Today, Nobel prizes are decided via nominations. Each Nobel Laureate is selected by his or her respective committee, and each committee usually consists of four or five elected members. In the first stage, several thousand people are asked to nominate candidates. These names are scrutinized and discussed by experts in their specific disciplines until only the winners remain. The names of the nominees are not announced, and neither are they told that they have been considered for a prize. Nomination records are sealed for 50 years.

Prize Winners

A Nobel Prize had launched many unknown winners into the celebrity spotlight, at least for a year, but often longer. Because of Nobel's name and the vast amounts of money awarded with the Laurels, the bestowments often receive wide media coverage. The Nobel Prize also produces much drama and debate, including commentary on those who have been ignored by the Nobel committee: for example, Leo Tolstoy, Bertolt Brecht, James Joyce, Virginia Woolf, and Mark Twain were never awarded a Nobel Prize in Literature. Still, the majority of award winners are well vetted and deserving of their prizes. For example, Jean-Paul Sartre was given the award for his work filled with the spirit of freedom and search for truth. Gao Xingjian won for his insights into universal linguistic ingenuity. Ivan Pavlov won for his work with digestion. Hans Krebs won for his work describing the citric acid cycle. Jane Addams was awarded the prize for her promotion of education, literacy, and social enlightenment of women. Recently, Wangari Muta Maathai won for her contribution to sustainable development, democracy, and peace.

Gregory Decker

See also Creative Productivity; Creativity in Science; Entrepreneurial Ability; Social Development; Social-Emotional Issues; Women, Gifted

Further Readings

Feldman, B. (2000). *The Nobel Prize.* New York: Arcade Publishing.

Gray, T. (1976). *Champions of peace.* Birmingham, UK: Paddington Press.

Sherby, L. (2002). *The who's who of Nobel Prize winners 1901–2000.* Westport, CT: Oryx Press.

No Child Left Behind

One of the most influential pieces of education legislation in the United States in recent years has been the No Child Left Behind Act (Pub. L. 107–110), otherwise known as the Elementary and Secondary Education Act of 2001. It has changed the environment and the content of school programs for all students, including gifted students.

Requirements

The avowed purpose of the legislation was to bring more accountability to the public schools. To achieve this purpose the law requires schools to show Adequate Yearly Progress (AYP), meaning that greater proportions of students will be judged *proficient* each year. Schools are required to embark on an extensive testing program that will document this progress.

Failure to meet these goals will be met with increasing levels of sanctions that would end, at the extreme, in dismissal of teachers and administrators and a takeover of low-performing schools by the state. This is the essence of high-stakes testing, meaning that important decisions will be made about the students (and teachers) as a result of these tests. There is an additional requirement that the gap between low-performing groups (minority, disability, and economically disadvantaged groups) and high-performing groups will be reduced over time.

Another requirement of the No Child Left Behind Act was that "highly qualified" teachers (teachers certified to teach in the subject area of their instruction) would be put in place in the schools by the 2006–2007 school year. As of 2008, this provision had not been met due to the lack of supply of "qualified teachers." Still other parts of the law stress early literacy and the increasing use of educational technology.

Schools have responded to these requirements by establishing comprehensive testing programs and by paying particular attention to the education of economically disadvantaged children and those students from recognized minority or ethnic groups.

The clear assumption behind this legislation is that the public schools have been performing poorly and that teachers have either been unprepared or inadequate, resulting in poor performance by their students. The solution presented for these assumed difficulties has been to enforce academic standards. Raising performance standards with accompanying sanctions would, therefore, be one strategy to *force* better performance from public schools. However, there are many more societal differences between students from low-income or ethnically different families and students from high-income mainstream families. These differences include student mobility, parental participation, peer group relationships, hunger and nutrition, television watching, and more, which also have proven to be related to school achievement. Unless these other factors are also changed, schools may have a difficult time reaching the school achievement goals set for them by this legislation.

Consequences for Gifted Students

A number of unintended consequences have occurred since the law was enacted that impact the education of gifted students. Primary among them has been the increased emphasis in the school on basic student competencies rather than excellence in performance. Gifted students have not often had the opportunity to use the extent of their talents in the regular classroom, and the No Child Left Behind Act seems to compound the problem.

One of the additional problems faced by students in public schools who are gifted and talented has been the new policy of *inclusion*. This policy, established for children with disabilities, has directed that all children will receive the best education in the regular classroom, instead of in resource rooms of special classes. Although this policy was not aimed at gifted students, many schools took inclusion as an overall policy, so gifted students were often placed in a classroom where the average student was two or three grades below the performance of the gifted student and the lessons were often pitched at a lower conceptual level. When added to the emphasis on basic learning stressed by the No Child Left Behind Act, school often became an unstimulating environment for the gifted student.

Another unintended consequence is that teachers are "teaching to the test," trying to prevent the failure of students and themselves. The result of this is gifted students in inclusive classrooms having to bear up under simplistic test item practices that do nothing for them or their interests.

The movement toward extensive testing has also had uncertain results for gifted students. The tests were often pitched at a basic level to check on mastery of basic academic goals and not aimed at a higher conceptual level for the gifted student. For example, a likely question would be, "Who won the battle of Gettysburg?" rather than, "Discuss the economic factors undergirding the Civil War."

Also, the personnel requirements for qualified teachers may well result in schools hiring remedial teachers to help borderline students rather than a gifted consultant who could raise the level and interest in the content.

Reauthorization

There has always been a tug-of-war between the interests of *equity* and *excellence* in the division of time and resources in the schools, and the No Child Left Behind Act leans toward equity. The law itself was scheduled for reauthorization hearings and amendments in 2008, but it was extended past the 2008 elections for a different Congress to take up the challenge of modifying this landmark legislation.

James J. Gallagher

See also Curriculum Models; High-Stakes Testing; Teacher Attitudes

Further Readings

Gallagher, J. J. (2004, September 18). No Child Left Behind and gifted education. *Roeper Review, 26*(3), 121.

Rawe, J. (2007, September 13). No gifted child left behind? *Time.* Retrieved December 21, 2008, from http://www.time.com/time/magazine/article/0,9171,1661701,00.html

Nonverbal Tests

Much ongoing controversy and debate exist about traditional intelligence tests and their validity and usefulness for making decisions in all educational settings (including gifted education, special education, higher education) and other settings (career, employment). Discussions of perhaps the most controversial topics revolve around the appropriateness of using tests standardized primarily on White and middle-class populations with culturally and linguistically diverse groups (Black, Hispanic, American Indian) and low socioeconomic status groups. Traditional intelligence/ability/cognitive tests have been charged with containing bias and being unfair; subsequently, they are thought to effectively limit the educational and vocational opportunities of diverse groups, especially African Americans. A central objection is that traditional intelligence tests have a high linguistic demand and high cultural demand, which serve to lower the test scores of diverse groups. On traditional intelligence tests, Black students, for example, tend to score one standard deviation (15 points) below White students. Opponents of using traditional intelligence tests with diverse groups are more likely to advocate for the use of culturally sensitive, bias-reduced measures.

Verbal and nonverbal tests are two different *ways* of measuring general ability. The verbal–nonverbal distinction refers to the *content* of the items on an intelligence test, not to the type of thinking or intelligence required. A nonverbal test measures intelligence in nonverbal ways (e.g., Raven's Progressive Matrices, the Naglieri Nonverbal Ability Test, Universal NonVerbal Intelligence Test, Comprehensive Test of Non-Verbal Intelligence). Essentially, nonverbal tests are paper-and-pencil or online tests designed to measure cognitive processes that do not involve verbal language. This does not mean that verbal instructions and strategies have been eliminated entirely; instead, it means that no words are included in the tests and no verbal responses are required. Such tests use shapes, patterns, diagrams, and sequences to measure general intellectual skills of a nonverbal nature. On these types of tests, Black students earn approximately the same score as White students; the one standard deviation gap is virtually eliminated.

Nonverbal tests have been used to measure general intellectual ability for many years; however, their use does not come without controversy. Debates exist about what types of skills nonverbal tests measure, whether they are more culturally fair than other tests, and whether they are less biased than traditional intelligence tests. Several theorists have offered insights into this type of measure. Charles Spearman proposed a two-factor theory of intelligence whereby all test questions contained a general intelligence factor known as *g* and another factor specific to each question. He proposed that this general intelligence (factor *g*) represents reasoning ability. Philip Vernon developed a hierarchical model of intelligence based on the earlier work by Spearman. Vernon proposed that the general intelligence factor *g* could be divided into two group factors, a spatial–mechanical–practical factor and a verbal–educational factor. It may be that tests that use pictures and visual stimuli may favor students with greater spatial–visual ability. J. P. Guilford adopted a model in which several equally important factors ran parallel with each other, with "general reasoning" being identified as one of these factors. Raymond Cattell defined nonverbal tests as measuring a "fluid-general intelligence," which involves the ability to reason with novel material, without the need to rely upon learned knowledge. Cattell contended that nonverbal tests were "culture fair," thereby providing a more appropriate measure of general intelligence, compared with verbal reasoning tests, for test takers not fluent in the language being used and those who were culturally diverse.

For persons whose first language is not English, the use of verbal tests poses problems if their English skills are poor. Both logic and research support the conclusion that they do poorly on English measures of general intelligence that contain verbal tests because of their limited English-language skills—not because of low intelligence or ability. This language barrier presents a solid rationale for having nonverbal measures as part of decision-making processes. Stated another way, because the test items do not require knowledge of words, nonverbal tests allow a fairer evaluation of individuals from different cultural and linguistic groups.

Although nonverbal tests are particularly useful for individuals with limited English-language skills, their value is not limited to that group. For example, individuals whose economic or social circumstances have limited their acquisition of knowledge and verbal skills may be better able to demonstrate their knowledge through this particular type of test. Nonverbal tests, being unlike most school-related tests, may not be as likely to induce stereotype threat. Taking nonverbal tests of intelligence will give these students the same opportunity to gain access to opportunities as other groups. Specifically, these students will have a better chance of being identified as gifted and talented.

In summary, nonverbal tests may provide a valid way to measure general ability for all populations. Nonverbal tests have several characteristics that are worth noting: (a) nonverbal content; (b) do not require written or oral responses; (c) tap cognitive processes less likely to involve verbal language; and (d) are more culturally fair, less culturally biased, than traditional intelligence tests that require verbal language and/or written responses.

Researchers have found that nonverbal tests identify similar proportions of Black and Hispanic/Latino children as gifted. This suggests that the problem of underrepresentation of minority children in classes for the gifted may be addressed by using such tests. Such tests provide information that can be used in conjunction with information from a variety of sources. Provided that nonverbal test scores are accepted or valued as a legitimate measure of intelligence, they have an important role to play in decision making and services. Given the increasing diversity of our nation and our schools, professionals can ill afford to continue using the same measures with all groups.

Donna Y. Ford and Gilman W. Whiting

See also Cultural Values; Diversity in Gifted Education; Intelligence; Naglieri Nonverbal Test of Ability; Raven's Progressive Matrices; Test Development

Further Readings

Bracken, B. A., & Naglieri, J. A. (2003). Assessing diverse populations with nonverbal tests of general intelligence. In C. R. Reynolds & R. W. Kamphaus (Eds.), *Handbook of psychological and educational assessment of children* (2nd ed., pp. 243–274). New York: Guilford Press.

Flanagan, D. P., & Ortiz, S. (2001). *Essentials of cross-battery assessment.* New York: Wiley.

Ford, D. Y., & Whiting, G. W. (2006). Under-representation of diverse students in gifted education: Recommendations for nondiscriminatory assessment (Part 1). *Gifted Education Press Quarterly, 20*(2), 2–6.

Naglieri, J. A., & Ford, D. Y. (2003). Addressing under-representation of gifted minority children using the Naglieri Nonverbal Ability Test (NNAT). *Gifted Child Quarterly, 47,* 155–160.

Whiting, G. W., & Ford, D. Y. (2006). Under-representation of diverse students in gifted education: Recommendations for nondiscriminatory assessment (Part 2). *Gifted Education Press Quarterly, 20*(3), 6–10.

Online Gifted Education

Online education involves instruction through electronic communications media to persons engaged in learning in a place or time different from that of the instructor or other students and in which online interaction accounts for at least 50 percent of the graded part of the course. *Online instruction, distance learning via the Internet, e-learning, Web-based learning, virtual learning,* and *e-studies* are the terms usually used, interchangeably, in programs and research studies to describe essentially the same type of instruction. At the same time, lack of conceptual distinction among the above-mentioned terms means that programs identified by the same terms may vary significantly, and programs with different names may be quite similar.

Online programs for gifted students are programs specializing in service to the gifted population and offering enrichment, Advanced Placement (AP), or acceleration courses in online format. Some educational institutions offer several online classes, and others serve as online schools, educational organizations that offer K–12 courses through Internet- or Web-based methods. The types of online schools include university based, state sanctioned, consortium/collaborative, charter, and private. Most programs use more than one type of technology and blend them together in ways that create an optimal mix for effective online learning.

General Online K–12 Learning

Distance learning in the form of correspondence courses appeared as an educational option more than a century ago. Computer-based instruction emerged in the 1960s. With the increase in the use of personal computers in recent years, and the exponential growth of the Internet, online education offerings have grown significantly in popularity. In recent years, online education went through several stages and has taken the form of virtual schools. Recent surveys show that K–12 online learning is a rapidly growing phenomenon. According to a report by North Central Regional Educational Laboratory, more than 500,000 K–12 students are currently enrolled in online classes in all 50 U.S. states. Enrollments in K–12 online courses showed steady increase over the past 5 years. As of November 2005, the North American Council for Online Learning reported that its database contains 157 unique K–12 online learning programs in 42 states (including 32 virtual charter schools, 3 online homeschool programs, and 53 public noncharter virtual schools that offer programs). Utah Electronic High School alone, the nation's largest online learning program, serves more than 35,000 students. Florida Virtual School (FLVS) is the second largest online learning program and serves around 33,000 students.

According to the U.S. Department of Education, during the 2002–2003 school year, 36 percent of U.S. school districts (5,500 out of 15,040) had students enrolled in distance-education programs, and 38 percent of public high schools (approximately 6,000) offered distance-education courses. Postsecondary institutions build on a long history of distance education and are the major providers of K–12 online learning. About 48 percent of public school districts reported an online education enrollment through a postsecondary institution in 2002–2003. According to J. Carl Setzer and Laurie Lewis, at least seven independent-study programs at universities have developed an online high school curriculum. Other postsecondary online K–12 learning programs originated in gifted education, dual enrollment, or early college credit.

Most attempts to define virtual schools distinguish them based on their operating unit. The problem, though, is that in such a way we miss a range of important elements and critical distinctions. Randall Greenway and Gregg Vanourek identified six defining dimensions of virtual schooling: comprehensiveness (complete program or discrete class offerings), reach (i.e., spanning over district, state, internationally), type (public, private, charter, contract, magnet, etc.), location (in school, at home, or a combination), delivery method (synchronous or asynchronous), and control (run by a school district, university, state, other provider, or combination). Another important dimension is type of interaction in online programs. It can be organized as independent study (one-on-one interaction between a student and an instructor) or group based (where in addition to interaction with the teacher, students participate in discussion groups with each other).

Online Learning for Gifted Students

Online education has emerged as an option for a number of special populations of learners whose needs are difficult to meet in the classroom. One such group is gifted students. In the past 10 years the online instructional methods have undergone some major changes, from simple downloading and posting of information to complex interactive courses and use of a wide range of multimedia. Online classes offer opportunities for learners whose needs are not met in the regular classroom but who are highly motivated to meet their educational goals—which describes nearly all gifted students. The literature shows that technology-enriched education of gifted students has been directed primarily to four types of experiences: (a) university-based programs, (b) specialized schools both private and public, (c) homeschooling, and (d) technology-based options. Del Siegle states that there are six different types of learning activities for gifted and talented students using the Internet: information resources, e-books, interactive projects, online classes, publishing platforms, and mentoring resources.

Literature on effective practices for working with gifted students shows that they need to learn at their own speed; skip over work they already know and understand; study topics of interest beyond basic schoolwork; and work with abstract concepts that require advanced thinking skills. The online environment provides them such an opportunity. Gifted learners like to take command of their own learning, master more things in shorter periods of time, and do not rely on being taught but like to take the initiative. From this perspective, such advantages of online instruction as flexibility of time and place of learning, more learner control, exposure to innovations, and optimization of learning rate make online classes appealing to gifted learners. In addition to the above-mentioned factors, one of the major advantages of online instruction is in reducing the social isolation of individuals who do not have gifted education programs in the area of their residence.

From the philosophy of different online education programs, it can be inferred that gifted students are expected to possess more self-motivation, and be able to take personal responsibility for learning. The need for self-direction is one of the biggest differences between a course offered in an independent learning environment and the course offered in the regular environment. More freedom and personal responsibility for the learning process and individualized attention are the things that most attract gifted students to such opportunities. Generally, distance education is seen as an opportunity to enhance student autonomy and the intellectual community and to create a self-paced, expert-directed, time/place independent environment for learning.

Online Programs for Gifted Students

Academically gifted children have the desire to learn beyond the level of instruction that many local school districts can offer. In response to their needs, several universities have initiated online learning programs to meet their unique needs. Such universities as Duke University, Johns Hopkins University, Northwestern University, the University of Missouri, Stanford University, and University of Iowa have online programs designed specifically for gifted and talented learners. Most of them offer independent study, AP, and enrichment online classes that have well-defined expectations for the participants in their program. Students use online courses to earn university credit before they begin their college education, earn extra credits in order to finish high school early, ease classroom scheduling conflicts, supplement schedules with courses not offered at their schools, enrich their high school experiences with more challenging courses, make up credits they lack to graduate on time, or even earn their high school diploma completely online.

Distance Education at the Center for Talented Youth, Johns Hopkins University

The Center for Talented Youth (CTY) at Johns Hopkins University, one of the pioneering programs in distance education for students of very high ability, opened its first distance education class in writing in 1984. Since then the program has grown to more than 6,000 enrollments per year and offers more than 45 courses in writing, mathematics, computer science, chemistry, physics, biology, psychology, and other subjects. Students who participate in CTY distance education classes come from all around the world. Mathematics courses are available to students beginning at age 5, and writing courses are open from Grade 5 and up. To become eligible to enroll in CTY's distance education, students need to show outstanding performance on above-grade tests in the subject of their strength. Students at CTY have many year-round options for advanced studies, including a wide range of AP courses, acceleration, and enrichment in the students' strongest areas.

The Center for Talented Youth, Talent Identification Program e-Studies, Duke University

The e-Studies Program at Duke's Talented Identification Program (TIP) is an online learning opportunity for students in Grades 8–12. In this program, gifted students connect with other students and TIP instructors to pursue advanced high school and university-level coursework. These e-studies courses are delivered through the Blackboard course management system. Students in the e-Studies Program read course materials, post completed assignments, and interact with their peers and their instructor through online discussions, virtual lectures, and real-time collaborations. A variety of online classes in chemistry, psychology, writing, advanced mathematics, economics, science, and technology are available. Students are admitted to the program based on their scores on either the SAT or the ACT. Admission to courses in mathematics, computer science, science, and economics is based on math scores; admission to courses in the humanities and social sciences is based on verbal and reading scores. Students are expected to be committed to spend 10–14 hours per week on one online course. Most of the interactions in Duke TIP e-Studies courses are asynchronous, which means that students can participate by accessing the course online at a time different from their instructor or other students. Creators of the program claim that e-Studies courses at Duke allow students to benefit from a high level of interaction, while also allowing flexibility not found in most face-to-face classes.

Gifted LearningLinks Distance Learning Program, Center for Talent Development, Northwestern University

The Gifted LearningLinks distance learning program (LL) in the Center for Talent Development at Northwestern University has been in existence since 1982. In recent years this program evolved into an interactive online program offering a variety of courses to students in Grades 3 through 12. These online options are designed for students who can work independently and want to move quickly to advanced levels of coursework. Flexibility of scheduling is one of the biggest advantages of the Gifted LearningLinks program. Students have an option to enroll throughout the year in online high school honors and AP courses, take enrichment courses in math, science, and humanities beginning in Grade 3, or enroll in 6-week online high school accelerated honors courses during the summer.

Education Program for Gifted Youth, Stanford University

Since 1990, the online Education Program for Gifted Youth (EPGY) at Stanford University has served more than 50,000 gifted students. In 2006, Stanford University also opened the first university-based high school designed specifically for the gifted population. The first 30 gifted students started their comprehensive program in the fall of 2006 and are expected to receive their high school diploma completely online.

Using a combination of asynchronous and synchronous technologies, EPGY offers computer-based courses to students in Grades K–8. EPGY also provides curricular and instructional support, trainings, and course materials for schools that want to add an online component for gifted and talented students throughout the United States.

Independent Study Program, University of Missouri

Originally formed as an independent study division in 1911, the Center for Distance and Independent Study (CDIS) at the University of Missouri is known throughout the nation for its pioneering efforts in the field of distance and continuing education. In recent years the University of Missouri's Independent Study Program created online courses to enhance the courses with new and promising interactive technologies. Among a variety of courses, CDIS offers several challenging independent study courses designed specifically for academically talented middle school and high school students. CDIS courses give gifted students an opportunity to take courses in their academic interest and to complete them at their own pace. Typically, it takes students from 6 weeks to 9 months to complete their course work. Gifted students work on a challenging curriculum that promotes the construction of new knowledge through technology-based interactions. Courses integrate the traditional study guides with the vast resources of the Internet and with supplementary technologies.

Iowa Online Advanced Placement Academy, University of Iowa

Established in 2001, the Iowa Online Advanced Placement Academy (IOAPA) delivers AP courses to high school students across the state of Iowa using Apex Learning online technology and the Iowa Communications Network. This program gives gifted high school students an opportunity to take college-level courses and exams. The focus of IOAPA is on helping accredited rural and small schools in Iowa. Students are eligible for enrollment in only one AP course per semester. The courses available are AP Calculus, AP Chemistry, AP English Language and Composition, AP English Literature and Composition, AP Physics, AP Statistics, and AP U.S. History.

Wisconsin Center for Academically Talented Youth

The Wisconsin Center for Academically Talented Youth (WCATY) is the North Central Association Commission on Accreditation and School Improvement accredited organization that has offered a versatile set of services to gifted children from elementary through high school statewide for almost 20 years. Among other year-round programs, WCATY offers district online cooperative courses (district Co-ops). District Co-ops combine online instruction and face-to-face workshops to allow academically talented students throughout a region or across a school district to learn together. District Co-op courses are run through the schools and school districts and are developed cooperatively. Co-ops can replace up to a quarter of the curriculum in the student's home school in one or more subject area. Co-ops typically run for 9 weeks and are designed to replace one hour of school each day. Students who take these online classes typically work independently in a resource room setting with Internet access, responding to assignments and classmates comments online, completing research, reading, and writing papers.

Future Directions

Rapid advancements in current computer technologies offer a lot of promising new directions for the online education of gifted students. Because the popularity of online classes among gifted students continues to grow, careful examination of current educational options for gifted students in the online environment needs to continue. Current online programs need to accumulate evidence of best practices for working with gifted and talented students in online environment.

With online learning expanding to the K–12 setting, there is also a pressing need for a scientific discussion on the necessity of a framework of standards to provide support for guidance and evaluation of online programs for gifted students.

Olha Skyba

See also Technology; Web-Based Learning

Further Readings

Center for Distance and Independent Study, University of Missouri: http://cdis.missouri

Center for Talented Youth, Talent Identification Program e-Studies: http://www.tip.duke.edu/e-studies

Education Program for Gifted Youth, Stanford University: http://epgy.stanford.edu/ohs/index.html

Greenway, R., & Vanourek, G. (2006). *The virtual revolution: Understanding online schools.* Retrieved April 4, 2006, from http://www.educationnext .org/20062/34.html

Iowa Online Advanced Placement Academy, the University of Iowa: http://www.education.uiowa.edu/ belinblank/programs/ioapa/index.html

Johns Hopkins University, Center for Talented Youth: http://cty.jhu.edu/cde/index.html

Northwestern University, Center for Talent Development: http://www.ctd.northwestern.edu

Setzer, J. C., & Lewis, L. (2005). *Distance education courses for public elementary and secondary school students: 2002–03* (NCES 2005–0 10). Washington, DC: National Center for Education Statistics. Retrieved October, 2006, from http://nces.ed.gov/ pubs200s/20050_10.pdf

Siegle, D. (2005). Six uses of the Internet to develop students' gifts and talents. *Gifted Child Today, 28*(2), 30–36.

Wallace, P. (2005). Distance education for gifted students: Leveraging technology to expand academic options. *High Ability Studies, 16*(1), 77–86.

Wisconsin Center for Academically Talented Youth: http://www.wcaty.org

Optimal Development

The optimal development of gifted and talented students has been a focus for theory, research, and practice since Lewis M. Terman's longitudinal investigation of the nature of giftedness and Leta Hollingworth's exploration of the differential needs of gifted students highlighted the importance of the relationship between social and emotional well-being and effective learning and functioning. Their common focus was a holistic understanding of giftedness and the realization of potential that has engendered an enduring emphasis on aspects of self-development (self-actualization) and social responsibility (interdependence), as well as high-level performance (productive achievement). Theories of giftedness have increasingly acknowledged that the realization of the intellectual potential of gifted students depends in part on optimal educational interventions so that the motivation for learning, training, and practice is maintained and the social and emotional needs of students are met.

Nicholas Colangelo has emphasized that such an approach is predicated on knowledge of both the affective and the cognitive needs of gifted students, and a view of giftedness as a challenge to be embraced as a natural function of the recognition of differences among students. All students require educational experiences that enable them to develop knowledge about and belief in themselves as effective lifelong learners, and this may be particularly important for gifted students whose beliefs about themselves may be influenced by their identity as learners from an early age. It is through effective learning that these students experience authentic motivational engagement. Students who have knowledge about and belief in themselves as learners, and who are able to pursue learning that enables them to experience authentic engagement, tend to apply their learning in ways that are productive and meaningful for themselves and their communities. Such engagement and connectedness are also correlated with mental well-being and healthy adjustment.

The primary goal of the developmentally oriented educator of the gifted is to establish an optimal environment that is conducive to students' educational growth. The work of Julian Stanley established that the pace of learning, as well as the breadth and depth of study in the context of strong academic programs, is vital to this growth process. The *optimal match,* a term first coined by Hal Robinson, therefore involves consideration of not only students' assessed ability and proven performance, but also students' motivation and other affective dimensions such as interests and learning preferences. Furthermore, Mihaly Csikszentmihalyi's research into intrinsic motivation suggests that optimal learning is facilitated when educational opportunities are responsive to a student's interests, abilities, and prior knowledge and actively promote cognitive growth through the intrinsic pleasure of developmentally appropriate learning experiences. In accordance with this approach, one of the most powerful tools for engaging intrinsic interest is providing a supportive learning context that affords opportunities to engage in sufficiently challenging experiences that, when mastered, make the student feel competent and help develop the coping strategies and resilience required to tackle future challenges.

Powerful connections have been identified between intimacy, self-esteem, and productive talent. Social relationships, particularly in late adolescence and early adulthood, greatly enhance self-esteem and may allow abilities to be realized as productive achievement. The task for educators of the gifted is, therefore, to create learning communities that enable students to experience academic rigor and complexity; to increase their intellectual interaction with like-minded others; and to foster collaborative and dynamic approaches to learning that enable students to build interdisciplinary connections and develop an integrated knowledge base. To facilitate optimal development, educators must foster a learning culture that provides opportunities to risk and experiment, and that directs the learning experience toward increased intellectual, social, and emotional engagement.

Students who demonstrate the goal of understanding rather than simple performance goals also show greater persistence and better achievement results. Similarly, students who have a positive self-concept, and believe themselves to be in control of their learning, are more likely to achieve in school. Albert Bandura has stressed that a major goal of education for all students should be to equip students with the intellectual tools, self-beliefs, and self-regulatory capabilities to educate themselves throughout their lifetime. Acquiring appropriate habits of mind, self-direction, and a healthy attitude toward lifelong learning are also, therefore, as desirable as the traditional emphasis on acquiring a sound knowledge base and sophisticated skills and processes. To implement this perspective within a school system, mediating developmental goals therefore also includes such important affective goals as learning goal orientation and a realistic and secure self-concept (academic and social).

Linda Silverman has emphasized that enabling gifted children to develop positive social adjustment, emotional maturity, and healthy self-concept depends to a great extent on a supportive environment. Indeed, an emerging pattern in the studies reporting that gifted students evidence better than average psychosocial development is the fact that in so many of the cases the gifted students are in special academic programs such as acceleration and ability grouping. Extensive literature reviews and meta-analyses conducted by Karen Rogers indicate a number of strategies that have been repeatedly identified as being particularly well suited to supporting gifted students to learn effectively; these include grouping with like-ability students, enrichment, acceleration, freedom to choose curriculum material, and access to mentors. These strategies have been shown to improve a number of motivational and well-being constructs, such as self-efficacy, control, optimism, intrinsic motivation, connection with others, and quality of school life. Time in specialized contexts may permit gifted students to establish their social competence in a safe environment. In such settings they may no longer worry about stigmatization, ridicule, excessive praise, or unfair expectations. Lawrence Coleman has suggested evidence of a learning context that enables gifted learners to develop their academic talents in ways that are challenging for them, without sacrificing peer acceptance, may be considered an important indicator of successful educational interventions that promote optimal development.

Counselors and psychologists who wish to contribute to gifted and creative students' optimal development may find the work of the various counseling laboratories for gifted and creative students useful. The Counseling Laboratory for the Exploration of Optimal States (CLEOS) provides counseling that has been found to promote engagement, purpose, and exploration and publishes its methods online.

Katherine Hoekman

See also Self-Actualization

Further Readings

Colangelo, N., & Davis, G. A. (Eds.). (2003). *Handbook of gifted education* (3rd ed.). Boston: Allyn & Bacon.

Counseling Laboratory for the Exploration of Optimal States (CLEOS): http://www.cleoslab.org

Csikszentmihalyi, M. (1992). *Flow: The psychology of happiness*. London: Ryder.

Kerr, B. A., McKay, R. A., & Hammond, D. (2008, August). *Increasing engagement of creatively gifted youth*. Paper presented at the annual meeting of the American Psychological Association, Boston. Available at http://www.cleoslab.org

Rogers, K. B. (2001). *Re-forming gifted education: Matching the program to the child*. Scottsdale, AZ: Great Potential Press.

Silverman, L. K. (Ed.). (1993). *Counseling the gifted and talented*. Denver: Love.

Originality

An idea or product must be original to be considered creative: Reproducing exact copies of paintings, verbatim quotes from poetry, or repeating scientific theories that others have already presented before the world cannot be considered creative. Definitions of *originality* usually focus on novel or unusual behavior and ideas, something or someone that does not imitate past action or practice. Originality involves escaping the obvious and commonplace, breaking away from habit-bound thinking. Originality—that is, novel or unusual behavior and ideas—is necessary for creativity. By itself, however, originality may characterize the bizarre and the inappropriate; therefore, originality is not sufficient for an idea or product to be deemed creative. Social value, aesthetic appeal, and appropriateness are also necessary.

Most measures of creativity assess originality by using the criterion of statistical infrequency or rarity of responses. The number of unique ideas is often used to score divergent thinking tests, which are the most commonly used estimate of creative potential.

Research findings support the existence of high correlations between originality and fluency on most measures of creativity. Fluency is the ability to produce many ideas; it enables the individual to formulate more ideas than others do. Paul Torrance found that a person who generates a large number of alternatives is more likely to produce original ideas, and Dean Simonton confirmed those findings, showing that a person's originality is a function of the number of ideas formulated. Measures of originality, however, usually predict creative behavior more accurately than do measures of fluency. Therefore, though fluency increases the chance that original ideas will be produced, it is not sufficient for generating original ideas.

For meaningful measurement, originality must be defined with respect to sociocultural norms. Ideas that may be original in one culture may be old news to members of another culture. Although originality is a hallmark of creativity, the determination of originality needs a comparative base, whether it is the repertoire of an individual or the norms of a population, society, or culture. At the highest levels of creativity, the comparative base is worldwide or historical.

To assess originality of thinking across cultures, Paul Torrance administered three nonverbal and six verbal tasks to students in Grades 1 through 6 in the United States, Australia, Germany, India, and Western Samoa. Some responses were common across all cultures, whereas others were common in one culture but were considered original in others. For example, on the Circles Task, baseballs, basketballs, hoops, doorknobs, doughnut holes, steering wheels, and satellites were common in the United States but were scored as original for other cultures. Boats, bowls, breadfruit, cats, and leaves were common in Samoa but were unusual—and therefore scored as original—in other cultures. Eggplants, melons, pomegranates, rackets, pitchers, and tables were common in India but original elsewhere. Butterflies and traffic signs were common in Germany and original in other cultures. Buttons, clowns' faces, targets, and tires were common in the United States and Germany but were original in other cultures. Goats, lollipops, pumpkins, and scissors were common in the African American students in the United States sample, but were original in other cultures, including the broader United States. The cultural specificity of originality has been confirmed by the experiences of various scorers of creativity tests, including the Torrance Tests of Creative Thinking (TTCT), using comparisons of American responses with the responses of people from other countries.

Originality scores on measures of creativity also change over time. Kyung Hee Kim questioned the reliability of originality scores from the latest version of the TTCT: It uses 1984 norms, and the frequency of different responses may well have changed since then. She suggests the creation and use of independent criteria for different times as well as cultures.

Mark Runco concluded that originality by itself is not a sufficient indicator of creativity, and that social value, aesthetic appeal, and appropriateness are also necessary. In fact, by itself, originality may characterize bizarre and obviously inappropriate work or behavior. Some researchers emphasize the fit or adaptiveness of creative ideas, and others define creativity in terms of originality and value, which includes intrinsic worth and/or pragmatic usefulness. An original idea or product is judged not by the originator but by its recipients; for instance, an original symphony that lacks beautiful or exciting themes and fails to make a deeper emotional connection with the audience lacks creativity when considering the criterion of adaptiveness.

Runco and his colleagues conducted a study to assess the relative contributions of originality and appropriateness to judgments of creativity. Their findings suggest that the best strategy for generating creative ideas or solutions focuses on originality because the judges in the study valued originality more than appropriateness.

Kyung Hee Kim

See also Creativity Assessment; Creativity Theories

Further Readings

Kim, K. H. (2006). Can we trust creativity tests? A review of the Torrance Tests of Creative Thinking (TTCT). *Creativity Research Journal, 18,* 3–14.

Runco, M. A. (1993). Operant theories of insight, originality, and creativity. *American Behavioral Scientists, 37,* 54–67.

Simonton, D. K. (1999). *Origins of genius: Darwinian perspective on creativity.* New York: Oxford University Press.

Torrance, E. P. (1963). *Education and the creative potential.* Minneapolis: University of Minnesota Press.

Torrance, E. P. (1979). *The search for Satori and creativity.* Buffalo, NY: Bearly Limited.

Out-of-School

Out-of-school activities can play an important role in the life of gifted youth. Parents and gifted youth educators, challenged to meet the unique needs of students using established school curriculums, often turn to out-of-school programs to support the enrichment needs of gifted youth. Unfortunately, only sparse empirical data exist that directly examine the impact of out-of-school activities on gifted youth, although several guides to opportunities for out-of-school activities for gifted young people have been published, including Julia Roberts and Frances Karnes's *Enrichment Opportunities for Gifted Learners.* Existing research on development of non-gifted youth who participate in out-of-school activities, however, provides compelling evidence for the benefits of participation in these activities for gifted youth; out-of-school activities can provide ideal conditions and opportunities to facilitate and meet specific needs and motivations that typify gifted youth. This entry summarizes the research on organized out-of-school activities and discusses how they are uniquely situated to meet the needs of gifted youth.

The Prevalence of Out-of-School Activity Participation

The term *out-of-school* typically refers to weekday hours when parents are at work and unable to directly supervise their children during the after school hours; recently, this time has been called the *after-3–hours.* It is estimated that about 25 percent of K–12 youth in the United States, approximately 14.3 million youth, are unsupervised during these after-3–hours, with the rate increasing to nearly one-third in families where both parents work or in single-headed families. Among older youth in Grades 9 through 12, the rate of unsupervised time during the after-3–hours is much higher, at around 60 percent. Although unsupervised time is not inherently detrimental, having large blocks of time without supervision is known to place youth at risk for behavioral and academic problems. Out-of-school activities provide important places where youth can spend time engaged in structured endeavors during the after-3 hours, providing a host of positive personal and social benefits while diminishing potential risks.

The Variety of Out-of-School Activities

In the United States there is a wide range of organized out-of-school activities from which youth can choose to participate. The term *out-of-school activities* is often used as the broader heading to which activities belong and is not related to where the activities occur, such as on school grounds or in a community center. The range of activities available to youth includes sports, arts, academic, service, and community-oriented and faith-based youth groups, although these categories are not the only way of grouping activities. Some researchers, for example, combine service and faith-based youth groups together. Research shows that sport activities draw the highest rates of participation among youth, followed by art activities; this includes school-sponsored activities and non-school activities. Based on a representative sample of 11th-grade youth, Reed Larson, David Hansen, and Giovanni Moneta reported that 87.7 percent of youth in their study participated in at least one of the categories of organized activities, and 70.3 percent participated in two or more activities concurrently. Thus, a large majority of youth in the United States regularly participate in organized activities. Although youth in the United States generally have a wide variety of activities to choose from, it should be kept in mind that the variety and availability of activities differ markedly by the geographic location (e.g., rural vs. suburb) and economic conditions of the community.

Youths' Time in Out-of-School Activities

The time youth spend participating in any single out-of-school activity can be considerable, depending on the type of activity. For example, youth in a sport activity spend on average between 10 and 20 hours per week participating; youth participating in academic activities report substantially fewer weekly hours, between 1 and 5 hours per week. Although many researchers assume that the amount of time youth spend in an activity influences their development, few studies have directly evaluated the effect of time or "dosage." Among the few studies that have evaluated "time," the findings suggest that a greater amount of time is related to higher rates of learning, providing preliminary support for researchers' long-held assumptions. The research, however, has not yet adequately examined whether there is a point at which too many hours of participation, such as 20 hours per week, leads to detrimental outcomes.

Developmental Conditions of Out-of-School Settings

Although youth participate in a variety of out-of-school activities and for considerable amounts of time, it is the result or the outcome of this participation that interests those concerned with the development of gifted and non-gifted youth. Research on out-of-school or organized youth activities suggests this setting provides a unique blend of conditions that facilitate growth and development: intrinsic motivation, challenge, and sustained effort. Theory argues that these three conditions are necessary for youth to develop *initiative,* the ability to use self-directed and sustained effort over time to achieve a challenging goal. Initiative (closely related to the concept of agency) is at the core of development for gifted youth; a consistent characteristic of gifted youth is an intense drive to master and achieve in a domain, such as arts, sports, music, or science.

Unlike many contexts in youths' lives, out-of-school activities are one area in which youth report feeling "alive"; that is, they report experiencing high levels of intrinsic motivation and concentrated effort as they participate in the activities of the program over time. By way of comparison, research shows that youth in a classroom experience low levels of intrinsic motivation and moderate levels of concentration; when with their friends, youth report high intrinsic motivation but low concentration. It is only in the out-of-school activity setting that youth report high levels of both motivation and concentration.

Implications

The function of out-of-school activities in the United States is typically to promote youths' engagement in learning. For gifted youth, these activities may take on an added dimension, providing an environment in which intense drives to achieve can be met. Within the out-of-school setting, challenges and a caring interpersonal environment cultivated by adults can encourage the creative expression of gifted youths' innate drive to excel. As research on participation of gifted youth in out-of-school activities increases, we will have a better understanding of the processes that best encourage the development of these youths' abilities.

D. M. Hansen and T. L. Arrington

See also Summer Camps; Summer Programs

Further Readings

Afterschool Alliance. (2005, March). *Working families and afterschool: A special report from America After 3 PM*. Retrieved June 15, 2008, from http://www.afterschoolalliance.org

Larson, R. (2000). Toward a psychology of positive youth development. *American Psychologist, 55*(1), 170–183.

Larson, R., Hansen, D., & Moneta, G. (2006). Differing profiles of developmental experiences across types of organized youth activities. *Developmental Psychology, 42*(5), 849–863.

National Institute on Out-of-School Time at Wellesley College. (2008). *Making the case: A 2008 fact sheet on children and youth in out-of-school time*. Retrieved June 15, 2008, from http://www.niost.org

National Research Council and Institute of Medicine. (2002). *Community programs to promote youth development*. Washington, DC: National Academy Press.

Roberts, J. L., & Karnes, F. A. (2005). *Enrichment opportunities for gifted learners*. Waco, TX: Prufrock Press.

Winner, E. (2000). The origins and ends of giftedness. *American Psychologist, 55*(1), 159–169.

Overexcitabilities

The concept of psychic overexcitabilities (OEs) emanated from Kazimierz Dabrowski's original concept of developmental potential, which he defined as a genetic endowment of traits that determine what level of moral development a person may reach under ideal circumstances. The five forms of OEs—psychomotor, intellectual, imaginational, sensual, and emotional—are considered types of increased psychic excitability and specific types of nervous energy Dabrowski witnessed in gifted and creative individuals. The OEs are described as a special kind of understanding, experiencing, and responding to the world. Michael Piechowski hypothesized that these overexcitabilities may be more prevalent in gifted and creative individuals than in the general population. The OEs are emerging as important components of giftedness and creativity, especially in light of the particular social and emotional needs of gifted individuals. The following sections further describe the specific OEs and the research that has been conducted on the OEs in typical and gifted school-age children, college students, and adults.

Overexcitabilities and Gifted Individuals

The psychomotor mode is one of movement, restlessness, action, excess of energy. The sensual mode relies on sensory contact and a need for sensory stimulation, including sensuality. The intellectual mode is characterized by analysis, logic, questioning, the search for truth, and a need for continuous and intense intellectual stimulation. The imaginational mode combines vivid dreams, daydreams, fantasies, images, and strong visualizations of experience. The emotional mode is expressed in attachments and bonds with others, and feelings of empathy, loneliness, and the happiness and joy of love.

Gifted, talented, and creative individuals are known to be energetic, enthusiastic, task committed, endowed with vivid imaginations, and strongly sensual, but they are also known to be emotionally vulnerable. Some are known to be aggressive, others to be morally sensitive. They may react strongly to aesthetic, intellectual, emotional, sexual, and other stimuli. According to Piechowski, the overexcitabilities feed, enrich, empower, and amplify talent, but they may also intensify emotional and intellectual insight, creating a tendency toward perfectionism, unrealistic expectations, and social and intellectual asynchrony.

Research

Michael Piechowski, Linda Silverman, Frank Falk, and Nancy Miller were instrumental in introducing the OEs to the gifted community through research studies utilizing various versions of the Overexcitability Questionnaire (OEQ), which has been used as an essay response instrument and as semistructured interview protocols. The most recent version of this instrument contains 21 questions such as, "Are you poetically inclined?" The instrument is holistically scored by trained raters. This line of research continues today and suggests that the overexcitabilities may be more prevalent among gifted, talented, or creative individuals, and that profiles of overexcitabilities differ among various groups. Researchers have found differences in the OEs among children and adolescents, with those identified as gifted scoring higher than those who are not identified as gifted. Some OEs were found to be strongest in artists when compared to the gifted and to have greater strength in more creatively gifted adolescents than less creatively gifted ones, but the artists in this study were self-identified, and not peer-recognized through the channels of the domain of visual arts. Other research has concluded that the Intellectual and Emotional OEs classified students as creatively or intellectually gifted and predicted group membership from among gifted, near-gifted, and non-gifted students. The authors of the original instrument found gender differences in which females had significantly higher emotional OE scores and males had higher intellectual OE scores. Others studied 9th- and 10th-grade gifted students enrolled in two private Catholic schools and found that they were differentiated from their non-gifted peers based on their higher psychomotor, intellectual, and emotional OE scores, with psychomotor providing the best predictor of giftedness.

More recent research, using a Likert-type instrument, the Overexcitabilities Questionnaire II (OEQII), found significant differences between males and females, gifted students and their parents, and gifted and typical students on the five OEs. Females scored higher than males on the Sensual and Emotional OEs. In addition, gifted students demonstrated higher Emotional and Intellectual OE scores, which may make them more insightful and volatile in their relationships with peers and others; this tension may also result in a discrepancy between how they perceive themselves and how they wish to be perceived. These two factors may help explain the asynchrony that gifted children often manifest when comparing themselves to their peers and to their imagined ideal selves.

The presence of high Psychomotor, Intellectual, and Emotional OEs in gifted students may be problematic because it may lead to diagnoses of attention deficit hyperactivity disorder (ADHD) and other behavior disorders. Gifted students with ADHD demonstrate behaviors such as daydreaming, incessant talking, inability to sit still, and social immaturity; all potential characteristics of the various manifestations of overexcitability. Researchers in the area of gifted students with learning issues found that gifted students with learning disabilities were typically the most disruptive students in their classes. Additional research suggested that gifted children with disabilities understand faster, ask more questions, hurry through math, and may be terribly disruptive. This evidence muddies the literature on gifted students with learning disabilities or ADHD because it becomes difficult to separate the characteristics of students with learning disabilities or ADHD from behaviors and characteristics often associated with gifted or creative children.

In a subsequent study using the OEQII, the researcher found significant differences between males and females, elementary and middle students, and typical and gifted students on the composite OE subscales. Mean OE subscale scores were relatively stable for typical students, but varied greatly for gifted students. Gifted elementary students scored higher on all five OE subscales, whereas typical middle school students scored higher on the Sensual and Imaginational OEs. Post hoc probing suggested that the mean Intellectual and Imaginational OE scores represented a majority of the difference between typical and gifted students. Finally, cross-cultural studies of the OEs continue today across Europe, Asia, and the Middle East.

Further research is needed into the construct of the OEs and the validity of results obtained from the OEQ instruments. Future research on the use of the OEs as a tool for discriminating among groups should focus on longitudinal patterns and differential manifestations of giftedness, because the literature suggests that highly gifted students may be more susceptible to social and emotional problems than those considered moderately gifted.

Finally, intervention research is needed to examine the OEs in school-age gifted children and to identify instructional strategies that may help gifted students understand and celebrate rather than disguise these intense behaviors and reactions.

Carol L. Tieso

See also Emotional Development; Emotional Intelligence; Existential Depression; Giftedness, Definition; Identification; Moral Development; Social-Emotional Issues; Supporting Emotional Needs of Gifted

Further Readings

Ackerman, C. M. (1997). Identifying gifted adolescents using personality characteristics: Dabrowski's overexcitabilities. *Roeper Review, 19*(4), 229–236.

Dabrowski, K. (1964). *Positive disintegration.* London: Little, Brown.

Falk, R. F., Lind, S., Miller, N. B., Piechowski, M. M., & Silverman, L. K. (1999). *The Overexcitability Questionnaire-Two (OEQII).* Denver, CO: Institute for the Study of Advanced Development.

Piechowski, M. M. (1999). Overexcitabilities. In S. R. Pritzker & M. A. Runco (Eds.), *Encyclopedia of creativity* (Vol. 2). San Diego, CA: Academic Press.

Piechowski, M. M. (2006). *"Mellow out," they say. If I only could: Intensities and sensitivities of the young and bright.* Madison, WI: Yunasa Books.

Silverman, L. K. (2008). The theory of positive disintegration in the field of gifted education. In S. Mendaglio (Ed.), *Dabrowski's theory of positive disintegration* (pp. 157–174). Scottsdale, AZ: Great Potential Press.

Webb, J. T., Amend, E. R., Webb, N. E., Goerss, J., Olenchak, F. R., & Beljan, P. (2005). *Misdiagnosis and dual diagnoses of gifted children and adults: ADHD, bipolar, OCD, Asperger's, depression, and other disorders.* Scottsdale, AZ: Great Potential Press.

Parallel Curriculum Model

The *parallel curriculum model* (PCM) is a comprehensive, concept-based approach to creating or revising curriculum. The model is intended to develop the strengths of a wide range of learners, including but not limited to those with high achievement and potential. PCM builds on previous theoretical beliefs concerning quality curriculum. The ultimate goal of PCM is to develop high-quality curriculum for the widest range of learners while still ensuring that the brightest learners are challenged. Through the use of the four parallels (Core, Connections, Practice, and Identity), either individually or in combination, PCM curriculum offers students opportunities to examine and engage the concepts and principles of a discipline in varied and compelling ways while growing toward expertise at an appropriately challenging level.

Theoretical Underpinnings

The model derives from the work of important theorists in the fields of psychology and curriculum and instruction to develop a rich and flexible approach to exploring and understanding the disciplines. Among the model's theoretical underpinnings are the following:

1. The key concepts and principles of a discipline represent the enduring knowledge of humankind. They are powerful in helping students understand what they study and in helping them organize, retrieve, transfer, and apply information. Concept-based curriculum leads to a depth of knowledge that is more powerful than the breadth without depth typified by a fact-based or coverage-based approach to curriculum.
2. Representative topics are those facets of a discipline that are highly reflective of other topics in the discipline. They are economical in helping students see how a discipline works and what it means. Representative topics enable students to study fewer topics in a discipline at much greater depth in order to see how the key concepts and principles make sense and how they govern the discipline as a whole. It is then possible for students to study subsequent topics with greater efficiency and effectiveness.
3. Process skills are central in powerful curriculum. Students learn more by doing than by listening and memorizing. Thus it is essential in curriculum design to engage learners' minds in a variety of kinds of thinking.
4. Knowledge is most useful when students can use what they learn to extend current knowledge and produce new knowledge. It is therefore important to teach students to work as much as possible like practitioners and problem solvers in a field would work.
5. Product-oriented curriculum enables students to draw on essential information, processes, and methodologies in a discipline in order to grapple with and ultimately address important issues and

problems. When students view themselves as producers of knowledge, they are more engaged in learning, find more satisfaction in their work, and have a more realistic opportunity to consider a range of possible futures for themselves.

6. Curriculum that serves as a catalyst for persistent movement toward expertise is necessarily concept based, process and method driven, and product oriented. To guide students toward increasing levels of expertise is to provide them with dynamic learning experiences and access to a promising future.

Curricular Parallels

PCM proposes four curricular parallels or ways of thinking about content. Each parallel can be used individually or in some combination with other parallels, and is unique in its intent and purpose. The four parallels are as follows: (1) The Core Parallel, which emphasizes the key concepts, principles, skills, information, and attitudes that shape a discipline; (2) the Connections Parallel, which helps students use the key concepts and principles of a discipline to make connections among and between various disciplines, time periods, places, and topics; (3) the Practice Parallel, which affords students opportunities to use the key concepts, principles, and methods of a discipline to engage in practitioner- and expert-like experiences that address key issues of a discipline; and (4) the Identity Parallel, which guides students in relating the key concepts and principles of a discipline to their own experiences, strengths, and goals.

The parallel curriculum model also encourages teachers to use key components of curriculum (e.g., content standards, assessments, introductory and closure activities, teaching methods, learning activities, grouping strategies, student products, resources, extension opportunities) as vehicles to ensure that students continue to focus on the key concepts, principles, and methods of a discipline as well as on the unique nature of a particular parallel. In addition, the model incorporates an approach to differentiating or personalizing instruction called Ascending Intellectual Demand (AID). AID guides teachers in examining a student's development in a particular segment of study and then adjusting the depth, breadth, pacing, and progression toward expertise as a means of providing optimum academic challenge.

Elements

Following is a brief examination of key PCM elements.

Core Curriculum

The Core Curriculum is designed to help teachers and students establish a framework of relevant knowledge, understanding, and skill that represents the nature and goals of a particular discipline. Although state and district standards play a key role in developing Core Curriculum, the main goal of Core Curriculum is to ensure that students develop a deep understanding of a discipline by coming to understand how experts in the discipline organize, make meaning of, and think about the discipline. Thus, in developing Core Curriculum, the teacher or curriculum developer ensures that content standards are organized conceptually in order to provide students with learning opportunities that help engage them in understanding the nature and structure of a discipline and to engage in complex thinking about the discipline.

Curriculum of Connections

Like the Core Curriculum, the Curriculum of Connections engages students in developing meaning based on the key concepts and principles of a discipline or topic. The Curriculum of Connections, however, helps students see how key concepts and principles reveal patterns and relationships across and among a variety of time periods, settings, cultures, events, people, and places. Thus, the Curriculum of Connections provides students, for instance, with opportunities to see meaningful relationships among topics being explored in U.S. history and in literature, in biology and in chemistry, in math and in art, in economics and in today's news, in the lives of "new world explorers" and lives of those who currently explore outer space. A heavy emphasis on subject-specific standards in schools makes this Parallel particularly useful in that it helps students organize discrete pieces of information around more meaningful concepts and principles and isolated skills into more purposeful tools.

Curriculum of Practice

As with the Core and Connections parallels, the Practice Parallel focuses on key concepts and principles of a discipline. The Curriculum of Practice, however, is intended to provide students with opportunities to take on the role of practitioner or expert in a discipline, seeing firsthand how experts use key concepts and principles to think about and address problems in the discipline. Further, this Parallel asks students to understand the methods, skills, habits of mind, and tools of production that experts in a discipline use. The Curriculum of Practice asks students to be disciplinarians—to "do" a discipline, rather than simply study it. Students thus address key issues and problems within a discipline as they seek solutions from the perspective of a practitioner in the discipline. The Practice Parallel provides students a window to the world outside of the classroom, making learning more compelling as students see real-world applications of classroom experiences, and leading to higher levels of student motivation.

Curriculum of Identity

The purpose of the Identity Parallel—also rooted in the key concepts and principles of a discipline—is twofold. First, students learn about the concepts and principles of a discipline or engage in expert-like activities. Simultaneously, however, the Curriculum of Identity helps learners see themselves in relation to the concept and principles and/or in comparison with practitioners. Students connect the discipline with their own lives, both now and in the future. Reflective opportunities simultaneously help students increase awareness of the nature of a discipline and of their own strengths, interests, and potential contributions to their world. The Curriculum of Identity is a means by which students can understand themselves more deeply as learners in relation to the concepts and principles of a discipline and in relation to the lives and work of those who practice that discipline.

Ascending Intellectual Demand

A goal of PCM is to ensure that virtually all students in a school are engaged with meaningful, high-quality curriculum. This does not suggest, however, that students should participate in one-size-fits all learning activities. Instead, an essential aspect of any PCM unit or lesson is to ensure that the unique needs of students are accommodated through a unique approach to differentiated instruction called Ascending Intellectual Demand (AID). AID both guides teachers in challenging students through more traditional differentiation and is based on students' personal growth trajectories as they move toward increasing expertise in a discipline. AID can be achieved (a) by offering students increasingly complex opportunities to work like experts in a discipline, (b) by using a set of AID prompts that help move students toward more advanced levels of expertise, and (c) by using rubric-like continuums that provide a learning progression from novice to expert in the disciplines.

Nonnegotiables

As is the case in implementation of any model or approach to curriculum and instruction, fidelity to the model's essential elements is imperative. The nonnegotiable elements of PCM include the following:

1. PCM curriculum is concept based and principle driven. That is, concepts and principles must be evident to and central in the work of students consistently and persistently.
2. PCM curriculum consistently reflects the "deep intent" of one or more parallels in the foreground of the unit. That is, it ensures students work to be able to answer the parallel's key questions, or other questions of equivalent importance and complexity.
3. PCM curriculum uses the curriculum components in a way that gives the unit coherence keeps the "deep intent" of the parallel(s) in the foreground of teaching, student work and thought, and class discussion.
4. PCM curriculum applies Ascending Intellectual Demand to extend student capacity by intensifying the "deep intent" of the parallels moving students progressively toward more expert-like ways of knowing, thinking, and working.

PCM curriculum should adhere to these guiding principles to ensure meaningful, high-quality learning experiences for students.

Implications

A fundamental assumption of PCM is that meaningful, high-quality curriculum should be available to virtually all students. In this way, PCM can simultaneously challenge advanced learners, serve as a catalyst for the recognition and identification of talent in groups of students who are traditionally underrepresented in gifted programs, and extend the abilities of many other students as well. AID is a novel way of looking at challenging students by meeting them at their appropriate readiness levels to help them progress toward expertise.

To these ends, PCM proposes the following:

1. There is no single "kind" of gifted learner. Students with high potential exist in all economic, racial, and ethnic groups—as well as in many facets of exceptionality—in far greater numbers than now recognized. It is important for the field of gifted education to embrace with equal energy and commitment both the extension of opportunity for high-performing students and the discovery and development of capacity in high-potential students.
2. Effective curriculum should be seen as a catalyst for both recognizing and developing high potential and for extending high performance.
3. Effective curriculum respects and responds to the unique characteristics and needs of individual students. Thus, effective curriculum provides support for students who encounter difficulty with content at a given time and for students who need to learn at a more rapid pace and at a greater depth. It attends to students' particular interests and encourages development of their particular talents.

PCM is thus intended to help those involved in educating gifted students play a more proactive role in the development of high-quality curriculum for the talents and abilities of a wide variety of students, including those who are identified as gifted and those who have undeveloped potential.

Carol Ann Tomlinson and Eric M. Carbaugh

See also Curriculum Models; Expertise

Further Readings

Tomlinson, C., Kaplan, S., Purcell, J., Leppien, J., Burns, D., & Strickland, C. (2006). *The parallel curriculum in the classroom, Book 1: Essays for application across the content areas, K–12.* Thousand Oaks, CA: Corwin Press.

Tomlinson, C., Kaplan, S., Purcell, J., Leppien, J., Burns, D., & Strickland, C. (2006). *The parallel curriculum in the classroom: Book 2: Units for application across the content areas, K–12.* Thousand Oaks, CA: Corwin Press.

Tomlinson, C., Kaplan, S., Renzulli, J., Purcell, J., Leppien, J., & Burns, D. (2002). *The parallel curriculum model: A design to develop high potential and challenge high ability learners.* Thousand Oaks, CA: Corwin Press.

Parental Attitudes

Parental attitudes about giftedness, which differ from one family to the next, are often affected by the many questions and concerns parents may have about how best to nurture and support their children's optimal growth. There is an ever-increasing wealth of information as people come to understand more and more about intelligence and giftedness, and ways to identify and address individual learning needs. Ongoing research in such domains as child development, neurological science, educational psychology, and other related fields continues to inform attitudes and perspectives on how children learn, how educators teach, and how parents can support their children both at home and at school. In addition, organizations of parents of gifted children have formed all over the world for the sharing of information and resources.

Underlying Factors

Feelings about a child's giftedness—and its many possible implications—can range from pure anxiety to confusion to unparalleled excitement, with infinite possibilities in between. Research shows that parental attitudes are often related to their socioeconomic status and knowledge about giftedness, with wealthier and more knowledgeable parents being more positive. Even those who understand the nature of giftedness may be daunted by the task of nurturing their child's abilities. For example, parents may wonder how to navigate the school system when dealing with matters that are seemingly complex. There are inevitably questions about individual developmental differences, identification measures, exceptional learning needs as they change over time, school-based programs, practices and policies, assessment methods, and advocacy channels. Parents' attitudes about the giftedness of their child may differ with the sex of the child, with sex-role stereotyping affecting parental attitudes. For example, finding out that a boy is mathematically gifted may be gratifying; finding out that he is a gifted dancer may be disturbing. Similarly, parents may have many questions about how and why gifted girls differ from average girls. What kinds of answers are parents receiving?

The research says that high-level ability comes in many forms, that there is no single gifted profile, and there is no educational or parenting approach that is suitable for every child. That means there are no easy answers. Moreover, in the whole scheme of things, there is still a lot to learn. Nevertheless, particular types of giftedness may require different resources and parenting skills.

Whether a child is formally identified as gifted or not, and regardless of the child's age, parents may perceive a mismatch between their child's diverse needs and the various learning opportunities being provided. Sometimes those learning opportunities require adjusting, whereas at other times what is warranted is a more thorough reevaluation and restructuring of the educational landscape. Finding a proper fit between a child and the educational system requires planning, time, solid information gathering, effort, collaboration, and thoughtful and targeted decision making on the part of many people.

Initiatives

Parents can begin by finding out all they can about child development issues, the nature of intelligence, and giftedness. It is important for parents to access pertinent and current information both proactively and reactively. It can be difficult to zero in on what is most essential to one's own particular needs or concerns because of the great proliferation of resource material to sift through, read, consider, and then apply. As such, it is helpful to work in concert with a child's teachers and, if necessary, with professional psychologists, determining needs based on the lived experience of the child, and then building a framework from which to address them. For example, parents may want to know what to do in relation to their child's achievement and aptitude, social and emotional well-being, school programming and placement, and domain-specific areas of strength and weakness. Parental attitudes about giftedness will be influenced by the type and accuracy of the resource material they acquire, reflect upon, and apply; the kinds and extent of support they are given by educators, counselors, and other professionals; the degree to which they network and share useful information with other parents; and the extent to which they are open-minded, flexible, and sensitive when confronting all the smooth and rough patches encountered over time at home, in school, and within society. Children's own attitudes, uncertainties, tendencies, assumptions, excitabilities, cognitive levels, concerns, and questions about giftedness are also some of the matters at the forefront of parents' investigative and advocacy efforts.

Support and Responsibility

Parental attitudes tend to be invigorated and made more positive when their understandings of giftedness and high-level ability are clarified, and when parents perceive success in finding and providing appropriate educational opportunities for their child's optimal development. Ultimately, parents who appreciate their children's uniqueness (including their different interests, experiences, learning preferences, and ways of functioning) are better positioned to provide the right influences and guidance along the way. It helps, also, for the family to work as a team, supporting each others' goals and giving each member both support and individual responsibility for learning. Nevertheless, misinformation and controversy about giftedness can be confusing, daunting, and even overwhelming. When parents (and others) understand "being gifted" as the identification of exceptional learning needs at a particular point in time, this serves to remove some of the elitism, mystery, and confusion often associated with the label, and much of the stigma frequently attached to it and to gifted education. Parents who cultivate inquiry, regularly access community support systems, and who have informed and positive mind-sets and understandings about giftedness from multiple reliable sources are attitudinally stronger and thereby better equipped to respond to their children's needs. This kind of acquired competence involves increasing one's familiarity with adaptive learning opportunities and environments; being attuned to children's abilities as they mature; helping children take some responsibility for their learning and to feel good about their accomplishments; learning about effective advocacy processes; and recognizing that one cannot categorize individual development, and that thus there is no predetermined path for any one child.

Parents of gifted/high-ability learners are positioned to help their children overcome difficulties that may accompany being perceived as "different" or "exceptional." Nurturing efforts should rest upon solid understandings of gifted-level development, open communication, love, and acceptance—and, most important, and unconditionally—an attitude that conveys respect for the intellectual and other domain-specific abilities and individual intricacies of the child, and all that he or she may come to be.

Joanne F. Foster

See also Attitudes Toward Gifted; Parenting; Student Attitudes; Teacher Attitudes

Further Readings

Begin, J., & Gagne, F. (1994). Predictors of general attitude toward gifted education. *Journal for the Education of the Gifted, 18*(1), 74–76.

Cross, T. (2005). *The social and emotional lives of gifted kids: Understanding and guiding their development.* Waco, TX: Prufrock Press.

Delisle, J., & Galbraith, J. (2002). *When gifted kids don't have all the answers.* Minneapolis, MN: Free Spirit Publishing.

Matthews, D. J., & Foster, J. F. (2005). *Being smart about gifted children: A guidebook for parents and educators.* Scottsdale, AZ: Great Potential Press.

Rogers, K. (2002). *Re-forming gifted education: Matching the program to the child.* Scottsdale, AZ: Great Potential Press.

VanTassel-Baska, J., & Stambach, T. (2006). *Comprehensive curriculum for gifted learners* (3rd ed.). Boston: Pearson Education.

Parenting

It has long been established that parents play an essential role in the development of gifted children. Twelve leading researchers, under the direction of Benjamin Bloom at the University of Chicago, studied the talent development of 120 children over a period of 4 years. In 1985, he reported in *Developing Talent in Young People* that parents played a crucial role in nurturing and encouraging these students. James Alvino's research indicates that caring, knowledgeable, and supportive parents can create a nurturing home environment that provides emotional support for students. This encouragement at home gives the child inner strength and a competent sense of self that enables the child to survive and even thrive. Linda Silverman's work in 1993 reinforces the concept that families who encourage and promote independence and exploration pave the way for a child's stable social and emotional development.

Traits that parents may have in common with their children include intensity, emotional involvement, acute sensitivity, high verbal ability, creativity and imagination, keen powers of observation, perseverance, and a tendency toward perfectionism. Thus parents have a need to meet with other parents of gifted to share experiences and learn skills to assist their children with issues such as stress, perfectionism, and friendships. Arlene DeVries and James Webb have proposed a guided discussion format that addresses social-emotional issues and parent relationships.

Parents as Advocates

Frances Karnes concludes in her studies that parents are powerful agents in advocating for appropriate educational placement for gifted children. When parents search for a school that provides a good educational fit, they need to consider whether their child's learning styles match that offered by the school; if there are provisions for the child to learn at his or her own pace; if the curricular content and extracurricular activities match the child's interests and talents; if there are opportunities for students to ask probing questions and explore various viewpoints; if creative thinking and problem solving are encouraged; if the social and emotional needs as well as the academic needs are addressed; and if parents and community members are involved in the education of the child. When a child has been placed in a classroom, an initial meeting with the teacher allows parents to share their child's strengths and any concerns they have about their child. It is helpful when parents share specific examples of student work, interests, or behaviors. When a new program or accommodation is introduced, following up in 2 to 3 weeks in person, by phone, or e-mail is useful for evaluating its effectiveness.

A 1994 research study of 3,554 elementary gifted students and their parents conducted by the Belin-Blank Center at the University of Iowa indicated that parents were appropriately involved in both the academic and the social lives of these high-achieving students. Effective advocates first establish rapport with the school by supporting current programs, volunteering, and sending appreciative notes to educators. These parents serve on district school boards, advisory committees, and parent–teacher organizations.

Knowledge about educational philosophy, district budgets, state mandates, district staff, gifted students, and current issues in gifted education enables parents to communicate with confidence. Parents and educators both want what is best for the child, but come with unique insights into the child's needs, aspirations, interests, and aptitudes. Communication, beginning with the classroom teacher before moving to the next person in command, is built on positives, is respectful, and diplomatic, yet persistent. Parents joining together can speak collectively for the needs of gifted children in the local district or at the state level. Local parent advocacy groups are often affiliated with a state gifted association for support.

Addressing Social and Emotional Needs

Stress

Because of gifted students' asynchronous development (the uneven way in which their physical, social, emotional, and intellectual states develop), Judy Genshaft and J. Broyles, in 1991, determined that these students are more susceptible to stress. When stress is ignored, physical and mental illness, including depression, can occur. Warning signs of excessive stress include change in sleeping or eating patterns, school avoidance, difficulty concentrating, stomachaches or headaches, major change in personality, and excessive lashing out or withdrawal.

Caring parents recognize when students feel the need to hide their abilities to be accepted; when they experience excessively high expectations from within and from others; when schoolwork is too easy or too overwhelming; when they have overcommitted themselves; when they are overly concerned about existential humanitarian world issues; and when they strive to attain unrealistic goals or perfectionism. Parents can assist students in recognizing the physiological and psychological symptoms associated with stress, and then support them in finding an appropriate coping plan such as the following: Remove themselves from the situation; alter the self-talk regarding the incident; express their emotions either verbally or through a physical activity; relax through deep breathing, creative visualization, reading, or listening to music; establish priorities; examine the problem objectively; devise a plan to resolve the conflict; and finally implement the plan. Successful families establish a calm, noncompetitive environment with quiet times and places; use light-hearted humor; implement personal journaling; and a have healthy stress-reducing diet that limits caffeine and sugar. When students are affirmed in their problem solving, in their successes and failures, a strong sense of self develops. This resilience allows students to cope with the stresses they encounter. Parents are role models in how they cope with the challenges and stresses in their lives.

According to research based on the National Education Longitudinal Study in a sample of 25,000 eighth graders, among four main areas of parental involvement—home discussion, home supervision, school communication, and school participation—home discussion was the most strongly related to academic achievement.

Perfectionism

Perfectionism among gifted students has been a major concern for parents and educators as reflected in studies of underachievement and emotional turmoil by Michael Pyryt. Research and clinical studies of gifted children and adolescents conclude that as a group gifted students are more perfectionistic than average-ability peers. Various professionals have estimated that as many as 20 percent of gifted children are perfectionists. Although parents might be concerned that they have created perfectionism in the child by having excessively high expectations, many children appear to have an inborn predisposition toward perfectionism.

D. E. Hamacheck views perfectionism on a continuum from healthy to unhealthy. A healthy pursuit of excellence means doing the best you can with what you have to work with, in the time you have; being satisfied with the results; and then moving on. Unhealthy perfectionists have an obsession with doing things perfectly, view themselves as "not good enough," often feel anxious and frustrated, and resort to procrastination and underachievement. Unhealthy perfectionists often try to imitate or live up to "perfect" standards as determined by others in society. Healthy perfectionists, on the other hand, can strive for excellence based on an intrinsic motivation to become truly themselves.

For unhealthy perfectionists, doing things perfectly is what one does to gain an identity and thus acceptance. When students lose one area of identity, such as being the "smart" student who always "gets it right," parents can assist them in finding another role. Parents can encourage them in a new hobby or extracurricular activity. They can also introduce them to an adult community or a family member who might become a role model for them in a new endeavor. In addition, parents can suggest they read biographies of successful adults in an area of their interest and discuss ways in which a character in a book overcame obstacles or failures. Parents can also share examples of when they took a risk in attempting a task in which they did not feel competent. When the student expresses a fear of risking a new undertaking, parents can be understanding and accepting.

The media and other societal influences that emphasize winning and being the "best" may contribute to students' inability to be less than perfect. The message can change from "Be the *best,*" to "Be the best *you* can be." Parents can commend students for the process or progress they make toward a goal, not just reward students for the finished product. They can help students set small manageable goals, establish priorities, and plan ahead. Students can work toward their personal best, but when they are pushed to extremes, it can cause frustration, anxiety, depression, and physical illness.

Friendships

Jonathan Plucker and Vicki Stocking in 2001 concluded that when students interact with others, they make assertions about their personal identity. Because they have diverse interests and think in ways that differ from their age-level peers, gifted children may have difficulty establishing friendships. Leta Hollingworth, in her studies as early as 1930, indicated that as IQ increased, so did difficulties with peer relations. Gifted children often are "off in their own world" and miss social cues in peer interactions. In 1942, Hollingworth indicated that highly gifted children tended to be solitary because they lacked available companions with similar interests or language abilities. Miraca Gross in 2001 concluded that most students tend to seek out friends of similar mental age rather than chronological age. It is the role of the parents to identify schools, extracurricular activities, community offerings, and gifted/talented summer schools and precollegiate programs where students will meet others with similar interests and abilities. Home can become a haven of acceptance for gifted children. Once they feel secure in the family, they are more willing to risk reaching out to others.

In her clinical observations of gifted students participating in programs of the Gifted Development Center in Denver, Colorado, Linda Silverman determined that among the highly gifted students, more than 75 percent were introverted in comparison to the 25 percent usually observed in the general population. She defines introverts as those who get energy from within compared to extraverts who are energized by interactions with others. For optimal development of predominantly introverted gifted children, parents need to respect their need for privacy. They need to give them advanced notice of changes in their routine. They can teach them new skills in private to avoid embarrassing them in public. Instead of pushing them to have many friends, parents can enable them to find one best friend and encourage that relationship. Extravert students, on the other hand, are more comfortable in new situations and parents can arrange for them to be part of group social activities.

Often it is difficult to determine if the student honestly prefers being alone, or if he or she lacks social skills and is retreating for fear of rejection. At times it may be necessary to "practice" social skills by doing role-plays at home. Parents can encourage children to be the first to reach out to another student. They can teach what it means to be a good listener and to inquire about the other's interests. While encouraging acceptance of others, parents can acknowledge there are certain friends they can do without. A parent who has encouraged positive self-esteem in the student feels confident that the student will refuse to join a peer group that engages in behaviors that are morally or physically destructive.

Supportive Parents

Gifted students have a "need to know." When they question authority and break traditions, parents can guide them in socially acceptable ways. Although these students have long attention spans, they are often dreamers and thinkers, and may be engaged in thoughts that tune out current realities. Parents need to establish a safe environment where children can express their ideas and feelings. In 2002, Nancy Robinson's study of 5,400 children in a Head Start Program showed that those who were high achievers by third grade had caretakers who displayed positive parenting attitudes and strongly encouraged their child's progress. Schools expect that parents will provide a wide variety of reading material, expose their child to the visual and performing arts, provide opportunity for physical activity, assist the child in goal setting and problem solving, expect the child to take responsibility for household tasks, avoid overprotecting the child by allowing consequences, balance learning and leisure, support and actively encourage the child's interests, and above all, value the child for who he or she is, not what the child does.

Arlene Rae DeVries

See also Depression; Family Achievement; Parental Attitudes; Social-Emotional Issues

Further Readings

Bloom, B. S. (1985). *Developing talent in young people.* New York: Ballantine Books.

DeVries, A., & Webb J. (2007). *Gifted parent groups: The SENG model* (2nd ed.). Scottsdale, AZ: Great Potential Press.

Neihart, M., Reis, S., Robinson N., & Moon, S. (Eds.). (2002). *The social and emotional development of gifted children: What do we know?* Waco, TX: Prufrock Press.

Peterson, J. (2007). *Talk with gifted/talented teens about self and stress.* Minneapolis, MN: Free Spirit Publishing.

Robinson, A., Shore B., & Emerson, D. (2007). *Best practices in gifted education.* Waco, TX: Prufrock Press.

Silverman, L. (1993). *Counseling the gifted and talented.* Denver, CO: Love Publishing.

Walker, S. (2002). *The survival guide for parents of gifted kids* (Rev. ed.). Minneapolis, MN: Free Spirit Publishing.

Webb, J., Gore, J., Amend, E., & DeVries, A. (2007). *A parent's guide to gifted children.* Scottsdale, AZ: Great Potential Press.

Parent Nominations

Parent nomination is a practice that provides opportunity for parents to recommend evaluation of their child for possible inclusion into gifted programs and solicits information about a child's potential need for gifted education. Gifted children often require educational services beyond those that can be provided within the regular classroom; however, to receive special services, these children must first be recognized as having special needs. Not all gifted students are identified through traditional means. This entry discusses the varieties of parent nomination methods and the benefits of, and concerns about, parents' input into identification of gifted students.

Many schools use a multistep, multiple measures approach for selecting students for gifted programs. Current practices generally employ a combination of objective and subjective assessments to identify high-ability students, rather than relying on scores from single tests of intelligence. Among the various subjective measures used, such as teacher nominations, peer nominations, and self-nominations, some districts reach out to parents through a formal nomination process. Other districts handle parent nominations on an informal, individual basis.

Parent nominations have been shown to be effective in identifying students who will benefit from gifted programming, because parents are frequently able to recognize and accurately describe aspects of their child's development. Despite this information, parent nomination is often used only as a secondary, alternative, or optional method for identification. There are no statistics on how many districts across the nation include various types of parent nomination in their assessment process.

Forms

Nomination forms for parents vary from location to location. They can be short and simple, such as four or five descriptive questions about how parents observe their child's response to academic activities, ability to adapt to novel situations, task persistence, and creative expression. More detailed nomination forms involve checklists concerning a child's intellectual curiosity, creativity, motivation, and social and emotional maturity.

Benefits

Young Children

What parents know about their child can help shape a successful learning environment. Because early experiences with learning influence later attitudes toward school and achievement, appropriately placing gifted children in stimulating programs is essential. An important first step to accurate placement is identification, yet the testing of young, gifted children remains problematic. Not all schools evaluate kindergarten and primary-age students. Even if a school is open to the assessment of a gifted young child, there are few valid and reliable instruments. In addition, when considering gifted programming options such as early entrance for a very young child, schools have very little, if any, achievement, ability, and observational data upon which to base their decision. Early entry requires parents to be proactive in contacting schools.

A majority of schools do not initiate the identification of gifted students nor program for them until third or fourth grade, which means that parent observation, documentation, and nomination can be crucial components in proper program placement during the primary grades.

Researchers have shown that parents do observe developmental differences among children and can provide insight into early signs of giftedness. Parents are likely to identify early readers accurately, as well as children with extensive and expressive verbal skills, strong memory, focus, imagination, curiosity, long attention span, logical reasoning skills, and creative problem-solving ability. When provided with clear checklists, even parents who are not well educated themselves are able to recognize characteristics of gifted learners. Nomination forms that solicit parent input also help parents become aware of the gifted identification process used by their child's school. In addition, the use of a parent nomination process encourages the sharing of useful anecdotal and developmental information with educators.

Older Children

Many variables, such as health, well-being, home environment, exposure to learning opportunities, and second language acquisition can impact how well a child scores on a test. Schools that limit identification for gifted programs to a single entry point undoubtedly overlook a number of high-ability students. The option for parent nomination provides another avenue for these children to be evaluated.

Twice-Exceptional Students

Parent nominations are useful in the case of children with multiple exceptionalities (high abilities in some areas along with learning deficits in others). These students present a complex set of learning needs that includes provision for opportunities for their gifts to develop, as well as remediation for any disabilities. Accurate recognition and identification of a twice-exceptional child may result only through parent nomination.

Diverse Populations

Gifted children from disadvantaged or diverse populations, who might not perform well on standardized tests or within regular classrooms, can be brought to the attention of teachers through parent nomination. Parents from disadvantaged situations are less likely to understand the necessity for advocacy when children need special academic services. Through a formal process that includes parent nomination, parents of at-risk students, particularly those from cultural backgrounds that discourage public discussion of a child's gifts or accomplishments, are informed and encouraged to advocate for appropriate school placement.

Concerns

There are several reasons why schools may be reluctant to include parent nomination as part of their identification process for gifted services. Current teachers rarely receive training in collaborating with parents, which can result in misunderstanding and heightened sensitivity about controversial topics such as inclusion in gifted programs. Often educators are not trained in either identifying gifted children or providing effective programs to support their intellectual and social-emotional development.

Lack of training for teachers about recognizing and understanding the needs of gifted students can lead to suspicions about parent motives for nominations. Educators can discount parent information, concerned that parents are seeking a distinctive label for their child. In some instances, parents do nominate their child without a clear understanding of the negative consequences, yet teachers who understand the confusion surrounding the wide range of definitions and programs for gifted students can often refocus parents in practical and meaningful discussion.

When parent nomination forms are used, schools may expect parents to be familiar with gifted characteristics and signs of intellectual abilities, skills that even trained educators may miss. Parents need training in noting key aspects of emerging giftedness and in supporting the development of their child's abilities. Without such background, parents may miss critical clues for the nomination process. In addition, there can be a misalignment of parental conceptions of giftedness and a school's operational definition. Clear definitions and terminology can help parent nominations be effective tools.

Final Thoughts

Parents have the ultimate responsibility for their child's education. They know their child's developmental history and can accurately document signs of possible giftedness. Parent and teacher observations of an individual child may differ, but each provides beneficial insights. Including parental nomination as a viable option for discovering gifted children broadens perspective of the assessment process for multiple populations of students.

Robin Schader

See also Early Entrance, Kindergarten; Early Identification; Identification; Iowa Acceleration Scale

Further Readings

Lee, S., & Olszewski-Kubilius, P. (2006). Talent search qualifying: Comparisons between talent search students qualifying via scores on standardized tests and via parent nomination. *Roeper Review, 28*(3), 157–166.

Rogers, K. B. (2001). *Re-forming gifted education: Matching the program to the child.* Scottsdale, AZ: Great Potential Press.

Sattler, J. M., & Hoge, R. D. (2006). *Assessment of children: Behavioral, social, and clinical foundations* (5th ed.). San Diego, CA: Jerome M. Sattler.

Schader, R. M. (2008). Parenting. In J. Plucker & C. Callahan (Eds.), *Critical issues and practices in gifted education: What the research says* (pp. 479–492). Waco, TX: Prufrock Press.

Perfectionism

Perfectionism is a widely studied construct in gifted education. As such, multiple perspectives on different types of perfectionism, its origins, its prevalence in the gifted population, and its effects on students are prominent in the literature.

Perfectionism Typologies

Various typologies of perfectionism have been proposed. Inherent within this discussion is the implicit understanding that different types of perfectionism are associated with varying attitudes and behaviors. Wayne Parker identified three groups of gifted students: nonperfectionists, healthy perfectionists, and dysfunctional perfectionists. Parker described the nonperfectionists as having low levels of conscientiousness, personal standards, parental expectations, and organization as well as an overall low score on the Multidimensional Perfectionism Scale (MPS)–Frost, a measure of perfectionism that breaks the construct into six factors: personal standards, organization, concern for mistakes, doubts about actions, parental expectations, and parental criticism. Healthy perfectionists were defined as having minimal concern for mistakes and doubts about actions, low perceptions of parental criticism, high organization, moderate personal standards, and a moderate overall score on the MPS. This group scored lowest on a measure of neuroticism, but highest on extraversion, agreeableness, and conscientiousness. Finally, Parker described dysfunctional perfectionists as having a high concern for mistakes, personal standards, and doubts about their actions. They perceived their parents as highly critical. They scored the highest on the MPS–Frost, and they scored the highest of all three groups on measures of neurosis and openness to experience, and lowest on agreeableness.

Other research also suggests typology frameworks corroborating Parker's findings of adaptive and maladaptive perfectionism. Kristie Speirs Neumeister used the Hewitt and Flett Multidimensional Perfectionism Scale (MPS–Hewitt), a measure that breaks the construct into three factors, including self-oriented (individuals who have excessively high standards for themselves), socially prescribed (those perceiving others to have excessively high expectations for their performance), and other-oriented perfectionism (individuals who have excessively high standards for others) to study gifted college students. She found that those scoring high on socially prescribed perfectionism tended to overgeneralize their failures, adopted performance goals, and perceived their parents as critical. In contrast, although the self-oriented perfectionists expressed frustration with failure, they were also more likely to adopt learning as well as performance goals and to perceive their parents as supportive. These findings support the notion that different types of perfectionism may be related to different perceptions, attitudes, and beliefs among gifted students.

Development

The literature also highlights several influences on the development of perfectionism. These influences include personality, parental modeling and styles, insecure attachment, and lack of challenge.

Prevalence

The results of some studies indicate a higher prevalence of perfectionism among gifted students, while others fail to show differences in the populations. Differences in how perfectionism was measured, the operationalization of giftedness, and the age of the students may account for the conflicting results.

Implications

Researchers have offered suggestions for working with perfectionistic students, including creating a classroom where students are challenged and learn to appreciate mistakes and examining the motives underlying perfectionistic behaviors to determine how to respond. Other suggestions include setting appropriate expectations, being mindful of modeling perfectionism, praising effort rather than ability, and demonstrating unconditional love. Barbara Kerr proposed a counseling strategy for perfectionists to retrain them in positive aspects of nonperfectionism.

As more research on perfectionism is completed, parents, teachers, and counselors will be able to guide gifted students more effectively toward adaptive thoughts and behaviors that facilitate, rather than inhibit, their talent development.

Kristie Speirs Neumeister

See also Achievement Motivation; Guidance; Parental Attitudes; Parenting; Social-Emotional Issues

Further Readings

Frost, R. O., Marten, P. A., Lahart, C., & Rosenblate, R. (1990). The development of perfectionism. *Cognitive Therapy and Research, 14,* 449–468.

Hewitt, P., & Flett, G. (1991). Perfectionism in the self and social contexts: Conceptualization, assessment, and association with psychopathology. *Journal of Personality and Social Psychology, 60,* 456–470.

Parker, W. D. (2002). Perfectionism and adjustment in gifted children. In P. Hewitt & G. Flett (Eds.), *Perfectionism: Theory, research, and treatment* (pp. 133–148). Washington, DC: American Psychological Association.

Speirs Neumeister, K. L. (2004). Understanding the relationship between perfectionism and achievement motivation in gifted college students. *Gifted Child Quarterly, 48,* 219–231.

Speirs Neumeister, K. L., & Finch, W. H. (2006). Perfectionism in high ability students: Relational precursors and implications for achievement. *Gifted Child Quarterly, 50,* 238–251.

Performing Arts

The performing arts use the artist's body, face, and voice to create "live art" that can be enjoyed by an audience. The performing arts require high levels of talent and creativity, requiring great physical and mental exertion during performances. The performing arts express human culture across a broad time span of human history. This entry discusses the nature of performing arts careers as well as the ways in which gifted students are involved in performing arts.

The performing arts involve the artist's own body, face, and physical presence. Performing arts include dancing, singing, acting, circus performances, theater, film, opera, music, and acrobatics. The performing arts take place before a live audience, and exist in real life for a finite amount of time. Artists who participate in the performing arts include actors, dancers, musicians, and singers.

The Western model of performing arts began during the 6th century BCE in Ancient Greece with Sophocles' tragic plays. During the 9th through the 14th centuries, performing arts in the Western world were limited to religious reenactments and morality plays. In modern times, the performing arts have expanded to include television and movie performances. New technologies allow viewers to see past performances that have been prerecorded, and in this day and age the performing arts are both a live and a historical art form.

The performing arts require a lengthy talent development process, a deep understanding of the art, and the ability to connect with a live audience on the stage. There are many exciting opportunities for gifted individuals in the performing arts, but hard work and perseverance are required for a successful career in this area. Performing artists can take lessons, practice their skills, work with mentors, and perfect their talent to a professional level.

Earning a living in the performing arts requires talent, hard work, and knowledge about a specific industry. However, many performing artists are able to create their own niche in the marketplace, finding audiences through unconventional methods ranging from word of mouth to reality television shows.

Gifted individuals who are exposed to the performing arts develop an understanding and appreciation of culture and become producers of art experiences. Individuals who have artistic talent can pursue careers in a variety of areas that are suited to their aptitude and natural talent.

Suzanna E. Henshon

See also Artistic Ability; Dance; Drama; Talent

Further Readings

Karnes, F. A., & Stephens, K. R. (2007). *A girl's guide to achieving in the arts.* New York: Royal Fireworks.

Pasternack, C., & Thornburg, L. (2000). *Cool careers for girls in performing arts.* Manassas Park, VA: Impact Publications.

Piirto, J. (1999). *Talented children and adults: Their development and education* (2nd ed.). Upper Saddle River, NJ: Prentice Hall.

Wright, B. (2002, Fall). Performing arts instruction for exceptionally and profoundly gifted children. *Gifted Education Press Quarterly, 16,* 4–5.

Personality and Intelligence

Intelligence refers generally to the capacity to collect, screen, process, and select information in an adaptive manner. It is commonly treated as a global capacity of the individual to deal effectively with his or her environment. However, it has been conceived alternatively as a set of specific capacities that are content, domain, or context dependant (social, emotional, academic, practical, creative, mathematic, linguistic, etc.).

Personality refers to the preferred ways that an individual behaves or interacts with the environment. Personality is classically associated with the notion of traits that are stable, preferred ways of being and acting across time and situations. Recent work taking an interactive *person–situation* approach has indicated the utility of considering that behavior may be codetermined by an individual's preferences and environmental features, which vary across situations.

Diverse theoretical positions relating personality and intelligence have been proposed. In general, intelligence and personality are currently considered as two separate psychological components. Nevertheless, it is not excluded that some personality traits favor intellectual activity and that some specific factors of intelligence favor the development of certain aspects of personality. Understanding the interplay between these two basic concepts in psychology is important for modeling complex phenomena such as giftedness, talent, and creativity.

Theoretical Articulation Between Intelligence and Personality

Intelligence as a Part of Personality

Kant separated the mind into three components: cognition, conation, and affect. Some personality theorists, such as Raymond Cattell, have suggested, however, that intelligence refers to a stable mode of functioning and should be included within the concept of personality. Based on a lexical approach according to which all human behavior is represented in language and more specifically in each language's adjectives, Cattell identified 16 primary factors of personality with 1 referring specifically to intelligence: contrasting lower general mental capacity and inability to handle abstract problems with abstract thinking, higher general mental capacity, and fast learning. In this perspective, intelligence and specifically fluid intelligence may be considered part of personality.

In a similar approach, George Welsh introduced intelligence as a personality dimension, *intellectance,* related to performance on intellectual measures. Intellectance refers to the level of investment in intellectual activities: the more an individual is invested and interested in a cognitive task, the more he or she could perform well and show intelligence in this task. Thus *intellectance* may be described as an intellectual ability trait that allows individuals to achieve their objective.

In this conception of intellectual ability as a trait, the psychological variable of prudence, referring to concerned choice, and action planning as the basis of balancing between personal interests and social concerns, has been proposed. This concept may partially relate to the notion of "wisdom," involving both personality and intelligence in the extent to which people use their intelligence for a social good.

More recently, John Mayer proposed that stable behavior, defined as a personality trait, inherently involves cognitive and affective features. For example, the trait of extraversion combines positive affect (an emotional mechanism), social affiliation (a motivational mechanism), and knowledge of how to socialize (a mental model concerning intelligence).

The concept of emotional intelligence, defined as a set of abilities to treat emotion and/or emotional information, has been developed. Two kinds of emotional intelligence models exist: One is a maximum-performance-based model, an ability-based approach, and the other is a trait-based model. Emotional intelligence measures range from performance-based tests to those that capture individuals' self-perception of their emotional intelligence. In this way, emotional intelligence may be defined as a tendency to deal adequately with emotions.

Intelligence and Personality as Two Independent Structures

Many current models of personality, such as the *Big Five model,* do not include intellectual abilities. Concerning the factors often studied—Neuroticism, Extraversion, Openness, Conscientiousness, and Agreeability—none is specially supposed to relate to differences in intellectual ability. In addition, dominant theories of intelligence do not include personality traits; they focus exclusively on performance-based abilities, which can be considered potentialities that may be developed and expressed as talent.

Within this "independence" view of intelligence and personality, cognitive styles are often considered to represent the interface between the two spheres. Cognitive style refers to preferred modes for using one's intellectual abilities. For example, according to Robert Sternberg's *mental self-government theory* of thinking styles, people may show preferences for either legislative thinking (inventing new rules and procedures), executive thinking (following established rules to reach a goal), or judicial thinking (evaluating procedures and productions). An individual may have any of these preferred modes of thinking, regardless of his or her level of intellectual ability. Another style dimension is "external–internal," referring to a preference for thinking in social, group settings versus thinking alone. This dimension connects the personality trait of extraversion–introversion with the realm of mental activities. It is postulated that a preference for the external or internal style should not lead to differences in intellectual performance in general across a wide range of tasks (a particular style may favor performance in a certain cognitive task, however). Many dimensions of cognitive styles have been proposed with some being specifically adapted to situations involving learning, decision making, creativity, or other kinds of mental activities.

Not Independence but Some Personality Characteristics May Favor the Fulfillment of Intellectual Potential

Some interactions between personality and intelligence have been suggested, particularly in developmental approaches. For example, some authors have emphasized the idea that intelligence is partly the result of investing in intellectual activities. Personality, interests, and motivation are considered important variables in the access to knowledge. Anxiety-trait may contribute to the observation of lower scores in intelligence tests. Concerning why some people have greater knowledge than others, intellectual openness, a facet of the personality trait of openness, reflects a general interest in learning and positively predicted engagement in information-seeking activities, which positively predicted knowledge of current events.

Empirical Data

Many studies have tested relationships between intellectual performances and personality traits. For example, a meta-analysis of studies examining relationships between anxiety and intelligence showed a significant negative relationship with a mean r of .23, indicating that the more individuals are anxious, the less well they perform. Another meta-analysis examined the degree to which personality traits (other than anxiety) and intelligence are related. Some personality traits tend to be positively correlated across ability, including Well-Being, Social Potency, Achievement, Social Closeness, Intellectance, Extraversion, and Openness to Experience. Personality traits that tend to be negatively correlated across ability traits include Stress Reaction, Alienation, Anxiety, and Psychoticism.

Recently, several studies have examined links between academic performance, intelligence factors and Big-Five personality traits. These studies showed a positive significant relationship of openness to experience with academic performance, but also with fluid intelligence. In fact, a causal association between openness and knowledge-based components of intelligence has been proposed whereby individuals with high levels of openness are more likely to "invest" in activities that stimulate the acquisition of knowledge. Moreover, it was observed that the trait of conscientiousness was negatively correlated with fluid intelligence. More precisely, conscientiousness was negatively linked to fluid intelligence but positively linked to exam grades (academic performance). These results support the idea of a "compensational function": lower fluid intelligence led to higher conscientiousness, which, in turn, led to higher academic performance. The trait of conscientiousness may compensate for lower cognitive ability.

Intelligence and Personality in Giftedness, Creativity, and Talent

Many theories of giftedness, creativity, and talent propose that both intellectual variables and personality factors are involved. For example, recent work on creativity suggests that a combination of intellectual abilities, such as divergent thinking, analogical-metaphorical thinking, and evaluation skills are necessary but not sufficient. There must be certain personality factors present to a sufficient degree to provide the right conditions to use the intellectual abilities. Risk-taking trait is often evoked in this context as a key element for creativity because novel thinking involves, by definition, breaking away from traditional ways of solving a problem or approaching a situation. However, it is difficult to break with tradition, in particular when these traditions serve as the basis of one's knowledge and expertise. Thus, in this context, the trait of risk taking provides the needed context in which intelligence can be turned to creative ends.

This example suggests that personality variables may provide a context for the use of intelligence. The opposite relationship has also been proposed within the context of giftedness, creativity, and talent. For example, the personality trait of tolerance of ambiguity has been found to be involved in creativity; tolerance of ambiguity trait allows one to explore potential avenues of a situation and ultimately to find a novel idea, because the problem solver avoids rapidly seeking closure and accepting a nonoptimal idea. Tolerance of ambiguity requires, however, noticing that there is some ambiguity. This awareness of ambiguity, which in turn may be tolerated to a greater or lesser degree, requires a sufficient level of intelligence. If an individual does not notice any ambiguity, the question of tolerating the ambiguity does not exist, and neither does the potential benefit of tolerating the ambiguity for creative thinking. Thus, complex phenomena such as giftedness, creativity, and talent most probably involve intelligence, personality, and their interactions.

Todd Lubart and Franck Zenasni

See also Creative Personality; Emotional Intelligence; Intelligence; Learning Styles

Further Readings

Ackerman, P. L., & Heggestad, E. D. (1997). Intelligence, personality, and interests: Evidence for overlapping traits. *Psychological Bulletin, 121,* 219–245.

Chamorro-Premuzic, T., & Furnham, A. (2006). Intellectual competence and the intelligent personality: A third way in differential psychology. *Review of General Psychology, 10,* 251–267.

Chamorro-Premuzic, T., & Furnham, A. (2008). Personality, intelligence and approaches to learning as predictors of academic performance. *Personality and Individual Differences, 44,* 1596–1604.

Hembree, R. (1988). Correlates, causes, effects, and treatment of test anxiety. *Review of Educational Research, 58,* 47–77.

Mayer, J. D. (2007). *Personality: A system approach.* Boston: Allyn & Bacon.

Sternberg, R. J., & Ruzgis, P. (Eds.). *Intelligence and personality.* New York: Cambridge University Press.

Playwrights

A playwright creates literature that is typically designed to be performed by actors on a stage. Because of the interactive nature of theater in general, a final dramatic piece may be the accumulation of creative contributions by the playwright, a director, a dramaturge, a choreographer, actors, reviewers, and sometimes the audience. Perhaps because playwrights produce a creative product that is a blend of individual creativity (such as that produced by a poet) and group creativity (such as that produced by an improvisational acting troupe), they have not inspired a great deal of psychological research. There are many studies of actors and performers, and there are many studies of poets or fiction writers. There is also an extensive literature on dramatic therapy—but the research on playwrights and playwriting is sparse.

Some of the research on playwrights focuses on the performing arts more broadly, touching on some of the characteristics that may also apply to playwrights. Nathan Kogan and Barbara Kangas, for example, looked at environmental and familial determinants of a career in drama. They found that most drama students did not have a parent who was professionally involved in theater, and students differed on both the age when they decided to become involved in the theater and in their schooling experiences.

Several studies, many including playwrights, have examined writers' longevity. James Kaufman, for example, found that poets tended to be more likely to have mental illness and were more likely to die at a younger age. In contrast, playwrights did not die notably young or have notably high rates of mental illness. Antonio Preti studied suicide rates in different types of artists, and also found that poets had higher rates of suicide, and visual artists had lower rates; playwrights were not exceptional in either direction.

James Pennebaker and Lori Stone studied the collected works of 10 well-known playwrights, novelists, and poets. They found that across most writers (regardless of domain), aging brought a number of linguistic changes in their work. Specifically, writers tended to use more positive affect and fewer negative affect words, fewer self-references, less past tense and more future tense verbs, and they demonstrated a general pattern of higher complexity in cognition.

Kogan notes the paucity of work on the dramatic arts, and makes a call for more research. He outlines some basic distinctions that can be made, such as separating the study of creators (which would include playwrights) and interpreters (such as actors). Although much of his article is more focused on the performing arts, he does offer a model of artistic development that could also be applied to playwrights.

James C. Kaufman and Bethany A. Pritchard

See also Eminent and Everyday Creativity; Emotional Intelligence; Everyday Creativity; General Creativity; Literary Creativity; Relationship of Creativity to Intelligence; Writers

Further Readings

Crimmens, P. (2006). *Drama therapy and storymaking in special education.* Philadelphia: Jessica Kingsley Publishers.

Kaufman, J. C. (2001). The Sylvia Plath effect: Mental illness in eminent creative writers. *Journal of Creative Behavior, 35,* 37–50.

Kaufman, J. C. (2002). Dissecting the golden goose: Components of studying creative writers. *Creativity Research Journal, 14,* 27–40.

Kaufman, S. B., & Kaufman, J. C. (Eds.). (in press). *Psychology of creative writing.* Cambridge, UK: Cambridge University Press.

Kogan, N. (2002). Careers in the performing arts: A psychological perspective. *Creativity Research Journal, 14,* 1–16.

Kogan, N., & Kangas, B. L. (2006). Careers in the dramatic arts: Comparing genetic and interactional perspectives. *Empirical Studies of the Arts, 24,* 43–54.

Pennebaker, J., & Stone, L. (2003). Words of wisdom: Language use over the life span. *Journal of Personality and Social Psychology, 85,* 291–301.

Perry, S. K. (1999). *Writing in flow.* Cincinnati, OH: Writer's Digest Books.

Piirto, J. (2002). *"My teeming brain": Understanding creative writers.* Cresskill, NJ: Hampton Press.

Preti, A., & Miotto, P. (1999). Suicide among eminent artists. *Psychological Reports, 84,* 291–301.

Sawyer, R. K. (2007). *Group genius: The creative power of collaborations.* New York: Basic Books.

Poets Laureate

The term *poet laureate* has existed since before 1619, when Charles I appointed Ben Jonson the first poet laureate in Great Britain. A poet laureate is a writer of poetry who receives honor for eloquence. The word *laureate* comes from the laurel, *Laurus nobilis,* a type of bay tree whose leaves are used to make an entwined crown as an emblem of victory or of distinction—in this case, in poetry. The laurel tree was, in Greek mythology, sacred to the god Apollo, who was the patron of poets. The poet laureate assumes an official position within a government, and is often called upon to write poems in honor of ceremonial occasions. Many countries, states, and cities have poets laureate. The custom seems to be more prevalent in English-speaking or British-influenced countries than in others in Europe, though Nazi Germany had a poet laureate (Hanns Johst). A Children's Poet Laureate has been funded by the Poetry Foundation of America.

The British poets laureate are salaried, and members of the royal household. They have been, since 1619, all males, including Ben Jonson, Sir William D'Avenant, John Dryden, Thomas Shadwell, Nahum Tate, Nicholas Rowe, Laurence Eusden, Colley Cibber, William Whitehead, Thomas Wharton, Henry James Pye, Robert Southey, William Wordsworth, Alfred Lord Tennyson, Alfred Austin, Robert Bridges, John

Masefield, Cecil Day-Lewis, Sir John Betjeman, Ted Hughes, and Andrew Motion. Students of British literature may recall having read the poetry of some, but not all of these poets laureate.

The United States has had poets laureate since 1937; they are attached to the U.S. Library of Congress and appointed to a one-year term, except for Joseph Auslander, the first poet laureate, who served from 1937 to 1941. The Library of Congress poets laureate have been mostly White male and female, with males outnumbering females. The first African American poet laureate was Robert Hayden. Currently, the position pays $35,000 per year. The poet serves as "official lightning rod for the poetic impulse of Americans," according to the Library of Congress. Each poet works on a special project designed to raise the awareness of Americans about poetry. Poets after Auslander were Allen Tate (1943–1944), Robert Penn Warren, Louise Bogan, Karl Shapiro, Robert Lowell, Leonie Adams, Elizabeth Bishop, Conrad Aiken (who was to serve two terms, 1950–1952), William Carlos Williams, Randall Jarrell, Robert Frost, Richard Eberhart, Louis Untermeyer, Howard Nemerov, Reed Whittemore, Stephen Spender, James Dickey, William Jay Smith, William Stafford, Josephine Jacobsen, Daniel Hoffman, Stanley Kunitz, Robert Hayden, William Meredith, Maxine Kumin, Anthony Hecht, Robert Fitzgerald, Reed Whittemore, Gwendolyn Brooks, Robert Penn Warren (second term), Richard Wilbur, Howard Nemerov, Mark Strand, Joseph Brodsky, Mona Van Duyn, Rita Dove, Robert Hass, Robert Pinsky (for 6 years), then Rita Dove, Louise Glück, and W. S. Merwin (who were the bicentennial consultants), Stanley Kunitz, Billy Collins, Louise Glück, Ted Kooser, Donald Hall, Charles Simic, and Kay Ryan.

Most states and the District of Columbia have a poet laureate. In some states the governor appoints the poet; in others it is the legislature. The selection processes vary. In some states the poets apply; in others, they do not. Poets have various backgrounds; some have advanced degrees in creative writing, others are self-taught. Some teach poetry in English departments at colleges and universities, others are poets who have widespread followings among the common people. Arizona, Hawaii, Massachusetts, Michigan, New Jersey, New Mexico, Ohio, and Pennsylvania have no poet laureate.

In 2008, the poets laureate for the other states were as follows. Alabama: Sue Walker; Alaska: Jerah Chadwick; Arkansas: Penny Vining; California: Al Young; Colorado: Mary Crow; Connecticut: Marilyn Nelson; Delaware: Fleda Brown; District of Columbia: Dolores Kendrick; Florida: Edmund Skellings; Georgia: David Bottoms; Idaho: Kim Barnes; Illinois: Kevin Stein; Indiana: Robert Dana; Kansas: Denise Low; Kentucky: Jane Gentry Vance; Louisiana: Brenda Marie Osbey; Maine: Betsy Sholl; Maryland: Michael S. Glaser; Minnesota: Robert Bly; Mississippi: Winifred Hamrick Farrar; Missouri: Walter Bargen; Montana: Greg Pape; Nebraska: William Kloefkorn; Nevada: vacant; New Hampshire: Patricia Fargnoli; New York: Jean Valentine; North Carolina: Kathryn Stripling Byer; North Dakota: Larry Woiwode; Oklahoma: N. Scott Momaday; Oregon: Lawson Fusao Inada; Rhode Island: Lisa Starr; South Carolina: Marjory Heath Wentworth; South Dakota: David Allan Evans; Tennessee: Margaret Britton Vaughn; Texas: Larry D. Thomas; Utah: Katharine Coles; Vermont: Ruth Stone; Virginia: Carolyn Kreiter-Foronda; Washington: Samuel Green; West Virginia: Irene McKinney; Wisconsin: Denise Sweet; Wyoming: David Romtvedt. Some states appoint poets each year; some have terms that are longer.

Other government entities also have poets laureate. For some, the selection process is quite elaborate. In Sonoma County, California, for example, the poet laureate is selected by a committee made up of representatives from many of the arts organizations and libraries. In Ohio, the selection of the Lucas County poet laureate (Joel Lipman) was made by a committee of poets. Boston has a poet laureate, although the state of Massachusetts does not. Denver has one (Chris Ransick), and so does San Francisco (Laurence Ferlinghetti).

Though most poets laureate serve out their terms without disagreement, some do not. One poet laureate wrote such a controversial poem that the position of poet laureate was cut from the state budget. This was the poem "Somebody Blew Up America," which the poet laureate of New Jersey, Amiri Baraka, wrote after September 11, 2001, suggesting that Israel had something to do with the World Trade Center attack. Tsegaye Gabre-Medhin, the poet laureate of Ethiopia until his death in 2006, had works banned by all the governments in his lifetime: Haile Selassie's, the Derg's, and the TDLF. In 2003, U.S. Library of Congress poet laureate Billy Collins declared his opposition to the war against Iraq, and an event where the First Lady Laura Bush was to appear was canceled by the White House. Collins's appointment was not without controversy among fellow poets; when he was appointed, poet Anselm Hollo declared himself the anti-poet laureate.

Jane Piirto

See also Eminence; Nobel Prize; Verbal Ability; Writers

Further Readings

McGuire, W. (1988). *Poetry's catbird seat: The Consultantship in Poetry in the English Language at the Library of Congress, 1937–1987*. Washington, DC: Library of Congress. (Library of Congress: http://www.loc.gov)

Political Leaders

Unlike what holds in the arts, sciences, chess, and sports, political leadership is not always counted as a major domain of giftedness or talent. Even so, several classic investigations included notable political leaders along with eminent scientists and artists. For example, Francis Galton's 1869 *Hereditary Genius* has a whole chapter devoted to prime ministers, presidents, and other heads of state, and Catharine Cox's 1926 *Early Mental Traits of Three Hundred Geniuses* examined illustrious politicians and revolutionaries among other professions. Whether or not political leadership can be considered as talent or giftedness depends on a scientist's stance on the causes of effective leadership. On the one hand, some investigators hold that political leadership depends on *being the right person*. On the other hand, some researchers defend the proposition that such leadership is actually contingent on *being at the right place at the right time*. The former position is sometimes called the *great man theory*, the latter the *Zeitgeist theory*. However, researchers in this area more often frame the debate as concerning the relative impact of individual and situational variables.

Individual Traits

If political leadership is a matter of being the right person, then it should be possible to identify one or more personal characteristics that correlate with the eminence or performance of political leaders. If it can also be shown that these predictive traits are inherited in some fashion (e.g., genetic endowment), then it is reasonable to speak of someone having a talent or gift for political leadership. For instance, psychometric studies have shown that leader effectiveness is positively correlated with general intelligence, and historiometric inquiries have indicated that intelligence is the trait that most strongly predicts achieved eminence or greatness as a political leader. Furthermore, general intelligence has one of the highest heritabilities of any individual-difference variable. Therefore, this trait can be taken as one component of political talent. Because most other personal predictors of leadership also feature a genetic contribution, talent in political leadership may be defined by a specific set of partially inherited traits.

Even so, several considerations render such talent much more complicated than in other domains of achievement. First, in some instances the traits have nonlinear associations with the success criterion. For example, political leadership can be a curvilinear inverted-U function of general intelligence. Second, sometimes a personal traits effect on leadership is indirect rather than direct. For instance, although leaders are more extraverted than introverted, extraversion does not predict performance but rather predicts policy stances that may or may not determine performance. Third, almost invariably individual traits have less predictive power than do situational factors. Although a politician must be the right person, it is even more important that he or she be at the right place at the right time.

Situational Factors

Political scientists are fond of enumerating all of the situational variables that influence leadership in governmental positions. These variables are not just political but also economic, military, and diplomatic. Not surprisingly, these factors tend to account for far more of the variation in leader performance than all the individual traits put together. Presidential leadership in the United States offers many examples: (a) voter approval ratings automatically go up when the nation is subjected to a surprise attack, (b) success in getting legislation through Congress is dependent on the president's party having majorities in both houses of the legislature; (c) the probability of getting reelected is lowered if an economic downturn takes place in the months leading up to the election, and (d) the president's ultimate greatness according to expert evaluations is enhanced if the chief executive just happens to get assassinated.

These situational influences are so powerful that they can convert an incompetent leader into a competent leader, and the reverse as well. An excellent example in U.S. political leadership is what has been called the *vice-presidential succession effect.* Presidents who enter the nation's highest office through the death or resignation of their predecessor—such as Andrew Johnson succeeding Abraham Lincoln and Gerald Ford succeeding Richard Nixon—encounter numerous problems dealing with Congress, and especially the Senate. For instance, they are more likely to have their appointments to the cabinet or the U.S. Supreme Court rejected, and they are more prone to having their vetoes overturned. Yet when "accidental presidents" manage to get reelected to a term in their right, these detriments immediately disappear. Apparently, elected legislators do not accept the legitimacy of a chief executive who was not really elected to that office—regardless of the politician's genuine talents.

Individual–Situational Interactions

Although situational factors are more crucial than individual traits in the achievements of political leaders, it is not always easy to separate out their effects. This difficulty results from the fact that interaction effects sometimes appear between the two sets of variables. In other words, it is often not just a matter of being the right person or at the right place and time, but rather it is important to be the right person at the right place and the right time. A person who has the constitution to be a very effective leader in one set of circumstances may be a very ineffective leader in another set of circumstances. Hence, political achievement may require just the right match between individual talents and the conditions under which those talents will be exercised. Thus, a wartime head of state needs to have different characteristics than a peacetime head of state. For example, Winston Churchill was far more effective when he served as Great Britain's prime minister during World War II than he was when his nation was no longer engaged in a military conflict. Specific personality traits that are assets in one situation may become drawbacks in another. To illustrate: Inflexible, even dogmatic presidents can be very effective if their political party controls Congress, but they can become very ineffective if their party is in the minority. A case in point is Woodrow Wilson, who did very well in the White House until the opposing party took over the Senate.

Because of such complexities, the talent underlying political leadership may be far more subtle than the talents providing the basis of most other domains of achievement. Indeed, in certain contexts a given talent may even cease to exist.

Dean Keith Simonton

See also Emotional Intelligence; *Genetic Studies of Genius;* Historiometry; Intelligence; Leadership

Further Readings

Ilies, R., Gerhardt, M. W., & Le, H. (2004). Individual differences in leadership emergence: Integrating meta-analytic findings and behavioral genetics estimates. *International Journal of Selection and Assessment, 12,* 207–219.

Simonton, D. K. (2001). Kings, queens, and sultans: Empirical studies of political leadership in European hereditary monarchies. In O. Feldman & L. O. Valenty (Eds.), *Profiling political leaders: Cross-cultural studies of personality and behavior* (pp. 97–110). Westport, CT: Praeger.

Simonton, D. K. (2008). Presidential greatness and its socio-psychological significance: Individual or situation? Performance or attribution? In C. L. Hoyt, G. R. Goethals, & D. R. Forsyth (Eds.), *Leadership at the crossroads: Vol. 1. Leadership and psychology.* Westport, CT: Praeger.

Polymaths

A polymath is an individual with unusual ability in more than one discipline. A classic example is Leonardo da Vinci—engineer, inventor, artist, gymnast, and entertainer. The existence of such Renaissance people in modern times has become a contentious issue of great significance to creativity studies.

The debate centers on whether creativity springs from intensive training and effort in a single domain or whether it results from combining talents and experience from several. Differing definitions of creativity complicate the matter. Some psychologists differentiate between personal or "little c" creativity and discipline-based on socially recognized "Big C" creativity. If creativity requires combining talents and experiences from several domains, "little c" creativity in one set of domains may foster "Big C" creativity in another. An associated issue is whether individuals can have general creative ability or whether creative ability, even in polymaths, is always specific to a single field.

The study of polymathy began in the 19th century. In 1878, J. H. van 't Hoff, who would be awarded the first Nobel Prize in Chemistry in 1901, noted that the greatest scientists, unlike their less able colleagues, displayed their imaginative ability outside of science as well as within it. Many were artists, musicians, poets, and even social and religious visionaries. Van 't Hoff himself was an accomplished flautist, a poet in four languages, and one of the founders of four new disciplines: stereochemistry, physical chemistry, geochemistry, and the history of science.

Subsequent research confirmed van 't Hoff's insight. Studies of mathematicians and physicists by Henri Fehr, Paul Julius Moebius, and Jacques Hadamard helped to establish the oft-repeated observation that mathematical ability is often associated with musical talent. Francis Galton and Wilhelm Ostwald both noted that eminent scientists were often successful artists, musicians, and craftsmen. Paul Cranefield found a direct correlation between the number of avocations that eminent scientists had and the range and importance of their discoveries. And Robert Root-Bernstein and his collaborators have shown that scientists who have the greatest impact on their fields are significantly more likely to have adult avocations (or even second vocations) in one or more arts.

More general psychological studies have confirmed what was first seen when scientists Lewis Terman, Robert K. White, and Catherine Cox surveyed hundreds of eminent historical figures: They concluded that the typical genius surpassed the typical college graduate in range of interests and ability. In prospective studies, Roberta Milgram has reported that the only significant predictor of career success in any field is having at least one intellectually intensive, long-lasting avocation.

Polymaths themselves have often commented on the essential connections between their professional and avocational activities. The Nobel Prize–winning physicist Max Planck, a concert-caliber pianist, argued that the creative scientist needs an "artistic imagination" and used musical theory in devising his concept of quantum mechanics. Santiago Ramon y Cajal, a Nobel laureate in neurobiology, painter, and pioneer of color photography, believed that polymaths developed useful skills and knowledge and employed their arts every day in their scientific studies. Writer and painter Henry Miller summarized this point of view by saying that, like the painter Ingres who was as devoted to his violin as to his paintbrush, every artist has a serious avocation.

Psychologists have recognized the validity of such individual insights. John Dewey noted that what distinguishes the most creative people are what he called "integrated activity sets" that make use of concepts, information, techniques, methods, and processes from multiple domains. Howard Gruber calls these sets "networks of enterprise," and Root-Bernstein "correlative talents." The key for all three is that the creative individual is not a dilettante, but explicitly recognizes and makes use of transdisciplinary thinking.

The major criticism leveled at the studies summarized above is that they do not really represent true polymathy. Some cognitive scientists insist that to qualify as a polymath, an individual must succeed at a very high professional level ("Big C" creativity) in two or more disciplines, which they argue does not and cannot happen in today's ultra-specialized and competitive world. There are two responses to these charges.

First, the intellectual or cognitive importance of avocational skills and activities need not depend on the extent to which that activity is professionalized or socially recognized. The point of integrated activity sets, networks of enterprise, and correlative talents is that knowledge and skills developed in one domain as "little c" activities are necessary ingredients for "Big C" creative success in another domain. Note, however, that this response depends explicitly on the transferability of concepts, knowledge, and skills from one domain to another, which is also a contentious issue in creativity studies. Some psychologists argue that all knowledge is domain specific. A long tradition of creativity studies stemming from Arthur Koestler and Albert Rothenberg, however, defines creativity as the useful combining of previously disparate concepts, processes, or objects. It follows that only those individuals who are capable of transferring experience between previously separated domains can be creative and that creativity can be recognized precisely because it results in new paradigms, disciplines, or domains.

Second, polymaths who have succeeded in multiple professions exist in droves. Van 't Hoff and Ramon y Cajal are two of hundreds of examples. Nobel Laureate Roger Guillemin (Physiology or Medicine) has an international reputation as an electronic artist; Oxford zoologists Desmond Morris and Jonathan Kingdon as internationally recognized painters. Miroslav Holub achieved international acclaim as both a poet and immunologist; Nobel Laureate (Literature) Vladimir Nabokov as a Harvard entomologist. The chemists Carl Djerassi ("father of the birth control pill") and Roald Hoffmann (Nobel Prize) are widely published and produced playwrights, novelists, and poets. Nobel literature laureates Derek Wolcott, Gao Xingjian, and Günter Grass all have second careers as fine artists. Composer Charles Ives not only revolutionized music but was a pioneer of the insurance industry. Composer George Antheil was hailed internationally for his revolutionary music and also for inventing (with actress Hedy Lamarr) the method of frequency hopping that underlies most secure electronic communications. Iannes Xenakis managed simultaneous careers in engineering, architecture, and composing, achieving international acclaim in the latter two.

The polymathic Renaissance person is very much alive, well, and capable of multiple forms of "little c" and "Big C" creativity.

Robert Root-Bernstein

See also Adult, Gifted; Artistic Ability; Eminent and Everyday Creativity; General Creativity; Genius; Scientists

Further Readings

Hjerter, K. G. (1986). *Doubly gifted: The author as visual artist.* New York: Abrams.

Milgram, R., & Hong, E. (1993). Creative thinking and creative performance in adolescents as predictors of creative attainments in adults: A follow-up study after 18 years. In R. Subotnik & K. Arnold (Eds.), *Beyond Terman: Longitudinal studies in contemporary gifted education.* Norwood, NJ: Ablex.

Root-Bernstein, R. S., Bernstein, M., & Garnier, H. (1995). Correlations between avocations, scientific style, work habits, and professional impact of scientists. *Creativity Research Journal, 8,* 115–137.

Root-Bernstein, R. S., & Root-Bernstein, M. (2004). Artistic scientists and scientific artists: The link between polymathy and creativity. In R. J. Sternberg, E. L. Grigorenko, & J. L. Singer (Eds.), *Creativity: From potential to realization* (pp. 127–152). Washington, DC: American Psychological Association.

Van 't Hoff, J. H. (1967). Imagination in science (G. F. Springer, Trans.). *Molecular Biology, Biochemistry, and Biophysics, 1,* 1–18.

Popular Culture

Once viewed as the antithesis of high cultural art forms (e.g., opera, literature, or classical music), *popular culture* was a term coined to describe the art and communication forms that were aimed at the masses. As such, popular culture includes forms such as newspapers, television, advertising, popular music, "low-brow" novels, film, and so on. Inherent in this delineation between high and low art is an assumption that the latter forms are of lesser quality. In the past couple of decades, however, a high level of academic interest has been directed to popular culture, which confirms the need for educators to seriously consider both the topic and its impact for young people.

Popular culture is an important topic in relation to giftedness because although a great deal is known about how parents, peers, teachers, and schools influence the development of talent, little is known about the role that popular culture plays in the realization of talent. This entry summarizes the relatively small quantity of research that has been conducted on giftedness and popular culture, most of which deals with the medium of television. The research literature has also been directed more toward gifted girls than boys. The entry concludes with recommendations for the type of research that is still needed on this topic.

Popular Culture and Giftedness

While there has been a significant quantity of scholarly research into popular culture in the context of general education, there is very little research that has considered the relationship between popular culture and giftedness. There are two main lines of research that could be taken on this topic. The first is to consider how giftedness, or gifted children and adults, are depicted in popular culture. Educators need to know what role models gifted students can access in popular culture texts because these depictions play a key role in the creation and maintenance of stereotypical notions of giftedness in the general population. The second line of research relates to the impact that popular culture has on gifted students. It is useful to know what they watch, read, and listen to and how they respond to the messages, particularly if those messages are negatively impacting their academic outcomes and their social-emotional well-being. Given their popular nature, television and other forms of popular culture have an important influence on other people's attitudes toward gifted students as well as on the gifted students themselves.

Television

Television has been the most commonly researched form of popular culture generally, but very little of this research has focused on gifted students. The debate on the value or danger of television viewing has occupied the attention of researchers for several decades. The majority of studies on television viewing and academic achievement, for example, are negative and argue that time spent in television viewing leads to reduction of time on reading and homework, and culminates in lower academic achievement. Nevertheless, some research points to the positive influences of good quality television on academic outcomes.

One example of the potential of television to shape the perceptions of its audience may be in the career aspirations of youth. Observers commenting on the current global decline in the numbers of young people studying science and a rise in boys wanting to be chefs instead, have suggested that this is a direct result of the influence of television, where there are many more cooking shows compared to portrayals of science other than forensics and medical doctors.

One of the earliest forays into the topic of giftedness and popular culture was a study of gifted children and television completed by Robert Abelman in the 1990s. This comprehensive research found that gifted children were attracted by television but preferred more complex programs compared to their peers. Interestingly, he observed that although gifted preschoolers tended to watch more television than their non-gifted counterparts, their consumption dropped markedly once they started school. Nevertheless, it remained an important influence in their lives.

Abelman's research also looked at depictions of gifted children in television in the United States. He indicated that the depiction of children in television shows is low overall, but the depiction of gifted children is even lower (less than 2 percent). Less than 11 percent of what children watch on television is specifically made for children. As a result, he argued that there are few role models for gifted children on television. More important, though, the portrayal of gifted youth is particularly poor at a time when they may be more susceptible to the messages contained in television programs. A national report in the United States also stated that the depiction of young women in television shows emphasizes appearance rather than intellect, with smart young women often portrayed as social misfits who are generally attractive only to gifted males who are also social misfits. Little has changed in television programming since these studies were undertaken.

Educators should not underestimate the influence of media such as television and film on young people. Research by Albert Ziegler and Heidrun Stoeger illustrated that even relatively short exposures to positive role models in film can influence young people's views about their own abilities in mathematics and science. In their study, the male students and the females who were interested in mathematics and science rated their own abilities higher after exposure to the film *IQ*, which depicts a lead character who is feminine and mathematically gifted. Students exposed to other films without such a role model did not rate themselves as highly.

Depiction of Intelligent Females

A key theme in the research on popular culture and giftedness has been the depiction of intelligent females in television and the potential this has for impacting the outcomes for gifted girls. Writers have suggested that issues and debates related to women's role in society—and particularly, the conflict between femininity and feminism—derive from the conflicting messages for girls presented in the mass media. Consequently, some studies have investigated the treatment of females in popular culture texts.

Wilma Vialle, for example, analyzed popular television programs *The Simpsons* and *Daria,* and the Harry Potter books and films to determine how giftedness was portrayed. She determined that there was a clear gender divide in how gifted children and youth were represented in these texts. Gifted girls, such as Lisa Simpson and Hermione Granger, were portrayed as studious, unpopular, and not interested in sports, whereas their male counterparts tended to be nonstudious or even mischievous and more interested in sports. Interestingly, these divisions parallel research that demonstrated that students and teachers most prefer adolescents who are average in ability, nonstudious, and athletic and least prefer those who are brilliant, studious, and nonathletic. Vialle also indicated that the gifted schools in the popular culture texts she examined were presented as privileged settings populated with "precious" characters. These images stand in stark contrast to the overwhelming research evidence on the value of grouping gifted students together, and may contribute to negative opinions among some educators toward homogeneous grouping.

Michele Paule extensively investigated gifted girls' reactions to television programs and indicated that there are conflicting messages of femininity versus intelligence for young women in these programs. Paule observed that giftedness was often subjugated by female characters for the sake of popularity or romantic success. The gifted girls in Paule's study recognized the stereotypes in television texts but did not necessarily believe that these reflected their own experiences. They also reported that in the absence of positive images of giftedness in television programs, they identified gifted traits in many of the female characters they viewed (e.g., Rachel, Phoebe, and Monica in *Friends*). Despite the mixed messages on television for gifted teens, there were good examples of female adult characters for whom giftedness was not a social handicap. Michele Paule proposed that there may be an element of delayed gratification for gifted girls in viewing these fictional gifted women.

A comprehensive treatment of giftedness and popular culture was recently released in the aptly titled *Geek Chic,* a collection of essays that explores the depiction and treatment of intelligent women in the media, ranging from real women such as Hillary Rodham Clinton to television characters such as Daria and the Gilmore Girls. A central tenet of all these essays is that popular culture endorses feminine stereotypes at the same time that it challenges the marginalization of intelligent women. The chapter by Paule in this volume, for example, explores the *super slacker girls,* a term coined to describe smart young female characters who opt out of academic success and career paths commensurate with their abilities; instead, through supernatural intervention, they take up altruistic roles. As such, they present a disturbing model of the underachieving gifted girl, one who does not fulfill her potential.

For gifted girls, the messages in popular culture, thus, are contradictory and highlight the dilemma experienced by many gifted youth in having to choose between their intellectual needs and the need for social acceptance. If popular culture is viewed as a reflection of society's beliefs and attitudes, it is hardly surprising that many gifted girls are constrained by expectations that are more aligned to their gender than their potential, as researchers such as Barbara Kerr have demonstrated.

Popular Music

It is somewhat surprising that there is not more research on giftedness and popular music, given that adolescents are by far the biggest consumers of popular music. Music is significant in the lives of young people, gifted or otherwise, not only for its entertainment value but also as a means of establishing a social identity.

A recent study, conducted by the National Academy of Gifted and Talented Youth, explored the musical preferences of more than 1,000 gifted adolescents in the United Kingdom. Six percent of these students ranked heavy metal as their first choice from the nine categories presented, and approximately 30 percent of the students ranked it in their top five. The researchers' findings seem to contradict the stereotypical negative images of the heavy metal fan and links that have often been made between this genre and rebelliousness, poor academic performance, and negative attitudes to school. The researchers then looked at the young people who had ranked heavy metal in their top five and found that they had slightly lower self-esteem and spent more time listening to music and playing computer games than those who did not rank heavy metal in their top five choices. In follow-up Web-based interviews, the research team explored the reasons that the gifted youth were attracted to heavy metal music. The students predominantly described it as a means to relieve stress and to work off their frustrations. Other students indicated that they appreciated the content of the lyrics in heavy metal songs, which provided cynical social and political commentary.

Future Directions

There is a strong need for further research into popular culture and giftedness. Although further research into the impact on gifted girls of popular culture is desirable, similar analyses of the treatment of gifted boys are particularly important. Finally, additional research is needed into popular culture forms other than television. Given the place of music in young people's lives, this would be a particularly fruitful area for additional investigation.

Wilma Vialle

See also Attitudes Toward Gifted; Eminent Women; Film and Film-Making Gifted; Girls, Gifted; Women, Gifted

Further Readings

Abelman, R. (1992). *Some children under some conditions: TV and the high potential kid.* Storrs, CT: National Research Center on the Gifted and Talented.

Cadwallader, S. M. (2007). *The darker side of bright students: Gifted and talented heavy metal fans.* Occasional Paper No. 19. Available online at http://www.nagty.ac.uk

Douglas, S. J. (1994). *Where the girls are: Growing up female with the mass media.* New York: Random House.

Inness, S. A. (Ed.). (2007). *Geek chic: Smart women in popular culture.* New York: Palgrave Macmillan.

Kerr, B. A. (1997). *Smart girls: A new psychology of girls, women, and giftedness.* Scottsdale, AZ: Gifted Psychology Press.

Steenland, S. (1988). *Growing up in prime time: An analysis of adolescent girls on television.* Washington, DC: National Commission on Working Women.

Positive Disintegration

The *theory of positive disintegration* (TPD) is Kazimierz Dabrowski's theory of individual personality development. According to Dabrowski, personality is shaped and created by each individual. The process of this development is called *positive disintegration.* It describes how people transform themselves from conforming and self-serving to introspective and self-directed individuals. Growth and development occur as a person moves from a lower level of integration to a higher level of integration through a series of psychological disintegrations and reintegrations that change one's view of self and the world. Dabrowski placed emotions more than intelligence at the heart of personality development and believed some individuals, especially gifted and highly creative people, possess higher levels of developmental potential. Overexcitabilties, the heightened sensitivity of the nervous system resulting in above-average responsiveness to stimuli, and dynamisms, the autonomous inner forces that control behavior and development, are key elements of developmental potential. According to this theory, these elements predispose gifted and highly creative people to experience life at a more intense level, resulting in frequent and often severe crisis or disintegrations.

Educators and administrators in gifted education have embraced Dabrowski's theory as a way to provide insight into the intense experiences of gifted students. The theory is difficult to study, given the problems with objectively assessing levels, investigating claims of neuropsychological bases of behavior, and empirically establishing links between Dabrowski's levels of functioning and giftedness. It is, therefore, the compelling metaphor and the explanatory power of the theory for gifted people that seem to account for the theory's popularity among educators of the gifted. This entry discusses the theory of positive disintegration, the stages and levels of positive disintegration, and the implications for gifted and creative individuals.

Personality Development

TPD believes that the journey from lower levels of mental functioning to higher levels comes as result of experiencing inner conflict. Therefore, negative emotions are an essential part of advanced personality development and should be welcomed as a sign of positive growth and development. The first part of the positive disintegration process is the dissolving of existing mental structures. Intense external and internal conflicts arise as one becomes aware of discrepancies between the world that is and the world that ought to be. The dynamisms of self-awareness and self-direction force the creation of a new higher-level and more-integrated mental structure that resolves the inner conflict.

Levels

Dabrowski grouped the disintegration/reintegration process into five levels. He cautions against treating levels as stages. A person can be at one level in one aspect of life and at a different level in another area of life. These levels are not universal. In fact, only a few individuals actually reach the last level of development. The five levels represent a general movement from egocentric, motivated by basic human drives, to altruistic, motivated by inner values and autonomy.

Level I. Primary Integration

A person at this level is focused on self-gratification, self-interest, and survival. There is little inner conflict. People at this level experience challenges and crises but are not transformed by them. They spend energy gaining advantage over others and quickly turn to the victim mentality of blame if something goes wrong. The two factors of biological impulse and social convention guide behavior.

Level II. Unilevel Disintegration

This is the beginning of disintegration, meaning development is occurring. Usually a milestone such as puberty, or a crisis such as a friendship ending trigger a sense of uncertainty, frustration, or despair. When a person does not have the mental structure in place to deal with the situation, the choice is reintegration back into the previous level or becoming motivated to find a solution and move to the next level. During Level II a person is pulled in many directions, becoming influenced by others and experiencing inner fragmentation and conflict. Level II is a transition phase. One cannot stay at this level for any length of time without dire consequences.

Level III. Spontaneous Multilevel Disintegration

The transition from Level II to Level III is a quantum leap that requires an extraordinary amount of energy. At this level, one spontaneously begins to examine beliefs, attitudes, and emotions and can see both higher- and lower-level alternatives. During this level, the vertical struggle between the "ideal" and the "real" changes the way one views the world and oneself. Instead of automatically adhering to social norms, one begins to develop a personal set of values to guide thinking and behavior. The dynamism of self-dissatisfaction dissolves as self-awareness increases. Level III is also a time of inner conflict.

Level IV. Organized Multilevel Disintegration

The conflict of Level III gives way to new dynamisms such as autonomy, self-education, and self-determination. People begin to make deliberate choices of higher values, pre-think actions, and exhibit a strong sense of responsibility for self and others. Social justice and empathic connections guide their interactions with others. At this level, people actively seek out information and pursue learning, thereby developing the necessary tools to guide themselves through times of crisis. Behavior moves from reactive to deliberate.

Level V. Secondary Integration

This is the peak of human development. A person becomes at peace with him- or herself. Life is driven by a constructed hierarchy of values. There is no inner conflict because the motivations causing inner conflict at lower levels have been destroyed.

Dabrowski believed that, at the lower levels of development, a person operated at the mercy of biological impulses (factor one) and social pressures (factor two). Once a person moved into Level III, multilevel development, he or she became more autonomous and was driven by self-determination (factor three). The goal of development is for ideals and actions to become one and the same.

Implications

The first implication of TPD for gifted and highly creative people is to understand the role emotions play in development. Focusing on the cognitive aspect with little or no attention to the emotional aspect of development is inadequate. A second implication is acknowledging that gifted and highly creative people will, by definition, experience internal conflict and struggle over the gap between what is and what ought to be. This is not a negative experience, but rather a positive indication of growth and development.

Joyce E. Juntune

See also Meaning of Life; Overexcitabilities; Personality and Intelligence; Social-Emotional Issues

Further Readings

Gifted and Talented Education Council. (2002). Dabrowski's theory of positive disintegration and gifted education [Special issue]. *AGATE, 15.* (Alberta Teachers' Association)

Mendaglio, S. (Ed.). (2008). *Dabrowski's theory of positive disintegration.* Scottsdale, AZ: Great Potential Press.

Poverty and Low-Income Gifted

Does being financially poor hurt creativity, talent, or giftedness? At first glance, one may immediately want to respond to this question negatively because of the belief that creativity, talent, and giftedness are innate, not something that can be taught. However, after consulting the literature and reflecting more carefully, one has to conclude that yes, in some ways being poor or living in a low-income family can hinder the complete development of an individual's abilities, talents, and skills. To quote Barbara Kerr when talking about women in her book, *Smart Girls Two,* "Another major barrier to achievement by gifted women is a lack of money" and the "scarcity of funds is the primary barrier between minority women and achievement" (p. 159).

According to the 2006 Census report, nearly 1 in 5 children under the age of 18, in the United States, live in poverty. Poverty can be defined not only as the deprivation of things such as food, clothing, safe drinking water, and shelter, but often individuals considered impoverished lack intangible items such as being educated, being properly socialized, being respected, and having opportunities for personal successes. Income level, for the purpose of this entry, is used as an indicator of whether a child lives in poverty. This entry discusses the impact of poverty on identification of gifted students; the difficulties of providing services to impoverished, gifted students; and the impact of poverty on career attainment, creativity, and personal strengths.

Identification of Gifted

This begs the question of whether the initial identification of giftedness and talent is related to family income. With such staggering numbers of children and adolescents living in poverty or below the median income level in the United States, it is important that educators look beyond the outward manifestations of income when identifying these special children. These outward manifestations may be related to poor hygiene, noncompletion of homework, and even acting-out behaviors that draw attention away from the child's or adolescent's unique talents and abilities. For example, Barbara Kerr and Robinson Kurpius found that when asked to identify adolescent girls who were at risk in some way and also talented/gifted, schools focused primarily on at-risk issues and were concerned with giftedness and talent second. Furthermore, the vast majority of these girls were living in what could be labeled poverty or low-income conditions. Family income influences teachers' perceptions of children and, therefore, may well influence their accurately placing these children in classes and other activities that would foster their creativity, talent, and/or giftedness.

Proper and equitable identification of persons chosen to participate in gifted and talented programs continues to be a problem. Underrepresentation of the poor, of minorities, and of the handicapped is particularly concerning. Perhaps this discrepancy is also related to the measurements currently in use. Typically, children are assessed using scales that address academic achievement and require a certain knowledge base. Children living in poverty or even in low-income families have many challenges just with basic survival. For example, according to Abraham Maslow's hierarchy, safety and security needs (food, clothing, shelter, safety) must be met before higher-level needs can be considered. Parents who make up "the working poor" may be so busy just trying to put food on the table that they don't have time to read to their small children; attend school events, which is often interpreted as parental support and concern; and may need to have older children miss school in order to care for younger siblings when the sibling is sick and the parent has to work. This certainly may hinder the academic achievement of gifted children if they are not in school where they can learn and expand what they know or if they are in families where books are not available nor is there time or support for them to visit local libraries. Even if these students check out books from the school library, expectation for helping at home may leave them little or no time to do homework, much less time to read extra books to expand their knowledge base and broaden their worlds. Although intellectual giftedness may be innate, it still needs to be nurtured and fostered so that it expands and develops as the child matures.

Service Difficulties

Mobility is an issue that contributes to difficulty in serving gifted children in poverty. Because single mothers and poor families must move often in order to secure better employment, housing, social services, medical care, or even food, their children must change schools. Different district policies make identification and placement in gifted programs spotty or nonexistent for poor, mobile children. Follow-up of student progress, grade reports, and portfolios get lost as students move about.

Social distancing is yet another hindrance affecting poor America, according to Dave Capuzzi and Douglas Gross. Bernice Lott notes that behaviors that manifest outwardly as classist discrimination, devaluation, separation, and exclusion on both a conscious and subconscious level exemplify the distance imposed by the nonpoor on the poor. This marginalization can perpetuate the view that the poor are uneducated, lazy, expendable, unpleasant, angry, and stupid. For example, classism in schools can be perpetuated by teachers treating children with disdain and not providing adequate encouragement. It is important to note, however, that children are incredibly resilient. Even with the enormous barriers that potentially thwart their successes, the majority still achieve academic, social, and personal success.

It should also be remembered that often the family living in poverty is a single-parent family, with a mother trying to support the family and raise children. According to Kerr, divorce is the quickest road to poverty; over 50 percent of marriages in America end in divorce, and 50 percent of remarriages also end in divorce.

Career Attainment

It should also be noted that there is a relationship between career attainment and poverty. According to Linda Gottfredson's *theory of circumscription and compromise,* individuals eliminate unacceptable occupations based on gender and perceived prestige of the occupation. The eliminating process is also influenced by socioeconomic status (SES) and ability. Individuals with higher SES tend to have higher career aspirations, and individuals with lower SES tend to have lower career aspirations. Therefore, it appears that low SES, as well as ability, imposes ceilings on what someone thinks of as a possible career.

Donating $200 million in cash and $200 million in computer equipment to libraries in low-income communities, Bill and Melinda Gates are trying to help bridge the gap in educational and career attainment related to level of income. The foundation's goal is "equal opportunity for all," regardless of income.

Creativity

When considering creativity, one needs to remember that children from all socioeconomic backgrounds often use creativity in play as an outlet for their thoughts, frustrations, anger, and imagination. Although researchers have struggled for decades to define creativity, literature on the construct suggests that creativity is product-, person-, or process-oriented. It is important to remember however, that intelligence and creativity are independent of one another and must, therefore, be measured independently. If creativity is being measured in an academic setting by the same measurements as intelligence, then it is not surprising that the outlying groups such as those living in poverty fail to be recognized and their creativity and talents fail to be encouraged and nurtured.

Researchers know a few things about what can be done to foster the creativity of children. Children can be provided with challenging environments, including developmentally stimulating toys, bright colors, and engaged parent–child and teacher–child interaction. Researchers know that creativity stems from the ability to build on past experiences. To that end, exposure to new sights, sounds, smells, tastes, and experiences is critical to the development of creative processes. This might be difficult when the family is focused on basic survival.

Benefits

Most programs and research seek to identify gifted, talented, and/or creative individuals as broadly as possible. This may require special attention when the child or adolescent comes from a low-income family. Maximizing the potential of all talented or gifted children not only benefits the individual, but society as a whole through the nurturing of one of its most precious resources.

Erin M. Carr Jordan

See also Diversity in Gifted Education; Multicultural Assessment; Resilience

Further Readings

Capuzzi, D., & Gross, D. R. (2008). *Youth-at-risk: A prevention resource for counselors, teachers, and parents* (5th ed.). Alexandria, VA: American Counseling Association.

Fisher, M. D. (2009, Winter). List of gifted programs and activities in need of federal, state and local funding [Editorial]. *Gifted Education Press Quarterly.*

Gates Foundation to invest $400 million in libraries. (1997). *American Libraries, 28(7),* 14.

Kaufman, J. C. (2006). Self-reported differences in creativity by gender and ethnicity. *Journal of Applied Cognitive Psychology, 20,* 1065–1082.

Kerr, B. A. (1994). *Smart girls two: A new psychology of girls, women, and giftedness.* Dayton, OH: Ohio Psychology Press.

Lott, B. (2002). Cognitive and behavioral distancing from the poor. *American Psychologist, 57,* 100–101.

Rostan, S. M., Pariser, D., & Gruber, H. E. (2002). A cross-cultural study of the development of artistic talent, creativity, and giftedness. *High Ability Studies, 13,* 125–156.

Practical Intelligence

Practical intelligence is one of the three forms of intelligence besides analytical intelligence and creative intelligence as theorized by Robert Sternberg in his *triarchic theory of intelligence.* Practical intelligence, also known as common sense or street smarts, is the intelligence that is highly valued in daily life, often more so than academic intelligence or book smarts. Specifically, practical intelligence is the ability that individuals have to adapt successfully to situations that arise in daily living with whatever knowledge and skills that they have to creatively overcome the problems facing them. Such situations include taking care of oneself; social interaction with others; and climbing the career ladder. Academic intelligence is useful in academic settings, especially in school, and it is rendered useless if one does not possess some practical intelligence for navigating the tasks of day-to-day living. The core component of practical intelligence, tacit knowledge; the distinction between academic and practical intelligence; and the value of practical intelligence across culture and age are discussed in this entry.

Academic intelligence is measured by many intelligence tests and is often reported in terms of intelligence quotient (IQ) scores. It marks an individual's ability to acquire quickly the kind of formal academic knowledge that is taught in schools. Tests of such intelligence are often of the paper-and-pencil kind (e.g., school exams). Practical intelligence, on the other hand, does not have any formal intelligence tests that are specifically designed to measure it, other than some tests that exist in the practical intelligence research circle. One way to measure a person's practical intelligence would be to assess the individual's ability to acquire tacit knowledge quickly. Tacit knowledge is the action-oriented knowledge that allows one to acquire personally valued goals. It is this tacit knowledge that is more valued in the real world—more so than formal academic knowledge that may not have a practical function in daily life.

Tacit knowledge has three distinct characteristics. First, it is procedural knowledge, which requires individuals to acquire it through action and experience. Second, it is highly connected to the achievement of intrinsic goals that are important to the individual. Third, it is self-acquired, not dependent on others to transmit the knowledge to the individual in question. Tacit knowledge is so named because it requires individuals to acquire it through inferences from personal experiences with little outside help from others who may not be invested in the resulting solution. Those who are able to gain tacit knowledge have an added advantage over those who are not, resulting in an extra knowledge base for these individuals when facing similar situations in the future.

Ulric Neisser outlined academic intelligence tasks (used in classroom and intelligence tests) as (a) formulated by others, (b) often of little or no intrinsic interest, (c) having all needed information available from the beginning, and (d) separated from an individual's ordinary experience. Robert Sternberg and Richard Wagner further include that these tasks (e) usually are well-defined, (f) have but one correct answer, and (g) often have just one method of obtaining the correct solution. In contrast, practical intelligence tasks or real-world tasks are often (a) self-formulated (arise from a situation that has to be put in a problem statement by the self), (b) high on intrinsic interest, (c) short of all the information needed for the solution, (d) connected with one's real-world experience, (e) ill-defined, (f) may have multiple solutions with each of their pluses and minuses, and (g) often have more than one method to figure out the correct solution.

Academic and practical intelligence may not always go together. A strict dichotomy between the two intelligences is seen in only the most extreme cases because most people have a mix of both intelligences and are able to navigate life sufficiently well.

Evidence of the difference between academic intelligence and practical intelligence can be seen in various cross-cultural studies. The ability of mechanics in developing countries to repair broken cars without advanced diagnostic systems; the skillful navigation of the Puluwat people in Micronesia without electronic ocean-navigation devices; and the speed and accuracy of young street merchants (kids under 12 years old in Brazil) to do math transactions are strong indicators of practical intelligence in place despite the lack of academic schooling to master basic math skills or advanced mechanical skills.

While academic knowledge declines over the years, as self-reported by older adults and verified through intelligence tests, practical knowledge remains stable or increases over the years with experience and age. It would be wrong to think that practical intelligence increases through experience and age alone; it requires the additional criteria that an individual also learn from experience for it to grow. As evidenced by early research into practical intelligence with academic psychologists, not all academicians rise through the ranks to become full professors with experience and age; it requires the extra know-how that is picked up through one's experiences or through learning of others experiences.

Success in life may depend on one's ability to maneuver deftly and to master the problems that arise in daily living and successfully turn these experiences into usable knowledge that is helpful in future dealings. As evidenced by research in practical intelligence, the focus on academic intelligence alone is not enough. More should be done to help students increase their practical intelligence so that they do not wind up being book smart but street silly.

Kai Kok "Zeb" Lim and Zi Ning Hor

See also Creative Problem Solving; Declarative and Procedural Memory; Factor Analyses Creativity; Fluid and Crystallized Intelligence; Intelligence; Out-of-School

Further Readings

Gottfredson, L. S. (2003). Dissecting practical intelligence theory: Its claims and evidence. *Intelligence, 31,* 343–397.

Sternberg, R. J., Forsythe, G. B., Hedlund, J., Horvath, J. A., Wagner, R. K., Williams, et al. (Eds.). (2000). *Practical intelligence in everyday life.* New York: Cambridge University Press.

Sternberg, R. J., Wagner, R. K., Williams, W. M., & Horvath, J. A. (1995). Testing common sense. *American Psychologist, 50,* 912–927.

Wagner, R. K. (2000). Practical intelligence. In R. J. Sternberg (Ed.), *Handbook of intelligence* (pp. 380–395). New York: Cambridge University Press.

Wagner, R. K., & Sternberg, R. J. (1985). Practical intelligence in real world pursuits: The role of tacit knowledge. *Journal of Personality and Social Psychology, 49,* 436–458.

Precocious Reading

Precocious reading occurs when very young children read in advance of their chronological-age peers. By the end of kindergarten, the typically developing child can identify letters and sounds at the beginning of a word, while the precocious reader is sounding out words and beginning to read. Typically, precocious readers are about 2 years ahead of their same-age peers on benchmarks of reading progress at the onset of formal schooling. Although the causes of precocious readers' abilities are yet undetermined, precocious reading has been defined by the Jacob K. Javits Gifted and Talented Students Education Act of 1988 as an example of giftedness, and it has been determined that these young readers require nurturing from their primary grades, teachers in order to develop their reading talent. This entry explores the characteristics of precocious readers, differentiates them from their typically developing peers, illustrates the influences of home and school environments, and gives recommendations for working with these learners.

Characteristics of Precocious Readers

Precocious readers learn letter–sound correspondence at a very young age. Their rapid advancements with language allow them to "break the code" and learn to read at a very young age. Breaking the code entails recognizing letters, identifying the corresponding sound for each letter, blending sounds to create words, and determining the sound that several letters in one word make when read together. This process of decoding, when used to create an understanding of text, is what is known as reading.

It seems that precocious readers, also called early readers, have varied strengths, weaknesses, and different orientations in their reading development. Some precocious readers decode rapidly and approach reading from a "text level" in which they think most about the decoding process as they read. Others approach reading from a "contextual level," determining whether words make sense—a process that aids them in decoding the words in any given sentence. These students use word meaning as a clue for detecting the words that belong in a passage.

Precocity in reading may be due in part to a combination of above-average intelligence and dynamic early-literacy experiences. The average IQ of precocious readers is 130, but individual IQ scores vary widely. Due to the fact that some precocious readers score well below average and others score at the highest levels, early reading and intelligence are only moderately related.

Early reading talent can present in combination with other advanced skills or appear alone. It is important to note that not all children with advanced verbal reasoning, or verbal precocity, will also read at a young age. Likewise, not all precocious readers demonstrate significantly advanced levels of verbal reasoning. Similarly, in some precocious readers, writing develops at a rate concurrent with their reading. In other children, reading and writing development are asynchronous, and writing development is on a more normal developmental pace.

These children usually have a firm grasp of the use of language and utilize expansive vocabularies to communicate ideas easily. They understand subtleties of language and enjoy using language for humor, as in creating puns.

Precocious readers usually enjoy the reading process; this may perhaps be because many have had pleasant early experiences reading with family members. These children often spend spare time engaged in reading or other literacy activities. These children also exhibit a wide variety of reading strategies and use them to create meaning from text. Even from a young age, these readers are able to integrate prior knowledge to create context for what they are reading. These readers think abstractly about their reading and can synthesize, analyze, and evaluate text beyond peers of their same chronological age. These students are also able to make inferences about characters and plot in the stories they read. Strategy use in reading is one of the determining factors in whether precocious readers become gifted readers over time.

In some circumstances children with average and below-average intelligence have also read precociously. A condition known as hyperlexia enables children to decode very early but with little sense of the meaning behind the text. These students have the ability to observe patterns that allow them to break the reading code. Hyperlexia is sometimes found in children with autism. These students usually do not remain above-average readers once peers are able to decode well and comprehension has increased significance in the ability to read well.

Comparison to Other Children

Precocious readers typically read about 2 years in advance of their chronological development. Though these children start with a lead, other children may eventually catch up to or even surpass the reading ability of the early reader. Generally, precocious readers continue to be above-average readers and do well as they progress through their school years. On the other hand, students who do not start out as precocious readers may later become gifted readers once they crack the reading code because high levels of verbal reasoning enable them to comprehend complex story lines and complicated nonfiction passages.

Although many of these students go on to be identified as gifted, not all precocious readers are good candidates for general gifted services. When programs heavily emphasize skills not associated with reading, students who lack these skills may become overwhelmed. Gifted programs that provide advanced reading experiences, or that are highly individualized may be appropriate for precocious readers with higher overall IQ scores.

Of those in generalized gifted services, about half read early. These students were typically able to identify letters around the age of 2. Neither reading nor language precocity, however, determines whether students will become gifted readers. The complexity of the findings about precocious reading has often led administrators to discount it as a sign of giftedness. This has had unfortunate consequences, particularly for gifted girls, whose parents may never again ask for special provisions for their child if persuaded that early reading is not a potential indicator of future giftedness.

Home Literacy Environment

Evidence shows that students' reading development is greatly influenced by their home literacy environments. Children who have had rich literacy experiences at home are more likely to read early. Language-rich homes are those where books are readily available, parents read regularly to their children, and family members engage in conversations concerning daily life. Parents of children who read early are usually involved to a great extent in their child's development. These children benefit from the fact that their parents are able to choose books that are appropriate and engage them in meaningful and pleasurable reading experiences. Most parents of precocious readers do not push their child beyond his or her desire or readiness to read, and many indicate that their child's reading was self-taught. Some parents are surprised when they learn that their child is significantly ahead of developmental benchmarks in reading. Still other parents spend significant amounts of energy coaching their children to read early; sometimes to no avail when children are not developmentally ready to begin reading. Experts agree that parents should follow the child's lead when it comes to literacy and should develop the child's interest in reading and other literacy activities. Although all young readers will benefit from these positive experiences, not all children raised in literacy-rich environments will become precocious readers. Thus, environment and nurturing alone will not produce precocious readers.

Early School Experiences

Early school experiences affect the continuous development of precocious readers. The developmental readiness of the child determines the pacing of school literacy experiences provided by the teacher, similar to the enriching home literacy experiences provided by parents.

Educators of early grades (including PreK–2) must be able to recognize precocity because early readers often enter school knowing how to read. Some young children will obscure their advanced ability in order to assimilate with the other children or because they are unfamiliar with the process of school and assume that everyone must learn the same thing at the same time, thus resigning themselves to the lack of challenge. It may also be difficult to identify reading precocity due to children's economic, cultural, or linguistic differences. For these reasons, early grades' teachers must assess the ability of their students to meet the individual needs of the students and can do so using story retellings and running records.

The ability of primary-grade teachers to differentiate the curriculum has a profound influence on the continued growth of the early reader. Though many primary-grade teachers use small groups or centers in their instruction, many do not alter the curriculum content to meet the varied needs of their learners, and these early readers have school experiences similar to those of their nonreading peers. Lack of stimulation and of rigorous content may reduce the progress of these students and cause them to make only minimal growth. On a long-term basis, this can cause young readers to become bored, frustrated, or complacent. Teachers who understand the reading process thoroughly are better able to provide differentiated experiences that will engage precocious readers and further their growth and development. These teachers understand that their precocious readers are already making the transition from learning to read to the process of reading to learn—a shift that usually occurs around third or fourth grade—and begin to provide experiences that will provide the readers with the appropriate reading instruction to help them make that shift.

Recommendations

Through support and challenge, advanced strategy instruction, and personalization of interest, teachers of precocious readers can create rich and challenging primary-grade experiences for advanced readers. The teachers must provide individualized work that will challenge the student, but must follow up with support of the student so that he or she is not working in isolation and without teacher guidance. Precocious readers will be unchallenged by the instruction and texts provided to their classmates. Teachers can model advanced reading strategies for these students and encourage them to utilize them in appropriately challenging books. Advanced readers should be guided to books that are just slightly above their current reading level and that offer rich language and advanced content, themes, and ideas. Some precocious readers may be adept at making appropriate book choices due to parental or sibling role modeling, but others may struggle to find an optimal match. Primary-grade teachers and librarians should support these students while they learn to make appropriate choices that will have sufficiently difficult text, but also appropriate content. Teachers should determine the areas of interest of their precocious readers and extend challenge through books and content in those areas.

Programmatic changes may also be necessary to accommodate the needs of precocious readers. When school administrators are aware of kindergarten children who are entering school with the ability to read, one way to meet their needs is to group them together in one classroom as a cluster group of precocious readers. This teacher will be better able to provide differentiated experiences and curriculum to a critical mass of early readers than will several teachers trying to provide these experiences to only one or two students in their classrooms. If reading talent is spread among several classrooms, however, it is possible to use cross-grade grouping as a way for talented young readers to come together to work with advanced texts and other differentiated curriculum. Evidence shows that precocious readers need to be able to interact with other readers on their cognitive level.

Elizabeth A. Fogarty

See also Elementary School, Literature Curriculum; Gifted Readers; Precocity; Prodigies; Talented Readers; Very Young Gifted

Further Readings

Catron, R. M., & Wingenbach, N. (1986). Developing the potential of the gifted reader. *Theory Into Practice, 25,* 134–140.

Dooley, C. (1993). The challenge: Meeting the needs of gifted readers. *Reading Teacher, 46,* 546–551.

Jackson, N. E. (1988). Precocious reading ability: What does it mean? *Gifted Child Quarterly, 32,* 200–204.

Jackson, N. E., & Roller, C. M. (1993). *Reading with young children* (RBBM 9302). Storrs, University of Connecticut, National Research Center on the Gifted and Talented.

Lamb, P., & Feldhusen, J. F. (1992). Recognizing and adapting instruction for early readers. *Roeper Review, 15*(2), 108–109.

Mills, J. R., & Jackson, N. E. (1990). Predictive significance of early giftedness: The case of precocious reading. *Journal of Educational Psychology, 82,* 410–419.

Stainthorp, R., & Hughes, D. (2004). An illustrative case study of precocious reading ability. *Gifted Child Quarterly, 48,* 107–120.

Precocity

Precocity is used to indicate an intellectually gifted child's advanced development in cognitive areas. Although the term can refer to advanced performance in any domain, it most frequently is used in conjunction with advanced language and thought. Historically, starting with Alfred Binet, precocity was sometimes expressed in terms of intelligent students having a higher mental age compared with their chronological peers. Precocity is sometimes also referred to as asynchronous development wherein gifted children's mental development surpasses their physical development. Precocious children's performance, on intelligence tests or at other tasks, matches that of older children. This entry explores behaviors that may demonstrate precocity, studies of precocious children, positive and negative adjustments precocity brings about, and ways of serving precocious children.

Behaviors

Precocity manifests itself in different ways in different gifted children. Some young gifted children will begin walking or talking by 6 months of age. Others will begin speaking later, but progress to using complete, and complex, sentences very quickly after that. Precocious children can sometimes produce identifiable pictures by 2-1/2 years of age, read at age 3, and read fluently by age 4. Demonstrated interest in and ability to solve mathematical problems or play musical instruments is also evidence of precocity. It is important to note that although early accomplishments are evidence of precocity, late acquisition of any of these skills is *not* necessarily an indicator of a lack of giftedness. History abounds, for instance, with examples of highly gifted individuals who struggled with reading, including such profoundly gifted exemplars as Winston Churchill, Albert Einstein, and Pablo Picasso. Children with exceptionally high-IQ scores are also considered precocious.

Studies

Precocity studies initially focused on children with extremely high IQ as measured by their scores on Lewis M. Terman's Stanford-Binet Intelligence Scale. In defining *intelligence,* Terman focused on children's ability to acquire and manipulate concepts. As a result of this focus, high-IQ students consequently show great adeptness with the symbols required for abstract thinking. Most studies of precocious students thus have used high IQ as a threshold for a child's inclusion. The *Talent Search/Study of Mathematically Precocious Youth* (*SMPY*) model uses diagnostic above-grade-level testing followed by prescribed instruction (DT → PI) to radically accelerate precocious children's education. The most well-known studies of precocity are those of Lewis Terman, Leta Hollingworth, Miraca U. M. Gross, Julian Stanley, Camilla Benbow, and Martha J. Morelock. Although conducted in different settings and across different decades, these studies share many similar findings.

Cumulatively, research has indicated that although no single characteristic can identify precocity in young children, the in-depth studies suggest that early talking and reading are the most consistent indicators of accelerated development. Precocious children demonstrate extraordinarily high abstract-reasoning capabilities and also tend to demonstrate advanced domain-specific skills. Precocity tends to allow children so identified to excel at, and be drawn to, a number of different domains, such as mathematics, languages, or science. The Talent Search/SMPY studies have shown that children who demonstrate proficiency on an above-level test, such as the SAT-I, the ACT, the School and College Abilities Test, or the Spatial Test Battery, are able to thrive in an accelerated program that can include, in addition to school-site acceleration, early entry to college. Precocious children with IQs in the 140 to 160 range tend to enjoy very successful careers as adults.

Adjustment

Precocious children with very high IQs, such as those above 180, demonstrated certain adjustment problems in research studies. First, many of these children failed to develop appropriate work habits, perhaps because they were placed in school settings geared to average children. The precocious students studied were found to spend much time off task and, as a result, learned to dislike school. Second, precocious students expressed difficulty in finding friends and playmates among their age peers and consequently felt isolated and alone. The children studied believed their chronological peers lacked common interests, vocabulary, and desire to engage in more complex activities. Third and last, precocious children often may demonstrate emotional vulnerability insofar that they can comprehend and are affected by major ethical issues before they are emotionally ready to deal with them. Adults who interact with children expressing such emotional vulnerability must be sensitive to the cause of these difficulties and provide necessary support to assuage the situation.

Precocity may cause issues to arise between precocious children and their families. Precocious children, for example, often are very sensitive to family values and themes. Their precocity allows them to more accurately notice, react to, and summarize these values and themes than their age peers. In addition, families that contain a precocious child often are more cohesive, insofar that family members help and support each other, and expressive, to the extent that members act openly and express feelings directly. Finally, birth order seems to influence precocity, as a disproportionately high number of children identified as profoundly gifted are firstborns. As a result, firstborn precocious children tend to define themselves more in terms of their thinking rather than their accomplishments.

Services

Precocious children should be provided with services that meet their cognitive and affective needs. Repeated studies have emphasized that providing *any* level of gifted education services to precocious children allows them to achieve at higher levels than their precocious peers who receive no services. Children who demonstrate behaviors that suggest precocity, including a very high IQ score, demonstrate strong indicators that they require gifted education services. School-based programming options that are especially appropriate for children demonstrating precocity include early entry to kindergarten, single-subject acceleration, grade skipping, honors classes, Advanced Placement or International Baccalaureate programs, or dual enrollment at area colleges. Parents and families can augment these services with Saturday and summer enrichment programs.

Stephen T. Schroth and Jason A. Helfer

See also Acceleration/*A Nation Deceived;* Acceleration Options; Asynchrony; IQ; Prodigies

Further Readings

Davis, G. A., & Rimm, S. B. (2004). *Education of the gifted and talented* (5th ed.). Boston: Allyn & Bacon.

Hollingworth, L. (1942). *Children above 180 IQ Stanford-Binet—Origin and development.* Yonkers-on-Hudson, NY: World Books.

Morelock, M. J., & Feldman, D. H. (2003). Extreme precocity: Prodigies, savants, and children of extraordinarily high IQ. In N. Colangelo & G. A. Davis (Eds.), *Handbook of gifted education* (3rd ed., pp. 455–469). Boston: Allyn & Bacon.

Schroth, S. T. (2007). Levels of service. In C. M. Callahan & J. A. Plucker (Eds.), *Critical issues and practices in gifted education* (pp. 281–294). Austin, TX: Prufrock Press.

Stanley, J. C., & Benbow, C. P. (1982). Educating mathematically precocious youths: Twelve policy recommendations. *Educational Researcher, 11*(5), 4–9.

Terman, L. M. (1925). *Genetic studies of genius: Vol. I. Mental and physical traits of a thousand gifted children.* Stanford, CA: Stanford University Press.

PRESCHOOL

Preschools provide a wonderful setting in which children, aged 3, 4, or 5, can develop their talents and pursue their creativity. There are skills that need to be learned because future success in school is dependent upon them, but they pale in importance compared to the understandings that children need to acquire about the learning process and their role in it. These are the years when children learn that learning is fun, that they are learners, and that they have a range of talents. Good preschools send children on a trajectory of exploration and success.

Characteristics of Preschoolers

Children usually come to preschool already brimming with the qualities that educators seek to have engendered by the time they graduate high school at age 18. Often preschoolers are excited about coming to school, even if some undergo a few days of tearful separation; they willingly learn with and from others; they are adventuresome in their explorations; they love to learn. To be fair, that is not true of every preschooler and not true of any preschooler in all situations. But by simply entering a classroom of 3-, 4-, or 5-year-olds and watching them busily exploring and learning, one can see that this is the norm. Most preschoolers think they're smart; they're proud of their talents; they willingly take risks to learn. Often, though, that begins to change when students enter "real" school in first grade. Why is this?

Preschools are designed to tap into and capitalize on students' strengths and interests. Preschool teachers focus on skills and understandings that are important and necessary, and their curriculum is rich and developmental. This is often in contrast with how education is approached beginning in first grade. As a result, too often "real school" means an exclusionary focus on skills and a narrow pathway for learning.

Managing Diversity of Talents

All children have a range of intelligences and interests. One way of managing this diversity of talents is to frame curriculum and instruction around Howard Gardner's *theory of multiple intelligences* (first described in his book *Frames of Mind*). Believing in multiple intelligences means understanding and accepting that children have strengths in many different areas. In preschool, the goal is not to create a hierarchy of learners or to identify what a student cannot do. Rather, when children are young, the focus is on their interests and talents; educators want them to make choices and use their burgeoning skills to learn and to solve problems, and ensure that they engage in joyful learning.

Learning How to Learn

On a practical basis, this means that teachers are going to challenge students by giving them a variety of ways to learn. At some times, all students will learn in the same way. In fact, learning how to learn while sitting and listening is an important skill and one that can be difficult for some children. Because that approach portends much for a child's future education, it is essential that a child learn how to do so. Likewise, it is important that children learn how to be good group members, and that means that they need to know how to be both leaders and followers. Though some children easily play one role, oftentimes it is difficult for a child to be able to do both. Promoting "active listening" and "being a good team member" are part of the routine of any good preschool teacher.

Beyond these basic requisites, children should be given options about how to learn (if not what to learn). A preschool teacher's first task is to ensure that the class's learning centers address all of the ways in which students can be talented. While still focusing on students learning how to read and write and calculate, learning centers to master the "scholastic intelligences" (as termed by Thomas Hoerr) must cover a far greater expanse of talent. Preschool teachers often create learning centers that tap into students' different intelligences. These are places where children can play dress-up and pretend, areas where they can run and throw, and settings in which they can tend to animals and touch nature. There may be art centers with paint or clay, or there might be musical centers with drums and horns. Perhaps there are teamwork centers, areas designed to teach students how to cooperate and share.

Creativity is developed and reinforced by the choices given students and by what is reinforced. If there's "one right way" or, even, "one best way," students will quickly know what it is and learn to pursue it. On the other hand, if there are many ways to show an answer, if there are a variety of ways to be correct, that will be known too. Creativity is developed when students are given different ways to solve problems and when out-of-the-box thinking is reinforced. Teachers need to show they value creativity by what they say, by what work they display, and by how they respond to students. Good teachers know that creativity is messy, and sometimes slow, and they enjoy that journey with their students.

It is essential to ensure that learning centers do more than occupy and entertain; they must also reinforce and challenge. When the centers are developmentally designed—constructed so that students can experience enough success to maintain interest and motivation but also challenging enough so that they will be stretched and pushed—children's gifts begin to unfold. This means, of course, that a classroom must have many centers and these centers must offer different levels of challenge. Good teachers steer children so that they are working at a level that nurtures them.

Student and Teacher Attitudes

The key factor in the success of this approach is the perspective of the preschool teacher. The teacher must know both the student's interests and talents, but that is not enough. The teacher must also understand the student's inclination to learn and ability to face frustration. Indeed, the student's attitude about learning is the major determinant in how much the student learns. Good preschool teachers tend to this attitude with much focus and energy.

But the greatest aspect of developing talents in preschool lies not with the centers or other aspects of curriculum, however developmentally appropriate and enticing they may be. It inheres in the attitude of the teacher toward student learning and in the teacher's understanding that all children have talents. In her seminal work, *Mindset,* Carol Dweck points out that how we define intelligence determines how intelligent we can become. Dweck says that if we have a "fixed mindset" perspective, we focus on preserving our successes and ensuring that we look smart. In contrast, a "growth mindset" perspective means that we view intelligence as evolving; this enables us to take risks and continue to learn. One way to engender the growth mind-set in students is to commend them on their effort and tenacity, rather than on how smart or talented they are.

Similarly, good preschool teachers cushion the falls but don't let children avoid them. The key is learning from new mistakes, not avoiding or repeating mistakes. Mistakes are an essential part of the creative process. If children are to grow and be creative, they must learn how to accept frustration and, sometimes, failure. Teachers need to create settings in which setbacks happen so that the student learns how to respond. Good teachers help students understand that making mistakes is part of the learning process.

Thomas R. Hoerr

See also Very Young Gifted

Further Readings

Dweck, C. (2006). *Mindset.* New York: Random House.

Gardner, H. (1983). *Frames of mind: The theory of multiple intelligences.* New York: Basic Books.

Hoerr, T. (2000). *Becoming a multiple intelligences school.* Alexandria, VA: Association for Supervision and Curriculum Development.

Preservice Education

Preservice education for prospective teachers provides research-based training from institutions of higher education using approaches, experiences, and materials to provide engaging curriculum content aligned with existing national standards to prepare preschool, elementary, or secondary teachers for initial teacher licensure. In most teacher training institutions, when trainees complete required courses on Exceptional Learners in the Classroom most of the instructional time is dedicated to learning about schoolchildren with various disabilities, the components of an Individual Education Plan, and the collaboration process to provide services to students with special needs. Although gifted and talented students, students from culturally diverse backgrounds, and students who are at risk are included in the broad definition of inclusion of students with special needs, courses in exceptionalities include increased awareness and understanding of the social, emotional, and behavioral concerns but often lack strategies to meet the needs of gifted and talented learners and their parents or guardians.

Understanding Characteristics of Gifted Learners

Merely distributing a packet of handouts on characteristics of gifted and talented learners and ideas for differentiation strategies is insufficient in creating interest or skills to teach gifted students. Certainly, engaging in lively class discussions, PowerPoint presentations, real-life stories, and knowing the state law are successful ways to engage teachers in addressing needs of gifted children in the regular classroom. However, several additional activities capture college students' attention.

One is using children's literature. Children's literature is a powerful teaching tool. For example, Roald Dahl has written a witty, fanciful tale about a precocious girl named Matilda who has highly advanced abilities in mathematics, vocabulary, reading, logic, and a knack for adventuresome activities. Matilda enchants her classmates and teacher, Miss Honey, while challenging her unengaged parents and rigid school authority. Students in a methods course might read this children's novel and then compare characteristics of giftedness in the general population to the central character, Matilda, using a variety of documents and activities to learn about giftedness. They discover that though Matilda seems unrealistically bright, there *are* precocious students with similar abilities, in comparison to their classmates, who require differentiated curriculum and emotional support to reach their potential.

A second approach is self-examination of attitudes toward gifted learners (Table 1). Using a modified survey ranging from 1 as *strongly agree* to 5 as *strongly disagree,* trainees reverse score the points on questions 1, 5, 6, and 9. A low score is a good score (see below). Questions include statements regarding preparation, instruction, policies, and tendencies to accommodate for the needs of gifted learners. Importantly, they learn of research that supports gifted education. They take the inventory prior to a discussion on gifted education, then again at the end of the semester as a way to reflect on attitudinal changes. Responses, kept in the hands of each student, are confidential for self-evaluation and growth. For whole class analysis, pre-and post-scores are collected anonymously, then compared to determine overall class growth related to understanding and providing experiences for gifted learners. Survey items generate lively discussion with opportunities to explore attitudes and future strategies for gifted learners.

Differentiation Strategies and Techniques

Typically, learning how to differentiate instruction for gifted students is a daunting expectation for preservice teachers as they design lesson plans for meaningful content, process, and products for elementary students they have not yet encountered. Preservice trainees need to learn at least five types of lesson plans, including direct instruction, presentation with advanced organizers, concept attainment, cooperative learning, and problem-based inquiry. Each of the five lesson plans should include a requirement to differentiate for special needs children who need time and attention, as well as for gifted learners who need a qualitatively differentiated program of instruction.

Excellent background explanation and an arsenal of strategies can be found in Carol Tomlinson's

Table 1 Examination of Attitudes Toward Gifted Learners

1	Gifted children need more attention than average children in the regular classroom.
2	When gifted children are excused to attend a pull-out class, they must make up all the work missed in their regular class.
3	Gifted children should do the same assignments as everyone else in the classroom.
4	Because gifted children often finish their work before their classmates, they should be given longer assignments or more of the same work.
5	Working with gifted children would be very stimulating.
6	Teachers of the gifted need additional release time for planning and developing instructional materials.
7	Gifted children can advance most rapidly in a regular classroom.
8	Disruptive behavior by gifted students would be eliminated by stricter discipline procedures.
9	Special materials, strategies, and curricula need to be provided for gifted learners.
10	It takes less time to prepare for gifted students than for below-average/challenged students.
11	Gifted children will succeed in life regardless of the school programming for high-ability learners.
12	Special classes for gifted foster elitism, because they think they are better than other students.
13	It would be embarrassing to have a gifted child correct me in front of the class.
14	I think all children are gifted.
15	Grouping gifted students together creates more problems than benefits.
Score:	
15–35	You are an advocate of gifted learners who understands the complexities of school gifted/talented concerns.
35–50	You have moderate understanding of issues and concerns of gifted learners. Keep reading and learning about gifted learners and their needs.
50–75	You need to revisit characteristics of gifted learners and ways to meet their educational needs.

Source: Revised by author (2001).

book, *How to Differentiate Instruction in Mixed Ability Classrooms*. Student trainees work in teams to develop lessons despite the fact that they do not have "real" classroom students whose needs they can identify. One might ask, "How would you design a lesson for Matilda if she were in your classroom?"

Research and Resources

Despite evidence of academic acceleration as best practice for many gifted schoolchildren, this strategy is often not employed in schools and districts. Preservice trainees learn the effectiveness of acceleration in *A Nation Deceived: How Schools Hold Back America's Brightest Students*. Resources from the National Association for Gifted Children (NAGC) Web site provide everything from a glossary of terms to resource directories and classroom resources and teaching for high potential. NAGC provides an invaluable collection of professional resources for teachers.

Frequently, the focus of preservice education on giftedness is how to challenge gifted learners. As a collaborative team, trainees can present research, resources, teaching strategies, and support for new elementary teachers to gain confidence in empowering gifted students to reach their potential. The team effort produces better-prepared teachers who have more than increased awareness and understanding. They become empowered themselves.

Sally R. Beisser

See also Competencies for Teachers of Gifted; Controversies in Gifted Education; Differentiation; Elitism; Teacher Attitudes

Further Readings

Colangelo, N., Assouline, S. G., & Gross, M. U. M. (2004). *A nation deceived: How schools hold back America's brightest students.* Retrieved August 27, 2008, from http://www.accelerationinstitute.org/Nation_Deceived/Get_Report.asx

Dahl, R. (1998). *Matilda.* New York: Puffin Books–Penguin Putnam.

National Association for Gifted Children: http://www.nagc.org

Tomlinson, C. A. (2001). *How to differentiate instruction in mixed ability classrooms* (2nd ed.). Alexandria, VA: Association for Supervision and Curriculum development.

Presidential Scholars

The Presidential Scholars Program is a recognition program honoring outstanding graduating high school seniors. It was put in place in 1964 by an Executive Order from President Lyndon Johnson. At that time, he emphasized that this program should do more than *reward* excellence. It should also be a means of *nourishing* excellence. The program was to be a way to stimulate achievement. It was hoped that having such a program would give students a goal to work toward during their high school years. This entry describes the Presidential Scholars Program's goals, the process of application, and the characteristics of Presidential Scholars.

Students who score extremely high on either the SAT or the ACT are invited to apply for the program. Candidates are evaluated on their academic achievement, personal characteristics, leadership, and community service activities. The Commission on Presidential Scholars selects one male and one female from each state, the District of Columbia, and Puerto Rico, as well as representatives from families of U.S. citizens living abroad. There are also 15 students chosen at large for a total of 121 Presidential Scholars. In 1979, President Carter expanded the program to include an additional 20 students in the arts. Students being considered for the Arts Program submit evidence of artistic accomplishment in the form of videos or manuscripts. They are judged in the categories of dance, music, music/jazz, music/voice, theater, photography, visual arts, and writing. The selected students are known as Presidential Scholars in the Arts. During the 1980s, President Reagan refined the selection process to emphasize the elements of leadership and community service.

The 121 Presidential Scholars receive a trip to Washington, D.C., in June to receive the Presidential Scholars Medallion at a White House ceremony. In 1969, it was decided that the design of the medallion would be the Great Seal of the Nation. Presidential Scholars Recognition Week activities include meetings with national and international leaders, discussions of relevant issues with government officials and elected leaders, meeting accomplished people in a variety of fields, participating in community service activities, and attending recitals and receptions. Time is also scheduled during the week to visit the various museums and monuments in the nation's capital. The week culminates with the White House Awards Ceremony. Even so, many Presidential Scholars will tell you that the best and most lasting part of the experience is the opportunity to exchange ideas with other accomplished and highly motivated peers. During the week together, many friendships develop that will last a lifetime. Students often refer to themselves as becoming members of the Presidential Scholars family.

For many years, the American Association for Gifted Children had a role in the Presidential Scholars Program. Their 1994 study of the Presidential Scholars suggested that the students developed their talents and abilities because of the encouragement of teachers and parents. All of the scholars are asked to nominate a teacher who inspired them and guided them in developing their talents and abilities. By 1998, the Distinguished Teacher award was renamed Presidential Scholars Program Teacher Recognition Award. This designation recognizes the educational excellence of outstanding teachers.

In 1981, Felice Kaufmann did a follow-up study on the Presidential Scholars of the mid-to late 1960s. She was wondering if the promise of youth lasted beyond their high school years. She found that 97 percent of the Presidential Scholars had received college degrees and slightly over 60 percent had earned a graduate degree.

Application Process

Students must be U.S. citizens to be considered for the Presidential Scholars Program. Students cannot initiate the application process. They must be invited to apply. Invitations are based on the student's test records on the SAT or ACT over a 2-year period of time. Students wanting to qualify for the Presidential Scholars in the Arts must participate in the youngARTS competition sponsored by the National Foundation for Advancement in the Arts (NFAA). This organization has been the exclusive nominating organization for the Presidential Scholars in the Arts since 1982. Approximately 2,700 students are invited to apply each year. After receiving an invitation, students send in self-assessments, school reports, a transcript, and a personal essay. The deadline for all application materials is usually in February. Semifinalists are chosen in March. The final decisions are made in April. In June, the new Presidential Scholars travel to Washington, D.C., for their Recognition Week.

The Applicants

This program recognizes young people who have learned multiple languages, worked for high-level organizations such as NASA, written scholarly papers, conducted research, held their own art exhibitions, performed concerts, or launched their own companies, all by the age of 17. Though they come from diverse backgrounds and situations, they share many qualities, such as a devotion to family and their heritage. They have often been at the forefront in their local schools, exhibiting spirit and taking on leadership roles in clubs and school-related activities. Their abundant supply of energy carries them into numerous activities within community and civic groups. They share the desire to turn their dreams for making the world a better place into reality. They go on to receive an education at some of the top schools in this country.

Today, the Presidential Scholars Program has an active and supportive alumni community. There are currently more than 5,000 Presidential Scholars. Following their recognition as Presidential Scholars, many have gone forward to impact our nation as scientists, artists, inventors, CEOs, stage and screen stars, attorneys, journalists, and teachers. They have joined the military, played in major symphonies, and become entrepreneurs. They have been awarded the Pulitzer Prize, the Rhodes Scholarship, the Marshall Scholarship, and Fulbright grants. This program illustrates the potential for education to open untold doors to the future. The Presidential Scholars continue to believe they can fulfill their dreams with passion and conviction long after the ceremony in the White House.

Joyce E. Juntune

See also Academic Talent; College Gifted; National Merit Scholarship Program; Talent; Valedictorians

Further Readings

Kaufmann, F. A. (1981). The 1964–1968 Presidential Scholars: A follow-up study. *Exceptional Children, 48*(2), 164–168.

Presidential Scholars Foundation: http://www.presidentialscholars.org

Problem Solving

Problem solving is the process of applying a complex set of thinking skills to resolve or complete a task. The ability to problem solve is thought to be the most important set of thinking skills students can learn to help them in their future lives. Problem solving involves both divergent and convergent thinking. Often linked to the literature on creativity, problem-solving skills include fluency, flexibility, originality, and elaboration of ideas.

To find a reasonable, viable, or acceptable solution to a problem, one must first generate many possibilities before evaluating the solutions that engage the higher-level thinking skills of synthesis, analysis, and evaluation. Curricula designed for gifted students often emphasize creativity and problem solving. The processes of problem solving can be domain specific such as in the field of physics, engineering, math, medicine, or business, as well as generic. This entry reviews processes, strategies, and curricula related to problem solving.

Processes

There are several articulated processes of problem solving in the literature related to psychology and creativity. Among the most frequently cited is the process for creative problem solving originally developed by Sidney Parnes and later disseminated by Donald Treffinger in the *creative problem solving model:*

Stage 1: Mess finding—Analyze and break down the big problem into smaller pieces

Stage 2: Data finding—Articulate and collect as much information as possible about the problem

Stage 3: Problem finding—Restate the fuzzy problem into a more manageable target to solve

Stage 4: Idea finding—Brainstorm as many ideas as possible to solve the problem

Stage 5: Solution finding—Select criteria to evaluate possible solutions

Stage 6: Acceptance finding—Articulate your best solution based on using the criteria above

Adhering to a process for problem solving enables students to practice specific thinking skills such as brainstorming, categorizing, comparing, contrasting, analyzing, synthesizing, and evaluating ideas as they proceed to find the most acceptable solution.

The Future Problem Solving Program International competition founded by E. Paul Torrance has students from all over the world engaged in selecting and solving problems whose solutions would better a global society. The Future Problem Solving Program International Fact Sheet describes the processes used in the problem-solving competition, which are similar to the creative problem-solving model described above:

1. Identify challenges related to the topic or future scene
2. Select an underlying problem
3. Produce solution ideas to the underlying problem
4. Generate and select criteria to evaluate solution ideas
5. Evaluate solution ideas to determine the better action plan
6. Develop the action plan

Although there are numerous versions of lists of skills and processes needed to solve problems, Robert Sternberg suggests that regardless of how they are labeled, the following six processes are used:

1. Identify the problem
2. Allocate resources
3. Represent and organize information
4. Formulate strategy
5. Monitor problem-solving strategies
6. Evaluate solutions (p. 40)

Problem-Solving Techniques and Strategies

The literature is filled with techniques and strategies to improve the thinking skills that are required to solve problems. To improve problem-solving skills, students must learn to deconstruct the characteristics of a difficult problem. As summarized by Joachim Funke, difficult problems lack clarity, have multiple goals, are complex, and have time considerations. Strategies such as "divide and conquer" to break the problem down into smaller parts, working backward, trial-and-error, experimentation, assumption reversal, and more are used to help give people the thinking tools they need to be better problem solvers.

Other problem-solving techniques may be found in the literature on creative thinking, such as incubation, which is described as putting the details of the problem in your head, and then allowing the subconscious mind to ponder them. Edward De Bono describes six different styles of thinking in his book, *Six Thinking Hats*. Each style presents a different perspective for examining important decisions or problems. Examining a problem from different points of view allows it to become less difficult to solve.

There are many commercialized programs that support the teaching of analytical thinking skills. Some are associated with specific fields. One such strategy used in business is the SWOT framework, whereby strengths, weaknesses, opportunities, and threats are examined to help make decisions and solve problems.

Problem-Solving Curricula

Technology has advanced ways to teach problem solving to young children. Gaming is becoming a 21st-century phenomenon, giving students opportunities to learn problem-solving strategies in virtual environments. In professional fields, too, technology enables scientists to use computer-generated models to solve both real and virtual scientific problems.

In addition to being domain specific, interdisciplinary problem solving is now found in learning standards across the United States. In Texas, as early as kindergarten, students are required to be exposed to problem-solving and decision-making processes. In New York, students are required to apply the knowledge of thinking skills of mathematics, science, and technology to address real-life problems and make informed decisions. Problem-based learning, often used with high-achieving students, provides an instructional framework for students to delve deep into a specific content area by solving real interdisciplinary and often ambiguous problems. Effective teaching practices for general and gifted education include infusing the teaching of problem-solving skills into the content and core curriculum. This includes giving students direct instruction on using thinking strategies, as well as opportunities to apply them in authentic contexts.

Nancy B. Hertzog

See also Creative Problem Solving; Creativity, Definition; Divergent Thinking; Future Problem Solving

Further Readings

Creative Problem Solving: http://www.mycoted.com/Creative_Problem_Solving_-_CPS

Csikszentmihalyi, M. (1996). *Creativity: Flow and the psychology and discovery of invention.* New York: HarperCollins.

De Bono, E. (1985). *Six thinking hats.* Boston: Little, Brown.

Frensch, P. A., & Funke, J. (Eds.). (1995). *Complex problem solving: The European perspective.* Mahwah, NJ: Lawrence Erlbaum.

Future Problem Solving Program International Fact Sheet: http://www.fpspi.org/PDF/FPSP%20Fact%20Sheet.pdf

Mind Tools: http://www.mindtools.com/pages/article/newTED_07.htm

Sternberg, R. J., & Grigorenko, E. (2000). *Teaching for successful intelligence.* Arlington Heights, IL: Skylight Training.

Treffinger, D., Isaksen, S. G., & Stead-Dorval, B. K. (2005). *Creative problem solving: An introduction* (4th ed.). Waco, TX: Prufrock Press.

Prodigies

Prodigies are those children, usually under 10 years of age, who exhibit an adult level of proficiency at various tasks, jobs, or work. A prodigy performs as an adult in a respected, highly demanding domain. Although prodigies can emerge in many fields, most demonstrate their abilities in music, chess, and mathematics. Prodigies have also demonstrated extraordinary abilities in art, languages, literature, mathematics, and science, but to a much lesser extent than in music, chess, and math. Historically, prodigies have been boys almost exclusively, but this has changed rapidly in recent years because the number of girls so identified has increased considerably. This entry provides a historical overview of conceptions of prodigies, reviews the research conducted on them, explores the relationship between prodigies and intelligence, examines how much of a child prodigy's talent is innate and how much due to environment, considers how teachers and families can support a child prodigy's development, and looks at how savants are sometimes confused with prodigies.

Historical Overview

Historically, prodigies' gifts were considered to be the result of supernatural causes. Over time, this view shifted and for much of the 20th century a very high IQ was seen as the basis of prodigious talent. Today, growing understanding about prodigies suggests that their talent develops through a confluence, the "co-incidence" of influences, with levels of nurture, training, and support prodigies receive as significant as any other factor. Providing this social support sometimes can be problematic because doing so requires a great degree of cooperation and coordination among different parties: quality teachers, conscientious parents, abundant opportunities for practice and performance, resources to provide lessons, access to publicity, and a certain degree of providence that allows the child to meet the domain's challenges. Prodigies are those who can negotiate these challenges and tests more rapidly than others. As a result, they enjoy eminence in the field at a much younger age than others. This level of prodigious talent raises several obstacles for children so endowed, each of which must be dealt with appropriately.

Research

Relatively few research studies have examined prodigies. At least part of the reason for the limited number of studies is the rareness of prodigies. Studies of prodigies have tended to be case studies of individual children or analyses of historically eminent individuals. The studies have shown that child prodigies generally have high, but not extraordinary, IQ scores. The child's prodigious ability is almost always limited to a specific domain, leading to gaps or discrepancies in abilities. For example, a musical prodigy may possess extraordinary pitch but poor fine motor skills; or a math prodigy may lag in other academic areas, for instance reading below grade level. Research suggests that almost all prodigies are performing at an adult level before the age of 10, which may be attributed to a coincidence of individual, environmental, and historical forces. *Individual* factors include the prodigy's talents, intelligence, and gifts. *Environmental* aspects comprise the existence of a highly developed field that can be taught to the prodigy. *Historical* aspects take into account the importance that society places on the domain in which the prodigy excels. This amalgamation of factors has been dubbed the *co-incidence* theory.

Relationship Between Prodigies and Intelligence

An IQ score of 120 serves more or less as the threshold for prodigious performance, with almost all prodigies having an IQ above that level. For many years it was thought that high IQ and occurrence of prodigy were related. More recently, however, the domain in which the prodigy excels is considered to be of more importance than the child's level of intelligence. Domains that produce prodigies tend to have several common aspects. First, they are highly rule bound in that a general consensus exists as to what constitutes a high level of performance. Second, the domains have relatively transparent knowledge structures that proceed in a logical and sequenced progression. Third, transmission of the domain's knowledge is demonstrated in a consistent and agreed-upon manner. Fourth, the criteria for what constitutes "excellence" are adequate, accepted, and acknowledged. Fifth and last, very young prodigies must be able to perform the tasks the domain demands.

Some prodigies not only are able to master the rules of a specific domain, but are also able to experiment with the skills and understandings that are so fluently developing. Though many children can replicate a notated musical composition or draw or paint, what sets the prodigious child apart is his or her need to play with the tools of a particular domain. This playfulness affords the prodigious child ample opportunities to gain a better understand of the rules of the domain as well as provides opportunities for the child to challenge the rules and potentially develop new ways of thinking and doing within the domain. Opportunities to play with the domain's tools also allow the prodigy to experience *fruitful asynchrony,* where the prodigy can continually challenge the rules and legitimated understandings of a domain. This challenging of the field is especially important for the prodigy because it helps support his or her continued development. Fruitful asynchrony sets the prodigy apart from other age peers. It is thus imperative that parents, caregivers, and schools that care for or work with prodigious children support this development.

Support

Children with prodigious ability require support from the home and school to develop their gifts fully. Supporting prodigies is challenging insofar as parents and schools may not have the necessary resources or expertise to support these children's learning needs. Parents and school personnel must be aware of, and have access to, resources that can best serve the child. This may mean allowing the child to work with an identified expert outside of school settings, or the child may engage in acceleration, including single-subject acceleration or, depending on the child, grade skipping within the school. No matter the choice implemented, it is imperative that these children have opportunities to work through and with the various structural principles within the domain and continue to refine and expand their content knowledge in authentic contexts. Parents, caregivers, and schools may be limited in the level of support they can provide. Thus, as the child's prodigious gifts mature, he or she often will need to seek the tutelage of an expert located outside the school or even some distance from the family home.

Early in his or her life, the prodigy's unusual gifts require an adult who can provide support. This adult must be able to ease the prodigy's way, supply opportunities, shield from critics, cushion through setbacks, and focus and channel talents in appropriate and productive directions, and otherwise act as a mentor. No matter how prodigious the child's talents, a mentor's guidance will be necessary to navigate the social intricacies of the domain. Though prodigies are often very gifted at mimicry, knowing what is taking place at the forefront of the domain and which conventional practices bear surpassing is dependent upon a knowledgeable and well-informed mentor. The mentor thus harnesses the prodigy's talent and provides the refinement and direction necessary to reach the next level. In addition, the social and emotional needs of the prodigious child must be supported by parents or other caring adults.

When prodigies are younger, their gifts tend to be most pronounced. During this period, caregivers, parents, or teachers must support the environmental, individual, and historical aspects of the specific domain in which a child is prodigious. In addition, prodigies must also have opportunity to understand how their prodigious abilities can be used to best serve the greater community as well as individual needs. The child's prodigious ability in a domain must thus be developed while the prodigy begins to understand and appreciate the limits and potentials of that ability. This understanding and appreciation is especially important as the child matures. As onetime prodigies grow into adulthood, they must compete with other masters of their domain, which may include age peers who have caught up with them in terms of skills and performance levels. This altered playing field inevitably results in a shock to the self-image of the former prodigy, one that occurs at the same time that he or she should be exerting personal career control and management. On the one hand, prodigies face a changed audience, one no longer amazed by their seemingly superhuman skills. On the other hand, prodigies may begin to face the reality that they have been the object of another's ambitions and goals, be it a parent, a teacher, or other mentor. This dual realization often causes some degree of distress, and may be one reason that many, if not most, prodigies do not fulfill their earlier potential. For those former prodigies who do make the transition to adult eminence in their field, their families are often the catalyst. Families of these individuals recognize the changing nature of their role, and allow the child to continue to grow while establishing a separate and autonomous life.

Ultimately the convergence of coincidence factors is required for prodigies to develop their gifts fully. Mozart, for example, is often portrayed as a child who received little or no tutelage in music. Mozart, of course, was a prodigy but he also had regular opportunities to see and hear the regular instruction his father provided to his sister. This training, albeit informal, was necessary for Mozart to reach his potential, as was his family's recognition and development of his prodigious gifts. Unlike most prodigies, Mozart also revolutionized the domain in which he performed. Though it is sometimes argued that prodigies are *not* creative, the speed and depth of their mystical capabilities suggest at least a close propinquity to creativity. However, because many prodigies' level of performance is what sets them apart from age peers, creativity must be looked at as a separate endeavor.

Savants

Savants are often grouped with high-IQ children and prodigies. "Idiot savants," a label originating in the 19th century, was used to describe mentally disabled persons who were able to display advanced levels of learning in certain areas. As with prodigies, savant syndrome is an exceedingly rare condition that occurs approximately 6 times more frequently in boys than girls. Savants differ from prodigies in that savants demonstrate only concrete and literal patterns of expression and thought, and show minimal abstract reasoning ability. Savants also tend to behave differently from children of the same age, with abstract expression often lagging behind that of others; moreover, they will not necessarily challenge the rules of a domain or develop refined skills and understandings. In all of these behaviors, the savant differs greatly from the prodigy, who exhibits behaviors much the same as his or her age peers with the exception of the area of prodigious talent. Current research suggests that savant syndrome is caused by a pre- or postnatal injury to the brain's left hemisphere, resulting in right hemisphere compensatory growth. No such brain abnormalities have been noted with prodigies.

Stephen T. Schroth and Jason A. Helfer

See also Genius; IQ; Mentoring Gifted and Talented Individuals; Precocity; Savants; Talent

Further Readings

Callahan, C. M., & Dickson, R. K. (2007). Mentoring. In J. A. Plucker & C. M. Callahan (Eds.), *Critical issues and practices in gifted education: What the research says* (pp. 369–382). Waco, TX: Prufrock Press.

Callahan, C. M., & Kyburg, R. M. (2005). Talented and gifted youth. In D. L. DuBois & M. J. Karcher (Eds.), *Handbook of youth mentoring* (pp. 424–439). Thousand Oaks, CA: Sage.

Cox, C. M. (1926). *Genetic studies of genius: Vol. 2. The early mental traits of three hundred geniuses.* Stanford, CA: Stanford University Press.

Davis, G. A., & Rimm, S. B. (2004). *Education of the gifted and talented* (5th ed.). Boston: Allyn & Bacon.

Feldman, D. H. (2007). Prodigies. In J. A. Plucker & C. M. Callahan (Eds.), *Critical issues and practices in gifted education: What the research says.* Waco, TX: Prufrock Press.

Gardner, H. (1993). *Creating minds: An anatomy of creativity seen through the lives of Freud, Einstein, Picasso, Stravinsky, Graham, and Gandhi.* New York: Basic Books.

Morelock, M. J., & Feldman, D. H. (2003). Extreme precocity: Prodigies, savants, and children of extraordinarily high IQ. In N. Colangelo & G. A. Davis (Eds.), *Handbook of gifted education* (3rd ed., pp. 455–469). Boston: Allyn & Bacon.

Professional Development

Professional development in gifted education is an elusive concept. Characterized simply as the "systematic development of professional skill" by Gloria Dall'Alba and Jörgen Sandberg (p. 383), the concept of professional development defies simplicity because of the widely varying ways individuals, schools, and districts envision and participate in systematic development. Professional development ideally begins at the preservice level, when undergraduates in teacher education programs receive an overview, or at least an introduction, to the nature and needs of the gifted learners they will encounter in the classroom. According to the 2006–2007 *State of the States in Gifted Education,* however, only 5 of 43 responding states require preservice hours in gifted education. The transmission of knowledge and skills in the field necessarily continues in formal ways within the school setting; known alternatively as staff development (e.g., Dettmer & Landrum, 1998) or as inservice or teacher training, learning experiences may be provided for all educators in a building or district by specialists brought in to facilitate such programs or by local staff members assigned to work with gifted students. Alternatively, the staff members assigned to work with gifted students may be the participants in these programs, or they may organize small communities of learning to further develop their abilities.

The process continues informally, as well, as individuals learn through their day-to-day interactions with gifted learners and independently seek answers to new challenges through reading, discussion, and reflection. All too often, educators of the gifted find themselves isolated in schools, and even in districts, as the only individuals dedicated to serving gifted and talented learners; these teachers are finding professional learning communities online, through Web sites dedicated to gifted education or through listservs in the field. Educators also can pursue continuing education, in person or through distance education, through colleges and universities; these efforts, largely funded by the individuals themselves, can result in endorsements in gifted education or in graduate degrees. Educators can attend state, regional, national, or even international conferences in gifted education, broadening their perspectives and enlarging their professional tool kits. The 2006–2007 *State of the States* reports that 6 of 43 responding states mandate some form of professional development in gifted education for the classroom teachers who spend the most time with gifted children; 15 states mandate certification or endorsement in the field.

Although systematic development as a process has defied implementation, both scholars and practitioners lack clarity about the meaning of "professional skill" in gifted education. Understanding the requisite skills required by teachers of the gifted is likely uncertain because the concepts of giftedness and talent are defined and operationalized in multiple ways. Nancy Bangel, Donna Enersen, Brenda Capobianco, and Sidney M. Moon suggest, however, that a consistent appraisal of teacher competencies emerged from the field of gifted education from the 1970s through the early 1990s. These include knowledge of both educational and affective needs of gifted children; skill in promoting high-level thinking and creative problem solving; ability to facilitate independent research; and ability to develop appropriate curricular units for the gifted. While many educators have concluded that these same competencies are evident in all effective teachers, outstanding teachers of the gifted indicate a specific preference for teaching gifted students, and they are willing to advocate for the gifted, even if it means challenging the status.

PreK–12 Standards

In 1998, the National Association for Gifted Children (NAGC) developed *PreK–Grade 12 Standards* that suggested that educators responsible for the successful implementation of gifted programs needed to be familiar with the following: *program design* based on "sound philosophical, theoretical, and empirical support"; *program administration and management,* "including developing, implementing, and managing services"; *student identification* "to determine appropriate educational services"; *curriculum and instruction* specifically for the "unique needs of the gifted child"; *socio-emotional guidance and counseling* "to recognize and nurture the unique socio-emotional development" of the gifted; *program evaluation,* studying "the value and impact of services provided"; and *professional development,* ensuring that those working with gifted learners "have specialized preparation in gifted education [and] expertise in appropriate differentiated content and instructional methods." Those accountable for program success should possess the professional skills and understandings to guide programs from minimal to exemplary competencies in each of these standards.

Initial Knowledge and Skill Standards for Gifted and Talented Education

In an effort to facilitate greater coherence in the professional development of educators of the gifted, The Association for the Gifted (TAG), a division of the Council for Exceptional Children (CEC), and NAGC promulgated *Initial Knowledge and Skill Standards for Gifted and Talented Education* to shape graduate programs in the field as well as district- or school-based decisions about personnel preparation. These standards, approved by the National Council for Accreditation of Teacher Education (NCATE), include broad areas essential for professionals in gifted education. These include the following:

- historical and philosophical foundations in the field;
- the development and characteristics of gifted learners, emphasizing comprehensive knowledge of individual cognitive and affective characteristics, as well as of developmental milestones, and the impact of family, community, and culture on development;
- individual learning differences honoring and integrating the full range of diversity in gifted education, including academic, affective, and cultural differences, into programs;
- instructional strategies, including a repertoire of curricular, instructional, and management

strategies to appropriately differentiate for the widely varying needs of all gifted learners;

- learning environments and social interactions focusing on interpersonal needs and interactions, and safe and supportive environments, necessary for optimal development;
- language and communication issues for contemporary students who come from diverse ethnic, cultural, and linguistic backgrounds, as well as those with language or communication disabilities;
- instructional planning that integrates a scope and sequence for differentiated learning into school, district, state, and national curriculum standards;
- assessment, identifying gifted learners and prescribing appropriate programming, as well as determining academic progress;
- professional and ethical practice, including competencies that facilitate the progress of gifted, talented, and creative learners from all walks of life;
- collaboration with all those who can enhance the educational experiences of gifted learners; and embedded throughout the standards,
- an emphasis on the critical importance of honoring and fostering diversity in gifted programs.

Research clearly has correlated the expertise of educators with excellence in student achievement—and inadequate professional performance with poor student achievement. The development and dissemination of national standards, both for programs and for personnel, may provide greater coherence for the systematic development of professional skill in gifted education. Within the context of standards, both individuals and systems will be able to measure current levels of proficiency and subsequently determine goals to enhance recommended skills, knowledge, and practices. As Robert Sternberg and Joseph Horvath aptly advocate, "If American public schools are to become centers of excellence, then their most important human resource (i.e., teachers) must be effectively developed" (p. 9).

Laurie J. Croft

See also Belin-Blank Center; Competencies for Teachers of Gifted; Council for Exceptional Children—The Association for the Gifted; Curriculum Models; Graduate Education; National Association for Gifted Children; Teachers of Gifted

Further Readings

Bangel, N. J., Enersen, D., Capobianco, B., & Moon, S. M. (2006). Professional development of preservice teachers: Teaching in the Super Saturday Program. *Journal for the Education of the Gifted, 29*(3), 339–361.

Council for Exceptional Children—The Association for the Gifted & National Association for Gifted Children. (2006). *CEC—NAGC initial knowledge & skill standards for gifted and talented education* (final version). Retrieved December 27, 2008, from http://www.gifted.uconn.edu/siegle/TAG/FinalInitialStandards4–14–06.pdf

Council of State Directors of Programs for the Gifted and National Association of Gifted Children. (2007). *The 2006–2007 state of the states in gifted education.* Washington, DC: National Association of Gifted Children.

Dall'Alba, G., & Sandberg, J. (2006). Unveiling professional development: A critical review of stage models. *Review of Educational Research, 76*(3), 383–412.

Dettmer, P., & Landrum, P. (1998). *Staff development: The key to effective gifted education programs.* Washington, DC: National Association for Gifted Children.

Gubbins, E. J. (2007). Professional development. In C. Callahan (Ed.), *Critical issues and practices in gifted education.* Washington, DC: National Association for Gifted Children.

National Association for Gifted Children. (1998). *Pre-K–Grade 12 standards.* Washington, DC: Author. Retrieved September 24, 2007, from http://www.nagc.org/index.aspx?id=546

Sparks, D., & Hirsh, S. (2000). *A national plan for improving professional development.* Oxford, OH: National Staff Development Council. Retrieved November 7, 2007, from http://www.nsdc.org/library/authors/NSDCPlan.cfm

Sternberg, R. J., & Horvath, J. A. (1995). A prototype view of expert teaching. *Educational Researcher, 24*(6), 9–17.

Wycoff, M., Nash, W. R., Juntune, J. E., & Mackay, L. (2003). Purposeful professional development [Electronic version]. *Gifted Child Today, 26*(4), 34.

Psychoanalytic Theories of Creativity

Psychoanalysis proposes two interrelated but distinctly different types of thinking. Sigmund Freud labeled these processes of thinking as primary and secondary to indicate chronological priority in that primary processes are assumed to be available at birth and secondary process occurs later as speech is developed. Secondary process can be conscious or unconscious and is characterized by logic and order. It functions in adapting to reality and relies heavily on verbal symbolism. The secondary process was seen by Freud as associated with the id and the reality principle. In contrast, primary process thought is characterized by visual imagery, symbolism, and displacement. It is largely unconscious and is the wellspring of the inner subjective world. Freud viewed the id and the pleasure principle to be associated with the primary process of thought. Primary process thinking is manifested through unconscious and conscious fantasy, daydreams, dreams while asleep, jokes, and artistic and creative expressions. Thus, psychoanalytic thought suggests that creativity springs from unconscious drives. Freud hypothesized that sensory data can be linked to words to be susceptible to conscious thought. However, others believe that in many creative processes, the sensory data become the form that is translated into a medium such as a painting or interpretative dance. Even if the medium is words, such as in the creation of poetry, the translation of the data is not used in the same way as in more traditional thinking. This entry discusses psychoanalytical theories and their application to understanding giftedness and creativity.

Various psychoanalytic schools of thought have different opinions on just how creativity comes from unconscious drives. Generally, psychoanalytic theory posits that early experiences with primary caregivers (typically mother and father) shape behavior extensively. Freud, for example, believed that creativity originates from conflicts resulting from wish fulfillment and biological drives. That is, in Freud's view, creativity is the sublimation of sexual drives.

Otto Rank initially embraced the Freudian view of the origin of creativity, but soon went beyond it. For Rank, creativity was at the center of personality development. That is, each person is an artist who fashions himself or herself. Thus, Rank saw the need for self-definition as universal for all human beings. It is from this self-definition that creative products can emerge.

Other psychoanalytic theories also recognize that in many creative activities there is a repetitive engagement with either a troubling (sexual or otherwise) or a soothing theme. For example, Edvard Munch's paintings are graphic representations of grief, depression, death, abandonment, and separation anxiety. His famous painting *The Scream* dramatically depicts the helplessness and hopelessness of severe separation panic. Munch suffered from depression and loneliness. His mother died when he was 5, and his childhood was plagued by personal illness. He was never able to commit to a relationship with a woman, and his life revolved around his painting. Munch expressed his conscious and unconscious pain through artistic expression, which is likely to have served as a defense mechanism.

Defense mechanisms are a means by which an attempt is made to protect the self from painful affect. Regression is a type of defense mechanism where the person returns to an earlier, more primitive form of mental activity. The ego uses regression in a variety of forms, such as some creative activities that are a more adaptive form of defense, that is, a controlled regression.

Art therapy is partially based on this idea. In addition, various types of assessment use art as a means for revealing aspects of the personality. An example is the use of drawings.

Creative inspiration is seen in psychoanalytic terms as sampling the depths of the unconscious, which is considered irrational though having some connection to reality. There is a risk of going "too far" in that the creative and psychotic modes are thought to be similar, according to psychoanalytic theory. Mental instability appears to occur in significantly higher rates among those who are highly creative than in the general population. However, there is a "chicken and egg" problem in that it is not clear which came first. Although most highly creative people are not mentally unstable and most mentally ill people are not highly creative, there seems to be a partial correlation. Ernest Hemingway and Virginia Woolf entered psychiatric hospitals and eventually committed suicide. Other creative individuals with turbulent lives include Georgia O'Keeffe, Jackson Pollock, and Sylvia Plath. Kay Jamison has written extensively about the link between mental illness, particularly bipolar spectrum disorder, and creativity.

Some types of personalities are also associated with creativity. For example, schizoid personality organization is a withdrawal into an internal world of imagination. Healthier schizoid people can convert this withdrawal tendency into works of art, scientific discoveries, and other types of creative endeavors.

Karen D. Multon

See also Creative Personality; Creative Process; Creativity and Mental Illness; Creativity Theories; Psychotherapy

Further Readings

Freud, S. (1971). The unconscious. In *The standard edition of the complete psychological works of Sigmund Freud* (Vol. 14, pp. 159–215). London: Hogarth Press. (Original work published 1915)

Jamison, K. R. (1993). *Touched with fire: Manic-depressive illness and the artistic temperament.* New York: Free Press.

Masterson, J. F. (1985). *The real self: A developmental, self, and object relations approach.* New York: Brunner/Mazel.

Milner, M. (1987). Psychoanalysis and art. In *The suppressed madness of sane men: Forty-four years of exploring psychoanalysis* (pp. 192–215). London: Tavistock. (Original work published 1956)

Rank, O. (1932). *Art and the artist.* New York: Knopf.

Rose, G. J. (1980). *The power of form: A psychoanalytic approach to aesthetic form.* New York: International Universities Press.

PSYCHOTHERAPY

Psychotherapy is a term originally meant to describe a method, closely related to psychoanalysis, for the treatment of patients with various forms of psychological illness. Today, the term has evolved to describe any method used by specifically trained therapists who use the relationship with their patients (sometimes referred as clients) and various techniques of verbal and nonverbal communication. Its purpose is to eliminate, change, or suppress psychological processes that interfere with psychological and personality development. Techniques may involve a combination of confrontation, clarification, interpretation, insight, advice, support, encouragement, guidance, and reassurance, as well as strategies for cognitive and behavioral modification.

There are no research studies that suggest standardized procedures or uniform approaches for the psychological treatment of gifted individuals. Nevertheless, clinicians are often faced with the need to help gifted individuals in psychological distress. A review of the limited psychotherapy literature may provide some useful insights.

A range of approaches is described. Cognitive and behavioral methods address conscious aspects of psychological difficulties. Psychoanalytic and psychodynamic methods address unconscious factors. One eclectic approach describes how both approaches are combined.

The literature includes a case report of the psychoanalysis of a young, gifted girl; clinical excerpts from the psychoanalysis of adolescents; a case report of the psychotherapy of a young boy. Other authors give general descriptions of the issues for both patient (or client) and therapist as they arise in psychotherapy. A recent unpublished manuscript gives a detailed description for how a traditional psychodynamic psychotherapeutic approach can be modified when treating exceptionally gifted adolescents and adults. The report also describes how their psychotherapy unfolded in predictable stages.

The Psychoanalysis of Gifted Children

Kerry Kelly's report is of the successful psychoanalytic treatment of a 4-1/2–year-old precocious child. Functioning at 2–3 years beyond her chronological age in many areas, she developed sleep difficulties, refused to read or write, and began to wet herself day and night. Her parents were psychologically deeply disturbed individuals unable to gratify each other in their marriage. Instead, focused on their daughter, they got great pleasure from her precocious accomplishments but were unable to nurture her more age-appropriate childish needs. The child's own self-criticism and high expectations caused feelings of intense inadequacy and poor self-esteem.

The clinical material is divided into four phases: oral, anal, phallic, and terminal. It provides an excellent example of how psychodynamic/psychoanalytic play psychotherapy works. In the sessions, the child acted out her unconsciously repressed wishes and conflicts and was allowed an opportunity to express her emotions freely. The patient used the therapist to act out different versions of important relationships while the therapist, at times, interpreted different levels of the unconscious meaning of these relationships as well as gratified some of the patient's basic needs. In this process, the patient found healthier solutions to painful conflicts—no longer needing symptoms to express herself. Of particular interest is a discussion of how psychoanalysis helped this young patient express her childish needs while simultaneously retaining her precocious level of functioning.

Psychotherapy of Children

William Dahlberg's case report is of the successful treatment of a profoundly gifted 9-year-old boy who entered psychotherapy because he had become suicidal and homicidal. Dahlberg's approach is a flexible one: Both parents, the patient, and his sister were treated individually. The parents were also seen as a couple.

The issues addressed in the psychotherapy were as follows:

- Parental misunderstanding of giftedness
- The patient's social isolation caused by
  a. Peer rejection
  b. An idiosyncratic, precocious intellect that permitted secretive, spiritual, and magical thinking
  c. An inadequate educational setting
  d. The parentification of the patient and his sister

The goals of the psychotherapy were to help the patient engage in age-appropriate social tasks and to find an appropriate setting for the full expression of his remarkable gifts.

The length of the psychotherapy, although not exactly specified, appears to have been relatively short term. Rather than terminate the psychotherapy, Dahlberg made himself available in an open-ended way so that all members of the family could and did request periodic consultations.

Psychoanalysis of Gifted Adolescents

Calvin Colarusso's case report is of the successful psychoanalysis of a twice-exceptional (gifted/learning disabled) 13-year-old boy. Clinical vignettes of major themes and conflicts are provided: The identification with a defective uncle, an oedipal conflict with the father, and learning as a homosexual submission because of passive identification with the father.

The patient was helped to explore the different levels of meaning of each of these conflicts and helped to express unconsciously repressed affects that accompanied each of these conflicts. Special mention is made of how frequently his underachievement and learning disabilities were used as unconscious mechanisms to express aggression toward his parents.

Leo S. Loomie, Victor H. Rosen, and Martin H. Stein's report on the Adolescent Gifted Project is perhaps the first report of a group examination of the creative process using full psychoanalytic clinical material. In what was described as a "clinical research project," a group of experienced analysts, led by Ernst Kris, met monthly to discuss the psychoanalytic treatment of "young people with creative gifts." Strict adherence to psychoanalytic principles was maintained for treatment parameters. Although labeled as "adolescent" gifted, the ages of patients ranged from 9 years to 36 years. They included a gifted sculptor, a writer, a painter, a composer, two mathematicians, a choreographer, and a dancer. The child had many musical, graphic, and literary talents.

The techniques of psychoanalysis were not described. The substance of the report concerns general observations that evolved from each patient's treatment:

- The nature of their unconscious conflicts;
- The special difficulties facing the analyst in attempting to understand highly specialized subjects;
- The process of sublimation in each of these patients did not involve complete repression of their instinctual material. At times, these gifted patients had easy access to it and this duality of partial repression and ready availability infused their creative work with remarkable vitality.

Psychotherapy of Gifted Adolescents and Adults

Diedra Lovecky describes five traits of giftedness that she encountered in her psychotherapy practice with gifted adults: divergent thinking, excitability, sensitivity, perceptiveness, and entelechy (the need for self-determination).

Her therapeutic work takes place in the cognitive, behavioral, and experiential realms. Cognitively, she helps clients learn strategies for working with these traits so they can be used more effectively. She helps them determine if and how to compromise in order to be effective in work and social situations.

Awareness of one's own limits and the limits of others is the key to higher levels of social connectedness and thus higher levels of self-esteem because isolation can be avoided.

Lovecky also describes certain difficulties that arise in the therapeutic process: Clients often have difficulty trusting the therapist and present ongoing challenges to therapeutic authority, expertise, and the basic premises of psychotherapy. Struggles also occur with the therapist when his or her empathy is perceived to have failed. She suggests setting short-term goals with clients when appropriate to avoid impatience with the therapy process.

Experientially, she suggests the use of shared intuition in the therapeutic process to help clients feel deeply appreciated for their special gifted traits.

Last, she describes psychotherapeutic work with gifted clients as an opportunity for the therapists to grow professionally as they develop new therapeutic techniques in working with these clients.

Jerome Oremland describes the successful psychoanalysis of a 20-year-old trombonist and composer. Only passing mention is made of Oremland's analytic techniques. Details are provided about how this man's talent as an instrumentalist and composer became enmeshed in conflicts about his biologically delayed adolescence and his deeply dysfunctional parents. Oremland discusses the specific conflicts that emerged in the different phases of this young man's treatment:

- His guilt when he discovered that he was more powerful than his alcoholic father.
- His disappointment when he realized that his mother cared more about his talent than about nurturing him.
- His continual struggle to limit his abilities so as to control his anger at his parents.
- His self-punishing behavior: He would permit his talent to gain him only admiration, but not intimacy.

As his delayed adolescence finally unfolded, he discovered that his talent also included an exceptional ability to compose. As a result, his self-esteem improved, which allowed him to develop intimate relationships.

Mary Elaine Jacobsen discusses how gifted adults can achieve what she describes as a "corrected personal history" by identifying as gifted, personality traits that were thought to be liabilities. She offers two case illustrations: A middle-aged man who achieved enormous success but felt increasingly empty and a professional woman whose extreme sensitivity and empathy for others' pain left her feeling depleted.

For Jacobsen, the psychotherapy process begins when the therapist examines patients' histories for gifted traits and unusual areas of interest and curiosity. In this early stage, the therapist may need to be intuitive, as adults rarely identify themselves as gifted. She also urges caution in this identification process so that client's chief complaints can be addressed first and to give clients an opportunity to work through negative connotations of giftedness. In addition, the client must be allowed to not explore giftedness even though it has been identified.

The working-through process requires a respect for the client's defenses. Appropriate but camouflaged stories of other clients can facilitate this process. Inquiring about unfulfilled purposes or dreams may enhance the therapeutic relationship.

Jacobsen suggests a number of other psychotherapeutic tasks:

- Follow a client's interests even though they may be complex or abstract.
- Be active.
- Avoid competing with the client.
- Be transparent about your own giftedness.
- Respect idiosyncrasies.
- Do not represent social norms.
- Confront self-destructive behavior.
- Give advice about enhancing energy, creativity, and self-realization.

Jacobsen also alerts therapists to expect a wide range of positive and negative feelings of their own, such as exhilaration, hurt, rejection, envy, and intimacy.

The most recent articles are by Jerald Grobman. His first report is about the psychodynamic psychotherapy of 15 adolescents—exceptionally gifted in arts, music, dance, writing, and science—who became underachievers primarily because of unresolved conflicts about their "inner experience of giftedness" rather than because of conflicts about school, work, peers, and family.

In each of his cases the psychotherapy unfolded in predictable ways. Once their presenting crisis was resolved and more practical concerns about school, peers, work, and family were successfully addressed, these patients began to accept that emotional conflict was a universal aspect of all growth and development. They also realized that having ambivalent feelings did not mean that they were weak or defective. These insights prepared them for deeper explorations about all the unconsciously conflicted aspects of their gifted endowment: their special sensitivities, sensibilities, the power of their curiosity and inner drive for mastery; their conviction about a grand vision and personal destiny to make valuable contributions as well as a feeling that they had become charismatic.

As these conflicts became conscious, open and frank discussion about them helped his gifted patients find more mature methods of conflict resolution, minimize underachievement, and integrate their giftedness with the other parts of their personality.

In an unpublished manuscript, Grobman presents an eclectic form of psychotherapy for exceptionally gifted individuals. His approach modifies traditional psychodynamic psychotherapy to include cognitive/behavioral techniques as well as "psychologically informed" mentoring, coaching, and advising. He discusses the issues that arise for patients in each stage of their psychotherapy and the corresponding challenges for therapists.

Crisis Intervention

In this stage an active, take-charge approach is required, and accurate symptom diagnosis ensures that medication will be used appropriately. Concrete stress management techniques are suggested. Taking an extensive history from all family members can establish a central dynamic formulation that will be used to guide the therapy.

Psychotherapy Proper

Beginning Phase

As patients settled into the early stages of psychotherapy, they began to resolve their guilt for being "given" more endowment than others. Later in this phase, psychologically informed mentoring, coaching, and advising helped each patient clarify a vision for his or her giftedness. A judicious use of therapeutic transparency was useful in this phase.

Middle Phase

In this phase, patients began to relinquish their exclusive need for autonomy and slowly came to accept the importance of relying on others for inspiration and guidance.

Late Phase

In this phase, patients identified their extracognitive capacities—inspiration, imagination, intuition, clairvoyance, curiosity, and special physical and aesthetic sensitivities and sensibilities—as the core of their exceptional giftedness. Experiencing the success of the therapist's intuitive interventions gave these patients permission to use their own extracognitive abilities in their therapy as well as in the outside world. They began to experience less conflict, less anxiety, and less need to deny, disavow, their exceptional giftedness or undermine it with underachievement and self-destruction.

Jerald Grobman

See also Adolescent, Gifted; Adult, Gifted; Career Counseling; Coaching; Precocity; Supporting Emotional Needs of Gifted; Underachievement

Further Readings

Colarusso, C. A. (1980). Psychoanalysis of a severe neurotic learning disturbance in a gifted adolescent boy. *Bulletin of the Menninger Clinic, 44*(6), 585–602.

Dahlberg, W. (1992). Brilliance—The childhood dilemma of unusual intellect. *Roeper Review, 15,* 7–10.

Grobman, J. (2006). Underachievement in exceptionally gifted adolescents and younger adults: A psychiatrist's view. *Journal of Secondary Gifted Education, 17*(4), 199–210.

Grobman, J. (2008). *A psychodynamic psychotherapy approach to treating underachievement in exceptionally and profoundly gifted adolescents and adults: A psychiatrist's experience* (unpublished manuscript). Retrieved January 20, 2009, from http://www.psychotherapyservicesforthegifted.com

Jacobsen, M. (1999). Arousing the sleeping giant: Giftedness in psychotherapy. *Roeper Review, 22*(1), 36–42.

Kelly, K. (1970). A precocious child in analysis. *Psychoanalytic Study of the Child, 25,* 122–145.

Lovecky, D. (1990). Warts and rainbows: Issues in psychotherapy of the gifted. *Advanced Development Journal, 2,* 107–125.

Oremland, J. D. (1975). An unexpected result of the analysis of a talented musician. *Psychoanalytic Study of the Child, 30,* 375–404.

Pull-Out Programs

See Acceleration/*A Nation Deceived;* Enrichment Triad Model

Purdue Model

Among models that have been developed to guide the development of educational programs for gifted and talented students, the *Purdue model* is one of the most flexible and powerful. It is a conceptual framework for both program and curriculum development in gifted education. The model is applicable to many settings and developmental levels; it develops creativity and academic talent, as well as motivational abilities such as persistence and long-term planning. Gifted students benefit from instruction based on the Purdue model, especially when they are grouped for instruction with other talented students who share their interests in advanced, interdisciplinary curriculum and self-directed learning.

The model was originally developed as a curriculum framework for undergraduate, university coursework. In 1978, John Feldhusen and Penny Britton Kolloff applied the model to gifted and talented education and developed the Program for Academic and Creative Enrichment (PACE), a pull-out enrichment program for talented elementary students. Later, the model was extended to secondary gifted students by Sidney Moon. This entry describes the Purdue model and provides examples of specific applications of the model in gifted education.

The Curriculum Model

The Purdue model offers a framework for the creation of curricular units in which each stage has a specific purpose intended to fit typical characteristics of academically gifted students and to develop their abilities further. The model focuses on creative and critical thinking skills, complex problem-solving abilities, and the ability to carry out independent projects. From a content area perspective, the model exposes students to advanced and interdisciplinary content on high interest topics such as inventors and inventions, architectural design, or forensic science. Each of the three stages has a specific process and content focus. During a particular unit of instruction, the stages build on each other, enabling students to become increasingly self-directed.

Stage I

In Stage I, learners participate in short-term creative and critical thinking activities that provide a motivating introduction to the unit topic. They also begin mastering content through experiences like reading, watching movies, taking field trips, and interviewing experts. In Stage I, most activities are teacher directed and relatively short term (5–30 minutes in length). Brainstorming ideas on some aspects of the unit topic represents a typical Stage I creative thinking activity. Another typical critical thinking activity might involve comparing two short, historical documents written from opposing points of view.

Stage II

Stage II focuses on complex problem solving; students are presented with challenging problems in the discipline(s) of study, which they solve using techniques similar to those used by professionals in those disciplines. Instructional content in Stage II is typically quite advanced—usually 2–3 years beyond the age of the students. Learners work in small groups on difficult problems that have been created by the instructor to develop specific understandings and skills. The teacher's role becomes more like a coach than a lecturer or director. The teacher encourages active thinking by asking probing questions and encouraging students to come up with new strategies and perspectives. Stage II activities take longer than Stage I activities to complete (1–5 hours). The types of problems utilized in this stage vary by discipline. In a mathematical problem-solving unit, students might be working on Model Eliciting Activities—problems where students are given data sets and must come up with a model that fits the data and solves a problem for a simulated client. In a creative writing unit, students might write specific types of poetry, such as haiku and sonnets.

Stage III

In the culminating stage of a Purdue model unit, students select an individual topic within the general unit, become an expert on their chosen topic utilizing tools of the discipline(s), and present what they have learned to others in a creative fashion. For example, in a unit on inventors for fourth and fiveth graders, students might study a particular inventor and produce an original invention to demonstrate what they have learned. A ninth-grade honors English class, studying the theme of identity, might produce Stage III projects that include original term papers on works of literature that address identity issues or original novelettes with an identity theme. In Stage III, students become self-directed, independent learners. The teacher's role is to connect students with resources that will facilitate their learning and to scaffold the development of independent research and presentation skills. Older students function much like professionals in Stage III.

The Programs

The Purdue model was designed to address the learning and social-emotional characteristics of gifted and talented students. Programs based on the model involve identifying academically talented students and grouping those students for Purdue model instruction. Goals of programs based on the model include (a) developing creative and critical thinking skills, (b) promoting positive social-emotional development by providing opportunities for interaction with other gifted students, (c) developing academic and motivational abilities by engaging students in challenging instruction, and (d) developing skills in self-directed learning through participation in independent study projects.

PACE is an example of a program for elementary students based on the model; it is the oldest application of the model in gifted education. PACE is a pull-out enrichment program for students in Grades 3–6. Creatively and intellectually gifted students meet with a trained enrichment teacher for a minimum of 2 hours a week and participate in units of instruction based on the Purdue model. PACE teachers emphasize the development of thinking, problem-solving, and independent learning skills. Other elementary applications of the model, especially those offered in university settings, focus on developing advanced content knowledge in specialized areas like electrical engineering or Incan art.

At the secondary level, the model has been used to develop interdisciplinary seminars, high school courses in particular subjects, and enrichment units for university-based summer programs. One of the most sophisticated secondary applications of the model was a science research class that required 2–3 years of high school to complete. In Stages I and II, talented science students worked with their teacher to develop skills in scientific research. The heart of the program, however, was an original, independent, scientific study conducted in collaboration with a professional research scientist. As a culminating activity, these talented students shared their findings with others via poster presentations at national conferences. Many students from this program went on to win national research awards for their work.

Sidney M. Moon

See also Academic Talent; Creative Productivity; Creativity in Engineering; Creativity in Science; Curriculum Models; Problem Solving; Saturday Programs; Thinking Skills

Further Readings

Kolloff, P. B., & Feldhusen, J. F. (1981, May/June). PACE (Program for Academic and Creative Enrichment): An application of the three-stage model. *Gifted Child Today, 5,* 47–50.

Moon, S. M. (1993). Using the Purdue three-stage model: Developing talent at the secondary level. *Journal of Secondary Gifted Education, 5*(2), 31–35.

Moon, S. M., Kolloff, P. B., Robinson, A., Dixon, F., & Feldhusen, J. F. (2008). The Purdue three-stage model. In J. S. Renzulli & J. Gubbins (Eds.), *Systems and models for developing programs for the gifted and talented.* Mansfield Center, CT: Creative Learning Press.

Raven's Progressive Matrices

Raven's Matrices are nonverbal measures for the assessment of general cognitive abilities. These measures, constructed by John Raven, have been available for a very long time. The Standard Progressive Matrices were first published in 1938 and are still a widely used psychometric instrument. Meanwhile, a further set of matrices has been compiled and presented as measures that apply to specific ability ranges or show other specific characteristics. The original measures were constructed as paper-and-pencil tests; at present they are also available as computerized tests. This entry describes the structure of Raven's Matrices, its uses, and research supporting its usefulness to educators of gifted students.

The individual matrices are incomplete patterns that have to be completed in such a way that a regular whole is achieved. Such a pattern is composed of nine parts, of which the last is missing. There is a set of eight alternatives from which the missing part has to be selected. The contents of the individual parts are simple figures. Comparing the simple figures of neighboring parts reveals the principles that guided the construction of the pattern. Completing a matrix problem requires the detection of these principles; the problem can easily be solved when the principles are known. The individual matrices are arranged in such a way that the degree of difficulty increases from one Matrices problem to the next Matrices problem. As a consequence, the cognitive demands on encoding and analyzing the patterns gradually increase. The principle of an increasing difficulty characterizes each one of the Matrices tests that are available.

Raven's Matrices have frequently been selected for the study of problem solving. Patricia Carpenter, Marcel Just, and Peter Shell showed that only a few simple principles are necessary for completing Matrices problems successfully, and also provided an explanation for the occurrence of individual differences in the ability to complete Matrices problems. According to the results of their research, the Matrices problems are especially demanding on working memory. Exceeding the capacity of one's working memory is the major source of failure in completing Matrices problems. Furthermore, the investigation of the demands characterizing Raven's Matrices reveals that completing Matrices problems means not only encoding and analyzing available information, but also the acquisition of a lot of external information. The more difficult the Matrices problems, the higher the demands on visual searches for helpful cues.

Charles Spearman's theory of intelligence provided the theoretical basis for the construction of Raven's Matrices. This theory distinguishes one general and a number of very specific factors of intelligence. According to this theory, two main abilities determine the general factor: the first one, which enables the clarity of thinking and the mastery of complexity, is denoted educative ability. The second one, which is essential for the storage and reproduction of information, is denoted reproductive ability. These abilities are assumed to be the true source of the performance stimulated by

Raven's Matrices and give reason for considering the Matrices as a measure representing the general factor (*g*). Despite theoretical and methodological advancements, even recent results support the notion that they are a good marker of *g*.

The model of the structure of intelligence has changed considerably since Spearman's time and, as a consequence, various modifications of the allocation of Raven's Matrices within the structure have been proposed. Raymond Cattell's model of intelligence, which emphasizes the difference between intelligence as biology-based ability and intelligence as culture-induced ability, suggests an association of Raven's Matrices and fluid intelligence because the influence of elaborate knowledge on the result of completing Matrices problems is limited. The basic processing routines stimulated by Raven's Matrices seem to demonstrate a dependence on biology-based properties. Therefore, it is no surprise that within the framework of Cattell's theory of intelligence, Raven's Matrices are also considered as the marker of fluid intelligence.

L. L. Thurstone's model is another formerly very influential model of the structure of intelligence. It assumes seven equally important abilities: word fluency, verbal comprehension, spatial visualization, number facility, associative memory, reasoning, and perceptual speed. In this model, the measures associated with the ability termed reasoning come closest to Raven's Matrices. As a consequence, this test can also be considered as a measure of reasoning. The demands of this test even seem to represent the rationale of reasoning especially well. Therefore, Raven's Matrices have frequently served as the example in studies of reasoning.

Because the modern hierarchical models of intelligence, for example, the *three stratum model of intelligence* and the *Cattell-Horn-Carroll model*, integrate some or all components of the previous models, there are different allocations for Raven's Matrices. In such models the component at the top level is associated with the *g* factor (G), fluid intelligence can be found at the subjacent level (F), and reasoning is assigned to the next level (R). Accordingly, in modern hierarchical models of intelligence, Raven's Matrices seem to be associated with a complex of abilities that range from the top level to the bottom level. Some justification for this GFR complex results from the observation that the corresponding abilities are especially closely related to each other, but other vertical associations of Carroll's three-stratum model of intelligence are not as close.

At present, Raven's Matrices are an accepted measure of fluid intelligence and reasoning. The popularity of this test results from its assumed independence of the testee's educational level because specific cultural knowledge is not necessary for completing the Matrices. Furthermore, because it is a nonverbal measure, it is considered culture fair. An interesting property of Raven's Matrices is that this test can be applied as a speed and power test. There is a high degree of objectivity because the influence of the experimenter is low. Various investigations have shown the Raven to have good to excellent psychometric properties; that is, it remains a valid and reliable measure of intellectual ability.

Karl Schweizer

See also Fluid and Crystallized Intelligence; Intelligence; Intelligence Testing; Problem Solving

Further Readings

Carpenter, P. A., Just, M. A., & Shell, P. (1990). What one intelligence test measures: A theoretical account of the processing in the Raven Progressive Matrices Test. *Psychological Review, 97,* 404–431.

Schweizer, K., Goldhammer, F., Rauch, W., & Moosbrugger, H. (2007). On the validity of Raven's Matrices Test: Does spatial ability contribute to performance? *Personality and Individual Differences, 43,* 1998–2010.

Reaction Time

The relationship between reaction time, or the speed at which individuals respond to sensory information, and intelligence has long been a topic of debate among researchers in the fields of education and psychology. Discussion on the topic dates back to Sir Francis Galton, who hypothesized that intelligence was a manifestation of efficiency in underlying motor and perceptual abilities. To test his hypothesis, he assessed the reaction times and sensory discrimination abilities of thousands of individuals in his laboratories. His work, though anecdotal and inconclusive, inspired American researcher James Cattell to incorporate speeded sensory discrimination tasks into his own research on intelligence. These tasks included purely physical reactions to stimuli, such as measuring how quickly subjects could respond to sound, and more mental tasks, such as measuring how quickly subjects could name colors as they were presented. Their combined work inspired a wave of interest in sensory/motor or psychophysical tests of intelligence that lasted until the early 20th century.

One of Cattell's own graduate students, Clark Wissler, is credited with striking a powerful blow to this line of inquiry. In 1901, Wissler published research suggesting little to no correlation between academic performance and reaction time. This finding was widely accepted, and helped to curtail interest in the topic of reaction time for a number of years. In the meantime, interest and support were on the rise for Alfred Binet's intelligence scales, further decreasing attention to chronometric measures of intelligence.

Since that time, however, various researchers have found support for a link between reaction time and cognitive ability, including Charles Spearman and Cyril Burt. Arthur Jensen, who has conducted numerous studies of reaction time, has been one of the best known proponents of this link. Jensen, like Galton, hypothesized speed and efficiency of underlying neurological mechanisms as key to the relationship between reaction time and intelligence. To study reaction time, Jensen created an apparatus that timed subjects' responses to various sized sets of stimuli. The apparatus had a home button on which the subject placed his or her finger, and buttons corresponding to eight different lights. When a light was activated on the panel, the subject moved his or her finger from the home button to the button associated with that light. Subjects were timed in their response to a single light, or asked to make a choice between multiple lights. The apparatus allowed Jensen to test the amount of time needed for removal of the finger from the home button (reaction time), and movement of the finger to the appropriate button (movement time). It also allowed measurement of differences in response time to one versus many stimuli. Subjects' times were correlated to their scores on intelligence tests.

Jensen found that reaction time was indeed significantly and negatively correlated with intelligence (i.e., faster response times equated to higher scores on IQ tests). Detailing his research, Jensen reports average correlations between reaction time and intelligence of −.19, −.21, −.24, and −.26, for no-choice, two-choice, four-choice, and eight-choice trials, respectively, on his apparatus. Other researchers have found average reaction time/intelligence correlations ranging from approximately −.22 for no-choice trials to −.40 for eight-choice trials. Most researchers accept the premise that reaction time increases as the complexity of the task increases; for example, people react more quickly to one light on Jensen's apparatus than to four lights. Some evidence has been found to suggest that more intelligent people require less additional time to respond to added information than do average individuals, creating a flatter slope to the linear relationship between reaction time and information. This finding, however, remains inconclusive and controversial.

A variety of other findings about reaction time and intelligence have emerged. Data suggest that reaction time increases as a function of age in childhood, and decreases as a function of age in adulthood. Gifted individuals have shown faster than average reaction times. There is research to indicate that men have faster reaction times than women; however, there is also research indicating the reverse. There is also research suggesting that the variability in an individual's reaction time across trials correlates with intelligence. In general, it is believed that variability correlates negatively with IQ.

One of the greatest sources of controversy in the discourse about reaction time and intelligence is research suggesting racial differences in mean reaction times. Many researchers, however, feel the evidence on this topic is inconclusive and potentially misleading. Moreover, interpretations of potential group differences in reaction time vary. Jensen has been strongly criticized for suggesting that group differences in reaction time may be genetically based. Other researchers have suggested that if intergroup differences in reaction time do indeed exist, they are likely due to environmental factors.

Also up for debate is the question of how information about reaction time may be usefully applied.

Some researchers suggest that there may be a place for reaction time tests in education, but others disagree. Proponents of the idea argue that reaction time tests are fast, simple, and content free—and thus may be more appropriate measures of intelligence than the lengthy psychometric tests widely used today. Others argue that reaction time measures are insufficiently reliable to replace current IQ testing methods. Moreover, many believe that speed of reaction is a necessary, but not sufficient, factor in intelligence. Advocates of this view note that although reaction time increases only up to between age 11 and 14, intellectual ability continues to improve. According to these individuals, measures of reaction time cannot capture the complexity of human intelligence and thus are inappropriate for assessing IQ.

Erin Sullivan

See also Intelligence; Intelligence Testing; Intelligence Theories

Further Readings

Cattell, J. M. (1890). Mental tests and measurements. *Mind, 15,* 373–380.

Deary, I. J. (1994). Sensory discrimination and intelligence: Postmortem or resurrection? *American Journal of Psychology, 107,* 95–115.

Jensen, A. R. (1987). Individual differences in the Hick paradigm. In P. A. Vernon (Ed.), *Speed of information processing and intelligence*. Norwood, NJ: Ablex.

Sheppard, L. D., & Vernon, P. A. (2008). Intelligence and speed of information processing: A review of 50 years of research. *Personality and Individual Differences, 44,* 535–551.

Regular Classroom

In contrast to the programs of the 1980s where gifted learners were pulled out of their classrooms to receive more advanced instruction, the focus shifted during the 1990s when fewer full-time and pull-out programs were implemented in favor of adjustments made in the regular classroom. The philosophy behind these types of programming options was that students could gain the benefit of a more challenging education without being pulled out. The strategies for teaching high-ability learners in the regular classroom drew on ideas and models that had existed in the field of gifted education for decades, and the move to present these ideas in a more accessible, user-friendly way better equipped some classroom teachers to meet the needs of their own gifted students. A volume of research exists that suggests that many classroom teachers do not know how to meet the needs of these students. Even when and if they have received professional development, many just do not find the time and resources to modify instruction and curriculum for gifted students in the regular classroom. Some teachers are effective in this task, but others feel the need to attend first and foremost to students who are below grade level in their achievement before any modification occurs in the curriculum for gifted students.

Curriculum Adjustment for Gifted Students

Many efforts have been offered during the past few decades to help classroom teachers adjust curriculum for gifted and talented students in the regular classroom. One of the first efforts was the creation of the Compactor Form, the core of curriculum compacting, developed by Joseph Renzulli and Linda Smith in 1978, that focused on having classroom teachers adjust regular curriculum in the classroom to challenge gifted students. In this respect, Beverly Parke was one of the first authors to write a book, in 1989, on challenging gifted students in the regular classroom. Previously, Joseph Renzulli had suggested the use of enrichment and independent study both in gifted programs and in the regular classroom in his work on the enrichment triad in 1977. Susan Winebrenner helped to make teaching the gifted in the regular classroom a more workable process through clearly articulated strategies for adjusting curriculum content, assessing student needs, and addressing special abilities and interests. Teachers who have little expertise in gifted education can implement these strategies with training. All students have the opportunity to prove their mastery in specific skills or knowledge areas. Learning contracts are key to the process of planning alternative trajectories for gifted students who need a different pace and level of instruction.

Joan Smutny, Sally Walker, and Elizabeth Meckstroth pursued similar practices for addressing the learning needs of *young* gifted children in kindergarten through the third grade classroom. They focused on the unique learning needs and circumstances of younger gifted children (e.g., *asynchronous development,* where a child's cognitive, physical, emotional, and social growth evolve at different rates), and provided a range of strategies teachers can use to create more appropriate educational experiences. Central to their ideas on adjusting the curriculum for the gifted is the importance of creativity as the most accessible resource for young students to draw upon in their earliest years of learning.

The push to teach the gifted in the regular classroom, occurring in the 1990s, contributed to current research and writing on differentiated instruction and the work of Carol Tomlinson. The strategies of all of these contributors have helped many classroom teachers to integrate this type of instruction into their classrooms. The goal is always to respond to the pace, level, and style of gifted children's learning ability—to release them from any lock-step structure that suppresses their natural gifts. At its most basic, the process involves the following steps:

- A pretest or other form of assessment to determine a child's level of mastery
- The planning of alternative learning in place of content already learned through contracts with the students that stipulate goals, activities, and time lines
- Follow-up assessment to evaluate progress and plan future adjustments

Strategies

The most effective strategies for teaching gifted students create flexibility in pacing and the possibility of in-depth learning that they need in order to learn in the regular classroom.

Curriculum Compacting

Compacting, a now familiar strategy developed by Renzulli, Smith, and Reis for differentiating the curriculum, enables gifted children to learn required content more quickly and eliminate review of what they already know through some form of preassessment. After proving mastery in some area, children either advance to more challenging content sequentially or divert from the path to investigate a related issue or idea.

Tiered Instruction

This strategy works well in mixed-ability classrooms where all students are working within the same unit. It enables teachers to accommodate gifted students by modifying the level (higher-level thinking, more difficult concepts) and pace (of reading, research). In a unit on the ecology of local forest preserves, for example, gifted students could research the introduction of the Asian long-horned beetle into the United States, analyze its impact on local flora and fauna, and evaluate current plans to eradicate it.

Clustering

James and Chen-Lin Kulik in 1991 published a study documenting the social-emotional and academic benefits experienced by gifted students in being grouped with gifted peers while working on assignments and projects. The most common form of grouping for gifted learners today is the *cluster group,* which pools advanced students from more than one class in a grade and keeps them together for the whole year.

Mentoring

A gifted child works with a mentor who can provide a much more advanced and rapid pace of instruction in a particular area of interest. Highly gifted, culturally diverse, disadvantaged, gifted girls and other underserved populations are ideal candidates for this option because the mentor can respond more specifically to their strengths, weaknesses, interests, and learning styles.

Independent Study

Most gifted children prefer independent study because it affords greater flexibility and independence than most other options. Suggested as a part of the enrichment triad in 1977, this option has become a mainstay of gifted programs. Often the format associated with mentoring and, to an extent, compacting, it helps gifted students create a systematic approach to exploring an interest by establishing realistic goals and learning objectives, and creating a time line and criteria for the successful completion of a project.

Creativity and the Arts

As a result of the early research of J. P. Guilford and E. Paul Torrance and of the models of creative thinking that have emerged since, the following processes have become commonly known in the schools and are applicable to gifted learners: *fluency* (generating many ideas); *flexibility* (creating different thought patterns); *originality* (producing unique, unexpected ideas); *elaboration* (extending ideas, embellishing, implementing ideas); *transformation* (changing/adapting an idea or solution into a different one); and *evaluation* (assessing the viability and usefulness of an idea). By using questioning techniques and creating open-ended, divergent-thinking assignments, teachers can accommodate the ability of their gifted learners to make discoveries and originate.

The net result of these strategies is that some gifted students can attend a regular classroom that serves their abilities and interests. Yet research also suggests that some teachers do not adequately meet the needs of gifted children in regular classrooms due to a lack of training, time, and resources, and so other services and levels of intervention may be necessary to challenge these students.

Joan Franklin Smutny

See also Differentiation; Effective Programs; Individualized Instruction; Talent Development

Further Readings

Renzulli, J. S. (1977). *The enrichment triad model.* Wethersfield, CT: Creative Learning Press.

Renzulli, J. S., & Smith, L. H. (1978). *The compactor.* Mansfield Center, CT: Creative Learning Press.

Smutny, J. F., Walker, S. Y., & Meckstroth, E. A. (1997). *Teaching young gifted children in the regular classroom.* Minneapolis, MN: Free Spirit Publishing.

Winebrenner, S. (1992). *Teaching gifted kids in the regular classroom.* Minneapolis, MN: Free Spirit Publishing.

Relationship of Creativity to Intelligence

The traditional approach to creativity can be characterized as the four-Ps approach, namely studying the *person,* the *process,* the *product,* and the *productive* conditions (or environmental *press*). In addition, there are a number of confluence theories of creativity, such as the *investment theory* of Robert Sternberg and Todd Lubart, as well as the *systems theory* of Mihaly Csikszentmihalyi. In these theories the general intelligence (*g*) of a person is a necessary component but not sufficient for Creativity (C) to manifest. In other words, a person with a high IQ would not necessarily have to be creative in work. Here Creativity ("Big C") is domain specific, and a creative product is one that causes a significant shift within a specialized domain of knowledge.

In the general literature on creativity, numerous definitions can be found. Anna Craft uses the term *lifewide creativity* to describe the numerous contexts of day-to-day life in which the phenomenon of creativity (C) manifests. Other researchers have described creativity as a natural survival or adaptive response of humans in an ever-changing environment. Ruth Richardson uses the term *everyday creativity* ("little c") to describe such activities as improvising on a recipe. It is generally accepted that works of extraordinary creativity can be judged only by experts within a specific domain of knowledge. For instance, Andrew Wiles's proof of Fermat's Last Theorem could be judged by only a handful of mathematicians within a very specific subdomain of number theory. More specifically, in the realm of educational psychology, one can also find a variety of definitions of creativity, such as the use of ordinary cognitive processes that result in original and extraordinary products. Sternberg and Lubart define creativity as the ability to produce unexpected original work that is useful and adaptive. Other definitions usually impose the requirement of novelty, innovation, or unusualness of a response to a given problem. Numerous confluence theories of creativity define creativity as a convergence of knowledge, ability, thinking style, motivational, and environmental variables in the evolution of domain-specific ideas resulting in a creative outcome. Most recently, Jonathan Plucker and Ronald Beghetto offered an empirical definition of creativity based on a survey and synthesis of numerous empirical studies in the field. They defined creativity as "the interplay between ability and process by which an individual or group produces an outcome or product that is both novel and useful as defined within some social context" (2004, p. 156).

Modern theories of intelligence can be traced back to the work of Francis Galton and Charles Spearman, who took the simplistic view that intelligence can be measured via a simple numerical score decomposable into general and specific components. Most modern intelligence tests measure components such as verbal ability, numerical ability, memory, spatial ability, and both general and deductive reasoning abilities. Psychometric approaches, however, such as those used to measure intelligence, have also been used to measure creativity. This entails quantifying the notion of creativity with the aid of paper-and-pencil tasks. An example of this would be the Torrance Tests of Creative Thinking developed by Paul Torrance, which are used by many gifted programs in middle and high schools to identify students who are gifted/creative. This test consists of several verbal and figural tasks that call for problem-solving skills and divergent thinking. The test is scored for fluency, flexibility, originality (the statistical rarity of a response), and elaboration. Sternberg claims that there are positive and negative sides to the psychometric approach of measuring creativity. On the positive side, these tests allow for research with noneminent people, are easy to administer, and are scored objectively. The negative side is that numerical scores fail to capture the concept of creativity because they are based on brief paper-and-pencil tests. Sternberg calls for use of more significant productions such as writing samples, drawings, and the like, to be evaluated subjectively by a panel of experts instead of simply relying on a numerical measure.

Sternberg's triarchic view of giftedness suggests that gifted individuals possess a varying blend of analytic, synthetic (creative), and practical giftedness. If we take any academic field, such as mathematics or science, as an example, then researchers within that field who are productive in their areas of research all have high levels of analytic and practical abilities. One can assume that all researchers within a given field have high levels of intelligence just by the evidence that they have succeeded academically. Practical abilities manifest in choosing researchable questions/problems that are accessible and publishable. Using the field of mathematics as a case study, Bharath Sriraman argues that truly creative individuals have much higher levels of synthetic abilities in comparison to the analytic and practical abilities in that their work opens up new research vistas for others in the field.

This leads to the question, What is the relationship between creativity and intelligence? The question is as yet unanswered in the domain of psychology. James Kaufman and John Baer ask whether these two constructs are "(a) two partially overlapping sets of abilities that share some common ground, (b) two sets of abilities that are distinct only in the sense of one being a subset of the other, or (c) a single set of abilities that have come to be known by different terms" (2004, p. 13).

There is general agreement that there is definitely an overlap between the constructs of creativity and intelligence. It is impossible to be creative without being intelligent; however, one can be intelligent but not necessarily Creative ("Big C").

Bharath Sriraman and Yasemin Kýymaz

See also Creativity Assessment; Creativity Theories; Flow; Fluid and Crystallized Intelligence; General Creativity; Intelligence Theories

Further Readings

Craft, A. (2002). *Creativity in the early years: A lifewide foundation.* London: Continuum.

Craft, A. (2003). The limits to creativity in education: Dilemmas for the educator. *British Journal of Educational Studies, 51*(2), 113–127.

Csikszentmihalyi, M. (1996). *Creativity: Flow and the psychology of discovery and invention.* New York: HarperCollins.

Gardner, H. (1983). *Frames of mind: The theory of multiple intelligences.* New York: Basic Books.

Kaufman, J., & Baer, J. (2004). Hawking's haiku, Madonna's math: Why it is hard to be creative in every room of the house. In R. J. Sternberg, E. L. Grigorenko, & J. L. Singer (Eds.), *Creativity: From potential to realization.* Washington, DC: American Psychological Association.

Plucker, J., & Beghetto, R. A. (2004). Why creativity is domain general, why it looks domain specific, and why the distinction does not matter. In R. J. Sternberg, E. L. Grigorenko, & J. L. Singer (Eds.), *Creativity: From potential to realization* (pp. 153–168). Washington, DC: American Psychological Association.

Richards, R. (1993). Eminent and everyday creativity. *Psychological Inquiry, 4*(3), 212–217.

Sriraman, B. (2005). Are mathematical giftedness and mathematical creativity synonyms? A theoretical analysis of constructs. *Journal of Secondary Gifted Education, 17*(1), 20–36.

Sternberg, R. J. (Ed.). (1999). *Handbook of creativity.* New York: Cambridge University Press.

Sternberg, R. J., Grigorenko, E. L., & Singer, J. L. (Eds.). (2004). *Creativity: From potential to realization.* Washington, DC: American Psychological Association.

Weisberg, R. W. (2006). *Creativity: Understanding innovation in problem solving, science, invention, and arts.* Hoboken, NJ: Wiley.

Research, Qualitative

Educational research is a wide-ranging field. The most common categorizations of research are quantitative and qualitative research. Both share the goal of increasing our understanding of educational policy, practices, and persons by engaging in systematic inquiry. Beyond this global statement, there are significant differences.

Three conventional notions about research are that methods of gathering, analyzing, and reporting data are equated with defining research; that research looks the same in all instances; and that research requires using numbers. These overly simplistic notions influence people to regard qualitative research as not being "true" research because the methods look different, are changeable, are situation specific, and rarely use numbers.

Differences Between Qualitative and Quantitative Research

Qualitative research, like quantitative research, its better known relative, has its own defining characteristics. Each genre of research originates from a scholarly tradition. Quantitative research (QR) grows from the natural sciences and agriculture, and qualitative research (QLR) from the social science and humanities.

In essence, the QLR tradition seeks to understand the perspective of participants in particular social and cultural contexts by discovering the meanings held by those persons; the QR traditions strive to produce highly generalizable statements of behavior and to predict future actions in situations. The two traditions take different stances in regard to data gathering, analysis, and validity. QR is very concerned with controlled data gathering using standardized measurement applied to persons who are representative of the population. Randomization is the tool for doing that, and distance between participants and researcher is carefully controlled. Objectivity is the global term summarizing that tradition. Findings are presented as statements of probability about the likelihood that, under certain conditions, something would not happen by chance.

In qualitative research, on the other hand, the investigator is at the center of the process as the data gatherer, analyzer, and interpreter of the findings. QLR believes subjectivity is always present and cannot be separated from the participants, situation, or researcher. Thus, the investigator's task is to manage bias so that participants' voices are revealed. A basic premise is that meaning is negotiated and constructed by people in social situations. Selection of participants is based on what they can reveal about the interactions going on in the situation. Description is important, but interpretation is the investigator's primary task. Claims that findings in one context are predictive of other situations are inappropriate. Each situation is unique. The results are presented so that the participants can understand and use the information.

Attributes of Qualitative Research

A list of attributes of qualitative research follows:

Insider perspective

Participant selection

Voice

Data collection—derivation of themes and discovery of process

Disclosure

Rich description (context, persons)

Interpretation

Alternate explanations-discrepant case

Triangulation/multiple sources, methods

Credibility and trustworthiness

Theory

The attributes of qualitative research in conjunction with the broad statements about QR and QLR underscore the outlines of the genre. Each is discussed below.

Insider Perspective

Describing a situation and its participants is a worthy but insufficient outcome of QLR. The goal is to capture the perspective of persons who live/work in a particular context. The meaningfulness of actions and words for insiders is not the same as for outsiders. For example, in a classroom, children can be heard saying, "I hate you" or "You loser"; yet looking inside reveals that the first means "I love you" and the second, "I notice and like you."

Participant Selection

A researcher's goal is to select informants who have data relevant to the phenomenon being investigated. Participant selection refers to persons as well as settings or context because meaning comes out of context. QLR prefers the use of a "purposive sample" or "theoretically relevant sample" and avoids convenience samples. Convenience and purpose may converge, but the scholarly reason for selection should trump the logistical reason. QLR researchers must provide enough information so the reader can understand the composition of the sample, the context, and the relevance to the research question.

Data Collection

Observing a phenomenon is at the center of every scientific inquiry, no matter the tradition. Three procedures are used in various forms of QLR: interviewing, observing, and collecting artifacts. The interviews are unstructured and open-ended. The observations are running narratives of the situation. The artifacts are papers, products, announcements, objects, and so forth, produced in accordance with the situation.

Data Analysis

The process is inductive, not deductive. Careful and repeated reading of transcripts, observation reports, and artifacts bounded by the research question reveal patterns of meaning in behavior and of relationship. These patterns, often called themes, are induced from the data, and interpretive assertions are made about the meaning and processes going on in the context. The idea is to discover what is happening beneath the surface of a particular situation.

Disclosure

The researcher is the primary research instrument. Data are collected and analyzed, filtered through the mind of the inquirer. The researcher has the obligation to report prior knowledge or assumptions about the phenomenon. The ideal is to "unpack" one's subjectivity so that the findings are happening in the situation and are not the invention of the investigator. Supplying the reader with information about what one brings into the situation, as well as the process used to arrive at a finding, allows the reader to judge the worth of the findings.

Interpretation

The outcome of any study is the interpretation of what is happening in that context with those participants. Interpretation goes beyond description and moves toward the discovery and uncovering of meanings beneath the surface of interactions. Following the elements described earlier validates the QLR process.

Voice

Revealing the voices of participants is a goal. Unearthing the tacit meanings of persons in context accomplishes this goal. The process of interacting is made apparent for the persons and others to hear. The actual meanings are created by the actors in the situation.

Rich Description

Situations are replete with subtle multiple variations and interpretations. Rich description gives the reader enough detail to enter the world of the participants, and the participants themselves would recognize the place.

Triangulation

Much like the captain of a ship at sea, the qualitative researcher uses data from multiple sources (e.g., people, newspapers, informal surveys) and multiple methods (e.g., interviews, videos, observations, artifacts) to locate the meaning in the situation. The more the interpretation can be anchored in the situation, the more the investigator validates his work.

Alternate Explanations

The researcher has an obligation to explore alternate explanations for what is uncovered. A recommended procedure is to look for a discrepant case or instance that does not match the findings and use that as a basis for reexamining the findings. Studies that offer no alternative explanation for findings and descriptions of how discrepancies were handled by the investigator are less valuable.

Credibility and Trustworthiness

Reliability and validity are parallel terms used in QR. The QLR researcher must tell the story of the participants and the situation in a manner that conveys credibility and trustworthiness. Credibility is enhanced by rich description, amount of time observing, voices of the participants, disclosure, and discrepant cases. Trustworthiness is providing information so that the reader can track how the interpretation was made. This can be done by establishing an audit trail; obtaining feedback from participants, called member checking; and asking others to examine the study.

Theory

Qualitative research is an inductive process. Theory that is produced is generally called "grounded theory" because it is derived from the soil of the situation. Theories of this type make sense to the participants, use language that is accessible, and provide information that they might use to change the situation should they wish to do so.

Given these descriptors, QLR is multifaceted and has the potential for taking multiple forms. Underlying all the potential variations is a habit of mind that seeks to study persons in social life in order to uncover meaning, reveal their voices, and discover the hidden processes of those situations.

Phenomenology, Ethnography, and Evaluation Research

Most of the attributes just enumerated are found in the research literature on gifted and creative studies. Within QLR, smaller groups of scholars implement studies in similar ways, yet not the same way as other groups. To illustrate the differences, generic studies three kinds of QLR—phenomenology, ethnography, and evaluation research—are presented. Notice that the interview or the observation or the artifact collection takes a different turn in each type.

Interviewing is used alone or with other techniques in many studies. Interviewing in QLR is open-ended and loosely structured. In phenomenological research the interview question are the most open, for example, What sticks out in your mind about (state the topic)? In an ethnography, the interview question might be, Take me through your typical day. In evaluation, the question is formulated on the basis of what objectives mean to various stakeholders. The question might be, How did you determine who should be assigned to independent study groups?

Observation takes different forms, also. In phenomenology, observation is infrequent and used to understand the participant. In ethnography, observation is at the heart of a study. Over a prolonged period the researcher inserts him- or herself into the context to experience directly what is happening and to develop interview questions relevant to the situation. In evaluation research, the observation is to see if what has been claimed to be going on is, and the manner in which it is executed.

Artifact collection is similar in all these forms. The goal is to collect information that illuminates the situation and participants. Examples of items might be birth certificates, knives, dishes, letters, videos, tape recordings, records, newspapers, and books.

Giftedness and Creativity Research

Qualitative inquiry has a history in gifted education. QLR has grown in popularity since 1990, although it is less frequently published than QR. The study of creativity and giftedness is dominated by psychologists and educational psychologists who have been trained in quantitative techniques and philosophy. Those fields publish fewer qualitative studies than quantitative studies. There is nevertheless a growing appreciation in the field of gifted education and the psychology of creativity for qualitative methodology as a way of enhancing the understanding of the perspective of gifted and creative individuals and the people who nurture and teach them.

A wide array of topics and research questions has been studied, including individuals, classrooms, programs, families, abilities, attitudes, and talents. The results have produced new theories and deeper understanding of the meaning of concepts dear to gifted education, like challenge, social systems in schools, and the experience of being gifted. The majority of the studies are case studies.

A relatively small handful of researchers have emerged who consistently use the genre. A kind of educational research has emerged called mixed methodology. Studies of this type employ quantitative and qualitative methods to answer the research question. It is debatable just how mixed the studies really are because most examples emphasize the quantitative research component over the qualitative component. Less than a handful use the methods in an equivalent manner, taking advantage of the strengths of each genre to understand a phenomenon. This situation is not unique to gifted and creative research. Furthermore, disagreement about the importance and utility of qualitative research is evident in gifted education. Although QLR is recognized as a form of research that can lead to new understandings, it is sometimes viewed as less valuable, being more suitable for discovering phenomena that could be better studied using quantitative research. Federal funding agencies favor this view.

Laurence J. Coleman

See also Action Research; National Research Center on the Gifted and Talented; Research, Quantitative; Twice Exceptional; Underrepresentation

Further Readings

Coleman, L. J. (2005.) *Nurturing talent in high school: Life in the fast lane.* New York: Teachers College Press.

Coleman, L. J., Guo, A., & Dabbs, C. (2007). The state of qualitative research in gifted education as published in American journals: An analysis and critique. *Gifted Child Quarterly, 51,* 51–63.

Denzin, N., & Lincoln, Y. (Eds.). (2000). *Handbook of qualitative research.* Thousand Oaks, CA: Sage.

Diezmann, C. M., & Watters, J. J. (2001). The collaboration of mathematically gifted students on challenging tasks. *Journal for the Education of the Gifted, 25*(1), 7–31.

Hertzog, N. B. (1997). Open-ended activities and their role in maintaining challenge. *Journal for the Education of the Gifted, 21*(1), 54–81.

Koro-Ljungberg, M. (2002). Constructions of high academic achievement through analysis of critical events. *Gifted Child Quarterly, 46*(3), 209–223.

Vespi, L., & Yewchuk, C. (1992). A phenomenological study of the social/emotional characteristics of gifted learning disabled children. *Journal for the Education of the Gifted, 16*(1), 55–72.

Research, Quantitative

How do gifted, creative, or talented children and adults differ from those not so identified? What instructional, identification, or parenting strategies are most effective with gifted, creative, and talented people? These are examples of basic research questions underlying the fields of giftedness, creativity, and talent. Quantitative research methods are required to answer these and derivative research questions; and finding these answers is imperative for the development of gifted education and related areas of study.

Quantitative research, often equated with scientific research, is a mode of controlled inquiry that reduces bias and advances knowledge. Quantitative research is based on the philosophical paradigm of positivism, or more accurately, postpositivism. Postpositivism holds that truth exists although it cannot be fully known, and that we strive for probabilistic statements instead of absolute statements. As such, quantitative research relies heavily on statistical analyses to arrive at probabilistic statements. Test theory, with its concepts of true scores, error, reliability, and validity also comes from this same philosophical position.

Quantitative Versus Qualitative Research

Hans Reichenbach identified two research contexts: the context of *discovery* and the context of *verification*. Qualitative research is best suited for the context of discovery or exploration. In contrast, quantitative research is best suited for the context of verification, or for testing whether things are related to one another (correlational research) or differ from one another (experimental research). Research accumulates slowly, often not being applicable to educational or other environments until several confirmatory studies have been done. Systematic reviews of an area provide the analysis and synthesis that often build a needed link between research and practice. The quantitative review procedure of meta-analysis summarizes effect sizes from a number of quantitative studies to provide an overall effect size that allows conclusions about an intervention or relationship. However, a meta-analysis can be only as good as the separate studies included in the analysis. Understanding and evaluating the research in giftedness, talent, and creativity are difficult tasks. Carolyn Callahan and Tonya Moon provide a useful guide for accomplishing this task.

Research on Giftedness, Creativity, and Talent

Reva Friedman-Nimz, Brenna O'Brien, and Bruce Frey studied publication trends related to the topics of gifted, creativity, talent, gifted and disabled, and gifted and disadvantaged by decade from the 1960s through the 1990s. They reported a major decrease in the percentage of quantitative research articles in educational, psychological, and special education journals over these decades (1960s = 62.3%, 1990s = 18.1%). Over this same period they observed a small increase in the percentage of qualitative research articles (from 14% to 20.5%). The major increase during this period was in the percentage of program description articles (1960s = 2.6%, 1990s = 37.8%). Thus, the issue is less whether one research paradigm (i.e., quantitative or qualitative) is replacing another, but more whether research is being supplanted by descriptions of untested procedures and programs. In 1990, Kyle Carter and H. Lee Swanson published an article examining the most frequently cited gifted journal articles since the Marland Report of 1972. They concluded from their review that information on gifted education was commonly unsupported by research and theory. Contributing to this problem is the lack of consensus on definitions and the tendency to develop new models rather that validate and refine existing models.

Notable exceptions to these trends do exist. Most of what is known, as documented by published research about giftedness, talent, and creativity, is the result of quantitative research. Francis Galton's effort to operationalize genius subsequently lead to his detailed description of five interlocking propositions: (a) A measure of an individual's genius can be derived from his or her degree of eminence; (b) on this eminence rests his or her reputation; (c) that this reputation, although based on contemporary critical opinion, is long term in character; (d) that critical opinion is focused on a real, extensively acknowledged achievement; and (e) that such achievement is the product of natural abilities that are made up of a blend of intellect and disposition (or what is now termed intelligence and personality), which provided a beginning point for quantitative research. The empirical studies that were spawned by this theory of genius provide an interesting picture of early research in giftedness. Subsequently, Lewis Terman and his longitudinal *Genetic Studies of Genius* also focused on the results of quantitative data analysis over time.

Besides seeking to understand genius and its dimensions, other important research areas that have directly impacted the directions taken by the fields of giftedness, creativity, and talent include the studies on creativity (e.g., Torrance); the meta-analyses of ability grouping conducted by James A. Kulik, Chen-Lin C. Kulik, and Karen Rogers; Ann Robinson's investigations of the effects of cooperative learning with gifted students; Nicholas Colangelo, Susan Assouline, and Miraca Gross's work on the effects of acceleration; Joseph Renzulli's *schoolwide enrichment model* (SEM); Joyce VanTassel-Baska's *integrated curriculum model;* and Julian

Stanley's Study of Precocious Youth (SMPY), which led to the *talent search model* at Johns Hopkins University and was subsequently expanded to other sites nationally.

Quantitative research indicates that creativity (e.g., divergent thinking, creative problem solving, creative performance, and creative attitude/behavior) can be enhanced through well-planned programs and techniques, such as grouping programs. Robinson's review of quantitative studies on cooperative learning points out continuing concerns with using heterogeneous cooperative learning groups with gifted students. Colangelo, Assouline, and Gross's important national report, *A Nation Deceived: How Schools Hold Back America's Brightest Students,* provides empirical support for grade-based acceleration, subject-based acceleration, early entrance into kindergarten and college, as well as other forms of acceleration. The SEM has been widely researched, resulting in revision and refinement of the model. These research studies have demonstrated that the SEM can be used in a variety of school settings and with diverse students, including high-ability students. Likewise, VanTassel-Baska provides evaluation research that supports use of the ICM in science and language arts courses. The SMPY made use of the *diagnostic testing–prescriptive instruction (DT–PI) model.* Used primarily in mathematics classes, the DT–PI model includes pretesting students to determine what they already know and what the next step in the learning process is. Class time is spent on concepts not yet mastered rather than on concepts already understood. Students take a posttest after studying a topic in order to demonstrate mastery. Research supports great success for this model. Participation in talent search programs through numerous universities has involved millions of students since 1972.

Challenges

Quantitative research models have become increasingly complex and sophisticated. Multivariate models recognize the complexity of the phenomena being studied. Studies that simply correlate two variables, while ignoring many other related variables, do little to help us understand gifted, talented, or creative children and adults. But, more complex statistical procedures (e.g., factor analysis, path analysis, structural equation modeling) require (a) researchers with advanced statistical skills, (b) members of editorial boards with advanced statistical skills, and (c) large samples.

In general, many graduates of educational psychology and related programs are well grounded in statistics and quantitative research methods. Graduates of educational leadership, curriculum, foundations of education, and other education-focused programs often emphasize qualitative research methods, sometimes with little background in statistics. Further, most of the major conventions in gifted studies/gifted education (e.g., National Association for Gifted Children, Council for Exceptional Children) are heavily attended by classroom teachers who have no quantitative research training beyond the normal curve and measures of central tendency and variability. Although a select few in the field who are committed to research attend the Special Interest Group (SIG) on Giftedness and Talent at the American Educational Research Association convention or the Wallace Symposium at the University of Iowa, the majority of those interested in gifted education are classroom teachers. As a consequence, because of the lack of advanced training in quantitative methods by bachelor's, master's, and doctoral graduates involved in gifted studies, the field is hampered by a lack of common research vocabulary and skill set.

Manuscripts using complex statistical procedures create problems for editors and editorial boards. Editors and editorial boards are typically established scholars, many of whom were well trained in quantitative methods; however, their currency with developing procedures may be problematic.

To study complex phenomena requires looking at interactions among multiple variables. The appropriate statistical procedures require large samples. This is increasingly difficult because of increasingly stringent regulations by institutional review boards, especially related to minors; reluctance of schools to participate in research; new Health Insurance Portability and Accountability Act (HIPAA) requirements; and the costs involved in large-scale research.

As discussed earlier, quantitative research has produced significant, applicable results. However, this research is the product of a relatively small number of highly productive researchers. Much of the research comes from the National Research

Center on the Gifted and Talented, which is supported by a federal grant. A cursory look at major journals in the field uncovers this cadre of researchers, and their graduate students, permeating the journals. While this group of researchers is to be commended, problems can accompany this pattern. Just as pharmaceutical companies researching their own products has led to abuses, much of the research on curriculum models, for example, has been conducted by the scholars who developed the model. And, like drug companies who are invested in good outcomes, research in support of a curriculum model or talent search program has economic consequences. With consultants in gifted education/gifted studies being paid thousands of dollars a day to implement a product, to present keynote addresses at state and national conferences often promoting their model, and with the pressure on faculty to obtain external grants related to a particular model, research supporting that product has significant economic consequences. These demand characteristics, usually unintentional, raise issues about the validity of some of the research in the field. The field needs replication of findings by independent researchers.

Quantitative research tests assumptions, offers opportunity to revise practices, and builds the knowledge base of a field. As evidenced by the research cited previously, quantitative methods have been the backbone of these research programs. However, some challenges still exist: developing a larger cadre of researchers with strong research design and statistical skills; using mixed research designs; and having research validated by independent researchers not affiliated with a particular model of intervention.

David N. Dixon and Felicia A. Dixon

See also Effective Programs; Factor Analyses Creativity; Gifted Education Centers; Intelligence; Meta-Analyses of Gifted Education; Research, Qualitative

Further Readings

Callahan, C. M., & Moon, T. R. (2007). Sorting the wheat from the chaff: What makes for good evidence of effectiveness in the literature in gifted education? *Gifted Child Quarterly, 51*(4), 305–319.

Carter, K. R., & Swanson, H. L. (1990). An analysis of the most frequently cited gifted journal articles since the Marland Report: Implications for researchers. *Gifted Child Quarterly, 32*(3), 116–123.

Colangelo, N., Assouline, S. G., & Gross, M. U. M. (2004). *A nation deceived: How schools hold back America's brightest students.* Iowa City, IA: Connie Belin & Jacqueline N. Blank International Center for Gifted Education and Talent Development.

Creswell, J. W. (2005). *Educational research: Planning, conducting, and evaluating quantitative and qualitative research.* Upper Saddle River, NJ: Pearson.

Friedman-Nimz, R., O'Brien, B., & Frey, B. (2005). Examining our foundations: Implications for gifted education research. *Roeper Review, 28*(1), 45–52.

Kulik, J. (2003). Grouping and tracking. In N. Colangelo & G. Davis (Eds.), *Handbook of gifted education* (pp. 268–281). Boston: Allyn & Bacon.

Lupkowski-Shoplik, A., Benbow, C. P., Assouline, S. G., & Brody, L. E. (2003). Talent searches: Meeting the needs of academically talented youth. In N. Colangelo & G. Davis (Eds.), *Handbook of gifted education* (3rd ed., pp. 204–218). Boston: Allyn & Bacon.

Olszewski-Kubilius, P. (2004). Talent searches and accelerated programming for gifted students. In N. Colangelo, S. Assouline, & M. U. M. Gross (Eds.), *A nation deceived: How schools hold back America's brightest students.* Iowa City, IA: Connie Belin & Jacqueline N. Blank International Center for Gifted Education and Talent Development.

Renzulli, J. S., & Reis, S. M. (2003). The schoolwide enrichment model: Developing creative and productive giftedness. In N. Colangelo & G. Davis (Eds.), *Handbook of gifted education* (pp. 184–203). Boston: Allyn & Bacon.

Robinson, A. (2003). Cooperative learning and high ability students. In N. Colangelo & G. Davis (Eds.), *Handbook of gifted education* (pp. 282–292). Boston: Allyn & Bacon.

Scott, G., Leritz, L. E., & Mumford, M. D. (2004). The effectiveness of creativity training: A quantitative review. *Creativity Research Journal, 16,* 361–388.

VanTassel-Baska, J. (2003). What matters in curriculum for gifted learners: Reflections on theory, research, and practice. In N. Colangelo & G. Davis (Eds.), *Handbook of gifted education* (pp. 174–183). Boston: Allyn & Bacon.

Resilience

In spite of existing research, the chameleon-like nature of what is meant by resilience is evident in attempts to define it. Resilience has been defined as a protective mechanism that modifies an individual's response to risk; as the tendency to spring back, rebound, or recoil; and as a child's ability to succeed contrary to predictions.

Resilience is not a fixed attribute, nor is successful negotiation of one stressful life event predictive of positive future adapting. Over the past several decades, resiliency has garnered the interest of researchers whose foci have included cognition, trauma, at-risk youth, as well as giftedness in children. The link between resilience and intelligence is found in longitudinal studies, among racial/ethnic groups, and among children from middle- and lower-class homes.

Characteristics of Resilient Individuals

According to Emmy E. Werner, individuals who are considered resilient typically possess (a) social competence—responsiveness, flexibility, empathy/caring, good communication, and a sense of humor; (b) problem-solving skills—thinking abstractly and reflectively, ability to plan, and flexibility; (c) autonomy—internal locus of control, sense of power and of self, and adaptive discipline; (d) sense of purpose—healthy expectations, goal directedness, success orientation, educational aspirations, persistence, hopefulness, hardiness, belief in a positive future, and a sense of meaning. Although resilient individuals may manifest all or few of these qualities, stressors during each life stage can trigger these qualities. In infancy, disruptive events include birth of siblings, separation from mother, and family disruption. During toddlerhood, stressors include maternal employment outside of the home, absent father, birth of siblings, and child/parent illness. During childhood, the child's perception of life, death of sibling, and crowding in the home can impact adaptive skills. Adolescent and adult stressors include teen pregnancy, financial problems, serious illnesses, or accidents. Although gifted/talented/creative students may encounter social and emotional difficulties due to their giftedness, L. C. Bland and C. J. Sowa postulated that gifted children have additional resources to overcome these difficulties. Internal resources common to resilient gifted individuals range from biological and psychological traits to self-taught coping strategies. Successfully coping with stressful life events can nourish one's resilience, which strengthens one's future resiliency.

Similar to other children who are resilient, gifted children may have specific genetic traits that foster resilience. For example, infants with an adaptable temperament tend to develop effective coping strategies earlier than infants with less easygoing personalities. Children with adaptive temperaments tend to develop interpersonal skills that contribute to an ability to cope with stressful situations. Biological factors, such as gender, have also been related to resiliency in gifted children, although whether these differences are due to environmental factors or genetic differences is not known. There are gender differences in how resiliency is fostered in girls and boys. Bruce Kline and his colleagues found boys tend to be more "at risk" than girls, but boys who are emotionally connected to a support network may have less difficulty overcoming barriers than their peers. In addition, Kline and colleagues found that ability to integrate an identity as a female and as gifted may be protective factors for young girls. Sharon Kurpius and Barbara Kerr studied risk and resilience extensively in talented at-risk girls and published their findings in a National Science Foundation report that includes their interventions to increase self-esteem, self-efficacy, and to reduce risk factors.

Personality characteristics have been linked to resiliency. Resiliency is impacted by how a child perceives himself or herself as a gifted individual. Gifted individuals who have higher self-esteem, confidence, optimism, motivation, and/or an internal locus of control tend to be more resilient in difficult situations than are peers without these characteristics. Talented children who have additional barriers (students of color experiencing oppression and racism) may develop stronger characteristics (e.g., motivation and internal locus of control) that assist in overcoming various barriers and contribute to resiliency. For example, Donna Ford found that gifted Black youth often use autonomy and bicultural coping skills when encountering difficult situations.

For gifted children, high intelligence alone does not reflect resiliency; it is, however, related to the ability to develop effective coping strategies. The ability to determine quickly whether a stressful situation is harmful is associated with mature adult cognitive processes. Gifted children use cognitive appraisal processes earlier, which may allow them to assess and predict stressful situations and either adapt behavior to alter the situation or adapt their perception of the situation (emotion-focused cognitions). Self-taught coping strategies also contribute to resiliency in talented children. This resiliency is demonstrated by choosing to withdraw from stressful or harmful situations or taking time out in order to think about how to respond or cope.

Fostering Resilience

Positive coping strategies and resilience can also be fostered by family and school. In addition to providing an organized, structured home environment, parents who are consistently nurturing, engender trust in others, modeling competence, and providing opportunities for confidence-building, foster resiliency in their children. While being emotionally responsive and expressive, these parents encourage involvement in challenging experiences and support their child in coping and mastery efforts. A close bond with at least one family member provides gifted children with stability, support, and attention. This person is often the mother, although the father can play an important role, particularly among girls and African American males. Grandparents can also play this role, particularly for children living in poverty.

Teachers, peers, and the church should also not be overlooked. The responsiveness and encouragement offered by individuals from these groups help to foster resiliency. Resilience is also enhanced by involvement in activities, both during and after school. Schools, families, and peers can support an environment for learning and effective coping that, in turn, contributes to and reinforces resiliency.

Sharon E. Robinson Kurpius, Marybeth Rigali-Oiler, and Erin M. Carr Jordan

See also Adolescent, Gifted; Boys, Gifted; Girls, Gifted; Self-Efficacy/Self-Esteem; Social-Emotional Issues

Further Readings

Bland, L. C., & Sowa, C. J. (1994). An overview of resilience in gifted children. *Roeper Review, 17,* 77–80.

Colbert, R. D., Hébert, T. P., & Reis, S. M. (2005). Understanding resilience in diverse, talented students in an urban high school. *Roeper Review, 27,* 110–120.

Ford, D. Y. (1994). Nurturing resilience in gifted Black youth. In Affective dimensions of being gifted [Special issue]. *Roeper Review, 17,* 80–85.

Gjerde, E., Block, J., & Block, J. (1986). Egocentrism and ego-resiliency: Personality characteristics associated with perspective-taking from early childhood to adolescence. *Journal of Personality and Social Psychology, 51,* 423–434.

Kitano, M. K., & Lewis, R. B. (2005). Resilience and coping: Implications for gifted children and youth at risk. *Roeper Review, 27*(4), 200–205.

Kline, B. E., & Short, E. B. (1991). Changes in emotional resilience: Gifted adolescent boys. *Roeper Review, 13,* 184–187.

Kline, B. E., & Short, E. B. (1991). Changes in emotional resilience: Gifted adolescent females. *Roeper Review, 13,* 118–121.

Kurpius, S. R., Kerr, B., et al. (2005). *Counseling women: Talent, risk, and resiliency.* Arlington, VA: National Science Foundation. Available from http://www.mtrworldwide.com/Default.aspx?tabid=25

Mandleco, B. L., & Peery, J. C. (2000). An organizational framework for conceptualizing resilience in children. *Journal of Child & Adolescent Psychiatric Nursing, 13,* 99–112.

Murphy, L. B. (1987). Further reflections on resilience. In E. J. Anthony & B. Cohler (Eds.), *The invulnerable child* (pp. 84–105). New York: Guilford Press.

Reis, S. M., Colbert, R. D., & Hébert, T. P. (2005). Understanding resilience in diverse, talented students in an urban high school. *Roeper Review, 27,* 110–120.

Sowa, C., & McIntire, J. (1994). Social and emotional adjustment themes across gifted children. *Roeper Review, 17,* 95–99.

Werner, E. E. (2000). Protective factors and individual resilience. In J. P. Shonkoff & S. J. Meisels (Eds.), *Handbook of early intervention* (2nd ed., pp. 115–132). New York: Cambridge University Press.

Revolving Door Identification Model

The enrichment triad model and the three-ring conception of giftedness were responsible in the

1970s and 1980s for opening gifted education to a much broader group of bright students than had been identified by intelligence tests alone. Nevertheless, Joseph Renzulli, Sally Reis, and Linda Smith found that there were still students with great potential for achievement who were being overlooked. The *revolving door identification model* (RDIM) was a response to this problem. This entry discusses the background, the various strategies of RDIM, and its advantages for increasing the talent pool.

Background

School personnel were routinely eliminating highly creative and productive students from participation in enrichment programs because they did not score in the top 1 to 3 percent of the population on either achievement or intelligence tests. Many of the same teachers who could not recommend these students because they did not meet a specified cutoff score believed the students would excel when they had the opportunity to become involved in high levels of creative, productive, and enriched work.

Teachers also failed to identify students who were reading and doing mathematics at an accelerated level who were missing the cutoff scores for inclusion in the gifted program by a point or two. Earlier research conducted by E. Paul Torrance had demonstrated that students who were rated highly on creativity measures achieved well in school and on achievement tests but were not selected for gifted programs because their scores were below the cutoff for admission. Research conducted by Sally Reis reported that when a broader pool of students of the general population, identified as the talent pool, was able to participate in Types I and II enrichment experiences, the quality of their completed Type III products was equal to that of students who were traditionally identified as gifted.

This research led Renzulli and his colleagues to field tests and trials with the RDIM in which a talent pool (10%–15%) of students receives regular enrichment experiences and the opportunity to "revolve into" Type III creative productive experiences. In RDIM, students were selected for participation in the talent pool on the basis of multiple criteria that included achievement scores, teacher nomination, creativity, and other locally selected indicators. Once identified and placed in the talent pool through the use of multiple criteria such as test scores; teacher, parent, or self-nomination; and/or examples of creative potential or productivity, students are observed in classrooms and enrichment experiences for signs of advanced interests, creativity, or task commitment. This part of the identification process, called *action information,* was found to be an instrumental part of the identification process in assessing students' interest and motivation to become involved in Type III creative productivity. Further support for this approach was contributed by Robert Kirschenbaum and Del Siegle, who demonstrated that students who are rated highly on measures of creativity tend to do well in school and on measures of achievement. The development of the expanded identification on the RDIM led to the need for new guidelines for how all of the components of the previous triad programs and the RDIM could be implemented. The resulting work, titled the *schoolwide enrichment model* (SEM), was developed by Joseph Renzulli and Sally Reis.

Considerations

Before listing the steps involved in this identification system, three important considerations should be discussed. First, talent pools will vary in any given school depending upon the general nature of the total student body. In a school with unusually large numbers of high-ability students, it is conceivable that talent pools will extend beyond the 15 percent level that is ordinarily recommended in schools and that reflects the achievement profiles of the general population. Even in schools where achievement levels are below national norms, there still exists an upper level group of students who need services above and beyond those that are provided for the majority of the school population. Some of the most successful RDIM/triad programs have been in inner-city schools that serve disadvantaged and bilingual youth; and even though these schools were below national norms, a talent pool of approximately 15 percent of higher-ability students needing supplementary services was still identified. Talent pool size is also a function of the availability of resources (both human and material), and the extent to which the general faculty is willing (a) to make modifications in the regular curriculum for above average ability students, (b) to participate in various kinds of enrichment and mentoring activities, and (c) to work cooperatively with any and all personnel who may have special program assignments.

A third consideration is the type of program for which students are being identified. The identification system that follows is based on models that combine both enrichment and acceleration, whether or not they are carried out in self-contained or pull-out programs. Regardless of the type of organizational model used, it is also recommended that a strong component of curriculum compacting be a part of the services offered Talent Pool students in the RDIM.

Test Score Nominations

If one were using nothing but test scores to identify a 15 percent talent pool, the task would be ever so simple. Any child who scored above the 85th percentile (using local norms) would be a candidate. In this identification system, however, the researchers have made a commitment to "leave some room" in the talent pool for students whose potentials may not be reflected in standardized tests. Therefore, they begin by dividing the talent pool in half and placing all students who score at or above the 92nd percentile (again, using local norms) in the talent pool. This approach guarantees that all traditionally bright youngsters will automatically be selected, and they will account for approximately 50 percent of the talent pool. This process guarantees admission to academically able students who are underachievers.

Any regularly administered standardized test (e.g., intelligence, achievement, aptitude) can be used for this purpose. This approach will enable students who are high in verbal or nonverbal ability (but not necessarily both) to gain admission, as well as students who may excel in one aptitude (e.g., spatial, mechanical). Programs that focus on special areas such as the arts, leadership, and athletics should use nontest criteria as major indicators of above-average ability in a particular talent area. In a similar fashion, whenever test scores are not available, or there is some question as to their validity, the nontest criteria recommended in the following steps should be used. This approach is especially important when considering primary-age students, disadvantaged populations, or culturally different groups.

The teachers should be informed of all students who have gained entrance through test score nominations so that they will not have to engage in needless paperwork for students who have already been admitted. This allows teachers to nominate students who display characteristics that are not easily determined by tests (e.g., high levels of creativity, task commitment, unusual interest, talents, or special areas of superior performance or potential). With the exception of teachers who are overnominators or undernominators, nominations from teachers who have received training in this process are accepted into the talent pool on an equal value footing with test score nominations. That is, students nominated by test scores are not referred to as the "truly gifted" and students nominated by teachers as the "moderately or potentially gifted." Nor are there any distinctions in the opportunities, resources, or services provided, other than the normal individualization that should be a part of any program that attempts to meet unique needs and potentials.

Alternate Pathways

Because all schools using this identification system make use of test score and teacher nominations, alternate pathways are considered to be local options, and are pursued in varying degrees by individual school districts. Decisions about the alternate pathways that might be used should be made by a local planning committee, and some consideration should be given to variations in grade level. For example, self-nomination is more appropriate for students who may be considering advanced classes at the secondary level.

Alternate pathways generally consist of parent nominations, peer nominations, tests of creativity, self-nominations, product evaluations, and virtually any other procedure that might lead to initial consideration by a screening committee. The major difference between alternate pathways on one hand, and test score and teacher nomination on the other, is that alternate pathways are not automatic. In other words, students nominated through one or more alternate pathway will be reviewed by a screening committee.

Special Nominations

Special nominations represent the first of two "safety valves" in this identification system. This procedure involves circulating a list of all students who have been nominated through one of the procedures mentioned above to all teachers within the school, and in previous schools if students have matriculated from another building. This procedure allows previous-year teachers to nominate students who have not been recommended by their present teacher, and it also allows resource teachers to make recommendations based on their own previous experience with students who already are in the talent pool, or students they may have encountered as part of enrichment experiences that might have been offered in regular classrooms. This step allows for a final review of the total school population, and is designed to circumvent the opinions of present-year teachers who may not have an appreciation for the abilities, style, or even the personality of a particular student. As with the case of alternate pathways, special nominations are not automatic. Rather, a case study is carried out and the final decision rests with the screening committee.

Action Information Nominations

This identification system may occasionally overlook students who, for one reason or another, are not selected for talent pool membership. To help overcome this problem, orientation related to spotting unusually favorable "turn-ons" in the regular curriculum is provided for all teachers. In programs following the schoolwide enrichment model, a wide variety of in-class enrichment experiences that might result in recommendations for special services is provided.

Action information can best be defined as the dynamic interactions that occur when a student becomes extremely interested in or excited about a particular topic, area of study, issue, idea, or event that takes place in school or in the nonschool environment. It is derived from the concept of performance-based assessment, and it serves as the second safety valve in this identification system. The transmission of an action information message does not mean that a student will automatically revolve into advanced level services, however; it serves as the basis for a careful review of the situation to determine if such services are warranted. Action information messages are also used within talent pool settings (i.e., pull-out groups, advanced classes, cluster groups) to make determinations about the pursuit of individual or small-group investigations (Type III enrichment in the triad model).

Approach Advantages

In most identification systems that follow the traditional screening-plus-selection approach, the "throwaways" have invariably been those students who qualified for screening on the basis of non-test criteria. Thus, for example, a teacher nomination is used only as a ticket to take an individual or group ability test; in most cases the test score is always the deciding factor. The many and various pieces of evidence that led to nominations by teachers are often ignored when it comes to the final (selection) decision, and the multiple criteria game ends up being a smoke screen for the same old test-based approach.

The implementation of the identification system described above has helped to overcome this problem as well as a wide array of other problems traditionally associated with selecting students for special programs. Generally, students, parents, teachers, and administrators have expressed high degrees of satisfaction with this approach, and the reason for this satisfaction is plainly evident. By "picking up" that layer of students below the top few percentile levels usually selected for special programs, and by leaving some room in the program for students to gain entrance on the basis of nontest criteria, this model has eliminated the justifiable criticisms of those persons who know that these students are in need of special opportunities, resources, and encouragement. The research underlying the three-ring conception of giftedness clearly tells us that such an approach is justified in terms of what we know about human potential.

Joseph S. Renzulli

See also Elementary Enrichment; Enrichment Triad Model; Giftedness, Definition; Schoolwide Enrichment Model

Further Readings

Kirschenbaum, R. J., & Siegle, D. (1993, April). *Predicting creative performance in an enrichment program.* Paper presented at the Association for the Education of Gifted Underachieving Students 6th Annual Conference, Portland, OR.

Reis, S. M., Burns, D. E., & Renzulli, J. S. (1992). *Curriculum compacting: The complete guide to modifying the regular curriculum for high ability students.* Mansfield Center, CT: Creative Learning Press.

Renzulli, J. S., & Reis, S. M. (1985). *The schoolwide enrichment model.* Mansfield Center, CT: Creative Learning Press.

Renzulli, J. S., & Reis, S. M. (1997). *The schoolwide enrichment model: A comprehensive plan for educational excellence.* Mansfield Center, CT: Creative Learning Press.

Renzulli, J. S., Reis, S. M., & Smith, L. H. (1981). *Revolving door identification model guidebook.* Mansfield Center, CT: Creative Learning Press.

Risk Taking

Four basic themes can be discerned in recent creativity research literature. First, it has been suggested that all people possess creative problem-solving abilities to some extent. Second, some people tend to be more creative than others. Third, creativity can be studied as a manifestation of cognitive skills that are developed within a creativity-fostering environment. Fourth, some authors propose that one should use a combination of these themes; for example, a holistic combined theory called the *investment theory.* One recurring perspective is that creativity commonly involves taking some risks.

Investment Theory

Robert Sternberg described investment theory as six interrelated resources: intellectual abilities, knowledge, styles of thinking, personality, motivation, and environment. All of these themes may have relevance in describing how an individual may be more or less creative. The creative individual is able to cope with novelty. Intellectual abilities refers to synthetic, analytic, and practical-contextual abilities. Knowledge is an ability to recognize which ideas are worth pursuing, and not be hindered by this knowledge. Personality refers to a willingness to overcome obstacles, take sensible risks, tolerate ambiguity, use self-efficacy, and defy the crowd. Thinking styles refers to the ability to think in new ways. Motivation involves receiving satisfaction from engaging in a creative act instead of focusing on the potential rewards. The environment needs to be supportive and rewarding of creativity so that creative ideas can be disseminated without stifling the individual. To take advantage of the market, the creative person must "buy low" and "sell high." Buying low is defined as investing in unpopular ideas with growth potential. Selling high refers to leaving the idea to others and moving on to new unpopular ideas.

Psychologists and philosophers who study the creative person, process, and product are in consensus that creativity requires novel and adaptive solutions to problems. It appears that openness to experience and a lack of conventionality are consistent characteristics of creativity in all domains. However, the creative person is always operating within a domain, discipline, or craft.

Domains

James Kaufman and John Baer with other authors discussed how creativity is demonstrated differently among domains, even among similar domains within the sciences and within the arts. Few people may be creative in two or more domains: One may have spatial skills and abilities in art and engineering, but it seems likely that there may be different requisites for being creative in engineering design versus in the fine arts. People may be more likely to take risks within their own domain where they have a higher comfort level.

Scientific creativity and artistic creativity have been explored separately as well in comparison with each other. Christine Charyton and Glenn Snelbecker investigated general, scientific, and artistic creativity among engineering students versus music students. Their research revealed differences but also some interesting similarities between engineers and musicians. Through studying scientific and artistic creativity, researchers may gain a clearer picture of what creativity entails in personality, processes, products, and fostering environments. For example, it may be that the risk of trying something new may involve similarities as well as differences across domains.

Cognitive Risk Tolerance and Creativity

Risk as a concept often is addressed in professional and mass media. Frank Farley has suggested that creativity and productive risk taking have been hallmarks of America from its beginnings. Individuals throughout history have encountered opposition as they try to develop novel approaches while confronting uncertainty about outcomes.

But only some aspects of risk, notably risk taking and risk tolerance, are likely to be relevant for creativity. Generally, risk involves making decisions though uncertain about outcomes. Sometimes people must cope with risk due to circumstances imposed on them. For example, individuals can be "at risk" of (a) a physical vulnerability to disease due to inherited attributes or (b) little likelihood of a good education due to poverty levels they cannot control and must endure. More relevant for creativity are instances where individuals have opportunities to make decisions that could lead to gains or benefits but also might risk dangers or losses from those decisions.

Risk as related to creativity often involves individuals facing conditions of uncertainty while making decisions with the potential for either losses or benefits. Commonly, such individuals could choose something conventional ("play it safe") versus trying new ideas or approaches while uncertain about outcomes.

Snelbecker and colleagues developed a risk tolerance model that includes a general factor along with context-specific aspects—financial, physical, social, and cognitive risk tolerance. Cognitive risk tolerance is defined as a tendency to express one's established beliefs and views for comments by other people or even to be open to new ideas or perspectives. Stated another way, instruments that were created in accordance with this model attempt to detect how comfortable a person is with voicing an opinion that may differ from that of other people. When a person interacts with others—such as in personal, educational, or business relationships—not all members of the group think the same way. Self-expression of an opposing viewpoint may result in resistance and ridicule. *Classical utility theory* addresses risk-averse versus risk-seeking approaches toward uncertainty. Risk aversion is a preference for a certain outcome over a gamble that possesses equal or higher expected value. Conversely, risk seeking is the rejection of a certain outcome in favor of a gamble of equal or lower expected value. Cognitive risk tolerance can also be considered as an attribute of general creativity and a positive psychology related construct. Just as creativity may take different forms, cognitive risk tolerance may be shared across domains yet be exhibited differently.

The creative person contributes through being novel in an applicable and useful area that is or becomes accepted. J. P. Guilford stated that higher-order transformation abilities are also an aspect of intelligence that contributes to creative behavior. Gifted people generally show superior intellect combined with a talent such as art, music, social leadership, foreign languages, science, mathematics, and creative writing—yet facility is not necessarily creativity. A person who is more likely to tolerate sensible, carefully thought-out risk prospects may also be more likely to demonstrate creativity.

Christine Charyton and Glenn E. Snelbecker

See also Creative Leadership; Creative Organizational Climate; Creativity, Definition; Domains of Talent

Further Readings

Charyton, C., & Snelbecker, G. E. (2007). General, artistic and scientific creativity attributes of engineering and music students. *Creativity Research Journal, 19,* 213–225.

Farley, F. (1991). The type T personality. In L. P. Lipsett & L. L. Mitnick (Eds.), *Self-regulatory behavior and risk taking: Causes and consequences.* Norwood, NJ: Ablex.

Kaufman, J. C., & Baer, J. (2005). *Creativity across domains: Faces of the muse.* Mahwah, NJ: Lawrence Erlbaum.

Snelbecker, G. E., Roszkowski, M. J., & Cutler, N. E. (1990). Investors' risk tolerance and return aspirations, and financial advisors' interpretations: A conceptual model and exploratory data. *Journal of Behavioral Economics, 19,* 377–393.

Sternberg, R. J. (2006). Creating a vision of creativity: The first 25 years. *Psychology of Aesthetics, Creativity, and the Arts, S,* 2–12.

Robotics

Robotics focuses science and technology on the creation of robots—artificially created mechanical devices that appear to have intent or agency of their own. Robotics education is frequently used as a source of enrichment for advanced students because it provides an excellent opportunity for students to use skills in technology, science, engineering, problem solving, and teamwork. This entry describes the history of robotics and robotics education programs.

History

Word Origin

The term *robotics* was unknowingly coined by Isaac Asimov, whose mid-20th-century science fiction short stories and novels popularized the notion of machines taking on human characteristics and fulfilling human roles. The root word *robot* is derived from the Czech word *robota,* meaning "forced labor." Josef Capek developed the term *robot,* which was used by his brother, Czech playwright Karel Capek, who wrote the play *R. U. R.—Rossum's Universal Robots* in 1920.

History of the Concept

Although it may seem that the idea of robots and robotics was an invention of 20th-century thinkers, the fascination with machines acting like humans had been sparking the imagination of creative, engineering minds long before the days of modern society. Even Leonardo da Vinci toyed with the idea of the robot, as documented through his drawings of a mechanical knight with the capacity to sit up, wave its arms, and move its jaw. There are even reports that the ancient Greeks and Chinese had conceptualized this idea of humanistic machines, as documented through ancient legends and writings.

First Robot

As 20th-century science fiction playwrights and writers began to popularize robots in the popular media, scientists and engineers were working to make robots a reality for industry. The first robot was revealed in 1954, when American George Devol created the first stationary industrial robot. This motorized lifting arm, dubbed Unimate, was eventually used by General Motors in its industrial plants. Since then robotics engineers have touched many facets of industry, including space exploration, medicine, industry, and entertainment. Robots such as R2D2 and the Roomba have become household names.

Laws of Robotics

Another important contribution to the field of robotics is the Three Laws of Robotics, authored by Isaac Asimov in his 1942 novel *Runaround.* These laws have come to be known as universal principles for engineers, writers, and philosophers alike. The three laws are:

1. A robot may not injure a human being, or, through inaction, allow a human being to come to harm.
2. A robot must obey the orders given it by human beings except where such orders would conflict with the First Law.
3. A robot must protect its own existence as long as such protection does not conflict with the First or Second Law.

Modern Robotics

These three laws, although the ideas of a science fiction writer, have guided robotics engineers through many modern developments. Robots are now a critical part of almost every field, including medicine, industry, space and underwater exploration, military combat, and many more. The technological advancements of the late 20th and early 21st centuries have facilitated an explosion of growth in the field. With so many possibilities, there seems to be a limitless amount of potential for the field and, therefore, an unprecedented need for talented minds to enter the field.

Robotics Education

Robotics education programs and competitions have been created by various organizations to increase the number of students who are channeled toward fields in science, technology, engineering, and mathematics (STEM). With the growth of programs and competitions since the late 1980s and the increased availability of robotics kits, robotics programming software, and curricular resources, K–12 educators now have a large body of resources from which to draw.

Tools

The basic tools of robotics education include a robotics building kit, software with which to program the robot, and a problem-based instructional design. A variety of robotics kits are available for school- and home use. Some of the most popular kits—the LEGO Mindstorms kits—have incorporated the familiar, easy-to-use LEGO building materials with simple, intuitive software to create robotics packages that are readily available for the mass market. Vex Robotics Design Systems offers a more advanced platform, providing a more complex approach to robot design.

Robotics Competitions

Arguably one of the most widely known competitions is the FIRST (For Inspiration and Recognition of Science and Technology) Robotics Competition, created by Dean Kamen in 1989 to attract young people to science and engineering. Kamen, whose company created such modern technologies as the Segway personal transporter and the IBOT—a wheelchair that can climb stairs and traverse rough terrain—had a vision for creating a program to attract young people to science and engineering. The FIRST Robotics League Competitions aim to give students opportunities to participate in fun, healthy competitions where they can put their engineering skills, creative ingenuity, and teamwork skills to the test. With programs now expanded to include students as young as 6, the FIRST program has more than 150,000 student robotics competitors in 33 nations each year. Other popular competitions and educational programs include Botball and the BEST (Boosting Engineering, Science, and Technology) competition.

Kristina Ayers Paul

See also Competitions; Creativity in Engineering; Creativity in Science; Extracurricular Activities; Inquiry; Technology

Further Readings

National Aeronautics and Space Administration. (2008). *Robotics curriculum clearinghouse.* Retrieved May 14, 2008, from http://robotics.nasa.gov/rcc

National Aeronautics and Space Administration. (2008). *The robotics alliance project.* Retrieved May 14, 2008, from http://robotics.nasa.gov/index.php

Robotics Institute at Carnegie Mellon University: http://www.ri.cmu.edu

US FIRST Robotics: http://www.usfirst.org

Rocketry

The opportunity to build and launch rockets has been a continuing success story in the area of hands-on science education, especially for gifted and talented children. Yet what do students actually learn from these experiences? This entry examines effective structuring of model rocket activity specifically, but also looks at the bigger picture of the structure of hands-on activities for gifted students.

A widespread interpretation of Piagetian theory favors an oversensitivity to the things a child cannot do cognitively rather than a more optimistic and challenging emphasis on what children could do easily with the proper instructional sequence, structure, and social support. This optimistic and empowering emphasis on the child's early competence and strength is both a more empowering basis for science instruction for the gifted child and is in accord with current learning theory. Moreover, much of this work looks upon the child in isolation rather than as a part of a community of learners like that in which rocket scientists engage in on a daily basis.

For instance, the scientist engages intellectually with colleagues at conferences, graduate students in labs, students in classes, and receives feedback on manuscripts from reviewers. What a rich community the rocket scientist belongs to. How can classrooms be structured to take advantage of these social practices of the rocket scientist?

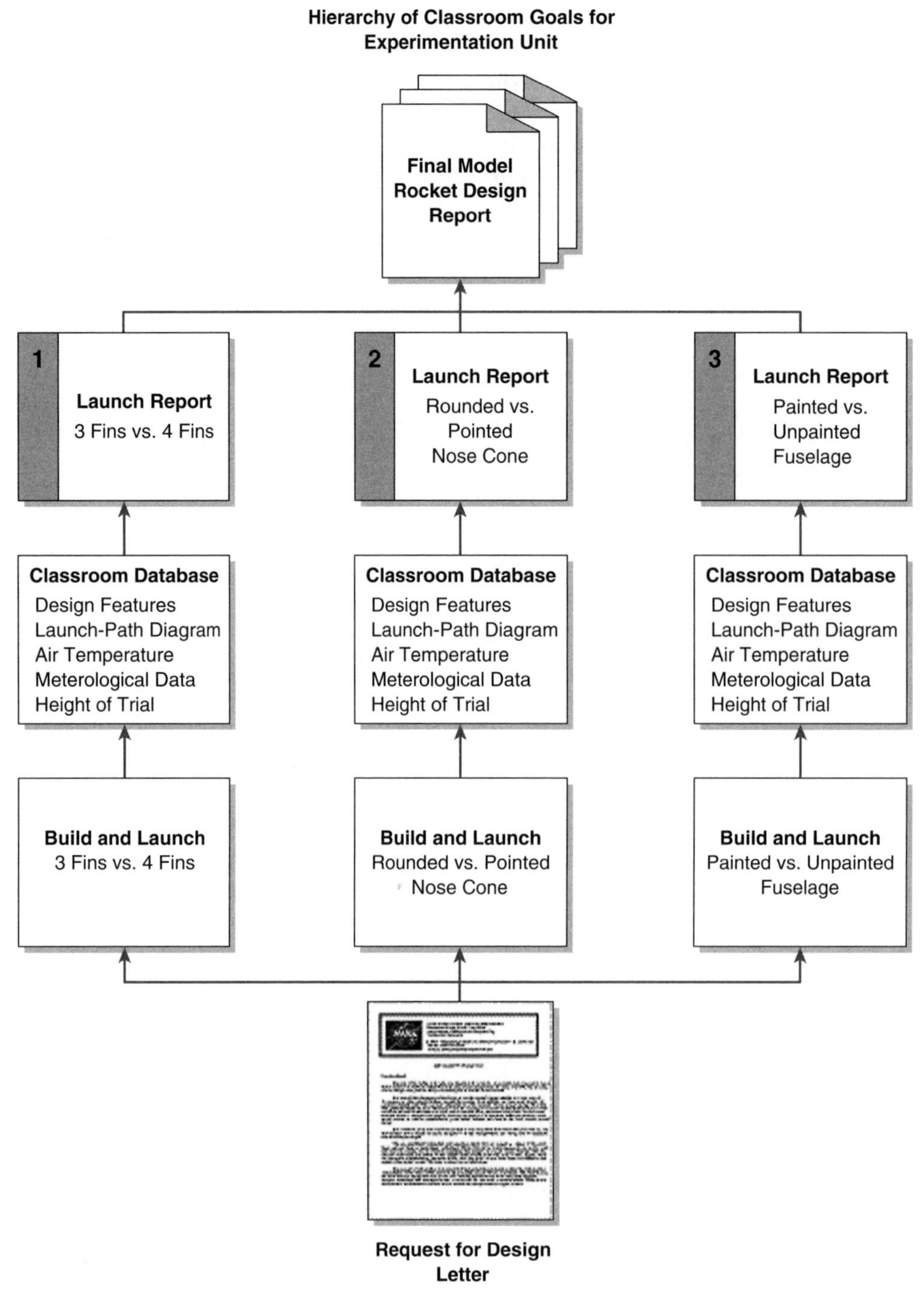

Figure 1 Activity Structure for Proposed Model Rocket Activity

Effective learning experiences are often organized around a driving question. Frequently, however, the question that drives a project is not crafted to make connections between activities and the underlying conceptual knowledge that one might hope to foster. Although the opportunity for deep learning is there, it often does not occur because of the tendency in these hands-on approaches to get caught up in the action without appropriate opportunities for reflection and revision. In such cases, the "doing" of an activity takes precedence over "doing with understanding." An example of the need for a well-crafted, driving question comes from projects in model rocketry. Thousands of classrooms throughout the country engage in similar types of activities. The opportunities to build and launch rockets have been extremely popular for students, teachers, and parents. Launchings frequently attract press attention, with footage shown on local news programs.

A great deal of recent research has explored whether it is possible to deepen students' understanding by creating the social structures of the scientists (this is sometimes called "participatory practices") without dampening students' enthusiasm. For instance, can students learn about experimentation and measurement if they have an appropriate driving question behind a model rocket project? To examine this issue, it is necessary to add a learning-appropriate goal to the standard model rocket project that motivates the use of scientific and statistical methods. Indeed, there are many reasons to proclaim such projects a success. But what do students actually learn from their experiences? Research has found that many students who completed the traditional rocket project learned relatively little from the hands-on activity of simply making and launching their rockets. They did not, for example, understand what made a better or worse rocket, and they did not understand how to evaluate the effectiveness of their rockets in any systematic way. One reason for this may be that the students did not have a driving question that could foster focused inquiry. For example, when students were asked what they thought about the purpose of the activity, a typical response was, "You know, to build them and see how high they will go."

More often than not, when rocketry is used in the classroom, teachers build the rockets, launch them, and then watch as the students run to catch the rockets as they fall to the ground. Students should be engaged in every phase of rocketry. In setting up this activity it is possible to use a design letter as an anchoring activity. An anchor is an activity that allows for continued and deepening exploration and that is designed to pose and solve complex, realistic problems. This letter not only calls for the building and launching of a model rocket(s) but also the measuring of the height it reaches, comparing effectiveness of various design plans, and a final written report. Moreover, the way this problem is set up, students do not compete, but rather cooperate as they attempt to figure out the best design attributes for reaching maximum height. The attributes that are compared are(a) nose-cone shape, (b) surface smoothness, and (c) number of fins (see Figure 1). In this way, students learn about experimentation as well as model rocketry.

Students are more likely to learn the design goals, and to learn important skills like controlled experimentation and methods of measurement that would help achieve these goals. Not only do students understand what they are trying to learn, but this knowledge appears to help them direct their learning. In addition, students may have an increased ability to generate their own questions to guide their scientific inquiry.

Anthony J. Petrosino

See also Elementary School, Science Curriculum; Middle School, Science Curriculum; Science, Curriculum; Scientists;

Further Readings

Barron, B. J., Schwartz, D. L., Vye, N. J., Moore, A., Petrosino, A. J., Zech, L., et al. (1998). Doing with understanding: Lessons from research and project-based learning. *Journal of the Learning Sciences, 7*(3), 271–3117.

Lehrer, R., Schauble, L., & Petrosino, A. (2001). Reconsidering the role of experiment in science education. In K. Crowley, C. D. Schunn, & T. Okada (Eds.), *Designing for science: Implications from everyday, classroom, and professional settings.* Mahwah, NJ: Lawrence Erlbaum.

Petrosino, A. J., Lehrer, R., & Schauble, L. (2003). Structuring error and experimental variation as distribution in the fourth grade. *Mathematical Thinking and Learning, 5*(2 & 3), 131–156.

Sneider, C., Kurlich, K., Pulos, S., & Friedman, A. (1984). Learning to control variables with model rockets: A neo-Piagetian study of learning in field settings. *Science Education, 68*(4), 465–486.

Roeper Review

The *Roeper Review* is one of the leading scholarly journals serving gifted education and related fields. George and Annemarie Roeper, holocaust survivors and founders of the innovative Roeper School in Bloomfield Hills, Michigan, founded the journal in 1978. Recognizing that exceptional human ability and compassion are needed in a world that occasionally gives rise to the horrors of war and other evils, the Roepers dedicated the Roeper School to discovering and nurturing the emotional, social, intellectual, and ethical development of bright young people. Roeper students are encouraged to become independent, self-aware, self-directed, curious, compassionate, and responsible individuals. The *Roeper Review* extends this vision and mission internationally while serving as a forum for leading research and theory pertaining to high ability. The journal is published quarterly by the Roeper Institute, which is a nonprofit corporation affiliated with the Roeper School. Recently, the Roeper Institute struck an agreement to transfer most of the production work to the Routledge publishing company. Routledge now produces and advertises the journal, although the Roeper Institute retains ownership and direction.

The *Roeper Review* is a juried scholarly publication, so submitted articles go through a blind review process involving three external reviewers and at least one internal reviewer. The review process is relatively expeditious, with most editorial decisions occurring within 8 weeks. Scholars who serve as reviewers must have considerable expertise and a recognized publication record in the appropriate area of expertise. More than 350 professionals are on the list of reviewers, and over 60 scholars who have extensive records of service to the journal and/or the field are listed as contributing editors. The latter are appointed by the editorial review board, which includes nine distinguished scholars of gifted education. The review board makes recommendations about the direction and content of the journal. Members of the board serve 3-year terms; their replacements undergo an intensive vetting process at periodic board meetings.

Contributing scholars follow the APA authorial style as outlined in the latest edition of the *Publication Manual of the American Psychological Association*. Submitted manuscripts typically are no more than 30 pages double spaced, including abstract and references. Most issues contain about seven articles plus special features.

Inquiry Topics and Cognitive Diversity

Primarily aimed at the needs of professionals and scholars in gifted education, articles in the journal address the interests of teachers, program developers, researchers, policymakers, and parents. In recognition that the field of gifted education is very diverse, somewhat fragmented, and contested at times, the *Roeper Review* addresses a wide array of topics. One of the key features distinguishing the *Roeper Review* from other academic journals is its mission to provide rich cognitive diversity for problem solving in the field. Cognitive diversity provides a significant advantage for those who engage in complex problem solving. A group attempting to grapple with very complex problems or issues establishes cognitive diversity if it collectively encompasses (a) diverse perspectives on problems or interpretations of issues, (b) diverse heuristics, and (c) diverse predictive models. Diverse perspectives or interpretations denote varied ways of perceiving, portraying, organizing, categorizing, or framing problems or issues. Diverse heuristics entail varied methods of problem solving. Diverse predictive models represent varied ways of inferring cause and effect.

Interestingly, cognitive diversity has been found to be at least as important as intelligence of the members for groups dealing with complex, multidimensional issues. The multidimensional nature of giftedness and the very large array of subtopics it entails make the study of high ability very complex; consequently, scholars and practitioners will understand more about giftedness if they capitalize on cognitive diversity in their research and theory development.

An academic journal that energetically strives to incorporate very diverse perspectives does much to generate the advantages of cognitive diversity within a field. The *Roeper Review* actively solicits diverse viewpoints, and the hundreds of authors who publish in the journal collectively provide considerable cognitive diversity. Taken together, they represent very diverse views on curricular and instructional issues, multicultural perspectives, research paradigms, and a wide range of cutting-edge theories.

Issues and Themes of Emphasis

Illustrating the cognitive diversity of the journal, recent topics have included conceptions of giftedness and talent; identification issues; the nuances of creativity; gender issues; curriculum development; the psychological dimensions of high ability; instructional issues at various age and grade levels; the nuances and advantages of various research methodologies; aspects of special education; developments in teacher education; testing, evaluation, and authentic assessment; program development; and of course the perspectives of gifted children themselves. Further enhancing its cognitive diversity, the journal runs periodic special issues on a variety of important topics. Examples of recently published and proposed special-theme issues include perspectives on intelligence; ability grouping and acceleration; underrepresentation in gifted education; the conceptual foundations for research and practice; analyses of Kazimierz Dabrowski's theory of positive disintegration; global awareness of the gifted; the history of gifted education as a field; specialized science, mathematics, and technology high schools; and the neuroscience of giftedness.

The journal also runs some special features, including interviews of prominent pioneers and current leaders in the field; periodic research commentary; point-counterpoint discussions in which leading scholars debate contentious, unsettled issues; and the column "According to Jim" in which James J. Gallagher, a giant in the field, dispenses probing insights about important issues.

Overall, the *Roeper Review* aims to push back the edges of the conceptual map that charts giftedness, talent, creativity, and various other dimensions of high ability. Its ultimate goal is to support educational professionals in their work of encouraging bright young people to become well-adjusted, self-aware, positive contributors to a complex, evolving world.

Don Ambrose

See also *Creativity Research Journal; Gifted Child Quarterly*; Research, Qualitative; Research, Quantitative

Further Readings

Borland, J. H. (Ed.). (2003). *Rethinking gifted education.* New York: Teachers College Press.

Page, S. E. (2007). *The difference: How the power of diversity creates better groups, firms, schools, and societies.* Princeton, NJ: Princeton University Press.

Tannenbaum, A. J. (1993). History of giftedness and "gifted education" in world perspective. In K. A. Heller, F. J. Mönks, & A. H. Passow (Eds.), *International handbook of research and development of giftedness and talent* (pp. 3–27). Oxford, UK: Pergamon.

Role Models

The impact of being gifted or talented on the development and well-being of individuals has been thoroughly discussed and speculated on by scholars, educators, and parents. Some believe that being gifted or talented leads to additional barriers that negatively impact well-being, while others believe that being gifted or talented is actually a protective factor for children and adolescents. Generally, the latter idea is more accepted within the psychology literature. Although gifted students encounter the same challenges as their non-gifted peers, in addition to other barriers specific to being gifted (i.e., feeling isolated in school, feeling unmotivated or unchallenged in course work, etc.), being gifted or talented provides children with more internal resources to cope with such barriers. Though gifted and talented children may have the internal resources, such as advanced problem-solving skills, environmental and interpersonal influences promote resiliency in children. Interacting with role models facilitates the growth of the positive intrapersonal factors that promote well-being among gifted and talented children.

Though there has been limited research on the impact of role models on well-being, self-efficacy, and self-esteem among gifted and talented children, Albert Bandura stressed the idea that general modeling and vicarious learning are part of *social learning theory.* He suggested that individuals learn behaviors based on what they observe from others, thus learning vicariously. His theory, developed to explain how self-efficacy (the confidence one has in successfully completing a task) influences career decisions, has been applied to career development and how role models influence one's decision to choose a specific career path through direct and indirect fostering of self-efficacy.

Role models can be defined as people who influence one's behaviors and/or beliefs. Role models tend to have three components that make them especially influential: (1) the individual perceives the role model to be similar to him or her, (2) role model behavior is imitated by the individual, and (3) the belief system of the role model is incorporated into the individual's own attitudes through the process of vicarious learning. Watching someone succeeding in a similar situation and facing similar challenges and barriers can have a profound impact on individuals who have lower self-efficacy in a given area, particularly if the role model is similar in gender, race/ethnicity, or other identifiable aspects. A role model with a similar racial/ethnic background and/or the same gender as the observer may be a protective factor against stereotypes related to these background characteristics that can negatively impact the observer. Furthermore, role models whose achievements were deemed attainable by the observer are more likely to have a positive impact on the observer's self-beliefs as compared to those role models whose accomplishments are perceived as too lofty for the observer to attain.

Being gifted often involves the skill of relating well to others, which makes role models especially impactful. Not only do role models promote understanding of academic and vocational information, they also have been found to help women develop more positive views on careers in which women are typically underrepresented. Exploring the factors influencing academic motivation in gifted children, scholars have found that family role models lead to more positive beliefs and behaviors related to motivation. Peers, parents, and teachers who are role models can have a positive influence on child and adolescent development.

Although there is evidence of the value of role models for gifted, talented, and creative children, appropriate role models may be scarce. First, this may be due in part to a disproportionate number of students of color and students from low socioeconomic status backgrounds being identified as being gifted, talented, or creative and then having these characteristics being nurtured so that these individuals one day can be role models for similar students. The resulting lack of representation of women, of racial/ethnic minorities, and of individuals with lower economic backgrounds in various careers also can lead to a smaller pool of available role models. Second, school curriculum promotes this disparity through a lack of multicultural focus and of limited lessons about the accomplishments and achievements of women and people of color. Third, disproportionate college attrition rates for students of color result in fewer academically qualified role models for overcoming barriers to persistence such as family unemployment and poverty. Racial identity, negative self-concept, experiences of discrimination, and peer relationships are often negative predictors of persistence decisions of racial/ethnic minority students. In contrast, having a role model who is a racial/ethnic minority may act as a protective factor for students facing racial backlash from peers, specific to the idea that achieving academically is "acting White."

It is clear that role models can serve as protective factors for gifted and talented children by promoting positive self-concepts and academic self-efficacy. Fostering role model relationships for talented and gifted children should be considered an important goal for educators, parents, and community leaders. The potential lack of available positive role models for students, especially those from diverse backgrounds, may provide challenges for teachers of gifted, talented, and creative children. It should be noted, however, that role models do not have to have a face-to-face relationship with a student: Modeling can be facilitated through various media and educational curricula. Having a person to look to as a model for achieving goals and overcoming barriers similar to those faced by the student may be the most important component of the role model relationship in regard to fostering self-efficacy and positive self-beliefs in gifted and talented children.

Marybeth Rigali-Oiler

See also Mentoring Gifted and Talented Individuals; Self-Efficacy/Self-Esteem

Further Readings

Clasen, D. (2006). Project STREAM: A 13-year follow-up of a pre-college program for middle and high school underrepresented gifted. *Roeper Review, 29,* 55–63.

Ford, D. (1994). Nurturing resilience in gifted Black youth. *Roeper Review, 17,* 80–86.

Karunanayake, D., & Nauta, M. (2004). The relationships between race and students' identified career role models and perceived role model influence. *Career Development Quarterly, 52,* 225–236.

Lockwood, P., & Kunda, Z. (1997). Superstars and me: Predicting the impact of role models on the self. *Journal of Personality and Social Psychology, 73,* 91–103.

Phillips, N., & Lindsay, G. (2006). Motivation in gifted students. *High Ability Studies, 17,* 57–73.

Pleiss, M., & Feldhusen, J. (1995). Mentors, role models, and heroes in the lives of gifted children. *Educational Psychologist, 30,* 159–169.

Quimby, J., & DeSantis, A. (2006). The influence of role models on women's career choices. *Career Development Quarterly, 54,* 297–208.

Reis, S., Cobert, R., & Hébert, T. (2005). Understanding resilience in diverse, talented students in an urban high school. *Roeper Review, 27,* 110–120.

Smith, W., & Erb, T. (1986). Effect of women science career role models on early adolescents' attitudes toward scientists and women in science. *Journal of Research in Science Teaching, 23,* 667–676.

Sowa, C., & McIntire, J. (1994). Social and emotional adjustment themes across gifted children. *Roeper Review, 17,* 95–99.

VanTassel-Baska, J., & Kulieke, M. (1987). The role of community-based scientific resources in developing scientific talent: A case study. *Gifted Child Quarterly, 30,* 111–115.

Rural Gifted

There is a lack of agreement on exactly what is meant by the term *rural.* A single designation may be used for an entire school district, even though the district may cover hundreds of square miles and include population groupings of various sizes. According to the National Center for Education Statistics, more than half of all school districts in the United States are in areas designated as rural, serving nearly a quarter of all students.

Since *rural* can be defined as not near a metropolitan area, the issue in the education of gifted learners is a lack of proximity to a broad selection of cultural events, lack of available mentors, distance from institutions of higher education, and the limitations of small schools in offering a broad and rigorous curriculum. Tracy Cross and David Dixon noted that developing the talent of these gifted students may also be complicated by limited access to academic materials and extended travel time to attend after-school opportunities. Different models, distance learning, or more purposeful planning for high-level cultural experiences may be required for gifted students in isolated rural environments.

Virginia Burney and Tracy Cross found comparatively little research specifically on students from impoverished backgrounds in rural areas. The strength of the academic preparation at the high school level, however, is a stronger variable than family income in explaining what makes a difference in college completion. Yet rigorous academic programming is one of the challenges of small rural schools. It was found in rural schools in one midwestern state that school personnel were less likely to have the special training required to plan for services for gifted learners; fewer advanced opportunities were available at any level, K–12; and students in rural schools achieved relatively fewer high scores on Advanced Placement exams than students in other locales. This is consistent with what high school counselors from small rural schools reported in the Javits-funded Project Aspire: It was uncommon for these schools to have had a student achieving at levels resulting in advanced standing when compared with able peers nationally from all locales.

Counselors in the Cross and Burney study reported that some of their able students in these rural schools were reluctant to take courses involving significant outside-of-class preparation; many were highly involved in activities, responsibilities, or part-time jobs and did not see the value or resented additional demands on their time. In addition, if Advanced Placement courses did not have the benefit of a weighted grade, the race for valedictorian resulted in some able students electing an easier program of courses for the more certain "A."

Adults in rural areas are less likely to have graduated from high school than are adults in metropolitan areas, according to the U.S. Census, 2000. The educational level of the community was found to be a significant variable in explaining the variance in high academic performance of a high school. Not only does this impact overall support for advanced academics in the rural community, but some parents without college experience are less supportive of the time required for advanced academics or going away for college and are less able to provide guidance for their students on the college-related processes or issues.

There are positives associated with rural areas for the gifted. A familylike atmosphere was described by gifted students in small rural schools. Gifted students in these rural high schools were less likely to experience the stigma of giftedness or to be categorized only as gifted, but to be appreciated for talents and their roles in multiple activities. The academic competition associated with the pursuit of being the valedictorian was viewed as positive in small rural schools and not as likely to be stressful, as reported by students in larger schools. Though gifted students may have fewer academic peers in small rural schools, they may have greater social latitude than might be experienced by gifted students in other environments because they are more likely to be treated as individuals. The challenge is to provide them with the rigor and breadth of opportunity needed to develop and nurture their giftedness. Online high school classes, Advanced Placement classes, and online college and university classes offer opportunities for gifted students to have appropriate education that was unavailable before the advent of widespread online teaching technology. In addition, summer camps and special gifted programs remain an important resource for youth isolated geographically to interact with their peers.

Virginia Burney

See also Online Gifted Education; Summer Camps; Summer Programs

Further Readings

Adelman, C. (1999). *Answers in the tool box: Academic intensity, attendance patterns, and bachelor's degree attainment.* Washington, DC: U.S. Department of Education, Office of Educational Research and Improvement.

Burney, V. H., & Cross, T. L. (2006). Impoverished students with academic promise in rural settings: 10 lessons from Project Aspire. *Gifted Child Today, 29*(2), 14–21.

Colangelo, N., Assouline, S. G., & New, J. K. (1999). *Gifted education in rural schools: A national assessment.* Iowa City, IA: Belin-Blank International Center for Gifted Education and Talent Development.

Coleman, L. J. (1985). *Schooling the gifted.* Menlo Park, CA: Addison-Wesley.

Cross, T. L., & Burney, V. H. (2005). High ability, rural and poor: Lessons from Project Aspire and implications for school counselors. *Journal of Secondary Gifted Education, 16*(4), 148–156.

Cross, T. L., & Dixon, F. A. (1998). On gifted students in rural schools. *NASSP Bulletin, 82*(595), 119–124.

Cross, T. L., & Stewart, R. A. (1995). A phenomenological investigation of the "lebenswelt" of gifted students in rural high schools. *Journal of Secondary Gifted Education, 6,* 273–280.

National Center for Education Statistics. (2003). *Participation in education: Concentration of enrollment by race/ethnicity and poverty. Condition of education, 2003.* Retrieved December 12, 2005, from http://nces.ed.gov/programs/coe/2004/section1/table.asp?tableID=38

U.S. Census Bureau. (2000). *Adults with a high school diploma or GED* [Summary File 3 (SF3) GCT-P11. Language, School Enrollment, and Educational Attainment: 2000]. Washington, DC: U.S. Census Bureau.

S

SAT

The SAT, described in this entry, is one of two major tests designed to help colleges make admittance decisions. The other is the ACT. Although scores from either test are acceptable to college admission offices, there are regional patterns, with the SAT more commonly taken by students on the East and West coasts and the ACT by students in the middle of the country. In the 2006–2007 school year, the SAT Reasoning Test was administered to approximately 1.5 million students.

Purpose and Uses

The purpose of the SAT as stated by its sponsoring organization, the College Board, is to help "college admissions officers make fair and informed admissions decisions." The College Board stresses that the SAT should not be used by itself, but as one part of the entire admissions record. A closely related use is for awarding scholarships. For example, the PSAT, a preliminary version of the SAT administered primarily to high school sophomores and juniors, is used as the National Merit Scholarship Qualifying Test. Individual colleges often use the SAT as part of the process for determining merit-based scholarships.

The SAT is also used by guidance counselors as part of discussions regarding high school course readiness and career exploration. Colleges use SAT scores for recruiting and marketing purposes.

History

Content

The SAT started in 1926 as a very different test than its current version. The 1926 SAT consisted of 315 verbal reasoning and mathematics items administered in 97 minutes. Few if any of the 8,000 young men who took the test were expected to have enough time to answer all the questions.

In 1928, 1929, and 1936–1941, the SAT contained no mathematics items. Throughout the early years, the verbal reasoning items required examinees to select the correct response, but math items required examinees to produce a short answer. Beginning in 1942, all items used the multiple-choice format, allowing for more efficient scoring. In 1994, (machine scorable) short answer questions were reintroduced to the math section of the SAT.

The most recent changes to the content of the SAT were introduced in 2005 and are described in a subsequent section of this entry.

Name

Between 1926 and 1990, SAT was an acronym for Scholastic Aptitude Test. In 1990, the words associated with the acronym were changed to Scholastic Assessment Test. In 1994, the name of the test was changed to SAT, the letters no longer standing for any words.

Test Description

The SAT Reasoning Test consists of three measures: Critical Reading, Mathematics, and Writing.

Critical Reading

The critical reading measure consists of 48 passage-based reading items (traditionally called reading comprehension items) and 19 sentence completion items. Most of the items (approximately 70 percent) are used to assess the ability of a student to reason about the material read. The remaining items measure literal comprehension and vocabulary in context. Examinees have 70 minutes to answer the 67 items.

Mathematics

The mathematics measure consists of 44 multiple-choice items and 10 student-produced items. Examinees have 70 minutes to respond to the 54 items. The items cover a variety of mathematics topics—numbers and operations, algebra and functions, geometry and measurement, and data analysis, statistics, and probability.

Writing

The writing measure consists of an essay in response to an assigned topic and 49 multiple-choice items. Examinees have 25 minutes to write their essays and 35 minutes to respond to the multiple-choice items. The multiple-choice items require examinees to select ways to improve sentences, identify sentence errors, and improve paragraphs. The essay is scored by two readers, rating the essay based on the quality of the development and expression of a point of view on an issue. According to the College Board, a top score on the essay requires the student to demonstrate the following characteristics:

- Effectively and insightfully develops a point of view on the issue and demonstrates outstanding critical thinking, using clearly appropriate examples, reasons, and other evidence to support the student's position
- Is well organized and clearly focused, demonstrating clear coherence and smooth progression of ideas
- Exhibits skillful use of language, using a varied, accurate, and apt vocabulary
- Demonstrates meaningful variety in sentence structure
- Is free of most errors in grammar, usage, and mechanics

Score Scales

Each measure of the SATs is reported on a 200–800 score scale. Scores are rounded to the nearest 10. Several steps are performed to produce these scaled scores. First, the number of correct answers is counted for a section. Then, for multiple-choice items, one-quarter point is subtracted for each wrong answer (no points are subtracted for omitted responses). This adjustment, known as formula scoring, is performed to discourage random guessing in the hope of producing scores that more accurately reflect student achievement. Finally, the resulting formula score is mapped onto the 200–800 scale using a process called equating, which adjusts for any differences in the difficulty of the items in the form of a test given at a particular administration.

In addition to the scores for critical reading, mathematics, and writing, two subscores are reported for the writing measure—one 2–12 score for the essay that is the sum of the two reader scores, and a 20–80 score based on the multiple-choice items.

The current SAT critical reading and mathematics score scales were developed in 1995 so that the mean score of recent college-bound seniors was 500. A similar approach was used for the writing measure in 2005. The average scores will change every year based on differences in the population of students taking the test and the quality of the education and life experiences they have had. For college-bound students graduating in 2007, the averages were 502, 515, and 494 for critical reading, mathematics, and writing, respectively.

Percentile ranks (the percentage of students scoring the same or lower) are also provided for each scale score.

Technical Quality

The SAT is one of the most researched education tests in existence. Currently, the College Board

Web site provides more than 100 downloadable research reports on the SAT. A significantly larger number of research studies have been conducted by independent researchers.

The two most important characteristics of test scores are validity (does the test measure what it is purported to measure) and reliability (essentially, are test scores for individuals likely to be consistent across test editions and across time). Evidence regarding validity is complex and cannot be adequately summarized in the available space, but can be found in some of the reports provided by the College Board.

Reliability is typically measured on a scale that ranges from 0 to 1, with a 0 indicating scores are randomly inconsistent and a 1 indicating scores are perfectly consistent. For the test editions administered between March 2005 and June 2006, average reliability estimates were about .91, .92, and .90 for the critical reading, mathematics, and writing measures, respectively. When a composite score is used (either by summing the three measure scores or using statistically determined weights), the reliability of that composite would be higher.

Uses With Gifted, Creative, and Talented

Individually administered intelligence tests, such as the Wechsler Intelligence Test for Children, Stanford-Binet, or Das-Naglieri Cognitive Assessment Series, may be highly appropriate for identifying gifted children, but they must be administered by highly trained examiners and thus are much more expensive than are group-administered tests. On the other hand, most group-administered tests were not designed to differentiate among the most able examinees—designing a test to do so would weaken its discrimination power for the much larger group of test-takers in the middle of the distribution.

An alternative that can identify highly gifted students is to administer a test intended for older students. This approach has been used since at least 1972, when Julian Stanley initiated the Study of Mathematically Precocious Youth at Johns Hopkins University, using the SAT mathematics score as one of the criteria for selecting participants.

To maximize the efficiency of talent identification, several gifted and talented programs have chosen to use a two-tiered process. First students who *might* be among the most gifted are identified (for instance, based on norm-referenced school-administered tests or parent recommendations). As an example, the Center for Talented Youth (CTY) program at Johns Hopkins allows students in Grade 7 or 8 to apply if they have scored at or above the 95th percentile on an age or grade level appropriate nationally normed standardized test (the program also provides alternative ways to demonstrate equivalent merit). For these students the second stage requires taking the SAT or ACT, tests typically taken by students 4 or more years older who are in 11th or 12th grade. The CTY program only considers critical reading and mathematics scores from the SAT because these are most closely related to reasoning ability rather than educational achievement. In 2008, 7th-grade students must achieve a score of 550 in critical reading or mathematics, and 8-grade students must attain a score of 600 in critical reading or mathematics to qualify. The scores required of 7th-grade students are higher than those achieved by about 63 percent of all SAT test-takers. The scores required of 8th-grade students are higher than about 88 percent of all high school seniors.

In 1985, more than 80,000 children 13 or younger took the SAT. Based on data from 1999–2000 and 2000–2001, about 100,000 seventh graders and 33,000 eighth graders took the SAT each year. This number is continuing to grow. Most if not all of these tests are given as part of searches to identify highly talented youth.

Other academic talent search programs—such as the University of Iowa's Belin-Blank Exceptional Student Talent Search, Northwestern University Center for Talent Development, University of Denver Rocky Mountain Talent Search, and Duke University Talent Identification Program—all use a similar two-tiered approach.

In 1985, ETS performed a survey of these young test-takers and their parents. At that time, the sample was predominantly White (90 percent) with 2 percent identifying themselves as Black and 1 percent as Hispanic. The gender breakdown was approximately equal—48 percent boys and 52 percent girls. Their parents tended to be highly educated (for example, 65 percent of their fathers had attained at least a bachelor's degree, as opposed to 33 percent in a subsample of National

Assessment of Educational Progress (NAEP) test-takers who identified themselves as White.

Even at this young age, their aspirations were high, with 94 percent expecting to go to college and 43 percent expecting to attend graduate or professional school. Compared with the previously mentioned NAEP sample, this group spent more time doing homework and less time watching television, and had taken more advanced courses in their schools.

Neal Kingston

See also Study of Mathematically Precocious Youth; Talent Searches

Further Readings

College Board: http://www.collegeboard.com

College Board. *About the SAT*. Retrieved from http://www.collegeboard.com/student/testing/sat/about.html

Olszewski-Kubilius, P. (1994). Talent search: A driving force in gifted education. *Understanding Our Gifted*, 6(4), 1–3.

Saturday Programs

Considering the unique needs of gifted students, researchers and educators alike have supported the need for special academic programming for them. As schools are often unable to provide for these needs, special programs are routinely offered outside the normal school setting. One type of programming that remains popular with students and their parents is the Saturday enrichment courses offered through schools and universities. According to John Feldhusen, the founder of Purdue University's Super Saturday program, schools are often not equipped to offer gifted students the educational opportunities needed to meet their academic and social needs. However, because of the narrow focus afforded special Saturday programs, instructors are better able to match their curriculum to the specific needs and abilities of their gifted students. In addition, the ability to interact in these programs with intellectual peers enhances the gifted student's self-confidence, self-esteem, and motivation. This entry describes structures and benefits of Saturday programs, as well as professional development for teachers.

Program Structures

A search of Saturday program opportunities reveals a vast array of alternatives. The styles and structures offered are as varied as the organizations providing the opportunities. Individual schools and school districts often offer a menu of Saturday enrichment choices. Often these programs are not designed specifically for high-ability students but are available to the school's entire student body. As enrichment, they often are seen as fun, engaging activities with little consideration given to the unique needs of gifted students.

A second source for Saturday enrichment programs has come through colleges and universities (e.g., Georgia State University, Northwestern University, Purdue University, University of Cincinnati, University of Southern Mississippi). Most often offered through the university's school of education, there is a greater acknowledgment and understanding of the need for specific programming for gifted students including faster pacing of instruction and more complex materials (both in depth and breadth).

Many university programs attempt to identify students who are most in need of specific services because of their advanced abilities. This is generally done through standardized test scores, IQ scores, evidence of prior participation in gifted programs, and letters of recommendation. The stringency with which programs adhere to individual standards varies according to the program's goals and organization. Although most Saturday programs offer a wide variety of enrichment courses focused on individual student interests, others are targeted toward a specific academic area (e.g., mathematics) using curriculum at an appropriate pace for gifted students.

Saturday programs are presented in a wide range of formats. Some offer one class for a few hours for a single Saturday with individual classes on consecutive Saturdays offering several different enrichment options for the students. Other programs offer one course taken over a more expansive period, generally a few hours each Saturday for 6 to 8 weeks. As all programs are unrestricted by a standardized school curriculum, the instructors are able to adjust their courses to meet the interests, ability, and pacing needs of their gifted students.

Benefits

Although research supports the positive effects in achievement for gifted students in other types of programs (e.g., pull-out and self-contained programs within the normal school setting and summer residential programs), a more limited body of knowledge is available concerning the specific benefits of Saturday programs. However, two recent studies, one that surveyed parents and the other that interviewed parents and students, indicated that students and parents felt students benefited from the challenge level of courses experienced in the Saturday programs. In addition, most parents believed the programs increased their children's motivation to learn as well as their academic confidence, especially as it applied to the specific subject matter studied. Parents also indicated that their children participated more in the Saturday classes than their regular classrooms and were more excited by the academic challenges offered. It was also noted that the variety of course offerings exposed the students to areas of study not found in the regular classroom.

Furthermore, many parents noted positive social and emotional outcomes of being with true academic peers. A small number of parents indicated that their children were not understood or accepted in the regular classroom, but identified with classmates in their Saturday programs. One parent went so far as to indicate that his daughter felt more "normal" in her Saturday classes. In addition, the students and parents emphasized the students' increased confidence in their academic abilities and the resulting increase in self-esteem.

Professional Development for Teachers

An added advantage to offering Saturday programming for gifted students is the practicum environment offered for teachers. Being exposed to the significant differences of gifted students as well as the opportunity to write curriculum that is appropriate for them affords teachers a strong professional development opportunity not found elsewhere. Some programs, such as the Purdue Super Saturday Program, offer this opportunity to preservice in addition to inservice teachers. The increased knowledge gained through the experience for the teachers is often translated into more appropriate experiences for gifted students in their standard classrooms.

Implications

High-ability students need access to curriculum that is appropriately challenging and paced. They also need to be exposed to peers who accept them and their abilities. Saturday programs afford a wealth of opportunities for students to grow academically as well as socially and emotionally. In addition, these programs offer practice in a unique environment in which teachers can become more aware of the needs of their gifted students.

Nancy J. Bangel

See also Academic Talent; Achievement Motivation; Creative Organizational Climate; Elementary Enrichment; Friendships; Middle School Enrichment; Parental Attitudes; Self-Efficacy/Self-Esteem; Teacher Training

Further Readings

Bangel, N. J., Enersen, D., Capobianco, B., & Moon, S. M. (2006). Professional development of preservice teachers: Teaching in the Super Saturday program. *Journal for the Education of the Gifted, 29,* 339–361.

Flack, J., & Friedberg, J. (1997). When children go to college on Saturday. *Teaching PreK–8, 27,* 44–46.

Olszewski-Kubilius, P., & Lee, S. (2004). Parent perceptions of the effects of the Saturday Enrichment Program on gifted students' talent development. *Roeper Review, 26,* 156.

Wood, B., & Feldhusen, J. F. (1996). Creating special interest programs for gifted youth: Purdue's Super Saturday serves as successful model. *Gifted Child Today, 19,* 22–25, 28–29, 40–42.

Savants

The term *savant* is borrowed from the French as a derivative of the verb *savoir,* which means "to know." *Savant* means "learned person" or "eminent scholar" and it has been in circulation in

English with a similar meaning since the 1800s. Its first use as part of the phrase *idiot savant* is jointly attributed to John Langdon Down, the physician who also identified the genetic disorder known as Down syndrome, and to Alfred Binet, the inventor of first intelligence test. Down first used the term *idiot savant* in 1887 to describe 10 cases of extraordinary individuals whom he encountered during his 30 years as the superintendent of London's Earlswood Asylum. In 1905, Alfred Binet also used the term *idiot savant* to describe cognitively impaired persons who showed an outstanding ability in a specific area. Even before the term *idiot savant* was used, however, there had been descriptions of savant skills in the scientific literature. As early as 1783, a German psychology journal published a case study of Englishman Jedediah Buxton's mathematical calculating skills, and in 1789, Benjamin Rush, founder of U.S. psychiatry, published a case study of the extraordinary calculating ability of his patient, Thomas Fuller.

Down used the term *idiot savant* to describe individuals of low cognitive functioning who carried a then-common clinical label "idiot," but who nevertheless possessed "savant" abilities in a certain area employing extraordinary memory. One of these cases was a cognitively disabled patient who could recite by heart Gibbon's enormous *Decline and Fall of the Roman Empire*. Down's original case studies have significance for our understanding of savant phenomena beyond their historical precedence; they also offer insight into the educational environment that may support savant talent. Earlswood Asylum under Down's leadership was an unusual place in an era when institutions served as holding facilities for the "feeble-minded," as cognitively disabled persons were called then. The residents of Earlswood were systematically educated, their special abilities nurtured, and they were treated by the staff with respect and were considered family members. Under these relatively favorable conditions, an extraordinary craftsman, James Pullen, called the "Genius of Earlswood," produced exquisite models and engravings of ships. In the United States, equally famous was Thomas "Blind Tom" Wiggins, a slave on a Georgia plantation, who in early childhood developed such an extraordinary musical talent that it brought him at age 11 to the White House to play the piano before President James Buchanan.

This entry describes the sociocultural context of savant ability, the nature and origins of savant skills, and future directions of savant research.

Sociocultural Context of Savant Ability

Until the Individuals with Disabilities Education Act of 1975 reshaped the treatment of persons with disabilities in U.S. life by requiring that they be educated in the least restrictive environment, most persons with cognitive disabilities spent their lives in institutions. Thus, the first cases of savant talent were usually described in an institutional context. Since 1975, the altered treatment context of disabled persons has had critical implications for understanding savant ability and developing educational approaches for individuals with savant talent. As children with savant skills grow up today as members of their families and the larger society, rather than as wards of institutions, educational approaches are much better suited to meet their complex special needs.

Nature and Origins of Savant Skills

Although the pejorative term *idiot savant* has given way to a more respectful *savant syndrome,* the definition continues to rely on a discrepancy-based model: to be diagnosed with a savant syndrome, one has to demonstrate intra-individual discrepancies in performance on standardized tests or common tasks across functional domains. For example, individuals are thought to have savant syndrome if they can carry out complex calendaric calculations but cannot solve simple arithmetic problems and have impaired communicative abilities. *Splinter skills* is another term used to describe such discrepancies in performance where functioning is dramatically uneven across different areas.

The five most common areas of savant skills are visual arts (drawing, painting, sculpture); music (composition and performance, most often on the piano); arithmetic (prime-number derivation); calendar (precise identification of the day of the week on which any date fell or will fall, regardless of the date's remoteness from the present); mechanics and space relations (special ability to memorize maps, directions, or to construct complex models or structures with great accuracy). The nonsymbolic, concrete, and directly perceived nature of these skills has led neuroscientists to propose that savant skills are right hemispheric in type, compared with the left-hemispheric skills that are predominantly symbolic and linguistic. One currently debated theory of the origins of savant syndrome is that savant abilities are the result of an injury to the left hemisphere with the right hemispheric overcompensating. Additional insights into the left-hemispheric origins of savant skills come from studies of previously nondisabled persons who develop new extraordinary abilities after a brain injury. Individuals with frontotemporal dementia, for example, often have no history of artistic ability yet develop remarkable artistic talent as the dementia progresses.

Because autism is a condition that often involves a discrepancy between areas of functioning, most commonly between verbal and performance IQ, it is more often associated with savant syndrome than are other neurodevelopmental conditions. Survey studies suggest that approximately half of all persons with savant syndrome also have autism, and the other half have other forms of developmental disabilities and disorders or injuries to the central nervous system. This does not mean, however, that many persons diagnosed with autism possess savant skills. The misconception that persons with autism commonly have savant skills was reflected in the 1988 Hollywood film *Rain Man*. These cultural misconceptions influence the lives of gifted individuals who have been diagnosed with autism spectrum disorders.

For example, young jazz musician Matt Savage, who was diagnosed with a nonspecific pervasive developmental disorder at age 3, has been called a "musical savant" by specialists, whereas a young person who shows a similar extraordinary musical talent in the absence of a clinical diagnosis would be called a "musical prodigy." A leader of a jazz trio and a prolific composer with eight music CDs to his credit, Savage has performed with such world-famous jazz musicians as Dave Brubeck and Wynton Marsalis. Savage's path to musical giftedness started with hyperlexia, a condition characterized by spontaneous and precocious mastery of single-word reading that emerges in advance of reading comprehension. Hyperlexia has been receiving increasing attention from researchers because it seems to provide a key to understanding the special skills of those affected by autism.

The estimated prevalence of those with savant skills among individuals with autism is approximately 9.8 percent, but prevalence among those with cognitive impairments is approximately 0.06 percent. A challenge to these estimations has come with the expansion of diagnostic criteria for autism in the past decade, which may have led to a diagnostic migration from other disorders to the autism spectrum. In addition, standardized testing does not usually offer adaptations for difficulties in reading comprehension, semantic processing, and for sensory-motor challenges. Such impairments may significantly distort the estimates of intraindividual functioning for some individuals.

Future Directions

The question researchers continue to struggle with is "how are savants different from normally developing gifted persons!" especially when savant talents and skills prodigiously manifest in childhood. Another important question raised in the savant syndrome field is whether savant talent can lead to lifelong achievement. The music played by Savage's jazz trio and the remarkable achievements of others with extraordinary talents accompanied by developmental challenges suggest a positive answer to this question. Another question awaiting further research is whether and how savant talent is different from giftedness or even genius in people without developmental disabilities. These questions are consequential because they provide the ideological and ethical foundation for educational practices and for expansion of learning opportunities for those with savant skills. These questions address the core dilemmas of how educational institutions regard the potential contribution of students with special needs to the intellectual and cultural life of society.

Olga Solomon

See also Asperger's Syndrome; Autism; Genius; Prodigies

Further Readings

Heaton, P., & Wallace, G. L. (2004). Annotation: The savant syndrome. *Journal of Child Psychology and Psychiatry, 45*(5), 899–911.

Miller, L. K. (1999). The savant syndrome: Intellectual impairment and exceptional skill. *Psychological Bulletin, 125*(1), 31–46.

Treffert, D. A. (2006). *Extraordinary people: Understanding savant syndrome.* Lincoln, NE: iUniverse.

Scholarships

A *scholarship* is defined as a financial grant awarded to a student so the student can attend an educational program. This entry focuses on the wide variety of scholarships available across educational levels and across international, national, state, regional, and local geographical locations. Public and private scholarships are open to students across K–12, undergraduate, graduate, dissertation, postdoctoral, early scholar, and grant awards. Awards are tailored to academic, athletic, the arts, and specific-talent domain areas.

A variety of scholarships from small to large financial awards are options to which students can apply or be nominated. Savvy scholarship seekers are aware of opportunities on the local, state, and national arenas and actively stay abreast of changes by scanning the print and online environment.

Financial awards increase accessibility to educational programs beginning with early education programs for young children and continuing through middle and high schools and beyond for cocurricular activities. For applicants, past success may breed future success and a record of previous attainment of merit awards may positively affect an applicant's future attainment of other awards.

Preparations for Applications

Well-known scholarship awards such as the Truman, Goldwater, Fulbright, and Rhodes prizes should be planned for. Being competitive for a selective scholarship requires the same kind of preparation necessary to be competitive for admittance to a strong school. Such preparation requires that applicants recognize the domino effect of their actions and that by laying a strong foundation for the career that they intend to pursue, they will likely be good candidates for scholarships in that chosen field of study.

Preparation also includes the need to start early in preparing to compete for scholarships. Some scholarships require extra preparation, and applicants may need several months in advance of submitting the actual award application to complete the application package. Students should make appointments to meet with school counselors, teachers, administrators, past recipients, and college recruiters to discuss scholarship opportunities early in the school year and create a personal timeline for application preparation and submission for the academic calendar year.

To be an eligible scholarship candidate and maximize chances of receiving an award, it is necessary to develop and follow a plan for targeting and pursuing scholarships. Although most scholarships may be open to applicants, some scholarships require nominations for consideration. In these instances, interested applicants may want to consider approaching a teacher or administrator for consideration. To prepare for comprehensive scholarship applications, students may choose to start and keep up a "resume" folder that provides a place for them to store and reference their activities and reflective experiences that they may choose to cite in essays that ask applicants to write about their learning experiences. Applicants may also want to compose and regularly revise their personal written goals. This allows for ongoing reflection as well as inputs that may be used in creating essay responses.

Because some applications require references, applicants should think of three to five people with whom they have close relationships to serve as references for them. References should know the applicant well to write a letter that will be meaningfully revealing to the scholarship selection committee.

The following are some preparation tips for students who are considering applying for scholarships:

1. Research scholarship possibilities.
2. Develop career goals.
3. Organize existing knowledge base.
4. Identify knowledge gaps and educational needs to pursue career goals.
5. Describe immediate educational needs, discuss preparations for the future and how the student

will contribute through his or her career, discuss technical assistance needed, describe the student's plan for how to make change and communicate those ideas.

6. Integrate both short-term decision making and long-range planning.
7. Demonstrate excellence daily and illustrate that excellence in a well-crafted application packet.

Scholarship Opportunity Examples

A wide variety of scholarships are available for high-ability students across the K–12 spectrum for participating in educational programs. Scholarship awards have a variety of requirements. Although some are competitive based on merit excellence in a specific subject area, some are noncompetitive, and some are based on financial need. The following two examples of scholarships for gifted students are intended to provide a stimulus for researching other awards specific to the reader:

> Annual award for a Texas graduating high school senior who is gifted and talented. Applicants must demonstrate outstanding leadership.
>
> Davidson Fellows Award applications available for $50,000 and $10,000 scholarships. Applications for the Davidson Fellows Award are available for students under the age of 18 who have completed a significant piece of work in science, technology, mathematics, music, literature, or philosophy. Individuals named as Davidson Fellow Laureates receive $50,000 scholarships and those named as Davidson Fellows receive $10,000 scholarships. These scholarships may be used for tuition and related expenses at accredited institutions of learning. To be eligible, applicants must be under the age of 18 and be U.S. citizens or permanent U.S. residents. There is no minimum age for eligibility. Each submission must be an original piece of work recognized by experts in the field as "significant" and have the potential to make a positive contribution to society.

Becoming a Good Candidate

To be a good candidate for scholarships, applicants must strive for excellence in their activities. Many Web sites discuss tips or advice for putting forth the best foot in an application process. Expanding one's personal knowledge base through work, internship, and volunteer experiences in a specific field and across a variety of settings will enhance and inform a candidate's application. Applicants can develop relationships with people in their chosen career paths to discuss the details of preparing for a career in a specific area. These relationships provide opportunities for mentoring, networking, and potential references. Getting involved in interesting extracurricular activities that are personally meaningful will enrich personal and professional perspectives and can be described in scholarship essays. Seeking leadership opportunities within activities that are personally and professionally important provides opportunities for individual growth and transformation. Finally, to be competitive for scholarships, applicants should stay informed about the latest views and opinions in their field of choice and be able to discuss varying viewpoints.

Specific strategies to increase the chances of an individual student winning a scholarship may include the following:

- Apply for both large and small scholarships.
- Submit essays to contests.
- Know the eligibility requirements and deadlines for various scholarships. Students should always allow plenty of time to write and review their applications before the due date.
- Work on communication skills. Many scholarships require interviews.
- Students should not give up if they are turned down. Many highly qualified people are turned down at some point but go on to find other awards or opportunities that suit their interests.

Bronwyn MacFarlane

See also Academic Advising; Academic Talent; National Merit Scholarship Program; Presidential Scholars

Further Readings

Davidson Fellow Scholarships: http://www.davidsongifted.org/fellows

Hoagies Gifted Education Page, College Scholarships: http://www.hoagiesgifted.org/scholarships.htm

Jack Kent Cooke Foundation:
http://www.jkcf.org/scholarships
Karnes, F., & Riley, T. (2005). *Competitions for talented kids*. Waco, TX: Prufrock Press.

School Attitudes

Gifted and talented students grow up in a world of mixed messages where their gifted behavior is both expected, yet often, unaccepted. It's no wonder there is still a great mystery about why the attitudes of gifted and talented students differ. Much of the conflict gifted students experience in schools is a consequence of their advanced developmental rate and the emergence of more complex abilities and interests, which causes them to be "different" from the "expected" behavior of non-gifted students of the same age. Questions such as, "Why does one gifted and talented student achieve and flourish in most traditional educational settings, and yet another not?" remain unanswered. Sometimes educators encourage their students to be creative and show what they know, but other times such intelligence and creativity are ignored or met with negativity. Many characteristics of the gifted, including persistence, criticalness, and the tendency to master generalizations at the expense of detail, pose a number of difficulties for the classroom teacher. This entry explores the attitudes of schools, teachers, parents, and curriculum toward gifted and talented students.

School Attitudes

The culture and climate of the school needs to create a learning environment where the philosophy is that all students should be expected to develop their strengths and weaknesses to the fullest. Gifted students will need a nurturing school environment that respects differences among its students and strives to develop the "whole" student with every learning opportunity.

Appropriate expectations and learning experiences in school depend on accurate recognition of a child's performance level or potential. Schools often hold beliefs and attitudes that result in actions that can be damaging to the optimal growth of gifted children. There is a need for schools to value uniqueness and talent in all children and to nurture and respect giftedness wherever it is found. To make a positive difference in what all human beings can be and how much of their potential they can develop and enjoy, the limiting ideologies that include the notion that gifted students will survive because of their intelligence must be dispelled. Schools need to recognize that gifted and talented students think differently than do most students their own age and require modifications to curriculum, organizational structure, teaching methods, and social constructs to maximize their learning potential.

Currently, most schools provide programming for gifted students that includes enrichment, acceleration, or special grouping in settings, or a combination of these program organizations. For these program options to be successful, the gifted students' strengths need to be encouraged and developed; the learning environment needs to provide alternative learning opportunities for expanding knowledge cognitively, emotionally, and socially; individual differences such as interests, abilities, learning rates, and learning styles need to be addressed; and gifted students need to have contact with other gifted students to provide opportunities where they are challenged by the thoughts of their peers.

Teachers' Attitudes

One of the most important factors affecting the success of gifted and talented students in schools is the selection of high-quality teachers who understand the unique needs and characteristics of gifted students. These teachers, as well as all other teachers, need to view gifted students as they would any other valuable natural resource: to be conserved, developed, and used for the good of all. Teachers need to recognize that there are multiple kinds of giftedness and that there is no one preferred teaching method to teach gifted students.

Gifted and talented students want teachers who understand subject matter, make students feel significant by taking time to talk, provide access to additional learning, show a sense of humor, set high standards, provide constructive criticism, are sensitive to their social and emotional needs, and see students for who they are. In addition, teachers who have no feelings of incompetence or failure if they do not know something about a gifted child's particular interests are more likely to be successful working with gifted and talented. The successful teacher is one who can allow the gifted student's intellect to fly higher than the teacher can ever hope to soar and take joy in playing a role in that effort. Being a continual learner is inescapable when teaching gifted and talented students.

Teachers of gifted and talented teachers also serve as the liaison between the school and the home. Many times when the school does not recognize the needs of gifted students, the teacher becomes the recipient of the parents' frustrations and quite often becomes the counselor for the parent with respect to recommending and suggesting what the parent should be doing at home to foster continued interest in school and encourage appropriate behavior in the classroom. Therefore, it is extremely important for teachers to become knowledgeable about coping strategies that can be applied both in school and at home to accommodate the behaviors and habits of gifted students that can become intolerable at times.

Parents' Attitudes

Parents have definite views on the learning needs of their children and understand that their child's learning needs are unique and different from the needs of their siblings. Parents also have opinions about how they can provide input into their child's education. This is why parents of gifted and talented students often become a strong "interest group" that applies pressure to local boards of education, school administrators, and teachers to provide what they believe are appropriate programs for their children and to have the opportunity to provide input before decisions are made that affect programs provided for gifted and talented students.

According to a study conducted by Nancy Hertzog and Tess Bennett, parents recognized that their children needed school environments that were challenging and stimulating and that their children needed opportunities to be creative. As a result, parents are often faced with having to make choices about their children's education (should the child attend the gifted pull-out program; should the child be accelerated, etc.). This same study also revealed that parents' perceptions of their child's needs are influenced by the availability of school and community resources, their values, and notions of giftedness. However, the data also showed that even though many programs for gifted and talented students focus on developing academics, parents were sensitive to the personal, emotional, and social needs of their child and would seek activities in art, music, drama, family trips and activities, and so on, outside the school to provide their child with well-rounded experiences.

Instructional Attitudes

The curriculum provides the framework for learning, and the curriculum shapes the organization and instruction that takes place in the classroom. The curriculum for gifted students must reflect what is happening in society and provide opportunities for students to apply what they are learning to real-life learning scenarios. Gifted students are often well read and are cognizant and knowledgeable about current events and what is happening in the world around them. Therefore, learning about current evens needs to be a part of the curriculum. Learning also needs to include the use of modern technology, reflecting what is being used in the "real world," so that students are prepared to acquire and evaluate information with expediency. Gifted students need to have a reason to become involved in the learning process or they will generally drift off on their own to find a purpose to pursue. Sometimes the curiosity of a gifted student enlisted by asking one essential question will be the driving force that takes the student far beyond the expectations of the learning scenario.

Successful teaching approaches for gifted students include activities where students must be creative, think critically, and be able to problem solve. Such activities should include the discussion of attitudes and values about self and social responsibility as well as incorporate research and study skills. Therefore, although many gifted students prefer to work independently of others in the class, they should at times work collaboratively with other students in cooperative learning groups. It is just as important for gifted students to develop appropriate social skills as it is for them to be challenged academically. Teachers of gifted students must suspend judgment and practice generating essential questions that will cause gifted students to continue their exploration of viable solutions to the problem presented.

Outlook

The attitudes of gifted and talented students require teachers and schools to modify and adjust teaching techniques and the school learning environment to meet each student's individual needs. In addition to the cognitive needs of gifted and talented students, schools must address their emotional, social, and psychological needs. To do so, resources and a variety of programs for gifted and talented students need to be expanded and enhanced. Rather than believe that gifted and talented students will do just fine because they have an innate ability to be successful if they want to be, schools and educators must recognize that gifted and talented students will not reach their maximum potential unless their giftedness is cultivated.

JoAnn P. Susko

See also Academic Talent; Adolescent, Gifted; Asia, Gifted Education; Attitudes Toward Gifted; Canada, Gifted Education; Giftedness, Definition; Teacher Attitudes

Further Readings

Ambrose, D., Cohen, L., & Tannenbaum, A. (2003). *Creative intelligence: Toward theoretic integration.* Cresskill, NJ: Hampton Press.

Coleman, L., & Cross, T. (2003). *Being gifted in school* (2nd ed.). Waco, TX: Prufrock Press.

Hertzog, N., & Bennett, T. (2004, Winter). In whose eyes? Parents' perspectives on the learning needs of their gifted children. *Roeper Review, 26*(2), 96–104.

Tomlinson, C. (1999). *The differentiated classroom-responding to the needs of all learners.* Alexandria, VA: Association for Supervision and Curriculum Development.

Tuttle, F., Becker, L., & Sousa, J. (1988). *Characteristics and identification of gifted and talented students* (3rd ed.). Washington, DC: National Education Association Press.

School Psychologists

School psychology is generally acknowledged as a general practice and health service provider specialty of professional psychology that is concerned with the science and practice of psychology with children, youth, and families; learners of all ages; and the schooling process. The basic education and training of school psychologists prepares them to provide a multitude of psychological services: psychological diagnosis, assessment, intervention, prevention, health promotion, and program development and evaluation services with a special focus on the developmental processes of children and youth within the context of schools, families, and other systems. School psychologists are prepared to intervene at the individual and system level, and to develop, implement, and evaluate preventive programs. In these efforts, school psychologists conduct ecologically valid assessments and intervene to promote positive learning environments within which children and youth from diverse backgrounds have equal access to effective educational and psychological services that promote healthy development.

School psychologists provide a variety of services for gifted, talented, and creative students. One of the most important is assessment. For schools that require intelligence testing for admission to gifted education programs, the school psychologist is usually the professional who administers and interprets the tests. In addition, school psychologists may be called on to consult with teachers and parents in designing individualized educational programs for gifted students who need special provisions to enhance their academic progress. Finally, twice-exceptional gifted students may need the services of school psychologists for the identification and treatment of and the referral for learning disabilities and psychological disorders.

This entry describes the background, education and training, and roles and functions of school psychologists.

Background

School psychology is not a new field. As early as 1898, the term *school psychologist* was used in print, with strong origins in Western Europe.

Alfred Binet's groundbreaking work on the development of mental ability in 1905, and the establishment of child development centers in the late 1890s and early 1900s in universities throughout Europe and North America spurred the emergence of school psychology as a discipline. In the mid-1950s, school psychology began to emerge as its own discipline, and in 1996, the International School Psychology Association (ISPA, founded in 1982) developed and adopted guidelines for the preparation of school psychologists.

International surveys of school psychologists reveal considerable diversity in how they are regulated and the orientation of their work. Recent data suggest that their diverse roles include focusing on a biologically based framework (providing basic care to children with severe mental or physical handicaps), efforts to socialize young children and provide vocational guidance to older individuals, educational and psychological assessments with an emphasis on special education issues, and the development and implementation of systems interventions (e.g., consultations, organizational development, research, and evaluation).

Education and Training

The academic and professional preparation and regulation of school psychologists varies considerably. In some countries, the equivalent of an undergraduate degree specializing in applied psychology is sufficient whereas in Canada and the United States more advanced graduate training is mandatory (there currently exists a controversy about whether a master's level or doctoral level certification should be required). Although the coursework and academic degrees needed to be recognized because school psychologists differ from country to country, the coursework and preparation has been quite similar. International guidelines for the preparation and certification of school psychologists have been proposed by the International School Psychology Association, the National Association of School Psychologists, and the American Psychological Association in the United States and the Canadian Association of School Psychologists and the Canadian Psychological Association in Canada.

The training of school psychologists draws from many different disciplines in both education and psychology: developmental psychology, psychopathology, personality, social psychology, biological and neurological bases of behavior, psychology of learning, clinical psychology, research and statistics, psychometry, psychiatry, early intervention, and curriculum design among others. Changes have occurred in diversity awareness, technological applications, increasing knowledge of cognitive science, and empirically based best practices in school psychology.

Roles and Functions

Much of the direct work and the roles and functions of school psychologists are often dictated by local job demands. Although most school psychologists work in educational environments (school systems with children and adolescents), others work in residential settings, mental health clinics, hospital or medical facilities, research units, universities, and state or federal departments of education.

A shifting of school-based psychological services appears to be occurring. In a recent report, the primary services provided by school psychologists included assessment (46%), consultation (16%), interventions (13%), counseling (8%), conferencing (7%), supervision (3%), parent training (3%), inservicing (2%), and research (1%). Today, most school psychologists appear to be engaged more often in consultation and other direct services than purely assessment work.

The changing roles and mandates of school psychologists parallel societal changes. Along with the emergence of special education services, school psychologists were required to play a diversified role. More than 70 percent of mothers of school-age children work outside the home and numerous parents of children of school age are divorcing; all of which are affecting the social and emotional development of their children. Technological and environmental changes have resulted in new childhood disorders (e.g., Internet addiction, gambling disorders). Significant legislative acts and ethical issues have similarly affected the roles and functions of school psychologists (especially in the applications of psychological assessments). All these changes have resulted in new challenges for school psychologists.

The school psychologist's role in helping serve students with special needs has not been diminished. Although the assessment function is abating in many jurisdictions, it nevertheless remains a principal role in identifying children with special needs. With respect to the gifted and talented, many school psychologists remain active in assessment strategies for placements, acceleration, or program development. Although the field of special education has witnessed a movement toward mainstreaming, children who are intellectually gifted and talented still require special services to optimize their educational, social, and emotional needs. School psychologists can play an important role in assessing intellectual giftedness, creativity, and talent as well as in providing support for the individual, the child's parent, and the educational system.

Jeffrey L. Derevensky

See also Administrative Attitudes; Guidance; Identification; Intelligence Testing

Further Readings

American Psychological Association. (2006). *Archival description of school psychology.* Retrieved from http:/www.apa.org/crsppp/schpsych.html

Cunningham, J. (2006). Centripetal and centrifugal trends influencing school psychology's international development. In S. R. Jimerson, T. D. Oakland, & P. T. Farrell (Eds.), *The handbook of international school psychology* (pp. 463–474). Thousand Oaks, CA: Sage.

Cunningham, J., & Oakland, T. (1998). International School Psychology Association guidelines for the preparation of school psychologists. *School Psychology International, 19,* 19–30.

Fagan, T. K., & Wise, P. S. (2007). *School psychology: Past, present and future* (3rd ed.). Bethesda, MD: National Association of School Psychologists.

Oakland, T. (2007). International school psychology. In T. K. Fagan & P. S. Wise (Eds.), *School psychology: Past, present and future* (3rd ed., pp. 339–365). Bethesda, MD: National Association of School Psychologists.

Reynolds, C. R., & Gutkin, T. B. (1999). *The handbook of school psychology* (3rd ed.). New York: Wiley.

Thomas, A., & Grimes, J. (Eds.). (2002). *Best practices in school psychology, IV* (Vol. 1 & 2). Bethesda, MD: National Association of School Psychologists.

Ysseldyke, J. E., Burns, M., Dawson, P., Kelley, B., Morrison, D., Ortiz, S., et al. (2006). *School psychology: A blueprint for training and Practice III.* Bethesda, MD: National Association of School Psychologists.

Schoolwide Enrichment Model

Joseph Renzulli and Sally Reis developed the *schoolwide enrichment model* (SEM) to encourage and develop creative productivity in young people. The SEM is based on Renzulli's *enrichment triad model* and it has been implemented in more than 3,000 schools across the United States and has continued to expand internationally. The effectiveness of the model has been studied during more than 30 years of research and field-testing about (a) the effectiveness of the model as perceived by key groups, such as principals; (b) student creative productivity; (c) personal and social development; (d) the use of SEM with culturally diverse or special-needs populations; (e) student self-efficacy; (f) the SEM as a curricular framework; (g) learning styles and curriculum compacting; and (h) longitudinal research on the SEM. This research on the SEM suggests that the model is effective at serving high-ability students and providing enrichment in a variety of educational settings, including schools serving culturally diverse and low socioeconomic populations. This entry describes the theoretical underpinnings of the SEM, identification of the talent pool, components of SEM, and Renzulli Learning.

Theoretical Underpinnings

The SEM is based on Renzulli's three-ring conception of giftedness that defines gifted behaviors rather than gifted individuals and the enrichment triad model. The SEM is currently used as the basis for many gifted programs, enrichment programs, magnet schools, charter, and theme schools. The original enrichment triad model is the core of the SEM. Type I enrichment is designed to expose students to a wide variety of disciplines, topics, occupations, hobbies, persons, places, and events that would not ordinarily be covered in the regular curriculum. Type II enrichment includes materials and methods designed to promote the development of thinking and feeling processes. Some Type II enrichment is general, consisting of training in areas such as creative thinking and problem solving, learning how to learn skills such as classifying and analyzing data, and advanced reference and communication skills. Type III enrichment involves students who become interested in pursuing a self-selected area and are willing to commit the time necessary for advanced content acquisition and process training in which they assume the role of a firsthand inquirer.

The SEM focuses on the development of both academic and creative-productive giftedness. Creative-productive giftedness describes those aspects of human activity and involvement where a premium is placed on the development of original material and products that are purposefully designed to affect one or more target audiences. Learning situations designed to promote creative-productive giftedness emphasize the use and application of information (content) and thinking skills in an integrated, inductive, and real-problem-oriented manner. In the SEM, academic gifts are developed because the role of the student is transformed from that of a learner of lessons to one in which she or he uses the modus operandi of a firsthand inquirer to experience the joys and frustrations of creative productivity. This approach is quite different from the development of giftedness that tends to emphasize deductive learning, advanced content and problem solving, and the acquisition, storage, and retrieval of information. In other words, creative-productive giftedness enables children to work on issues and areas of study that have personal relevance to them and can be escalated to appropriately challenging levels of investigative activity.

Identification of Talent Pool

The SEM has three major goals that are designed to challenge and meet all of the needs of high-potential, high-ability, and gifted students and, at the same time, provide challenging learning experiences for all students. In the SEM, a talent pool of 10 to 20 percent of above-average ability/high-potential students is identified through a variety of measures including the following: achievement tests, teacher nominations, assessment of potential for creativity and task commitment, and alternative pathways of entrance (self-nomination, parent nomination, etc.). High-achievement tests or IQ test scores automatically include a student in the talent pool, enabling those students who are underachieving in their academic schoolwork to be included.

Components

The SEM has three components that provide services to students: the Total Talent Portfolio, Curriculum Modification and Differentiation, and Enrichment (see Figure 1). These three services are delivered across the regular curriculum, a continuum of services, and a series of enrichment clusters. Once students are identified for the talent pool, they are eligible for these services. First, interest and learning styles assessments are used with talent-pool students, in the development of a total talent portfolio for each student. Style preferences include projects, independent study, teaching games, simulations, peer teaching, programmed instruction, lecture, drill and recitation, and discussion.

Second, curriculum compacting and other forms of modification are provided to all eligible students for whom the regular curriculum must be adjusted. This elimination or streamlining of curriculum enables above-average students to avoid repetition of previously mastered work and guarantees mastery while finding time for more appropriately challenging activities. A form, entitled the Compactor, is used to document which content areas have been compacted and what alternative work has been substituted.

Third, a series of enrichment opportunities organized around the *enrichment triad model* offer three types of enrichment experiences through various forms of delivery, including enrichment clusters. Types I, II, and III enrichment are offered to all students; however, Type III enrichment is usually more appropriate for students with higher levels of ability, interest, and task commitment.

In the SEM, teachers are encouraged to work with students to help them better understand three dimensions of their own learning: their abilities, interests, and learning styles. This information, focusing on their strengths rather than on deficits, is compiled into a total talent portfolio that can be

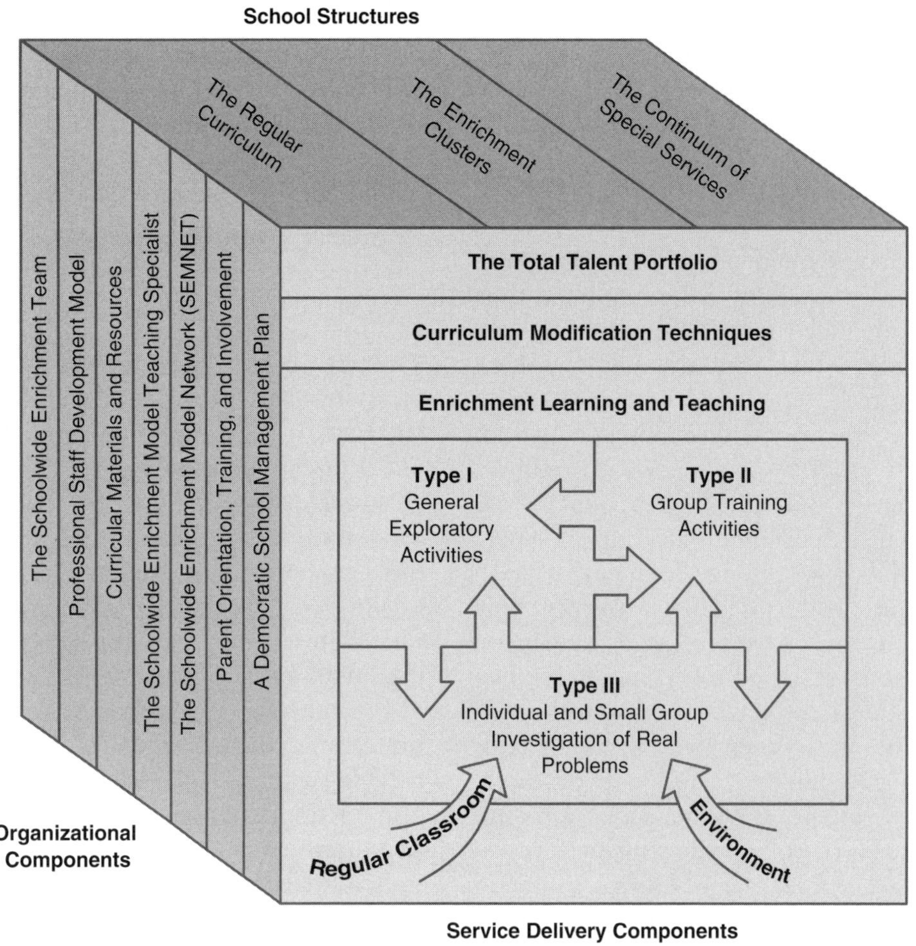

Figure 1 The Schoolwide Enrichment Model

Source: Renzulli, J. S., & Reis, S. M. Available from http://www.gifted.uconn.edu/sem/semexec.html

subsequently used to make decisions about talent development opportunities in regular classes, enrichment clusters, or in the continuum of special services. The ultimate goal of learning that is guided by these principles and the SEM is to replace dependent and passive learning with independent and engaged learning. The three service delivery components of the SEM (total talent portfolio, curriculum compacting, and enrichment teaching and learning) are applied to three school structures: the regular curriculum, enrichment clusters, and a continuum of services.

The Regular Curriculum

The regular curriculum consists of everything that is a part of the predetermined goals, schedules, learning outcomes, and delivery systems of the school. The regular curriculum might be traditional, innovative, or in the process of transition, but its predominant feature is that authoritative forces (i.e., policymakers, school councils, textbook adoption committees, state regulators) have determined that the regular curriculum should be the centerpiece of student learning. Application of the SEM influences the regular curriculum in three ways: through processes such as curriculum compacting and textbook content modification procedures; systematic content intensification procedures used to replace eliminated content with selected, in-depth learning experiences; and the types of enrichment recommended in the enrichment triad model that can be integrated selectively into regular curriculum activities.

The Enrichment Clusters

The enrichment clusters, a second component of the SEM, are nongraded groups of students who share common interests, and who come together during specially designated time blocks during school to work with an adult who shares their interests and who has some degree of advanced knowledge and expertise in the area. Enrichment clusters usually meet for a block of time weekly during a semester. All students complete an interest inventory developed to assess their interests, and an enrichment team of parents and teachers tally all the major families of interests. Adults from the faculty, staff, parents, and community are recruited to facilitate enrichment clusters based on these interests, such as creative writing, drawing, sculpting, archaeology, and other areas. Training is provided to the facilitators who agree to offer the clusters, and a brochure is developed and sent to all parents and students that summarizes student choices of enrichment clusters. Students select their top three choices for the clusters and scheduling is completed to place all children into their first or, in some cases, second choice. Like extracurricular activities and programs such as 4-H and Junior Achievement, the main rationale for participation in one or more clusters is that students and teachers want to be there. All teachers (including music, art, physical education) are involved in facilitating the clusters, and their involvement in any particular cluster is based on the same type of interest assessment that is used for students in selecting clusters of choice.

The Continuum of Special Services

A broad range of special services is the third school structure targeted by the SEM. Although the enrichment clusters and the SEM-based modifications of the regular curriculum provide a broad range of services to meet individual needs, a program for total talent development still requires supplementary services that challenge the most academically talented young people who are capable of working at the highest levels of their special interest and ability areas. These services, which cannot ordinarily be provided in enrichment clusters or the regular curriculum, typically include the following: individual or small group counseling, various types of acceleration, direct assistance in facilitating advanced level work, arranging for mentorships with faculty members or community persons, and making other types of connections between students, their families, and out-of-school persons, resources, and agencies.

Direct assistance also involves setting up and promoting student, faculty, and parental involvement in special programs such as Future Problem Solving, Odyssey of the Mind, the Model United Nations program, state and national essay competitions, and mathematics, art, and history contests. Another type of direct assistance consists of arranging out-of-school involvement for individual students in summer programs, on-campus courses, special schools, theatrical groups, scientific expeditions, and apprenticeships at places where advanced-level learning opportunities are available. Provision of these services is one of the responsibilities of the schoolwide enrichment teaching specialist or an enrichment team of teachers and parents who work together to provide options for advanced learning.

Renzulli Learning

Renzulli Learning is a new, interactive online program that helps the implementation of SEM by matching student interests, expression styles, and learning styles with a vast array of enrichment educational activities and resources, designed to enrich gifted and high-potential students' learning process. Using Renzulli Learning, students explore, discover, learn, and create using the SEM married to the most current technology resources independently and in a safe environment.

Renzulli Learning has simple online tools that relate to SEM. The Renzulli Profiler is an interactive assessment tool that identifies students' talents, strengths, interests, and preferred learning and expression styles to provide a comprehensive student learning profile. The Renzulli Enrichment Database is an information warehouse containing more than 35,000 carefully screened, grade-level appropriate, child-safe enrichment opportunities, which are regularly monitored, updated, enhanced, and expanded at a rate of more than 500 per month. The Wizard Project Maker is an online project tool that helps students create their own high-interest projects and store them in their own talent Portfolios. More than 100 Super Starter

Projects have been added to the Project Maker to enable students to begin the process of doing projects on a small-scale basis, and then after students have learned how to do short-term projects, they will be able to do projects more independently.

Collectively, the components of Renzulli Learning correlate with the SEM to provide both students and teachers with unique educational experiences, directly suited to their unique learning profiles, while giving parents insights about their child's enrichment needs. Renzulli Learning also helps all teachers better understand and know their students and meet their diverse needs. Perhaps the most significant aspect of the Renzulli Learning system is its emphasis on a student's strengths. Many adjunct educational programs focus on finding and correcting weaknesses and liabilities. Renzulli Learning celebrates and builds on students' strengths, abilities, and interests, in the tradition of SEM. This Web-based online program matches students' interests, learning styles, expression styles, abilities, and grade level to thousands of opportunities designed to provide enriched, challenging learning. It gives teachers a virtual equivalent of multiple "teaching assistants" in their classrooms—each and every day—to implement the SEM. Other resources to implement the SEM are available online at Creative Learning Press, where how-to books have been collected to make the implementation of SEM easier.

Sally M. Reis

See also Creative Productivity; Elementary Enrichment; Enrichment Triad Model; Talent Development

Further Readings

Creative Learning Press: http://www.creativelearningpress.com

Reis, S. M., Burns, D. E., & Renzulli, J. S. (1992). *Curriculum compacting: The complete guide to modifying the regular curriculum for high ability students.* Mansfield Center, CT: Creative Learning Press.

Reis, S. M., & Renzulli, J. S. (2003). Research related to the schoolwide enrichment triad model. *Gifted Education International, 18*(1), 15–40.

Renzulli, J. S., Gentry, M., & Reis, S. M. (2002). *Enrichment clusters: A practical plan for real-world, student-driven learning.* Mansfield Center, CT: Creative Learning Press.

Renzulli, J. S., & Reis, S. M. (1994). Research related to the schoolwide enrichment triad model. *Gifted Child Quarterly, 38*(1), 7–20.

Renzulli, J. S., & Reis, S. M. (1997). *The schoolwide enrichment model: A comprehensive plan for educational excellence* (2nd ed.). Mansfield Center, CT: Creative Learning Press.

Renzulli Learning: http://renzullilearning.com

Science, Curriculum

Science curriculum is the portal through which everyone achieves the basic science literacy required for life in our increasingly technological world. Curriculum, often defined as a course of study or set of courses, is the result of a design process that includes all of the methods, materials, and media used to transmute raw scientific knowledge, the content, into a set of learning experiences. As cognitive psychologists and neuroscientists have shown, learning is a change that occurs when people experience events that forge new neural pathways and change the structure of their brains in ways that enable them to accomplish tasks they were previously incapable of performing. Learning literally changes the physical structure of students' brains.

One of the most important breakthroughs in learning has been the research on experts and how they gain their expertise. The development of expertise serves as a good model for science curriculum for gifted students for two main reasons. First, the study of experts shows what successful learning looks like. Experts are, by definition, people who function at a high level within a domain of knowledge. Implicit within this idea is an emphasis on actively solving problems or designing new creations, rather than merely answering questions of the type that appear on standardized tests. After all, a scientist is someone who discovers something new.

Also, the expertise research lifts the focus of curriculum to the development of process skills and metacognitive skills (i.e., thinking about thinking), which form *procedural knowledge,* what cognitive psychologists term how-to-do-it knowledge.

Procedural knowledge, the cognitive backbone of expertise, is the knowledge of how to accomplish key tasks and goals, which has become so deeply ingrained as to become an automated and unconscious skill. Procedural knowledge, developed through years of challenging deliberate practice sessions, is estimated to account for 50 to 90 percent of the performance of experts. This is the skill of the major league outfielder who, hearing the crack of the bat, races for the fences and catches the ball over his shoulder on the run.

Most curriculum and most state standards focus on *declarative knowledge,* the term for the conscious knowledge of the facts, concepts, and principles of a domain, the knowledge that allows us to answer test questions. This is why many students who have scored highly on science tests in high school encounter serious difficulty in college lab courses that require facility with lab equipment and science process skills. Expertise is the development of extensive networks of procedural knowledge in a domain, guided by highly developed metacognitive skills or the executive control functions, and richly studded with extensive declarative knowledge and cross-linked to be available when needed. To be most effective, this declarative knowledge must be linked to the key points on the procedure where they will be applied. This expertise is exemplified in the movie *Apollo 13* by the skill of the NASA engineers, who were told, "Houston, we have a problem" and creatively solved the air quality crisis, along with many others, to bring the spacecraft home safely.

An ideal curriculum for gifted, creative, and talented students develops the ability to systematically test hypotheses and construct explanations, along with a solid grasp of the main theoretical frameworks of the physical sciences, the life sciences, and the earth sciences. For all students, this forms the basis of scientific literacy, a core of knowledge, skills, and attitudes that will enable them to function at a high level in a society built on scientific knowledge and the technological products of that knowledge. For other students, scientific literacy is the starting point in a career-long quest to add to scientific knowledge or to develop that knowledge in some way to meet the needs of humanity.

An ideal science curriculum organizes and sequences a powerful set of transformative learning experiences into an effective and efficient overarching architecture of cognition. Although there is much to say about good curriculum and good science curriculum, two key ideas form twin pillars, each supporting the other and both constituting a foundation for an ideal curriculum. One idea, differentiation, comes from exceptional teachers, curriculum developers, instructional designers, and leading educators. The other, inquiry science, emerges from the work of master science teachers, scientists, and science educators. Both are rooted in our scientific knowledge about human learning and exemplified by the learning of experts, which is not the goal for everyone, but a path all can follow as long as desired. This entry describes these aspects of an ideal science curriculum

Inquiry Science

Experienced science teachers, scientists, science educators, and science curriculum developers generally agree that the best way to learn science is by doing science. This general approach, called for in the National Science Education Standards, is called *inquiry science.* Inquiry science seeks to emulate the processes of investigation used by scientists and focuses on teaching students to use those processes, practices, principles, and tools. Although students read and write in inquiry science, the main emphasis is not on reading chapters of a textbook and writing the answers to the questions at the end of the chapter. Reading books about the strategies, techniques, rules, and history of basketball is useful to a player, but no substitute for the core of the game, which is playing. The same is true of science.

Inquiry science also goes beyond a merely hands-on approach to science, where students engage in science activities using the tools and materials of science, but do so with little critical or creative thought. Inquiry includes asking questions, creating tests to answer those questions, running those tests and collecting the data, analyzing the data, and proposing explanations for what has been discovered, all in the context of comparing ideas and findings to those of others within a framework of logic and evidence. Inquiry science is centered on conducting experiments and investigations to answer questions.

Inquiry may best be thought of as a continuum of scaffolded processes and habits of mind, beginning with young children in preschool exploring how balls roll down ramps to see what happens, through middle school students investigating Newton's laws of motion by measuring velocity and a mass of balls rolling down ramps, to graduate students participating in original research projects with their professors mapping differences in the earth's gravity field. The key to inquiry science is a talented teacher who has both deep scientific knowledge in say, physics, for example, and extensive pedagogical content knowledge about how students learn physics, what their common misconceptions are, multiple content representations, cool demonstrations, and a ready supply of answers to frequently asked questions. Though inquiry science will be centered on the investigation, rather than on the textbook, the lecture, or the test, talented teachers may make use of textbooks, lectures, and tests as part of a broader approach to inquiry.

Differentiation

A differentiated science curriculum is designed to meet the range of needs and abilities of the students in the classroom. A differentiated curriculum offers an extensive and rich "network" of science content with variety in the level of difficulty of the content modules, pathways through that content, methods to explore that content, and means to assess learning outcomes. For example, a differentiated science curriculum unit might allow a student to move through the unit learning modularized chunks of content at his or her own pace, rather than moving in lockstep with every other member of the class.

Furthermore, different students might start in different places along the curricular path because their prior knowledge or experience would allow them to demonstrate their mastery of certain content modules. One hallmark of a differentiated curriculum is placing students at the appropriate level in the content material. Going farther still, this differentiated science curriculum might not be a simple linear set of content modules leading to mastery of a single set of learning goals, but it might be a true network of modules with more than one module covering certain content objectives in different ways and in different depths. This would open the possibility of different pathways through the curriculum; each student would not work in all the modules in the network, but would make choices based on her or his needs, abilities, and learning profile. For example, in a middle school chemistry curriculum unit, the base level expectation would be that each student would master the concept of *concentration of a solution* and would either work with that module or demonstrate mastery, perhaps by "testing out."

Some students, those who might want to delve as deeply as possible in chemistry, might work with a module introducing the Avogadro's number and the concept of the mole. These might be students who quickly worked through the base level module or those who skipped the base level module because they already knew the material. This also implies differentiation in learning outcomes. This would mean that although a base level of learning outcomes or standards for all students was defined for a grade level, different students would be free to achieve as far beyond that base level as their ability and interest could take them. Different students always learn different amounts of material in every classroom; a differentiated curriculum might make this different explicitly and plan for it, rather than ignoring it or pretending everyone learned exactly what the state or district standard said they should, no more and no less.

In conceiving a differentiated science curriculum as a large network of learning modules or lessons, the need for both articulation and integration are obvious. *Articulation* refers to the linkage between succeeding levels in the curriculum, as when the fourth-grade life science curriculum dovetails neatly with the fifth-grade life science curriculum, with just enough overlap to make the connection and no gaps where fifth-grade students are presumed to know something that has not been covered in earlier curricula. Textbook series often perform this role, but an inquiry-centric curriculum needs to make an independent check for articulation.

Likewise, a differentiated science curriculum can provide a sound basis for integrating learning areas. *Integration* can be thought of as the linkage among curriculum areas, such as the chemistry and biology, for example. Ultimately, integration seeks to link all the curricular areas, including language arts, social studies, and even physical education with the sciences. Some curricular areas are so closely related that many programs build on those relationships, such as the science, technology, engineering, and mathematics (STEM) programs. Integrating the humanities with the sciences works well when exploring the logical connections between the disciplines, such as investigating the effects of families, communities, and governments on global climate change and vice versa. Integration requires much planning by curriculum developers and teachers, and requires much classroom time to make effective linkages. However, research on learning shows that although an alarming amount of what is taught in school is soon forgotten, one of the factors that increases the retention is packaging learning experiences to touch multiple knowledge areas or integration.

Inquiry and Differentiation: Complementary Practices

Inquiry and differentiation share many common features. Both require identifying learning goals and relevant educational standards for a range of student outcomes at the outset to guide instruction. Both require instructionally useful assessment methods that measure student progress not only at the end of instruction, but along the way to adapt instruction to meet student needs. An emphasis on mastery learning and a bias for depth of learning over thinly "covering" the "standard of the day" are philosophically compatible with both inquiry and differentiation.

Teaching with inquiry naturally tends to differentiate instruction for students, and differentiation naturally tends toward inquiry. Use of a wide range of media and computer technology, along with the authentic tools and techniques of science support both these practices. Both are challenging to implement and require effective classroom management practices, as well as strong, experienced teachers. Each of these systems exists along a continuum practice, and each is most successfully implemented in stages. Both inquiry and differentiation evolved to align with our knowledge of how people learn and about the most effective instructional techniques. Finally, working together, each will strengthen and improve the other, as well as better gifted, talented, and creative students.

Fred Estes

See also Brain-Based Research; Chemistry Curriculum, Gifted; Cognition; Curriculum Models; Declarative and Procedural Memory; Differentiation; Expertise; Inquiry; Learning; Parallel Curriculum Model

Further Readings

Bransford, J., Brown, A., & Cocking, R. (Eds.). (1999). *How people learn: Brain, mind, experience, and school.* Washington, DC: National Academy Press.

Estes, F. (2007). Inquiry science for young gifted students: The pleasure of finding things out. *Gifted Education Communicator, 38*(4), 3–5.

Flick, P., & Lederman, N. (Eds.). (2006). *Scientific inquiry and nature of science: Implications for teaching, learning, and teacher education.* New York: Springer.

Jarrett, D. (1997). *Inquiry strategies for science and mathematics learning: It's just good teaching.* Portland, OR: Northwest Regional Educational Laboratory.

Olson, S., & Loucks-Horsley, S. (Eds.). (2000). *Inquiry and the national science education standards: A guide for teaching and learning.* Washington, DC: National Academy Press.

Tomlinson, C., Kaplan, S., Renzulli, J., Purcell, J., Leppien, J., & Burns, D. (2002). *The parallel curriculum: A design to develop high potential and challenge high-ability learners.* Thousand Oaks, CA: Corwin Press.

VanTassel-Baska, J., & Little, C. (Eds.). (2003). *Content-based curriculum for high ability learners.* Waco, TX: Prufrock Press.

Wiggins, G., & McTighe, J. (2005). *Understanding by design* (2nd ed.) Alexandria, VA: American Society for Curriculum Development.

Science Talent Search Winners

The Science Talent Search (STS), America's oldest and most prestigious nationwide precollege competition, was initiated in 1942 by the Society for Science and the Public (called Science Service until 2008). The Society for Science and the Public is a nonprofit organization dedicated to the advancement of scientific knowledge through publications and educational programs such as science fairs and scholarship competitions.

Watson Davis, former director of Science Service beginning in 1928 and publisher of *Science News,* wanted to bridge the gap between the scientific community and the general public. To do this, Davis collaborated with the American Institute of the City of New York in 1941 to organize 800 existing science clubs throughout the country. Science Service linked these science clubs with museums, and other educational and scientific institutions and societies, resulting in expansion to 25,000 clubs. Various national meetings of regional and local science fair winners evolved into the STS competition and the International Science and Engineering Fair, also organized by the Society for Science and the Public.

In 1998, Intel took over support of the competition from Westinghouse, and has now involved more than 120,000 students looking to pursue careers in science, mathematics, engineering, and medicine. Academically gifted high school seniors compete for more than 3.8 million dollars in scholarship funds as well as financial assistance for college tuition. This entry describes the selection process, outcomes, the role of STS in gifted education, and research conducted on winners.

Selection Process

In November, students submit an entry form consisting of advisor recommendations, high school transcripts and test scores, and a research report. The research report describes an independent research project that is designed to display students' creativity and enthusiasm for one or more of 16 selected areas of science: behavioral and social sciences, biochemistry, bioinformatics and genomics, botany and plant science, chemistry, computer science, earth and planetary science, engineering, environmental science, mathematics, medicine and health, microbiology, materials science, physics, space science, and zoology and animal sciences.

Students entering the STS must be seniors in high school in the United States, Puerto Rico, Guam, Virgin Islands, American Samoa, Wake, the Midway Islands, or the Marianas. Contestants can also be enrolled in a foreign school as an exchange student or because their parents are temporarily working or living abroad. Students cannot be the children of any STS employee, evaluators, or judges or have previously entered the STS.

The first round of STS involves selecting 300 semifinalists based on project reports evaluated by three or more scientists, mathematicians, or engineers. Those 300 papers are then narrowed down to 40 finalist papers. In March, the 40 finalists participate in a Science Talent Institute in Washington, D.C., all expenses paid. Finalists undergo an ultimate evaluation process that includes extensive interviews and a presentation of their research before judges that include top scientists from a variety of disciplines. Candidates are also given the opportunity to display their projects at the National Academy of Science in front of thousands of visitors, governmental heads, and scientific figures. In the past, contestants have met with the president as well as presidential candidates. At the conclusion of the contest, the top 10 finalists are announced at a banquet honoring the contestants.

Outcomes

STS winners have gone on to receive more than 100 honors in mathematics and science. By 2007, these included 6 Nobel Prizes, 2 Field Medals (the Nobel's equivalent in mathematics), 3 National Medals of Science, 56 Sloan Research Fellowships, and 12 MacArthur Foundation's genius awards. In addition, by 2007, 32 winners had been elected to the National Academy of Sciences as well as 5 to the National Academy of Engineering. According to data collected by Science Service, more than 95 percent of former finalists pursued careers in science, more than 70 percent go on to receive M.D.s and Ph.D.s, and many are engaged in research at top universities and colleges.

Roles in Gifted Education

Gifted education has three major strands. One is focused on addressing the school-based needs of students who are performing beyond their classmates in academic subjects. A second addresses the needs of students who score highly on tests designed to measure intellectual or academic potential. A third strand that has been of increasing interest in recent years is on talent development in specific domains. The talent development literature focuses on talent identified on the basis of a challenging apprenticeship, coaching, or mentorship in a specific domain. The STS personifies this process by engaging young scientists to work in a mentored apprenticeship on a scientific paper. Some participants submit projects they have developed entirely on their own, but most work in a laboratory or other venue with professionals becoming socialized into the scientific enterprise. Even those who submit solo papers work with teacher assistance on the technical aspects of writing the paper. Another component of talent development is engaging with a challenging peer group. STS provides such a peer group to finalists by way of the Science Talent Institute week in Washington.

Research Conducted on Winners

Most of the research published on STS winners has been conducted by Rena Subotnik and her colleagues, and by Gregory Feist. The following paragraphs review briefly the outcomes of their work.

Subotnik and her colleagues, Karen Maurer and Cynthia Steiner, identified the variables that led to the retention and attrition in science of the 1983 winners of the Westinghouse Science Talent Search. The results of three earlier collection points established patterns of external and internal influences on participation in either the research sciences, into applied sciences (e.g., medicine, engineering), or out of the field altogether. At age 34, a disproportionate number of participants had left science altogether, especially the women. Some of the key reasons for the attrition, and conversely for retention, included these:

- Availability of mentors who could provide intellectual challenge, role modeling, professional connections, and tacit knowledge.
- View of the lifestyle associated with science as either one of isolation, brutal competition, and dead ends—or one of excitement, competition, and collegiality.
- Effects of time and place in history can ensure or prevent the existence of available positions in academe and industry that are challenging, creative, and well funded.

Feist conducted a comparison study of samples from four cohorts of Westinghouse winners and members of the National Academy of Sciences. As in the Subotnik study, women were more likely to leave science careers than were men. However, the cohorts that Feist reviewed were more likely to continue in science careers than the 1983 cohort investigated by Subotnik. In educational accomplishment, 91 percent of the men and 74 percent of the women earned doctoral degrees. Most intriguing is the association Feist found between immigrant status and scientific achievement in both prestigious study samples, with children of recent immigrant families disproportionately represented.

Rena F. Subotnik and Cari McIntyre

See also Scientifically Gifted; Scientists; Talent Development; Talent Searches

Further Readings

Feist, G. (2006). The development of scientific talent in Westinghouse finalists and members of the National Academy of Sciences. *Journal of Adult Development, 13,* 23–35.

Mlot, C. (1997). Is science talent squandered? How future scientists can come undone. *Science News, 51,* 338.

Society for Science and the Public: http://www.societyforscience.org

Subotnik, R. F., Maurer, K., & Steiner, C. L. (2001). Tracking the next generation of the scientific elite. *Journal for Secondary Gifted Education, 13,* 33–43.

Scientifically Gifted

In the post-*Sputnik* years of the 1960s and 1970s, a surge of interest in science education dominated, along with mathematics, the federally funded mandates in curriculum and pedagogy in the United States and by other governments internationally. Not entirely inconsequentially, the emergence of international comparison testing of student performance in mathematics and sciences has become an industry in and of itself. A nation's relative and absolute rankings on tests of math and science achievement carry the status level of award programs on a par with the entertainment industries. These rankings have become a fairly stable mechanism for predicting surges in fiscal support for mathematics and science education expenditures by national governments. In the United States, issues of pipeline recruitment of high-ability, gifted, and talented, or highly interested science students has generated much interest, with institutions of higher learning and federal science agencies convening regular panels, councils, interagency working groups, or U.S. commissions to study and recommend solutions and treatments. Nevertheless, the study of, identification of, and response to the needs of students with high interest, ability, or talent in natural sciences remains critical and challenging. Among the challenges, merely defining scientific giftedness is a complex endeavor. This entry describes research relating to the scientifically gifted.

The research is increasingly clear that scientific giftedness is a complex phenomenon—distinct from problem-solving ability in, say, chemistry or physics, as it was frequently defined in the earlier years of study. Giftedness in scientific thought or activity is increasingly considered distinct from the mathematical-scientific continuum that was the hallmark of the earliest studies, which failed to disaggregate scientific curiosity and scientific aesthetics from the logico-empirical problem-solving approach to knowledge management. Moving away from achievement or IQ-driven definitions of scientific and scientific giftedness, most comprehensive efforts of the last 50 years suggest that scientific or scientific giftedness includes a variety of social, personal, behavioral, ethical, aesthetic, and complex identity components.

The seminal internally framed psychosocial treatment of scientific or scientific giftedness was Louis Fliegler's delineation in 1961. He carefully distinguished mathematical reasoning from scientific curiosity in gifted individuals. Fliegler developed a checklist of science domain-specific characteristics of gifted individuals that included early interest in science, curiosity, and early ability to understand abstract concepts, a love of collecting natural objects, and creativity in science projects in early school experiences. Further, as later researchers observed, Fliegler noted the ability of truly gifted individuals to assimilate marginally related ideas along similar concept and relational lines.

Among the recent characterizations of scientifically gifted individuals, one group of researchers has found that scientific accomplishment, leadership, creativity, morality, motivation, and cognitive experimentalism are measurable characteristics of scientifically gifted students. To these characteristics, other researchers add a heightened ability to transfer learning across concept sets, the ability to infer concepts from less specific and more loosely delineated objective data, and a heightened ability to make connections outside of the formal curriculum. Nevertheless, these studies continue to pose scientific giftedness nearly as a subset of problem solving and the ability to develop and apply complex conceptual information to linear problem resolution.

Perhaps the most important definitional paper of recent years was that of Gino Innamorato, who surveyed a broad summary of the components of scientific ability, inquiry, creativity, and identification issues. This paper adds analogical reasoning ability, creativity, independence, divergent thinking, efficiency in memory, genetics, intuition, and the ability to shift thinking across cognitive domains fluidly to the characteristics of the scientifically gifted student.

Outside the mathematical, problem identification/resolution framework, an additional foundational effort at defining the scientifically gifted individual was Howard Gruber's work on Charles Darwin and on Jean Piaget. Gruber describes the aesthetic experiences of scientific exploration and discovery, suggesting characteristics of the field of scientific inquiry or of the natural world, which may correspond in some manner to the gifted individual him- or herself. These characteristics included orderliness, universality, inevitability/law, simplicity, unity, balance, equilibrium, and invariability. These seemed to appeal, for Gruber, to an aesthetic psychological dimension embedded between the cognitive and emotional areas of the individual. Gruber's work was a substantive methodological improvement on many earlier studies (and many since) in that he used ethnography and detailed life study to describe the complex nature of scientific giftedness in individuals. And indeed, the life study, believed to capture both internal and external characteristics of the gifted individual in an embedded, environmental context, is broadly used in sociological and psychosocial research on gifted students today, such as in Jane Piirto's extended and unique treatment of creative individuals.

The most recent emerging set of characteristics related to scientific giftedness concerns the heightened sensitivity to environmental ethic, the interconnectivity of human life and the natural world, and the evolution of a global, environmental stewardship and self-concept. Beginning in the early 1990s and continuing, the construct of environmental stewardship as a worthwhile characteristic of scientifically literate citizens became a hallmark of the U.S. federal science agencies. Research conducted on high-ability science students in secondary-level educational competitions in the United States has consistently revealed a link between exemplary performance in science accomplishments at an early age with a heightened awareness of global environmental systems and environmental and ecological stewardship concepts and ethical systems. Further research in this area focused on the pipeline recruitment of scientifically gifted secondary students has further linked environmental ethic with persistence in science coursework and selection of science-related college majors. Although research is inconclusive regarding the balance of internal and external factors that either reveal or result in these scientific ethical systems in the individual, these ethical characteristics are both strong and unique concerns of scientifically gifted and oriented students.

Howard D. Walters

See also Creativity in Science; Science, Curriculum; Science Talent Search Winners; Scientists

Further Readings

Fliegler, L. A. (1961). *Curriculum planning for the gifted.* Englewood Cliffs, NJ: Prentice Hall.

Gruber, H. E. (1981). *Darwin on man: A psychological study of scientific creativity* (2nd ed.). Chicago: University of Chicago Press.

Gruber, H. E., & Voneche, J. J. (1977). *The essential Piaget.* New York: Basic Books.

Innamorato, G. (1998). Creativity in the development of scientific giftedness: educational implications. *Roeper Review, 21*(1), 54.

Ngoi, M., & Vondracek, M. (2004). Working with gifted science students in a public high school environment: One school's approach. *Journal of Secondary Gifted Education, 15*(4), 141–147.

Park, S-K., Park, K-H., & Choe, H-S. (2005). The relationship between thinking styles and scientific giftedness in Korea. *Journal of Secondary Gifted Education, 16*(2/3), 87–97.

Piirto, J. (1998). *Understanding those who create* (2nd ed.). Scottsdale, AZ: Great Potential Press.

SCIENTISTS

Scientist comes from the Latin root *scientia,* which means knowledge or understanding, and generally refers to one who helps build an organized system of thought about the nature of the world. Scientists study natural phenomena using disciplined and systematic methods. Through logical and objective application of these methods, they gain understanding about living or nonliving things, and often work to improve the human condition through careful application of what is known. Their work covers an enormous range of fields. The National Institutes of Health listed more than 125 major science careers. The huge range of careers is categorized into two major branches that vary depending on the source but generally include the natural sciences (study of living and nonliving things), and the social sciences (study of people and society). The branches are also categorized along lines of the formal sciences (mathematics, logic, and statistics) and the applied sciences (engineering and technology). In a conceptual sense, scientists use objective methods to observe and explain the world. More specifically, they use detailed prescriptive methods to outline a series of steps that consider prior knowledge and assumptions, ensure careful data collection and analysis, and result in meaningful reporting and further study. This series of specific strategies is commonly referred to as the *scientific method* and is the process that helps bind together a large number of people involved with disparate areas of science and wide-ranging expertise. This entry describes the scientific method and science performance.

Scientific Method

The scientific method is a set of objective processes by which scientists, collectively and over time, gain accurate insight about the world in which we live. Most scientists rely on quantitative methods that generally include some variation of the following steps: (a) observe a phenomenon or a cluster of phenomena; (b) articulate a hypothesis that explains the phenomena; (c) design a study, including analyses to test the hypothesis; (d) conduct the study; (e) collect data; (f) analyze data; (g) draw conclusions regarding the hypothesis, particularly whether the results of the study support it or not; and (h) report the completed study, including all of these steps as well as limitations of the study and questions for further research. Scientists, however, are making increased use of qualitative methods that supplant or augment existing quantitative methods and in general rely on the following steps: (a) participate in the setting of inquiry and observe the context; (b) observe the phenomenon directly; (c) collect observational data and verbal data via interviews and focus groups; (d) analyze observations, verbal data, and other materials; (e) allow emergent themes to guide the next steps.

Scientists acknowledge that personal and cultural beliefs can alter both perceptions and interpretations of natural phenomena. Those with certain beliefs may sometimes see things as reinforcing their beliefs, even when they do not; this is called the confirmatory bias. Scientists must guard against this and other biases—for example, cultural bias—by using procedures specifically designed to minimize them when testing a hypothesis or formulating a theory. Such procedures are central to the scientific method.

Science Performance

The No Child Left Behind and other policy reports purport that the United States is behind other nations in science and that students from the United States lack the basic skills to become scientists and meet the needs of a technological society. Major institutions such as the U.S. National Academics, National Aeronautics and Space Administration, and the National Science Foundation have also expressed concern about declining performance of students in the United States on measures of science proficiency. Such institutions have called for improved K–12 education in science, technology, engineering, and mathematics (STEM); improved training for STEM teachers; and increased numbers of college graduates with STEM degrees. Those conclusions, however, have been challenged by Harold Salzman and B. Lindsay Lowell, who pointed out statistical errors with the comparison data. Their reevaluation of the data used for international comparisons led them to conclude that students in the United States perform as well as many of their international counterparts on average, but that STEM educational improvements should be aimed primarily at low performers.

Scientists directly affect the quality of life. To maintain or improve the world's economy, security, and health, it is important to prepare a diverse citizenry that is literate not only in scientific concepts and facts as well as in the scientific method as ethically executed.

Jan B. Hansen

See also Critical Thinking; Multicultural Creativity; Research, Qualitative; Talent Development

Further Readings

Bernstein, L., Winkler, A., & Zierdt-Warsha W, L. (1996). *Multicultural women of science.* Maywood, NJ: Peoples Publishing Group.

Donovan, S., & Bransford, J. D. (2005). *How students learn: History, mathematics, and science in the classroom.* Washington, DC: National Academies Press.

Horowitz, M. C. (Ed). (2003). *New dictionary of the history of ideas* (Vol. 1–6). Charlottesville, VA: Electronic Text Center.

Salzman, H., & Lowell, B. L. (2007). *Into the eye of the storm: Assessing the evidence on science and engineering education, quality, and workforce demand.* Retrieved from http://ssrn.com/abstract=1034801

Scope and Sequence

Within an educational context, *scope* refers to the expansiveness or comprehensiveness of a curriculum, and *sequence* refers to the order in which content standards, concepts, and skills of a comprehensive curriculum are taught. Thus, a curriculum scope and sequence is a framework that school faculty and leaders may design and implement as a guide that systematically outlines when and which content, concepts, and skills are taught. A scope and sequence serves as an institutional map for educators and administrators to use as they plan appropriate instruction and curriculum options for their students. This entry provides an overview of scope and sequence, particularly as it relates to the gifted.

Overview

Historically, scope and sequence became popularized after Ralph Tyler published his seminal text entitled *Basic Principles of Curriculum and Instruction* in 1949. Tyler proposed that a curriculum must provide useful learning experiences, organized through appropriate learning objectives and consistently evaluated and revised based on data. In 1962, Hilda Taba also alluded to the need for organizing the curriculum into a cohesive system and outlined a need for sequencing how the curriculum should be taught. In 1971, Tyler further emphasized the need for defining which skills and information need to be taught to students and how those skills and information should be ordered as evidenced by a scope and sequence. School districts began to design scope and sequence frameworks that continue to be emphasized as maps for planning and guiding instruction throughout a child's PreK–12 school career.

Sometimes a scope and sequence is misinterpreted as a list of curricula to be taught in each subject area and at each grade level. Instead, a scope and sequence is a deliberate outline of goals and outcomes that build on others in a cohesive way so that at any given time within a child's school career, schools can confidently outline what a child should know and be able to do. Therefore, a scope and sequence must be articulated to school personnel and faithfully adhered to. Educators must have a conceptual understanding of how their current grade-level curriculum connects with the previous and future content standards students have mastered or will attain at varying grade levels. For example, a scope and sequence would outline what students are required to know at various stages in their school careers and how and when they should obtain that knowledge. Metaphorically, this is the same as planning a trip. One must know where one is going before one can arrive. Just as a map provides a conceptual guide for progressing from point A to point B, a scope and sequence provides an instructional guide for educators to use to help students move from one conceptual understanding to another, in a seamless, cohesive manner. Without a conceptual plan that spans all grade levels, curriculum and instruction becomes fragmented and hinders optimal learning opportunities.

Scope and Sequence for Gifted

Although scope and sequence designs are more common as part of an overall district framework for the general population of students, both June Maker and Joyce VanTassel-Baska have consistently outlined the need for a scope and sequence to be designed specifically for gifted students. In 1982, Maker suggested that gifted students be provided a differentiated scope and sequence based on their unique characteristics and ability to learn advanced content at faster rates. In 1988, VanTassel-Baska prescribed a process for designing a scope and sequence for gifted learners as part of curriculum development and differentiation standards. By designing a scope and sequence for gifted learners, educators have a method of relating curricula and instructional emphases to various stakeholders, ensure methods for demonstrating how districts are differentiating instruction for gifted learners, and outline the importance of specific content emphasis at various grade levels. In 1988, VanTassel-Baska explained the following key considerations as part of a scope and sequence development as follows: (1) Could all students meet this goal or objective or is it appropriately advanced for gifted learners? (2) How are the objectives more sophisticated as they move from each grade-level cluster (e.g., K–2, 3–5, 6–8, 9–12)? (3) Do the objectives include a broad scope of conceptual information and knowledge inclusive of the skills required of gifted students? (4) Are the objectives logically sequenced so that the goals of the scope can be attained? (5) Are the objectives developmentally appropriate for gifted learners?

Gifted students learn at faster rates and have the ability to understand abstract ideas at earlier ages, so a scope and sequence for these special learners should introduce more complex conceptual understandings earlier in their school careers and include accelerated content standards at least one or two grade levels beyond their chronological ages. Moreover, the expected goals and outcomes should be higher levels in terms of expected content understandings and outcomes. For example, in mathematics, a typical scope and sequence objective may require students to perform simple computations such as adding, subtracting, multiplying, and dividing one-, two-, and three-digit numbers by the end of fifth grade. A scope and sequence for gifted learners would require students to solve complex problems by applying the appropriate computation(s) rather than simple calculations only, and at an earlier age.

Overall, scope and sequence is a useful tool that, when articulated and well-planned, will guide educators in teaching appropriate content at the appropriate times. By designing a scope and sequence, educators can determine what and when students are taught specific content. This reduces the overlap of goals and standards within and across grade levels and prevents gaps in instruction. When planning a scope and sequence for gifted learners, educators should be sure that the scope and sequence is fast-paced enough to challenge gifted learners, provides advanced outcomes such as reflective and critical thinking, and is developmentally appropriate.

Tamra Stambaugh

See also Curriculum Models; Giftedness, Definition; Instructional Management

Further Readings

Maker, C. J., & Nielson, A. B. (1996). *Curriculum development and teaching strategies for gifted learners* (2nd ed.). Austin, TX: Pro-Ed.

Taba, H. (1962). *Curriculum development: Theory and practice*. New York: Harcourt, Brace & World.

Tyler, R. W. (1962). *Basic principles of curriculum and instruction*. Chicago: University of Chicago Press.

VanTassel-Baska, J. (2003). *Curriculum and instructional planning and design for gifted learners*. Denver, CO: Love Publishing.

Secondary School, Literature Curriculum

Novelist Fyodor Dostoyevsky understood gifted adolescents as he wrote of the tremendous power given to those who are gifted. He did warn that the more power given, the greater the responsibility to use it wisely. Truly gifted adolescents at the secondary level seek, choose, and decide what to do and how to do it. If they are given appropriate choices in a constructivist classroom atmosphere, they can achieve great things, possibly reaching their potential. In English classes, these great accomplishments can occur in their writing, in their choice of reading material, and in their oral expressions—discussions, speeches, debates, and role-plays in class. Indeed, the power of the teacher in a secondary literature classroom, whether it is Advanced Placement or not, is a considerable power. The level of thought encouraged, the trust in the students to be more than passive recipients, and the choice of meaningful curriculum—all factor into the type of class the teacher decides to teach or organize. This entry focuses on secondary literature curriculum as a way to meet the needs of gifted adolescents.

In choosing a meaningful curriculum for gifted students, Judith Halsted suggested a list of activities designed to address the characteristics of high-ability students. To challenge verbal abilities, gifted students need to do the following:

- Use their full vocabulary and develop it further with intellectual peers.
- Read books at an appropriate intellectual and emotional level.
- Be introduced to books that represent a variety of literary conventions and styles and that use language gracefully.
- Express ideas verbally and in depth by writing or speaking with others who challenge and thus refine their views and concepts.

Gifted students must be challenged with rigorous content, process, and products designed to meet the students at their cognitive levels. Because classical literature focuses on the larger issues and themes of humanity, it provides good choices on which to base curriculum for gifted adolescents. However, other issues prevail as well in choosing appropriate literature. For example, multicultural themes, interdisciplinary themes, and challenging vocabulary are essential in choosing appropriate reading material. Gender balance—both in protagonist in the novel and author of the novel—is important to consider. If a curriculum is constructed from works of all "dead White males" in this era, there is a problem, and gifted students will be the first to note and voice the problem. Current events or local issues may make particular works of literature more attractive and meaningful for gifted students. Required material for students to read and process must be carefully examined for the ideas conveyed, the language used to convey these ideas, and the discussion and thought levels tapped by this content. The English teacher should not censor material for gifted students. They are able to see through artificial barriers themselves and often are insulted by school systems that do not think they can understand sophisticated issues and language well advanced of their age. However, the message must always provide the rationale for the use of a controversial piece in any educational setting. Gifted students will read literature both inside and outside of school, so an assignment must consider the value and worth in that context of each piece of literature assigned.

Writing is absolutely essential and valued in a well-developed secondary-literature curriculum. Students must respond by writing in reflective journals, writing persuasive pieces, and writing long research pieces. In addition, creative choices offer students the chance to integrate their own ideas with forms that express these ideas both responsively and originally. Poetry, screenplays, interviews, and original drama are wonderful ways for gifted students to add their own voices to the literature they read.

In addition, secondary gifted students must be encouraged to have a voice in a literature class. Understanding a critical analysis of a work assigned and presented relative to the study of the original piece is a thought-provoking and challenging task. However, assigning students the task of constructing their own critical analysis, unraveling metaphor and working through the large issues presented in several works studied invites students to express ideas while forging connections between their own thoughts and those other voices in the texts read. Couple this with active discussion in which they listen to other active, gifted minds, and the secondary literature class becomes a language laboratory in which thought is encouraged to flourish.

The value of literature in a liberal education cannot be overstated. Dostoyevsky, who was mentioned at the beginning of this entry, noted the importance of the power of decision making. Wise teachers of gifted secondary adolescents must keep continually challenging students to make wise decisions. Barbara Taylor stated that we look to literature as a source of collective wisdom, for insights into our muddled human condition, to be reassured by the record of human heroism or restrained by the corrective drama of human folly. We look to literature for experience that enlarges understanding—understanding accessible only through experience. Indeed, understanding is supposed to be the desired end of all teaching, the goal of all learning.

As in all meaningful curricula for gifted learners, the assessment for the unit must make sense and be in concert with the activities assigned. Critical thinking reigns supreme in such curricula and assessment must match the task and strategies used. Writing persuasive essays is catalytic, as is assessing the level of discussion that transpires in the class. The discussion format for assessment—even in examinations—makes good sense for classes that are heavily discussion oriented. The use of the discussion examination requires the teacher to be knowledgeable in the assessment procedure used. Felicia Dixon advocates a rubric adapted from Bloom's Taxonomy. A knowledge of these levels of thought and ready access to listening and noting them is essential.

Finally, the well-educated person has a knowledge of important literature. The archetypes prevalent in enduring literature convey the essence of humanity for all times. Teachers must model reading and discuss what they are reading and what meaning it has for them along with the discussion of the assignments of the course. Leaving the curriculum all up to Advanced Placement or International Baccalaureate does not work well when working with secondary gifted adolescents. They need more than acceleration; they also need the enrichment that is inherent in a well-developed humanities curriculum. Challenging reading and discussion that tap depth of thought, the opportunity to express connections in writing, and an environment that invites synthesis among all disciplines are characteristics of the curriculum that must be present in secondary literature classes for gifted students.

Felicia A. Dixon

See also Adolescent, Gifted; Secondary School, Writing Curriculum; Secondary Schools

Further Readings

Dixon, F. A. (2000). The discussion examination: Making assessment match instructional strategy. *Roeper Review, 23,* 104–108.

Dixon, F. A. (2006). Secondary English for high ability students. In F. A. Dixon & S. M. Moon (Eds.), *The handbook of secondary gifted education* (pp. 363–391). Waco, TX: Prufrock Press.

Dostoyevsky, F. (1950). *The brothers Karamazov.* New York: Modern Library.

Halsted, J. W. (1994). *Some of my best friends are books.* Dayton: Ohio Psychology Press.

Taylor, B. A. (1996). The study of literature: Insights into understanding. In J. VanTassel-Baska, D. Johnson, & L. Boyce (Eds.), *Developing verbal talent* (pp. 75–94). Boston: Allyn & Bacon.

Secondary School, Mathematics Curriculum

Multiple definitions of *curriculum* contribute to the complexity in defining the secondary school mathematics curriculum. A simplistic definition of curriculum is a sequence of courses. Another definition is that which is taught in schools. A more comprehensive definition is the total set of experiences students encounter in schools. For purposes of this entry, the secondary school mathematics curriculum refers to the total set of mathematics middle and high school students experience in schools, including the content, sequence of courses, and extracurricular opportunities.

Mathematics is recognized as a gatekeeper for advanced courses and areas of study. The type of mathematical experiences gifted, creative, and talented students encounter in schools is of utter import, particularly considering continual efforts to enhance international competitiveness in the fields of science, technology, engineering, and mathematics (STEM). Examination of the secondary school mathematics curriculum can assist in determining how mathematics school experiences can be improved. This entry explores the basis for an appropriate mathematics curriculum for advanced learners, the secondary mathematics course-taking pipeline, and extracurricular mathematics opportunities.

Ideal Mathematics Curriculum for Advanced Learners

The mathematically gifted or talented learner is different from other students. These students are different in the pace with which they learn, the depth of their understanding, and the interests they hold. As such, an appropriate mathematics curriculum for advanced learners is one that is challenging, provides opportunities for extension, and connects to other disciplines. It also allows for depth and complexity, focuses on problem solving and higher-order thinking skills, and incorporates abstraction.

Appropriate experiences for advanced learners in mathematics should include compacting and differentiating the curriculum. Opportunities for acceleration and enrichment should be present, where acceleration refers to the faster pace with which the curriculum is covered and enrichment refers to the deeper level with which the curriculum is covered. Ideally, advanced learners should experience acceleration and enrichment, not one or the other.

Pre-assessment and diagnostic testing should be used for placement to ensure that advanced students have the opportunity to experience exciting and new curriculum. In addition, students should participate in regular, ongoing summative and formative assessments, some of which are authentic. Inquiry-based and open-ended problems should be incorporated that allow for multiple solutions and multiple methods of solution. Students should have the opportunity to integrate technology and manipulatives to enhance learning and support multiple representations. The type of secondary school mathematics curriculum described here is rich, deep, and accelerative. This curriculum, however, is not the reality for many advanced mathematics learners.

Mathematics Course-Taking Pipeline

The reality of the secondary school mathematics curriculum differs greatly from the idealized one described. Most secondary schools address the mathematics curriculum for advanced learners through acceleration only. Students experience advanced mathematics through honors courses, the Advanced Placement program, or the International Baccalaureate program. Although honors, Advanced Placement, and International Baccalaureate courses represent the only option in some schools, these programs are not specifically designed for gifted, creative, and talented mathematics learners. In other districts, particularly urban and rural districts, schools are unable to offer students a variety of advanced or accelerative mathematics options.

Although course titles and the sequence of courses may differ from school district to school district, the typical mathematics course-taking pipeline includes Algebra 1, Geometry, Algebra II, Precalculus/Trigonometry, and Calculus. Before a student can complete calculus in high school, he or she must have taken Algebra I by the eighth grade. Students must take Algebra I even earlier if they are to experience more advanced mathematics courses such as a second year of calculus or linear algebra. Some students who are capable of successfully completing Algebra I in the earlier grades are not provided that opportunity. Some school districts lack a formal acceleration policy. Other school districts allow students to accelerate, but run out of courses to offer because of a lack of funding or adequately trained personnel.

Extracurricular Mathematics Opportunities

A viable outlet for advanced mathematics learners is participation in mathematical clubs, contests, and competitions. These activities expose advanced learners to rich mathematical experience and provide students the opportunity to work with peers of similar interests. Some of these competitions include American Mathematics Competition (AMC, AMC 10, and AMC 12), MATHCOUNTS, Mathematical Olympiad, and Mathematics Pentathlon.

With advancements in technology, students can access advanced mathematics course offerings through distance learning programs. This allows students attending schools with limited offerings to take advantage of advanced coursework offered in other cities and states. Many universities such as Carnegie Mellon, Duke, Johns Hopkins, Northwestern, and the University of Iowa offer talent search programs; some even offer distance learning courses. Through Massachusetts Institute of Technology (MIT) OpenCourseWare, students can access free, online materials to more than 1,800 MIT courses. These extracurricular and off-site opportunities can potentially enhance the mathematical experiences for many gifted, creative, and talented mathematics students.

Valija C. Rose

See also Advanced Placement; Honors Programs; International Baccalaureate; Mathematical Talent; Mathematics, Curriculum; Middle School, Mathematics Curriculum

Further Readings

Assouline, S., & Lupkowski-Shoplik, A. (2005). *Developing math talent: A guide for educating gifted and advanced learners in math.* Waco, TX: Prufrock Press.

Chamberlin, S. A. (2006). Secondary mathematics for high-ability students. In F. A. Dixon & S. M. Moon (Eds.), *The handbook of secondary gifted education* (pp. 461–479). Waco, TX: Prufrock Press.

Johnson, D. T. (2003). Adapting mathematics curricula for high-ability learners. In J. VanTassel-Baska & C. A. Little (Eds.), *Content-based curriculum for high-ability learners* (pp. 161–190). Waco, TX: Prufrock Press.

Sheffield, L. J. (Ed.). (1999). *Developing mathematically promising students.* Reston, VA: The National Council of Teachers of Mathematics.

Secondary School, Social Studies Curriculum

According to the National Council for the Social Studies (NCSS), social studies curriculum encompasses course offerings from an array of related disciplines. Although the primary focus at the secondary high school level is on history, civics, and geography courses, high schools also may offer courses in anthropology, archaeology, economics, philosophy, psychology, religion, and sociology. NCSS maintains that the purpose of social studies is to prepare students for active and effective citizenship in a democratic society and to preserve democratic traditions. Research and literature related to gifted education and secondary social studies curriculum focus also on the importance of meeting and challenging the intellectual, social, and emotional capacities of gifted students. The integrated nature of social studies courses and the practice of infusing social studies lessons with examples from the humanities and the arts make the courses a natural fit for many gifted adolescents. Gifted students, who aspire to leadership positions and to careers in one of the social studies professions, particularly benefit from high-quality social studies curriculum. Examination of the links between gifted, creative, and talented students and social studies; and current research on the teaching and learning of social studies through a gifted education lens further highlights the importance of social studies education in the intellectual and social development of gifted students. This entry describes characteristics of gifted students and the social studies, high school offerings, curriculum for future thinkers and leaders, and benefits of secondary-school social studies curriculum.

Characteristics of Gifted Students and the Social Studies

The interdisciplinary nature of the social studies mirrors the way many gifted students view the world. Michael Piechowski explored the importance that gifted adolescents place on discerning connections underlying concepts, and on pursuing, uncovering, and creating meaning in their lives. A relentless quest for and relishing of complexity mark the intellectual and emotional life of many gifted students. At the same time, heightened sensitivity to ethical questions, moral issues, and social justice concerns tend to develop at a young age and lead in the high school years to intense passions for humanitarian causes and justice concerns. The study of secondary-school social studies can outfit gifted students with practical knowledge and skills that will sustain their pursuit of meaningful political and social activities throughout their lives.

High School Offerings

Twenty-first-century high school reform movements are generating multiple options for advanced learning in all subject areas. In the social studies, opportunities range from honors classes, Advanced Placement courses, both virtual and on-campus, and International Baccalaureate courses, to dual enrollment options, that is, college courses taught in high schools by college instructors. In addition, historical and governmental institutions, such as the National Archives and the Library of Congress, offer online learning experiences, and institutions of higher learning, such as the Massachusetts Institute of Technology (MIT) and Yale University, offer courses without charge to all students with Internet access. In a more traditional vein, secondary schools continue to provide enrichment opportunities to engage students in active problem solving and real-world learning through the Future Problem Solving International Program (FPSIP), Community Problem Solving (CmPS), and simulated experiences, such as Model United Nations and Model Judiciary.

Social studies curriculum specifically designed for gifted students offers more than acceleration and advanced coverage of content. It also ensures that gifted students understand and can engage in skills that will help them frame their own questions and acquire research skills and tools in areas of the social sciences that are important to them. To build this expertise, students work with practicing historians, government officials, politicians, and other community members who exemplify the work of professionals in their disciplines, either in person, through their teachers, virtually through Web-based learning, or some combination of all three. Teachers of gifted students continually strive to increase their knowledge of scholarship in their fields. They engage with students as coaches, guides, and mentors of future scholars, leaders in democracies, and citizens. Social studies teachers understand that democratic leadership abilities are learned, not natural skills. Many gifted students by virtue of their abilities to organize and inspire will become leaders in their professional and social lives. Hence, it is critical that they develop habits of personal reflection; engage in conscious practice of democratic skills, such as respect for minority views; observe good role models of democratic thought, discourse, and action; and appreciate the complexity of historic events. High-quality social studies curriculum for gifted students is key to the perpetuation of individual freedoms, rights, and responsibilities in democratic societies.

Curriculum for Future Thinkers and Leaders

Current social studies education research emphasizes the acquisition of inquiry and reasoning skills in the development of thoughtful and effective citizens. Many social studies resources are available to support this goal, in print and through the Internet. Several examples embody best practices in the teaching of social studies. Through the U.S. Department of Education Teaching American History grants program, teachers have opportunities to strengthen their power as bridges between professional historians and students. In collaboration with professionals from regional academic and arts institutions, teachers learn to model professional thinking about challenging social studies content. For those who prefer published curriculum for gifted and advanced learners, the William and Mary social studies units provide teachers and students with content and reasoning models that are applicable to a wide range of inquiry. Another option, historicalthinkingmatter.org, the result of a collaborative project between scholars at George Mason University and Stanford University, is an example of a high-quality online curriculum option. An examination of these offerings clarifies what good social studies curriculum for gifted students looks like.

Teaching American History Grants

Exposure to the disciplines of social studies from the perspectives of professionals in the field gives gifted students the kinds of school experiences that nourish natural interest and stimulate independent research. Since 2001, the Department of Education has awarded 660 Teaching American History grants to school districts in partnerships with universities, nonprofit history or humanities organizations, museums, and libraries to improve history teaching and student achievement. Rachel Ragland of Lake Forest College reported on the results of a program for teachers who participated in a collaborative project in a Midwest school district. Through the program, teachers significantly added to their repertoire of teaching skills and went from initially using lectures, worksheets, some music, and popular film to rethinking their own conceptualization of history and history teaching. Their understanding of history as a discovery process grew as they worked side by side with historians. Teachers incorporated the use of primary sources and artifacts, multiple perspectives, critical thinking and analysis, and conceptual and thematic questions into their lessons and conveyed to their students the experience of doing history that they enjoyed through the Teaching American History project. Although the Department of Education continues to fund the program for more teachers across the United States, curriculum units, such as the William and Mary units, are available that incorporate the principles of the programs and are ready for immediate classroom use.

The William and Mary Social Studies Units

The design of the William and Mary social studies units is based on the *integrated curriculum model* developed by Joyce VanTassel-Baska, the executive director of the Center for Gifted Education at the College of William and Mary. The integrated curriculum model is a framework that focuses on student outcomes related to advanced content and higher-level thinking processes of reasoning, inquiry, and document analysis developed in the context of rich, overarching concepts or themes. The units incorporate strategies recommended by both practicing professionals in the social studies disciplines and by educators of the gifted. Models of reasoning, research, vocabulary, writing, and concept development are illustrated and explained in detail in each curriculum. Because the models are used throughout all the William and Mary units, students have multiple opportunities, through practice during the school year, to develop expertise as thinkers, researchers, and writers.

At the heart of the William and Mary units are gifted students, with their particular intellectual, emotional, and social makeups. Students' natural curiosity and passion for questioning are refined through an interdisciplinary approach that recognizes the importance of documents and artifacts; incorporates important aspects of geography, psychology, economics, and other fields of intellectual pursuit; and builds appreciation for the contribution of the humanities to self-understanding and deeper knowledge of the social studies. Students learn how to think critically about social studies content and to practice reasoning skills while making personal connections to the material. The interplay of content, reasoning, and reflection on their thoughts and feelings gives students opportunities to deepen their understanding of themselves as effective citizens, democratic leaders, and emerging scholars.

Historicalthinkingmatters.org

Historicalthinkingmatters.org is another resource dedicated to the development of historical thinking. The Web-based resource presents units of study using a framework of analysis that again matches the way historians work as they construct historical narratives. Modules for teachers support the development and refinement of critical inquiry skills for those who are not practicing historians themselves and demonstrate scaffolding techniques using visual and auditory media that teachers can replicate in their teaching. Investigations begin with a provocative question, such as "Why did the Montgomery bus boycott succeed?" and provide students with opportunities to practice historical thinking skills. Students begin to think like historians as they identify the source of documents and artifacts, recognize and understand the time and place in which a document or artifact originated, read and question material closely with thoughtful attention to details, and corroborate information from different sources and different perspectives.

All the examples of good curriculum practice focus on students' growth as inquirers, thinkers, and active participants in the world, with the support of thoughtful and knowledgeable teachers. Although they understand gifted students' strong need for autonomy and independence, teachers recognize the importance of their own roles as mature guides to intellectual and social growth. Social studies teachers and those who support their development play important roles in the development of active citizens and scholars, and in the preservation of a nation's democratic ideals and practices.

Benefits

Secondary-school gifted students who experience the social studies through curriculum that is driven by universal concepts, thoughtful questions, and committed professionals become educated in much more than content knowledge. Through practice of careful reasoning, consideration of differing perspectives, reliance on document and artifact analysis, facility with conceptual thinking, construction of personal connections, and engagement in personal reflection, gifted, talented, and creative students develop skills and expertise as citizens and leaders in democratic societies. Together, researchers and practitioners, using contemporary resources and technology, create rich curriculum at the secondary level. In so doing, they contribute to students' appreciation of the social sciences in high school, assist students' entrée into the world of higher social studies education, and build habits of lifelong respect for the traditions of democratic societies.

Joanne Russillo Funk

See also Adolescent, Gifted; Advanced Placement; Brain-Based Research; Character and Moral Development; Creative Problem Solving; International Baccalaureate; Leadership; Social Studies, Curriculum

Further Readings

Bransford, J., Brown, A. L., & Cocking, R. R. (2000). Effective teaching: Examples in history, mathematics, and science. In J. D. Bransford, A. L. Brown, & R. R. Cocking (Eds.), *How people learn, brain, mind, experience, and school* (Expanded ed., pp. 155–189). Washington, DC: National Academy Press.

Center for Gifted Education. (2006). *Guide to teaching social studies curriculum.* Dubuque, IA: Kendall/Hunt.

Center for Gifted Education. (2006). *Primary sources and historical analysis.* Dubuque, IA: Kendall/Hunt.

Martin, D., Wineburg, S., Rosenzweig, R., & Leon, S. (2008). Historicalthinkingmatters.org: Using the Web to teach historical thinking. *Social Education, 72*(3), 140–43.

Mayer, R. H. (1998). Connecting narrative and historical thinking: Research-based approach to teaching history. *Social Education, 62*(2). Retrieved May 7, 2008, from http://members.ncss.org/se/6202/620207.html

National Council for the Social Studies. (Updated 2008, February). *Curriculum guidelines (for social studies teaching and learning).* Retrieved May 4, 2008, from http://www.socialstudies.org/positions/curriculum

Piechowski, M. M. (2006). *"Mellow out," they say. If I only could.* Madison, WI: Yunasa.

Ragland, R. G. (2007). Changing secondary teachers' views of teaching American history. *History Teacher, 40*(2), 221–246.

Stepien, W. J., & Stepien, W. C. (2006). "Pulling the cat's tail" in social studies and history classrooms. In F. A. Dixon & S. M. Moon (Eds.), *The handbook of secondary gifted education* (pp. 393–426). Waco, TX: Prufrock Press.

Secondary School, Writing Curriculum

A challenge in designing a writing curriculum is that the writing process is a subjective area of teaching. Yet, the research on teaching writing offers insight into how student written improvement is best accomplished with an array of strategies for teachers to use with talented writers. These insights on writing can be coalesced into a curriculum scope and sequence at the secondary level that is appropriate for gifted students, as described in this entry.

The four dominant approaches to the K–12 vertical articulation of teaching writing include (1) *presentation:* the teacher explains what good writing is and gives examples; (2) *natural process:* the teacher has students engage in a great deal of free writing, individually and in groups; (3) *focused practice:* the teacher structures writing tasks to emphasize specific aspects of writing; and (4) *skills:* the teacher breaks down writing into its component parts and then provides practice, sometimes in isolation, on each part. Of the four approaches, the focused practice approach has produced the strongest learning effects among student writers whereas the remaining three approaches resulted in weaker effects.

Instructional Strategies

The three processes identified as being critical to effective writing instruction are planning, writing, and revision. It is important for teachers to have opportunities to learn more effective procedures for teaching writing to apply the most effective strategies in their classrooms. The direct teaching of focused and intensive writing techniques appears to be more successful than is relying on general process techniques. When the organizational skills necessary for successful writing were emphasized throughout a unit, increases in students' scores on the organizational quality of their essay writing from the pretest to the posttest assessments have been found especially for students who received low scores on the pretest.

Good writers apply a rich vocabulary and correct grammar to convey their written point to their readers. Before students can write descriptively, they must possess a rich vocabulary. An extensive vocabulary is one of the characteristics that is most highly correlated with intelligence. A comprehensive vocabulary development program should be integrated into a secondary writing curriculum and include regular emphasis on interesting words encountered, direct instruction of techniques or procedures to develop a varied vocabulary, connected learning, and practice and repetition. Vocabulary development is enhanced through excellent reading instruction and diverse reading resources.

Writing is an advanced language task and is taught naturally and most effectively when integrated with reading instruction. Interrelated activities organizing instruction into broad, thematically based clusters of work through which reading, writing, and speaking activities are integrated promotes understanding of ideas. Furthermore, a balanced teaching of critical reading and writing skills can be embedded in the context of total language learning through direct instruction. Writing journals have been found to be valued by teachers and students alike for helping in various other aspects of the English curriculum.

Another instructional emphasis that enhances writing is the use of metacognitive strategies.

Ample guided practice should be provided by having students use metacognition control strategies for as many appropriate tasks as possible, providing reinforcement and feedback on how students can improve their execution of the strategies. Students need to practice self-monitoring of their performance when using the strategies, and teachers need to encourage generalization of the strategies by having students use them with different types of materials in a variety of content areas. Moreover, all students need teachers to explain writing task expectations clearly and fully.

Writing fosters learning in all disciplines. It is a tool for thinking, which makes it integral to every subject at every scholastic level. Skill in writing is developed and refined through practice, which means students should have frequent opportunities to write across the curriculum. The integration of reading and writing tasks has produced learning benefits for students. Specifically, the combination of incorporating inquiry through advanced questioning, analyzing and responding in writing to literature, prewriting, and communicating specific criteria as expectations for learners have been found to be effective curriculum strategies that produce higher achievement gains in learners. Inquiry learning is particularly important for gifted students, who thrive on accelerated learning opportunities and on learning that requires greater depth and complexity of thinking.

A field study of eight high schools contrasted four schools that had a senior writing project that included the program components of a research paper, product, portfolio, and presentation with that of four schools that did not have a senior writing project. A variety of measures, including focus groups, writing assessments, achievement test scores, and surveys were used to examine possible differences between schools with the senior project and schools without. Results of the study indicated several significant differences between the two sets of schools. Students in schools that incorporated the senior writing project across the curriculum indicated a more positive association with the following specific skills than did their counterparts at the control schools: writing a research paper, preparing and presenting a speech, carrying out a plan, and conducting interviews. Moreover, students in schools with the senior writing project perceived the skills of preparing and presenting a speech, conducting research, and locating appropriate references to have been reinforced more in their classes than the students at control schools did.

Despite identified practices that have been investigated in empirical studies to measure increased student achievement, the effective teaching of writing at the secondary level has continued to be found lacking in the literature. Although national writing assessments have exhibited student gains at earlier ages, no significant change was detected in the performance of 12th graders between assessment years.

Varied packaged programs to teach writing are readily available for schools to use and have yielded impressive gains for consistent use. Research-based teaching units produced by the College of William and Mary Center for Gifted Education have been found to show significant achievement gains in both gifted and non-gifted students at the secondary level in the area of persuasive writing, using performance-based assessments, modeled after National Assessment of Educational Progress (NAEP) assessment measures.

The integration and use of technology into the writing curriculum should be expanded in developing young writers. Distance learning opportunities have dramatically increased options for meeting the needs of gifted students in writing with online high school and college courses that provide challenging curriculum opportunities for students who demonstrate proficiency with grade-level material. The use of laptop computers most directly affects writing skills followed by communication and presentation skills.

Writing is a metacognitive thinking process, so rigorous writing experiences provide gifted students with opportunities to develop competence in their ability to think as well as to write. Fundamental skills associated with a process writing approach that should be used with gifted learners at all stages of development include (a) prewriting, (b) paragraph development, (c) theme development (literary generalizations), (d) development of introductions and endings, (e) work on supporting details, (f) effective use of figures of speech, (g) editing, (h) teacher and peer conferencing, (i) revising, and (j) rewriting.

Consideration also needs to be given to the type of writing that gifted students are encouraged to master. There should be a planned balance between creative writing forms and analytic expository writing forms, including persuasive writing. Writing with gifted students should include exposure to good writing through extensive reading, critique of others' writing, and many opportunities to practice their own writing skills.

Various studies have shed light on which teaching techniques specifically work well with teaching writing to gifted secondary students. The use of strategy instruction and self-regulation to improve gifted students' creative writing, following application of a writing instructional package, has been found to result in students writing longer stories, increasing their writing fluency, including more story elements, and writing higher quality stories. Students whose teachers had special training in writing instruction performed significantly better than do students with untrained teachers. When a graphic organizer was used to teach persuasive writing, explicitly using a rubric, and teacher feedback was consistently provided, gifted learners showed significant improvement in persuasive writing at secondary levels from Grades 6 through 11.

However, extensive studies examining the effective teaching of writing methods to gifted students at the secondary level is limited. Although use of packaged writing programs, technology tools, and having an abundance of opportunities to write using a structured model and receiving teacher feedback have all been found to be effective in increasing writing skills among all students, evidence does not suggest that teaching writing to the gifted should be perceived as a different enterprise from teaching it to all learners. Differentiation appears to be most needed in diagnosing the level of written proficiency at the beginning of instruction and providing follow-up assistance appropriate to that knowledge of functional level. Moreover, the personalization of the writing process through the feedback that teachers provide allows individual differences to be accommodated.

An emphasis on the writing process is a researched best practice strategy in improving writing. By stressing the processes of composing (planning, drafting, revising, sharing, and publishing), these sequential processes contribute to improved competence in writing ability among students. Twenty-five years of research on the compositional process has helped identify the various stages of writing. In the classroom, the complete process of written composition involves a series of recursive and interlocking stages, each of which should be discussed with students so they understand its value and place in the process. Longitudinal improvement in writing competence at the secondary level depends on students' understanding the processes they are involved. Furthermore, frequent practice in the classroom of the various stages of the writing process is necessary for student writing to improve. Such practice requires the devotion of regularly scheduled class time to the process. This time can be especially effective when structured as a writing workshop across a double period in which the teacher can provide guidance. Writing conferences have also been effective with developing written compositions. It is important for secondary gifted students to recognize and understand that written perfection is not achieved with the first draft of a manuscript but that rather, multiple drafts are standard and necessary to achieve a well-written document. This strategy matches the synthesis (high) cognitive domain as students create and compose using the writing process strategy.

The College of William and Mary Center for Gifted Education regularly assesses the effectiveness of instructional methods in curriculum research studies. The William and Mary teaching models that focus on developing student cognitive facility with higher-order thinking strategies have been found in multiple studies to be effective in increasing student performance in language arts. Use of the William and Mary teaching models strategy aligns cognitively with the analysis taxonomical domain, also at a high cognitive level, as gifted students analyze relationships and categorize relevant and irrelevant information using and automatizing critical thinking processes with specific graphic organizers.

The *hamburger model* uses the familiar metaphor of a sandwich to help students construct a paragraph or essay. The *Dagwood model* is the extended version of the sandwich metaphor that is especially appropriate for use with secondary students developing their persuasive writing skills. Richard Paul's *elements of reasoning* model for critical thinking emphasizes eight elements to process an idea: the issue, purpose, point of view, assumptions, concepts, evidence, inferences, and implications or consequences. The graphic organizer

"Reasoning About a Situation or Event," is also based on the elements and concept of the Paul model, this reasoning model should be used when analyzing a specific event where two or more people or groups of people are in conflict with one another and have a vested interest in the outcome of the event. Teachers should encourage students to actively use the terms and the model in approaching problems and issues to develop an understanding of reasoning through a situation and apply these elements to their written compositions.

Writing Assessment

A survey of writing assessment activities found a mix of traditional paper-and-pencil activities and formal writing assignments. Although paper-and-pencil activities appeared to dominate the classroom in regular and routine use, writing activities carried more weight when teachers computed course grades. Writing portfolios were not found to be in general use. In an NAEP survey for teachers and students, the technique of peer review was reported to be a common writing assessment practice in more than two-thirds of eighth-grade classrooms.

Researchers have known for a long time that testing drives the school curriculum and that writing is not immune to this reality. An analysis of writing assessments across five states through the use of interviews with educators, examination of materials related to assessment used at the local and state levels, and writing assessments across 43 states found that writing assessments stipulate the kinds of writing that should be taught, set standards for what counts as good writing, and set the conditions under which students must demonstrate their proficiency and what they should learn. Also found was the great variability in writing assessments used, from 40-minute assessment prompts in one state to portfolio assessments in another state. Although testing ensures that what is tested is taught, the tests cannot ensure that things are taught well. For teaching of writing to improve, states will have to intervene to provide teachers more opportunities to learn effective procedures for teaching writing.

The importance of teacher feedback about student writing on student learning does not correlate with the degree of feedback offered to students. Data collected from 55 middle school English classes indicated that incidents of high-quality instructional feedback and individualized instruction occurred in a small number of smaller classrooms and never occurred in larger classrooms. Teacher qualifications (years of experience and credential status) were unrelated to this teaching practice, nor did reduced class sizes directly affect the use of this teacher practice in secondary classrooms.

Gifted Students

Writing instruction for gifted students must be tailored to their unique needs. Using both collaborative and direct instructional approaches, writing programs should include the writing conventions of various disciplines, writing for the general public, writing across the curriculum, technical writing, expressive writing, and persuasive writing. Writing competitions are readily available for secondary students online and in reference materials.

Teachers need opportunities to learn more effective procedures for teaching writing. High-stakes testing can shift instruction away from the all-important feedback and revision aspects of writing, thereby leading to a reductive approach to writing in the curriculum. Key enabling structures and standards for implementation of the instructional strategies discussed include increased professional development training for teachers on the effective delivery of the strategies, increased time (scheduling of double-blocks) for student writing with valuable teacher feedback built in, and the increased use of flexible grouping strategies when peer review strategies are used with students to heighten the degree of meaningful peer feedback. These elements of effective writing instruction must be integrated in a systemic and regularly consistent manner across the secondary writing curriculum.

Bronwyn MacFarlane

See also Literary Creativity; Verbal Ability; Writers

Further Readings

Appleman, D. (2000). *Critical encounters in high school English: Teaching literary theory to adolescents' language and literacy series.* New York: Teachers College Press.

Black, S. (1999). Alternate doorways: Teaching writing to children with varied gifts. *Gifted Child Today Magazine, 22*(3), 18–22.

Carlin-Menter, S., & Shuell, T. (2003). Teaching writing strategies through multimedia authorship. *Journal of Educational Multimedia and Hypermedia, 12*(4), 315–335.

College of William and Mary Center for Gifted Education: http://www.cfge.wm.edu

Hillocks, G. (2002). *The testing trap: How state writing assessments control learning.* New York: Teachers College Press.

Hillocks, G. (2003). Fighting back: Assessing the assessments. *English Journal, 92*(4), 63–70.

Ketter, J., & Pool, J. (2001). Exploring the impact of a high-stakes direct writing assessment in two high school classrooms. *Research in the Teaching of English, 35*(3), 344–393.

Langer, J. A. (2001). Beating the odds: Teaching middle and high school students to read and write well. *American Educational Research Journal, 38*(4), 837–880.

Marzano, R. J., Pickering, D., & Pollack, J. (2001). *Classroom instruction that works: Research-based strategies for increasing student achievement.* Alexandria, VA: Association for Supervision and Curriculum Development.

Scherff, L., & Piazza, C. (2005). The more things change the more they stay the same. *Research in the Teaching of English, 39*(3), 271–304.

Schunk, D. H., & Swartz, C. W. (1993). Writing strategy instruction with gifted students: Effects of goals and feedback on self-efficacy and skills. *Roeper Review, 15*(4), 225–230.

VanTassel-Baska, J. (2002). Assessment of gifted student learning in the language arts. *Journal of Secondary Gifted Education, 13*(2), 67–72.

VanTassel-Baska, J., & Stambaugh, T. (2006). *Comprehensive curriculum for gifted learners* (3rd ed.) Boston: Pearson, Allyn & Bacon.

VanTassel-Baska, J., Zuo, L., Avery, L. D., & Little, C. A. (2002). A curriculum study of gifted-student learning in the language arts. *Gifted Child Quarterly, 46*(1), 30–44.

Secondary Schools

Secondary schools can be defined as broadly as Grades 6 through 12, or as narrowly as Grades 10 through 12, depending on the placement of students during early adolescence in middle schools, junior high schools, or K–8 schools. In this entry, secondary schools mainly refer to 3- or 4-year high schools because middle schools generally have different approaches to nurturing academic giftedness. Secondary-school programs include honors courses, Advanced Placement (AP) courses, and the International Baccalaureate (IB), all of which are geared toward college-bound students. In addition, some high schools provide special seminars for gifted students that focus on further enrichment with such things as special topics, social and emotional issues, and career development. Such programs in secondary schools can play a key role in preparing students with the academic skills they will need to be competitive for college admission and scholarships, as well as preparing them for success in college, as this entry describes.

The difference between primary and secondary education is that most students begin to take courses with teachers who specialize in specific content areas (e.g., mathematics). Consequently, students begin to rotate among teachers, allowing students to structure individual schedules and enroll in courses different than their peers.

In Grades 6 through 8, gifted students begin to show their interest and aptitude in different content areas more clearly. They may start taking courses on a precollege preparatory track that prepares students to be competitive for college admission in a variety of areas. In mathematics, this may mean that students complete Algebra I by the end of eighth grade to ensure they have taken calculus before graduating high school. For those wanting to attend elite universities (e.g., Ivy League schools), this may also mean completing Geometry or Algebra II before entering high school and several AP mathematics courses (such as AP statistics, AP calculus) before graduation.

In addition to advanced course completions, honors courses are one way students receive enriched curriculum beyond the standard curriculum. Secondary schools vary in the honors courses they offer, but they often cover all core content areas (English, mathematics, science, and history). These courses, designed for students who can work at a fast pace, typically cover a broader range of topics compared with nonhonors courses. In many high schools, honors courses are weighted so that they count extra toward a student's grade-point average (GPA). This weighted grade provides students in honors courses an opportunity for a higher GPA than the standard 4.0 scale. This higher GPA increases a students' likelihood of earning top rankings in their graduating classes, thus making them more appealing to highly selective 4-year colleges or universities.

Like honors courses, AP courses at the secondary level also include rigorous curriculum across all content areas as developed by the College Board. Although some sixth- through eighth-grade programs offer honors or faster-paced courses, AP courses are only offered in high school. These courses can also be weighted, and in some schools, the weighting for AP courses is greater than for honors courses. The primary difference between honors and AP courses is that AP courses can count toward college credit. Students in AP courses take exams at the end of the course, and a score of 3 or better is accepted in most colleges as general education credit. Taking and passing AP exams gives students an academic advantage when starting college—they can move on to more advanced courses because they have already received credit toward their basic college requirements through AP.

Another secondary program offered is the International Baccalaureate (IB), a program that prepares students for competitive university life outside of the United States. There are only 750 schools in the United States offering IB programs at the secondary level. There is an IB program for middle years (defined as ages 11–16, or equivalent to sixth grade through sophomore year), and the diploma program, which can be mapped to the last 2 years of high school. Students study eight different subjects in the IB middle-year program, including two languages, mathematics, humanities, technology, science, arts, and physical education. In the diploma program, students study six different subjects, including two languages, mathematics and computer science, individuals and societies, experimental sciences, and the arts. Students may be enrolled concurrently in honors, AP, and IB programs as long as the school can overlap the courses.

Special seminars for gifted students often round out their education with emphasis on developing a sense of identity and purpose. Discussions of literature, philosophy, or current events help students to discover personal meaning in classroom material, and guidance activities help students with career and personal development.

Secondary-school students enrolled in honors, AP, or IB are involved in a college preparatory curriculum that will exceed the minimum requirements for high school graduation. As such, courses in secondary schools play a prominent role in how well students are prepared for college. Students may begin coursework that allows them to complete advanced courses, such as AP and honors, before high school graduation. Weighted grades allow them to have a higher academic ranking within their high school. They may receive college credit even before students enroll in college. For some, this rigorous academic path makes them highly competitive for coveted scholarships and admission into top universities. For others, gifted education in high school provides an opportunity for personal challenge, engagement with learning, and guidance for the academic paths they choose.

Pamela L. Paek

See also Achievement Motivation; Advanced Placement; Honors Programs; International Baccalaureate

Further Readings

Adelman, C. (1999). *Answers in the tool box: Academic intensity, attendance patterns, and bachelor's degree attainment.* Washington, DC: U.S. Department of Education.

Adelman, C. (2006). *The toolbox revisited: Paths to degree completion from high school through college.* Washington, DC: U.S. Department of Education.

Ewing, M. (2006). *The AP program and student outcomes: A summary of research.* New York: College Board.

SELF-ACTUALIZATION

Although popularized by Abraham Maslow, the concept of "self-actualization" was originally introduced by Kurt Goldstein, a physician specializing in neuro-anatomy and psychiatry in the early half of the 20th century. As conceived by Goldstein, self-actualization is the ultimate goal of all organisms. It is the process of an organism fulfilling all of its capacities to become what it is biologically intended to be. Goldstein saw all behaviors and drives as manifestations of this overarching motivation.

Maslow defined self-actualization more narrowly and diverged from Goldstein in his conception of when and how self-actualization can emerge as a motivator. Similar to Goldstein, Maslow sees self-actualization as the fulfillment of one's greatest potential. In his discussions of self-actualization, however, he is referring solely to people, rather than all organisms. In addition, his theory asserts that the drive to self-actualize will only emerge as a motivator once a variety of more basic needs are met. This entry describes Maslow's hierarchy of needs and self-actualization.

Maslow's Hierarchy of Needs

As noted, other needs must be met before self-actualization becomes a dominant motivator of behavior. Self-actualization is at the pinnacle of what Maslow defined as a hierarchy of human needs. In this hierarchy, lower needs (described as "pre-potent" needs) typically must be met before higher needs emerge. Physiological needs are the most primary in this hierarchy. Although Maslow himself declined to make a list of physiological needs, citing the nearly endless contributors to physical homeostasis, "food" is his prime example of this type of need. Maslow suggests that if an individual is starving or near starving, he or she is essentially defined by that hunger. In most cases, an individual with extreme hunger will eschew higher needs, such as love and belonging, to fulfill the body's need for nourishment.

Once physiological needs are met, the next level of need—safety—immediately rises to consciousness and begins to drive behavior. Interestingly, Maslow suggests that these new needs arise and that physiological needs, once fulfilled, are nearly forgotten. Thus, the need for food may suddenly seem trivial compared with the need for physical protection—provided the individual continues to have a steady food supply. This cycle of need, fulfillment, and forgetting occurs at every stage of the hierarchy.

Maslow asserts that average adults in affluent, organized societies have few safety needs under typical conditions. Most have little need to worry about physical attacks, fires, and so forth. Thus, safety needs in these individuals are expressed in subtle ways, such as the desire for savings accounts and steady jobs. However, Maslow notes that safety needs drive individuals in less stable conditions, such as those living in low-socioeconomic conditions, or under wartime conditions. He also suggests that certain mental health conditions reflect, in part, safety needs. He argues that individuals with neurotic or compulsive tendencies are psychologically similar to children in their sense of danger. However, although children truly are dependent on others for safety, the neurotic individual only feels as if this is the case. Likewise, just as children seek to avoid unpredictable events because of the danger they might present, people with compulsive behaviors try to make the world orderly and predictable to avoid perceived danger.

Love needs are next in Maslow's hierarchy. These include friendship, family, and sexual love, as well as the desire to be accepted by peer groups and to receive affection. To meet our love needs, we must be positioned to both give and receive love. Maslow, like many theorists, psychologists, and psychiatrists, suggests that the failure to fulfill love needs is at the root of much psychopathology seen today. Near the top of Maslow's hierarchy are esteem needs. These needs include the desire for competence, high self-regard, respect, a sense of strength, and general self-worth. Maslow notes that if these needs are not met, an individual either becomes deeply discouraged or develops maladjusted methods for coping with feelings of inferiority and worthlessness. Only after these needs—physiological, safety, love, and esteem—are met can an individual begin to be motivated by the need for self-actualization.

Maslow's Concept of Self-Actualization

Maslow argues that, to be truly happy, painters need to paint; writers need to write; musicians need to play. This is self-actualization. However, he also notes that even if all other needs are met, self-actualization does not emerge as a motivator in all cases. When it does, it can take many forms, depending on individual talents, values, and so on. Often the urge is creative, as in the case of artists or writers; however, it might also take the form of maximizing the quality of one's relationships, or to perfect the physical form through athletics and good health. Maslow notes that self-actualization is one of the least studied and understood needs, because of its relative rarity. It is the exception, rather than the rule, he states, for an individual's other needs to be so sufficiently met that self-actualization can emerge as a motivator.

In considering Maslow's conception of self-actualization, certain arguments spring readily to mind. There are numerous examples of individuals living in states of poverty, loneliness, low self-esteem, and so forth, who nonetheless seem to self-actualize through their work. Examples include Vincent Van Gogh, whose life and suicide suggest a deep well of unmet needs, and Anne Frank, whose universally acclaimed diary was written in, and facilitated by, conditions of extreme danger. Maslow's theory is not insensible to these obvious exceptions. He notes that in certain people the creative urge is so strong that it outweighs other needs, including those considered to be pre-potent in most individuals. He does not go so far as to say that in some cases self-actualization occurs because of hardship, but admits that it may occur despite unmet needs. Questions remain, then, about individuals who seem to self-actualize in direct response to need-threatening conditions. Researchers in the psychology of giftedness and positive psychologists have much to explore in future work in the area of self-actualization.

Erin Sullivan

See also Creativity, Definition; Optimal Development; Spirituality

Further Readings

Daniels, M. (1982). The development of the concept of self-actualization in the writings of Abraham Maslow. *Current Psychological Reviews, 2*(1), 61–75.

Maslow, A. H. (1943). A theory of human motivation. *Psychological Review, 50,* 370–396.

Maslow, A. H. (1967). Self-actualization and beyond. In J. F. T. Bugental (Ed.), *Challenges of humanistic psychology* (pp. 279–286). New York: McGraw-Hill.

Self-Contained Classroom

Philosophy and pragmatism are two determinants used to initiate, sustain, or negate self-contained classrooms for gifted students. References to self-contained classrooms are defined as programmatic models or organizational structures and are labeled in a variety of ways: special day classes, full-time ability groups, homogeneous classrooms, and accelerated or enriched classrooms. Traditionally, self-contained classrooms were associated with secondary education by subject to achieve particular goals or outcomes. Regardless of the specific label attributed to this teaching and learning environment, the common features across all the terms is that a self-contained classroom provides for special grouping of students with like ability or aptitude within or across grade levels. This entry describes the history, curriculum and instruction, affective and social outcomes, and debate regarding self-contained classrooms.

History

Assigning gifted students with like abilities to the same classroom has been met with controversy throughout history. Abraham Tannenbaum stated, "No other specific grouping of children have been alternatively embraced and repelled by so much negativism by educators and laypersons alike" (p. 16). In an interview, A. H. Passow confirmed that if grouping gifted students was administered as a means to avoid assuming responsibility to attend to the issues of general education for all students, it was elitist. Across the eras, James Kulik identified educational, national, and social issues that have caused educators and communities to posit positive or negative reactions to grouping patterns. Issues noted by Kulik that have influenced the establishment or dissolution of self-contained classrooms over time can be defined to include the following: the development of sophisticated measurement instruments, technological and economic global competitiveness, and concerns for social justice denied by equity and access. Statements by Jeannie Oakes that juxtaposed ability grouping and tracking caused strong negative reactions among educators and laypersons and caused policymakers to reconsider providing self-contained classrooms. Robert Slavin's work that articulated the need for students to work cooperatively with peers, representing economic, cultural, linguistic, and academic diversity also created concern for the implementation of self-contained classrooms. The shifts in perspectives regarding the self-contained classroom consistently brought about national and local changes in curriculum, instruction, professionalism, class size, and allocation of resources for gifted students.

Curriculum and Instruction

The self-contained classroom has been legitimized by the concept that it provides the opportunity to respond to the needs, interests, and abilities of gifted students. The dual demands of the classroom wherein the teacher must respond to the specialized and general needs of students continues to affect decisions about grouping. Carol Ann Tomlinson described heterogeneous classes as a "one-size-fits-all" unless differentiation of instruction has taken place within the context of that classroom. Tomlinson stated that advanced learners were intellectually thwarted by work that they already had accomplished and were possibly "ignored" because they had achieved their designated proficiency levels. However, just grouping students of like ability is insufficient, according to Barbara Clark. Karen Rogers supported this idea by stating that one of the flaws in the studies regarding full-time grouping has been the emphasis placed on grouping rather than on analyzing teaching differences.

In his meta-analytic review of grouping programs, Kulik stipulated key distinctions among grouping programs that were related to curriculum adjustments. Whether the self-contained classroom was for purposes of acceleration or enrichment, the curricular adjustments within these classes were fundamental to their outcomes. Accelerated classrooms adjusted the pace of the presentation of the curriculum; the enrichment classrooms provided learning experiences that extended the basic or core curriculum. Kulik found that there was a relationship between the degree of curriculum adjustments in both the accelerated and enrichment self-contained classroom configurations and the gifted students' academic performance; the more the curriculum was modified, the greater and more positive the impact on gifted students' achievements. Marcia Delcourt, Brenda Loyd, Dewey Cornell, and Marc Goldberg also found that gifted students' academic performance was rated higher than that of gifted peers who were not enrolled in separate day classes. According to the Delcourt study, gifted students in separate classes achieved at a higher level than did their gifted peers assigned to any type of within class or other grouping pattern.

Basic to the curriculum modifications in self-contained classrooms are issues relevant to the following: assessment of the gifted students to define the curriculum most developmentally appropriate; culturally responsive curriculum to meet the diverse needs of the student population; acknowledgment of variations of abilities within the gifted population; and sufficient differentiation. Joyce VanTassel-Baska outlined a set of key characteristics that are important to the differentiated tasks gifted students should be taught: use a variety of resources, study topics from multiple perspectives, engage in open-ended learning experiences, meet more complex and conceptually oriented content, and engage in analytic and interpretative thinking opportunities.

Sidney Moon, Melanie Swift, and Ann Shallenberger studied a fourth- and fifth-grade self-contained classroom and articulated the following features that were important to the attainment of academic success and goal attainment in this setting: challenging environment, differentiated instruction, and development of learning skills.

Affective and Social Outcomes

Rogers identified the attributes of gifted students who benefited most in full-time grouping situations: students who were academically motivated, students who functioned above grade level, students who had a preference to be challenged and to learn at a faster rate of speed, and students who enjoyed academic endeavors or work. Delcourt reported that the gifted students' perceptions of themselves in self-contained classrooms were lower than those of their peers involved in other types of grouping patterns. The students were also more teacher-dependent than were their gifted peers in other classroom settings.

The Debate

The long-standing arguments of the efficacy and effectiveness of self-contained classrooms most likely will continue. Ellen Winner addressed the case against and for ability grouping. She noted support for ability grouping has been built on lowering standards and omitting challenge whereas the case against ability grouping focuses on the emergence of elitism and arrogance. Kulik stated that the advantages of self-contained classrooms include such items as better preparation for advanced classes in high school and a single teacher continuously assigned to instruct the same class. Also noted by the same author were the disadvantages of the self-contained classroom including funding, depriving the heterogeneous classroom of gifted student to "enrich" the class, and parents who resist the traveling that might be necessary to transport student to the school where self-contained classes are housed. The controversies surrounding self-contained classrooms have not been resolved and continue to be debated.

Sandra N. Kaplan

See also Controversies in Gifted Education; Curriculum Models; Group Dynamics

Further Readings

Clark, B. (2008). *Growing up gifted.* New York: Merrill Prentice Hall.

Delcourt, M., Loyd, B., Cornell, D., & Goldberg, M. (1994). *Evaluation of the effects of programming arrangements in student learning outcomes.* Storrs, CT: National Research Center on Gifted and Talented.

Kirschenbaum, R. J. (2004). Interview with Dr. A. Harry Passow. In J. VanTassel-Baska (Ed.), *Curriculum for gifted and talented students.* Thousand Oaks, CA: Corwin Press.

Kulik, J. A. (1992). *An analysis of the research on ability grouping: Historical and contemporary perspectives.* Storrs, CT: National Research Center on the Gifted and Talented.

Kulik, J. A., & Kulik, C. C. (1992). Meta-analysis findings on grouping programs. *Gifted Child Quarterly, 36,* 73–77.

Moon, S., Swift, M., & Shallenberger, A. (2002). Perceptions of a self-contained class for fourth- and fifth-grade students with high to extreme levels of intellectual giftedness. *Gifted Child Quarterly, 46*(1), 64–79.

Oakes, J. (1986). *Keeping track: How schools structure inequality.* New Haven, CT: Yale University Press.

Rogers, K. (2002). *Reforming gifted education.* Scottsdale, AZ: Great Potential Press.

Slavin, R. (1995). *Cooperative learning: Theory, research and practice* (2nd ed.). Boston: Allyn & Bacon.

Tannenbaum, A. (1983). *Gifted children.* New York: Macmillan.

Tomlinson, C. A. (1999). *The differentiated classroom: Responding to the needs of all learners.* Alexandria, VA: Association for Supervision and Curriculum Development.

VanTassel-Baska, J. (2003). *Curriculum and instructional planning and design for gifted learners.* Denver, CO: Love Publishing.

Winner, E. (1996). *Gifted children: Myths and realities.* New York: Basic Books.

Self-Efficacy/Self-Esteem

"I want to do it myself!" "I can do it!" Anyone who has been around young children has heard these two statements. Statements such as these reflect children asserting their independence and reflect children's sense of self. Children believe in themselves. Only as they grow older and interact more with their environment and with others do children start to have self-doubts that challenge their self-esteem and self-efficacy. *Self-esteem* is a global concept that has been defined as one's general feelings of self-worth, and Albert Bandura coined the term *self-efficacy* to describe one's belief in his or her ability to do a specific task. This entry describes self-efficacy in relation to gender and race/ethnicity, positive self-esteem, talented and gifted students, and fostering positive self-beliefs.

Gender and Race/Ethnicity

A landmark study by the American Association of University Women examined the self-esteem of a large, national sample of boys and girls from childhood through adolescence. As young children, both boys and girls were positive about themselves; however, as they matriculated from

4th grade to 12th grade, girls experienced a dramatic decline in their self-esteem, whereas the self-esteem of boys seemed to get stronger. Carol Gilligan suggested that girls enter adolescence feeling strong, wise, and capable, yet during adolescence they start to hide their "true self," which leaves them feeling less confident and having more negative views of themselves. Indeed, this negative view of self is also reflected in girls, regardless of giftedness, starting to develop negative self-perceptions with respect to their body images, another aspect of self-esteem. Another possible explanation for the negative shift in girls' self-esteem is that girls experience an increase in depressive affect during adolescence. By late adolescence, girls experience more depression than do boys their age. Sex-role development and the socialization for females to be communal and for males to be competitive also affects self-esteem. As noted in the National Council for Research on Women report, *The Girls Report & What We Need to Know About Growing Up Female,* twice as many girls as boys are depressed, and self-esteem is a strong correlate of depression.

In a longitudinal study, researchers found that change in self-esteem among women was related to interpersonal characteristics that included nurturance and warmth, whereas changes in self-esteem among men was strongly linked to self-focused qualities such as managing social anxiety. Self-esteem is important in that it is positively related to an individual's ability to cope with stress and is negatively associated with depression, stress, and suicidal ideation. Furthermore, race/ethnicity interacts with self-esteem with Hispanic, Asian American, and Native American adolescents, particularly girls, having lower self-esteem than do Euro-American adolescents.

Positive Self-Esteem

Positive self-esteem has been consistently linked with creativity, talent, and giftedness. An important aspect of creativity is motivation. Intrinsic motivation (being driven by personal interest, gratification, challenge, or fulfillment) is associated with increases in self-esteem and creativity; however, extrinsic motivation (being driven by external rewards, evaluation, and competition) negatively affects creativity and self-esteem. Creative students who did not receive rewards or evaluation during or after completing a task have been found to be more creative than are the students who received rewards or evaluations. Also, persons with high self-esteem are not as vulnerable to environmental factors as those with low self-esteem. Thus, self-esteem is a protective factor against the negative external influences that constrain creativity.

Talented and Gifted Students

Talented and gifted students perceive and are affected by their abilities differently. For example, when asked to compare self-esteem levels with those of their non-gifted peers, gifted students report having an average or above average self-esteem. There are also gender differences in how the self-esteem of gifted boy and girl students is influenced. Higher mathematical ability is positively associated with the self-esteem of girls, but not of boys. In contrast, the self-esteem of gifted boys has been linked to their having higher levels of athletic and skill expectations. Despite the environmental factors that can negatively influence gifted students' self-esteem, talented young people enjoy their enhanced academic or athletic abilities, which fosters increased self-esteem and self-efficacy.

Although both self-esteem and self-efficacy are self-beliefs, they are different concepts. *Self-efficacy* is typically discussed as one's confidence that one can do behaviors related to accomplishing a specific task, such as school self-efficacy or career self-efficacy. Among bright, talented girls, school self-efficacy was found to be positively related to course taking, particularly math and science courses, and to future aspirations. Those who had higher self-efficacy also were more likely to be willing to pursue careers in math, science, or engineering. As Bandura stressed, those individuals who are higher in self-efficacy make heightened and sustained efforts in the face of failure to reach their goals. Rather than quitting, they are more likely to blame setbacks on lack of necessary knowledge or skills or insufficient effort. This is particularly true when gifted children are faced with challenging school tasks. They typically do not quit but instead problem solve to figure out what they need to accomplish the task. They have high self-efficacy (or self-confidence) that they will succeed. This belief, combined with their intrinsic motivation, propels them to continue until they accomplish their goal. Gifted children expect to succeed and when they do, this reinforces their self-efficacy as well as their self-esteem.

Fostering Positive Self-Beliefs

Support from others fosters positive self-beliefs. Mothers and fathers, when they provide a healthy family environment that is caring and structured with boundaries for behaviors, can enhance and reinforce children's and adolescents' self-beliefs. Teachers who provide gifted and creative students with challenges appropriate to their abilities and then let them struggle to be problem-solvers foster self-esteem and self-efficacy. Individuals who have positive self-beliefs, who believe in themselves, have the potential to become our future leaders.

Sharon E. Robinson Kurpius, Sarah K. Dixon, and Erin M. Carr Jordan

See also Resilience; Social Development; Social-Emotional Issues

Further Readings

Amabile, T. M., Goldfarb, P., & Brackfield, S. C. (1990). Social influences on creativity: Evaluation, coaction, and surveillance. *Creativity Research Journal, 3,* 6–21.

American Association of University Women (AAUW). (1991). *Short-changing girls, short-changing America.* Washington, DC: Author.

Bandura, A. (1993). Perceived self-efficacy in cognitive development and functioning. *Educational Psychologist, 28,* 117–148.

Block, J., & Robins, R. W. (1993). A longitudinal study of consistency and change in self-esteem from early adolescence to early adulthood. *Child Development, 64,* 909–923.

Ellis, C. J., Riley, T. L., & Gordon, B. (2003). Talented female athletes: Are they going for the gold? *Journal of Secondary Gifted Education, 14,* 229–242.

Field, T., Harding, J., Yando, R., Gonzalez, K., Lasko, D., Bendell, D. C., et al. (1998). Feelings and attitudes of gifted students. *Adolescence, 33,* 331–343.

Garber, J., Robinson, N., & Valentiner, D. (1997). The relation between parenting and adolescent depression: Self-worth as a mediator. *Journal of Adolescent Research, 12,* 12–33.

Solano, C. H. (1983). Self-concept in mathematically gifted adolescents. *Journal of General Psychology,* 33–42.

Wilburn, V. R., & Smith, D. E. (2005). Stress, self-esteem, and suicidal ideation in late adolescents. *Adolescence, 40,* 33–45.

SERVICE-LEARNING

Connecting schools to community service is known as *service-learning.* Service-learning, described in this entry, is a method by which students learn and develop through curriculum integration and active participation in thoughtfully organized service experiences that address actual needs in the community. Providing structured time for students to think, talk, and write about their experiences during a service activity, service-learning provides students with opportunities to use their skills and knowledge in real-life situations in their own communities. These experiences enhance learning, especially for the gifted, by extending student learning into the community and helping to foster a sense of caring for others. Service-learning, tracing its roots to community service, has been shown to be an effective, differentiated methodology in the education of the gifted by encouraging creativity and collaboration, enhancing critical thinking skills, and further developing students' character and individual talents.

People helping others in their community is a tradition in the United States. Over the generations, Americans have answered the call to service offering their time, their efforts, and, most importantly, their compassion. In the early years when the United States was primarily an agrarian society, people helping others was an integral part of the social fabric. Young people were aware of their roles and learned early to contribute to their communities. In 1933, President Franklin Roosevelt launched the Civilian Conservation Corps (CCC), which helped pull the country out of the Great Depression. Millions of the unemployed served their country building bridges, national parks, and buildings in this country until 1942.

Progressives such as John Dewey encouraged schools to include the value of social reform and emphasize social and cooperative activities.

Connecting schools to community service was also encouraged by William Kilpatrick during World War II when he suggested that learning should take place in settings outside classroom walls and should include experiences to meet real community needs.

The first service-learning legislation was signed into law in November 1990 by President George H. W. Bush. This legislation, the National and Community Service Act of 1990, created the Commission on National and Community Service. In 1993, President Bill Clinton championed the National and Community Service Trust Act creating the Corporation for National and Community Service, which continues to support service-learning through its Learn and Service America program. Supported by liberals and conservatives alike, service-learning continues to generate much interest and support.

Classifications of Service-Learning

Jann Bohnenberger and Alice Terry developed the K–12 Developmental Service-Learning Typology, which identifies three levels of service-learning: community-service, community-exploration, and community-action. In Community-Service service-learning, students participate primarily in volunteerism; they perceive issues that are individual rather than societal. Although tied to the school curriculum and involving a high degree of service, this level involves a lesser degree of learning. Activities at this level include activities such as tutoring and serving in soup kitchens. Community-Service service-learning is appropriate for younger gifted students as a way to experience service to others, as an entry-level service-learning experience.

The next level of service-learning is Community-Exploration. At this level, the students explore, research, and connect a classroom topic to their community. Community-Exploration service-learning includes activities such as internships, high-level community research, and outdoor and environmental education.

Community-Action service-learning is the highest and most appropriate level for gifted students, especially adolescents. In Community-Action service-learning, students analyze a challenge in their communities, generate new ideas, and implement a plan of action to address the community challenge. They work in self-selected collaborative groups based on their interests, skills, and talents. At this level, the students develop complex problem-solving skills, advanced communication skills, the ability to connect knowledge across the disciplines, and the perseverance to overcome obstacles. Activities can include civic reform and community enhancement. Community-Action service-learning encourages gifted students to explore societal concerns; it involves a high degree of service, producing a broader community impact and the highest degree of learning.

Service-Learning in the Education of Gifted Students

Involving gifted students in service-learning is beneficial to the students and to the communities they serve. Participation in high levels of service-learning is advantageous for gifted youth because of their potential for advanced social, emotional, moral, and ethical development. The gifted tend to have a more highly developed sense of social justice, fairness, ethics, concern for others, and interest in global issues than do their non-gifted peers. Service-learning has the potential to help gifted students become more sensitive to community concerns and to develop socially, emotionally, and ethically.

In addition, high-level service-learning experiences can help gifted students develop advanced problem-solving skills, critical and creative thinking skills, and leadership skills. Service-learning has the potential to help gifted students reach their creative potential as they seek creative solutions to society's ever-increasing problems. It is also an effective, differentiated methodology for the gifted that can help gifted students develop greater self-esteem and self-efficacy as well as help them stretch toward self-actualization. Advanced levels of service-learning have been shown to provide gifted students with opportunities to demonstrate high levels of creativity, responsibility, reflective judgment, self-awareness, empathy for others, and autonomy of thought and action, in addition to other characteristics of self-actualization. The Future Problem Solving program's Community Problem Solving component has proven to be an excellent avenue for helping teachers incorporate effective Community-Action service-learning into their classrooms.

Alice Wickersham Terry

See also Character and Moral Development; Creative Problem Solving; Critical Thinking; Differentiation; Future Problem Solving; Problem Solving; Self-Actualization; Self-Efficacy/Self-Esteem

Further Readings

Corporation for National and Community Service, Learn and Service America: http://www.learnandserve.gov

Renzulli, J. S. (2002). Expanding the conception of giftedness to include co-cognitive traits and to promote social capital. *Phi Delta Kappan, 84,* 33–58.

Terry, A. W. (2003). Effects of service learning on young, gifted adolescents and their community. *Gifted Child Quarterly, 47,* 295–308.

Terry, A. W., & Bohnenberger, J. E. (2003). Service learning: Fostering a cycle of caring in our gifted youth. *Journal of Secondary Gifted Education, 1,* 23–30.

Terry, A. W., & Bohnenberger, J. B. (2007). *Service-learning . . . by degrees: How adolescents can make a difference in the real world.* Portsmouth, NH: Heinemann.

Sex Differences in Creativity

Most research conducted on creativity and productivity in adult life has concentrated on men. It has been noted in the research on sex differences in creativity that men produce more creative work in research publications than women do and that cumulatively, men earn more degrees, produce more works of art, and make more contributions in professional fields. Even in areas such as literature, in which both younger boys and girls believe that women excel, adult men are more productive in their professional accomplishments. For many years, for example, more men than women have been recipients of grants from the National Endowment Fellowships in Literature.

Recently, a few researchers including Jane Piirto and Sally Reis have questioned why so few eminent women creators exist. Little research has been completed and little is known about creative women, their creative processes, and the decisions they face about their own creative productivity, and therefore how creativity can be developed and promoted in diverse girls and women. The social and political movement focusing on women during the past five decades has provided some understanding of women's creative processes as well as the creative roles that women have played in our society and the forces that shape those roles. When one reflects on what has been learned about creativity during the last 50 years, one is forced to acknowledge that a gap exists in one major area. Little research has been completed and little is known about diverse, creative women, the choices they make, and the decisions they face about creative productivity in their lives.

Despite limited research on highly creative women, some explanations have been offered for the small number of women recognized as highly creative in certain domains. Piirto suggests that one reason for the absence of many famous women artists is how intensely they pursue their passions for art. But how intensely do creative women pursue other fields? Isaac Asimov's *Biographical Encyclopedia of Science and Technology* is subtitled "The Lives and Achievements of 1510 Great Scientists From Ancient Times to the Present, Chronologically Arranged." Of the 1510 scientists included in the book, only 14 are women. When Barbara McClintock won the Nobel Prize in Physiology and Medicine in 1983, she was only the fifth woman to receive this award in the eight decades since it was established. Research by Reis on the creative processes and personalities of creative girls and women has demonstrated that gender stereotyping throughout their lifetimes, as well as both internal and external barriers in their education, marriage, and family lives, affect their creative productivity. The choices that some highly creative women make willingly, or are forced to make, profoundly affect both the quantity and direction of their creative output. These choices affect the focus of their creativity, either as applied to work or to other essential components of their lives, including family, relationships, personal interests, and work related to family and home.

The social and political movement focusing on women during the past five decades has provided some understanding of women's creative processes as well as the creative roles that women have played in society and the forces that shaped those roles. Research focusing on the development of women's creativity can be classified into three major themes, which are presented in the remainder of this entry.

Theme One: Personality Characteristics of Creative Women and Their Barriers to, and Supports for, Creative Work

The first theme relates to the personality characteristics of highly creative women, the internal blocks that may prevent them from creating, and the study of these characteristics as a means of helping other women with creative potential to develop their creativity. Research in this area generally falls under the umbrella of either historical views or more modern explanations. To explore historical issues, researchers use retrospective analyses to investigate how creativity evolved in eminent women. Studies have been conducted, for example, on famous writers, scientists, and artists to attempt to identify factors characterizing the lives of talented, creative women of the time. These have generally included the following: the ability to overcome challenges or problems, the need for or absence of support, the opportunity to learn independently in the absence of formal education, and the willingness to live a different life from their peers or counterparts.

Rena Subotnik and Karen Arnold investigated women in science, generally finding what has been noted in previous research, that creative women scientists appear to be motivated largely by deep intellectual engagement and the recognition associated with influential discoveries. The degree to which women scientists resemble or differ from this largely male-derived profile has not been extensively researched. Subotnik and Arnold found, however, that a potential mismatch existed between the single-minded devotion to science, characteristic of eminent researchers, and the desire to balance family and career that appears so prevalently in reports of professional women. Ravenna Helson compared a sample of highly creative women mathematicians with a sample of other women mathematicians. The two groups differed only slightly on measures of intelligence, cognition, and masculine traits, but the creative mathematicians had more research activity, were highly flexible, original, and rejected outside influence. Half of the creative women were foreign born, and most had professional men as fathers. Compared with creative men mathematicians, the creative women had less assurance, published less, and occupied less prestigious positions. Helson also found differences between creative and comparison subjects in background and personality, perhaps indicating that their personality characteristics were powerful determinants of creativity of women mathematicians. The traits most characteristic of these creative women were (a) rebellious independence, introversion, and a rejection of outside influences; (b) strong symbolic interests and a marked ability to find self-expression and self-gratification in directed research activity; and (c) flexibility, or lack of constriction, both in general attitudes and in mathematical work. Helson attributed differences in creative productivity between men and women after graduate school to social roles and institutional arrangements.

Research with creative women has demonstrated that internal personal barriers often exist in the process of completing creative work. The way women have been raised and the cultural messages they encounter seem to result in these internal barriers and failure to develop the belief in self that is necessary for a commitment to highly creative work. Instead, Reis has found that some creative women remain in the background, in a less "center stage" position, as implementers of the ideas of others. Creative potential in some women may be directed to lower-profile work. Although their male counterparts produce plays, write articles or books, undertake large deals, and are viewed as creative high achievers, many highly creative women make conscious or unconscious decisions to work in a more facilitating role, often implementing the creative ideas of others.

Many women do not perceive themselves as creators, follow their interests into career preparation, or place importance on the works they produce. For example, one study of men and women at the School of the Art Institute of Chicago, one of the premier schools of art, found that men more often referred to themselves as "artists" and women referred to themselves as "students," indicating differences in identity development. The problem may be further exacerbated when women do produce original, creative works, as some researchers have found that women are more conscious of criticism than men and find it more difficult to deal with negative perceptions of their work.

Highly creative women who are able to capitalize on their creative potential often display single-minded purpose, make difficult choices about personal lives, and have support systems to enable their creativity to emerge. These support systems include supportive spouses, or choices made about personal life that have been considered nontraditional in the past, such as remaining unmarried, choosing not to have children, living alone or with a partner, or any combination of these. A recent National Science Foundation Study found that neither talent nor achievements but, rather, the nature, size, and timing of marriage and childbirth distinguished between women who achieved tenure, promotion, and highest ranks. Highly creative women make decisions that support the adaptation of a life style conducive to the production of highly creative work.

Theme Two: Societal Factors That Facilitate or Impede the Development of Women's Creativity

A second theme in research relates to the societal factors that facilitated or became an impediment to the development of women's creativity. Research in this area is generally divided into either historical or more modern explanations, focusing on why there were so few eminent women creators (scientists, composers, and artists). Researchers who study the history of women's achievement have shown that creative works produced by women are often underrated or ignored in history. Historical research indicates that although intellectual stimulation in the home seems to play a major role in the development of creative ability, many girls were typically not encouraged or even allowed to engage in intellectual pursuits by their families or peers. They traditionally received less education than did boys, and society often denied women access to certain cultural materials and teachers. In the past, women, and especially culturally diverse women, undoubtedly received little encouragement, stimulation, and access to tools necessary for building intellectual skills and developing the ability to create something of cultural value. Moreover, women were regarded as less able than were men to use their intellectual skills creatively. Women who have the need to create may also experience constraints on their personal lives.

Other explanations of why there are so few eminent women creators have to do with time commitments. Researchers who have offered "historical" explanations about the limited number of women creators argue that women were burdened with family responsibilities, child bearing, and limited educational opportunities. Contemporary researchers argue that creative women may have too many demands on their time, feel guilty if they attempt to do creative work in time that should be spent with their family, or in some cases, dislike working alone for the periods necessary for creative accomplishment. Some researchers have noted that the same years in which Harvey Lehman found the height of men's creative productivity to coincide with the peak period of women's responsibilities to children. Some contemporary researchers have noted that in our society, exceptionally able women experience considerable stress related to role conflict and overload, which may reduce creative urges.

Theme Three: Gender and Cultural Differences in the Creative Process and Product

A third theme relates to the notion that gender differences exist in creativity and the creative process. A growing number of researchers have called for changes in the paradigm of how women and creativity are viewed, and the need for changes in society that could facilitate the development of creativity in women. Women have made, and continue to make, many creative contributions that are different from the creative accomplishments made by men, yet men's creative accomplishments seem to be valued more by society. The creative accomplishments of women are regarded as more modest and do not reflect the types of creative productivity that result in awards, prizes, books, articles, art, patents, professional stature, and financial gain. Rather, as Reis pointed out, their creative efforts were diversified over several initiatives, and their creative products were different than those listed.

Several researchers have argued that gender differences exist in creativity among men and women. Some researchers perceive that at least some women perceive creative phenomena differently from men. Women's experiences and situations in society have been vastly different from men's, so one would expect differences in perception to emerge, for perception cannot be separated from learning and experience. Perhaps the most controversial issue related to women and the creative process is the claim that there may be a potential mismatch between the single-minded devotion necessary for creative accomplishment and the desire to balance family and career that appears so frequently in research about creative women. Actually, many women do have the potential to display single-minded devotion to their work, but they also choose to diversify their creative efforts.

The creative process in women may emerge differently than in men, and in some people, it may not exist. Women's perceptions of the creative process in art as well as other areas have been filtered through male perspectives and the cultural roles developed for women but not by women. Therefore, women writers, artists, scientists, and creators in all domains deal with men's conceptions of creativity and a creative process that has been accepted as the standard within that domain, but may only be standard for men creators. Again, more research is needed in this area.

Sally M. Reis

See also Creative Productivity; Eminence; Girls, Gifted; Talent Development

Further Readings

Helson, R. (1996). In search of the creative personality. *Creativity Research Journal, 9*(4), 295–306.

Kerr, B. A., & Larson, A. (2008). How smart girls become talented women. In S. Lopez (Ed.), *Positive psychology: Exploring the best in people* (pp. 131–167). Westport, CT: Praeger.

Ochse, R. (1991). Why there were relatively few eminent women creators. *Journal of Creative Behavior, 25*(4), 334–343.

Piirto, J. (1991). Why are there so few? (Creative women: Visual artists, mathematicians, musicians). *Roeper Review, 13*(3), 142–147.

Reis, S. M. (1998). *Work left undone.* Mansfield Center, CT: Creative Learning Press.

Reis, S. M. (2002). Toward a theory of creativity in diverse creative women. *Creativity Research Journal, 14*(3 & 4), 305–316.

Subotnik, R. F., & Arnold, K. D. (1995). Passing through the gates: Career establishment of talented women scientists. *Roeper Review, 18*(1), 55–61.

Sex Differences in Mathematical and Spatial Ability

In the United States, there is a dearth of women at the top of mathematically intensive fields. Is this an indicator of a lack of aptitude, perhaps because of biological causes? Or are there fewer women because of sociocultural or historical reasons? This entry describes cognitive sex differences among the highest performers and explores biological and sociocultural explanations. Evolutionary, brain-based, and hormone-based accounts of sex differences in mathematics are inconclusive. Differences in interests clearly exist, but their etiology is unclear. The current sex difference in representation at the top of math-based fields in the United States may not reflect the difference in the number of men and women who are innately gifted in math. It may, instead, largely reflect a combination of a pipeline effect and differences in interests (whether driven by genetic or sociocultural factors).

Background

Camilla Benbow and Julian Stanley in 1983 created a controversy when they published their findings concerning the top-scoring students in their mathematics talent search, who were disproportionately men. Benbow and Stanley suggested men's superiority in mathematical reasoning as one hypothesis to explain their findings. Indeed, at the top 50 universities, the proportion of full professorships held by women in math-intensive fields (engineering, mathematics, physics, computer sciences, chemistry) ranges between 3 percent and 15 percent. Does this underrepresentation reflect innate differences in some kinds of ability, or are nonability accounts such as culture, differential interests, or discrimination to blame? This entry, based on the past few decades of analyses of sex differences research, explores the issues pertinent to answering these questions.

In 1995, Larry Hedges and Amy Nowell examined six studies, each based on a national probability sample of adolescents and young adults. They found that the cognitive ability distributions for men and women differed substantially among the top and bottom 1, 5, and 10 percent: Men excelled over women in science, math, spatial reasoning, and social studies as well as in various mechanical skills. Women excelled over men in verbal abilities, associative memory performance, and perceptual speed. The means for men and women were usually similar, but men's scores had greater variability, which led to large asymmetries at the highest and lowest tails of the distribution. As one of Hedges and Nowell's more dramatic findings, despite only small differences at the midpoint of the distribution, men outnumbered women in the top 1 percent of mathematics and spatial reasoning by a ratio of seven to one.

These findings were consistent with those of many other studies. For example, Benbow and Stanley had reported men–women ratios among the top 0.1 percent of adolescents (i.e., one in a thousand) on the SAT–Mathematics of approximately 10-to-1 and in Stanley's seminal work with 12- to 14-years-olds who were recommended for a gifted program at Johns Hopkins University (the Study of Mathematically Precocious Youth, or SMPY), the highest-scoring girl's score was surpassed by 43 boys.

Biological Explanations

There are some grounds for positing a biologically based account for this apparent sex difference in mathematical giftedness, whether caused by innate differences in ability or other factors such as interests.

Evolved Ability

David Geary suggested that evolutionarily important behaviors such as male–male competition involve greater reliance on the ability to represent three-dimensional space geometrically; thus, 3-D spatial ability may underlie advanced mathematics.

Brain Structure and Functioning

Many studies by neuroscientists demonstrate sex differences in brain structure and functioning. Ruben Gur and Raquel Gur argued that men's brains are optimized for enhanced connectivity *within* hemispheres, whereas women's brains are optimized for communication *between* the hemispheres, especially in language processing and posterior brain regions, as indicated by the larger callosal splenia. Relatedly, Karin Kucian and colleagues found that, for spatial tasks, better performance of men when solving the harder problems was associated with more focal activation of right visual association areas of the brain whereas women recruited additional regions bilaterally for these tasks. Also, Richard Haier and his colleagues used magnetic resonance imaging to investigate whether brain structure, especially the amount of gray and white matter in different brain areas, was related to general intelligence, as determined by standard IQ tests. Apparently, it is. There are structures distributed throughout the brain where the amount of gray matter or white matter predicts IQ scores. Specific areas associated with language in the frontal and parietal lobes seem especially important. Other researchers have shown that the volume of these same brain areas appears to be under genetic control. The amount of gray and white matter in the frontal areas seems more important in women, and the gray matter in the parietal areas seems more important in men, suggesting that men and women achieve the same cognitive capability using different brain architectures.

Hormones

Prenatal and postnatal hormones may play a role, particularly in spatial cognition: numerous studies show that male hormones—up to a certain level—benefit spatial reasoning. Doreen Kimura reviewed this evidence and suggested that prenatal androgen levels are a major factor in the level of adult spatial ability, and even in adulthood variations (across the menstrual cycle in women and across seasons and time of day in men) are associated with variations in cognitive abilities. She further noted that such sex differences are seen early in life, before the environments of boys and girls diverge. In addition, she noted that sex differences in humans parallel differences found in nonhumans, where social influences are minimal (e.g., male rats are superior to female rats in learning spatial mazes, and these sex differences can be reversed by hormonal manipulation or castration of male rats).

Interests

Simon Baron-Cohen argued that girls come into the world with an orientation toward people whereas boys come with an orientation toward objects, which leads them down differing paths of interests. As adults, men and women tend to prefer different careers and lifestyles that are said to be based on these early tendencies. Sex differences exist in occupational preferences occuring along a "people-to-object" dimension: Women are more likely to pursue people-oriented or organic fields, whereas men with similar mathematics and science abilities tend to pursue object-oriented fields. Sex differences on the people-to-object dimension are quite large, and they are longitudinally stable, according to Richard Lippa. Sex differences in occupational preference are more predictive of later careers than is the SAT-M or GRE-Q: in their tracking study of 1,100 high-mathematics aptitude students who expressed a goal of majoring in mathematics and science in college, many students later switched to nonmathematics majors, and they were more likely to be women. Although all of these 1,100 students came from the top 1 percent in mathematics aptitude, they manifested both ability and interest differences that were evident long before they began taking different courses that led to different college majors. One determinant of who switched out of math and science was the asymmetry between their verbal and mathematics abilities. Women's verbal abilities were nearly as strong as their mathematics abilities (only 61 points difference between their SAT-V and SAT-M), leading them to enter professions that prized verbal reasoning (e.g., law), whereas men's verbal abilities were 115 points lower than their mathematics ability, possibly leading them to view mathematics as their only strength. Numerous surveys show that women, regardless of their mathematical aptitude, prefer careers that emphasize living things (e.g., medicine, biology, veterinary medicine, law) over mechanical phenomena (computer science, engineering, chemistry, physics).

Environmental Explanations

There are also persuasive grounds for explaining the math sex differences by nonbiological causes. This research takes issue with claims of biological causation, and points to environmental bases of sex differences.

Evolved Ability

Nora Newcombe criticized evolutionary accounts of sex differences in 3-D reasoning on numerous grounds, and Diane Halpern and colleagues pointed out that the available evidence is insufficient to determine the impact that evolutionary pressures have had on sex differences in cognitive ability, although they present intriguing suggestions. Such explanations are further challenged by Jacqueline Eccles's model of early socialization differences that lead to adult differences, and by findings by Janet Hyde and others showing that sex differences can be sensitive to context, and that women from some nations outperform U.S. and Canadian men on mathematical aptitude tests, often by greater margins than U.S. men outperform U.S. women. If ability differences are the result of evolution, they should not be affected by culture. On the other hand, if cultural beliefs about men's superiority are a major cause of women's underperformance, then men's overrepresentation in mathematics and science should be greater in countries low on egalitarian gender beliefs, such as Turkey and Korea, than in the United States and United Kingdom, and this is indeed generally the case. Consistent with this, the math gender gap disappears among 15-year-olds in countries viewed as highest on gender equality: for example, answering negatively questions such as "When jobs are scarce, should men have more right to a job than women?" Countries high in equality such as Iceland, Sweden, and Norway have virtually no math gap, even among those scoring above the 99th percentile—whereas countries such as Turkey, that rank low on gender equality, have math gaps in favor of men. In addition, the ratio of men-to-women in the gifted mathematics range has changed dramatically over time, from 10 to 1 in the early 1980s to less than 3 to 1 in 2008, illustrating malleability, and thus arguing against genetic causation. Further, the meaningfulness of test scores as an accurate indicator of ability has been challenged by stereotype threat research that suggests that it can undermine test performance for some women, perhaps especially those who are mathematically talented. Paul Davies and Steve Spencer found that women who marked the box corresponding to their gender *after* completing the SAT Advanced Calculus test scored significantly higher than did their women peers who checked their gender *before* starting it, presumably because directing attention to women's gender at the start of the exam causes anxiety that impedes performance, a phenomenon known as stereotype threat. Identifying their gender *after* the AP Advanced Calculus exam would add nearly 3,000 women eligible to begin college with advanced credit for calculus.

Brain Structure and Functioning

Brain differences may indeed exist, but some brain differences may be experience-based rather biologically based. For example, juggling practice can increase gray-matter density in the temporal cortex. Similarly, taxi driving experience has been found to correlate with hippocampal volume.

Hormones

Interpretation of the extensive and complex literature on the effects of sex hormones on spatial abilities is not straightforward. Positive findings are often offset by studies representing challenges or problems. Animal studies show the most pronounced hormone effects, but they are less applicable to humans. Lacking are large-scale, representative human studies of individuals at the right tail of the ability distribution that unequivocally demonstrate the predicted pattern. Clinical studies of individuals of unknown representativeness are fascinating bases for generating hypotheses, but must await randomized experiments and large-scale population studies that report data for right-tail groups. Also, inconsistencies need to be reconciled.

Interests

Elizabeth Spelke refuted the claim that there exist sex differences in infants' people-versus-object orientation, based on a review of extensive evidence. Therefore, she suggests, the observed post-infancy sex differences in interests are more likely to be caused by sociocultural forces and, hence, malleable.

Others have addressed the issue of sex differences in math ability by observing that there may not be as much to explain as some suggest. First, the number of women at the top now may be an outdated indicator, given historical changes and the pipeline effect. When individuals now at the peak of their careers were growing up, there were fewer high-math-scoring women, presumably because of sociocultural factors. The proportion of women earning bachelors degrees in scientific and engineering fields has increased without interruption every year since 1966. Women are also attaining doctoral degrees in scientific and engineering fields in growing numbers: By 2001, women earned 37 percent of Ph.D.s in scientific and engineering fields, up from just 8 percent in 1966. Second, given the data showing a dearth of women scoring in the top 1 percent on mathematics tests even today, one might imagine that few women would succeed in mathematically intensive baccalaureate and graduate programs, but this is not the case. By 2001, the number of women earning degrees in the United States actually exceeded the number of men earning degrees in some science, technology, engineering, and medical fields. There are no longer gender differences in the number of demanding mathematics courses taken in U.S. high schools, and girls do better than boys in these courses. Men and women get equal grades in U.S. college math classes that are of comparable difficulty, and women now earn 48 percent of bachelor's degrees in mathematics. If the ability to master new, challenging mathematical material over extended periods is the criterion for ability, then U.S. college men and women show equal aptitude for mathematics. Further, in transnational comparisons, sex differences in mathematics and science performance are sometimes nonexistent or even favor women. Men's superiority is not ubiquitous.

Research Results

Evolutionary, brain-based, and hormone-based accounts of sex differences in mathematics are inconclusive. Differences in interests clearly exist, but their etiology is unclear. The current sex difference in representation at the top of math-based fields in the United States may not reflect the difference in the number of men and women who are innately gifted in math. It may, instead, largely reflect a combination of a historical factors and differences in interests (whether driven by genetic or sociocultural factors). Other noncognitive factors common to all fields, such as time spent raising families, likely also play a role.

Stephen J. Ceci, Wendy M. Williams, and Susan M. Barnett

See also Boys, Gifted; Girls, Gifted; Mathematical Talent; Men, Gifted; Sex Differences in Creativity; Women, Gifted

Further Readings

Achter, J. A., Lubinski, D., Benbow, C. P., & Eftekhari-Sanjani, H. (1999). Assessing vocational preferences among gifted adolescents adds incremental validity to abilities. *Journal of Educational Psychology, 91,* 777–786.

Baron-Cohen, S. (2007). Sex differences in mind: Keeping science distinct from social policy. In S. J. Ceci & W. M. Williams (Eds.), *Why aren't more women in science? Top researchers debate the evidence* (pp. 159–172). Washington, DC: American Psychological Association.

Benbow, C., & Stanley, J. (1983). Sex differences in mathematical reasoning ability: More facts. *Science, 222*(4627), 1029–1031.

Ceci, S. J., Williams, W. M., & Barnett, S. M. (2009). The underrepresentation of women in science: Sociocultural and biological considerations. *Psychological Bulletin.*

Geary, D. C. (1998). *Male, female: The evolution of human sex differences.* Washington, DC: American Psychological Association.

Guiso, L., Monte, F., Sapienza, P., & Zingales, L. (2008). Gender, culture, and math. *Science, 320,* 1164–1165.

Halpern, D. F., Benbow, C. P., Geary, D., Gur, R., Hyde, J. S., & Gernsbacher, M. A. (2007). The science of sex differences in science and mathematics. *Psychological Science in the Public Interest, 8,* 1–51.

Hedges, L. V., & Nowell, A. (1995). Sex differences in mental test scores, variability, and numbers of high-scoring individuals. *Science, 269,* 41–45.

Hyde, J. S. (2005). The gender similarity hypothesis. *American Psychologist, 60,* 581–592.

Lubinski, D. S., & Benbow, C. (2007). Sex differences in personal attributes for the development of scientific expertise. In S. J. Ceci & W. M. Williams (Eds.), *Why aren't more women in science? Top researchers debate the evidence* (pp. 79–100). Washington, DC: American Psychological Association.

Spelke, E. S. (2005). Sex differences in intrinsic aptitude for mathematics and science: A critical review. *American Psychologist, 60,* 950–958.

Sibling Relationships

In an effort to help parents encourage the development of their gifted child, research and literature has been aimed at the parental relationship of a gifted child, giving advice and support and showing the link between the parents' actions and the child's ability to capitalize on his or her gifts. But little attention has been paid to the role of the sibling relationship on a gifted child's development. More recent research on sibling dynamics has highlighted the importance of the sibling relationship throughout the life span.

Siblings are our closest genetic matches; they are with us from either birth or very young and will likely remain in our lives longer than any other family relationship, including our spouse. In childhood, siblings spend more time with one another than with either peers or parents. It is no surprise that they have an influence on our lives. The nature of the influence is still being examined. Specifically the nature of sibling influence on gifted children has been under-examined. This entry describes sibling relationship as they relate to the gifted.

Gifted Family Description

Although giftedness is an individual label, researchers have sought to understand the family background of precocious children. Studies have shown that giftedness runs in families. Often when a gifted child is labeled, parents realize their own giftedness that may not have been identified when they were children. Therefore, a child is more likely to be surrounded with gifted siblings and parents than to be the sole gifted person in the family.

Gifted Sibling Relationships

Labeling a child gifted can have some implication for the adjustment of siblings that may later affect the sibling relationships within the household. There are incidents of individual children being labeled gifted but another is not, and many studies focus on the relationship consequences of this disparity. The problems that manifest when one child is labeled gifted and another is not likely stem more from the parents' reactions to this. If parents pour attention and energy into the labeled child at the expense of other children, sibling rivalry and resentment will more likely occur. Other research indicates that relationships among gifted siblings are more adjusted than are their counterparts across the general populations. Nicholas Colangelo and his colleagues discovered that although there is an initial, slightly negative reaction of siblings to one of them being labeled gifted, this effect diminishes with time, with attitudes becoming positive or neutral.

Current Research of Personality and Interests of Siblings

Although birth order is an often-researched area when looking at individual differences in personality and interests, results have been inconclusive and inconsistent. Variables such as age spacing between siblings and intermarriage of families confound the generalizability of any birth-order relationship with personality that has been garnered.

Several theories of learning and development may inform subsequent research; two of these are *social learning theory* proposed by Albert Bandura and *sibling de-identification,* attributed to several different theorists including Alfred Adler.

Social Learning Theory

Social learning theory is often used to describe similarities in attitude, personality, and interests, and most especially behavior within families. Bandura explains that children will model behavior when they have the following assumptions about the person and activity they are modeling: The modeled behavior will result in outcomes that the child values, and the child must identify the person they model as similar to themselves and as having valued status. It would make sense, then, that an older sibling would commonly be an identified model for a younger child. This would be especially true when the older sibling is exhibiting socially valued behaviors, and not true when the older sibling is exhibiting antisocial behaviors.

Sibling De-Identification

Sibling de-identification theory is another developmental theory that attempts to explain differences in personality and interests among siblings. This theory states that siblings compete to gain parental love and attention. In an effort to minimize sibling conflict and competition and to gain independence and parental favor, each child endeavors to establish his or her own valued niche within the family. Specifically, the theory states that the differentiating process appears to be strongest when siblings are more similar in qualities such as sex, age, and appearance.

Sibling Influence on Creativity

In an effort to address the question of sibling influence on creativity, Mary Givens conducted a preliminary investigation into the subjective experience of sibling influence on creative adolescents. Eighty-six participants in a career development workshop for creative adolescents were surveyed about the influence of a sibling on their interests, personality, and creativity. Responses to the survey questions were analyzed using grounded theory.

Themes that emerged for older siblings indicated they were experiencing no influence by younger siblings on their interests and being a leader or role model. Themes for younger siblings included the following: introduction by an older sibling to an activity or interest, learning social skills from an older sibling, and encouragement and support of creative gifts from an older sibling.

A second analysis was conducted to determine if social learning theory or sibling de-identification theory better described the phenomenon of creative sibling influence. Social learning theory emerged as the single predominant theory for this sample.

Implications

The contradictory findings of studies on sibling influence and birth-order comparison indicate that sibling relationships are complex and cannot be summed up easily, nor have they been fully researched. Much of the research has focused on the gifted family as a whole or on interfamilial conflict surrounding the labeling of giftedness. A review of the research literature written during the last 20 years indicates that researchers continue to focus on negative aspects of sibling relationships, such as sibling rivalry. Few researchers focus on the influential relationship siblings can have on the development of creative lives. There is much yet to be discovered about the intricacies of a relationship that will span the lives of many of our creative students. The hope is that the information garnered about these relationships that shape the lives of creatively gifted children can be used to create more effective interventions and dialogue with these students.

Mary Givens

See also Family Creativity; Mentoring Gifted and Talented Individuals; Personality and Intelligence

Further Readings

Chamrad, D. L., Robinson, N. M., Janos, P. M. (1995). Consequences of having a gifted sibling: Myths and realities. *Gifted Child Quarterly, 39*(3), 135.

Cicirelli, V. G. (1967). Sibling constellation, creativity, IQ, and academic achievement. *Child Development, 38*(2), 481–490.

Colangelo, N., & Brower, P. (1987). Labeling gifted youngsters: Long-term effects on family. *Gifted Child Quarterly, 31*(2), 75–78.

Givens, M. (2008, August). *Siblings of creatively gifted.* Paper presented at American Psychological Association, Boston.

Yewchuk, C. R., & Schlosser, G. A. (1996). Childhood sibling relationships of eminent Canadian women. *Roeper Review, 18*(4), 287–292.

Single-Sex Schooling

Single-sex schooling refers to the provision of education to children in an environment consisting solely of members of the same gender, that is, all-boy or all-girl classes or schools. Renewed interest in single-sex schooling revisits questions of appropriate curriculum for students according to their performance, abilities, and talents as well as their gender. Since 2002 and the implementation of the No Child Left Behind Act, single-sex schooling has emerged as a potential means of enhancing student performance. Understanding the potential implications of single-sex schooling for gifted students requires a grasp of the historical background of the reform, as well as an awareness of research that has explored the effectiveness and the perceived benefits of creating single-sex classes and schools, as described in this entry.

Historical Background

Coeducational classes are a relatively new development in U.S. education and education in general. Throughout the early days of U.S. education, single-sex schools were the norm in secondary schools. At that time, however, only students of above-average ability and above-average income attended secondary schools, that is, primarily upper-class White boys. During the 1920s, Progressive policymakers created comprehensive coeducational high schools to offer a wide range of courses and theoretically to provide access to the entire curriculum to all students, particularly girls, who had previously been afforded limited opportunities, particularly in math and science. Then, in 1975, Title IX legislation specifically forbade single-sex physical education classes because of inequitable resources and facilities for women athletes. Title IX did not include academic classes, but, confused over both the spirit and the letter of the law, schools then steered clear of single-sex classes in all subjects until Title IX was essentially changed by the implementation of the No Child Left Behind Act.

Rhetoric about the effectiveness of single-sex classes dominated the early years of the 21st century, with conflicting opinions about whether boys or girls benefited, if at all, by the arrangement. In 2002, an amendment to No Child Left Behind legislation opened the door for schools to experiment with single-sex classes as a means of improving educational outcomes for all students, with no special emphasis on those who readily achieved or exceeded mastery. Education policymakers looked to single-sex classes as a solution for declining achievement in specific content areas, such as mathematics and science for girls and language arts and reading for boys. Schools that attempted to implement single-sex classes frequently experienced conflicts between policymakers and educators over ideology and resources, as well as concerns about equity and stereotypical attitudes

In 2006, the U.S. Department of Education confirmed the legality of single-sex arrangements. This decision emerged in the midst of the proliferation of such classes in school districts that had already begun experimenting with the model. Since 2006, the number of single-sex classes and schools has increased exponentially. Many of these arrangements have been ideologically driven without the benefit of research-based foundations. Limited attention has been paid to the efficacy of single-sex schooling for gifted students, although the particular learning needs of gifted girls have merited scrutiny.

Effectiveness

In the United States, the debate about gender differences continues to fuel interest in single-sex classes and schools. In the 1990s, research focused on inherent inequities for girls in mixed classrooms and that girls often choose, with permission and even encouragement from school authorities, to take less demanding courses. The American Association of University Women originally endorsed single-sex classes, but ultimately reversed its stance because of the slippery slope that might result in inequitable curriculum offerings for girls, reversing the gains of the past 50 years. At the beginning of the 21st century, attention turned to underachievement among boys across all ethnicities. Some proponents of brain-based differences argue that the specific needs of boys and girls are best addressed only in single-sex classes and schools. More temperate brain-based theorists strongly suggest that the professional development of teachers must focus on specific strategies for teaching each gender, regardless of whether they are segregated from each other.

Assessing the effectiveness of single-sex classes is problematic. In the United States, single-sex arrangements are often part of multifaceted educational reform, including changes in curriculum delivery. Therefore, it is difficult to attribute student success to any one variable. Educators in the international arena have also weighed in on the effectiveness of the single-sex classes, but their findings have been largely inconclusive. As single-sex schools and classes have increased in number, so have the efforts of researchers to examine the phenomenon. A large meta-analysis of studies on single-sex education was commissioned in 2005 by the U.S. Department of Education. After excluding the many studies that lacked appropriate research design and controls, researchers found moderately positive or neutral impact of single-sex schools on student achievement in concurrent programs and neutral effects on social and emotional development.

Perceived Benefits

The benefits of single-sex schooling for gifted students remain open to discussion. For example, no conclusive evidence exists that single-sex classes increase girls' participation in Advanced Placement calculus classes, but some evidence indicates that girls' academic engagement does increase in single-sex classes. Sex differences in mathematics and science among the gifted and talented continues to dominate discourse about appropriate curriculum for gifted students. Most importantly, differences have surfaced in teacher and student interactions in single-sex and mixed classes, specifically in student competition for both boys and girls in single-sex classes, with different manifestations for boys versus girls. Some studies have shown that women who have attended single-sex schools have had more opportunity for leadership and more mentoring than have women in coeducational programs.

The question remains whether single-sex classes should be offered as a viable choice for gifted students and their parents. Some teachers strongly favor single-sex schooling and want to teach in all-girl or all-boy classes. Given adequate professional development of such teachers, both in appropriate strategies for boys and girls, as well as in differentiated instruction for the gifted students, single-sex classes can potentially provide one way of addressing the cognitive and social development of students who choose them.

Frances R. Spielhagen

See also Boys, Gifted; Classroom Practices; Girls, Gifted; Parental Attitudes; Sex Differences in Creativity; Sex Differences in Mathematical and Spatial Ability

Further Readings

Datnow, A., Hubbard, L., & Conchas, G. (2001). How context mediates policy: The implementation of single-sex public schooling in California. *Teachers College Record, 103*(2), 184–206.

Gurian, M. (2002). *Boys and girls learn differently! A guide for teachers and parents.* San Francisco: Jossey-Bass.

Reis, S. M., Callahan, C. M., & Goldsmith, D. (1996). Attitudes of adolescent girls and boys toward education, achievement, and the future. In K. Arnold, K. D. Noble, & R. F. Subotnik (Eds.), *Remarkable women* (pp. 209–224). Cresskill, NJ: Hampton Press.

Salomone, R. (2003). *Same, different, equal: Rethinking single sex schooling.* New Haven, CT: Yale University Press.

Siegle, D., & Reis, S. M. (1998). Gender differences in teacher and student perceptions of student ability and effort. *Gifted Child Quarterly, 42,* 39–47.

Spielhagen, F. (Ed.). (2007). *Debating single-sex education: Separate and equal.* Baltimore: Rowman & Littlefield Education.

U.S. Department of Education. (2005). *Single sex versus coeducational schooling: A systematic review.* Washington, DC: Author.

Social Development

As one examines the social development of a gifted child, it is important to remember that each child is unique, respect the basic nature of the child, and remember that cognitive abilities are just one part of the child's identity influencing social development. Erik Erikson's theory of psychosocial development suggests that all individuals, including those with exceptional abilities, must move through eight developmental stages, five of which occur before adulthood:

1. Infancy: trust versus mistrust
2. Toddler: autonomy versus shame and doubt
3. Preschooler: initiative versus guilt
4. Elementary school age: industry versus inferiority
5. Adolescence: identity versus identity confusion

Within each of these stages, the child will face a crisis that must be resolved. If the child is successful in meeting these challenges, then basic strengths or virtues will emerge. However, if the child is unsuccessful in negotiating the different stages effectively, these issues will be carried forward as the child seeks to establish his or her social identity. How gifted children learn to explore their environments during these formative years will affect how successful they are in moving through these developmental stages, described in this entry. Lack of proper identification may, in turn, impede a gifted child's social development because the child will not be receiving appropriate educational services.

One of the greatest challenges to a gifted child's social development is an ill-fitting environment. Gifted children are often bombarded with mixed messages. This is particularly true when the child reaches school age. Gifted students who were thriving as very young children may suddenly be faced with a host of new contradictory expectations. Parents and teachers may place expectations on the child based on what they perceive the child's strengths to be. However, some gifts take time to develop and may only surface if the child is allowed to experiment and explore different possibilities. Furthermore, each of the adults is observing the child through a distinctive lens. Therefore, the child's perception of himself or herself may be remarkably different from those of the adults.

Other factors in a child's environment may have a profound effect on the child's social development as well. Children from low socioeconomic backgrounds are at the greatest risk for underachievement. Gender may play an important role in social development. Some gifted girls report concern that there will be negative social consequences as a result of their academic successes. In a 1999 study by Sylvia Rimm of 1,000 successful women, many reported paying a further social price for their academic success; many reported feeling isolated from their peers as children. Cultural expectations can also influence a gifted child's social development and peer expectations can have an intense impact as well.

Many gifted children develop asynchronously, so that their cognitive development quickly surpasses their development socially. This unevenness sometimes makes it more challenging for gifted students to find friends who share their interests and perspectives. Hence, some gifted kids feel that they do not quite fit with either their cognitive-related peers or age-related peers.

In *Schooling the Gifted,* Laurence Coleman offers a *stigma of giftedness paradigm,* as follows:

1. Gifted children want to have normal social interactions.
2. They believe that others will treat them differently if they learn of their giftedness.
3. Gifted students learn that they can manage information about themselves in ways that enable them to maintain greater social latitude. (p. 36)

Gifted kids should feel valued and have the opportunity to complete meaningful and challenging work both inside and outside the classroom. Without these opportunities, gifted children may never acquire perseverance, empathy toward peers, or sound learning strategies to cope with life's challenges. Participating in activities such as band, theater, or sports can help foster a gifted child's social development. It is important that the activity is self-selected and the child is doing something where relative success is likely. Such activities, which allow gifted students to follow their passions, can act as stress relievers and provide opportunities for the gifted youth to grow in new ways.

Children learn best from those with whom they have a positive caring relationship; every gifted child needs at least one caring adult to help navigate life's challenges. There are many divergent views concerning how a gifted child should behave. Having someone who will allow gifted children to consider those differing views and express their opinions honestly can be beneficial to the child in their social development. This adult mentor can also help the gifted child build positive relationships with others. Because gifted children tend to see the world from a slightly different perspective, gifted children should be given opportunities to interact with a wide variety of people from diverse backgrounds. This will enable them to learn to understand and appreciate their own gifts and talents, as well as appreciate what can be learned from the diversity of others.

Patricia Gillespie

See also Emotional Intelligence; Social-Emotional Issues; Socioeconomic Status

Further Readings

Coleman, L. J. (1985). *Schooling the gifted.* Menlo Park, CA: Addison Wesley.

Cross, T. L. (2004). *On the social and emotional lives of gifted children* (Academic ed.). New York: Bantam Dell.

Neihart, M., Reis, S. M., Robinson, N. M., & Moon, S. M. (Eds.). (2002). *The social and emotional development of gifted children: What do we know?* Waco, TX: Prufrock Press.

Santrock, J. W. (2004). *Life-span development* (2nd ed.). Boston: McGraw-Hill.

Social-Emotional Issues

Affective qualities play an important role in realizing extraordinary potential. In his groundbreaking study of highly intelligent children and youth, Lewis M. Terman discovered that although intellectual potential was relatively homogeneous among his subjects, life achievements were much more variable among the men in the study. He pinpointed affective qualities that differentiated between (relatively) high- and low-achieving men: "persistence in the accomplishment of ends, integration toward goals, self-confidence, and freedom from inferiority feelings. In the total picture the greatest contrast between the two groups was in all-round emotional and social adjustment, and in drive to achieve" (p. 148). An extensive body of longitudinal or retrospective analyses of factors that distinguish between extraordinarily able individuals who perform highly throughout their lives and others who falter and often fail to actualize their abilities now supports his conclusions. These studies, albeit descriptive, indicate that social-emotional issues must be addressed before individuals with high intellectual ability can navigate the shoals of personal development and successfully sail the seas of high performance.

Three issues complicate professionals' ability to identify social-emotional issues and related affective needs unique to gifted and talented learners: the talent-blindness of current research, measurement concerns, and developmentally insensitive research on high-potential individuals. Specifically, it is generally accepted that a key developmental task for all youngsters is to know, understand, accept, and value oneself, but it is unclear relative to the degree to which high intellectual or creative abilities affect this task. Empirically defining social-emotional issues, manifested in affective needs that accompany high potential has been elusive. Instruments related to affective variables such as self-concept, self-esteem, and motivation are not built on theories that include giftedness, and they are too easily "faked" in that test-wise respondents can create profiles that indicate higher functioning than is actually the case. Last, much of the talent-focused research in the affective domain has been conducted with adults. Their retrospective descriptions are filtered through decades of experience. Developmental theorists agree that the child is not a precise predictor of the adult, yet only a handful of studies are longitudinal.

Despite these limitations, four areas of affect appear important to address with youngsters having high intellectual potential: understanding giftedness (self-concept), disengaging self-worth from achievements (self-esteem), initiating tasks and persevering until the work is completed at an appropriate level of accomplishment (motivation), and functioning in a variety of contexts (using resources effectively). This entry describes these areas, then methods for addressing affective needs.

Self-Concept

Gifted/creative/talented young people need to understand their abilities as a multidimensional phenomenon that changes over time and in different contexts. Thus, youngsters can develop the ability to analyze their profiles of strengths and needs and thereby set goals based on realistic self-assessments. A solid sense of self permits more flexibility and less compulsiveness to achieve at all costs. A differentiated strengths profile is also associated with perceiving oneself as less ipsative. An ipsative view of ability would mean that one's abilities are a fixed sum. To be highly able in one arena would necessarily mean that there is less ability available for other arenas of endeavor. A less ipsative self-concept has profound implications for self-esteem and motivation.

Self-Esteem

When bright, sensitive youngsters learn to separate self-worth from extraordinary achievements valued by others, they permit themselves the opportunity to learn from setbacks as well as successes, a hallmark quality of successful, highly able adults. The core self also maintains its mental health through the uncontrollable ups and downs of life. A higher self-esteem results in a more internal standard of assessing one's work and less sensitivity to peer pressure in academic as well as social realms.

Motivation

The two aspects of self profoundly affect how individuals explain success and failure and their willingness to attempt tasks that carry some risk of failure and to persevere through a learning period. When gifted and talented youngsters see themselves as unable to improve through effort, they exhibit less resilience, a greater inclination to underperform, and more self-sabotaging behaviors such as procrastination, cheating, and undershooting goals. Bright youngsters who see themselves as improving their skills and abilities through deliberate practice are more optimistic, more likely to undertake tasks that carry some risk of failure, more able to regroup and persevere after a setback, and more able to work patiently in stages to achieve goals.

Using Resources

Children born in high-risk environments who learn even as infants to elicit caregivers' positive attention demonstrate the ability to use resources effectively. Accessing resources such as helpful adults, and intellectual peers who promote self-valuing and the acceptability of being bright is crucial to the life success of high-potential youngsters. In contrast, children who receive attention and assistance only when they act out or display helplessness are much more likely to underachieve, to engage in risky behavior, and to fail to actualize their potential. The ability to recognize and either select or modify the social context to provide needed resources (identified on the basis of realistic self-knowledge) is demonstrated repeatedly in the lives of successful, high-achieving adults.

Methods for Addressing Affective Needs

Two categories of interventions promote meeting affective needs: methods that address needs directly, and methods embedded in curriculum. Teaching bright students about their abilities, about the effects of self-concept, self-esteem, motivation, and resources on one's ability to "think and act smart"—in short, the qualities that make key differences in the lives of high-potential individuals—can demystify giftedness and promote a more realistic sense of control over important goals. This kind of teaching can take place in special seminars for gifted students, as part of an enriched curriculum, or in out-of-school opportunities as part of gifted education conferences, camps, or summer learning programs.

Narrative approaches are somewhat less direct and could be more engaging for a complex thinker. These methods characteristically draw on social learning principles such as vicarious reinforcement through learning from the lives of symbolic models and are typified in bibliotherapy, cinematherapy, and drama therapy. Contact with exemplary models through interviews, shadowships, or internships also allow the gifted learner to identify with the talented adult in real time as that individual articulates setting goals, tackling difficult tasks, persevering through setbacks, and so on.

Curriculum-based approaches are the most indirect. Project-based learning in which the gifted and talented students learn to think, act, and feel as the adult creative, talented individual producing high-level, unique work provides a real-life context for the youngster to process more abstract constructs such as motivation or self-esteem. Creating open dialogues about the affective foundations of intellectual work is important to fully plumbing the potential of this approach.

Finally, counseling and guidance that is targeted for gifted students is available in a number of university-based settings, such as the counseling program at the University of Iowa's Belin & Blank Center or the Counseling Laboratory for the Exploration of Optimal States at the University of Kansas. In addition, the Social and Emotional Needs of the Gifted (SENG) program maintains a list of counselors, psychologists, and other practitioners with a special interest, specialized knowledge, and a special concern for gifted students.

In considering the qualities identified as critical in the successful development of talented individuals, it is important to consider the social effects of addressing particular social-emotional issues for all youngsters. Perhaps the needs mentioned in this entry are universal, but they are critical to life success and fulfillment for individuals with extraordinary ability.

Reva Friedman-Nimz

See also Emotional Development; Emotional Intelligence; Motivating Gifted Students; Personality and Intelligence; Self-Efficacy/Self-Esteem

Further Readings

Amabile, T. M. (1989). *Growing up creative: Nurturing a lifetime of creativity.* Buffalo, NY: Crown.

Bain, S. K., & McBell, S. M. (2004). Social self-concept, social-attributions, and peer relationships in fourth, fifth, and sixth graders who are gifted compared to high achievers. *Gifted Child Quarterly, 48*(3), 167.

Bandura, A. (1982). Self-efficacy mechanism in human agency. *American Psychologist, 37*(2), 122–147.

Dweck, C. S. (2006). *Mindset: The new psychology of success.* New York: Random House.

Gottfried, A. E., & Gottfried, A. W. (2004). Toward the development of a conceptualization of gifted motivation. *Gifted Child Quarterly, 48*(2), 121–132.

Hoge, R. D., & Renzulli, J. S. (1993). Exploring the link between giftedness and self-concept. *Review of Educational Research, 63*(4), 449–466.

Kerr, B. A. (1991). *A handbook for counseling gifted and talented.* American Association for Counseling and Development. Retrieved from http://www.cleoslab.org

Masten, A. S. (2001). Ordinary magic: Resilience processes in development. *American Psychologist, 56*(3), 227–238.

Neihart, M. (1999). The impact of giftedness on psychological well-being: What does the empirical literature say? *Roeper Review, 22*(1), 10–17.

Sternberg, R. J., & Spear-Swerling, L. (1998). Personal Navigation. In M. D. Ferrari & R. J. Sternberg (Eds.), *Self-awareness: Its nature and development* (pp. 219–245). New York: Guilford Press.

Terman, L. M. (1959). *Genetic studies of genius* (Vol. 5). Stanford, CA: Stanford University Press.

Yong, F. L. (1994). Self-concepts, locus of control, and Machiavellianism of ethnically diverse middle school students who are gifted. *Roeper Review, 16,* 192–194.

Zimmerman, B. J. (2000). Self-efficacy: An essential motive to learn. *Contemporary Educational Psychology, 25,* 82–91.

Social Studies, Curriculum

The primary goal of social studies curriculum is to equip students with the knowledge and skills to become active participants in society. Citizenship education is a common thread transcending different perspectives on social studies curriculum, though there has been long-standing disagreement on the definition of the phrase as it relates to curriculum and instruction. The Goals 2000: Educate America Act passed by Congress in 1992 called for the development of national standards in many areas of education but omitted social studies from its list. The National Council for the Social Studies (NCSS), founded in 1921, and a group of educators responded by advocating for and eventually adding social studies to the agenda for the development of national standards. A task force of social studies curriculum and instruction experts assembled and developed the 1994 publication *Expectations of Excellence: Curriculum Standards for Social Studies.* The 10 main themes that serve as the basis for the national standards outlined in this publication are as follows:

- Culture
- Time, continuity, and change
- People, places, and environment
- Individual development and identity
- Individuals, groups, and institutions
- Power, authority, and governance
- Production, distribution, and consumption
- Science, technology, and society
- Global connections
- Civic ideals and practices

The development of national standards in the educational content areas has been viewed by many as a response to the 1983 publication *A Nation at Risk.* This publication drew attention to the mediocre status of curricula in the United States and indicated that the percentage of students taking general courses instead of college-track courses had increased dramatically from 1964 to 1979. Gifted learners in particular are affected by such nonrigorous curricula and are capable of learning more material, often at accelerated rates than those of their peers. Even with national standards in place, social studies curriculum and instruction must be adapted and modified to meet the needs of these high-end learners.

NCSS defines the academic purview of social studies as "the integrated study of the social sciences and humanities to promote civic competence" (National Council for the Social Studies, 2008, p. 211). This broad context incorporates an array of subjects, stemming from the traditional topics of history, geography, and political systems to less prominent fields such as economics, philosophy, religion, psychology, and anthropology. Armed with such a vast body of material to explore and to process, the social studies curriculum offers the gifted learner a wealth of intellectual stimuli and fertile opportunities for research, evaluation, and application. In addition, the social studies curriculum carries the NCSS mandate to guide the development of young people by fostering their abilities to make informed decisions and to participate actively in culturally diverse societies. With this aim of building informed and proactive global citizens, the gifted learner is challenged by social studies to develop an enlightened mind-set and to attain a collection of strategies and skills to achieve a high level of citizenship and real-life engagement in world affairs. This entry describes textbooks and other curricular resources along with curricular adaptations and modifications for gifted learners.

Textbooks and Other Curricular Resources

Despite the adoption of NCSS standards at the national level, the social studies curriculum of each school district is often primarily influenced by the content of current textbooks, which are not necessarily based on national standards. Analyses of social studies textbooks have demonstrated that each book's content is subject to authors' biases and often reflects the values of consumers rather than providing accurate, multicultural perspectives of events. In addition, the difficulty level of textbooks has steadily declined during the past few decades, a process referred to as "dumbing down" by former Secretary of Education Terrel Bell. Textbooks are designed to give broad content overviews, and some have been criticized for their biased viewpoints of events of historical and cultural significance. To provide in-depth, detailed accounts from multiple perspectives, social studies curriculum experts suggest the inclusion of additional resources and materials.

According to subject experts, a key component of any social studies curriculum is the investigation of primary source material. For the gifted learner, it is essential that ample opportunities be provided to explore, contemplate, interpret, debate, and respond to primary documents and other authentic objects and artifacts. The advanced learner can develop higher-order reasoning, abstract conceptualization, and an awareness of bias and alternate perspectives through the dissection and explanation of primary materials and their themes. Gifted learners, who are often capable of absorbing and processing content at a faster pace and more sophisticated level than are their peers, should be engaged with primary source materials as an effective way of addressing this pedagogical challenge. Working independently under the supervision of the teacher, the gifted learner can establish his or her own plan of research, pursue individual interests, generate written pieces and other forms of assessment, and develop essential social studies skills such as critical thinking, document analysis, and the synthesis of multiple sources and perspectives.

Curricular Adaptations and Modifications for Gifted Learners

Though research on effective implementation of social studies curricula with gifted learners is limited, the theories and recommended practices from gifted and talented educational researchers can often be applied across content areas. The National Association for Gifted Children (NAGC) recognizes the special needs of gifted learners and has developed standards designed to help schools meet the needs of these students. In its standards, the NAGC calls for each content area to have well-defined national standards spanning prekindergarten through Grade 12. This goal is often neglected in social studies as districts sacrifice this subject in the early grades to provide additional time for the more heavily tested areas of mathematics and reading. Early school engagement with a vibrant social studies curriculum can meet the challenges of developing the intellectual curiosities and defining the academic capacities of the gifted learner. The wide variety of subject areas encompassed by the social studies curriculum provides teachers with an assortment of topics for evaluating and developing core skills while generating meaningful discovery activities. The practice of exposing students to multiple subject areas within social studies and basing activities and experiences on their strengths and interests is supported by gifted education theory, including Joseph S. Renzulli's work on the enrichment triad model. The young gifted learner should be offered opportunities for self-directed exploration and the chance to pursue individual fields of interest. From the hands-on research and open-ended speculation offered by the areas of anthropology and archaeology, to the authentic interaction with primary source materials contained in the study of history, geography, politics, and economics, the social studies curriculum can expose the gifted learner to a wealth of intellectual stimulation and valuable skill development. Particularly within the gifted and talented student population, the young learner must be presented with opportunities to explore and to define his or her personal interests and to investigate material in an independent but supported manner. Natural curiosity, especially prominent in the gifted learner, should be fueled by a rigorous and diverse social studies curriculum.

The social studies curriculum provides the gifted learner with multiple opportunities for authentic research. Through engagement in inquiry activities, the gifted learner can pursue investigations into historical topics and contemporary issues on a self-directed and individually paced basis. During inquiry projects, the complexity of content and level of expectations can be monitored and adjusted by the teacher to accommodate different learning styles and abilities, an essential concern of gifted education. Although employing technology to access a variety of primary and secondary source materials, the gifted learner can achieve the key social studies goals, including student investigation of original documents, critical analysis of multiple sources, and consideration of bias, fact versus opinion, and alternate viewpoints. Finally, independent inquiry can enable the gifted learner to engage in higher-order reasoning, to tailor intellectual pursuits to personal interests and proclivities, and to consider historical themes balanced against modern interpretations and culturally diverse perspectives.

In addition to inquiry research, the social studies curriculum provides the gifted learner a variety of ways to explore historical topics and contemporary issues, to demonstrate the accumulation of knowledge and skills, and to explore real-world applications of content. The gifted learner should be given the chance to express knowledge of social studies materials in personalized formats and through cooperative learning experiences. For example, the gifted learner often interprets material in unusual and unpredictable fashion because of his or her advanced intellectual abilities. Suitable outlets for demonstrating knowledge should consider these individual differences. Instead of simply writing a generic letter to a congressperson, a standard approach employed in the average social studies classroom, alternate assessments such as drafting authentic legislation, creating a Web site to promote a social cause, or interviewing local politicians to produce an informational video can be employed. Gifted learners are often isolated because of their advanced abilities in misguided efforts to meet their special needs. This approach can alienate students and stigmatize both a gifted learner and his or her classmates. A stated purpose of social studies education is to build citizenship, so the gifted learner should be given appropriate opportunities to build leadership skills and to work collaboratively with peers. Through presentations, multimedia productions, mock trials, debates, and other classroom activities, the gifted learner can develop strong citizenship and leadership abilities while learning to work effectively with peers.

Product differentiation and inquiry research are typical methods of differentiating social studies curricula for gifted learners, but may not be sufficient for students who have already mastered the content of a particular course or unit. Research on curriculum compacting done by the University of Connecticut's National Research Center on the Gifted and Talented (NRC/GT) found that as much as 50 percent of content can be eliminated for high-ability students in different content areas. The curriculum compacting process consists of identifying the subject area objectives and selecting a pretest that matches the stated objectives. Based on pretest results, the curriculum can be modified and compacted for students who have mastered some or all of the objectives. These students work independently on projects and assignments focused on the nonmastered objectives, and then pursue enrichment or acceleration activities on successful completion of the unit test. Of the five subject areas examined in the research study, social studies was compacted least frequently.

The PreK–12 social studies curriculum for the gifted learner demands challenge, customization, and effective teaching. With appropriate adaptations and modifications, it provides avenues to meet all of these goals. The diversity of content within the social studies orbit provides ample material for authentic research and numerous opportunities for real-world applications. Through inquiry and other social studies approaches, the gifted learner's academic pursuits can be tailored to his or her personal interests, intellectual levels, and particular learning styles. Differentiation strategies from gifted education curricular experts can be used to modify existing social studies curricula to meet the needs of advanced learners.

Shelbi K. Cole and Conan A. Schreyer

See also Curriculum Models; Differentiation; Elementary School, Social Studies Curriculum; Individualized Instruction; Secondary School, Social Studies Curriculum; Service-Learning

Further Readings

Little, C. A., & VanTassel-Baska, J. (1991). *Content-based curriculum for high ability learners.* Waco, TX: Prufrock Press.

National Commission on Excellence in Education. (1983, April). *A nation at risk.* Retrieved June 13, 2008, from http://www.ed.gov/pubs/NatAtRisk/index.html

National Council for the Social Studies. (1994). *Expectations of excellence: Curriculum standards for social studies.* Washington, DC: Author.

National Council for the Social Studies. (2008). Curriculum guidelines for social studies teaching and learning: A position statement of National Council for the Social Studies (NCSS Position Statement). *Social Education, 72*(4), 211–212.

Parker, W. C. (1991). *Renewing the social studies curriculum.* Alexandria, VA: Association for Supervision and Curriculum Development.

Reis, S. M., & Renzulli, J. S. (1992). Using curriculum compacting to challenge the above-average. *Educational Leadership, 50*(2), 51–57.

Ross, E. W. (2006). *The social studies curriculum: Purposes, problems, and possibilities* (3rd ed.). Albany: State University of New York Press.

Thornton, S. J. (2004). *Teaching social studies that matters: Curriculum for active learning.* New York: Teachers College Press.

Troxclair, D. A. (2000). Differentiating instruction for gifted students in regular education social studies classes. *Roeper Review, 22*(3), 195–198.

Socioeconomic Status

The abilities of privileged children can appear magnified beyond actual proportions, whereas the abilities of many economically deprived children can be suppressed or never recognized. The fertile advantages and social networks of privilege account for much undue magnification, and oppressive, socioeconomic barriers to aspiration, talent discovery, and achievement account greatly for suppression and disregard. Most people assume that free-market, democratic societies are meritocracies in which the gifted and talented rise in status, wealth, and achievement according to their individual abilities. This is true to some extent. Nevertheless, "merit" can be misunderstood because face-value merit, reflecting the advantages of birth into privileged socioeconomic status, often is confounded with the broader, truer merit of one's actions in the world. As a result, upper-middle class and elite children tend to enjoy much more undue credit and reward, or undeserved merit, at the outset of life's journey than do children of low socioeconomic status.

There is some disagreement about the extent, and even the existence, of socioeconomic barriers to achievement. For example, sociologists investigate the nature of social, cultural, and economic contexts and the barriers they pose to the poor. In contrast, neoclassical economists and the social scientists they influence tend to ascribe success or failure to individuals themselves because these individuals are assumed to be self-interested actors in a level, free-market playing field. Nevertheless, evidence accumulates on the pernicious effects of impoverishment, although neoclassical economic theory faces stronger challenges for overlooking socioeconomic inequality. This entry describes socioeconomic barriers, international differences, and true merit.

Socioeconomic Barriers

Sociologists and educational researchers have revealed troubling dimensions of the barriers that can suppress ability and crush aspirations. Material deprivation, segregation, and stigmatization in racist and classist societies represent the most serious barriers. Among other sources, deprivation can arise from the following problems: (a) weak educational experiences in underfunded, inner-city and rural, school systems; (b) poor nutrition, (c) inadequate early child care; (d) a U.S. health care system that leaves many children and their families without basic health care; (e) lack of employment opportunity for impoverished parents; and (f) economic globalization's undermining of lower-class wages and employment security, which enables corporations to move capital around the globe for cheap wages and weak employment regulations.

As for segregation, contrary to popular belief, the U.S. Civil Rights Movement did not solve the problem of partitioning populations by race and class. Despite progress made in de-institutionalizing racial segregation, de facto segregation by race, ethnicity, and class persists. Deprived children who are segregated sometimes lack the cultural capital and social networks that are especially needed by the gifted, as they discover high aspirations and develop talents for pursuing lofty dreams. Advantaged children's cultural capital provides them the insider knowledge and dispositions that are associated with the approving linguistic and cultural labels, such as "giftedness." Segregation can also lock children into dangerous, violent, and toxic environments where the gifted and talented, for lack of legitimate opportunities, may turn toward criminal pursuits and gang leadership.

One other barrier posed by segregation is environmental racism, the location of toxic industries in poor neighborhoods that lack the political clout to resist. Bright children growing up in industrial areas may face the burden of environment-borne illnesses, making their aspirations far less attainable than are those of their more fortunate peers.

Stigmatization is an even less-appreciated barrier to the development of high ability. Poor children often face indirect, sometimes even blatant, vilification through media outlets and through everyday social interactions. Psychologists also have revealed detailed accounts of the denigration faced by poor rural populations. Derogatory terms such as *cracker, linthead, ridge runner,* and *white trash* often appear in the popular culture. Compared with a child from a privileged background, a gifted child whose identity group is persistently denigrated is less likely to view lofty life goals as reasonable.

International Differences

International comparisons of socioeconomic contexts for child development reveal some additional dimensions of these issues. Economists have compared nations according to social distance, which is the extent to which nations are willing to tolerate income gaps between the rich and poor. The United States and the United Kingdom have the largest income-based social distance measures of the developed nations. Further aggravating this inequality is the gap between the asset accumulation of the poor and the asset accumulation of the rich, which differs greatly in highly stratified nations such as the United States.

The severe deprivation associated with income and wealth inequality damages deprived children's life opportunities. But there is an additional dimension of the problem. Nations vary considerably in the extent to which they invest in public goods that support child development. Public goods are government-provided resources made available to all. Examples include government-funded universal health care, free and equitable public education, early child-care programs, and other social safety nets. Compared with other developed nations, highly unequal nations, such as the United States, invest relatively little in public goods. Consequently, in highly stratified nations, bright young children in lower socioeconomic strata face the dual liability of minimal access to public goods and severely limited private income and asset accumulation.

Seeking True Merit

True merit, as opposed to unearned, inherited, face-value merit, will emerge more often when citizens and policymakers recognize the effects of socioeconomic deprivation, stigmatization, and segregation on gifted and talented children's development. However, educators can seek out and implement promising educational intervention programs aimed at recognizing talent discovery and development among deprived populations.

Don Ambrose

See also Achievement Motivation; Aspiration Development and Self-Fulfillment; Classroom Practices; Rural Gifted; Self-Efficacy/Self-Esteem; Underachievement; Underrepresentation

Further Readings

Ambrose, D. (2002). Socioeconomic stratification and its influences on talent development: Some interdisciplinary perspectives. *Gifted Child Quarterly, 46*(3), 170–180.

Arrow, K., Bowles, S., & Durlauf, S. (Eds.). (2000). *Meritocracy and economic inequality.* Princeton, NJ: Princeton University Press.

Borland, J. H., Schnur, R., & Wright, L. (2000). Economically disadvantaged students in a school for the academically gifted: A postpositivist inquiry into individual and family adjustment. *Gifted Child Quarterly, 44,* 13–32.

Fischer, C. S., Hout, M., Jankowski, M. S., Lucas, S. R., Swidler, A., & Voss, K. (1996). *Inequality by design: Cracking the bell curve myth.* Princeton, NJ: Princeton University Press.

Rainwater, L., & Smeeding, T. M. (2003). *Poor kids in a rich country: America's children in comparative perspective.* New York: Russell Sage Foundation.

VanTassel-Baska, J., & Stambaugh, T. (Eds.). (2007). *Overlooked gems: A national perspective on low-income promising learners.* Washington, DC: National Association for Gifted Children.

Specialized Secondary Schools

One possibility for meeting the unique educational needs of gifted secondary students is through specialized schools. These schools may be private or public. Public school services may be provided at the district or the state level. They may be magnet schools, charter schools, and residential schools. These schools may provide a specialized curriculum focusing on one academic area, or they may provide a more general educational background. These schools typically focus on acceleration of content areas, but may also provide enrichment and greater depth of learning in combination with acceleration of instruction.

There are a variety of options in the form of specialized schools for gifted learners, although magnet schools are typically under the guidance of a school district and may provide specialized and advanced instruction in talent areas of gifted students, such as technology, sciences, or the fine arts. Charter schools are not under the direct guidance of a school district but, rather, operate under their own "charters" and are accountable to the sponsoring organizations. Some charter schools specialize in the unique needs of gifted and talented secondary students. Finally, state-sponsored schools for the gifted typically offer advanced coursework and accelerated curriculum for talented students. There is, however, a paucity of research available on the efficacy of these programs for gifted learners. This entry describes these types of specialized secondary schools.

Magnet Schools

Many local school districts choose magnet schools as a way to offer greater choice to students and parents. Rather than the typical assignment to a secondary school based on geographic location, students may choose to attend a magnet school that specializes in an area of interest or instructional strategy or pedagogical theory. Unlike the other types of specialized schools, magnet schools remain under the supervision of a school district. They operate bureaucratically in the same fashion as typical high schools in the school district, but magnet schools differ from typical high schools in their instructional strategies, course offerings, and specialized programming. For example, some magnet schools focus on Montessori techniques, and other magnet schools focus on mathematics and science, the performing or visual arts, or gifted programming. Admission to magnet schools is varied, some have strict admissions criteria, and others operate on a first-come, first-serve policy or a lottery system.

Magnet schools have their origins in the late 1960s and early 1970s to promote academic desegregation. Their goal was to open enrollment to students from diverse geographic locations to increase diversity in school populations by offering high-quality instruction in specialized areas. Therefore, diversity is often an explicit goal of many magnet schools.

Many magnet schools have additional funding that allows them to spend more money per student than traditional high schools spend. This may allow the school to provide additional resources such as lab equipment, art studios, or technology. Magnet schools report higher attendance, higher graduation rates, more professional development opportunities for teachers, and greater levels of parent involvement.

Magnet schools vary in their appropriateness for gifted learners. Although some magnet schools are specifically developed for gifted and talented students, not all programs have such a focus. Admission criteria, programming choices, and curricular options provide the foundation for appropriate curriculum for gifted learners. Specialized schools in the sciences, fine arts, or gifted programming often have more selective admission criteria and target talented students for enrollment.

Charter Schools

Charter schools are typically more innovative schools that operate independently from traditional school district policies. These schools submit a "charter" to their sponsoring organization (typically either state or local school system) that documents their purpose, goals, assessment, and measurement of success. Thus, they have autonomy in how they implement educational policies, but remain accountable for progress. Typically, charters last from 3 to 5 years, at which time they may be renewed by the sponsoring agency.

Some evidence indicates that charter schools may increase student achievement and close the achievement gap between low-income and culturally diverse students. However, there is little research on the effectiveness of charter schools for the gifted population. Specifically, relatively few charter schools focus on the unique needs of gifted learners or learners talented in a particular content area.

State-Sponsored Schools

State-sponsored schools, sometimes called governor's schools, for the gifted are another option for gifted students. These schools are currently operating in 13 states and include both residential and nonresidential programs. Residential schools typically recruit students from across the state and diverse geographic locations, but nonresidential schools may be located throughout the state to draw local students in several geographic locations. The Virginia system is one example of nonresidential governor's schools.

The state-sponsored schools may have a content area focus, such as science and mathematics or humanities, or they may have a more general focus on advanced content in many areas. These schools may offer a prescribed curriculum, or they may offer greater choices for students. Some of these schools are housed on university campuses, whereas other schools operate on independent campuses. Several of the schools on university campuses use the university faculty and courses as the courses for their students, but others operate more independently.

The admissions processes at the schools typically have selective guidelines. These schools typically require SAT or ACT scores that are competitive with those of entering college students, even though the students applying are between 2 and 4 years younger than graduating seniors. In addition, students are typically required to submit essays and teacher recommendations along with the application materials. Admissions officers look for advanced academic achievements and for emotional maturity to handle the residential school setting and task commitment needed to be successful with the additional course requirements. In addition to written materials, many state-sponsored schools also require on-campus interviews to secure a place at the school.

The curriculum at state-sponsored schools for the gifted is varied. The curriculum at all of these schools, however, is focused on advanced content and acceleration for the state's most academically talented students. In addition, many of these schools offer enrichment opportunities such as mentorships and research opportunities for students. In addition, the curriculum is more closely aligned with a college model, rather than a typical high school. For example, student schedules for classes may be on a college schedule, rather than a typical eight-period schedule of a high school.

In the cases of some schools, such as the Texas Academy of Mathematics and Science, the courses are entirely offered at the college campus. Students at the academy are enrolled in classes at the University of North Texas, and are required to take specific courses to meet the requirements for graduation, including chemistry, biology, and physics. Students may also take a variety of elective courses from the university, provided that they have the requisite grade-point average set by the academy. Thus, students graduate from the academy with a high school diploma as well as 2 years worth of college credits.

Other state-sponsored schools operate under different models. Some schools offer high school credit along with an associate's degree. Other schools housed at university campuses use many of the facilities of the university, but the classes are specifically for academy students, and thus students do not necessarily earn college credits. These classes are typically at the college level of content and offer students opportunities to explore content at an advanced level and in greater depth than in typical high schools.

The faculty at the state-sponsored schools have varying levels of expertise and qualifications. Many of these teachers hold advanced or terminal degrees in their content areas. At schools such as the Texas Academy, teachers are university faculty and thus typically hold terminal degrees in their subject area. Typically, state-sponsored schools for the gifted do not require teaching certification or advanced coursework in gifted education, maintaining the focus of recruitment of teachers on advanced knowledge of the content area. Some schools, however, do request previous teaching experience and work with gifted learners.

One major concern of these schools is the student life. These schools work to provide extracurricular activities for students in addition to the advanced level of content in the curricular domains. These schools offer academic clubs, such as Mu Alpha Theta and Literary Society, service organizations such as Key Club, leadership opportunities such as Student Council, and opportunities in the fine arts. In addition, many of these schools continue to provide typical high school activities such as prom and homecoming. There are also numerous athletic organizations on campus, either as intramural sports or as competitive teams. However, these organizations might not provide the same level of opportunities as the typical high school.

Various research has documented the academic, social, and emotional outcomes of attending specialized schools. Research has shown that there are few psychosocial differences between students who attend state-sponsored schools and typical high school students, using the Minnesota Multiphasic Personality Inventory for Adolescents (MMPI-A) and the Myers-Briggs Type Indicator (MBTI). Qualitative research, as well, has shown that students are able to adapt to the differing social complexities of the environment. Some research, however, indicates that students may have difficulty adjusting to the increase in academic rigor of the coursework. Social structures of family, school, and peers help students to adapt to the new environment.

The academic benefits of attending a state-sponsored school have also been examined by the research. Graduates from these schools report satisfaction with their academic experience, as well as continued academic gains as a result of their attendance. However, many of these studies do not include an adequate control group, so conclusions based on this research are difficult to interpret. A large number of graduates from these schools go on to obtain graduate and advanced degrees in majors related to their areas of academic expertise.

Hope E. Wilson

See also Adolescent, Gifted; College Gifted; Governor's Schools; Secondary Schools; Summer Programs

Further Readings

Boothe, D., Sethna, B. N., Stanley, J. C., & Colgate, S. D. (1999). Special opportunities for exceptionally able high school students: A description of eight residential early-entrance programs. *Journal of Secondary Gifted Education, 10,* 195–202.

Cross, T. L., Adams, C., Dixon, F., & Holland, J. (2004). Psychological characteristics of academically gifted adolescents attending a residential academy: A longitudinal study. *Journal for the Education of the Gifted, 28,* 159–161.

Jarwan, F. A., & Feldhusen, J. F. (1993). *Residential schools of mathematics and science for academically talented youth: An analysis of admissions programs.* (Collaborative Research Study, CRS93304). Storrs: National Research Center on the Gifted and Talented, University of Connecticut. (ERIC Document Reproduction Service No. ED379851)

Jones, B. M., Fleming, D. L., Henderson, J., & Henderson, C. E. (2002). Common denominations: Assessing hesitancy to apply to a selected residential math and science academy. *Journal of Secondary Gifted Education, 13,* 164–172.

Magnet Schools of America: http://www.magnet.edu/modules/content/index.php?id=88

National Association of Schools of Art and Design: http://nasad.arts-accredit.org

National Consortium of Specialized Secondary Schools in Mathematics, Science and Technology: http://www.ncsssmst.org

U.S. Charter Schools. (2006). *Overview of charter schools.* Retrieved April 26, 2008, from http://uscharterschools.org

What is a magnet school? (2003). *Public School Review.* Retrieved April 25, 2008, from http://www.publicschoolreview.com/articles/2

Spiritual Intelligence

What is spirituality? What kinds of experiences are considered to be spiritual? What does it mean to "be" spiritual? Are there neurological sites of spiritual activity? Is spirituality a form of intelligence? If so, how might it be defined and measured? Does it enhance emotional and physical health, psychological development, and moral and ethical awareness? These and related questions are at the heart of a burgeoning conversation among psychologists, religious scholars, and neuroscientists who are seeking to understand the role of spirituality in human evolution.

Spiritual experiences are complex phenomena with cognitive, emotional, biological, cultural, and religious components. These kinds of experiences are ubiquitous and have been reported in every culture and era. They are extremely diverse and unavoidably subject to individual interpretation. Some involve contact between individuals and the sacred, or what they perceive to be God, the Creator, or ultimate reality. Others are more prosaic, and include extrasensory perceptions, dreams, and altered states of consciousness, such as shamanic and out-of-body experiences. These phenomena arise in a plethora of ways and contexts, including meditation, contemplation, listening to music, being in nature, attending religious services, psychological and physical trauma, sensory deprivation, and the ingestion of psychoactive plants or drugs.

Spiritual experiences are precursors to spiritual intelligence, which is described in this entry. Two contemporary psychologists, Robert Emmons and Kathleen Noble, have argued that spiritual intelligence has both theoretical validity and practical implications. Emmons delineated five characteristics that he considers to be at the core of spiritual intelligence: the capacity for transcendence; the ability to enter into heightened spiritual states of consciousness; the ability to invest everyday activities, events, and relationships with a sense of the sacred; the ability to use spiritual resources to solve problems in living; and the capacity to be virtuous and to engage in virtuous behavior. Noble added two additional features: the conscious recognition that physical reality is embedded within a larger, multidimensional reality, and the choice to develop psychospiritual awareness to promote the health of both the individual and the global community. Her research suggests that in order for spiritual experiences to evolve into spiritual intelligence, an individual must seek to understand the meaning of those experiences and mindfully integrate them into the totality of his or her personal and community life. Intelligence, she argues, is critical to this process because the experiences can have profound effects biologically, psychologically, intellectually, and interpersonally. Further, individuals must learn to tolerate uncertainty and paradox, and recognize that all religions, wisdom traditions, and spiritual experiences contribute important and unique insights into the larger phenomenon of ultimate reality.

The theory of spiritual intelligence is controversial. Two psychologists, John Mayer and Howard Gardner, disagree with the concept albeit for different reasons. Mayer proposes that spirituality is a heightened consciousness rather than an intelligence, and that the paradigm of intelligence is too limiting because spirituality is more than abstract reasoning, a core feature of intelligence. Further, he does not distinguish spiritual intelligence from spirituality itself. Gardner, however, disputes the concept of spiritual intelligence partly because it cannot be supported by experimental psychological investigations or psychometric findings, two of his criteria for distinguishing an independent intelligence.

Can spiritual intelligence be empirically measured? At this time, the answer is no. Part of the difficulty lies in defining what a spiritual experience might be. Different cultural and religious traditions have unique vocabularies for depicting what could be identical experiences, and there is much disagreement about what constitutes a spiritual experience. Quantitative measures of the incidence and prevalence of spiritual experiences have been developed, although each uses its own definitional and metaphorical language. Numerous studies that have used one or more of these instruments suggest that significant numbers of people, both children and adults, have had what they consider to be a spiritual experience. Other studies have used qualitative methods, such as phenomenology, grounded theory, and narrative history, to explore the ways in which individuals experience spirituality and how these experiences inform their daily lives. Unfortunately, research in this area is limited by the small number of investigators who study these questions. Spiritual experiences and the concept of spiritual intelligence are irreconcilable with the materialist models of reality employed by contemporary Western science. Consequently, researchers who explore these questions are often subjected to marginalization and derision within their professional arenas. Building on Noble's work, Barbara Kerr has suggested a way out of this dilemma by operationalizing spiritual intelligence as the deliberate management of consciousness states in the service of one's own growth and that of others. This definition, however, leaves out some of the richness of qualitative conceptualizations and may be only useful when psychophysiological instruments such as fMRI are sophisticated enough to capture the suppleness of the consciousness of spiritually intelligent people.

Nonetheless, neither the experiences nor the questions they inspire are likely to go away. The possibility of spiritual intelligence has great relevance to the study of creativity, consciousness, and human psychological development. Emmons, for example, wonders whether there is an optimal level of spiritual intelligence, whereas Noble hypothesizes a continuum of spiritual intelligence such as those that exist for other forms of intelligence and suggests that an individual could be developmentally delayed or advanced in spiritual terms. How to account for the fact that spiritual experiences can be and have been used in the service of heinous and destructive human behavior is also of grave concern. The study of spiritual intelligence is a theoretical nodal point at which many disciplines meet. It has profound implications for biomedical research and neuroscience, peace studies, deep ecology, and the training of professionals in the health and educational professions. It also has great potential for helping address the seemingly intractable problems of ethnic and religious strife and the unending quest for social justice.

Kathleen D. Noble

See also Attitudes Toward Religion and Spirituality; Existentially Gifted; Multiple Intelligences; Spirituality; Spiritual Leaders

Further Readings

Emmons, R. A. (2000). Is spirituality an intelligence? Motivation, cognition, and the psychology of ultimate concern. *International Journal for the Psychology of Religion, 10*(1), 3–26.

Halama, P., & Strizenec, M. (2004). Spiritual, existential or both? Theoretical considerations on the nature of "higher" intelligences. *Studia Psychologica, 46*(3), 239–253.

Kerr, B., & McAlister, J. (2001). *Letters to the medicine man: The shaping of spiritual intelligence.* Cresskill, NJ: Hampton Press.

Mayer, J. D. (2000). Spiritual intelligence or spiritual consciousness? *International Journal for the Psychology of Religion, 10*(1), 47–56.

Murphy, M. (1992). *The future of the body: Explorations into the future evolution of human nature.* Los Angeles: Jeremy P. Tarcher.

Noble, K. D. (2001). *Riding the windhorse: Spiritual intelligence and the growth of the self.* Cresskill, NJ: Hampton Press.

Spirituality

The origins of spirituality are found in our evolutionary history, starting from shamanistic and animistic traditions in numerous societies, to pantheistic and monotheistic religious traditions that characterize the world today. According to Robert Bellah, a prominent U.S. sociologist, the term *spirituality* was always a subdomain of religion and the two are historically compatible. However, Bellah claims that since the 1970s, societal use of the word *spiritual* is used to connote something other than being religious. A common remark one hears today is, "I am not religious, but I am spiritual," which is a relatively new sociological phenomenon. The late 20th century was a time of renewed interest in spirituality around the world, with many people exploring indigenous spiritualities of Native Americans, Aboriginals, and West Africans as well as the mystical practices linked to the world religions. This entry discusses the many meanings and expressions of spirituality, as well as its importance in the lives of gifted and creative individuals.

The adjective *spiritual* has a long list of meanings, the most common of which are pertaining to (a) spirit; (b) soul; (c) moral, devotional, or religious nature; (d) ethereal or supernatural; (e) mind or consciousness; (f) sacred; and (g) ecclesiastical. In other words, being spiritual means trying to reach a higher plane of consciousness, having a heightened self-awareness, having empathy for humanity, or achieving oneness with a deity or the universe. Spirituality is an important dimension of giftedness given the research-based evidence that the social-emotional characteristics of gifted individuals includes a heightened awareness of existential questions, inequities, fairness, and moral and ethical dilemmas, as well as concern for larger societal and planetary problems such as world hunger, exploitation of workers by multinational corporations, fair trade policies, third world debt, poverty, and world peace. The spiritual development of gifted young people takes place mainly outside of school, where wise and caring adults are needed to provide guidance on reading, experiences, and spiritual practices that can enhance the young person's understanding of self and capacity for self-transcendence.

The dominant religious traditions of the world today, such as Christianity, Hinduism, Islam, Buddhism, and Judaism, have consisted of individuals universally agreed to be spiritual leaders because of their ability to receive insights or revelations beyond the cognitive, sensual, and affective capacities of normal human beings. Examples of such spiritually gifted individuals are Jesus of Nazareth, the Rishis of the Vedas, the prophet Mohammed, Gautama Buddha, and the prophets in the Old Testament. All these religions also consist of strands or offshoots viewed as mystical traditions, such as the Sufism in Islam; Kabbalism in Judaism; Victorines, Rhineland, and Flemish mystics within Christianity; the Vedic tradition in Hinduism; and Taoism, Zen, and Tibetan Buddhism. These mystical traditions are similar in their quest to seek oneness with God or unity with the cosmos through yogic practices, meditation, dance, poetry, or chanting to transcend dualistic dilemmas, reductionism, and infinite regressions that characterize logic, language, and empiricism.

The branch of philosophy known as metaphysics is an intellectual tradition that attempts to transcend the limitations of science and the empirical traditions within science. Metaphysics concerns itself with the study of notions such as existence, ontology, causality, space, and time, and consists of contributions from the eminent thinkers within theology and philosophy of religion (the Buddha, Adi Shankara, St. Augustine of Hippo, Hildegard of Bingen, Jiddu Krishnamurti), philosophy (Plato, Spinoza, Nietzsche, Kant, Sartre, Levinas), and science and mathematics (Descartes, Newton, Leibniz, Russell), among others.

Spirituality is closely linked with a highly evolved sense of ethics, altruism, and morality, so it is natural to question whether there are any evolutionary explanations for our spiritual tendencies. Charles Darwin, in *The Descent of Man,* posed the question whether the phenomenon of moral behavior in humans could be explained in evolutionary terms, namely, natural selection. However, the evolution of social systems (religious, ideological, political) of various kinds is not explainable strictly in Darwinian terms. One of the most interesting but controversial theories proposed to explain social evolution is that of Herbert Spencer, better known for his population-pressure theory. Spencer paid attention to the phenomenon of warfare and its role in shaping human progress, namely raising the consciousness of organizations to a higher more evolved plane. History shows examples of this evolution of consciousness after conflicts; for example, Asoka's embracing of the peaceful doctrines of Buddhism after the carnage at Kalinga; the Icelanders' conversion to Christianity as a means to end internal strife among warring clans in the year 1000 and to work toward the common good of their isolated society. The Icelandic Parliament is in fact more than 1,000 years old. August Comte proposed a stage theory for our social evolution in which humanity moves from a theological stage onto a metaphysical stage onto a "positive" stage, where we reject absolutism of all kinds.

Pierre Teilhard de Chardin, an early 20th-century paleontologist and a Jesuit priest, believed humanity is collectively moving toward a shared collective consciousness and spirituality via socialization, personalization, and *planetization* despite recurring international political conflicts and socioeconomic strife. Teilhard de Chardin defined *planetization* in three phases, the first of which consists of population expansion and *divergence* of human species followed by a phase where humanity undergoes differentiation characterized by racial, social, and cultural differences, followed by a third phase of planetization in which global *convergence* occurs where people share their knowledge and ideas. In his view, past socioeconomic strife and political ideologies are simply evolutionary "birth pangs" of a coming new age of collective global organization and consciousness. Stephen White writes that Teilhard de Chardin's global vision is grounded on the realization that just as humans have a common biological and psychic history, likewise they have a common collective future. Future progress is dependent on the collective consciousness of a common planetary citizenship.

Bharath Sriraman

See also Aspiration Development and Self-Fulfillment; Consciousness; Spiritual Intelligence; Spiritual Leaders

Further Readings

Bellah, R. (1970). *Beyond belief: Essays on religion in a post-traditional world,* New York: Harper & Row.

Comte, A. (1972). Das Drei-Stadien-Gesetz. In H. P. Dreitzel (Ed.), *Sozialer Wandel* (pp. 95–111). Neuwied and Berlin: Luchterhand.

Darwin, C. (1871). *The descent of man.* London: John Murray.

Dawkins, R. (1976). *The selfish gene.* Oxford, UK: Oxford University Press.

Spencer, H. (1857). Progress: Its law and cause. In J. D. Y. Peel (Ed.), *Herbert Spencer and social evolution* (pp. 38–52). Chicago: University of Chicago Press.

Spencer, H. (1873). *Descriptive sociology.* New York: Appleton.

Sriraman, B., & Adrian, H. (2004). The use of fiction as a didactic tool to examine existential problems. *Journal of Secondary Gifted Education, 15*(3), 96–106.

Sriraman, B., & Benesch, W. (2005). Consciousness and science: An Advaita-Vedantic perspective on the theology-science dialogue. *Theology and Science, 3*(1), 39–54.

Teilhard de Chardin, P. (1995). *The future of man.* New York: Harper & Row. (Original work published 1959)

Teilhard de Chardin, P. (1999). *The human phenomenon* (S. Appleton-Weber, Trans.). Brighton, UK: University of Sussex Press. (Original work published 1955)

White, S. R. (2008). Multicultural visions of globalization: Constructing educational perspectives from the east and the west. *Interchange, 39*(1), 95–117.

Spiritual Leaders

Spiritual leaders are spiritual pathfinders who aspire to achieve the highest measure of what it means to be human, and use their spirituality in the service of others. Spiritual leaders demonstrate behaviors and beliefs that Dorothy Sisk and E. Paul Torrance in *Spiritual Intelligence: Developing Higher Consciousness* proposed as spiritual intelligence. These individuals speak and act in accordance with perceptions and values that reflect a larger perspective, and their words and actions awaken in others the recognition of universal truths. They demonstrate the power of one person being able to reinvigorate a community or a nation to restore hope and raise expectations. Through lives of service, spiritual leaders transform biological reality into a transformation of the spirit. They transform the conditioning forces of ethnicity, gender, socialization, or political that constrain them. One major characteristic of spiritual leaders is their sense of purpose and otherworldliness, being in the world, but not of it.

Spiritual leadership is manifested in the wisdom of the ages, and their lives leave footprints on the sands of time. Spiritual leadership is imbedded in spirituality, but there is a distinction between spirituality and religion. The Dalai Lama in *Ethics for the New Millennium* offered this clear distinction:

> Religion I take to be concerned with faith in the claims of one faith tradition or another, an aspect of which is the acceptance of some form of heaven or nirvana. Connected with this are religious teachings or dogma, ritual prayer, and so on. Spirituality I take to be concerned with those qualities of the human spirit—such as love, compassion, patience, tolerance, forgiveness, and contentment. A sense of responsibility, a sense of harmony—which brings happiness to both self and others. (p. 22)

A number of spiritual leaders manifested spirituality at an early age, and many were in hopeless situations; yet, they were able to find ways to make a difference. The spiritual leaders presented in this entry represent people of integrity who inspired others with their ideals. They made things happen that others thought were impossible and created new ways for society to be.

Nelson Mandela

Nelson Mandela was born in 1918 in a small village in the Transkei region. His birth name was Rolihlahla, meaning pulling the branch of trees. At age 7, he enrolled in a local Methodist school, and had to change his name, spoken language, and even the clothes he wore. Early on, he became convinced that education was the road to success, and later enrolled in the all-Black University College of Port Hare with 150 students representing the brightest youth of South Africa. He dedicated himself to work for racial equality in South Africa using peaceful protests through the African National Congress (ANC). Mandela finished a law degree, and he started his own law firm with Oliver Tambo. In 1955, the ANC drafted a Freedom Charter stating, "the people shall govern, all national groups shall have equal rights, the people shall share in the country's wealth, and the land shall be shared among those who work it."

Mandela was invited to the Pan African Freedom Movement meeting in Algeria, and spent 7 months of travel outside South Africa. During that time, he was viewed as a symbol of resistance and dangerous to the South African government. When he returned, Mandela was charged with inciting people to strike and with leaving the country illegally. During his trial, Mandela aired the grievances of Black Africans.

Mandela was given a sentence of life in prison, and spent 27 years in prison. On his release, he praised the heroism of students who had resisted, and the international community for its sanctions against South Africa. He was elected president of the ANC, and showed little or no revenge, focusing on what was best for the future of the country. Mandela and President Frederik de Klerk of South Africa were awarded a joint Nobel Peace Prize for their efforts in South Africa. In 1992, Mandela became the first Black president of South Africa. Mandela demonstrated spiritual leadership in instilling a sense of peace and forgiveness in the people of South Africa.

Mother Teresa

Mother Teresa was born Agnes Gonxha Bojaxhiu in Skopje, Albania, in 1910. As a young girl, Agnes demonstrated strength, character, and purpose; joined a student group in her local parish; and became interested in the work of missionaries. At age 18, she joined the Irish order of the Sisters of Loreto, taking the name of Teresa after St. Theresa, a Carmelite nun. Mother Teresa's dream was to go to India, and after learning English, she transferred to Calcutta to teach English at St. Mary's high school, eventually becoming the principal. During World War II, she contracted tuberculosis. She went to the Himalayas to convalesce, and during the trip, heard a voice directing her to leave the school and live among the poorest of the poor.

Mother Teresa identified six steps in creating peace: Silence, Prayer, Faith, Love, Service, and Peace. She called this the simple path. Over the years, thousands of people have been inspired by her work, and these people take the vows of poverty, chastity, obedience, and service to the poor, and undergo rigorous training to become members of the order established by Mother Teresa, the Missionaries of Charity.

The Children's Home in Calcutta feeds more than 1,000 people daily, mostly beggars from the street, and cares for more than 2,500 patients in one week. Mother Teresa's leadership continues even after her death in 1997, with requests for opening new homes all around the world. The Missionaries of Charity have AIDS homes in Spain, Portugal, Brazil, Honduras, and the United States, including the cities of New York, Washington, D.C., Baltimore, Dallas, Atlanta, and San Francisco. Mother Teresa won the Nobel Prize for compassion without condescension. Mother Teresa tirelessly worked for peace and was an exemplar of spiritual leadership, living a life of service to others, based on love and compassion.

Mohandas Gandhi

Mohandas Gandhi was born in 1869 in Porbandar, India. As a child, he was quiet and contemplative, and early on, read the *Bhagavad Gita*, which became his calling to undertake his "battle of righteousness." Two major beliefs directed Gandhi's life: holding firmly to the deepest truth and soul force, and nonviolence to all living things.

He graduated from law school and went to South Africa to practice law, where he experienced considerable discrimination. These experiences helped him resolve to fight for social justice. Gandhi spent 23 years in South Africa fighting injustice, and returned to India in 1930. When he was age 61, he and his followers marched 240 miles in 24 days to make their own salt from the sea, an act in defiance of British colonial laws. When they reached the sea, thousands of people had joined in the march, and more than 60,000 people were arrested, including Gandhi.

Gandhi was a powerful political force in India, and a spiritual leader for people throughout the world. Gandhi was convinced that mass noncooperation could achieve independence, and that one cannot be dominated unless one cooperates with one's dominators. His vision of independence was never realized during his lifetime, for two nations; Pakistan and India were formed out of colonial India. Civil war broke out between the Hindus and Muslims, and Gandhi was killed by a Hindu fanatic. Gandhi's spiritual leadership influenced other spiritual leaders. Gandhi is held in universal esteem as a spiritual leader, and a living model of nonviolence.

Martin Luther King, Jr.

Martin Luther King, Jr., was born in 1929 in Atlanta, Georgia. He became motivated to fight racial prejudice as a boy of 6, when the mother of his two best friends who were White, told King that when they began school, he could no longer play with her sons. This stimulated his conviction that people should not be judged by the color of their skin. King was a gifted student, accelerated three grades, and graduated from high school at age 15. He followed in the footsteps of his father and grandfather and was ordained as a minister at the age of 18. He earned a doctorate at Boston University where he studied nonviolent leaders, particularly Gandhi.

During the 1950s, King became a powerful leader in the Civil Rights Movement, and during that time, he received numerous threats to his life. In 1963, a civil rights demonstration was held in Washington, D.C., and King spoke to more than 250,000 people, delivering his "I Have a Dream" speech. In 1964, he was awarded the Nobel Peace Prize, the youngest person to win the prize, and he donated the prize of $54,000 to the Civil Rights Movement.

King was convinced change comes from within, from believing in one's self, and one's strength and courage. He was shot in 1968 while working with a group of Blacks protesting in Memphis concerning the rights of workers. His tombstone reads, "Free at Last, Free at Last, Thank God Almighty I'm Free at Last."

Dorothy Sisk

See also Spiritual Intelligence; Spirituality

Further Readings

Dalai Lama. (1999). *Ethics for the new millennium.* New York: Putnam.

Isaacon, W. (1999, December 31). Who mattered and why. *Time,* 52.

King, C. (1983). *In the words of Martin Luther King, Jr.* New York: Newmarket Press.

Mandela, N. (1986). *Long walk to freedom: The autobiography of Nelson Mandela.* Boston: Little, & Brown.

Mother Teresa. (1967). *In the heart of the world.* Novato, CA: World Library.

Sisk, D., & Torrance, E. P. (2001). *Spiritual intelligence: Developing higher consciousness.* Buffalo, NY: Creative Education Foundation Press.

Time-Life. (2000). Martin Luther King Jr., consciousness of a nation. In *People who changed the world* (p. 50). Alexandria, VA: Time-Life Publications.

Vardey, L. (1995). *Mother Teresa: A simple path.* New York: Ballantine Books.

Stanford-Binet

Stanford-Binet refers to a widely used intelligence test that dates back to 1905. Although other intelligence tests are available, the Stanford-Binet is preferred in high-ability testing because it can differentiate the degree of giftedness at a very high level (IQ > 160) compared with other intelligence tests. The history; the theoretical foundation; the general descriptions; the psychometric properties; the strengths and weaknesses; and the clinical application for gifted assessment of the Stanford-Binet are discussed in this entry.

History

In France, the Stanford-Binet started life as the Binet-Simon Intelligence Test in 1905, a test developed by psychologist Alfred Binet and physician Theodore Simon to diagnose schoolchildren with mental retardation for placement in special education classes. At Stanford University in 1916, with the publication of *The Measurement of Intelligence: An Explanation of and a Complete Guide for the Use of the Stanford Revision and Extension of the Binet-Simon Intelligence Scale,* by Lewis Terman, the original test gained a new life as the Stanford-Binet.

The translations and adaptations of the original French test items, along with the addition of new items by Terman plus the use of normative studies and rigorous methodological research contributed to the continued success of the Stanford-Binet today. Terman and colleagues conducted research on the Stanford-Binet with the specific intention of identifying extremely gifted children who would earn the label *genius*. This research is well-documented in Terman's five-volume, *Genetic Studies of Genius*, making the Stanford-Binet the intelligence test of choice to identify highly gifted (145–159 IQ), exceptionally gifted (160–179 IQ), and profoundly gifted (180+ IQ) children. In the years from the first edition Stanford-Binet in 1916 to its current fifth edition revision, which was completed in 2003, there have been continued changes made to both the norms and the subtests.

Theoretical Foundation

The Stanford-Binet Fifth Edition (SB5) has a strong theoretical foundation; it uses the Cattell-Horn-Carroll (CHC) theory of cognitive abilities to guide its test development. SB5 uses five factors—Fluid Reasoning, Knowledge, Quantitative Reasoning, Visual-Spatial Processing, and Working Memory—of the list of 8 to 10 factors of the CHC theory to derive a general intelligence (*g*) factor. These five factors were selected based on research on school achievement and on expert ratings of the importance of these factors in intellectual assessment drawn from advisory panels of prominent researchers and practitioners; from contracted consultants; from workshops on assessment of gifted individuals and from key experts in the field of intelligence theory such as John Carroll, John Horn, Richard Woodcock, and Kevin McGrew. These five factors also emphasize the reasoning abilities of the CHC model that can be easily administered within a 1-hour assessment period without the use of specialized timing or test apparatus such as the tape recorder.

General Description

The SB5 is an adaptive test, with the examiner using information about the examinee to determine the appropriate testing point to reduce the time to administer the test and to decrease the frustration that may be experienced by the examinee when tested with items that are either too easy or too hard. The test provides norms for examine between ages 2 through 85 or more years for the Verbal IQ (VIQ) and Nonverbal IQ (NVIQ) scores as well as the Full Scale IQ (FSIQ) scores. The test items cover items in both the nonverbal and verbal domains that allow the test to be accurate and fair for assessing a range of intelligence from low-end functioning, to normal intelligence, all the way to high levels of giftedness.

Psychometric Properties

The SB5 standardization involves extensive studies of reliability, validity, and fairness. The internal-consistency reliability ranged from .95 to .98 for IQ scores and from .90 to .92 for the five Factor Index Scores (e.g., Fluid Reasoning and Knowledge). Test-retest and interexaminer reliability studies that were conducted showed the stability and consistency of SB5 scoring. The SB5 has correlations of .84 with the Wechsler Intelligence Scale for Children–Third Edition (WISC-III) FSIQ, correlation of .83 with the Wechsler Preschool and Primary Scale of Intelligence–Revised (WPSSI-R) FSIQ, and correlation of .90 with the Woodcock-Johnson III Tests of Cognitive Abilities (WJ III COG; five factors), showing that the SB5 is valid for intelligence testing. In addition, positive correlations between the SB5 and two major achievement batteries—the Woodcock-Johnson III Tests of Achievement (WJ III ACH) and the Wechsler Individual Achievement Test–Second Edition (WIAT-II)—provides strong evidence for comparing intellectual and achievement scores of examinees. For norming purposes, 4,800 subjects aged 2 to 96 years old, chosen from a stratified sample approximating the U.S. Census Bureau 2000 population served as a norm group that includes gender, geographic region, ethnicity (African American, Asian American, European American, Hispanic or Latino/Latina American, Native American, and Other), and socioeconomic levels (years of education completed or parents' education level) were used. The SB5 was developed with the goal of creating a fair test with little bias related to religious perspectives, ethnic, gender, and disability groups such as deafness.

Strengths and Weaknesses

The strengths of the SB5 relevant to giftedness assessment includes being a culture-fair test for minority gifted populations; use of content-validity studies of CHC-aligned factors; use of standard deviation of 15 instead of 16 in alignment with other intelligence test for easy comparison; optional new scoring with Change-Sensitive Scores (CSSs) that allows for better tracking purposes when individuals are tested multiple times across the years; inclusion of extended IQ scores; and use of colorful toys, blocks, and illustrations to test young gifted children. The weaknesses of the SB5 relevant to giftedness includes not covering all possible factors in the CHC model, limited gifted population samples data, conventional scaled scores and IQ ceiling of 160 IQ on the non-extended test, and use of the Nonverbal Knowledge (Picture Absurdities) subtest and other nonverbal subtests that require some level of language abilities and expressive abilities that may be unfair to minority gifted individuals who have limited language abilities.

Clinical Application

Selected clinical applications of the SB5 for gifted evaluation allow the examiner to evaluate examinees for giftedness while considering gifted individuals' characteristics such as being deliberate in reasoning. Special composite scores such as the "Intellectual Giftedness" composite, derived from selected SB5 subtests allow the examiner to evaluate individuals who are referred for gifted evaluation. This composite score also allows identification of twice-exceptional gifted individuals, individuals who are both gifted and diagnosed with attention-deficit hyperactivity disorder, learning disabilities, or autism-spectrum disorders. In addition, the new feature of Extended IQ (EXIQ) scoring (permits scores between 161 and 225 IQ) allows the examiner to assess exceptionally and profoundly gifted examinees, providing an FSIQ score of up to 225.

The Stanford-Binet Fifth Edition bears little resemblance to its original, the Binet-Simon Intelligence Test (1905). However, the original test created an important foundation for the development of an intelligence test that allows for testing of high-ability individuals. The continued revision of the Stanford-Binet highlights the importance of continued development and testing of an intelligence test to serve the needs of those who are of high-level intellectual functioning, as well as low-level intellectual functioning individuals, to accurately identify and serve their needs.

Kai Kok "Zeb" Lim

See also Cognitive Abilities Test; Fluid and Crystallized Intelligence; History of Gifted Education in the United States; Intelligence Testing; IQ; Kaufman ABC Tests; Terman's Studies of Genius; Wechsler Intelligence Scale for Children–Fourth Edition; Wechsler Preschool and Primary Scale of Intelligence–Third Edition

Further Readings

Alfonso, V. C., Flanagan, D. P., & Radwan, S. (2005). The impact of the Cattell-Horn-Carroll theory on test development and interpretation of cognitive and academic abilities. In D. P. Flanagan & P. L. Harrison (Eds.), *Contemporary intellectual assessment: Theories, test and issues* (2nd ed., pp. 185–202). New York: Guilford Press.

Becker, K. A. (2003). *History of the Stanford-Binet intelligence scales: Content and psychometrics.* (Stanford-Binet Intelligence Scales, Fifth Edition Assessment Service Bulletin No. 1). Itasca, IL: Riverside Publishing.

Roid, G. H., & Barram, R. A. (2004). *Essentials of Stanford-Binet intelligence scales (SB5) assessment.* Hoboken, NJ: Wiley.

Roid, G. H., & Carson, A. D. (2003). *Special composite scores for the SB5.* (Stanford-Binet Intelligence Scales, Fifth Edition Assessment Service Bulletin No. 4). Itasca, IL: Riverside Publishing.

Ruf, D. L. (2003). *Use of the SB5 in the assessment of high abilities.* (Stanford-Binet Intelligence Scales, Fifth Edition Assessment Service Bulletin No. 3). Itasca, IL: Riverside Publishing.

State Associations

State associations for the gifted are collaborative efforts of parents, educators, and other interested parties, usually as nonprofit organizations. Many associations were originally established in the

1950s and 1960s, when gifted education as it is known today was in its infancy. These associations typically have a mission of advocacy and support for educators and parents of gifted children. Forty-seven state associations are currently members of the National Association for Gifted Children (NAGC). The focus in this entry is on consistencies across most state associations, while acknowledging the individuality of each association, based on the state's size, history, needs, and resources.

Many state associations provide self-published educational materials, such as statewide or regional newsletters, or professional journals. Newsletters provide educational materials in the form of articles and research reports and communicate information about upcoming events and legislative actions. Associations also act as dissemination sites for other resources concerning gifted education, through online connections, publishing of white papers and fact sheets, or providing an access point for journals and books on gifted education. Most state associations have Web sites that serve as clearinghouses of local resources as well as connections to national information regarding gifted education.

Influencing public policy as it applies to gifted education is an ongoing goal of virtually all state associations. The state associations have members in advisory groups for state departments of education, collegiate programs for gifted education, and local school districts. Members of state associations work with local and state legislators in developing and supporting public policy to benefit gifted children and educators. Each association sets its own legislative priorities and strategies. Legislative concerns addressed through state association advocacy work can include funding of gifted education; teacher training, including prelicensure and postlicensure; and meeting the programming needs of gifted children, including acceleration and identification policies. In addition, some state associations have been instrumental in establishing public policy on educational options for students that reflect current trends in gifted education, such as programs or schools for science, technology, engineering, and mathematics, or for fine art.

State associations also provide educational experiences in the form of conferences, workshops, online courses, or continuing education courses for educators. Typically, each state or regional area provides an annual conference for educators and parents with up-to-date information on the best practices in gifted education. Workshops and seminars may focus on specific topics of importance in gifted education and provide timely presentation of research. Many state associations provide continuing education credits to meet the certification requirements of their state for teachers and gifted specialists and coordinators. Lists of speakers on current topics in gifted education who have expertise in those topic areas are generally distributed by the state associations.

Support for parents, educators, and students takes many different forms among the state associations. In addition to providing information and guidance on topics of gifted children, associations work to promote the development of innovative programs at the school and regional levels. Scholarships are often provided for educators and students, and in many cases, educators are supported through mini-grant opportunities to refine their knowledge base regarding best practices in gifted education. Students are frequently supported to attend academic classes and summer programs designed specifically for gifted students. In addition, in some states, students may apply for mini-grants for personal research, or creative projects that reflect their gifts and talents. Outstanding contributions by educators, parents, and students are recognized through a variety of awards, providing opportunity to identify excellence or creativity in teaching or exhibition of student talent. The Nicholas Green Award through the NAGC is a common form of recognition for student achievement by a state association.

State associations are primarily designed to provide leadership in advocating for changes in public policy, developing a knowledge base in best practices for teaching gifted students, and promoting understanding of the complex and specialized needs of the gifted child. Although varied in their approaches and accomplishments, all associations share a commitment to improving the learning opportunities and lives of gifted children.

Teresa Argo Boatman

See also Asia, Gifted Education; Canada, Gifted Education; Europe, Gifted Education; State Offices of Gifted

Further Readings

National Association for Gifted Children, NAGC State Affiliate Associations: http://www.nagc.org/index.aspx?id=609&gbs

State Offices of Gifted

State offices of gifted education oversee state involvement in the education of learners whose exceptionally high abilities or potentialities require differentiated instruction and systems of support beyond those provided in traditional classrooms to ensure appropriate instructional opportunities. Because there is no federal mandate to serve gifted and talented students, there is a wide range of policies and practices affecting gifted students implemented and overseen by the state offices. This entry describes national standards, local control, the state of the states, and further indicators of differences.

Although the federal definition of gifted and talented students is not binding on the states, many state definitions are modeled after a federal definition that first came into used in the 1970s. The No Child Left Behind Act of 2002 modified previous federal definitions of gifted and talented students, children, or youth as those "who give evidence of high achievement capability in areas such as intellectual, creative artistic, or leadership capacity, or in specific academic fields, and who need services or activities not ordinarily provided by the school in order to fully develop those capabilities."

National Standards

Prekindergarten through Grade 12 Gifted Program Standards, published by the National Association for Gifted Children (NAGC) in 1998, addresses standards in seven program areas for gifted learners, and Teacher Preparation Standards in Gifted Education, published by NAGC and the Council for Exceptional Children, define teacher candidate knowledge and skill competencies determined by the field of gifted education. NAGC, working with the Council for Exceptional Children, has revised the standards, which are used by the National Council for the Accreditation of Teacher Education to accredit college and university teacher preparation programs in gifted education. National standards have not been developed for state offices of gifted.

Local Control

State and local entities are responsible for gifted and talented education funding initiatives. With neither a national mandate nor a federal funding stream, the depth and breadth of services varies greatly throughout the United States. Sole responsibility rests upon each state to develop policies and procedures that recognize and respond to the needs of this unique population. Differences in laws and regulations regarding the definition of giftedness, mandates to identify and serve gifted learners, programs and services, personnel preparation, accountability, allocation of funding and human resources reveal a considerable diversity of state perspectives. Numerous states assign the responsibilities for key decisions of these areas to local education agencies.

In 1993, all 50 states had policies recognizing the needs of gifted learners, according to A. Harry Passow and Rose A. Rudnitski as reported in a 1993 collaborative study with the National Research Center on the Gifted and Talented. By 2007, nearly all states had a state office of gifted providing information, consultation services, and some level of advocacy on behalf of gifted learners residing in their state. Additional roles and responsibilities of state offices of gifted differ and are significantly influenced by the structure of their state education agency.

Local education agency control prevails in many states, such as California, Connecticut, Delaware, Illinois, and Minnesota. Florida, Indiana, Kentucky, Oregon, and Virginia are among the states that have highly prescriptive legislation, which defines identification, service, educational placement, procedural safeguards, and support services for gifted and talented learners.

State of the States

In the 2006–2007 biannual report, *State of the States in Gifted Education,* a joint publication by the NAGC and the Council of State Directors of Programs for the Gifted, respondents were asked to identify their reporting structure for gifted and talented education. Of the 43 respondent states, most housed gifted and talented with curriculum and instruction, followed by special education, exceptional students, and general education. Arizona and Massachusetts were the only states with a special section or department for gifted education.

The *State of the States in Gifted Education* report identifies the provision of technical assistance as the single most time-consuming activity performed by state education agency personnel. Technical assistance by phone was named in the top three activities by 30 of the 43 states. Additional high-ranking activities included responding to parental questions, providing technical assistance to local education agencies in the field, providing professional and staff development, monitoring program compliance, and grants management.

At least one full-time education agency person was allocated in more than half of the responding states. A part-time person devoted to gifted education was common in the remaining states. Most directors of state offices of gifted had responsibilities including special programs or other projects not specifically related to gifted education.

Further Indicators of Differences

Though a paucity of evidence exists regarding the role of state offices of gifted, most states locate the offices of gifted and talented education within other areas of educational focus. Additional data was gleaned from a 2008 independent survey of state directors of gifted programs conducted by the Minnesota Department of Education (MDE). Thirty-eight states responded to the MDE survey, identifying agency placement, personnel preparation, roles, collaboration, and data collection.

The survey revealed a correlation between the director's personnel preparation and the office of gifted education's placement within the agency. Most state directors held gifted education certificates, master's degrees in gifted education, or doctorates in gifted education. Many held advanced degrees in educational leadership or a specific content area, and several had degrees in special education. All had substantive knowledge and experience in curriculum and instruction.

Respondents named the provision of on-site technical assistance, administration of grants, or monitoring as their primary and secondary roles. Creation of resources and staff development followed.

State directors collaborate most often with content specialists in elementary and secondary education. Advanced Placement/International Baccalaureate/College Level Examination Program specialists and the office of Special Education were listed third and fourth. Outside the agency, the top-ranked organizations listed for collaboration were advocacy groups, followed by districts/schools and postsecondary institutions. Collaboration with charter schools and psychologists occurred in a few of the states surveyed.

Joyce VanTassel-Baska defines educational policy as an adopted course of action by a governing board, motivated by the existence of an educational problem or issue. The MDE survey found that state directors had various roles of influence in state policy. When asked to identify their role in state policy, creation in collaboration with stakeholder groups, revision of policy, and creation on behalf of the agency were the most common roles cited. Seven of the respondents reported their offices had no role and influence in the creation or revision of policy.

Data collection was common among state offices with responsibilities for monitoring elements of gifted education. The survey results revealed the number of gifted learners, program demographics, and academic performance in school by gifted learners as the most frequently culled components of state data-collection systems.

Wendy A. Behrens

See also Differentiation; Giftedness, Definition; National Association for Gifted Children

Further Readings

National Association for Gifted Children and Council of State Directors of Programs for the Gifted Programs. (2007). *State of the states in gifted education 2006–2007.* CD-ROM. Washington, DC: NAGC.

National Association for Gifted Children Standards. Retrieved February 12, 2008, from http://www.nagc.org/index.aspx?id=546

No Child Left Behind Act, P.L. 107–110 (Title IX, Part A, Definitions (22) (2002); 20 U.S.C. Sec.7802 (22) (2004).

Passow, A. H., & Rudnitski, R. A. (1993). *State policies regarding education of the gifted as reflected in legislation and regulation* (No. CRS 93302). Storrs, CT: National Research Center on the Gifted and Talented, Collaborative Research Study.

VanTassel-Baska, J. (2006). State policies in gifted education. *Designing services and programs for high-ability learners* (pp. 249–261). Thousand Oaks, CA: Corwin Press.

Stereotype Threat

Stereotype threat situations occur when one is in jeopardy of confirming a negative self-referent stereotype in an achievement context. Often, preoccupation with a threat results in dampened performance, and repeated threat situations theoretically can lead to disassociation from the relevant domain. The effects of stereotype threat may exacerbate the aptitude-performance gap and relatively lower attainment observed among African Americans in intellectual domains and U.S. women in math and science domains, for example. Thus, unmitigated stereotype threat can interfere with the development and expression of talent, particularly the talent of underrepresented group members. However, educators can take steps to prevent stereotype threat from affecting performance, as described in this entry.

The first description and studies of stereotype threat came from Claude Steele and Joshua Aronson who were concerned with the underperformance of African Americans in academic contexts. These researchers found that African American students and their White counterparts performed equally well except when the stereotype of African Americans' intellectual and academic inferiority to Whites was made salient. African Americans' underperformance occurred when a task was described as diagnostic of intellectual ability (rather than nondiagnostic) or when participants were asked to report their race before the task. Stereotype threat effect evidence has been collected with stereotypes based on gender, race, age, socioeconomic status, sexual orientation, and academic major; in a variety of contexts including general intelligence, memory, math skills, verbal skills, political knowledge, child care ability, and athleticism; and with student populations from elementary through graduate school. However, researchers warn against interpreting stereotype threat theory as the cause for achievement gaps and a few investigations have resulted in a lack of support for the theory.

Underperformance on a task is one outcome of stereotype threat; however, other outcomes have been detected. Performance on subsequent tasks may suffer when those tasks draw on cognitive resources similar to those required for the initial task. Also, under stereotype threat conditions, individuals tend to downplay their interest in the domain and their interest in other relevant areas. For example, African Americans under stereotype threat conditions will report lower levels of interest in stereotypically African American interests such as basketball and jazz music, compared with African Americans under neutral conditions. Another outcome of stereotype threat is stereotype lift—salience of positive stereotypes along with social identity can bolster performance. For example, when men are reminded of the gender and math stereotype, they experience slightly improved math performance.

Several conditions influence whether stereotype threat affects performance. Stereotype threat affects people who care about and identify with the domain of interest or who value the social identity of interest. Women math majors are more likely to be susceptible to stereotype threat than are women humanities majors because of their motivation to disprove the stereotype. Stereotype threat can occur at all levels of attainment but requires tasks that challenge individuals' abilities. The quantitative SAT will not prompt a math graduate student to question the veracity of the stereotype. However, the same test may prompt a mathematically gifted middle school girl to wonder whether the difficulty she is facing is because boys really are better at math.

Finally, personal endorsement of the relevant stereotype is not required; rather, there must be an awareness of the relevant stereotype in the culture. As stereotypes differ between cultures, the groups of people vulnerable to stereotype threat as well as the domains in which the threat may occur also differ between cultures. For example, Asian American women are less vulnerable to stereotype threat in the math domain because although U.S.

residents hold a stereotype that women are inferior in math, U.S. residents also hold a stereotype that Asians are superior in math. In contrast, Canadians do not hold a stereotype about Asians and math so Asian Canadian women are as vulnerable to stereotype threat as are any other Canadian women.

Stereotype threat is frequently studied in laboratory experiments and numerous triggers of stereotype threat have been identified through this work. These triggers vary in their degree of subtlety but all can occur in natural achievement settings. Blatant reminders of the stereotype can induce threat conditions. In experimental studies, such reminders have included video perpetuating the stereotype and research articles supporting the veracity of the stereotype. However, even subliminal priming has been shown to create stereotype threat effects. Many laboratory stereotype threat conditions are derived from typical testing conditions. Test description can create stereotype threat conditions when a test is described as diagnostic of ability or as having shown differences in scores along group lines in the past. Also, stereotype threat effect can occur when test-takers are asked to report their group membership (gender, race) before the test.

Several hypothesized mechanisms of stereotype threat effect have been tested with few clear results. For example, anxiety has been shown to mediate stereotype threat effect through biological measures (blood pressure and heart rate variability) and through behavioral measures (observed fidgeting), but not through self-report of anxiety. Some evidence supports the hypothesis that stereotype threat increases intrusive negative thoughts, which decreases working memory capacity. Stereotype threat may also induce prevention focus, increasing risk aversion, whereas positive stereotypes induce promotion focus, increasing creativity. Neurological investigations have provided support for a combination of these factors as stereotype threat mediators. Compared with positive stereotypes, stereotype threat activates the right amygdala, which is associated with emotional arousal and fear conditioning, as well as the ventral prefrontal cortex, which is associated with simple working memory. Positive stereotypes activate complex working memory processing regions (anterior prefrontal cortex) as well as regions related to task procedures.

Although stereotype threat creates biological effects, improving performance expectancies can ameliorate the performance effects of stereotype threat. One way to diminish stereotype threat is to weaken the strength of group membership. This has been accomplished by discussing the social construction of social groups such as race, listing similarities between groups in the performance domain, and individuating—describing one's personal traits or opinions. Alternatively, the applicability of the stereotype can be challenged. This can be accomplished by highlighting achieved subgroup membership through a counterstereotype. An example of a counterstereotype is that students at elite colleges are less vulnerable to stereotype threat than are those at less prestigious colleges. This may or may not be true, but the sentiment can protect students from stereotype threat effects if they have attained acceptance to an elite college. The stereotype can also be challenged by the presence of role models who debunk the stereotype (e.g., a high-achieving woman mathematician). Finally, individuals can be convinced that the evaluator will not be swayed by stereotypes if the evaluation criteria are clear and objective and if the evaluator conveys a belief that all the students can succeed at the task regardless of group membership.

Anne S. Beauchamp

See also Academic Self-Concept; Classroom Practices; Intelligence Testing; Underrepresentation

Further Readings

Jordan, A. H., & Lovett, B. J. (2007). Stereotype threat and test performance: A primer for school psychologists. *Journal of School Psychology, 45*, 45–59.

Steele, C. M., & Aronson, J. (1995). Stereotype threat and the intellectual test performance of African Americans. *Journal of Personality and Social Psychology, 69*, 797–811.

Stigmatization

The psychosocial experience of giftedness is also a rich area of inquiry. There are a myriad of messages and expectations about giftedness in the general population. Gifted youth can be buffeted by these sometimes unrealistic, incompatible messages. What's more, the paradox of being both lauded and spurned for the same behaviors is a source of conflict for these children. They are left to wonder how best to please themselves and others. Tracy Cross and Laurence Coleman have suggested that the social cognition of gifted youth deserves attention.

Social cognition is manifested in the integration of social experiences with behavior. Social cognition describes the way people think and reason about social situations as they observe the social world around them. People use social cognitive processes to gather information about the social setting. This information can influence social interactions with others. It is important to attend to the social cognition of gifted youth in school because school environments teach gifted youth what their giftedness means.

Many gifted children and adolescents speak of feeling different from their peers. Often this feeling of differentness is a result of being labeled *gifted*. In the course of navigating the social world of schools, this differentness can cause gifted youth to feel they stand out so much that their uniqueness is stigmatizing. Erving Goffman, the creator of stigma theory, defined stigma as the process whereby a person deemed deviant is subject to global devaluation. He further contends that stigma resides in the gap between a person's virtual reality and actual identity. Cross and his colleagues reason that this discrepancy between virtual and actual identity is a subjective judgment of a privileged in-group. A person comes to be stigmatized upon the failure to live into expectations of suitability and normalcy, as this entry describes.

However, giftedness is not a "visible" stigma, like gender or ethnicity or physical ability. So, rather than compete with "myths" others create about giftedness, gifted youth may choose to control the information others have of them. According to Goffman's theory, this is a way of managing the influence of stigmatization. Though children in elementary school make such decisions, the lived reality of gifted adolescents encourages them to be especially judicious about information about them in circulation in a school setting. This is largely because of the importance of peer groups and identity development during adolescence. Adolescents can be hypervigilant about how they are perceived. Erik Erikson notes that teens are heavily invested in how they appear to others and give less credence to a personal sense of individuation.

Not all gifted youth feel they need to censor what others learn about them. Moreover, giftedness as a social stigma is situation-specific. Readers should not overgeneralize about the stigmatization of giftedness presented here to such a degree that they divorce this aspect of a gifted youth's social cognition from context. In addition, not all gifted youth are surrounded by peers and adults who make them feel giftedness is so strange or worrisome that it affects them socially. That being said, Cross and Coleman suggest that the *stigma of giftedness paradigm* can be a constructive frame for the school-based social cognition of gifted youth. The three tenets to the paradigm are as follows:

1. Gifted and talented students want to have normal social interactions.
2. They believe that people treat them differently when aware of their giftedness.
3. They can influence how others interact with them by manipulating the information others have about them through various coping strategies.

By being aware of how gifted students might feel stigmatized and the coping strategies they use to deal with stigmatization, counselors, teachers, and parents can assist gifted students in finding constructive and positive ways of thinking about their giftedness and interacting with others.

Tracy L. Cross and Andrea Dawn Frazier

See also Academic Advising; Anti-Intellectualism; Attitudes Toward Gifted; Cultural Conceptions of Giftedness

Further Readings

Coleman, L. J., & Cross, T. L. (2005). *Being gifted in school* (2nd ed.). Waco, TX: Prufrock Press.

Cross, T. L., & Coleman, L. J. (1993). The social cognition of gifted adolescents: An exploration of the stigma of giftedness paradigm. *Roeper Review, 16*(1), 37–40.

Cross, T. L., & Coleman, L. J. (1995). Psychosocial diversity among gifted adolescents: An exploratory study of two groups. *Roeper Review, 17*(3), 181–185.

Cross, T. L., Coleman, L. J., & Terharr-Yonkers, M. (1991). The social cognition of gifted adolescents in school: Managing the stigma of giftedness. *Journal for the Education of the Gifted, 15*(1), 44–55.
Erikson, E. H. (1979). *Dimensions of a new identity: The Jefferson lectures in the humanities.* New York: W. W. Norton.
Goffman, E. (1963). *Stigma: Notes on the management of spoiled identity.* Englewood Cliffs, NJ: Prentice Hall.
Manor-Bulock, R., Look, C., & Dixon, D. N. (1995). Is giftedness socially stigmatizing? The impact of high achievement on social interactions. *Journal for the Education of the Gifted, 18*(3), 319–338.
Swiatek, M. A. (1998). Helping gifted adolescents cope with social stigma. *Gifted Child Today, 21*(1), 42–46.

Storytelling

Storytelling is a communication process in which at least one person tells a story to at least one listener using oral or signed language. Storytellers usually narrate stories in person directly to an audience although they can also do so indirectly through media such as radio, TV, computer, CD, and DVD. Storytelling calls into play visual, cognitive, and emotional content in the minds of both storyteller and audience, giving teachers a flexible tool for engaging students and allowing gifts, creativity, and talent to surface.

The word *storyteller* can designate a teller of a people's history or a performer who seeks to elevate narration to an art form by using verbal and nonverbal communication skills and carefully chosen language, sometimes improvised. The nonverbal communication aspects (gestures, postures, sounds, facial and vocal expression) play a large part in communicating meaning interpreted by the teller for an audience. For these reasons, a writer who writes for a reader is a storywriter rather than a storyteller. This entry describes the roots and renaissance of storytelling, and discusses storytelling in education

Roots of Storytelling

Stories can be true or fictional, exaggerated, humorous, fantasies, personal accounts, and traditional tales such as legends, myths, epics, fables, folktales, and fairy tales from various cultures. Elders across the ages have relied on oral tradition to transmit from one generation to the next the collective learning, wisdom, and histories of their people. Religions of the world have relied on stories and parables told by their shamans, priests, healers, rabbis, and ministers to convey deeply held spiritual roots. Rural villagers still gather to listen to tales that entertain and convey important information and moral codes, which have guided people throughout the ages. Traditionally, in Ghana, West Africa, a griot, the storyteller-historian, helps villagers preserve storytelling. Teachers and parents everywhere use storytelling to help children develop empathy and to recall content by using stories in various formats.

But in 20th-century United States, with the advent of television and access to books, the live storyteller lost prominence, except for some librarians and rural tellers. Storytelling appeared destined to become a quaint folk art. In the 1970s and 1980s, however, storytelling began a rebirth.

Storytelling Renaissance

Jimmy Neil Smith, a teacher of journalism, grasped the value of storytelling as an art form and as a tool for literacy and cultural transmission. In 1973 in Jonesborough, Tennessee, Smith organized the first National Storytelling Festival, which signaled a national movement to preserve and perpetuate the art of storytelling. During the 1990s and 2000s, festivals and competitions expanded rapidly and included more diverse voices. Although storytelling was considered a form of theatrical arts, professional storytellers along with the help of the National Storytelling Network and the International Storytelling Center claimed storytelling an art form in its own right. The oral tradition began to be included in school-enrichment clusters, artist-in-education programs, and several graduate college curriculums. A National Youth Storytelling Showcase gave students a stage on which to perform their stories. Yet, the larger promise of storytelling as a fertile resource for identifying and supporting students' creativity, talent development, and learning was only beginning to be studied and understood.

Storytelling in Education

The national definition of gifted and talented students includes categories for talent in leadership, specific academic areas, creativity, intellect, and artistic abilities. Storytelling allows students to find and develop talents in the performing arts, creative use of language, and leadership. Students use visual-spatial intelligence in mapping or sketching scenes to aid retelling without reading aloud. In the process of performing a story, students explore communication and thinking skills they will use in their careers. For example, students learn to adapt their range of vocal and physical expressiveness for various audiences. The process of storytelling also invokes higher-order mental activities such as analysis, synthesis, evaluation, visualization, improvisation, prediction, inferential thinking, humor, perspective taking, and problem solving. For creative, gifted, and talented students disenchanted with schooling, the art of storytelling can serve to capture attention and, in some cases, keep students in school.

There are no ceilings on the creativity, vocabulary, amount of detail, or expressiveness, so teachers can use storytelling as an alternate way to discover students' gifts and talents. Teachers observe students as they engage their kinesthetic, musical, and linguistic intelligences to find the best words, sounds, and gestures to convey the meaning of their stories. In addition, the human reservoir of stories is so vast and diverse that virtually any subject can be enriched by a teacher's modification of the curriculum through the artistic use of storytelling. From the physical and mathematical to the social sciences and humanities, to professional studies such as business and law, most subjects are enriched through stories that teachers and students tell to engage minds and memories.

Joseph Renzulli and Sally Reis, researchers from the National Research Center on the Gifted and Talented, encourage teachers to create interest-development centers and enrichment clusters, which promote students' exploration of the literature, methods, and materials of practicing professionals. Student storytellers participate by collecting oral histories or stories, performing, teaching, and helping organize festivals and competitions. Regional, state, and national forums exist that offer aspiring tellers venues to share stories and interact with peers and professionals. In this way, creative, gifted, and talented youth become engaged and challenged inside and outside the classroom, achieving excellence in accordance with professional standards and their own interests.

Gail N. Herman

See also Enrichment Triad Model; Multiple Intelligences; Performing Arts; Talent Development

Further Readings

Hamilton, M., & Weiss, M. (2005). *Children tell stories: Teaching and using storytelling in the classroom* (2nd ed). Katonah, NY: Richard C. Owen.

Mello, R. (2001, February). The power of storytelling: How oral narrative influences children's relationships in classrooms. *International Journal of Education & the Arts,* 2(1). Retrieved July 1, 2008, from http://ijea.asu.edu/v2n1

National Storytelling Network: http://www.storynet.org, http://www.storynet.com

Norfolk, S., Stenson, J., & Williams, D. (2006). *The storytelling classroom: Applications across the curriculum.* Westport, CT: Libraries Unlimited.

Renzulli, J. S., & Reis, S. M. (1997). *The schoolwide enrichment model: A how-to guide for educational excellence* (2nd ed.). Mansfield Center, CT: Creative Learning Press.

Structure of Intellect

The *structure of intellect* (SI) model of intelligence, described in this entry was developed by J. P. Guilford and his associates in the Psychological Laboratory at the University of Southern California. Guilford disagreed with the makers of the major intelligence tests that intelligence was one broad unitary ability. Guilford defined intelligence as a collection of abilities for processing different kinds of information in a variety of ways. Using factor analysis to isolate various components of intelligence eventually led to a three-dimensional model of intellectual abilities called the *structure of intellect* (SI). Guilford's SI model extended Louis Thurstone's theory of 7 primary abilities of intelligence, into 120 separate components or factors.

The three dimensions (operations, content, and products) of the SI model form the various factors of intelligence. Guilford believed every mental task always involved one kind of operation performed on one type of content resulting in one kind of product. Therefore, each factor within the model is characterized by one element from each area: one operation, one kind of content, and one product.

The operations dimension of the original SI model involved five kinds of intellectual operations: cognition, memory, divergent production, convergent production, and evaluation. Guilford considered cognition to be the first and most basic of the operations. Cognition is the ability to discover, comprehend, and understand information. The memory process is used to store information in the brain. Memory is one of the oldest and best known of the intellectual operations. Memory involves the storage of information as well as the ability to retrieve the information later. Guilford characterized the process of retrieval as either narrow or broad and called the broad retrieval process divergent production because one is searching for a variety of alternative ideas and building on information to create new ideas. Divergent production is knowledge generation or construction. The narrower retrieval process is called convergent production—the search to find a particular item. In convergent production, the goal is to locate the "best" idea or the idea that meets the criteria. Convergent thinking is a rigorous activity that moves beyond memory retrieval. In convergent thinking, one has to search systematically and follow principles when converging for the "right" solution. The last of the operations is evaluation—the determination of the accuracy, validity, or suitability of information.

The content dimension illustrates the broad types of information to which the operations are applied. There are four types of content: figural, symbolic, semantic, and behavioral. Figural content is information in its visual form. This type includes shapes, objects, and forms. Symbolic content is information in the forms of letters, numbers, or the use of codes as in music. Semantic content is information in the form of words or ideas that are associated with abstract meaning. Finally, behavioral content refers to content in the form of actions and expressions.

The product dimension describes how content is organized. The six product areas listed in order of increasing complexity are units, classes, relations, systems, transformations, and implications. A *unit* is a single piece of information—a letter, a word, a number. *Classes* is used to describe how items of information belong together, the grouping together of units that share common characteristics and knowing why each item belongs in the group. *Relations* is the finding of connections or associations between items of information, differentiating information based on differences, linking information into a sequence, or creating analogies to describe the information more clearly to others. *Systems* is a sense of ordering information for a specific purpose such as putting words together to build sentences or language structures. Mathematical symbols and numbers are put together to form equations or represent problems that need to be solved. *Transformations* is an abstract ability. A transformation task involves redefining and modifying original information to create new information. The last product is implications, the most abstract of the abilities. *Implications* is the ability to see consequences, to make inferences, and to generalize and apply learned information to new situations.

In the early 1980s, Guilford separated figural content into the two areas of visual, information gained through seeing, and auditory, information gained through hearing. This separation brought the number of factors of intelligence to 150. A year later, he separated memory into memory recording (encoding) and memory retention (recall), increasing the number of different intellectual factors in the SI model to 180.

Guilford's contribution goes beyond redefining intelligence more broadly. He also brought a focus to the understanding of creativity. Guilford saw creativity as a part of intelligence, so it had a prominent place in his SI model. His model for divergent thinking within the SI model is quite comprehensive. When one combines the process (operation) of divergent production across the model with different content categories and different products, 24 different factors emerge. Then, add in the additional combinations built on the product area of transformation, which Guilford felt was essential to creative thinking, and the number of factors increases. Several creativity tests are built on Guilford's conception of divergent production.

By 1969, Mary Meeker had taken on the task of applying the Guilford SI model to educational problems ranging from a better understanding of learning disabilities to improving reading comprehension in the classroom. Her work refers to the *structure of intellect model* as the SOI model.

Guilford's work is not without critics of both his initial theory and his method for determining the factors of intelligence. However, the SI model did open the field of intelligence to thinking about newer models of intelligence

Joyce E. Juntune

See also Divergent Thinking; Intelligence Theories; Relationship of Creativity to Intelligence

Further Readings

Guilford, J. P. (1977). *Way beyond IQ*. Buffalo, NY: Creative Education Foundation.

Meeker, M. N. (1969). *The structure of the intellect: Its interpretation and uses*. Columbus, OH: Charles Merrill.

Sternberg, R. J., & Grigorenko, E. L. (2000–2001). Guilford's structure of intellect model and model of creativity: Contributions and limitations. *Creativity Research Journal, 13*(3 & 4), 309–316.

Student Attitudes

Attitude is the gifted student's visible manifestation of inner adaptation to the environment. Although much research describes factors that can lead to gifted students' negative attitudes toward school, there is also a great deal of evidence that many gifted students are well adjusted and, therefore, quite likely to demonstrate positive attitudes toward school. This entry describes characteristics and attitudes of gifted students, factors that influence attitude, and implications.

Characteristics and Attitudes

Lewis Terman, in his 1925 classic longitudinal study of gifted individuals, found that 60 to 80 percent of his research subjects had qualities of humor, truthfulness, conscientiousness, and leadership. Furthermore, these characteristics carried into adulthood. In a review of research in gifted education that spans 70 years, Linda Silverman found that in addition to positive characteristics similar to Terman's findings, as a group, gifted children show diminished tendencies to boast, engage in delinquent activity, aggress, withdraw, or be domineering.

In research with gifted students in rural areas and small towns, Virginia Burney and Tracy Cross found that despite the challenges these students encountered with limited academic course offerings and few academic peers, many had positive attitudes toward school. Gifted students often described their small schools as having a family-like atmosphere. They experienced little stigma from being academically gifted and they had many opportunities for extracurricular activities that allowed them to be seen as more than a single dimension of giftedness.

Others find evidence of a positive attitude even when it is partially hidden in underachievement. Betsy McCoach and Del Siegle researched the differences between high- and low-achieving gifted high school students using the School Attitude Assessment Survey-R. They assessed five factors that include academic self-concept, attitudes toward school, attitudes toward teachers, motivation/self-regulation, and goal valuation, which means the value students' place on academic goals or school assignments.

In four areas, attitudes toward school, attitudes toward teachers, self-regulation, and goal valuation, McCoach found significant differences between the achieving and underachieving students. However, there was no significant difference in the academic self-concept factor. Regardless of differences found in the other factors, these students demonstrated a positive attitude about their learning abilities. Both groups were equally confident in their own intellectual abilities and inwardly maintained positive attitudes toward themselves as learners.

In Maureen Neihart's review of the literature on social adjustment in gifted students, she found most studies revealed high to normal levels of adjustment among the subjects. In reviewing discreet categories of adjustment, however, she found a correlation between the thinking processes of those with certain psychiatric disorders and highly creative adults. However, she cautioned against extrapolating the results obtained with adults to creatively gifted children in the midst of development. Neihart pointed out that the psychological well-being of a gifted child is related to the type of giftedness, the educational fit, and the child's personal characteristics such as self-perceptions, temperament, and life circumstances.

Factors That Influence Attitude

Attitudes of the gifted toward school are as diverse as gifted children. Some of the factors that can influence the attitudes of gifted students toward school include age, type and level of giftedness, disability, gender, race, teachers, and curricula.

Age, Type, Level of Giftedness, and Disability

Attitude depends on the student's intellectual and emotional interaction with factors within the environment. Age, type, and level of giftedness can influence the attitude of gifted students from the youngest through the college level. In gifted children, mental age can be seriously out of sync with chronological age, causing frustration for the child in a classroom where the content, processes, and pace are not commensurate with his or her capabilities.

Silverman points out that there are many variations within the construct of asynchrony. The discomfort of asynchrony is more acutely felt by the most highly gifted children with IQ 160 and higher. Leta Hollingworth noted that children between the ages of 4 and 9 feel the social isolation most intensely, but when they were allowed to move to an appropriate grade level, the loneliness and social isolation disappeared. Neihart cautions, however, against assuming that children with IQs at 160 and above will necessarily experience social and emotional difficulties. She points out that, as with highly creative children, appropriate educational placement is essential.

Children who are both highly gifted and have learning and emotional disabilities experience a more extreme form of asynchrony that can affect attitude. Although these students show high ability in abstract verbal reasoning outside the classroom, they may exhibit difficulties within the classroom with auditory and visual processing, handwriting, perceptual motor problems, dyslexia, or emotional challenges. When emotional and learning disabilities mask giftedness, the student acutely feels the frustration caused by the discrepancy between expectations, both personal and external, and actual achievement.

Gender and Race

There is a large amount of research on how gender influences the gifted throughout school and into adulthood. Barbara Kerr explored gifted girls' shifting attitudes toward their own giftedness in Smart Girls. Kerr and her colleagues also found that girls perceived giftedness to be more of a social liability than boys did, but that boys and girls were both positive about the academic benefits of being labeled as gifted. Yet, for gifted minority students, especially young Black men, complex issues of racial identity further confound attitude in the area of academic performance. John Ogbu suggests that underachievement in school is related to peer influence. Some young African Americans interpret academic achievement as a betrayal of their cultural group and adopt an oppositional social identity in a response to racism and prejudice. Shaun Harper, however, found in his interviews with 32 high-achieving Black men undergraduates at six major predominantly White universities that they felt supported in their leadership and academic pursuits by other Black men students.

Educational Fit

Gifted children's cognitive needs are closely and visibly interwoven with emotional well-being, so attitude in school is most often a function of appropriate educational fit. Full-time self-contained gifted classrooms, part-time pull-out programs, and curriculum differentiation within the general education classroom are all structures used to provide gifted students with more appropriate educational environments.

Recent research on acceleration shows that acceleration is a valuable option in serving the needs of gifted students. A wide variety of acceleration alternatives have been examined including early school entry, grade skipping, and early entrance to college with a variety of ways each method can be carried out. Concerns about the social-emotional effects of acceleration were found negligible in comparison with the positive academic effect.

A better educational fit is often needed to alleviate the boredom in an unchallenging classroom that can lead to underachievement. Lannie Kanevsky and Tacey Keighley investigated what boredom meant to 10 underachieving gifted students who were selected by school counselors in a suburban Canadian school district. These researchers uncovered pedagogical practices that these underachieving students felt would provide a better educational fit within their classrooms.

Like McCoach and Siegle, Kanevsky and Keighley found that these students were confident in their academic learning abilities. The students articulately described their learning needs in terms of five C's that represent control, choice, challenge, complexity, and caring. The students wanted choices about the content they were required to study and more experiences grounded in the real world. They wanted hands-on assignments and processes that included high levels of thinking and involved their emotions and interests. The students wanted an increased pace of learning with fewer repetitions and more choice in the learning environment. They wanted choice in assignments, flexible time to explore a topic in depth, and an opportunity to select members for group work. The students wanted caring teachers who showed respect for them as learners.

Implications

Gifted children are diverse and complex individuals. Many are well-adjusted hard-working students who achieve their academic and personal goals. Some are, as James Delisle describes, gifted nonproducers who are confident of their abilities but choose not to do schoolwork that they consider inappropriate and irrelevant. Still others underachieve because of low self-esteem, lack of independence, and physical, emotional, or cognitive circumstances that affect learning. Yet, research studies that concern attitudes of gifted students toward school consistently point to a universal need for classrooms with knowledgeable, caring, observant teachers. Such teachers are aware of the learning needs of all students, including gifted students. These teachers are able to design curriculum that meets both the intellectual and social-emotional needs of students and can recognize the need for appropriate placements that support each student in reaching his or her full potential.

Christy T. Folsom

See also Academic Self-Concept; Asynchrony; Emotional Development; Guidance; Teacher Attitudes

Further Readings

Burney, V. H., & Cross, T. (2006). Impoverished students with academic promise in rural settings: 10 lessons from Project Aspire. *Gifted Child Today, 29*(2), 14–21.

Folsom, C. (2008). *Teaching for intellectual and emotional learning: A model for creating powerful curriculum*. Lanham, MD: Rowman & Littlefield Education.

Gibson, M. A., & Ogbu, J. U. (Eds.). (1991). *Minority status and schooling: A comparative study of immigrant and involuntary minorities*. New York: Garland.

Harper, S. R. (2006). Peer support for African American male college achievement: Beyond internalized racism and the burden of "acting White." *Journal of Men's Studies, 14*(3), 337–358.

Hollingworth, L. S. (1942). *Children above IQ 180: Their origin and development*. New York: World Book.

Kanevsky, L., & Keighley, T. (2003). On gifted students in school: To produce or not to produce? Understanding boredom and the honor in underachievement. *Roeper Review, 26*(1), 20–28.

Kerr, B.A. (1997). *Smart girls: A new psychology of girls, women, and giftedness*. Scottsdale, AZ: Great Potential Press.

McCoach, D., & Siegle, D. (2003). Factors that differentiate underachieving gifted students from high-achieving gifted students. *Gifted Child Quarterly, 47*(2), 144–153.

Neihart, M., Reis, S. M., Robinson, N. M., & Moon, S. M. (Eds.). (2002). *The social and emotional development of gifted children*. Washington, DC: National Association for Gifted Children.

Robinson, N. M. (2004). Effects of academic acceleration on the social-emotional status of gifted students. In N. Colangelo, S. G. Assouline, & M. U. M. Gross (Eds.), *A nation deceived: How schools hold back America's brightest students*

(Vol. 2, pp. 59–67). Iowa City, IA: Connie Belin & Jacqueline N. Blank International Center for Gifted Education and Talent Development.

Silverman, L. K. (1997). The construct of asynchronous development. *Peabody Journal of Education, 72*(3/4), 36–58.

Study of Mathematically Precocious Youth

The Study of Mathematically Precocious Youth (SMPY), described in this entry, is a large-scale longitudinal project devoted to understanding the characteristics and needs of talented individuals—as children and adults—and the determinants of their varying paths of development and achievement throughout the life span. (Indeed, "SMPY" is something of a misnomer because the project has always focused on abilities in mathematics and science and has come to include verbal and spatial abilities, as well. Nevertheless, the project's name was maintained for the sake of consistency.) SMPY was begun in 1971 by Julian C. Stanley at Johns Hopkins University and is currently directed by Camilla P. Benbow and David Lubinski at Peabody College of Vanderbilt University. When completed, the study will span 50 years and include 5,000 individuals in five cohorts, individuals who were identified between the years 1972 and 1997.

SMPY is premised on the idea of *appropriate developmental placement,* in which students are presented with a curriculum tailored to their rate of learning and intellectual curiosity. Most precocious students prefer an accelerated curriculum and one with greater breadth and complexity to maintain their interest and motivation to learn. Of course, precocious students are not a single type; they exhibit great variability in cognitive and noncognitive characteristics. Like other students, their talents fall in some areas but not in others, and the level and pattern of their abilities need to be assessed, as well as their particular constellation of interests and values. SMPY has introduced and provided empirical support for a model showing how abilities and personal preferences can be used together to understand the student's developmental path and achievements.

Four of SMPY's five cohorts were created by talent searches of students at age 13 that were conducted in the periods 1972–1974, 1976–1978, 1980–1983, and 1992–1997. The talent searches were conducted using *above-level testing,* in this case, by administering college entrance examinations, such as the SAT, to seventh and eighth graders who scored in the top 3 percent, approximately, on conventional achievement tests administered in their schools. Individuals in these cohorts vary between the top 3 percent and the top .01 percent in quantitative or verbal reasoning ability. A fifth cohort consisted of first- and second-year graduate students in top U.S. mathematics or science programs in 1992. This cohort is used primarily to assess the generalizability of SMPY's model for identifying mathematic and scientific potential. Benbow and colleagues and Lubinski and colleagues conducted 20-year longitudinal follow-ups on SMPY's first three cohorts, as part of the larger plan to follow up the first four cohorts at ages 18, 23, 33, 50, and 65. The fifth cohort has been followed up at age 35 and will be again at ages 50 and 65. So far, seven books and more than 400 articles have been based on SMPY; many recent articles are found on the SMPY Web site.

SMPY findings have shown that students' accelerated learning is associated with both achievement and satisfaction in later life. The findings attest particularly to the importance of assessing individual differences *within* the top 1 percent of ability. Individual differences at this level affect the prediction of significant achievement (e.g., publishing a novel, achieving tenure at a major U.S. university, earning a patent). Not surprisingly, individual differences in ability *pattern* (e.g., salient verbal abilities relative to quantitative and spatial abilities manifested in early adolescence) affect the prediction of the specific nature of achievements in later life (e.g., excelling in the humanities versus science). Thus, those with comparatively greater talent in mathematics or science are said to have a *mathematic* or *scientific tilt* and tend to seek educational and career experiences in science, technology, engineering, and mathematics (STEM), and those with a *verbal tilt* seek corresponding experiences in the humanities. In 2007 and 2008, Greg Park, Lubinski, and Benbow provided empirical examples of the importance of ability level and pattern in predicting achievement.

SMPY's longitudinal findings during the past 35 years point to the importance of specific abilities beyond IQ. But they also suggest that traditional intellectual assessment in quantitative and verbal reasoning can be improved. The current view is that there are *three* content domains in the intellectual repertoire: verbal, quantitative, and spatial reasoning. This suggests that spatial reasoning measures should be added to talent search assessment procedures. It is estimated that approximately half of those in the top 1 percent in spatial ability are missed by talent searches restricted to verbal and quantitative reasoning. This neglected student population could be much better identified and served. The school curriculum could be expanded beyond its current verbal and quantitative emphases, to prepare students better for specialized training and careers in such fields as architecture, engineering, and the physical sciences. This is quite possibly the largest resource of unidentified human capital in the United States, such that the area is in need of investigation.

SMPY will soon begin conducting its first follow-ups of 50-year-olds. As its cohorts mature, SMPY will focus increasingly on the development of eminence, as well as on what experiences are needed to promote achievement in adulthood. This is a relatively unexplored time of life, especially for intellectually talented women who until recently were excluded from many educational and career opportunities. The developmental patterns of intellectually talented women have not been fully explored, and SMPY plans to contribute in this area.

David Lubinski and Camilla P. Benbow

See also Acceleration/*A Nation Deceived;* History of Gifted Education in the United States; Learning Styles; Mathematical Talent; Talent Searches; Verbal Ability

Further Readings

Benbow, C. P., Lubinski, D., Shea, D. L., & Eftekhari-Sanjani, H. (2000). Sex differences in mathematical reasoning ability: Their status 20 years later. *Psychological Science, 11,* 474–480. Retrieved from http://www.vanderbilt.edu/Peabody/SMPY/SexDiffs.pdf

Benbow, C. P., & Stanley, J. C. (1996). Inequity in equity: How current educational equity policies place able students at risk. *Psychology, Public Policy, and Law, 2,* 249–293. Retrieved from http://www.vanderbilt.edu/Peabody/SMPY/InequityInEquity.pdf

Lubinski, D., & Benbow, C. P. (2000). States of excellence. *American Psychologist, 55,* 137–150.

Lubinski, D., & Benbow, C. P. (2006). Study of mathematically precocious youth after 35 years: Uncovering antecedents for the development of math-science expertise. *Perspectives on Psychological Science, 1,* 316–345. Retrieved from http://www.vanderbilt.edu/Peabody/SMPY/DoingPsychScience2006.pdf

Lubinski, D., Benbow, C. P., Webb, R. M., & Bleske-Rechek, A. (2006). Tracking exceptional human capital over two decades. *Psychological Science, 17,* 194–199. Retrieved from http://www.vanderbilt.edu/Peabody/SMPY/PsychScience2006.pdf

Park, G., Lubinski, D., & Benbow, C. P. (2007). Contrasting intellectual patterns for creativity in the arts and sciences: Tracking intellectually precocious youth over 25 years. *Psychological Science, 18,* 948–952.

Park, G., Lubinski, D., & Benbow, C. P. (2008). Ability differences among people who have commensurate degrees matter for scientific creativity. *Psychological Science, 19*(10), 957–961.

The Study of Mathematically Precocious Youth: http://www.vanderbilt.edu/Peabody/SMPY

Wai, J., Lubinski, D., & Benbow, C. P. (in press). Spatial ability for STEM domains: Aligning over fifty years of cumulative psychological knowledge solidifies its importance. *Journal of Educational Psychology.*

Webb, R. M., Lubinski, D., & Benbow, C. P. (2007). Spatial ability: A neglected dimension in talent searches for intellectually precocious youth. *Journal of Educational Psychology, 99,* 397–420.

Substance Abuse

Substance abuse among young children and adolescents has proven to be a rapidly changing phenomenon. Beginning in the 1960s, the use of illicit drugs and alcohol significantly increased among adolescents. From a public health perspective, the rise and incidence of substance abuse (e.g., amphetamines, methamphetamines, hallucinogens, barbiturate sedatives, cocaine, opioids, ecstasy, heroin, crystal methamphetamine, cannabis, inhalants, and excessive use of over-the-counter and prescription drugs), cigarette smoking, and alcohol use among teens has been the focus of considerable international attention. Such behaviors often begin during adolescent and young adulthood. Beginning in 1975, the use of a variety of substances among adolescents has been systematically tracked. Both the U.S. National Institute on Drug Abuse and National Institutes of Health has tracked this behavior through the *Monitoring the Future* annual survey of high school students. The increased use of substances by adolescents has been noted in many countries throughout the world. Significant policy changes and programs have been implemented as a result of the rising problems associated with substance use. This entry provides an overview and discusses risk factors and consequences of substance abuse, along with its implications for highly creative and talented individuals.

Overview

The most recent Monitoring the Future Study published in 2006 in the United States provides a disturbing picture of adolescent drug use. Historically, although there has been a decline since the 1970s in the percentage of adolescents reporting experimentation and ingestion of a variety of substances, there seems to be a relative plateauing of the use of many substances during the past few years. However, new recent findings suggest an increase in some substances, including hallucinogenic drugs such as psilocybin (mushrooms), mescaline, and crystal methamphetamine. Equally disturbing are the findings of an increase in binge drinking among young adults, although recent data from the Monitoring the Future study has suggested alcohol use and binge drinking may have leveled off for adolescents and are significantly below the levels of the 1980s.

The Monitoring the Future study also points to the high numbers of young people using prescription-type medications. The increase in use of sedatives, antidepressants, and other nonheroin-based narcotics has been associated with an increase in the use of other psychotherapeutic drug use.

Although a large percentage of youth report experimentation with drugs and alcohol and are not likely to have substance abuse problems, certain groups are more likely to report heavy excessive use, multidrug use, and social and economic problems resulting from substance use, with some experiencing substance abuse and dependence. Emerging evidence seems to indicate that adolescents may be engaging in regular substance use as a self-medicating means of coping with untreated trauma, to change one's level of consciousness, and to help relieve underlying psychological disorders or stress.

Risk Factors

Strong empirical support indicates that substance use increases with age during adolescence, peaks during the mid- to late-20s, and then gradually declines during adulthood (inhalant use is the exception—typically decreasing during adolescence). Gender is also an important risk factor, with men typically engaged in more substance use and abuse. However, several recent empirical studies suggest that girls are similar to boys in their drinking of alcohol, binge drinking, getting intoxicated, smoking, and use of illicit drugs. The trends with respect to smoking among teens are encouraging in that there was a significant decrease in daily use. Nevertheless, nearly half of all adolescents have reported smoking cigarettes with approximately one-fifth of adolescents being current daily or occasional smokers.

Substance abuse and dependency among many adolescents remains sufficiently widespread to merit serious attention. Almost half of all teens (48 percent) are reported to have experimented with an illicit substance by the time they complete high school. Risk factors include inaccurate perceptions of the perceived risks and benefits associated with substance use; impulsivity and sensation- seeking behaviors; psychological disorders; poor parental and familial bonding; past or current sexual, physical, or psychological abuse; poor academic performance and failure; an inability to live up to expectations of others; ease and accessibility of substances; and societal values and cultural norms.

Consequences

Alcohol use among adolescents remains extremely widespread. The Monitoring the Future study suggests that approximately three-quarters of high school students have consumed alcohol by the time they leave school, with 56 percent of adolescents in Grade 12 and 20 percent of eighth graders reporting getting drunk. Repeated intoxication resulting from excessive alcohol consumption often results in significant self-injury, school truancy, and legal, familial, and academic problems.

Ample evidence indicates that substance abuse and dependency often lead to a multiplicity of physical, neurological, psychological, interpersonal, and social problems. Prolonged cigarette, alcohol, and substance abuse have been associated with a wide variety of diseases including cancer, respiratory problems, cardiovascular diseases, cognitive problems, liver disease, hypertension, neurological problems, and self-injurious behaviors.

Highly Creative and Talented Individuals

Although no strong data suggests that intellectually gifted adolescents deviate from typical teen norms in either direction with respect to substance use, individuals identified as highly creative and talented have often been associated in the public mind with a culture of drug use, rehabilitation, and in some cases, overdosing on a variety of substances. Hollywood is replete with promising young stars succumbing to the allure of the fast fix, excessive alcohol and substance use, and the need for instant gratification and exhilaration. Some evidence indicates that European and North American pop stars are at increased risk for a substance overdose related to a chronic drug or alcohol problem (25 percent of music stars' deaths were caused by excessive drug or drug-related behaviors).

The history books are replete with musicians, actors, authors, scientists, astronauts, and politicians having admitted to having significant alcohol or drug problems at some point in their lives. Nevertheless, a study of writers at the leading Iowa Writers Workshop, of artists at the School of the Art Institute of Chicago, midwestern popular musicians, and a comparison group of community college adults found that creative adults did not differ significantly in their use of substances from noncreative adults, and that students and apprentices in the arts were much more likely to abuse substances than were practicing creative writers, artists, and musicians.

Additional Considerations

Prevention and treatment programs targeting substance-abusing adolescents have resulted in variable success. A greater understanding of the risk factors associated with multiple forms of substance abuse will help clinicians, parents, and educators develop more effective strategies. Substance abuse among teenagers is an evolving phenomenon with new forms of drugs replacing old ones and remains an important public health and public policy problem. Substance use among gifted and creative students may lead to many of the problems that other twice-exceptional gifted experience—isolation, underachievement, and failure to fulfill dreams and goals.

Jeffrey L. Derevensky

See also Adolescent, Gifted; Adult, Gifted; Twice Exceptional

Further Readings

Adalf, E. M., & Paglia-Boak, A. (2005). *Drug use among Ontario students: Detailed OSDUS findings, 1977–2005*. Toronto: Centre for Addiction and Mental Health.

American Psychiatric Association. (2000). *Diagnostic and statistical manual of mental disorders: DSM-IV-TR* (4th ed.). Washington, DC: Author.

Bellis, M. A., Hennell, T., Lushey, C., Hughes, K., Tocque, K., & Ashtan, J. R. (2007). Elvis to Eminem: Quantifying the price of fame through early mortality of European and North American rock and pop stars. *Journal of Epidemiology & Community Health, 61*, 896–901.

Johnston, L. D., O'Malley, P. M., Bachman, J., & Schulenberg, J. E. (2007). *Monitoring the future national results on adolescent drug use: Overview of the key findings, 2006* (NIH Publication No. 07–6202). Bethesda, MD: National Institute on Drug Abuse.

Kerr, B. A., Shaffer, J., Chambers, C., & Hallowell, C. K. (1991). Substance use patterns of talented adults. *Journal of Creative Behavior, 25*, 145–154.

Paglia-Boak, A., & Adlaf, E. (2007). Substance use and harm in the general youth population. In Canadian Centre on Substance Abuse, *Substance abuse in Canada: Youth in focus*. Ottawa, Ontario: Canadian Centre on Substance Abuse.

Romer, D. (Ed.). (2003). *Reducing adolescent risk: Toward an integrated approach.* Thousand Oaks, CA: Sage.
Schuckit, M. A. (2000). *Drug and alcohol abuse: A clinical guide to diagnosis and treatment* (5th ed.). New York: Kluwer Academic.

SUICIDE

Are gifted and talented children and adolescents more prone to suicide than their non-gifted peers are? Presently, this question has proven difficult to answer. Tracy Cross and his colleagues have found that this is because of the complexity in defining giftedness, the lack of a designation of giftedness in data colleted on suicide, confidentiality diminishing access to information, psychological autopsies being expensive and time consuming, and the lethality of suicide causing certain information to be collected after a suicide completion. That being said, it can be assumed that gifted youth complete suicide at rates commensurate with the general population, at the minimum. Suicide is listed as the third leading cause of death in adolescents between the ages of 15 and 24. For youth ages 10 to 14, suicide rates increased by 51 percent between 1981 and 2004, according to the American Association of Suicidology. Internationally, suicidal rates are 0.5 for girls and 0.9 for boys per 100,000 in children between the ages of 5 and 14. It increases to 12.0 for girls and 14.2 for boys per 100,000. No matter what country a young person may call home, suicide is listed as a common cause of death in adolescents. This entry discusses suicide risks and warning signs, along with theories of suicide and possible interventions, with regard to youth in general and gifted youth in particular.

Risks

The typology of suicide behavior includes ideation, gesturing, attempts, and completions. Youth who ideate think about killing themselves. Gesturors engage in nonserious suicide attempts. Attemptors involve themselves in bona fide, but unsuccessful, suicide attempts, and completers take up behaviors that end their life. Gifted adolescents who may be at a heightened risk for attempting suicide are youth with prior history of a psychological disorder. Other risks identified by Lucy Davidson and Markku Linnoila include a history of drug or alcohol use, lethal weapons in the home, genetic factors, gender (boys are four times more likely to complete suicide than are girls; girls are three times more likely to attempt suicide than are boys), homosexuality, impulsiveness, and aggressiveness. Risk factors that may be particular to gifted youth consist of perfectionism, sensitivity, social isolation caused by extreme introversion, Kasimierz Dabrowski's five overexcitabilities, and inappropriate educational accommodations.

Philip Rutter and Andrew Behrendt warn that overemphasizing demographic variables in discussions of suicide risk can obscure who truly in the population is in peril. For example, current studies about suicide in young people focus on White youth. Consequently, intervention strategies may be tailored to this population. Suicide rates for African American, Native American, and Latino youth have mushroomed during the past decade. Focusing on demographic variables may misidentify some and underidentify others from these populations. Moreover, the intervention strategies proposed may be inappropriate or ineffective. Rutter and Behrendt thus urge the consideration of the combination of hostility, a negative self-concept, isolation, and hopelessness as conducive to accurately identifying which youth may be at risk for suicide.

Warning Signs

Young people who evince warning signs for suicide can be said to be ideating about suicide at the minimum. Some warning signs include prior attempts to take one's life; an increase in the use of alcohol and drugs; loss of interest in work, school, and personal hobbies; giving away cherished possessions; and preoccupation with death and dying. Several warning signs particular to gifted students may include an abrupt change in school performance; complete engrossment in schoolwork; lack of social participation; difficulties in relationships with significant others, especially when these peers are similar in ability; and a difficulty delineating the difference between fiction and fact. One should not assume a list will be created that captures all the ways young people may communicate that they are considering suicide. Moreover, Cross, Karyn Gust-Brey, and P. Bonny Ball cautioned against equating giftedness with being troubled. It would be better to err on the side of caution and assume that troubles in a gifted young person's life require attention.

Theories

Several theories by suicidologists, or researchers who study suicide, have been advanced that explain how a person comes to consider suicide as a viable alternative. Two theories highlighted here are Edwin Schneidman's four elements of suicide and Judith Stillion and Eugene McDowell's suicide trajectory model. Schneidman argues that the path to suicide begins with intensified inimicality or an increase in the ways that a person can be self-punishing. A feeling of being ill at ease is worsened. Thinking becomes highly constrained and polarized. Young people can ignore how others may be affected by their suicide and block memories from their pasts. The fourth element to Schneidman's theory about suicide is cessation. Young people come to feel that the only way they can end their pain is to end their life.

Stillion and McDowell combined work from several schools of thought about suicide as the basis for their suicide trajectory model. The model posits that there are four primary areas of risk: cognitive (rigid thinking, poor problem solving), biological (manic depression, gender), environmental (weapons in the home, life stressors), and psychological (feelings of hopelessness, low self-concept). The risk areas play a role in young people coming to ideate about suicide, and they affect each other, such that a young person who does not solve problems well may come to feel hopeless. Stillion and McDowell conclude that to understand suicide as an ultimate decision, one must understand how life experiences manifest the previously mentioned risk areas.

These theories encourage a holistic approach to understanding why youth commit suicide, as Rutter and Behrendt so urge. Psychological autopsies of youth who commit suicide serve just such a function. Though intended for investigating mysterious deaths, psychological autopsies have come to be used to explain suicides. Cross, Gust-Brey, and their colleagues used this data-gathering procedure to explore, posthumously, the environmental, psychological, and social influences in the suicide of Reed Ball, a gifted college student. The researchers hoped that the story of Ball would help reduce the likelihood of suicide in gifted adolescents and young adults.

Cross, Gust-Brey, and colleagues concluded that risk factors and warning signs for suicide in youth in the general population can serve as risk factors and warning signs for gifted youth. Cross and colleagues urge parents, teachers, friends, and counselors to not equate giftedness with aberrant behavior and belief systems. Moreover, relationships can serve as safeguards in the face of the tendency by suicidal youth to isolate themselves.

Interventions

The preceding analysis of the literature allows one to conclude that suicide is far from being the result of an invisible progression of events or circumstances. There are many places of entry, and thus intervention and prevention, to reduce suicide completions in gifted youth. As expected, parents and schools can serve pivotal roles.

Mirjami Pelkonen and Mauri Martunen report that youth sought help from parents and friends rather than counselors before a potentially deadly suicide attempt. Indeed, it is imperative for parents to heed talk of suicidal thoughts when their children share them. As a parent, is it seductive to pacify oneself with the rationales that a child is too young to take his or her life or the child is not serious? Parents who chose this path rather than action on behalf of their child and as a consequence lost their child to suicide were deeply remorseful and were eloquent in their plea that parents not do as they did. As mentioned previously, a persistent parent can stand in the way of a suicidal youth seeking to isolate herself or himself, and parents are often the ones most likely to connect their child with the requisite counseling. Finally, parents may need to decode behavior as a precursor to having conversations with their child about suicide. Therefore, parents should make themselves aware of the warning signs and risks of suicide in children and youth, according to Cross, Gust-Brey, and colleagues.

Schools can serve this educative function for parents, teachers, and peers. Though school officials are urged to proceed cautiously with suicide awareness programs, they have been proven effective interventions in certain cases. Schoolwide intervention programs incur the risk of normalizing suicide. Educators are encouraged to emphasize the message that suicidal thoughts are an abnormal way of grappling with life stressors to allay this risk.

School environment can also serve as an intervention. Denise de Souza Fleith encourages the development of school environments that facilitate rewarding social relationships, honest discussion of fears and dreams, and the bolstering of student strengths, abilities, and interests. Moreover, Laurence Coleman and Cross argue that schools need to establish holistic guidance program at the elementary and secondary levels for gifted youth. These guidance programs would have as their theoretical basis an understanding of universal child development and domain-specific atypical growth and change. The guidance program would also help gifted youth apprehend their environment in such a way that they can think their way through their worries. This aspect of the guidance program recognizes that thinking and emotion are interconnected.

Tracy L. Cross and Andrea Dawn Frazier

See also Emotional Development; Guidance; Life Satisfaction; Stigmatization

Further Readings

Coleman, L. J., & Cross, T. L. (2005). *Being gifted in school* (2nd ed.). Waco, TX: Prufrock Press.

Cross, T. L., Cook, R. S., & Dixon, D. N. (1996). Psychological autopsies of three academically talented adolescents who committed suicide. *Journal of Secondary Gifted Education, 7*(3), 403–409.

Cross, T. L., Gust-Brey, K., & Ball, P. B. (2002). A psychological autopsy of the suicide of an academically gifted student: Researchers' and parents' perspectives. *Gifted Child Quarterly, 46*(4), 247–264.

Davidson, L., & Linnoila, M. (Eds.). (1991). *Risk factors for youth suicide.* New York: Hemisphere.

Delisle, J. R. (1982). Striking out: Suicide and the gifted adolescent. *Gifted Child Today, 13,* 16–19.

Fleith, D. S. (1998). Suicide among talented youngsters: A sociocultural perspective. *Gifted Education International, 13*(2), 113–120.

Fleith, D. S. (2001). Suicide among gifted adolescents: How to prevent it. Retrieved March 5, 2007, from http://www.gifted.uconn.edu/nrcgt/newsletter/spring01/sprng012.html

Hayes, M. L., & Sloat, R. S. (1989). Gifted students at risk for suicide. *Roeper Review, 12*(2), 102–107.

Rutter, P. A., & Behrendt, A. E. (2004). Adolescent suicide risk: Four psychosocial factors. *Adolescence, 39*(154), 295–302.

Schneidman, E. (1996). *The suicidal mind.* New York: Oxford University Press.

Stillion, J. M., & McDowell, E. E. (1996). *Suicide across the life span.* Washington, DC: Taylor & Francis.

Summer Camps

The defining element of a summer camp is outdoor adventure. Although all of the camps described in this entry are open to academically gifted students, most are not solely focused on the academically gifted. For the adventurous student, a multitude of locations around the continental United States, as well as in Alaska and Hawaii, are available. There are also outdoor summer adventure camps in countries such as Canada, Norway, Costa Rica, Panama, Ecuador, British Columbia, Mexico, and many others. Each of these camps provides opportunities for students to grow and develop in unique ways.

The Gifted Question

Gifted abilities involved in adventure camps are both physical and mental. Some of these adventure camps focus almost entirely on physical development, but others emphasize intellectual as well as physical development. Most of these camps do not have specific intellectual requirements, such as high grades or high-IQ scores. Many camps work with students on team building, as well as on social and leadership skills. Service-learning projects are also a large part of some of the camps, particularly those that are based in foreign countries. Adventure camps often focus on developing a sense of community responsibility among participants, as well as developing physical abilities, leadership capabilities, artistic talents, and mental acuity. These camps generally aim to maximize all aspects of student potential. In the list later in this entry, camps that have a gifted and talented criterion, that information is listed in italics on the line with grade or age parameters.

Adventure Camp Activities

The adventure camps feature a wide range of highly physical land and water activities. In some camps, students may spend large amounts of time in water activities such as white-water rafting, swimming, snorkeling, kayaking, canoeing, sailing, scuba diving, and photographing undersea life. There are equally as many, if not more, land activities such as mountain climbing, backpacking, rock climbing, mountain biking, archery, ropes courses, and fishing. In addition to this array of physical activities, some camps offer arts and crafts, language immersion, leadership training, the study of marine animals, and conservation service projects.

Age Requirements

Most of the highly physical adventure camps require students to have completed sixth grade. However, a few adventure camps tailor their activities to allow children in first or second grade to attend.

Questions to Ask

Before choosing a summer experience, one should carefully consider the aspects of several programs, and the attending student should assist in the decision-making process. For example, people who are considering what summer experience is best for their students should consider the following questions:

1. What do I want my student to gain from this experience?
2. What does my student hope to gain?
3. Does my student want to go?
4. Has my student had some enjoyable and successful experiences with outdoor activities?
5. Might my student need some other kinds of outdoor experience before this one?
6. Do I want my student to go?
7. What is the student to instructor ratio?
8. How long has the camp been in operation?
9. What is the experience level of the staff?
10. Does the camp give me sufficient evidence of monitoring the safety of students?
11. Is the length of the experience right for my student?
12. What are my student's strengths?
13. What might my student need to develop?
14. What kinds of supervision are in place at different times of the day and evening?
15. Is the potential benefit of this experience worth the financial cost?
16. Is my student mature enough to handle this experience?
17. Do I feel comfortable that the camp is a good match for my student?

Specific Outdoor Summer Adventure Camps

Listed alphabetically is a sample of summer adventure camps. The list is far from exhaustive but does give an overview of the location of the camp, special camp features, specific activities, age groupings, and contact information. Only further searching and questioning will help determine if an outdoor adventure camp is right for a particular student.

Adventure Treks

Dates: June–August

Ages: 13–18

Locations: Northern California, Alaska, Pacific Northwest, British Columbia

Special features: Camping out each night, teamwork, and community building

Activities: Backpacking, white-water rafting, sea kayaking, mountain climbing, rock climbing, canoeing, sailing, mountain biking

E-mail: info@adventuretreks.com

Web site: www.adventuretreks.com

Aquatic Sciences Adventure Camp

Date: June–August

Ages: 9–15

Location: Texas State University–San Marcos, Texas

Special features: Learning basic principles of water chemistry and aquatic biology in a university setting

Activities: Scuba diving, rafting, tubing, swimming, snorkeling, and trips to Sea World

E-mail: LG16@txstate.edu

Web site: www.eardc.txstate.edu/camp.html

Camp Broadstone's Summer Enrichment Program for Gifted Youth

Dates: June and July

Grades: 4–8 *Gifted*

Location: Appalachian State University, North Carolina

Special features: Blend of morning enrichment classes and afternoon adventures

Activities: Canoeing, rappelling, high-ropes course, hiking, and camping trips

E-mail: bevanjk@appstate.edu

Web site: www.campbroadstone.com

Camp Nor'wester

Dates: June–August

Ages: 9–16

Location: Roche Harbor, Washington

Special features: Experience designed to build a spirit of community by learning camping and outdoor skills such as living in tents and building fires

Activities: Nature studies, archery, sailing, kayaking, canoeing, arts and crafts, music, bicycling, northwest native focus, singing, and drama

E-mail: norwester@rockisland.com

Web site: www.norwester.org

Camp Yunasa

Dates: July–early August

Ages: 10–14

Location: Camp Copneconic on Lake Copneconis, Fenton, Michigan

Special feature: Aimed at integrating intellectual, emotional, social, physical, and spiritual aspects of students

Activities: Swimming, canoeing, campfires, archery, ropes courses, and arts and crafts

E-mail: IEAgifted@educationaladvancement.org

Web site: www.educationaladvancement.org

Catalina Sea Camp

Dates: July–August

Ages: 8–12, 1 week; ages 12–17, 3 weeks

Location: Catalina Island, California

Special feature: Exploration and study of the marine science and island ecology of Catalina Island including seafood cookery and arts and crafts

Activities: Scuba diving, sailing, surfing, wall climbing, snorkeling, ocean kayaking, underwater video and photography, plus the study of fish, sharks, plankton, algae, marine mammals, and island biology

E-mail: info@guideddiscoveries.org

Web site: www.catalinaseacamp.org

Cottonwood Gulch Foundation

Dates: June–August

Ages: 10–18

Location: New Mexico

Special features: Wilderness expeditions that explore the natural sciences and cultural history of the Southwest and explore the 540-acre ecological preserve where the camp is located

Activities: Backpacking, canoe trips, animal tracking, Native American history and art, plus the study of ornithology, geology, anthropology, and archaeology

E-mail: amy@cottonwoodgulch.org

Web site: www.cottonwoodgulch.org

Crow Canyon Archaeological Center

Dates: Summer

Grades: 6–12

Location: near Cortez, Colorado, in one of the richest archaeological regions in the United States

Special features: Scenic 170-acre campus

Activities: Study of archaeology in the large wilderness area near Mesa Verde National Park

E-mail: ttitone@crowcanyon.org

Web site: www.crowcanyon.org

Deer Hill Expeditions

Dates: June–August

Grades: 7–12

Locations: U.S. Southwest, including Colorado, Utah, Arizona, and New Mexico, and Costa Rica,

Special features: Interaction with native cultures, cross-cultural community service projects with Navajo, Hopi, Zuni, or the Tico people of Costa Rica

Activities: Rafting, canoeing, kayaking, backpacking, mountain biking, leadership development, Spanish language immersion, and conservation service projects

E-mail: info@deerhillexpeditions.com

Web site: www.deerhillexpeditions.com

Grand Canyon and Four Corners Adventure—Travel Quest

Dates: Summer

Grades: 7–12 *Academically Gifted*

Location: Begins in Albuquerque, New Mexico, and ends in Las Vegas, Nevada

Special features: Historic tour includes Santa Fe, Mesa Verde, Grand Canyon, Hoover Dam, Durango, and Crow Canyon Archaeology Center in Cortez, Colorado

Activities: Hands-on approach to learning, and the study of archaeology

E-mail: tours@ailteam.com

Web site: www.ailtours.com

Green River Preserve

Dates: June, July, August

Grades: 2–12

Location: Near Brevard in Western North Carolina

Special Features: A natural sciences and environmental camp in a nature preserve. Activities: Hiking, exploring, swimming, canoeing, backpacking, kayaking, rock climbing, crafts, fishing, natural arts, archery, pottery, and creative writing

E-mail: missy@greenriverpreserve.org

info@greenriverpreserve.org

Web site: www.greenriverpreserve.org

Marine Quest Summer Camps at University of North Carolina at Wilmington

Dates: Summer

Ages: 5–16 *Gifted and Talented*

Locations: Bimini, Bahamas, and Curacao, Netherlands Antilles, off north coast of Venezuela

Special features: Hands-on ocean and marine life educational programs

Activities: Age-appropriate exploration of barrier islands, where all U.S. Coast Guard safety requirements are enforced

E-mail: marinequest@uncw.edu

burnettj@uncw.edu

Web site: www.uncw.edu/marinequest

Mercersburg Academy Adventure Camps

Dates: June–August

Ages: 7–16

Location: Mercersburg, Pennsylvania

Special features: Amusement park trips

Activities: Kayaking, horseback riding, overnight campouts, baseball games, and river rafting

E-mail: summerprograms@mercersburg.edu

Web site: www.mercersburg.edu

Outward Bound Wilderness

Dates: Summer

Ages: 12 and older

Locations: Various locations across the United States

Special features: The program emphasizes personal growth and challenge in a variety of wilderness situations such as leading a mountain-peak ascent or navigating a boat through rapids

Activities: Students may attend who have had no previous wilderness experience, as they gain skills, they move through a series of progressively more difficult challenges; students also learn to communicate, to lead, and to work as a team

Web site: www.outwardboundwilderness.org

The Road Less Traveled

Dates: 1- to 6-week sessions in summer

Ages: 13–19

Locations: Western United States, Alaska, Norway, Costa Rica, Panama, Guatemala, Peru, Spain, Hawaii, Azores Islands, France

Special features: Wilderness expeditions, community service, and language immersion

Activities: Rafting, kayaking, rock climbing, backpacking, ice and snow mountaineering

Web site: www.theroadlesstraveled.com

Sail Caribbean

Dates: June–August

Ages: 13–18

Locations: British Virgin Islands, Leeward and Windward Islands

Special features: The Eleuthera program combines marine biology study with youth outreach and environmental conservation projects in the British Virgin Islands

Activities: Sailing instruction, marine biology camps, wide variety of scuba diving courses, teen sailing adventures, cultural immersion, marine biology, and community service projects

E-mail: info@sailcaribbean.com

Web site: www.sailcaribbean.com

Science Camp Watonka

Dates: June–July, July–August

Ages: 7–15 for boys only

Location: Paupack, Pennsylvania

Special features: Daily science laboratory experiences in astronomy, robotics, chemistry, physics, and earth sciences

Activities: Climbing, windsurfing, ropes, swimming, riflery, mini-bike riding, sailing, crafts, woodworking, archery, arts and crafts, magic shows, overnight camping, rocketry, and waterfront safety

E-mail: mail@watonka.com

Web site: www.watonka.com

Seacamp–Seacamp Association Incorporated

Dates: June, July, August

Grades: rising 7–12

Location: Big Pine Key, Florida

Special features: Opportunities to explore the sea plant and animal life of the coral reefs, mudflats, tidal pools and grassy areas of the waters of the Lower Florida Keys under the guidance of marine science instructors

Activities: Basic and advanced courses in scuba diving, sailing, windsurfing, camp newspaper, arts, and crafts

E-mail: info@seacamp.org

Web site: www.seacamp.org

SEACAMP San Diego

Dates: June–August

Grades: 7–12

Location: San Diego, California

Special features: Innovative, hands-on, interactive marine education in three unique camps—SEACAMP I, SEACAMP II, and SEACAMP III—that study invertebrates, fish adaptations, night adaptations, marine mammals, and shark ecology

Activities: Snorkel excursions, kayaking, boogie boarding, boat trips, from a private supervised beach

E-mail: seacamp@seacamp.com

Web site: www.seacamp.com

Sea Camp—Texas A&M University at Galveston

Sea Campus Kids

Dates: Summer

Ages: 6–11

Location: Galveston, Texas

Sea Camp for Older Students

Dates: Week-long summer adventures June–August

Ages: 10–18

Locations: Texas coast, Belize

Special features: Marine biology and ecology, study of marine mammals in their habitats, coastal camping, ecotourism in Belize

Activities: Use of oceanographic equipment and laboratories, firsthand encounters with reef fish, coral, and mangroves

E-mail: seacamp@tamug.edu

Web site: www.tamug.edu/seacamp

Student Hosteling Program—American Camping Association

Dates: June–August

Grades: 8–12

Location: Conway, Massachusetts

Special features: During these teenage biking tours, students stay in campsites, hostels, and other modest facilities

Activities: Small groups of 8 to 12 students make bike touring trips in the countryside and in cultural centers

E-mail: shpbike@aol.com

Web site: www.bicycletrips.com

YMCA Camp Flaming Arrow

Dates: June–July

Ages: 8–15

Location: Hunt, Texas

Special features: A variety of camp clubs, such as Saddle Club, Crafts Club, Varsity Club, and others from which to choose

Activities: Wall climbing, fishing, hiking, nature studies, archery, canoeing, arts, and crafts, horseback riding, river swimming, overnight campouts, high and low-ropes course, basketball, volleyball, campfires

Web site: www.ymcacampflamingarrow.org

Online Information

A vast amount of adventure camp information is available online. Many of those are well-established commercial enterprises, others are university-based programs, and others are nonprofit.

Patricia L. Hollingsworth

See also International Schools for Gifted; Saturday Programs; Summer Programs

Further Readings

Duke University Talent Identification Program, Educational Opportunity Guide Online: http://www.duketipeog.com

Duke University Talent Identification Program, Summer Programs: http://www.tip.duke.edu/summer_programs

MySummerCamps.com: http://www.mysummercamps.com

Simmons, E. J. (2006). *Educational opportunity guide: A directory of programs for the gifted.* Durham, NC: Duke University Talent Identification Program.

Summer Programs

Summer programs for the gifted are broad in scope, content, focus, and format. These include talent searches, summer institutes, workshops, and conferences. They tend to be more focused on reaching the specific academic needs of gifted students than are summer adventure camps. Many of these programs are specifically designed for gifted and talented students, and several of them are described in this entry.

More than a decade ago, researcher Donna Enerson found that summer programs had positive effects on gifted students. More recent investigations by Paula Olszewski-Kubilius have similar positive findings. Gifted students find challenging course work with a group of intellectual peers to be satisfying and meaningful. For gifted and talented students, being able to attend a summer program with a group of intellectual peers can be a life-changing experience. They are in classes with other gifted students and are given the opportunity to pursue the subject matter of their choice. For some students, this will be the first time that they have found a group where they belong.

Talent Search Programs

Talent search programs provide qualified seventh-grade students with the opportunity to take either the ACT or SAT college entrance exams. These scores are then used to qualify them for an array of exceptionally interesting and challenging summer school programs, as well as, some outstanding school-year programs. There are four regional talent search programs in the United States: Duke University Talent Identification Program; Johns Hopkins Center for Talented Youth; Northwestern University Center for Talent Development; and University of Denver—Rocky Mountain Talent Search.

These talent search programs identify academically talented students and offer them an assortment of summer programs. Students may select to apply to the summer programs in any of these regions.

Test scores are often listed as part of the requirements for Talent Search Summer Programs. These generally refer to ACT, SAT, or PSAT exam scores, but some programs may require others. Going to specific Web sites will provide more specific information regarding all the requirements.

Duke University Talent Identification Program

Requirements: Test scores, gifted and talented

Grades: 4–12

Special features: The Duke program is a long-standing leader in programming for gifted students. Programs include workshops in creative writing, drama, film studies, and scientific field studies in a wide variety of locations, such as the Smoky Mountains, New Mexico, Costa Rico, and Italy.

E-mail: QandA@tip.duke.edu

Web site: www.tip.duke.edu

Johns Hopkins University—Center for Talented Youth (CTY)

Requirements: Test scores for 7th–12th grades

Grades: 2–12

Special features: Programs are offered for 2nd through 6th graders in the Baltimore and Washington, D.C., area as well as in West Los Angeles and Pasadena, California. For 7th through 12th graders, a variety of CTY courses are offered, including Civic Leadership for 10th–12th graders, and programs in Madrid, Spain, and Monterrey and Puebla, Mexico, for 7th–12th graders. There is also a program in historic Nanjing, China, for 10th–12th graders.

E-mail: ctyinfo@jhu.edu

Web site: www.cty.jhu.edu

Northwestern University—Center for Talent Development

Requirements: Application, transcript, recommendations, test scores, GPA, writing sample, gifted and talented

Grades: 4–12

Special features: Students going into 5th and 6th grades may be in the Apogee enrichment program. Spectrum is for students completing 7th, 8th, or 9th grades. Equinox is a 3-week program for academically talented students completing 9th through 12th grades. The Civic Leadership Institute is a service-learning program for high school students.

E-mail: ctd@northwestern.edu

Web site: www.ctd.northwestern.edu/summer

University of Denver—Rocky Mountain Talent Search

Dates: June and July

Requirements: Test scores, portfolio of student work

Grades: 7–10

Special features: Students from 4th through 6th grades are in the 1-week residential program called Discovery that focuses on enrichment and exploration. Students from 6th though 8th grades are in a 2-week residential program called Frontier that helps students move from enrichment activities to more intense studies. The Pioneer Program is a 3-week residential program for mature 8th through 10th graders who focus on one intense course of study for 7 hours a day.

E-mail: rmts-info@du.edu

Web site: http://www.du.edu/city/programs/academic-year-programs/rocky-mountain-talent-search/; www.du.edu/city/programs/summer-programs

Duke Talent Identification Program Institutes

The Duke Talent Identification Program (TIP) Institutes are designed to meet the needs of academically exceptional high school students who want real-world experiences. The Leadership Institute helps students develop their leadership potential. The Pre-Law Institute is designed to aid students in the understanding of the criminal justice system in the United States. The Computational Science Institute provides students with outstanding teachers and many hands-on experiences.

Duke University Talent Identification Program International Field Studies

There are at least three staff members in each group of 20 to 25 students who are selected to participate in individual international field studies.

The following field studies are available for 10th- through 12th-grade students:

- China: *A Leader in the Global Economy,* held in Shanghai, Xian, and Beijing
- England: A Diplomat's Perspective on World Politics, held in London
- France: *Paris through the Eyes of Its Greatest Minds*
- Italy: *Architecture and Art History,* held in Rome and Florence
- Costa Rica: *Tropical Ecology,* held in La Selva, Monteverde, and Palo Verde
- Costa Rica: *Tropical Medicine and Ethnobiology,* held in Las Cruces

Examples of Specific Talent Search Camps

Language Immersion Programs, Hampshire College, Amherst, Massachusetts

Dates: June–July

Requirements: Test scores

Grades: 6–9

Special features: 4-week language immersion programs in Arabic, Chinese, French, and Spanish

Activities: Cultural events, trips, and activities available in the cultural context of the language being studied

Web site: www.cty.jhu.edu/summer/immersion

Reel Expressions: Filmmaking—Chapman University, Orange, California

Dates: June–July

Requirements: Test scores

Grades: 9–12

Special features: Students learn the basics of filmmaking and complete two original films during their 2-week stay at film school.

Activities: Learning the basics of storytelling, filmmaking, and editing; trips to movie studios, visiting famous sites in Hollywood

Web site: http://www.tip.duke.edu/summer_programs/arts/index.html#film

Summer Institute for the Gifted (SIG)

The SIG summer programs are sponsored by outstanding colleges and universities around the country. Amherst College, Bryn Mawr College, Emory University, University of California at Berkeley, University of California at Los Angeles, University of Michigan–Ann Arbor, University of Texas at Austin, and Vassar College provide residential programs for 4th- through 11th-grade gifted students. Princeton provides a residential program for 7th though 11th graders.

Day programs for kindergarten through sixth-grade students are provided by Bryn Mawr College, Fairfield University, Manhattanville College, Moorestown Friends School, and Stuart Country Day School. All of these programs are for students with high academic ability and achievement.

Web site: http://www.giftedstudy.com

Southern Methodist University Talented and Gifted Summer Programs, Dallas

Southern Methodist University located in Dallas, Texas, provides summer programs for middle and high school students with high academic potential. Courses are offered in science, art, and the humanities. Students live on campus and may earn college credit for their summer work.

E-mail: gifted@smu.edu

Web site: www.smu.edu/ce

Writer's Art: Creative Writing— Ghost Ranch, New Mexico

Dates: June

Requirements: Test scores

Grades: 9–12

Special features: The site of this camp is the former home of painter Georgia O'Keeffe. Professional writers work with students to help them develop their own writing styles and abilities.

Activities: Journal writing, creative writing, swimming, hiking, and field trips to cultural centers

Web site: http://www.tip.duke.edu/summer_programs/arts/index.html#film; http://ghostranch.org/index.php?Itemid=&option=com_search&searchword=wri

Other University-Based Academic Programs

California State University, Fresno, Summer Animation Workshop

The animation workshop will focus on creating digital characters that can perform as a real actor with attitude, style, and appeal. Students will learn to scan and rig a three-dimensional character. They will study motion technology and learn to apply this movement to their 3-D characters.

E-mail: rvertolli@csuchico.edu

Web site: http://www.animationnation.com

Goucher College, Baltimore, Maryland, Summer Arts Institute

The Goucher College Summer Arts Institute provides opportunities for serious young artists (ages 12–18) to study with professional artists. Students may choose from computer music, dance, jazz music, or drums and percussion. Computer music students will use the latest technology to write and orchestrate their own original compositions. Dance students may have instruction in ballet, jazz, tap, and modern dance. Jazz students will play in small and large ensembles as well as having individual instruction. Students studying drums and percussion will be exposed to such instruments as African and Brazilian drums, as well as dance accompaniment.

E-mail: linda.garofalo@goucher.edu

Web site: http://www.goucher.edu/x7545.xml

University of California at Berkeley— Lawrence Hall of Science Summer Camps

The Lawrence Hall of Science Camps are for students from ages 10 to 18. There are two residential camps, each 1 week in length. In each camp, students may take either the wildlife biology, marine biology, or mountain ecology while backpacking in the Sierras.

E-mail: lhsinfo@uclink,berkeley.edu

Web site: www.campchannel.com/camps/1925.html

University of Nevada, Reno—
THINK Summer Institute

The THINK Summer Institute, sponsored by the Davidson Institute, is a 3-week residential program for exceptionally gifted students from ages 13 to 16. Courses are taught by college professors, and students may earn as many as seven college credits.

E-mail: Think@ditd.org

Web site: www.ditd.org

University of Northern Colorado, Boulder—
Summer Enrichment Program

The Summer Enrichment Program (SEP) is a 2-week residential program that has provided enrichment courses for gifted students for 30 years. Courses that may be offered are art, creative writing, debate, dance, mathematics, music, technology, cultures, drama, history, and science. After class, students may be involved in sports, recreation, crafts, and library research.

E-mail: sep@unco.edu

Web site: www.unco.edu/sep

Washington University in St. Louis

Current high school juniors, who are 16 or older, may attend Washington University to get a head start on earning college credits and learning about college life. They may study a wide variety of courses including biology, ecology, foreign languages, literature, journalism, mathematics, history, and visual and performing arts. Students may earn as many as seven college credits during the summer.

E-mail: mhussung@wustl.edu

Web site: http://summerscholars.wustl.edu

Western Kentucky University, Bowling Green—
The Center for Gifted Studies

The Summer Program for Verbally and Mathematically Precocious Youth (VAMPY) is a 3-week academic program sponsored by the Center for Gifted Studies that provides students with the opportunity to learn from a wide variety of academic disciplines. Classes that have been taught are ancient civilizations, chemistry, Civil War, genetics, humanities, mock trial, physics, Shakespeare, and psychology.

E-mail: gifted@wku.edu

Web site: www.wku.edu/Dept/Support/AcadAffairs/Gifted

Summer Arts Programs

Blue Lake Fine Arts Camp, near
Muskegon, Michigan

Blue Lake Camp is in the middle of 1,300 acres of preserved forest in the Manistee National Forest on the shore of Little Blue Lake just north of Muskegon, Michigan. There are more than 275 buildings, shelters, and cabins on the campus. Annually the camp serves more than 5,000 gifted elementary, middle, and high school students. Students study music, art, drama, and dance and give more than 175 performances during the Summer Arts Festival. Other activities include dances, talent shows, concerts, carnivals, campfires, and recitals, as well as sports such as basketball, soccer, volleyball, and swimming.

Web site: www.bluelake.org/programs.html

Idyllwild Arts Summer Program,
Idyllwild, California

The Summer Program provides intensive workshops in the visual arts for students from ages 9 to 18. There are 2-week workshops in ceramics, computer animation, drawing, painting, jewelry-making, photography, and portfolio preparation.

E-mail: summer@idyllwildarts.org

Web site: http://www.idyllwildarts.org

Choosing a Summer Program

Making a choice from so many options may be difficult. One of the big decisions is between residential and nonresidential programs. A few summers spent at programs close to home can make a smooth transition to a residential program.

Attending a residential program requires student maturity, some experience in living away from home, and desire by the student to try this adventure. If a student and the student's parents are comfortable at all these levels, then a residential program can be an extremely positive experience. Having the student involved in all steps of the decision making will more likely make it a positive experience.

Patricia L. Hollingsworth

See also International Schools for Gifted; Saturday Programs; Summer Camps

Further Readings

Duke University Talent Identification Program, Educational Opportunity Guide Online: http://www.duketipeog.com

Duke University Talent Identification Program, Summer Programs: http://www.tip.duke.edu/summer%5Fprograms

Enersen, D. L. (1993). Summer residential programs: Academics and beyond. *Gifted Child Quarterly, 37*(4), 169–176.

MySummerCamps.com: http://www.mysummercamps.com

National Association for Gifted Children: http://www.nagc.org

Olszewski-Kubilius, P. (2007). The role of summer programs in developing the talents of gifted students. In J. VanTassel-Baska (Ed.), *Serving gifted learners beyond the traditional classroom: A guide to alternative programs and services* (pp. 13–32). Waco, TX: Prufrock Press.

Simmons, E. J. (2006). *Educational opportunity guide: A directory of programs for the gifted.* Durham, NC: Duke University Talent Identification Program.

Supporting Emotional Needs of Gifted

As the field of giftedness education grows, educators and parents are getting better at meeting the academic needs of the gifted children under their care; however, the social and emotional needs of the gifted are still lacking understanding and support. The prevailing myth that gifted children are smart and are able to take care of themselves is a major reason gifted students flounder socially and emotionally. This entry addresses the social needs and emotional needs of gifted students and provides some tips for educators, parents, and professionals on how to support the gifted. Supporting Emotional Needs of the Gifted (SENG), a nonprofit organization established in 1981, is highlighted as an organization in which educators, parents, and professionals band together to better facilitate the exchange of research and best practices to help both gifted children and adults cope with their social and emotional needs.

Social Needs

To meet the social needs of the gifted, concerned adults need to be aware of the role of introversion, availability of mental-age peers, and image control of gifted students that could affect the social development of these students.

Introverts are individuals who prefer the internal world of ideas and concepts within their heads, get their energy by being alone, and become drained when surrounded by others. This is different from being lonely, where one does not have any friends to belong to or share experiences with. Therefore, one should not push introverted gifted students to socialize unnecessarily because this may hamper the pursuit of interest and talent refinement during the student alone time.

Gifted students who were not in accelerated programs may lack the companionship of high-ability peers who are able to comprehend and understand the interests and abilities that they possess. Being more intellectually advanced than their same-age peers, gifted students may be seen as different and be rejected. Opportunities for social involvement exist in many avenues beyond the classroom, however, development of the natural talents of the gifted students should not be stopped for concern of lack of social interactions with the same-age peers.

The macho culture that is highly valued during adolescence may influence gifted boys to underachieve because academic success does not rank highly among their peers. Gifted girls similarly may play down their intelligence, dress and act in a manner consistent with the adolescent female culture to belong with their peers at the expense of their gifted and talented area performances. To overcome these cultural expectations, gifted students need successful role models who overcame similar situations to help them.

Emotional Needs

To meet the emotional needs of the gifted students, concerned adults should watch for the role of perfectionism, self-esteem issues, moral sensitivity and emotional intensity, and gifted learners feeling different from their same-age peers.

Many gifted learners have a perfectionist streak, expecting A's and superior performance in the tasks that they undertake to the point of not challenging themselves in academic or extra cocurricular activities that they believe or know that they are not superior in. This fear of failure may help these students to excel at a high level of performance compared with their cohort, but the extreme of this behavior could cause students to lose sight of what is important in their lives and spend inordinate amounts of time pursuing unattainable perfection. Consistent superior performance in one's life without the occasional failure that affects everyone could make the gifted students less resilient in facing normal challenges in life. Gifted students may already suffer from a loss of their social self-esteem, because of the inability to connect well with their same-age peers and to conform to the cultural norms of their peers; when compounded with a fear of academic or talents failure, this could lead to a sharp drop in self-esteem and self-confidence in gifted students. Self-esteem increases from one's ability to rise above challenges; therefore, experiencing failure from everyday life experiences is also essential so these gifted students can lead normal lives.

Moral sensitivity refers to the heightened sense of honesty, fairness, morality, global concerns, and sensitivity toward others, and *emotional intensity* refers to the different ways of experiencing the world that is more vibrant, gripping, intense, encompassing, multifaceted, and powerful than what would be experienced by the non-gifted. Moral sensitivity and emotional intensity add another layer of complexity to the experiences of the gifted learners who are already superior in their talent areas compared with their cohorts. This feeling of being different from the rest of their peers could alienate or isolate the gifted from the everyday experiences of their same-age peers, further compounding the difficulty of the gifted to socialize with others, leaving these students emotionally dejected. This problem is further compounded if gifted students do not understand that moral and emotional sensitivity may be natural for them.

Finally, twice-exceptional gifted students—those who are gifted and also must deal with Asperger's syndrome, attention deficit hyperactivity disorder, bipolar disorder, obsessive compulsive disorder, or other psychological disorders—are often misdiagnosed and underserved in gifted education programs. Concerned adults must learn how to identify and seek appropriate guidance for twice-exceptional students.

Serving Gifted Students

Some ways that educators, parents, and professionals can help gifted students include (a) providing validation of students' social and emotional struggle and offering appropriate support, (b) using bibliotherapy and cinematherapy to help gifted students find role models in the media, (c) teaching coping strategies such as calming techniques, (d) offering social skills training to those who need it, (e) enrolling students in summer and out-of-school gifted programs that have peers with similar abilities and interests, (f) seeking professionals who have experience working with the social and emotional needs of the gifted, (g) helping students learn creative problem-solving skills to tackle their challenges, (h) presenting appropriate modeling on how to cope with life's challenges and setbacks, and (i) teaching mood management skills for coping with troubling feelings.

Although this list is not a comprehensive list of what to do to help gifted students cope with their social and emotional needs, it does provide some basic ideas about how to support gifted students. Gifted students are naturally smart and talented; helping them leverage their innate abilities and skills to overcome their own problems helps them build their self-esteem and self-confidence and overcome obstacles in their lives. A little support and feedback from wise adults in their lives are still invaluable for these students.

SENG was formed in 1981 as a reaction to the lack of programming available to serve the social and emotional needs of gifted children at that time. SENG was founded by James T. Webb as part of the School of Professional Psychology at Wright State University but was reestablished as a non-profit organization in 2001. Although establishing SENG was discussed in 1980, the 20,000 calls and letters from audience members confirming the ongoing myths and misunderstanding about gifted children and their families that resulted from a discussion on an episode of *The Donahue Show* between host Phil Donahue, Webb, and a few parents of gifted children who had committed suicide reinforced the need for SENG.

SENG's mission is "to inform gifted individuals, their families, and the professionals who work with them about the unique social and emotional needs of gifted persons with the goal of empowering caring families and communities to influence more positively and effectively the development of giftedness in those individuals entrusted to their care." Supporting programs that empower gifted individuals to develop and express their innate abilities and talents fully are part of SENG's mission. To this end, SENG has been convening with its own SENG Conference yearly where the programming primary focus is on the social and emotional development and needs of the gifted. The recent 25th Silver Anniversary SENG Conference—held July 18 through July 20, 2008 in Salt Lake City, Utah—shows, through its longevity, the importance of such a conference to educators, parents, and professionals who serve the gifted. SENG also provides continuing education courses; facilitates the establishment of SENG–Model Parent Support Groups; provides suggested reading lists on various topics on giftedness; maintains an electronic article database on giftedness drawn from professionals in the field; and offers a free monthly e-mail newsletter to help parents, educators, and professionals keep abreast of new resources and issues affecting the social and emotional needs of the gifted.

Educators, parents, and professionals all have important roles in providing for the social and emotional needs of the gifted students. The highlighted social and emotional concerns of the gifted are interchangeable and represent a subset of the concerns that are exhibited by the gifted. Smart and talented students need just as much support and guidance from experienced elders in their lives to flourish in their academic and personal lives as other students do. Most people would consider it a great waste of talent if the gifted are groomed to excel in their aptitude areas but left to struggle alone socially and emotionally. The existence of SENG provides much awareness, hope, and empowerment for educators, parents, and professionals to offer much needed social and emotional support to the gifted students based on established research and practice.

Kai Kok "Zeb" Lim and Adeline Low

See also Asynchrony; Attitudes Toward Gifted; Emotional Development; Friendships; Perfectionism; Positive Disintegration; Problem Solving; Resilience

Further Readings

Cross, T. L. (2005). *The social and emotional lives of gifted kids: Understanding and guiding their development.* Waco, TX: Prufrock Press.

Delisle, J., & Galbraith, J. (2002). *When gifted kids don't have all the answers: How to meet their social and emotional needs.* Minneapolis, MN: Free Spirit Publishing.

Moon, S. M., & Reis, S. M. (Eds.). (2004). *Social/emotional issues, underachievement, and counseling of gifted and talented students (Essential readings in gifted education series).* Thousand Oaks, CA: Corwin Press.

Neihart, M., Reis, S. M., Robinson, N. M., & Moon, S. M. (Eds.). (2001). *Social and emotional development of gifted children: What do we know?* Waco, TX: Prufrock Press.

Supporting Emotional Needs of the Gifted (SENG). Retrieved July 29, 2008, from http://www.sengifted.org

Synectics

Synectics, described in this entry, belongs to a broad set of techniques that help users produce new ideas and new idea combinations as part of creative thinking or problem solving. It is an approach for generating ideas through use of unusual connections uncovered in metaphor and analogy. One explanation of the term *synectics* is that it comes from the Greek *syn,* which means to bring together, and *ectos,* or external things. Consequently, the idea of synectics is to join different and often diverse items in ways that explore or solve a problem. To use a synectics approach to a problem, the individuals involved identify a problem owner and use direct, personal, fantastic, or symbolic analogies to develop insights into creative solutions. These are then applied to the problem at hand, and solution paths are identified. The problem owner makes the evaluative judgments about the usefulness of the solutions along the way.

The synectics method was created by William Gordon and his colleagues beginning with their work on a psychology of problem solving in the 1940s. In 1961, he published *Synectics,* in which he described its central concept as trusting things that are alien and alienating things that are trusted. These iconoclastic juxtapositions open the individuals involved to ideas that might not have emerged otherwise and help them avoid premature closure or settling for the first or more obvious answers or approaches.

Synectics used as a complete process is useful as an approach to creative thinking or problem solving. The component parts from the overall synectics approach are individually applicable in many creative-thinking or problem-solving situations. Synectics resembles brainstorming and other techniques that generate fluent, flexible, original, and elaborative ideas. Synectics, though sharing commonalities with the other brainstorming techniques, brings to the creative problem-solving session its own unique approaches to the generation and combination of ideas. Brainstorming or other generative techniques may bog down after the obvious ideas are expressed. Synectics is a way to move beyond the obvious or to jump-start the creative process and allow fresh or unusual ideas to emerge and be tested.

Sometimes the synectics process is described as making the strange familiar or making the familiar strange. The synectics process begins with a group analysis, definition, and description of the issues involved. This part of the process is described as making the strange familiar. It is an analytical phase where participants try to better understand the problem and its nuisances. Those participating might recall how each has experienced the issues, the background, what has been tried, and the possible scope of action. The group then sums up their discussion by expressing the problem in one or more definitions or wishes.

When generating a lot of ideas through brainstorming, attribute listing, idea checklists, and so forth, in a classroom or with a team, each person who has put forth an idea feels some ownership of the final solution. This lack of a single evaluator of the goodness of any solutions may cause trouble at those points in the creative process when a judgment or evaluation is required. In synectics, this problem is avoided by identifying one problem owner before the session begins. The other class or team members are there to help the owner solve his or her problem. Several individuals can take ownership at different times in the synectics process. Typically, the members do not know as much about the issue or problem as the owner does; although this lack of knowledge might appear problematic, it is useful in synectics. The relative lack of knowledge or experience in the problem area encourages the suggestions of wild or crazy ideas that people might otherwise unconsciously avoid because the ideas may appear silly or distracting. On closer examination, however, these wild ideas might not be so ridiculous or they might suggest to others new ideas that prove more effective.

Next, one or more analogies are used to explore the problem or wishful statements. Here, participants take an excursion or begin to make the familiar strange. Through use of analogy, they distort, invert, transpose, and rearrange the everyday elements and ways of looking and responding. In using direct analogies, participants discuss and explore ways similar problems are solved. For example, how do animals solve a similar problem? How would the problem be solved in the Old West? How might an astronaut in space solve a similar problem?

Another analogical approach is to identify the problem with oneself. In personal analogies, the respondents imagine they are some component of the problem or wished-for situation. How would you feel if you were a rabbit who was trying to get away from a fox? What would you do? Where would you go? Who could help you? How does it feel to be an abstract piece of art? An impressionist painting? A Goya print? Personal analogies often provide new perspectives as the users become part of the problem or desired outcome.

Fantasy analogies have the users explore the images that come into their minds as they would solve the problem in some wild fantasy or within some fantastical world. Gordon claimed fantasy analogies worked because they fulfilled a deep unconscious wish by the participant. Questions that stimulate fantasy ideas are many. Can this problem be made to solve itself? How do the Jetsons keep their house clean? How would the big-bad wolf get dressed in the morning? How could Frodo or Bilbo use the magic ring to help them get their work done quickly and efficiently?

Symbolic analogy, sometimes called book titles, use pairs of words that seem to be contradictory or opposite for making the familiar strange. Examples include "steaming cold," "gorgeous ugliness," or "peaceful rebellion." These strange combinations of common things or ideas are sometimes useful in looking at problems in new ways and coming up with unusual solutions. "Steaming cold" might be used as an analogy for a hot beverage that does not require a stove or heat source to warm it and that could be used while walking in a cold winter forest.

Synectics succeed partly by slowing down the creative process, like a stream that comes to a wide spot. Its excursions and analogies provide time to linger in the outrageous stages before the class or team needs to create practical solutions about which the owner can make choices as to which are the most feasible today.

Michael F. Sayler

See also Creative Problem Solving; Creative Process; Creativity Training; Divergent Thinking

Further Readings

Gordon, W. J. J. (1961). *Synectics.* New York: Harper & Row.

Nolan, V. (2003). Whatever happened to synectics? *Creativity and Innovation Management, 12,* 34–38.

Prince, G. M. (1970). *The practice of creativity: A manual for dynamic group problem solving.* New York: Harper & Row.

T

Talent

Talent, like *giftedness,* is a term that lacks common understanding and agreed-upon meaning. *Talent*'s original meaning was that of a weight, especially of gold or silver. Talent's original meaning is ancient and describes a unit of mass, value, weights, or money. The word derives from the Latin *talentum,* which in turn comes from the Greek τάλαντον, meaning scale or measuring balance. Usually *talent* was used to describe a talent's worth of gold or silver, which was about that of an average person's weight in one of these precious metals. This term for large quantities of monetary riches became associated with human performance later in history.

In common usage, talent and giftedness mean essentially the same thing. The national definition is an example of this commingling of the terms. Other conceptions of talent distinguish it from gifts in terms of the domain where the high-level performance occurs. For some, *talent* refers to artistic, creative, intellectual, or athletic excellence whereas *giftedness* in this conception is defined as the overall ability of the person. Talent then would develop in areas of specific aptitude that were valued and rewarded by society and where significant practice occurred to develop high-levels of specific performances. Others see talent as the outcome of developed natural abilities regardless of the talent domain. Talent has been proposed as a more useful and less offensive concept than giftedness. Talent seems to reflect hard work over time, whereas giftedness suggests unearned largess. Talent in this understanding can be defined in terms of performance criteria whereas giftedness is seen as a personal characteristic. This entry describes various aspects of talent, especially in comparison with giftedness.

Talent and Genius

Louis Terman's first work on understanding human genius began by seeking individuals who excelled in specific talent areas such as music, art, mechanical ingenuity, and inventiveness. In his initial search, he did not first test these individuals for high intelligence test scores. Terman eventually gave up the search for talent independent of ability because he could not find viable instruments to distinguish between levels of talent. Also, those children he found who excelled in talent performance also had high intelligence scores when measured later.

At about the same time, Leta Hollingworth distinguished talent from genius. She initially defined *genius* as having a wonderful capacity for mental perfection and *talent* as a remarkable ability, but falling short of genius. Later, she modified this definition and suggested that the term *talent* be used to describe specialized aptitudes such as music or art. In this conception, she was defining *talent* as similar to high levels of Charles Spearman's specific (*s*) factors and giftedness as similar to high levels of Spearman's general (*g*) factor.

National Definition

In 1972, a national definition of talent and giftedness was created in the Marland report and then repeated in P.L. 103–382. This definition did not make clear distinctions between the two words. "The term 'gifted and talented' when used in respect to students, children, or youth means students, children, or youth who give evidence of high-performance capability in areas such as intellectual, creative, artistic, or leadership capacity, or in specific academic fields, and who require services or activities not ordinarily provided by the school in order to fully develop such capabilities" (P.L. 103–382, Title XIV, p. 388).

Classifications and Differentiations

In 1983, Abraham Tannenbaum suggested more specific meanings with four categories or classifications of talent: scarcity, surplus, quota, and anomalous talents. *Scarcity talents* are those in short supply, but that benefit and are needed by society and all peoples. Scarcity talents include high-level performances in areas such as innovations that make the world safer, healthier, easier, and more understandable. *Surplus talents* are those talents that are desired by society, but not essential to its survival. Musicians, artists, actors, and writers fit in this category. Tannenbaum was not calling surplus talents unimportant or superfluous; they made significant contributions to society. Their contributions, though, were not at the same critical level as medical breakthroughs, solving world hunger, or curing mental illness. *Quota talents* are those somewhere between surplus and scarcity talents. They are specialized, high-skill-level performances for which the market is limited. In quota talent performance, it is clear how the individual attains top-level performance and no creative breakthroughs are required. Physicians, teachers, lawyers, engineers, business leaders, and public officials work in quota talent areas. Tannenbaum's final talent area is *anomalous talent*. These talents are exceptional feats that sometimes have a practical value but in other cases only provide entertainment or amusement. Anomalous talents include speed readers, mountain climbers, Broadway singers, gourmet chiefs or cooks, and anachronistic manual craftsmen.

The uncertainty about the differences between gifts, aptitudes, talents, and performances is understandable because all are closely related. Francoys Gagné suggested a differentiation that clarified the differences between gifts and talents. Aptitudes can be thought of as capacities to learn, underlying potential, or natural ability. Giftedness can be thought of as high levels of aptitude.

These could be seen as gifts to the individual because only small increases were possible after conception and birth. *Talents,* however, were defined as high levels of developed abilities or performances. The assessment of talent must be defined and measured in real-world terms and performances. This is not true of aptitude measures that are assessed indirectly with field performance tasks unique to the assessment and not directly measuring any real-world performance.

Catalysts

Talents or high-level performance do not follow automatically from gifts. An individual may be born with high-level aptitudes, which are latent talents, but without the proper dispositions, education, and environments the talents may remain latent. Gagné proposed two broad categories of catalytic factors that sped up or slowed down the transformation of gifts into talents. One category of catalysts is those things internal to the person. These intrapersonal catalysts include things such as motivation and temperament. There are also catalysts external to the person, or environmental catalysts. These environmental catalysts include their surroundings, the people, places, events, and opportunities that exist for them. Gagné also includes chance factors that are more random and uncontrollable but, like intrapersonal and environmental catalysts, may speed up or slow down the individual's talent development.

Talent Searches

Other uses of the term *talent* are common. Since the mid-1970s, millions of young people have participated in talent searches sponsored by various regional talent search centers. Individuals who are in middle school and sometimes younger qualify for participation through high performance on standardized tests or with parent nomination. These then sit for the SAT or the ACT program exams. Both of these assessments are normally given to college-bound high-school seniors. Data from the above-level tests are used to identify high levels of talent and suggest appropriate educational interventions.

Talent Development

Benjamin Bloom defined and studied talent in the 1980s by looking for world-class performance in relatively young individuals from a variety of talent domains. Although not limiting talent only to world-class performance, this research paradigm provided opportunities to talk to talented individuals and their mentors, coaches, teachers, and parents to better understand the process of talent development. The results suggested world-class talent performance required significant investment of time and efforts by individuals and their families along with experiences of success and acclaim, increasingly longer and harder practice, and mentoring, teaching, or coaching at ever more sophisticated levels.

More recently, talent has been proposed as a more useful and less offensive concept than giftedness is. Giftedness suggests a single intellectual capacity over which the individual, parent, and educator have little or no control. Talent implies performance that is the result of hard work, good education, appropriate opportunities, and personal motivation; things individuals, parents, and educators or mentors and coaches can influence. One concern with the current distinction is that it can lead to the inaccurate assumption that anyone can become anything if they just work hard enough or have the right training. In reality, talent development is the result of a match between above-average natural abilities and a talent domain with the interventions and catalytic effects of education, training, resources, hard work, motivation, and a sense of purpose.

Michael F. Sayler

See also Academic Talent; Eminence; Expertise; *Genetic Studies of Genius;* Talent Development; Talented Girls, Mathematics; Talented Readers; Talent Identification Programs

Further Readings

Bloom, B. (1985). *Developing talent in young people.* New York: Ballantine Books.

Gagné, F. (2005). From gifts to talents. In R. Sternberg & J. Davidson (Eds.), *Conceptions of giftedness* (2nd ed., pp. 98–119). New York: Cambridge University Press.

Hollingworth, L. S. (1926). *Gifted children: Their nature and nurture.* New York: Macmillan.

Marland, S. P., Jr. (1972). *Education of the gifted and talented: Vol. 1. Report to the Congress of the United States by the U.S. Commissioner of Education.* Washington, DC: U.S. Government Printing Office.

Renzulli, J. S., & Reis, S. M. (1998). Talent development through curriculum differentiation. *NASSP Bulletin, 82*(595), 61–74.

Tannenbaum, A. (1983). *Gifted children's' psychological and educational perspectives.* New York: Macmillan.

Terman, L. M. (1925). *Genetic studies of genius: Mental and physical traits of a thousand gifted children.* Stanford, CA: Stanford University Press.

Treffinger, D. J., & Feldhusen, J. F. (1996). Talent recognition and development: Successor to gifted education. *Journal for the Education of the Gifted, 2,* 181–193.

Talent Development

The process of talent development within specific domains is one that has fascinated teachers, parents, and psychologists during the last century. How is it that some extremely smart children end up dropping out of high school and failing to realize their promise and potential? Why is it that some prodigies grow up to be quite average in the fields in which they showed such promise when they were young children? Why do other traits—described by Joseph Renzulli as cocognitive traits—appear to be so important in talent development when combined with potential in a particular domain? This entry discusses these questions.

Researchers have long studied these questions and others related to talent development in an attempt to identify factors that contribute to high achievement in adulthood. For example, Benjamin Bloom and colleagues closely examined 120 individuals who excelled in academic, artistic, or athletic pursuits before age 35. The researchers conducted interviews with these accomplished individuals, exploring both how home and school contributed to the resulting international success demonstrated by participants. They found that the development of talent occurred most often when family members had a personal interest in the talent field and gave strong support, encouragement, and rewards for developing the talent. Parents, in particular, provided both high levels of support and resources. Most families assumed that the talent would be developed as part of the family's life. Individualized instruction in the talent field both at home and at school also correlated with later success.

Other researchers interested in talent development include Rena Subotnik who interviewed master creators in a variety of fields and Howard Gardner who studied the lives of pivotal figures through the lens of his life's work in multiple intelligences.

Longitudinal Studies

It is undeniable that retrospective studies, such as those discussed earlier, have contributed substantially to our knowledge of talent development. However, this type of research is subject to bias. Memory is notoriously unstable and subject to interpretation and reinterpretation based on current circumstances and beliefs. Thus, accomplished people may remember early influences on talent development differently than they might if they had not ultimately succeeded in their chosen domains.

Longitudinal research, which is free from this type of bias, is therefore crucial to the exploration of talent development. Longitudinal studies have been part of gifted education for decades. The most famous of these is Lewis Terman's seminal longitudinal study of gifted students, which still affects research. Subotnik and colleagues, for example, conducted a follow-up of the graduates of Hunter College Experimental School and compared their accomplishments and life choices with those of Terman's subjects.

In other longitudinal research, Barbara Kerr studied the participants in a *Sputnik*-era program for academically gifted students to investigate gender differences in outcomes. Marcia Delcourt studied students who had formerly participated in a pull-out program based on Renzulli's enrichment triad model. Although the students in this study were still in college and had not yet started their careers, they had identified long-term goals that dovetailed with their "passions" as identified and developed in the enrichment program. In addition, all but one of the students reported completing at least one in-depth project in the 3 years since leaving the program.

In addition to these studies of general academic ability, longitudinal studies have targeted programs that develop specific gifts and talents in areas such as math and science. Two of the most well-known programs in this category are the Westinghouse (now Intel) Science Talent Search and the Study of Mathematically Precocious Youth (SMPY). Subotnik and her colleagues investigated graduates of the Westinghouse Talent Search to discover the means by which students talented in science persisted or failed to persist in science. The SMPY is ideal for a longitudinal study because it is a national program with a clearly defined definition of giftedness and a specific methodology for meeting the needs of qualifying students. The SMPY embeds longitudinal research within its program design by sending periodic follow-up questionnaires to participants, and numerous longitudinal studies have been conducted on this project. Collectively, these studies have found that acceleration worked well for participants and caused neither gaps in knowledge nor burnout in the field of study. Most accelerated students report that they were satisfied with their experience of being accelerated.

Both SMPY and the Westinghouse competition found that most of the winners from the 1983 Westinghouse competition and SMPY students chose to remain in science and math following their participation in the program. Moreover, most of those who had "left science" as a discipline reported that they did so because they had found a mentor in another domain, not because they lost interest in the original field. This finding of the importance of a supportive environment or presence as key in the development of talent echoes findings by Mihaly Csikszentmihalyi and Bloom, both of whom have noted the importance of cultural values on the development of talent.

A number of interesting implications emerged in examining the outcomes of these talent development and enrichment programs. For example, most of the former participants in the programs reported success and satisfaction in a chosen discipline, but not at the level that may have been expected, given their early potential. Subotnik addressed this issue directly in comparing the responses of the graduates of the first 12 classes of Hunter College Experimental School with those of Terman and Melita Oden's subjects on the midlife questionnaire instrument used by Terman and Oden. Although many individuals in both groups did achieve midlife stability and success in both their personal and professional lives, none of them had made original contributions in a domain, perhaps because they had not found anything they loved enough to jeopardize the stability and well-rounded conventional success they enjoyed.

Other Studies

In their study of talented teenagers, Csikszentmihalyi, Kevin Rathunde, and Samuel Whalen conducted a 5-year longitudinal study addressing how and why some teenagers become committed to the development of their talent but others become disengaged from their talent. The authors found that children must first be recognized as talented before they can fulfill their potential. Thus, students who committed to their talents tended to have skills valued by their culture. They also demonstrated personality traits such as concentration, endurance, openness to experience, awareness, and understanding. In addition, teens who had habits conducive to cultivating talent, such as spending time in challenging pursuits with friends, focusing attention, and spending time alone, instead of wasting time, were more likely to have developed their talents. Talented teens were also more conservative in their sexual attitudes and aware of the possible conflict between productive work and relationships.

Similar to the Bloom study, this group of researchers found that talented teens had families that provided both support and challenge to enhance the development of talent. Talented teenagers were also positively influenced by teachers who were supportive and modeled enjoyable involvement in a field. Talent development, according to this study, was found to be a process that requires both expressive (evoking positive feelings) and instrumental (useful to future goals) rewards. The last finding in this study related to how talents developed, and the researchers found that talent development is more likely to occur if it produces optimal experiences in teenagers. Memories of peak moments motivated students to continue to work to improve in the hopes of achieving or replicating the same intense experience again.

What Teachers and Parents Can Do to Develop Talents

Parents and teachers can and should actively help students to develop their gifts and talents. Unfortunately, traditional methods of schooling often fail to provide the types of broad, rich experiences that encourage talent development in young people. Renzulli believes that the field of gifted education has been a laboratory for the many innovations that have become mainstays of the U.S. educational system. Practices promoted in gifted education suggest that, rather than merely being sources for the acquisition of information, schools can and should be places where students learn who they are and how to make the most of the gifts they have been given.

How can educators help develop the talents of gifted, creative, and talented children? In a period in which fast is good and faster is better, how can educators help children to learn to think creatively and to value opportunities for quiet reflection and creative work of their choice? Some previous evidence suggests that gifted education programs help children to develop their abilities, creativity, and task commitment. A central premise of gifted education is this: If educators give children opportunities to become involved in talent development opportunities in school, these experiences will increase the likelihood that students will emerge as talented and creatively productive adults in whatever area they select for their future work.

The research reviewed on studies of talent development suggests several factors that contribute to this complicated process. Research suggests that recognition of talent promotes talent and that cultural values affect whether a talent is rewarded. Certain personality traits also seem to accompany talent development. These factors coupled with individualized instruction in the talent field, both at home and in an educational setting, seem to produce good results. Talent development is also more likely to occur if the process results in optimal experiences.

Memories of peak, exciting experiences such as starring in a drama production or publishing a story or book can help motivate students to replicate the intense experience again. Perhaps the most important finding of research on talent development is that there is no common path that enables individuals to fulfill their potential. Fate, support, environment, family climate, the right teachers, and the desire to work hard all play important roles in determining whether talents can and will be developed.

Sally M. Reis

See also Eminence; Giftedness, Definition; Intelligence; Talent

Further Readings

Bloom, B. S. (Ed.). (1985). *Developing talent in young people.* New York: Ballantine Books.

Csikszentmihalyi, M., Rathunde, K., & Whalen, S. (1993). *Talented teenagers: The roots of success and failure.* Cambridge, UK: Cambridge University Press.

Delcourt, M. A. B., Loyd, B. H., Cornell, D. G., & Goldberg, M. D. (1994). *Evaluation of the effects of programming arrangements on student learning outcomes.* Storrs: National Research Center on the Gifted and Talented, University of Connecticut.

Feldman, D. H., with Goldsmith, L. T. (1991). *Nature's gambit: Child prodigies and the development of human potential.* New York: Teachers College Press.

Gardner, H. (1993). *Creating minds.* New York: Basic Books.

Kerr, B. A. (1997). *Smart girls: A new psychology of girls, women, and giftedness.* Scottsdale, AZ: Great Potential Press.

Subotnik, R. F., & Arnold, K. D. (Eds.). (1994). *Beyond Terman: Contemporary longitudinal studies of giftedness and talent.* Norwood, NJ: Ablex.

Talented Girls, Mathematics

Although the field of mathematics, a traditionally men-dominated field, has seen an increase in participation by women, research continues to document differences in performance and participation for mathematically talented women. As minorities in the field, mathematically talented women are confronted with issues that relate to their domain-specific talent, to gender issues, and to the interactions of their mathematical talent with biological, physiological, and societal aspects of being women. This entry describes some of these issues.

Discrepancies for Men and Women

Although mathematics performance before high school is comparable for boys and girls in the general population, this is not the case for mathematically talented boys and girls. Even in elementary schools, more boys than girls earn top scores on standardized mathematics assessments, particularly on above-level assessments that reduce the ceiling-effect for mathematically talented students. Similarly, significantly more boys than girls are identified as "mathematically precocious" through national talent-search programs, such as the Study for Mathematically Precocious Youth (SMPY), which reported a 17-to-1 ratio of preadolescent boys to girls scoring above 700 on the mathematics section of the SAT.

Several claims about biological bases of these discrepancies have been made. More attention in recent years has fallen on spatial abilities. Although research results are conflicting and inconclusive on gender differences in spatial abilities, evidence showing a connection between gender differences in mathematical achievement and gender differences in *certain* spatial skills is accumulating. Although in the early years of schooling the focus is on encoding and retrieving information from long-term memory, the later years include more visual-spatial problems that require constructing and transforming visual-spatial representations within one's working memory. Because girls excel at cognitive processes like those on which the early schooling years focus, they have the advantage in the early years. However, gender differences in visual-spatial working memory favoring boys can be found as early as preschool, and boys have the advantage later in school. In fact, mechanical and visual-spatial skills are a stronger contributor to gender differences on Trends in Mathematics and Science Study (TIMSS) items than mathematics self-confidence is. Infant studies, however, have shown for more than three decades that there are no sex differences at birth in orientation toward spatial skills.

Another claim for the existence of sex differences in mathematics ability has involved the evidence that boys outperform girls is mathematics fact retrieval. By fourth grade, boys in the top half of the speed distribution are faster at mathematics fact retrieval than are similar girls, and they are equally accurate. This is significant because speed of mathematics fact retrieval is a statistically significant predictor of mathematics test performance in middle school and college, affecting later scores and decisions to pursue higher-level mathematics. This may be one reason that overall gender differences on the mathematics portion of the SAT are eliminated when the time limit is removed. On the other hand, it has been found that many categories of items that favor girls have been removed from the SAT–M, and that when SAT–M scores are considered with regard to their power to predict college achievement in advanced mathematics, gifted girls' achievement is significantly under-predicted by these tests. This, and the fact that findings of extreme gaps in SAT–M performance at the highest levels are based on samples in which boys represent a much more selective sample than girls do, leads Elizabeth Spelke and other researchers to believe that the SAT–M may not be an appropriate measure of talented girls' true abilities to achieve the highest levels of mathematics performance; the SAT–M's tendency to overestimate boys' abilities and underestimate girls' abilities makes it suspect as evidence of biologically based sex differences.

A third claim was that the attainment of fewer degrees in mathematics by women than men at all levels (bachelors, masters, and doctorates) was evidence of sex differences in ability. Research, however indicates that psychological and sociological influences as well as biological influences affect these performance and participation discrepancies in mathematical talent development. In fact, the mathematics achievement gap is rapidly closing, with as many women as men taking calculus and achieving high scores, majoring in college mathematics, and graduating with degrees in mathematics. Even among the girls of the original study of mathematically precocious youth, those who were encouraged by accelerated instruction in mathematics attained the same proportion of high-level positions in mathematics and science as boys did.

Influences on Discrepancies for Men and Women

More commonly studied and accepted than biological influences are the psychological influences on the discrepancies between men's and women's mathematics talent development. Many researchers have argued that men and women have equal aptitude for mathematics and equal cognitive ability, although with somewhat different profiles, so there is no genetic basis for cognitive sex differences. However, confidence in one's mathematical abilities is strongly correlated with mathematics performance and achievement. Men consistently exhibit more confidence in their mathematics abilities than women do, and women's lack of confidence has a negative impact both on their mathematics achievement and on their decisions to take further mathematics courses.

Men and women also differ in their locus of control. Although men tend to attribute their success in mathematics to their mathematical ability and their failure in mathematics to a lack of effort, women are more likely to attribute their success in mathematics to hard work and their failure in mathematics to lack of mathematics ability. This holds true for all achievement levels, including for mathematically talented populations. Although men's locus of control enhances their academic self-efficacy, this does not appear to be true for women. Instead, women's locus of control may decrease their persistence in mathematics, which has been shown to be necessary for mathematics talent development.

Talented and eminent women struggle for self-esteem, and they struggle against the societal influences on their mathematical talent development, including the conflict they experience between their gender roles and career options, particularly in the domains of mathematics and science. Research has shown that because mathematically talented women have less belief in their intellect and mathematics abilities and more concern about balancing family and career than men do, they do not aspire to achieve at the highest levels in their professions. These struggles within mathematically talented women and with societal expectations cause many women to devalue their mathematics abilities and achievements. Thus, women's psychological and biological profiles interact with societal expectations, and together these influence women's decisions to or not to develop their mathematical talent and the career path they choose.

Besides influencing women's decisions about which career to pursue, societal expectations and gender roles also influence young girls as they make decisions about which courses to participate in and whether to display their mathematics talent or not. Teenagers associate mathematics with masculinity, causing some mathematically talented women to hide their talent, to choose not to perform well in mathematics, or to choose not to pursue mathematics studies further.

In addition to their peers, mathematically talented women also are influenced by the perceptions and expectations of their parents and teachers. Unfortunately, research has shown that parents exhibit gender stereotypes, such as mathematics being for boys, when conveying their expectations to their children and that teachers provide boys more attention and opportunities for participation. These behaviors are particularly damaging to girls' mathematical talent development because they are more influenced by and more likely to pay attention to the expectations and advice of their teachers and parents than boys are.

Future Outlook

Researchers in gifted education, mathematics education, and gender studies continue to study mathematically talented women, providing new insights into their performance and participation in mathematics as well as the interaction of the domain-specific nature of their talent and their gender on their talent development. Resources are available to parents and educators interested in encouraging mathematically talent girls, helping them address and overcome the conflicts they are presented with, and realizing their potential.

Jill L. Adelson

See also Girls, Gifted; Mathematical Intelligence; Mathematically Precocious; Mathematical Talent; Self-Efficacy/Self-Esteem; Sex Differences in Mathematical and Spatial Ability; Study of Mathematically Precocious Youth; Women, Gifted

Further Readings

Arnold, K. D., Noble, K. D., & Subotnik, R. F. (Eds.). (1996). *Remarkable women: Perspectives in female talent development.* Cresskill, NJ: Hampton Press.

Fennema, E., & Leder, G. C. (Eds.). (1990). *Mathematics and gender.* New York: Teachers College Press.

Gallagher, A. M., & Kaufman, J. C. (Eds.). (2005). *Gender differences in mathematics: An integrative psychological approach.* Cambridge, UK: Cambridge University Press.

Reis, S. M., & Park, S. (2001). Gender differences in high-achieving students in math and science. *Journal for the Education of the Gifted, 25,* 52–73.

Spelke, E. (2005). Sex differences in intrinsic aptitude for mathematics and science? A critical review. *American Psychologist, 60,* 950–958.

Subotnik, R. F., & Arnold, K. D. (Eds.). (1995). *Beyond Terman: Contemporary longitudinal studies of giftedness and talent.* Norwood, NJ: Ablex.

Talented Readers

Identifying the characteristics of and defining talented readers is challenging because no consensus exists. Research indicates that not all academically gifted students are talented readers, and not all talented readers are identified as academically gifted perhaps because of the wide variation of abilities in this population. This widely known research has had the result of precocious reading not being taken seriously by educators, who often believe that early reading is just decoding without comprehension. Many of these early readers are likely gifted but are overlooked for gifted education programs. Most current research suggests that gifted students' general learning characteristics differ from average learners in several ways: They usually learn faster than others; have the capacity to find, solve, and act on problems more readily; have a developed use of thinking skills; and understand and make connections about abstract concepts ideas more easily. Less is known about the characteristics of talented readers. This entry describes issues relating to talented readers.

Characteristics of talented readers have been described anecdotally, but little research has focused on these populations. They have been described as having exceptional reading ability and the capacity to understand textual information well above what would be expected of other students in their age group. Talented readers are often defined as reading approximately 2 or more years above grade level as measured by some reading assessment. Work in the last two decades has focused on identifying some of the characteristics of this group, although no common list of research-based characteristics exists. Sally Reis and a team of researchers at the University of Connecticut reviewed recent work that suggests that many talented readers read earlier than their peers, read at least two grade levels above their chronological grade placement, begin to read early and may be self-taught. It also suggests that some of these students are avid, enthusiastic, voracious readers who use reading differently for different purposes, spend more time reading than their peers, and read a greater variety of literature into adulthood. In addition, it has been suggested that they automatically integrate prior knowledge and experience into their reading; use higher-order thinking skills such as analysis, synthesis, and evaluation; and communicate these ideas. Several researchers indicate that talented readers display verbal ability in self-expression, use colorful and descriptive phrasing, demonstrate advanced understanding of language, have an expansive vocabulary, perceive relationships between and among characters, and grasp complex ideas.

Other anecdotal information suggests that talented readers possess an unusual capacity to process information as well as an ability to process thoughts at an accelerated pace, synthesize ideas in a comprehensive way, perceive unusual relationships and integrate ideas. Some may display an advanced ability to understand a variety of texts and have other language-related abilities, such as the ability to retain a large quantity of information, as well as advanced comprehension, varied interests and curiosity in texts, and high level language development and verbal ability. Talented readers understand that books can help them acquire information, clarify ideas, stimulate the imagination, and deepen understanding, and many highly able readers often have preferences for science, history, biography, travel, poetry, and informational texts such as atlases, encyclopedias, and how-to books. Advanced reading is a complex process made up of many subskills that vary within the advanced-reader population. Talented readers' skills are usually considered advanced only as relative to their peers and a common definition is challenging as peer groups vary. Judith Wynn Halsted identified a pattern for young talented readers that may change throughout their academic lives, finding that they initially teach themselves how to read before they start school, are independent readers by second grade, know their favorite authors by third grade, and have well-established reading patterns by fifth grade. Unfortunately, their reading level may drop off by the time they reach middle school as a result of increased participation in extracurricular activities or an absence of challenge in reading in school.

Little research has focused on identifying and teaching talented readers to ensure that they can make continuous progress in reading. Recently, Reis and others synthesized research that found that talented readers can be defined by four characteristics: reading early and at advanced levels, using advanced processing in reading, reading with enthusiasm and enjoyment, and demonstrating advanced language skills (oral, reading, and written).

Talented readers need appropriately challenging instruction and curricular content that helps them make continuous progress in reading. They have differentiated talents and instructional needs that require advanced learning opportunities to challenge and extend their abilities and enable them to read content above their current reading level, to engage and think about complex texts, and to extend conventional basal reading instruction, which is usually below their chronological grade level. Talented readers are placed at risk in many schools simply because they are not challenged and therefore their reading development can be delayed or even halted. If reading instructional and independent materials are not above the students' level of knowledge or understanding, learning is less efficient and reading development may be delayed or stopped. Some talented readers never learn to exert effort in reading and, consequently, acquire poor work habits.

A summary of information on the current classroom reading experiences of talented readers suggests that although they can benefit from appropriately challenging levels of reading, they seldom receive it. Methods for differentiating curriculum and instruction for talented readers exist, and teachers can learn to differentiate. Some research supports the effectiveness of specific instructional and curricular strategies with talented readers, particularly curriculum compacting, grouping, acceleration, the use of advanced literature and challenging reading, and using the schoolwide enrichment model–reading approach developed by researchers at the University of Connecticut. Without these challenges, some talented readers grow accustomed by third or fourth grade to expending minimal effort and learn few self-regulation strategies and few advanced reading strategies. If talented readers are going to be challenged, it will require more professional development, new curricular and instructional options, and the use of materials that eliminate or extend basal reading programs and provide high levels of challenge. To challenge talented readers, educators must compact their regular reading instruction, provide challenging alternate materials, give opportunities for acceleration, and find other ways to stimulate their potential. Promising strategies do exist, but they must be more widely implemented.

Sally M. Reis

See also Gifted Readers; Precocious Reading; Verbal Ability

Further Readings

Halsted, J. W. (1994). *Some of my best friends are books: Guiding gifted readers from pre-school to high school.* Dayton: Ohio Psychology Press.

Jackson, N. E. (1988). Precocious reading ability: What does it mean? *Gifted Child Quarterly, 32,* 200–204.

Reis, S. M., Eckert, R. D., Jacobs, J., Coyne, M., Richards, S. Briggs, C. J., et al. (2005). *The schoolwide enrichment model—Reading framework.* Storrs, CT: National Research Center on the Gifted and Talented.

Reis, S. M., Gubbins, E. J., Briggs, C., Schreber, F. R., Richards, S., Jacobs, J., et al. (2004). Reading instruction for talented readers: Case studies documenting few opportunities for continuous progress. *Gifted Child Quarterly, 48,* 309–338.

Talent Identification Program

Duke University's Talent Identification Program (TIP), described in this entry, was founded in 1980 by a grant from the Duke Endowment. One of four university-based talent search programs in the United States (the others are Johns Hopkins University's Center for Talented Youth, Northwestern University's Center for Talent Development, and the University of Denver's Rocky Mountain Talent Search), the TIP has served more than 1.8 million gifted students, in a geographical area focused on 16 states in the South and Southeast. Duke TIP was first created to identify gifted students and help serve their educational needs through partnerships with local gifted and talented programs. Since its first talent search in 1981, which focused on seventh-grade students, Duke TIP has expanded its offerings to include a twice-yearly fourth- and fifth-grade talent search, summer programs, school-year programs, e-studies, and independent learning opportunities.

Talent Search Programs

Talent Searches

In a typical talent search program, students who score in the top 5 percent on a standardized achievement test are invited to take one of the two main college entrance examinations, either the SAT or the American College Testing program (ACT). Based on their test results, students are then offered access to various services provided by the particular talent search program. The reasoning behind using the above-level testing to identify gifted and talented students is that most grade-appropriate tests would have too low a ceiling, resulting in a lower, inaccurate picture of the student's true abilities.

Duke TIP Seventh-Grade Search

When TIP originated in 1980, it was in the form of a talent search program that served seventh-grade students. The first talent search, which was held in 1981, identified about 8,700 students. Currently, approximately 6,000 middle and junior high schools participate each year in the seventh-grade search. Once the students take their examination (ACT or SAT), they are provided with feedback about their abilities, and how they performed in comparison with other similar students. Students and their parents receive materials about further educational enrichment opportunities, receive a certificate of merit, and are typically invited to participate in an awards ceremony.

Duke TIP Fourth- and Fifth-Grade Search

Originally called Motivation for Academic Performance, the fourth- and fifth-grade talent search was started by Duke University in 1994. By 2005, more than 41,000 students participated in the lower-level talent search. Students who qualify for admission receive educational materials, a certificate of achievement, and the opportunity to take an achievement test developed by the ACT for an eighth-grade population, the EXPLORE.

Beyond the Talent Search

Once students have been selected for admission through the talent search process, Duke TIP offers may different opportunities to enrich each student's education through multiple programs. Some programs are offered only during the summer, and others are offered throughout the year. Some programs require an overnight stay, but others can be experienced from the home.

Summer Studies Programs

Duke TIP started its Summer Studies program in 1981, serving 151 students on the Duke University campus. Currently, Duke TIP offers two varieties of summer study programs, with the difference based on the student's level of achievement on the talent search admission test. The Academy for Summer Studies programs, currently offered on four college campuses (Appalachian State University, University of Kansas, Duke University Marine Lab, and Texas A&M University), serves students who have lower qualifying scores on either the SAT or ACT. The Center for Summer Studies programs, currently offered on five college campuses (Davidson College, Duke University East Campus, Duke University West Campus, Duke University Marine Lab, and Wake Forest University), serves students who score higher qualifying scores on the SAT or ACT. Both programs accept students in the 7th through 10th grades.

These programs are 3-week-long residential programs, where each student takes one fast-paced college-level course that meets for approximately 40 hours per week, Monday through Saturday. Students typically live in the college dorms in residential groups based on gender and age. Classes tend to be mixed both in gender and grade level, so any class may contain 7th, 8th, 9th, and 10th graders. Classes tend to be offered based on the individual campus specialties, so universities with a strong veterinary program might offer Introduction to Veterinary Medicine, but another university with a strong aerospace program might offer Aerospace Engineering. While not in classes, students participate in evening review sessions, as well as social and recreational activities that range from sports to games to crafts to movie viewing. Two sessions are offered each summer on most campuses.

Field Studies

Field studies are offered both nationally and internationally to qualifying students in the 9th through 12th grades (international programs start in 10th grade). These residential programs last 2 weeks and cover a variety of interests, from Astronomy at an observatory in North Carolina to Architecture in Italy. Each program typically serves 20 to 25 students and is staffed by three adults, one of whom is the instructor while the other two are assistants. As with the Summer Studies programs, the instructors tend to be college professors, graduate students, or teachers, and the assistants tend to be undergraduate college students. Only one field study program of each type is offered per summer.

Institutes

Duke TIP offers three institutes for students in Grades 9 through 12, with two new institutes offered this year. Each program focuses on a different area of interest, from leadership to computational science to prelaw. Students live on Duke University's East campus, in residential groups. Twenty-five to 35 students are selected for each 15-day residential program. Only one of each institute program is offered each summer.

School-Year Programs

Duke TIP also offers Scholar Weekend programs during the school year for qualified 8th through 11th graders, although some campuses accept 12th graders. These programs offer a short but intense course in topics usually not available in the students' home school. These courses, similar to the summer studies courses but shorter in length, offer students a chance to explore a topic of interest in depth for a fast-paced weekend, and provide a brief experience of college life. Scholar Weekends are offered on seven university campuses, and cover topics ranging from Anatomy to Fairy Tales to Criminal Trial Advocacy.

E-Studies and Independent Learning

For students who prefer to work from home, TIP offers e-studies and independent learning opportunities. E-studies courses offer a distance-learning environment, run by a TIP instructor over the Internet. These courses typically allow students to work at their own pace, in collaboration with other gifted students from around the world. Courses are 16 weeks long and are offered once per year. The courses are available for students in Grades 8 through 12.

The TIP Independent Learning Programs provide offerings for students in Grades 4 through 12. These programs are CD-ROM based, not requiring the use of the Internet. In the Learn On Your Own Courses, students in Grades 4 through 12 work through a workbook and CD-ROM with a local mentor. In the CD-ROM Enrichment Courses, students use a multimedia CD and workbook to learn. The Enrichment Courses are offered to students in Grades 7 through 12. The Learn On Your Own Courses tend to cover topics found in the normal school, and the CD-ROM Enrichment Courses offerings cover topics not usually found in middle and high schools.

Carol A. Carman

See also ACT College Admission Examination; Center for Talent Development; SAT; Study of Mathematically Precocious Youth; Summer Programs; Talent Searches

Further Readings

Talent Identification Program. (2009). *Educational opportunity guide.* Durham, NC: Duke University. Retrieved from http://www.tip.duke.edu/resources

VanTassel-Baska, J. (1984). The talent search as identification model. *Gifted Child Quarterly, 28*(1), 55–57. Retrieved from http://www.gt-cybersource.org/Record.aspx?NavID=2_0&rid=11227

Talent Searches

The talent search method was developed by Julian C. Stanley (Johns Hopkins University) to assess the ability of students with academic performance far above that of most others their age. In 1969, Stanley evaluated a 13-year-old boy by using tests designed for college students. Current talent searches around the world trace their history back to this assessment. This entry discusses at-level testing, above-level testing, talent searches, extracurricular opportunities, educational planning, and future directions of talent searches

At-Level Testing

Standardized achievement tests typically are used *at-level* (also called *in-grade*). They are given near the end of the school year and present material at a student's grade level to determine how well the student has mastered what was taught. For most students, this approach is effective. For someone achieving a high score, however, important questions remain unanswered. Does the student know higher-level material than that covered on the test—and, if so, at what level is the student functioning?

At-level testing cannot answer these questions because of a *ceiling effect*—the tests do not include items of sufficient difficulty. Including only grade-level material means that someone who knows grade-level material as well as more advanced material will obtain the same score as someone who knows grade-level material only. To accurately assess gifted students' abilities, an assessment method must raise the ceiling by providing higher-level material.

Above-Level Testing

In *above-level* testing, standardized tests are administered to students younger than those for whom the tests were designed, but for whom the ceilings on at-level tests are too low. Because this method tests students on information they have not been taught, the results indicate reasoning ability, rather than retention. The use of existing, published tests ensures test security, appropriate standardization and content, good psychometric properties, and valid comparisons of the gifted student's performance with that of other students at a similar academic level. Above-level testing provides a more accurate assessment of a high-achieving student's ability than is possible with at-level testing, and scores predict performance in advanced classes, higher education, and careers.

Talent Searches

The results of Stanley's initial above-level testing were extremely useful in developing appropriate educational plans for highly able students. In 1972, the first talent search was conducted; the mathematics portion of the SAT was administered to 450 gifted seventh- and eighth-grade students from the Baltimore, Maryland, area. In 1973, the verbal portion of the SAT was added. Later, this original talent search expanded its coverage beyond Baltimore, and other regional talent searches were developed. Currently, several state-based programs also exist, and talent searches have been established outside the United States. Presently, the major regional talent searches in the United States are as shown in Table 1.

Over time, talent search programs have expanded beyond the SAT to include the American College Testing Program (ACT) for seventh- and eighth-graders and talent searches for elementary school students. To qualify, a student must obtain a score at or above the 95th percentile (97th percentile for the youngest students in some programs) on the national norms of an in-grade standardized achievement test. Once talent search results are in, programs provide information about interpreting the scores and using them for educational planning, as well as opportunities for students to take special classes outside of school.

Extracurricular Opportunities

Many talent searches offer classes for students who earn high scores in talent search testing. Some classes are accelerative and can replace classes students typically would take in school; others are enrichment-based and offer a chance to explore a topic in more depth or breadth than is possible in school. All classes provide important opportunities for students to interact with others who have similar abilities and interests. Students have reported significant benefits from the social interaction, as well as the academic challenge, provided by these classes. In many cases, however, extracurricular classes are not enough; highly gifted students also require academic interventions within their school settings.

Table 1 Regional Talent Search Programs in the United States

Program	*States Covered*	*Grade Levels Served*
Center for Talented Youth (CTY) Johns Hopkins University, Baltimore, MD www.cty.jhu.edu	AK, AZ, CA, CT, DE, DC, HI, ME, MD, MA, NH, NJ, NY, OR, PA, RI, VT, VA, WA, WV	2–8
Midwest Academic Talent Search (MATS) Center for Talent Development (CTD) Northwestern University, Evanston, IL www.ctd.northwestern.edu	IN, IL, MI, MN, ND, OH, SD, WI	3–9
Rocky Mountain Academic Talent Search (RMATS) Center for Innovative and Talented Youth (CITY) University of Denver, Denver, CO www.du.edu/city/programs/academic-year-programs/rocky-mountain-talent-search/index.html	CO, ID, MT, NV, NM, UT, WY	3–9
Talent Identification Program (TIP) Duke University, Durham, NC www.tip.duke.edu	AL, AR, FL, GA, IA, KS, KY, LA, MS, MO, NE, NC, OK, SC, TN, TX	4–7

Educational Planning

Because students who obtain high scores in talent searches function at an advanced level, acceleration often is appropriate. Acceleration involves academic work at an advanced grade level. One means of accomplishing this is to allow a student to skip material that already is known. The high ceilings of above-level tests allow accurate assessment of what is known, so talent search results can be used to identify students who may benefit from acceleration. Standardized tests may not be perfectly aligned with a school's curriculum, however, so talent search results often are used as a screening tool, after which above-level administration of a school's own assessment tools (e.g., end-of-year exams) can determine the most appropriate placement for a given student within the school's curriculum.

Future Directions

Hundreds of thousands of students have participated in talent searches since 1972, but there is a need to reach more eligible students. Currently, talent searches are conducted by independent programs and charge fees to participants. Although financial aid is provided, the cost and the need to become involved outside school may discourage some families from participating. For students who do participate, there is a need to ensure a match between ability and education. Too often, schools fail to follow up on talent search results with appropriate educational plans. Talent search programs are actively working to address these concerns.

Mary Ann Swiatek

See also Center for Talent Development; Midwest Academic Talent Search; Study of Mathematically Precocious Youth; Summer Programs; Talent Identification Program

Further Readings

Olszewski-Kubilius, P. (2003). Special summer and Saturday programs for gifted students. In N. Colangelo & G. A. Davis (Eds.), *Handbook of gifted education* (3rd ed., pp. 219–228). Boston: Allyn & Bacon.

Stanley, J. C. (1996). In the beginning: The study of mathematically precocious youth. In C. P. Benbow & D. Lubinski (Eds.), *Intellectual talent: Psychometric and social issues* (pp. 225–235). Baltimore: Johns Hopkins University Press.

Swiatek, M. A. (2007). The talent search model: Past, present, and future. [Special issue: Best practices in gifted education.] *Gifted Child Quarterly, 51*(4), 320–329.

Teacher Attitudes

A considerable body of literature in gifted education espouses teacher qualities that promote talent development. A perusal of approximately 20 references, from the 1950s to date, reveals more than 140 different characteristics desirable for gifted education teachers. A closer examination finds lists consist predominantly of knowledge and skills. Knowledge includes anticipated areas such as the nature and needs of students and differentiated instruction, but also specifically test construction. Some lists speak to knowledge of creativity; some do not.

An abundance of skills are suggested, such as being able to understand giftedness, think complexly, and use questioning techniques. Developing a suitable environment is named in approximately half of the time; however, this might be described in terms of safety, warmth, caring, learner-centeredness or even permissiveness. Differences surface as authors include the ability to teach creativity and problem solving, but others do not mention this trait. The extensiveness expands to possessing skills in training others and being organized and well prepared. However, little in the literature described the desired attitudes of teachers concerning beliefs toward students, instruction, or teaching. This entry describes intelligence as a criterial quality, the lack of framework for teacher preparation, attitudes that make a difference, and application of teacher attitudes.

Intelligence as a Criterial Quality

The most frequently cited quality necessary to teaching bright students successfully is the teacher's superior intelligence or intelligence similar to the students they teach. This quality is proffered in more than half of the references reviewed spanning 1954 to 2004. In approximately a third of the references, others similarly assert gifted education teachers need to possess advanced subject matter knowledge; however, neither assertion is supported by empirical evidence.

Lack of Framework for Teacher Preparation

Although the gifted education field is replete with frameworks for conceptualizing giftedness, identifying students, and programming for these learners, there has not been a parallel development of conceptual frameworks for preparing their teachers. It is generally agreed that gifted education teachers need specialized training or licensure. Frameworks for this training have been lacking, yet talented teachers continued to be touted as the most important means of reaching gifted and talented students. Guidance from empirical research is needed for those who prepare teachers to work with gifted and talented students.

Attitudes That Make a Difference

Studies reviewed did not specifically delineate between knowledge, skills, and attitudes of teachers nor was there an accepted framework by which to analyze attitudes of gifted education teachers who taught with reputational expertise. Instead, lists of characteristics and competencies were vague, diverse, and occasionally contradictory. Many studies were considered only secondary sources, only citing other authors. Of the more than 20 studies uncovered in a comprehensive search of the extant literature, few employed actual interviews of gifted education teachers. Others used checklists and student or teacher surveys. Methodology employing direct observation of teachers in action in the classroom was rare. In two qualitative studies found, one examined a single teacher; the other a specialized setting with teachers as facilitators. Lack of research and only vague standards to describe the attitudes related to teachers who possess reputational expertise calls for rigorous research using direct observation and personal reflection.

A Phenomenological and Ethnographic Study

Critical to the field was a phenomenological and ethnographic study to examine the beliefs of teachers more closely. Intensive case studies, including observations of teaching, planning, and thinking aloud–style reflections about gifted education offered a new method to define behaviors and attitudes of teachers possessing reputational expertise. Observations encompassed elementary through high school teachers and documented occurrences seen as sufficiently evident behaviors from which deductions concerning attitudes could be made. Think-aloud reflections strengthened the deductions as these individuals expounded on their thinking and beliefs accompanying the incidents. Units of information from stories, explanations, and quotes were then categorized and sorted into the conceptual framework.

Reputational Expertise Qualities

Defining belief systems of teachers of the gifted who displayed reputational expertise were (a) displaying enthusiasm and insatiable curiosity, (b) learning continuously, and (c) showing firmness in their belief system. In addition, they held their commitment so strongly to these beliefs that the teachers felt compelled to promote and encourage students to value them as well. In practice, teachers used and modeled the techniques and engaged students in metacognitive discussions and reflections to encourage them to adopt the behavior.

Enthusiasm and Insatiable Curiosity

Instructional goals encompassed inherently and intrinsically motivating, stimulating, and inspiring activities and projects because teachers recognized if they were bored with assignments or curriculum, students must be as well. Sparking creativity and developing passion was viewed as strengthening student investment in learning. Enthusiasm and insatiable curiosity fueled teaching and learning.

Continuous Learners

Teachers displaying reputational expertise exhibited lifelong learners traits and encouraged students to embrace this as well. Viewing themselves as facilitators of learning eliminated the need to be seen as an expert and enabled teachers to learn and become enlightened along with students. Students were encouraged to think, challenge, and find out. Understanding the perspectives of others, reflective thinking, and learning to question were practiced pathways. Values centered on learning autonomously and taking responsibility for one's own growth. Taking risks and experiencing failure were part of the process; personal, in-depth reflections were encouraged, and a desire to improve was promoted. Teachers personally embraced the same philosophies.

Firm in Their Belief System

Teachers who displayed reputational expertise exemplified strong commitment to their belief systems. Responses to questions were pensive and replete with signs of prior evaluation and reflection. Conviction and commitment flowed effortlessly as teachers explained rationales and values.

The Policy Attribute

As evidence of conviction, teachers with reputational expertise attempted to teach and pass on these behaviors to students. Accompanying commitment to their own personal lifelong learning led the teachers to consciously share this value with students. Holding strong beliefs about the benefits of thinking interdependently found students actively using the strategies but also learning how to apply them to their lives. Teachers developed these skills in their students rather than merely exposing students to these skills.

Application

Teacher training and professional development can use desired qualities espoused in the literature and offer practitioners time to discuss and examine implications for the classroom. Students and practicing teachers could articulate and define other behaviors that blended with qualities in the literature. Specialization in the field is validated. It provides opportunities to think interdependently about attitudes encompassing the desirable characteristics and promotes understanding, reflection, and application of the examined traits. Intense study and a desire for continuous improvement will better allow teachers to walk the talk.

Marcia Dvorak

See also Professional Development; Research, Qualitative; Teachers of Gifted; Teacher Training

Further Readings

Colangelo, N., & Davis, G. A. (Eds.). (2003). *Handbook of gifted education* (3rd ed.). Boston: Allyn & Bacon.

Coleman, L. (1992). The cognitive map of a master teacher conducting discussions with gifted students. *Exceptionality, 3*(1), 45–53.

Heath, W. J. (1997). *What are the most effective characteristics of teachers of the gifted?* ERIC Document Reproduction Service: ED 411 665. EC 305 858.

Robinson, A., & Kolloff, P. (2005). Preparing teachers to work with high ability youth at the secondary level: Issues and implications for licensure. In F. Dixon & S. M. Moon (Ed.), *The handbook of secondary gifted education* (pp. 581–610). Waco, TX: Prufrock Press.

Robinson, A., Shore, B. M., & Enersen, D. L. (2007). *Best practices in gifted education: An evidence-based guide.* Waco, TX; Prufrock Press.

Story, C. M. (1985). Facilitator of learning: A micro-ethnographic study of the teacher of the gifted. *Gifted Child Quarterly, 29,* 155–159.

Teacher Nominations

Teacher nomination has been found to be a valuable method to use to identify students for gifted and talented programs. The use of teacher nomination, described in this entry, has been compared with other independent variables such as peer and parent ratings and evaluations of work samples and is considered a standard practice in the identification of academically gifted and talented students. However, only a small number of teacher nomination instruments have been developed for rating the characteristics of high-ability students, and only a few studies have investigated the technical aspects of most scales. Several researchers have investigated the effectiveness of teacher nominations of students for gifted programs during the last few decades and their findings suggest that when specific rating criteria exist, teachers are able to identify talented students in their classrooms.

Teacher nominations are often completed when teachers use either rating scales or checklists of known characteristics and behaviors of gifted and talented children, and teacher nominations can be an important procedure in identifying gifted and high potential students. Teacher nominations can help identify students who do not excel on standardized tests; teachers often are able to identify characteristics such as creativity, leadership, motivation, and other specific talent areas such as music, art, and drama.

When nominations are sought from multiple sources, students who are nominated by teachers or others can be considered for gifted program participation. The following tools are often used in the nomination of gifted students: standardized achievement test scores; aptitude or other tests; grades, state achievement tests, behavioral inventories, or checklists; the nomination of a previous or current teacher; classroom observations; portfolio or student work submissions; parent nomination; self-nomination; and peer nominations.

When classroom teachers nominate students for participation in gifted programs, their nominations are often considered along with other assessment information that has been gathered. For example, many teacher nominations are not considered unless students also achieve a certain cutoff score on aptitude or achievement tests. In the Joseph Renzulli and Sally Reis talent pool identification approach that is a part of the *schoolwide enrichment model,* teacher nominations are more important. In this approach, teacher nominations are the second phase of identification and are considered an automatic pathway as part of the procedure. In this approach, all teachers are informed about the students who have gained entrance through test score nominations so that they will not have to engage in needless paperwork for students who have already been admitted. In the second step of the schoolwide enrichment model, teachers nominate students who display characteristics that are not easily determined by tests (e.g., high levels of creativity, task commitment, unusual interest, talents, or special areas of superior performance of potential). With the exception of teachers who are overnominators or undernominators, nominations from teachers who have received training in this process are accepted into the talent pool in the schoolwide enrichment model on an equal value with test score nominations.

Teacher nominations in other identification systems may be informal, as some nomination procedures simply ask teachers to consider which students in the class might benefit from a gifted program. Others ask teachers to "think about a few students in your class that might qualify for the gifted program." Others are more formal and include objective checklists with specific forms that teachers are asked to complete.

Teacher nominations are part of many identification systems for gifted and talented programs, although this method does have some inherent problems, such as a potential for teacher bias. Some teachers may nominate only students who display academic giftedness in all content areas all of the time. Some teachers may not consider nominating students who speak English as a second language or those with high potential but who underachieve in school. One way to eliminate bias in teacher nomination is to use a series of scales or checklists to make the nomination process more formal and less subjective.

Research conducted on teacher nomination has found that professional development provided to teachers on characteristics of giftedness can help increase the reliability of teacher nominations. This research suggests that, with additional training in gifted and talented education, teachers can improve their nomination and the subsequent identification of gifted students that they have nominated. Teachers who nominate students for placement in gifted programs usually consider the following characteristics:

- Achievement in content areas such as reading and mathematics at 1 or more years above current enrolled grade level
- Strong ratings on teacher checklists of gifted learner characteristics
- Scores on individual achievement or aptitude tests

Most school district personnel use some type of district or school screening instrument that can be completed by classroom teachers in the spring of the school year so that teachers can nominate students who have been in their classrooms for a year. This nomination form usually enables teachers to nominate students whose performance exceeds expected grade-level norms in one or more content areas. After teachers have completed a nomination form and a referral is made, additional information is usually collected. This information generally includes standardized achievement or aptitude tests, grade averages, learning characteristics checklists, information from parents, and work products or other creative product ratings. Then, in most school districts, a committee reviews the data and decides which students will be subsequently identified as gifted.

Joseph S. Renzulli

See also Giftedness, Definition; Identification; Schoolwide Enrichment Model; Teacher Rating Scales; Teacher Training

Further Readings

Johnsen, S. (Ed.). *Identifying gifted students: A practical guide.* Waco, TX: Prufrock Press.

Renzulli, J. S., & Reis, S. M. (1997). *The schoolwide enrichment model: A comprehensive plan for educational excellence.* Mansfield Center, CT: Creative Learning Press.

Renzulli, J. S., Reis, S. M., & Smith, L. H. (1981). *Revolving door identification model guidebook.* Mansfield Center, CT: Creative Learning Press.

Siegle, D., & Powell, T. (2004). Exploring teacher biases when nominating students for gifted programs. *Gifted Child Quarterly, 48,* 21–29.

Teacher Rating Scales

Many researchers suggest the use of teacher rating scales as one way to help identify gifted and talented students. The use of reliable and valid teacher rating instruments and scales can aid teacher nomination and may result in the inclusion of more students in gifted and talented programs. Only a handful of teacher rating instruments have been developed for rating the characteristics of high-ability students, and only a few studies have investigated the technical aspects of most scales. Several researchers have investigated the effectiveness of teacher ratings of students for gifted programs and results collectively suggest that when specific rating criteria are used, teachers can and do identify gifted and talented students in their classrooms. Other studies have examined the construct validity or criterion-related validity of teacher judgment instruments for high-ability students and generally supported some instrument developers' assertions that the instruments do examine the hypothetical construct(s) being measured. This entry describes various types of teaching rating scales.

Teacher Rating Instruments and Scales

Researchers have developed different observation and nomination scales for teachers, parents, and others for many years. These rating scales can and do provide valuable information about specific strengths of students. The Scales for Rating the Behavioral Characteristics of Superior Students (SRBCSS) by Joseph Renzulli and his colleagues was the first published instrument with available reliability and validity information in 1976, with 10 scales to identify student strengths in the areas of learning, motivation, creativity, artistic, musical, dramatics, communication-precision, communication-expressive, and planning. It was subsequently revised, and scales were added in the areas of reading, mathematics, technology, and science. The scales were developed for teachers and other school personnel to rate students for specialized programs using a six-point rating: *never, very rarely, rarely, occasionally, frequently,* and *always*. The most widely used scales in the SRBCSS are those dealing with learning, motivation, leadership, and creativity and these three scales were subsequently revised. An independent summary review of SRBCSS from the Buros Mental Measurements Yearbook explained that the SRBCSS represented a significant advancement in the expansion of the methodology for identifying intellectually gifted, creative, or talented youth.

The Gifted Education Scale, Second Edition, developed by Stephen McCarney and Paul Anderson is another scale used for the screening and identification of children and youth in kindergarten through Grade 12. This scale includes 48 items across five areas: intellectual ability, creativity, specific academic aptitude, leadership, and performing and visual arts, with an optional scale on motivation.

The Pfeiffer-Jarosewich Gifted Rating Scale (GRS) developed by Tania Jarosewich and Steven Pfeiffer is also used to identify students in preschool kindergarten and school-aged children and includes subscales focusing on intellectual, academic, creative, and artistic talent and motivation. The data support the intended use of the instrument as a screening measure or as part of a comprehensive battery to determine whether a student qualifies for gifted programming.

The Scales for Identifying Gifted Students (SIGS) include seven abilities: General Intellectual Ability, Language Arts, Mathematics, Science, Social Studies, Creativity, and Leadership. Both a school version and home version are available, and those completing the form are asked to provide examples for any subscale with six or more high responses. The Buros summary of the SIGS included some cautions, however, about the technical adequacy of the SIGS.

The Gifted and Talented Evaluation Scales (GATES) developed by James Gilliam, Betsy Carpenter, and James Christensen were also designed to identify gifted students from ages 5 to 18. The GATES are based on the current federal and state definitions of giftedness, including intellectual ability, academic skills, creativity, leadership, and artistic talent. Teachers, parents, and others who are knowledgeable about the child may complete the GATES for nomination for gifted and talented programs. The Buros commentary on the GATES suggests that its validity and the value-added role of the GATES remain unclear and suggests that more research would be needed to provide a stronger justification for using this product.

Any teacher rating scale or instrument should be cautiously used as a part of an identification plan for gifted students. Rating scales should be used as a part of a comprehensive battery of assessment techniques—the Buros reviews indicate that the psychometric properties of these scales are mixed. For example, there may be lower reliability when SRBCSS is compared with an intelligence test such as the Wechsler Intelligence Scale for Children—Revised (WISC–R) because it was designed to identify characteristics that are not often measured in intellectual assessments. Some instruments seem to load on one factor. For example, the Buros reviews of the Gifted Evaluation Scale (GES) suggest that the five behaviors the test purports to measure load primarily on one "general academic" factor, with leadership and arts as subfactors. A comparison of independent reviews of these rating scales as reported in the Buros Mental Measurement Yearbook would be an important step for any educator interested in using any of these scales. Teacher rating scales that are both valid and reliable can aid identification initiatives for high-ability students in and help their teachers to be more objective in nominating them for gifted and talented programs.

Joseph S. Renzulli

See also Giftedness, Definition; Identification; Teacher Nominations

Further Readings

Gilliam, J. E., Carpenter, B. O., & Christensen, J. R. (1996). *Gifted and talented evaluation scales.* Austin, TX: PRO-ED.

Jarosewich, T., Pfeiffer, S. I., & Morris, J. (2002). Identifying gifted students using teacher rating scales: A review of existing instruments. *Journal of Psychoeducational Assessment, 20,* 322–336.

McCarney, S. B., & Anderson, P. D. (1998). *The Gifted Evaluation Scale: Technical manual* (2nd ed.). Columbia, MO: Hawthorne Educational Services.

Renzulli, J. S., Smith, L. H., White, A. J., Callahan, C. M., Hartman, R. K., & Westberg, K. L. (2002). *Scales for rating the behavior characteristics of superior students* (Rev. ed.). Mansfield Center, CT: Creative Learning Press.

Ryser, G. R., & McConnell, K. (2004). *Scales for identifying gifted students: Ages 5 through 18.* Waco, TX: Prufrock Press.

Teachers of Gifted

In gifted education as in other disciplines the teacher has been found to be the most influential factor in student achievement and satisfaction. Effective teachers are well prepared to teach in their area, have common personality traits, use a wide range of pedagogical strategies in their teaching, and view parents as partners. There is no "one right way" to teach gifted children. Different teachers use different strategies at different times. Effective teachers respond to the individual child and the circumstances and choose strategies and activities based on their individual teaching strengths and styles, as well as their students' learning profiles, readiness levels, and interests. Whereas it was assumed by Lewis Terman and other early scholars of the gifted that teachers of gifted students should be gifted themselves, little research has been done in this area. Instead, research has focused on training and preparation, and this research shows that teachers trained in gifted education are more effective in teaching these students, as described in this entry.

Preparation

Teacher preparation in gifted pedagogy is essential to ensure that students are provided with appropriately challenging learning experiences. The National Association for Gifted Children (NAGC) and the Council for Exceptional Children (CEC) worked together to develop Teacher Preparation Standards in Gifted Education, which were adopted in 2006 by the National Council for Accreditation of Teacher Education (NCATE), the professional organization that accredits teacher education programs at colleges and universities. These research-based standards clarify the knowledge and skills needed to be an effective teacher of the gifted. The NAGC-CEC standards are intended as guidelines for training teachers of the gifted in teacher preparation and in district-based professional development programs. Such training is designed to extend that which is delivered in initial teacher licensure instruction. Training gives teachers an understanding of the cognitive needs of the gifted, as well as giving teachers insight into the social and emotional development of gifted students. Teachers with minimal or no training in gifted education are less likely to differentiate the curriculum and have lower expectations than do those who have received training, thereby limiting the learning opportunities for gifted youth. Students of teachers who had received training in gifted education pedagogy reported higher levels of thinking and discussion in their classrooms and, in addition, their teachers were less likely to lecture, and more likely to engage students in discussions and activities that challenge students to work at high levels of cognitive processing. Educated and experienced teachers are more likely to implement a wide variety of curricular models.

Gifted education coursework grounded in the NAGC-CEC standards encompasses a wide range of topics related to gifted education. The standards go beyond the development and delivery of appropriate curriculum to include knowledge and skills in the areas of the cognitive and affective development of gifted children, cultural diversity, and foundational knowledge. The foundational influences including key theories, philosophies, and models are the basis for Standard 1. In addition to historical influences, the importance of social, economic, and cultural factors are also stressed, as are research-based constructs. Standard 2 explains the importance of understanding the development and characteristics of gifted children, their idiosyncratic ways of thinking and learning, and the similarities and differences between gifted youth and their chronological peer group. The influence of culture and the environment on the development of individuals with gifts and talents in all domains—intellectual, academic, creative, leadership, and artistic—is underscored. Individual learning differences is the topic of Standard 3 with a special focus on diverse groups of learners. Standard 4 stresses the importance of using evidence-based curriculum and instructional strategies to differentiate for individuals with gifts and talents. Critical and creative thinking, problem solving, and performance skills are to be used in conjunction with differentiated instruction to provide properly paced activities. Learning environments and social interactions are the topics of Standard 5. Self-awareness and the development of self-advocacy skills are imbedded in instruction focused on a thorough understanding of cultural diversity. Standard 6 is centered on the role of language and communication in talent development. The need to develop oral and written communication skills may necessitate the use of assistive technologies for English language learners or students who have concomitant learning disabilities. Instructional planning is discussed in Standard 7. The importance of planning differentiated curricula for gifted students consisting of in-depth activities that are conceptually challenging and include complex content is stressed. The value of incorporating academic and career guidance into gifted students' educational experience is also noted. Standard 8 emphasizes the need to integrate assessment into the decision-making process when determining the appropriate placement and instructional steps for gifted children. Professional and ethical practices are the subject of Standard 9. Teachers of the gifted need to strive for continuous improvement by participating in continuing professional development as a means to remain cognizant of current evidence-based practices. Standard 10 focuses on collaboration. Teachers of the gifted should collaborate with fellow educators, as well as work with families, professionals, and community workers as they advocate for their gifted students.

Personality

Effective teachers of the gifted share common personality characteristics including empathy, openness, patience, curiosity, a sense of humor, and a positive sense of self. Teachers who excel in working with gifted children understand the inner workings of the child, both the cognitive and emotional aspects. They empathize with the child and are able to imagine how the child thinks and feels about situations and topics. These teachers have an openness that results in their being sensitive to and accepting of all children. Curious about many topics themselves, teachers of the gifted are enthusiastic about students with diverse interests even when the areas of passion for the students are not aligned with the curriculum. Being socially responsive and culturally sensitive, teachers of the gifted are able to bridge the fields of gifted education and multicultural education. A strong sense of humor coupled with a positive sense of self allows these teachers to easily laugh at themselves and laugh with others. As a result of their comfort level with their own identity, effective teachers of the gifted are willing to make mistakes and have a sense of comfort with ambiguity and not knowing "all of the answers." Having a sincere interest in the whole child, not just academic prowess, these teachers focus on student strengths and interests and create a secure classroom environment.

Pedagogy

Teachers of the gifted choose strategies and activities based on their individual teaching strengths and styles, as well as their students' learning profiles, readiness levels, and interests. They rarely teach something the same way twice because their students' academic needs vary widely, and they have an extensive repertoire of strategies from which to draw. Essential pedagogical strategies to be used by the educator of the gifted include culturally responsive teaching, creativity, flexibility, student-centered approaches, and high expectations. Teachers of the gifted recognize the effects of culture and environment and acknowledge the importance of using culturally sensitive techniques to frame instruction. Educators of the gifted think creatively, and they bring an aspect of creativity to their teaching. Creative, flexible, and differentiated approaches to curriculum development and delivery allow students to learn content through relevant activities and at an appropriate pace. Student-based strategies including curriculum compacting, inquiry-based instruction, problem-based learning, open-ended activities, and independent and small-group investigations increase the level of expectations. Planned instruction revolves around open-ended activities that necessitate the use of critical and creative thinking. These activities move students away from the misconception that excellence in education is manifested by being able to recite one correct answer and on to the realization that new discoveries and true learning are multidimensional. Effective teachers model excellence through their own high achievement orientation and commitment to personal intellectual growth. Exemplary teachers of the gifted act as facilitators and allow students to become active seekers of knowledge and take charge of their own learning. These teachers pass on their own enthusiasm for lifelong learning and share their broad interests with their students.

Parents

Extending their reach beyond the students, effective teachers of the gifted work with the parents of their students to support them in their efforts to nurture their children. As the teacher works collaboratively with the parents, he or she is better able to understand the child's strengths, relative weaknesses, and interests. In return, the teacher is able to provide the parents with a support system through conversation, literature recommendations, and advocacy resources on topics such as overexcitabilities, perfectionism, and underachievement. Educators of the gifted can provide parents of gifted children with the knowledge and skills that will nurture the intellectual growth, as well as the social and emotional development of the child. Working together, parents and teachers can help students understand their cognitive, emotional, and social needs and assist them as they develop self-advocacy skills to be used in efforts to have their needs met.

Exemplary teachers of the gifted understand and empathize with their students. Such teachers have an appreciation of their students' strengths, relative weaknesses, and interests. These teachers have a keen awareness of the knowledge and skills they want their students to acquire and can easily adapt instructional techniques and the curriculum to meet their students' needs. Their repertoire of teaching strategies and instructional activities is extensive and allows them to develop high level learning experiences for their students. Teachers of the gifted share their students' enthusiasm for learning and curiosity about the unknown. While raising student expectations, these teachers are able to create nonthreatening learning environments through an acceptance of all students, an awareness of their students' needs and interests, and a confidence in their own abilities.

Rebecca L. Mann

See also Best Practices; Effective Programs; Teacher Attitudes

Further Readings

Bishop, W. E. (1980). Successful teachers of the gifted. In J. S. Renzulli & E. P. Stoddard (Eds.), *Under one cover: Gifted and talented education in perspective* (pp. 152–160). Reston, VA: Council for Exceptional Children.

Callahan, C., Cooper, C., & Glascock, R. (2003). *Preparing teachers to develop and enhance talent: The position of national education organizations.* (ERIC Document Services No. ED477882)

Davalos, R., & Griffin, G. (1999). The impact of teachers' individualized practices on gifted students in rural, heterogeneous classrooms. *Roeper Review, 21*(4), 308–314.

Eyre, D., Coates, D., Fitzpatrick, M., Higgins, C., McClure, L., & Wilson, H., et al. (2002). Effective teaching of able pupils in the primary school: The findings of the Oxfordshire effective teachers of able pupils project. *Gifted Education International, 16*(2), 158–169.

Ford, D. Y., & Trotman, M. F. (2001). Teachers of gifted students: Suggested multicultural characteristics and competencies. *Roeper Review, 23,* 235–239.

Hansen, J. B., & Feldhusen, J. F. (1994). Comparison of trained and untrained teachers of gifted students. *Gifted Child Quarterly, 38,* 115–121.

Lewis, J. F. (1982, May/June). Bulldozers or chairs? Gifted students describe their ideal teacher. *Gifted Child Today* (23), 16–19.

Rash, P. K., & Miller, A. D. (2000). A survey of practices of teachers of the gifted. *Roeper Review, 22,* 192–194.

Renzulli, J. S. (1968). Identifying key features in programs for the gifted. *Exceptional Children, 35,* 217–221.

Stephens, K. R. (1999). Parents of the gifted and talented: The forgotten partner. *Gifted Child Today, 22*(5), 38–43, 52.

Stronge, J. (2002). *Qualities of effective teachers.* Alexandria, VA: Association for Supervision and Curriculum Development.

Whitlock, M. S., & DuCette, J. P. (1989). Outstanding and average teachers of the gifted: A comparative study. *Gifted Child Quarterly, 33,* 15–21.

Teacher Training

Teacher training may be perceived as somewhat of an intangible construct because it presumes to cover a lot of ground, takes on many forms, and pertains to different kinds of participants. There are teachers from preschool through graduate studies; in homes, resource centers, schools, and alternative educational settings; in various stages of professional careers; and in the throes of juggling many administrative, instructional, learning, and other kinds of responsibilities. As understandings evolve as to the magnitude of who teaches, and what teaching encompasses, so, too, do our understandings broaden regarding the training that is necessary to do the job (in all its multifaceted complexity) *well*.

Training implies learning and development in any number of capacities, personal and professional, but given the breadth of whom and what is at issue with respect to training processes within an educational framework, it is impossible to detail all the elements here. This entry will specify the two predominant types of teacher training thrusts (preservice and inservice), and many important aspects and considerations involved therein, and as they apply to gifted education.

Initial Teacher Training

Preservice training is designed for individuals who have chosen to enter the teaching profession. This training for certification generally includes work that addresses theoretical perspectives, pedagogical practice, and educational psychology (such as the study of cognitive development, identity formation, strategies for classroom management, and suitable means of fostering and sustaining motivation). There is a practicum component to preservice education whereby teacher candidates learn "on the job" and receive feedback from experienced associates. Prospective teachers are encouraged to share their various learning experiences with their colleagues-in-training through discussion, meaningful activities, and online venues. Preservice offerings may or may not have a special education thrust, an umbrella under which the "gifted exceptionality" would likely fall. The amount of attention directly paid to gifted learning needs varies greatly from one preservice program and geographical locale to the next, although much of the literature in the field of gifted education argues for more, better, and appropriately targeted training provision in gifted-related matters. Initial teacher training programs often focus on subject-specific domains grounded in curricular requirements at various grade levels, prescribed standards of practice, familiarity with current research findings and resource materials, assessment procedures, relevant legislative matters, and how to facilitate a good learner-learning match for all students. Professionalism, a solid grasp of principles underlying learning and teaching, and an appreciation of diversity in context and how best to address it, are the cornerstones of such programs. Some preservice programs are longer than others, and they can range from a minimum of 10 months of training through to several years depending on the selected program of study. When there is a particular focus, such as gifted education, then the course would be geared to pertinent material to better equip teachers to address the needs of the target population. Ideally, those who provide this training are current, knowledgeable, and master teachers in their own right—effectively trained to train effectively. There are postgraduate level certification and advanced degree programs in place for educators who want to take on this sort of leadership role—and some teacher trainers will have been exposed to a rather generalized orientation with respect to topics such as child development, and how to differentiate for exceptionalities, whereas others will have received more of a gifted focus.

Teacher Training for Experienced Educators

Inservice training is designed for practicing educators. Whereas preservice training provides the fuel and momentum required to become an effective teacher, inservice training replenishes and sustains practicing educators. Training often takes the form of professional development sessions, one or more specifically targeted presentations, or additional qualification or degree courses that are formally offered through colleges and universities. It may also involve consultation, reflection, hands-on group activities, case study work, visitations and careful observation, documentation and analysis of current practice, and action research. Sometimes grants are available for research and advanced training initiatives. Some teachers go on sabbatical, others take time off to extend their knowledge base in the field of education, and many continue to work in classrooms.

Like its preservice counterpart, inservice training is variable in design, extent, and the nature of core elements. For example, training might focus on enhancing or honing educators' pedagogical, technological, or communication skills; on inquiry-based processes; or on the application of specialized procedures. Generally speaking, teachers learn how to better identify and address learning problems, develop curriculum and instruction, acquire a foundation of information on a range of strategies for appropriately responsive teaching, and engage in collaborative practices in and beyond schools. This, in turn, makes them stronger in an ever-changing educational environment, enabling them to contribute more meaningfully to the learning community while raising the bar for others. At the same time, teacher training reinforces the importance of continued, constructive, and collegial learning for students, and because it requires time, commitment, and effort, this, too, sends a positive message to youngsters. The nature of inservice training tends to be flexible and fluid, and commonly boils down to whatever a particular individual, group, administrative body, or school district deems important to its optimal functioning at any point in time. However, inservice training builds from two premises: that teachers have a basic understanding of educational theory and of what underlies best practice, and that their participation in the training process is predicated on a desire to improve, update, and evaluate what they do. Teacher training moves in different directions from there, sometimes formal and sometimes informal in nature, with learning opportunities more or less available depending on such factors as accessibility, funding, demand, need, and even whim.

Teaching Training in Gifted Education

Teacher training in gifted education may or may not be part of the short-term or overall professional development plan for any one person, department, school, or district. Far too often, things "gifted" do not rank high on a priority list, and many administrators do not consider it essential given numerous other competing issues and demands for limited time and educational funding allocations. However, it is important for teachers to recognize the importance of gifted issues, for administrators to do their part to promote increased understanding about high-level development, and for parents to advocate for their highly able children. This could have a strong and advantageous effect on the teacher training impetus, increasing the availability and caliber of professional development offerings on giftedness. As it is, the paucity of teachers actually receiving training in gifted education is problematic, especially when one considers that there are high-ability learners who are going unrecognized, and whose diverse learning needs are not being met. When teachers are offered and choose to avail themselves of opportunities to think constructively about giftedness and issues pertaining to high-level development, and to develop sound approaches for working with exceptional learners—and when they are administratively supported in this regard—the system and everyone in it stands to benefits.

New and seasoned educators can access teacher training, collaboratively or independently, in many ways. Several associations, college faculties, and university-affiliated organizations disseminate information about giftedness, thereby heightening awareness and promoting the appropriate address of exceptional learners' needs. Teachers can form study groups, partner with professional networks (industry, business committees, corporations), and enroll in distance education programs. Some professional consultants make it their business to crisscross the world offering teacher training programs in gifted-related topics including social-emotional concerns, talent development, subject-specific curriculum, differentiated programming models, identification procedures, and so on. Countless resources are available online, at bookstores, and in conference exhibit halls, and one can also access gifted chat rooms, advocacy organizations, and lectures on gifted-related topics of interest. Although teacher training for certification purposes is generally structured by an overseeing body in accordance with set standards, teacher training for the sake of professional growth—designed to help one become a more competent and effective educator—is, as noted at the outset, an evolving and both a personal and professional endeavor.

The field of gifted education is now formally recognized as having its own training standards as approved by the National Council for Accreditation of Teacher Education (NCATE) in the United States. These standards outline many specific areas of knowledge and skill requirements, and focus on important matters such as diversity, assessment features, instructional strategies, and collaborative endeavors. At the same time, there is an emphasis on the importance of coursework, clinical practice, and field experience among teacher candidates in gifted education at both the undergraduate and graduate levels, and among more experienced teachers as well. Targeted resource material that represents research-based and standards-based practices in gifted education is increasingly available for use by professors, course developers, accreditation coordinators, and professional development leaders, and use of these resources helps build coherence and ensure educational quality across programs, districts, and countries. Two guidebooks of particular note are *Gifted Education Standards for University Teacher Preparation Programs* and *Using the National Gifted Education Standards for PreK–12 Professional Development.*

Conclusion

The nature of any teacher training offered and the challenges of the learning process itself will vary from one trainer, teacher, context, and area of focus to the next. There is much more to teaching than the day-to-day goings-on in any given classroom, school, or other educational setting. Regular, appropriately designed, and effectively delivered training is essential for teachers so they can consolidate and build on their understandings, develop the tools and the competences they need to address diversity in today's student population, and support and champion lifelong learning.

Joanne F. Foster

See also Competencies for Teachers of Gifted; Effective Programs; Preservice Education; Professional Development

Further Readings

Dettmar, P., & Landrum, M. (Eds.). (1998). *Staff development: The key to effective gifted education programs.* Waco, TX: Prufrock Press.

Johnsen, S., VanTassel-Baska, J., & Robinson, A. (2008). *Gifted education standards for university teacher preparation programs.* Thousand Oaks, CA: Corwin Press.

Kitano, M., Montgomery, D., VanTassel-Baska, J., & Johnsen, S. (2008). *Using the national gifted education standards for PreK–12 professional development.* Thousand Oaks, CA: Corwin Press.

Landrum, M. S., Callahan, C. M., & Shaklee, B. D. (Eds.). (2001). *Aiming for excellence: Annotations to the NAGC PreK–Grade 12 gifted program standard.* Waco, TX: Prufrock Press.

Matthews, D. J., & Foster, J. F. (2005). Teacher development. In *Being smart about gifted children: A guidebook for parents and educators* (pp. 337–362). Scottsdale, AZ: Great Potential Press.

National Association for Gifted Children. *NAGC Standards: Professional development.* Retrieved September 15, 2008, from http://www.nagc.org

Technology

In this entry, *technology* refers to computer technologies and peripherals, which require technical skills to operate and evaluative skills to determine which computing functions are most appropriate to accomplish a goal. Technology has received greater emphasis in educational settings during the last 20 years, especially with the advent of the Internet, affordable pricing of computers for the general public, and widespread use of technology in business, industry, and academia. Computer technologies are recognized as both learning tools and as a content area in gifted education, each of which should be included in the curriculum for gifted to appropriately address gifted students' intellectual, creative, academic, psychosocial, and leadership needs. This entry presents accepted standards and educational goals for using technology in educating gifted learners, considers the implications of technology for educators, and discusses the literature dealing with the role of technology in gifted education.

Standards and Educational Goals

Technology is a tool that fits well with the precepts of gifted education, especially as a means of solving problems, but also because gifted learners should also explore the philosophical aspects of technology—including its effects on society and problems generated through society's use, dependence, and need for technology. Two guiding bodies have developed standards, which, in concert with the PreK–12 Gifted Program Standards developed by the National Association for Gifted Children (NAGC) and national content-area standards, can assist educators in conceptualizing and developing appropriate learning challenges for the gifted in using technology or considering its role from a systems approach. The Technology Standards for Students developed by the International Society for Technology in Education (ISTE) and the Technology Content Standards developed by the International Technology Education Association (ITEA) are seminal works in education because each establishes benchmarks in the study and use of technology in all grade levels and disciplines with the goal of developing technologically literate students.

Today's K–12 gifted learners have known a world that uses technology for social and academic pursuits—unlike the world many veteran teachers knew, which had little to no exposure to computers during their schooling. Gifted learners often come to school with advanced technology skills and can quickly and efficiently use digital cameras, e-mail, word processors, and games. Teachers, on the other hand, may require professional development to understand the functions of computers and their connections to learning, especially because the K–12 classrooms of their childhood may not have offered the infusion of these tools or models of how to integrate them into the curriculum.

Although gaining the necessary technical expertise requires practice, educators must think beyond the mere inclusion of gadgets and gizmos to a more holistic understanding of information technology, including a systems perspective and a practical design perspective. This understanding, based on the sound philosophies generated by ITEA, is centered on providing students opportunities to think critically about (a) the influx of these technologies in our world; (b) how these tools enhance or diminish communication, relationships, business, and government; and (c) the historical, present-day, and future issues and concerns posed by the ever-changing world of technology. The approach to studying technology offered by ITEA is similar to the best practices and recommended instructional approaches for working with gifted learners. As the NAGC standards and other seminal resources in the field indicate, gifted learners should regularly engage in discussions and experiences focused on social issues and recognizing how innovations may affect the world. The emphasis of the ITEA standards is to build students' awareness of technology and its impact on life, which allows students to use many higher-level thinking skills, including analysis, synthesis, evaluation, and reflection.

The ITEA's standards outline educational goals and outcomes that are similar to gifted education, including problem-solving skills; preparing students to become independent, lifelong learners and informed, judicious consumers of information; maintaining technology equipment; and the interdisciplinary nature of technology as a tool to assist students in learning about other content areas, including math and science as well as the arts. The expectations for what teachers should know and be able to do with respect to technology are outlined in a set of standards provided by ISTE. Then, teachers must remain current with the evolution of computers and related peripherals and learn how to modify instruction so that students with advanced technology abilities are provided appropriately challenging learning opportunities in the classroom.

The sophisticated uses of computers are especially important for gifted students because their curricular experiences should include cognitive challenges that can be facilitated through information technology, including all phases of research and project development, such as concept mapping; data gathering; analysis of appropriate and credible electronic sources; communication with experts via e-mail, blogs, chats, or wikis; synthesis of ideas using word-processing tools; and digital presentations in the form of electronic portfolios, Web sites, or presentation media, to name a few.

Although the study of technology and the use of technology with gifted learners seem to be a natural fit, the relationship between these fields has received little attention thus far in the literature. This gap may be because research has only recently addressed the role of technology in student learning gains, and definitive answers to questions about whether technology can, in fact, increase achievement, remain. Extant literature in gifted education supports the design of learner-centered experiences, opportunities for creative problem solving, and maximizing these thinking processes through the sophisticated application of technology. Project-based learning—which promotes higher-level thinking—is ideal for gifted learners because information technology can facilitate concept mapping through graphics such as Inspiration© and Kidspiration©; research through databases and the Internet; electronic processing of data through spreadsheets; word processing for written explanations; and graphics, digital videos and pictures, and electronic portfolios for developing products.

Implications for Educators

Just as educators should provide students with opportunities to think about the role of technology, teachers must learn how to adjust their teaching methods. Just as educators of the gifted are expected to differentiate learning so that instruction meets the needs of gifted students and the range of abilities presented, learning can be differentiated according to a student's technological proficiency so that individuals are provided opportunities to advance from novice to expert levels of use. Furthermore, teachers can sculpt learning experiences to address individual learning interests as well as flexible and accelerated pacing through the use of technology. Accelerated learning software, digital simulations, WebQuests, and electronic classrooms can open up a gifted student's world and be helpful tools for teachers in responding to the needs of students.

Information technology can also be a great tool for teacher planning through electronic resources for teachers. Thematic units that integrate multiple disciplines are available online, and lesson plans and units specific to technology infusion can be obtained free of charge for teachers at all grade levels and content levels—sometimes even with recommended modifications for the gifted. Ethical uses of technology are identified in the ISTE standards for students and delineate considerations teachers of the gifted should discuss with gifted students, including societal issues surrounding licensing, copyrights, hacking, gaming, virtual spaces, and related philosophical, legal, and moral issues.

As educators become more aware of the educational possibilities technology offers, virtual classrooms and distance learning will become more prominent features of gifted education. Gifted learners may spur the influx of these electronic classroom options, so schools will be increasingly expected to implement learning opportunities that address these expectations. For students without local access to Advanced Placement courses or dual enrollment opportunities, online course delivery will grow in its availability, cost effectiveness, and sophistication. Concurrently, the demand for K–12 educators skilled in developing and delivering online courses will likely increase, requiring educators to further develop their knowledge about effective distance-learning teaching practices for working with gifted children.

As schools have increased spending on hardware and software, teacher training has also become a related consideration because seasoned educators likely had little exposure to computer technologies during their preservice teacher training programs—a trend that is rapidly being replaced by teacher preparation programs that emphasize technology integration. Many of the recent teacher graduates have used such technologies as students themselves and, thus, may have more positive attitudes toward infusing computers into classroom learning experiences.

Current and Future Research

The research guiding gifted education in understanding the role of technology in learning is largely derived from the general education literature, especially given the recent influx of technology in education. Research indicates that teachers' views of the influx of computer resources are central to how these tools are incorporated into the curriculum. Prior investigations have documented the key role attitudes play in educators' acquisition, adoption, and sustained use of technology in the classroom, all of which can also affect students' use of technology.

To date, most of the literature about technology in gifted education has been theoretical, though there has been a dramatic increase in the number of published articles in gifted education that focus on various technologies to challenge the gifted, most of which are framed around growth in academic pursuits and technology skill acquisition. During the last few years, a variety of articles have provided teachers with guidance in using computers in classroom instruction; these works have addressed presentation software, Internet use, blogs and Webcasts, and global positioning systems. Innovative approaches to thinking about the role of technology in gifted education have also been suggested.

Though the focus of most of the technology literature focuses on academic needs, the role of technology in addressing social-emotional needs has also been established. Tracey Cross examines the psychosocial connection gifted learners have with communication technologies, especially as e-mail, instant messaging, chat rooms, social networking and other communication devices are frequently used by students, often for the emotional support and assistance that may not be available to students in their schools or communities. Mentoring can also be facilitated through online supports, whereby a student communicates regularly with a designated adult who guides the learner, provides feedback to questions about careers, personal challenges, schooling, social skills, and identity development.

With the influx of technology in education, the field of gifted education has included information technology in the standards developed by the NAGC. The current K–12 Gifted Program Standards recommend that schools have state-of-the-art technology. With the proliferation of computers and related tools, additional emphasis on learning with technology and about technology may be warranted, as will recognition of the specialized learning needs of technologically gifted learners, according to Del Siegle. A sign of the times is the addition of a technology checklist in one of the most widely used instruments for screening gifted learners.

Though computers are now regular fixtures in classrooms, homes, and businesses, there is a paucity of research in gifted education about the value these technologies bring to the lives of gifted learners and the ways in which students and teachers use technology. One recent empirical work by Elizabeth Shaunessy provides a statewide picture of the attitudes about technology among teachers of the gifted; findings indicate teachers with more training and exposure to computers tend to have more positive feelings about these tools than do their colleagues with fewer opportunities to experiment with technology.

Robert Abelman's work sheds light on computer usage among achieving and underachieving gifted learners and indicates the latter use the Internet significantly more often than do achieving and average-ability learners. Likewise, parents of underachieving gifted learners monitored their child's electronic pursuits to a greater degree than did parents of achieving gifted and academically average learners. Future research should address the efficacy of instruction using technology, technology as a motivational tool for learning, the connection with individuals from around the world (including experts and other students), and the correlation between computer use and learning gains.

Elizabeth Shaunessy

See also National Association for Gifted Children; Online Gifted Education; Web-Based Learning

Further Readings

Abelman, R. (2007). Fighting the war on indecency: Mediating TV, Internet, and videogame usage among achieving and underachieving gifted children. *Roeper Review, 29,* 100–112.

Cross, T. L. (2004). Technology and the unseen world of gifted students. *Gifted Child Today, 27,* 14–16, 63.

Cross, T. L. (2007). The changing life metaphor of gifted youth. *Gifted Child Today, 30,* 14–16, 65.

International Society for Technology in Education (ISTE). (2000). *National educational technology standards for students: Connecting curriculum and technology.* Eugene, OR: Author.

Landrum, M. S., Callahan, C. M., & Shaklee, B. D. (2001). *Aiming for excellence: Gifted program standards.* Waco, TX: Prufrock Press.

Shaunessy, E. (2007). Attitudes toward information technology of teachers of the gifted: Implications for gifted education. *Gifted Child Quarterly, 51,* 119–135.

Siegle, D. (2004). Identifying students with gifts and talents in technology. *Gifted Child Today, 27,* 30–33, 64.

Technology for All Americans Project, & International Technology Education Association. (2000). *Standards for technological literacy: Content for the study of technology.* Reston, VA: International Technology Education Association.

Terman's Studies of Genius

Lewis Terman was fundamental in establishing the empirical study of precocious children and contributed to the modern conception of the "gifted" child. He dispelled many of the popular misconceptions that gifted children were ultimately disadvantaged physically, socially, or professionally. Through his research on intelligence and testing, he provided the instruments that became the foundation of the study of gifted children and the educational policies that affected them for decades. Commonly referred to as "the father of gifted education," he is often credited as the first psychologist to empirically study gifted children and adults. This entry describes Terman's background and his studies of genius.

Background

Terman was born on the January 15, 1877, on a small farm in Johnson County, Indiana. Terman displayed an aptitude for school at an early age, quickly finishing the rural schools and entering a teacher's college at the age of 15. Terman taught for several years to earn enough money to permit graduate study and ultimately earned an M.A. from Indiana University at Bloomington in 1903 and a Ph.D. in psychology from Clark University in 1905. After graduation, Terman was employed as a school principal for San Bernardino, California, and as a professor at the Los Angeles Normal School in 1907. In 1910, Terman became a professor at Stanford University, where he remained until his death in 1956. During his career, he was elected as the president of the American Psychological Society and served as the editor of six professionally reviewed journals.

Intelligence Testing

Terman's interest in intelligence developed early in his academic career, as evidenced by his doctoral thesis entitled, "Genius and Stupidity: A Study of the Intellectual Processes of Seven 'Bright' and Seven 'Stupid' Boys." Interestingly, his most famous contribution to the field of intelligence came from adapting a French intelligence test developed by Alfred Binet and Theodore Simon in 1906. Terman translated the measure to English, revised or removed some of the tasks, and added several additional tasks developed for his doctoral thesis. To develop statistical norms for U.S. populations, Terman undertook the arduous task of organizing the testing of more than 1,000 California schoolchildren. Although this sample was not representative in race and socioeconomic status, it is widely considered revolutionary in its attempt at rigorous empirical controls. In 1916, Terman published the Stanford Revision of the Binet-Simon scale, or the *Stanford-Binet.*

Though it is possibly now the most famous test from that era, the Stanford-Binet was not the only mental test available during the 1920s. Many other intelligence and achievement tests had been developed, and an English translation of the Binet-Simon scale had already been developed by Henry H. Goddard in 1908. However, Terman's empirical standardization, combined with effective marketing by its publisher World Books, led to his measures being some of the most popular instruments of academics and school administrators. A school district in San Jose, California, became the first to develop a tracked system to accelerate students or offer remedial work based on the Stanford-Binet in 1921 and was quickly emulated by school systems around the nation. The Stanford-Binet is still one of the most commonly used measures of intelligence. Though the current edition has been thoroughly updated, many test items from the 1916 revision are still employed. Similarly, scores on intelligence tests like the Stanford-Binet are still one of the main criteria for receiving special education services in many states.

Terman's instrument to measure intelligence was a tremendous contribution to the empirical study of gifted individuals. The development of the Stanford-Binet provided researchers with a seemingly scientific and objective way to identify and categorize intelligence. Although other methods, such as accomplishments, academic progress, or evaluations by teachers or family were viable options, their obvious vulnerability to subjective bias caused the apparent impartial precision of the Stanford-Binet to be one of the preferred instruments in the boom of research on precocious children during the 1920s and 1930s. Many of the most prominent contemporary figures in gifted education, including Lulu Stedman, Leta Hollingworth, and Guy Whipple, used the Stanford-Binet as a central component in identifying gifted children for their research.

However, the popularity of Terman's instruments within the study of gifted education also had several negative impacts. Most notably, the selection of items and standardization procedures resulted in severe disadvantages for children who were racial minorities or came from low socioeconomic backgrounds on his tests. The consequential racial and class differences found using his instruments resulted in an underrepresentation of minorities within the research on gifted education and were used as evidence for the eugenics movement. Although some critics challenged his research in the 1920s—most notably Walter Lippmann, William C. Bagley, and John Dewey—not until the Civil Rights Movement of the 1960s were many of the biases in intelligence testing and, thus, the conceptualization of the gifted child, rectified.

Research on Gifted Individuals

Before the 1920s, precocious children were viewed by many educators as being physically frail and socially maladjusted. There was a strong belief in the common saying "early ripe, early rot," which was supported by many anecdotes of individual children who showed great success in childhood but did not exhibit any success as adults and of slow children who went on to great accomplishments. Possibly motivated by his own precocious background, Terman started a program of research to investigate, and ultimately dispel, many of these assumptions.

In 1921, Terman began his legendary longitudinal study of highly intelligent children. Terman organized the testing of more than 250,000 school children on the Stanford-Binet intelligence test, from which he identified a core group of 1,528 children who scored within the top 1 percent of the population (corresponding to an IQ of higher than 140) with the goal of tracking them as they developed into adults. Data was collected regarding their physical, academic, social, and familial characteristics. The results were initially published in 1922, and follow-up studies were conducted in 1929, 1950, 1955, 1960, and 1972. The volumes were called the *Genetic Studies of Genius*. Terman revealed that, on average, these highly intelligent children, nicknamed "Terman's Termites," lived slightly healthier, happier, and more successful lives then the average child. Although it is difficult to determine if these children were truly better off than their counterparts, the study did provide strong evidence that many precocious children do go on to lead perfectly normal lives. In addition, although constrained by the rigid sex roles of the time, Terman's women went on to college and professional work in much greater numbers than average women did. The men went on to higher status positions and many accomplishments, and their success led most subsequent researchers to conclude that high intelligence was associated with greater success in school, college, and graduate and professional work.

Ryan Hansen

See also Eugenics; Hollingworth's Studies of Highly Gifted Students; Intelligence; Intelligence Testing; Stanford-Binet

Further Readings

Brim, O. G., Glass, D. C., Neulinger, J., & Firestone, I. J. (1969). *American beliefs and attitudes about intelligence.* New York: Russell Sage.

Fancher, R E. (1985). *The intelligence men: makers of the IQ controversy.* New York: W. W. Norton.

Jolly, J. L. (2005). Pioneering definitions and theoretical positions in the field of gifted education. *Gifted Education, 28*(3), 38–44.

Kimble, G. A., & Wertheimer, M. (1991). *Portraits of pioneers in psychology* (Vol. 4). Washington, DC: American Psychological Association.

Minton, H. L. (1987). Lewis M. Terman and mental testing: In search of the democratic ideal. In M. Sokal (Ed.), *Psychological testing and American society: 1890–1930.* New Brunswick, NJ: Rutgers University Press.

Minton, H. L. (1988). *Lewis M. Terman: Pioneer in psychological testing.* New York: New York University Press.

Terman, L. M. (1919). *The intelligence of school children.* Boston: Houghton Mifflin.

Test Development

A *test* refers to the systematic procedure by which a sample of behavior is measured. Tests are used as part of the measurement process and constitute one way of making attributes observable. In this respect, *tests* can refer to a process or tool by which data is collected with regard to a defined attribute of interest. The subset or sample of behavior measured should be representative of the entire domain of interest. With a subset of information tested, an inference can be made about an individual's true status with regard to the attribute of interest.

The process of test development can be complex and meticulous, as described in this entry. However, if it is well-documented and comprehensive, a test can become a valuable tool for measuring traits and skills of various kinds. Although educational tests have historically been used for assessing general traits of collectives, they are also applicable to the assessment of individuals and hard-to-define constructs such as in the case of giftedness, creativity, and talent.

Purpose and Content Defined

The first and most important step in the test-development process is to establish the purpose of the test. In other words, the construct of interest must be identified and well defined. For instance, tests may be developed for the purposes of identification and placement, to measure progress of a skill or ability, or to assess potential. The purpose of any test will be based on the inferences the test developer intends to make from the results of that test. The intended use of any test should guide all subsequent steps in the test-development process.

Content should be developed based on a theoretical knowledge and understanding of the construct of interest. The realm of content included may belong to a general subject area such as math, science, or art, it may comprise items from multiple disciplines, or it may be a set of attitudinal items. The content that is chosen will be based on the purpose and objectives of the test. For instance, when evaluating giftedness in mathematics, it is probably not necessary to include items that peers are able to answer correctly. The purpose of the test would be better served if the content was more challenging and allowed students to demonstrate their unique abilities and skills.

Test Specifications

Test specifications describe how the content will be converted into test format. These specifications are often referred to as the test "blueprint." It contains every detail and direction necessary for the development of that test. Test specifications should be sufficiently detailed to provide different developers enough information that they could create parallel forms based only on those specifications. Test specifications should include, at a minimum, content objectives and details, a description of the test type, item type used, and the reporting design.

Content Objectives and Details

The objectives of test content should express where subject change or differences are expected. The goal is to understand these variations through responses to the content. Thus, objectives need to be observable and measurable. Content objectives define the test blueprint and therefore need to be explicitly stated in the specifications.

Test specifications also need to outline details concerning the content that will be included on a test. For instance, the test developer must decide how items should be balanced in content and item difficulty. It may be of interest to place items of similar content together on a test, whereas in other situations, similar items may need to be balanced throughout. Typically, items are ordered in a test to increase the level of difficulty. Once again, the ordering of items is based on the intended use of the test. All things being equal, test content should not be ambiguous; it should be practical, realistic, and appropriate for intended examinees. Finally, test content should be appropriate in length and difficulty for the time that will be allocated to administer the test, unless the purpose states otherwise.

Type of Test

Tests can be divided into two main categories known as maximum performance assessments and typical behavior assessments. In general, tests belong to one of these two categories based on what the examinee is instructed to do on the test. If the directions on a test indicate that examinees should do their best at choosing the correct answer, then it is a maximum performance test. If the directions indicate that examinees should express their opinions, values, attitudes, and so on, and that there is not a correct or incorrect answer, then it is a typical behavior test.

Maximum Performance Tests

Several distinctions can be made among maximum performance assessments. One common distinction is made between achievement and ability (aptitude) tests. Achievement tests measure that which has already been learned within a domain of knowledge, and ability tests measure one's facility for learning new material. Even though a distinction is made between these two test types, tests often contain elements of both.

Tests of creativity can be thought of as ability tests in that they assess one's aptitude for producing novel ideas, works of art, or any other type of original creation. Creativity tests often require the use of divergent thinking in that multiple "correct" answers are usually sought. The ability to draw on one's imagination and creativity to develop solutions and answers in an innovative and unique manner is the main focus of creativity tests.

A distinction can also be made between power tests versus speed tests. Speed tests consist of items that most students would be able to answer correctly. However, because of the lack of time allowed to complete the test, most students would not be able to finish the entire test. In this case, testing speed becomes part of the construct of interest. Power tests typically comprise only a few relatively challenging items. A sufficient amount of time is allocated to take the test. However, because of the level of item difficulty, most students are not able to complete it.

Another common distinction that is often made among maximum performance assessments is between summative and formative tests. Summative tests are typically administered at the end of an instructional period and assess what students have learned throughout that period. Formative tests are used during the instructional process and are intended to provide feedback to be used for improving the teaching and learning process. The main difference between these types of assessment is the point in time at which they are administered.

The nature of any test will be defined by the intended uses of the test and the content objectives. Assessing giftedness, talent, and creativity requires techniques that are both innovative and diverse. Use of multiple methods or nontraditional assessment may optimize the identification and evaluation process of a small number of gifted individuals or the assessment of a large number of talented and creative individuals.

Typical Behavior Tests

Tests of typical behavior can be subdivided into tests that measure constructs such as personality, interests, and attitudes. Personality tests measure individuals' traits, dispositions, and behaviors that define constructs such as leadership, extraversion, and self-discipline. Interest inventories are typically used for occupational purposes and measure the degree to which individuals prefer certain activities over others. Tests can also be used to measure individuals' positive or negative tendency toward some thing such as an object, a person, an event, or a product. These attitudinal tests measure both agreement and disagreement with the attitude of interest.

Item Types and Cognitive Levels

Item format will determine the level(s) of cognitive ability that the test will be able to capture. Item types can measure several different levels of cognitive complexity (based on Bloom's Taxonomy). However, each item type may or may not efficiently lend itself to the various cognitive levels. Following is a description of the cognitive levels measured well or poorly by four different item types.

1. *Matching:* Matching items can be written to measure basic knowledge of a construct, some areas of comprehension (e.g., organization of information), and quantitative application abilities. Higher-order cognitive levels are difficult to measure using matching items.

2. *True/False:* Because of the 50 percent chance of guessing the correct answer, true-false questions are best suited for measuring basic knowledge of a construct.

3. *Multiple Choice:* Multiple-choice questions can readily measure basic knowledge, comprehension, and application abilities. With practice, these items can be skillfully written to measure all high-order cognitive levels.

4. *Open-Ended Performance:* Items that require a constructed response can readily test higher-order

thinking abilities, including the abilities to analyze, synthesize, and evaluate information that is difficult to measure with other item types.

Report Design

An essential component of deciding the purpose behind a test is determining how the scores of that test will be interpreted. There are two main types of test interpretation: norm-referenced tests and criterion-referenced tests. Norm referencing provides meaning by comparing examinees' scores relative to a well-defined, meaningful comparison group. Data on groups is gathered from a representative sample and is subsequently used to determine how new examinees compare with these norms. For example, norm-referenced tests can be used to evaluate students' achievement levels as they compare with students across the nation. These tests can also be used to compare results on typical behavior assessments to characteristics of reference groups. Alternatively, criterion-referenced tests provide meaning by describing what an examinee with a certain score can do. For instance, criterion-referenced tests can be used to determine a student's level of mastery of a specified content domain. They can also be used to assess an individual independently of others, such as in the evaluation of personality traits.

Standardization and Objectivity

Standardization refers to the extent to which test content, administration, and scoring procedures are the same for all students who receive scores that may be compared. Standardization is on a continuum where standardized and nonstandardized tests are on the two ends of the spectrum. A well-standardized test will have tight content specifications to ensure that multiple forms of the test cover the same content. There will be instructions for test administrators so that similar testing experiences will be provided for all examinees. It has been argued that standardization discriminates against anyone who is not considered part of the norm (e.g., those with different cognitive and perceptual, and learning methods and styles). For these reasons, it may be more appropriate, when attempting to identify and assess giftedness, creativity, and talent, to administer tests that are less standardized. In any case, the purpose behind any test will determine the degree to which it should be standardized.

The word *objective* refers to that which can be measured and observed without the influence of personal opinion or judgment. Conversely, the word *subjective* refers to an opinion or judgment that cannot be readily observed or measured. All other things being equal, tests should be as objective as possible and free from subjective opinion. However, there are many sources of subjectivity—every time a decision is made in the test development, scoring, and reporting of test scores there is some element of subjectivity—all subjectivity cannot be avoided in any testing context. In the area of giftedness, creativity and talent subjectivity may be more acceptable in the assessment process. That is, the judgment of well-qualified educators in the identification and assessment of either a small number of gifted students or the talent of a large number of average students might provide a more accurate depiction of these constructs than might an objective measure that does not allow for such personal opinion.

Reliability and Validity

The landmark of any well-developed test is the degree to which it is both reliable and valid. Reliability refers to the consistency of scores or results that a test produces across multiple administrations. Validity refers to how accurately a test measures the intended construct of interest. Although these two concepts are frequently discussed independently, they are directly related to each other. Reliability is a necessary but not sufficient condition of validity. That is, a valid measure must produce consistent results, but those results must also reflect the intended construct. The key to developing a reliable and valid test is to link all steps in the test-development process back to the original intent and purpose behind the test.

John Poggio and Brooke Nash

See also Aptitude Assessment; Artistic Assessment; Cognitive Abilities Test; Creativity Training; High-Stakes Testing; Identification; Intelligence Testing

Further Readings

Anastasi, A., & Urbina, S. (1997). *Psychological testing* (7th ed.). Upper Saddle River, NJ: Prentice Hall.

Bloom, B. S. (1954). *Taxonomy of educational objectives.* Boston: Allyn & Bacon.

Cronbach, L. J. (1990). *Essentials of psychological testing* (5th ed.). New York: Harper & Row.

Domino, G. (2000). *Psychological testing: An introduction.* Upper Saddle River, NJ: Prentice Hall.

Downing, S. M., & Haladyna, T. M. (2006). *Handbook of test development.* Mahwah, NJ: Lawrence Erlbaum.

Friedenberg, L. (1995). *Psychological testing: Design, analysis, and use.* Needham Heights, MA: Allyn & Bacon.

Gregory, R. J. (2007). *Psychological testing: History, principles, and applications* (5th ed.). Boston: Allyn & Bacon.

Test Preparation

In the 21st century, we are living in a world of tests; many important educational decisions are made based on results of tests—for example, whether or not one will receive a high school diploma, a scholarship, or an admission to a university. Test performances can be improved by appropriately using test preparation activities. Providing practice tests for the students, teaching students test-taking skills, or offering classes for students to learn particular subject matter more in depth for a test are all examples of test preparation.

Previous studies have found a statistically significant relationship between test preparation and performance on a high school graduation test. In particular, the strongest relationships are found for mathematics, where the relative effect size, phi (ϕ) was approximately 0.25 and somewhat less for other subject areas. The patterns of the relationships between test preparation and test performance were generally consistent across subgroups related to gender and ethnicity. What has been found to date by independent researchers are weak-to-modest positive relationships between preparation and performance. So the next questions are, what kinds of activities are appropriate for administrators and teachers to prepare examinees for a test? And, what should be considered when developing test preparation activities?

Before answering the questions, the meaning of test preparation needs to be discussed. Although there is no exact definition for *test preparation* in the literature, the general idea of test preparation is to assist students or test-takers to improve their test performance through a variety of activities, tools, or aids. Test preparation activities and materials can range from simple practice to in-depth instruction, but most of these activities use some form of subject-matter reviews, tests familiarization, practice with feedback, and test-taking skills.

To determine the appropriateness and suitability of particular test preparation activities, administrators and teachers should consider ethical issues related to test preparation. Test preparation should not violate ethical standards of the educational profession. For instance, leaking test questions, stealing a test, cheating, violating state-imposed security procedures regarding the content of high-stake tests, or artificially increasing students' test scores on a test without increasing students' mastery of the domain knowledge and skills are all violations of ethical standards.

Administrators, teachers, or test-givers are often in the position of developing test preparation activities. This entry describes five common activities that capture most of the important test preparation options available to the administrators, teachers, and test-givers.

Teaching the Content Domain

Teaching students the content domain of the test is the first step for test preparation. However, instruction should not be limited to the content areas that teachers know will be tested. Teachers should assess students on various aspects of the content domain and should expose students to all curriculum objectives to be mastered at their grade level. For instance, in preparing for a mathematics test, teachers should not only emphasize the content domains that are sampled on the test, but also ensure their students can use mathematical concepts and procedures, such as number and computation, algebra, geometry, and data analysis, in a variety of situations.

Providing Information for Test Format

Test format can affect students' test performance directly. Students may spend extra time on becoming familiar with the test format before they actually start to answer the questions, or students may get nervous when they are taking a test with an unfamiliar test format. Teachers can provide students information about what the test looks like before testing, for example, a description of the item types (multiple-choice items or constructed-response items), the number of items, the number of parts in the test and the testing time. Not providing this information may affect test results negatively.

Teaching Test-Taking Skills

Although teachers should not focus mainly on teaching students how to take a test, students' test performance can be improved by teaching them appropriate test-taking skills. One critical test-taking skill is time management; teachers can teach students how to finish a test within time limits. For instance, teachers can teach students (a) to work on easy questions first and come back to hard questions later on, (b) to spend more time on hard questions, but less time on easy ones, and (c) to skip the questions that they don't know or are uncertain of the answer, and come back to them later on. Teachers can also teach students how to transfer answers to separate answer sheets, and how to eliminate obviously incorrect distracters to choose the best answer for the question.

Providing Test Practice

Preparing students for tests by conducting practice on items from parallel forms of the test can provide students with the opportunity to learn test content and vocabularies, can integrate teaching of test-taking skills, and can ensure students have had prior experience with the testing format being used. For instance, formative assessments (in class questioning, pretests, and classroom/local assessments) are provided to students to act as test practices in state assessment.

Raising Students' Morale

Teachers can let students know their belief about testing is that students' performance is mediated by students' engagement and effort and not subject to direct teacher or school control. The most important thing that teachers can do is to try to exhort students to do their best on the test. Also, teachers can encourage students to get a good night's sleep and eat a light breakfast before the test, leaving time for a last quick review of the major content areas.

Although test preparation can help students develop the skills they need to do well on tests, it is a learning tool, instead of a shortcut for students to simply receive high scores on tests. Teachers should not over-rely on the test preparation activities and put too much effort on teaching students how to take a test. Instead, teachers should focus on teaching students curriculum objectives and make sure students can master the domain of knowledge or skills that the test is supposed to reflect. Finally, we should note that test preparation activities need to be affordable and equally available to the students. There should be no limitation or restriction regarding students' socioeconomic status or ethnicity for receiving test preparation materials or resources. In some situations, lower-income students may not have the means to afford test preparation and thus are denied this opportunity. Whereas test performance is only partly correlated to test preparation, there is some advantage to having the experience. Therein may lay the greatest bias and inequity of test preparation.

John Poggio and Pui Chi Chiu

See also Curriculum Models; High-Stakes Testing; No Child Left Behind; Student Attitudes; Teacher Attitudes; Test Development

Further Readings

Gulek, C. (2003). Preparing for high-stakes testing. *Theory Into Practice, 42*(1), 42–50.

Norton, S. M., & Park, H. S. (1996, November). *Relationships between test preparation and academic performance on a statewide high school exit examination.* Paper presented at the annual meeting of the Mid-South Educational Research Association, Tuscaloosa, AL.

Popham, W. J. (1991). Appropriateness of teachers' test-preparation practices. *Educational Measurement: Issues and Practice, 10*(4), 12–15.

Smith, M. L. (1991). Meanings of test preparation. *American Educational Research Journal, 28*(3), 521–542.

Thinking Skills

Thinking is as natural a part of our lives as breathing, blinking, or swallowing. It would be logical to assume that everyone understands what is meant by the word *thinking* because we do it all the time. However, depending on the person and the context, thinking means different things to different people in different places. Change, progress, and innovation all depend on flexibility of thought. Thinking also underlies the basic elements of everyday communication: speaking, listening, reading, and writing. It is the engine of learning.

Thinking skills may refer to skills used and honed during daily goings-on, such as inquiring, problem solving, reflecting, being creative, critiquing, and so on. There are low-order thinking skills, such as remembering, comprehending, and actively listening and processing information. There are high-order thinking skills whereby people intricately question, interpret, construct, and then evaluate new knowledge. For gifted or high-ability learners, this is especially important. Educators and parents can focus on helping high-ability learners build diverse and more complete understandings of the world, giving them the skills so they can challenge their surroundings and their minds, while teaching them to formulate more complex thinking processes. This entry discusses learning and metacognition and gifted education strategies in relation to thinking skills.

Learning and Metacognition

There are various views of what constitutes learning, yet they all relate to thinking in some meaningful way. An individual acquires knowledge based on myriad experiences involving active construction within one's own mind, as it might apply to such activities as the reconstruction of prior knowledge, practical application, guided practice, technological endeavors, and collaborative effort. Each of these activities requires thinking, and this effort may take such forms as reflecting, researching, interacting with others, drawing conclusions, and building new ideas. When skills become well learned and fairly automatic, they are often transferred to new situations, thus enabling more thinking and learning to take place.

Adults can teach thinking by modeling good thinking processes, encouraging practice, and providing targeted lessons in such skills as drawing comparisons, synthesizing ideas, weighing alternatives, making decisions, and changing perspectives. Careful thinkers employ many skills: For example, they ask pertinent questions, examine beliefs and assumptions, define criteria for analysis and evaluation, assess arguments, seek proof, look for solutions, and show a willingness to adjust their viewpoints.

There are also established models of thinking instruction (for example, Benjamin Bloom's Taxonomy, Edward deBono's thinking skills program, Robert Sternberg's triarchic model). These can be employed in ways that align with learners' interests and mastery of a subject area, and at a pace that is commensurate with their abilities. The learning can be integrated into curriculum-based activities and resources, with support and guidance involving a flexible approach, collaborative endeavors, and ongoing communication.

Being able to capitalize on knowledge efficiently and insightfully demands thinking about issues, events, acquired information, and problems in intricate ways, by distinguishing relevant information, and also combining and applying it meaningfully. Goal-directed thinking (which focuses on a desired outcome while working to comprehend, assess, or resolve matters) may involve such skills as focusing on reason, being precise, distinguishing between fact and opinion, seeking knowledge, and being aware of one's own biases. Scientific thinking (which demands such specific skills as drawing hypotheses, analyzing data, finding patterns, and devising recommendations based on solid evidence) empowers one to make discoveries by vision and logic, or creating order from chaos. Metacognition, or thinking about thinking, can also be taught. By monitoring and self-regulating one's cognitive processes, and by sharing and valuing one's own thoughts and proficiencies (e.g., memory, comprehension, elaboration, and other processes), one can become a developer, a gatekeeper, a collaborator, and a dreamer—in short, someone better able to tap into curiosity and both explore and extend the sense of wonder, linking ideas to experiences, informational sources, perspectives, and other modes of thought. Perhaps this is thinking at its finest.

Gifted Education: Strategies for Parents and Teachers

Adults who live and work with gifted or high-ability learners should consider their own reasoning, and plan how they want to teach and promote thinking skills—in various settings, both in isolation and as part of more general educational approaches. They can reflect on specific elements of programming such as structure, scaffolding, task design, risk-taking, and assessment elements and figure out how best to integrate choice and authentic (real world) issues to stimulate thought. They can also foster reflective habits of mind by encouraging children to engage in inquiry. (How can I be sure? What are the consequences? What if I tried this instead? When/why is it necessary to? Where can I find out more?) Adults can teach children to be convergent thinkers (learning how to narrow possibilities), divergent thinkers (devising many possible solutions to problems), and lateral thinkers (moving away from one way of looking at things). Another strategy is to encourage subject-specific thinking (skills consciously applied to a specific area or topic) and more wide-range thinking (where the whole world awaits one's exploration and introspection). Adults can also help children learn about self-assessment, and guide them so they can make explicit connections to previous experiences and knowledge bases. In this way, children can learn to set and monitor performance goals for themselves, and they will be well on their way to being able to think more broadly, reflectively, and astutely. These are prerequisites for high-level expertise.

Joanne F. Foster

See also Cognitive Abilities; Creative Problem Solving; Creativity Training; Critical Thinking; Divergent Thinking; Triarchic Theory

Further Readings

Dweck, C. S. (2006). *Mindset: The new psychology of success.* New York: Random House.

Matthews, D. J., & Foster, J. F. (2005). *Being smart about gifted children: A guidebook for parents and educators.* Scottsdale, AZ: Great Potential Press.

Woolfolk, A. E., Winne, P. H., & Perry, N. E. (2005). *Educational psychology* (3rd Canadian ed.). Boston: Pearson Custom Publishing.

Torrance Center for Creativity and Talent Development

In 1966, E. Paul Torrance returned to his home state of Georgia to take up the mantle of department head of the newly merged department of Educational Psychology, Research, Measurement, and Statistics at the University of Georgia. He brought with him his extensive work in creativity and the renamed Torrance Tests of Creative Thinking née Minnesota Tests of Creative Thinking. During his time at the University of Georgia, he continued and expanded his work in creativity, developing the following four areas of inquiry: the Future Problem Solving Program, the incubation model of creative teaching, the eponymous tests, and the international collaborations with others interested in creativity research.

In 1984, when Torrance retired, Mary Frasier, a colleague of Torrance's, founded the Torrance Center for Creative and Future Studies in the College of Education at the University of Georgia. The center was established to carry on Torrance's work of identifying and developing creativity, giftedness, and talent in individuals. The Center, which was renamed in 2001 as the Torrance Center for Creativity and Talent Development, has served many students, families, teachers, schools, and scholars in its trifold mission of education, service, and research, as described in this entry.

In 2003, when he passed away, Torrance left money to the center to enable it to continue its work. He established separate funds for the center's operation, the annual lecture, and an endowed professorship. Housed in the Department of Educational Psychology and Instructional Technology, the Torrance Center works through the department and college to serve a local, state, national, and international constituency.

The programs that are supported by the Torrance Center include direct service programs for children from kindergarten through high school. These programs, which are held on weekends and in the summer, comprise a variety of offerings for students of various ages, interests, and talent levels. Each program charges tuition, but there are full and partial scholarships available. From the

Challenge Program, which offers enrichment opportunities to elementary students, to the Talent Identification Program (TIP), which offers challenging classes on the university campus, students are given opportunities to study topics and in ways that they would not ordinarily do in the regular classroom. In spring 2009, the Torrance Center started offering Saturday programs, called Academic Adventures, for students who have participated in the Duke fourth- and fifth-grade Talent Search. The Torrance Center now has a coordinator of educational programs, Elizabeth Connell, and additional programs are in development.

In addition to serving children and their families, the educational programs serve as a training ground for potential teachers and researchers who aspire to work with such students. University students and faculty from throughout the university participate in teaching the children and adolescents and investigating better ways to identify and nurture their talents.

The center also conducts regular training to prepare and update educators on skills such as administering and scoring the Torrance Tests of Creative Thinking, or the various components of coaching students in the Future Problem Solving Program, both creations of Torrance. Longer-term training sessions, each lasting for several weeks, have educated teachers from Korea about identifying and teaching gifted and creative students.

The Torrance Center sponsors a yearly Torrance Lecture, which has brought outstanding national and international speakers to the University of Georgia campus to discuss current creativity research and practices. Recent lecturers have included Dean Keith Simonton, Joseph Renzulli, June Maker, Mark Runco, and Terry Kay.

In the interest of sharing existing knowledge and creating new knowledge, the center maintains a small library with tests, articles, and books related to creativity. It also supports a visiting scholar program for individuals from around the world to work with faculty and resources in the center as well as the much larger collection of resources established by Torrance and housed in the Hargrett Rare Books Library of the University of Georgia main library. Scholars have come from Russia, Korea, Portugal, Egypt, and Turkey in recent years.

In 2008, the center hosted its first international creativity conference at the University of Georgia's Costa Rica campus. For 5 days, individuals from around the world and the United States shared insights, research, and programs related to creativity at an ecological campus on the edge of the cloud forest. This conference is planned to be a biennial event held during universities' winter break in January.

Also in 2008, the Torrance Center was able to hire the first endowed E. Paul Torrance Professor of Creative Studies and Gifted Education, Mark Runco. Runco, who is also the Torrance Center Director, has bolstered the research power of the Torrance Center with his role, which is strongly dedicated to research and development. As founder and editor, he has moved the *Creativity Research Journal* to the Torrance Center.

Bonnie Cramond

See also Creativity, Definition; Torrance Tests of Creative Thinking

Further Readings

Cramond, B. (in press). The life and contributions of E. Paul Torrance. In T. Coste (Ed.), *Recreating creativity.* Austin, TX: American Creativity Association Press.

Hébert, T. P., Cramond, B., Millar, G., & Silvian, A. F. (2002). *E. Paul Torrance: His life, accomplishments, and legacy* (RM02152). Storrs: National Research Center on the Gifted and Talented, University of Connecticut.

Millar, G. (2007). *E. Paul Torrance, "The creativity man": An authorized biography.* Bensenville, IL: Scholastic Testing Service.

Torrance, E. P., & Safter, H. T. (1990). *The incubation model of teaching: Getting beyond the aha!* Buffalo, NY: Bearly.

Torrance Center for Creativity and Talent Development: http://www.coe.uga.edu/torrance/index.html

Torrance Tests of Creative Thinking

The Torrance Tests of Creative Thinking (TTCT), described in this entry, are a battery of tests that are designed to assess creative thinking abilities in individuals from kindergarten to adulthood.

Published since 1962 by Scholastic Testing Service (STS), the figural and verbal tests are more than tests of divergent thinking. They also assess creative strengths and dispositions that may be expressed through the activities. These strengths and dispositions include humor, resistance to premature closure, and emotional expressiveness, among others. The tests do not measure motivation, skill, temperament, or any number of other factors that play a part in creative productivity. However, the same could be said of other aptitude and achievement measures. IQ tests certainly do not measure motivation to use the intelligence.

What *is* important is how well the tests measure what they purport to measure and how useful they are to educators and researchers. Several studies affirm the TTCT's predictive validity, most recently the results of the 40-year follow-up of elementary children given the tests in 1958 who were contacted in 1998 to assess their creative achievements in adulthood. So, evidence indicates that they are useful as predictors of creativity. Also, the reliability of the tests indicates strong internal consistency. Interrater reliability studies that are routinely performed in the STS Scoring Center and by the Torrance Center illustrate that trained scorers routinely obtain reliability coefficients showing agreement of greater than 90 percent. Finally, in the 50 years since they were created, the TTCT have been translated into more than 35 languages and have been used around the world. Their lasting and widespread use is further evidence of their efficacy.

To further make the case for the usefulness of the tests, we can look at E. Paul Torrance's reasons for developing them. In 1943, Torrance was a counselor and high school teacher, he read *Square Pegs in Square Holes* by Margaret Broadley, and he was struck by her description of children who don't fit into the school environment as "wild colts" who must have their energy directed toward positive pursuits. She wrote that unless this energy is used and directed into the right channels, it is a problem, but well-directed and developed, the aptitude can lead individuals in outstanding creative work. Torrance's career was interrupted by military service in the U.S. Army. He was appointed to head a task force to study factors in fighter interceptor effectiveness in Korea with particular emphasis on the jet aces, and he found that the outstanding aces were also like wild colts but had learned discipline to adapt successfully in the Air Force and learn how to survive. Seven years of experience in Air Force survival research gave Torrance many insights about creativity and training to behave creatively in response to emergencies and extreme conditions.

Moreover, Torrance believed that everyone has creativity, and it can be nurtured. When U.S. education was making its first response to *Sputnik,* he was designing tests to measure this special ability, creativity. Torrance was concerned that creative individuals are being overlooked and even undermined psychologically for lack of widespread use of creativity detection instruments. Thus, he designed the tests to measure creative thinking abilities so that they could be enhanced in everyone. The TTCT, especially the figural, are culture-fair tests that can be administered to individuals of all ages, cultures, and socioeconomic statuses to highlight their abilities. The tests were seen as a means of assessing the effectiveness of creativity training, understanding the human mind, and assisting with curriculum design and psychotherapy.

The verbal tests consist of six activities that take approximately one hour to administer. The respondents are requested to ask questions, guess causes, predict consequences, improve a product, think of new uses for a common object, and reason in a hypothetical situation. The figural tests consist of three activities and take approximately 45 minutes to administer. The respondents are given 10 minutes each to add details to black-and-white shapes and abstract line drawings to make something out of them. The instructions for the activities are designed to motivate the respondents to give creative responses by instructing them to give many, unusual, detailed ideas. Torrance found that performance on the verbal and figural tests show almost no relationship, which indicates that the verbal and figural tests measure different areas. In addition, Torrance has developed other creativity tests to measure creativity in other areas such as *Thinking Creatively With Sounds and Words* (TCSW) and *Thinking Creatively in Action and Movement* (TCAM).

Among Torrance's creativity tests, the TTCT, the TCSW, and the TCAM are in widespread and worldwide use because they have good reliability, have proven validity, are easy to use, and are neutral regarding a wide variety of factors such as gender, race, community status, language, and culture. The TTCT are most often used as part of a multiple criteria approach to identifying students for gifted programs. The recent and growing emphasis on identifying a broad array of talents in a diverse population of students has increased interest in assessments such as the TTCT. Also, because Torrance was originally interested in creative students, wild colts who were often in trouble in schools, the TTCT may be particularly useful for discovering and redirecting such children's energies and talents toward more positive pursuits.

Torrance's creativity tests are useful to assess creativity in a wide variety of situations and for a wide variety of age groups from as young as age 3 to adults. The TTCT, the TCSW, and the TCAM are good measures for identifying and educating the gifted and for discovering and encouraging creativity in everyday life in the general population.

Bonnie Cramond and Kyung Hee Kim

See also Creative Productivity; Creativity Assessment; Creativity Training; Torrance Center for Creativity and Talent Development

Further Readings

Cramond, B., Matthews-Morgan, J., Bandalos, D., & Zuo, L. (2005). A report on the 40-year follow-up of the Torrance Tests of Creative Thinking: Alive and well in the new millennium. *Gifted Child Quarterly, 49,* 283–291.

Millar, G. W. (2007). *E. Paul Torrance, "The creativity man": An authorized biography.* Bensenville, IL: Scholastic Testing Service.

Scholastic Testing Service: http://www.ststesting.com

Torrance, E. P. (1966). *Torrance tests of creative thinking: Norms-technical manual* (Research ed.). Princeton, NJ: Personnel Press.

Torrance, E. P. (1971). Are the Torrance Tests of Creative Thinking biased against or in favor of "disadvantaged" groups? *Gifted Child Quarterly, 15,* 75–80.

Torrance, E. P. (1977). *Discovery and nurturance of giftedness in the culturally different.* Reston, VA: ERIC Clearinghouse on Handicapped and Gifted Children. (ERIC document Reproduction Service No. ED145621)

Torrance, E. P. (1995). Rationale of creativity tests. In E. P. Torrance (Ed.), *Why fly? A philosophy of creativity* (pp. 83–99). Norwood, NJ: Ablex.

Torrance, E. P. (2008). *Torrance Tests of Creative Thinking: Norms-technical manual.* Figural (Streamlined) Forms A&B. Bensenville, IL: Scholastic Testing Service.

Torrance, E. P. (2008). *Torrance Tests of Creative Thinking: Norms-technical manual.* Verbal Forms A&B. Bensenville, IL: Scholastic Testing Service.

Transpersonal Psychology

Transpersonal is defined as extending or going beyond the personal and individual. As described in this entry, transpersonal psychology grew out of humanistic psychology, which emphasized positive psychological health and self-actualization, that is, the realization of human potential. Self-actualization is much more than self-fulfillment. Abraham H. Maslow introduced it as the ideal norm of robust mental health, contrasting it with the norms based on what is average, which he found deficient. He described the characteristics of self-actualizing individuals in rich detail. Among the most salient are the following: problem centering (focusing on problems outside oneself); autonomy and will (independence of culture and environment); the mystic experience and the peak experience; *Gemeinshchaftsgefühl* (a sense of fellowship with all human beings); democratic character structure (some basic respect for all human beings); discrimination between means and ends ("they do right and they do not do wrong"); resistance to enculturation and the transcendence of any particular culture. The transpersonal component is represented by mystical and peak experiences: uplifting experiences of expanded consciousness of "limitless horizons," connectedness, loss of self (transcendence), and unity of everything. In other words, these transpersonal experiences go beyond self-actualization, beyond the personal and individual.

Maslow suggested transpersonal psychology as a field that would explore these "far reaches of human nature." Transpersonal psychology was founded in 1969 with the launching of the *Journal of Transpersonal Psychology.* The field is devoted to bringing together Western and Eastern psychologies (especially through the work of Ken Wilber), exploring varieties of spiritual experiences, methods of healing, and meditation techniques.

William James can be said to be the forerunner of transpersonal psychology. From his study of spiritually gifted people, James concluded that the visible world is part of an invisible spiritual universe. Communion with that universe gives zest, infusion of energy and enthusiasm, and a loving attitude toward others. Consequently, although the spiritual universe remains unseen, it nevertheless produces real observable effects. Therefore, if the unseen can produce real effects, it must be real, too.

One of the founders of transpersonal psychology was Roberto Assagioli who developed psychosynthesis in contrast to psychoanalysis. Psychoanalysis is limited to investigating the subconscious and unconscious layers of the psyche, so Assagioli stressed that the psyche also had a higher, superconscious sphere and within it the individual's higher self as the source of energy and creativity. Assagioli developed techniques for personal and spiritual growth designed to bring about the integration of disparate parts of the psyche expressed as different facets of personality, or to use his word, "subpersonalities."

Assagioli designed numerous scenarios for guided imagery. His work has been extended by Piero Ferrucci. Psychosynthesis techniques have been also adapted for young children.

Psychosynthesis techniques may work well with gifted children and adolescents who have the capacity for concentration, vivid visualization, and absorption in the imaginal experience. Imaginal experience is visualization with a full spectrum of sensory experience. In other words, the act of imagining oneself riding a horse cantering on a beach creates all the sensations of feeling the horse, smelling its scent and the sea, feeling the water splashed on one, hearing the sound of the horse's hoofs on the sand, the sound of the ocean waves, feeling the warmth of the sun, the wind, and so on.

Gifted children may be capable of having transpersonal experiences when they become deeply absorbed in experiential exercises or when they participate in a visualization. On such occasions, spiritual experiences may take place involving an encounter with a wise person or a spiritual figure. Another kind of imaginal experience is shapeshifting—experiencing oneself as something else. Consciousness seems to transfer into an animal or natural object (e.g., water, air, a tree) and the individual experiences things as that animal or object. For example: "When I became the water I traveled fast through the canal and could feel myself partially scraping against the sides and the bottom of the wet soil. To come back I had to come back to myself from where it was I first became the water. My soul then transferred back to my body."

Psychosynthesis exercises and guided imagery for gifted children and adolescents may enable them to exercise their imagination in an atmosphere of acceptance.

Michael M. Piechowski

See also Self-Actualization; Spiritual Intelligence; Spirituality

Further Readings

Assagioli, R. (1965). *Psychosynthesis*. New York: Viking.

Ferrucci, P. (1982). *What we may be: Techniques for psychological and spiritual growth through psychosynthesis*. New York: Jeremy P. Tarcher.

Hart, T., Nelson, P. L., & Puhakka, K. (Eds.). (2000). *Transpersonal knowing: Exploring the horizon of consciousness*. Albany: State University of New York Press.

James, W. (1902). *The varieties of religious experience*. New York: Longmans.

Maslow, A. H. (1970). *Motivation and personality* (2nd ed.). New York: Harper & Row.

Piechowski, M. M. (2006). *"Mellow out," they say. If I only could. Intensities and sensitivities of the young and bright*. Madison, WI: Yunasa Books.

Wilber, K. (1986). *Up from Eden: A transpersonal view of human evolution*. Boulder, CO: Shambhala.

Triarchic Theory

The *triarchic theory of successful intelligence* represents a way of understanding intelligence in broader terms than is the case for traditional theories of intelligence. The theory is called "triarchic" because, as explained in this entry, it has three parts, or subtheories. The theory views intelligence as a synthesis of analytical, creative, and practical skills.

Defining Intelligence

Intelligence is the ability to achieve success in life as defined by one's personal standards, within one's life context. The field of intelligence has, for the most part, produced tests that stress the academic aspect of intelligence, as one might expect, given the origins of modern intelligence testing in Alfred Binet and Theodore Simon's work at the beginning of the 20th century in designing an instrument that would distinguish children who would succeed from those who would fail in school. But the construct of intelligence needs to serve a broader purpose, accounting for the bases of success in all of one's life. Joseph Renzulli has pointed out that many children are gifted in school, but not in life. It is therefore important to define intelligence and giftedness in intelligence in the broader context of potential life, rather than just school, accomplishments.

One's ability to achieve success depends on one's capitalizing on one's strengths and correcting or compensating for one's weaknesses. Theories of intelligence typically specify some relatively fixed set of abilities. Such a specification is useful in establishing a common set of skills to be tested. But people achieve success, even within a given occupation, in many different ways. For example, successful teachers achieve success through many different blendings of skills rather than through any single formula that works for all of them. One teacher might excel in lecturing, another in leading seminars, another in supervising independent projects, another in raising students' self-esteem, and so forth. There is no one fixed set of abilities that constitutes the basis for giftedness in teaching. Different teachers bring different gifts to their teaching and excel in different ways.

Balancing of abilities is achieved to adapt to, shape, and select environments. Definitions of intelligence traditionally have emphasized the role of adaptation to the environment. But intelligence involves not only modifying oneself to suit the environment (adaptation), but also modifying the environment to suit oneself (shaping), and sometimes, finding a new environment that is a better match to one's skills, values, or desires (selection). For example, when someone takes a new job, that person is selecting a new environment in which to work. One needs to adapt by figuring out the rules and customs in the new employment setting and how to make oneself fit with them. But a person likely also wants to shape the environment, and make it a better place for himself or herself and others. For example, the person might have suggestions about how the work environment could be made a more rewarding one for himself or herself and other employees.

Success is attained through a balance of analytical, creative, and practical abilities. Analytical abilities are the abilities primarily measured by traditional tests of abilities. But success in life requires one to analyze one's own ideas as well as the ideas of others and to generate creative ideas and persuade other people of their value. This practical necessity occurs in the world of work, as when a subordinate tries to convince a superior of the value of his or her plan; in the world of personal relationships, as when a child attempts to convince a parent to do what he or she wants or when a spouse tries to convince the other spouse to do things his or her preferred way; and in the world of the school, as when a student writes an essay arguing for a point of view. People who are extremely gifted in one way but lacking in other abilities may be at risk in their life courses. For example, no matter how creative one is, if one cannot persuade others of the value of one's ideas, one may find oneself being frustrated in attempts to achieve acceptance of one's ideas.

Information-Processing Components

According to the triarchic theory of successful intelligence, a common set of mental processes underlies all aspects of intelligence. These processes are viewed as universal. For example, although the solutions to problems that are considered intelligent in one culture may be different from the solutions considered to be intelligent in another culture, the need to figure out the nature of the problems facing one and to devise strategies to solve these problems exists in all cultures.

Metacomponents

Metacomponents, or executive processes, plan what to do, monitor things as they are being done, and evaluate things after they are done. Examples of metacomponents are recognizing the existence of a problem, defining the nature of the problem, deciding on a strategy for solving the problem, monitoring the solution of the problem, and evaluating the solution after the problem is solved.

Consider an example. Suppose someone's car is not working well, despite having put a lot of money into repairing it. Recognizing the existence of the problem means that the person knows that he or she has a problem, namely, that the investments in the car are not paying off. Defining the problem means figuring out why: Is it a bad car-repair shop, or is the car just too old to be repaired properly, or are the weather conditions unusually harsh, or what? Deciding on a strategy means figuring out what to do: keep trying to repair the car, perhaps at a new car-repair shop; buy a new car; buy a used car; lease a car; and so forth. Monitoring the solution means that, as one tries to solve the car problem, one continually asks oneself whether one is on the right track. Evaluating the solution means looking at how whatever one has decided to do has worked. For example, if the decision is to keep the car, will that mean continuing to pay a lot for repairs? If the decision is to buy a new car, is the new car working better?

Performance Components

Performance components execute the instructions of the metacomponents. For example, inference is used to decide how two stimuli are related, and application is used to apply what one has inferred. Other examples of performance components are comparison of stimuli, justification of a given response as adequate although not ideal, and actually making the response. For example, in deciding between two cars a person is considering buying, she likely will compare them in some detail. She may also infer things about the cars, such as how likely she is to enjoy driving them. In the end, she might decide that neither car is ideal, but that given her budget, she cannot afford the ideal car. So she might attempt to justify to herself that the car she is buying is the best she can do, given her financial circumstances.

Knowledge-Acquisition Components

Knowledge-acquisition components are used to learn how to solve problems or simply to acquire knowledge in the first place. Selective encoding is used to decide what information is relevant in the context of one's learning. Selective comparison is used to bring old information to bear on new problems. And selective combination is used to put together the selectively encoded and compared information into a single and sometimes insightful solution to a problem.

For example, suppose someone is about to take a written driver's test. He realizes that he cannot memorize everything in the driver's information book. So he selectively encodes what information he believes is most important and that therefore he is most likely to be tested on. He might also selectively compare what he read to what he already knows, especially if he has moved from one state to another. Sometimes, there are differences in laws from one state to another, and keeping track of changes might help him to avoid committing infractions in the new state that would not have been infractions in the former state.

Although the same processes are used for all three aspects of intelligence universally, these processes are applied to different kinds of tasks and situations depending on whether a given problem requires analytical thinking, creative thinking, practical thinking, or a combination of these kinds of thinking. In particular, analytical thinking is invoked when components are applied to fairly familiar kinds of problems abstracted from everyday life. Creative thinking is invoked when the components are applied to relatively novel kinds of tasks or situations. Practical thinking is invoked when the components are applied to experience to adapt to, shape, and select environments.

For example, someone may be good at solving textbook mathematics problems, but have more difficulty applying the principles to real-life math problems, or vice versa. The person thus might be better at the analytical aspect or the practical aspect, with the difference reflected in which kind of problem the person finds easier to solve. Jean Lave has found that housewives who are able to compute which of two products in a supermarket is a better buy are not necessarily able to do the same computations when they are presented in a paper-and-pencil, academic format.

What Does the Theory Predict?

A reasonable question to ask would be whether the theory actually can predict anything useful.

Researchers have done many different kinds of investigations to address this question.

For example, in one set of studies, people around the world were queried about what their beliefs are regarding the nature of intelligence. It turns out that different cultures, and even different ethnic groups within a culture, often have quite different conceptions of what it means to be intelligent. In many countries, especially in the developing world, social and practical skills are considered much more important to intelligence than are academic skills. These views may reflect less emphasis on academic training. But they also may reflect an awareness that performance in real-world jobs is not fully predicted by academic success.

Robert Sternberg and his colleagues studied performance in diverse real-world jobs in the United States. They were particularly interested in the relationship of both academic and practical kinds of skills to job performance. Like Frank Schmidt and John Hunter, Sternberg and his colleagues found that the kinds of more academic skills measured by conventional ability tests matter for real-world job performance. But they also found that practical aspects of intelligence predicted job performance, independently of more academic skills. Understanding other people and how to relate to them, for example, are important for job success, but are not measured by conventional ability tests.

In another set of studies, Sternberg and his colleagues asked how adding creative and practical predictors might affect the college-admissions process. They tested more than a thousand high school seniors and college freshmen, assessing creative and practical in addition to analytical skills. For example, in assessments of creative skills, students might be asked to write a story with a title such as "Beyond the Edge" or "The Octopus's Sneakers," be asked to tell a story about a picture of athletes, or be asked to caption a cartoon. In assessments of practical skills, the students might be asked how to solve an everyday problem, such as what to do if one eats in a restaurant and then finds one does not have the money to pay for the meal, or how to get a bed up to a bedroom when the bed does not fit up a winding staircase. The results showed that using such assessments doubled prediction of freshman grade-point average, and substantially reduced differences in test scores between members of diverse ethnic groups, such as African Americans, Anglo Americans, Hispanic Americans, and Asian Americans.

In sum, the triarchic theory of successful intelligence provides a broader framework in which to understand human intelligence. It does so by considering the analytical abilities measured by traditional tests, as well as creative and practical abilities. A gifted individual can be gifted by virtue of excellence in any one or more of these three abilities, or by virtue of having found a way of particularly well capitalizing on strengths and/or compensating for or correcting weaknesses.

Robert J. Sternberg

See also Academic Talent; Aptitude Assessment; Creative Process; Critical Thinking; Intelligence; Intelligence Theories; Thinking Skills

Further Readings

Cianciolo, A. T., & Sternberg, R. J. (2004). *A brief history of intelligence.* Malden, MA: Blackwell.

Hunter, J. B., & Schmidt, F. L. (1984). Validity and utility of alternative predictors of job performance. *Psychological Bulletin, 96.*

Sternberg, R. J. (Ed.). (2000). *Handbook of intelligence.* New York: Cambridge University Press.

Sternberg, R. J. (2003). *Wisdom, intelligence, and creativity synthesized.* New York: Cambridge University Press.

Sternberg, R. J. (Ed.). (2004). *International handbook of intelligence.* New York: Cambridge University Press.

Sternberg, R. J., & Grigorenko, E. L. (2007). *Teaching for successful intelligence* (2nd ed.). Thousand Oaks, CA: Corwin Press.

Twice Exceptional

Although there is no formal, agreed-upon definition of *twice exceptional,* this term is commonly used to refer to children who have two seemingly contradictory sets of traits: those related to their high intellectual or artistic abilities, and those related to their limitations or deficits. Another term often applied to this group is *gifted/learning disabled,* although not all twice-exceptional children are formally diagnosed with learning disabilities. Those who are may have one or more diagnoses such as dyslexia, central auditory-processing disorder, visual-processing disorder, attention deficit disorder (with or without hyperactivity), Asperger's syndrome, obsessive/compulsive disorder, sensory-processing disorder, and Tourette's syndrome.

The exact number of twice-exceptional children is unknown. Estimates vary greatly, from 2 to 5 percent of all gifted children to as high as 20 percent. This entry discusses twice-exceptional children.

Characteristics

Because the causes of twice exceptionality are so varied, there can be no single profile of a twice-exceptional child. Children identified as twice exceptional can exhibit a wide range of traits, many of them typical of gifted children. In general, those who are twice exceptional, like other gifted children, show greater asynchrony than average children (that is, a larger gap between mental age and physical age). They are often intense, with a highly developed sense of curiosity and an unusual sense of humor. Also like other gifted children, they tend to be highly sensitive to their emotional and physical environments, and to display keen observation skills, an ability to remember large amounts of information, and advanced vocabularies and use of language.

Along with these traits, twice-exceptional children have deficits that may interfere with their ability to perform the tasks that classroom learning requires. Among the deficits may be the following:

- Limited short-term memory
- A poor sense of time and difficulty following a schedule
- Language-based disorders that can interfere with some or all of the following: reading, writing, verbal expression, and mathematics
- Difficulty focusing attention on subjects or tasks not of their choosing
- Fine or gross motor skills that are not well developed
- Processing disorders that make it hard to interpret visual or auditory information
- An inability to correctly interpret social cues, such as facial expressions and tone of voice
- Sensory processing difficulties that make it hard to organize and interpret information received through the senses of touch, taste, smell, sight, and sound, as well as through the placement and movement of their bodies.

Combination of Strengths and Weaknesses

The combination of exceptional strengths and weaknesses in a single individual results in inconsistency and often leads to a child who is misunderstood. His grades can alternate between high and low, sometimes within the same subject. She might have plenty to say but is unable to organize and express those thoughts on paper. He might do careful artwork but turn in assignments that are sloppy or illegible. She might complete assignments but is unable to keep track of them and remember to turn them in.

A disadvantage that twice-exceptional children face is that their disabilities or deficits are often not apparent to those around them. The twice-exceptional student may appear to be uninterested, lazy, distracted, or disruptive. He or she might present any of the three profiles that researcher and educator Susan Baum has identified: bright but not trying hard enough, learning disabled but with no exceptional abilities, or just average. In each situation, the twice-exceptional student's strengths are helping compensate for deficits; the deficits, however, are making the child's strengths less apparent.

It can be easy to assume that these children could do better if they tried. The reality for many twice-exceptional children is that they may be working as hard or even harder than others, but with fewer results to show for their efforts.

This struggle to accomplish tasks that appear easy for other students can leave twice-exceptional children with little enthusiasm or energy for schoolwork, and it can lead them to become frustrated, anxious, and depressed. Furthermore, because these children rarely meet the expectations others have for them, and that they may have for themselves, their self-esteem often suffers.

Identification

When their children are young, parents are often unaware that they have a twice-exceptional child. At home, many of these children seem bright, with varied interests and advanced vocabularies. School is usually where problems first appear.

Teachers may notice social difficulties first. The twice-exceptional child may find it hard to make friends and fit in. Academic problems, however, may not arise until later. Transitions are common times for children to be identified as twice exceptional, such as entering third grade—when reading, writing, and organization skills become more important—or entering middle school, high school, or even college. As work demands increase, teachers may see a drop in performance or an increase in problem behaviors. Assignments may be inadequate, late, or missing. Neatness, organization, and poor time management may become obstacles to good grades. Behavior issues may surface or increase. Teachers might see that the child is unable to sit still and work quietly, plays the class clown, or has trouble controlling anger or frustration; or teachers might see that the child has withdrawn, showing reluctance to speak out or take other risks in class.

These difficulties spread from classroom to home, as parents start to see disappointing report cards and requests for teacher/parent conferences. A common result is that parents take on new, and often stressful, roles: academic tutor, behavior coach, or homework supervisor.

If these difficulties persist, school personnel or parents may decide that testing and evaluation are necessary to determine the cause. This assessment may be done by school district personnel, or parents may choose to have it done by independent professionals. In either case, it is important that the professionals who take part in the process are knowledgeable about giftedness. Some characteristics of giftedness can look much like those of a learning disability or disorder and, as a result, gifted children are sometimes incorrectly diagnosed.

Assessment may include achievement tests to assess strengths and weaknesses in subject areas such as reading, math, and spelling; and IQ testing to identify strengths and weaknesses in cognitive areas. The process might also include neuropsychological evaluation to examine multiple areas of functioning such as memory; executive function; visual, perceptual, and motor functions; and language function. Social-emotional testing may also be included. In addition, functional behavioral assessment may be performed to look at causes of, and ways to address, problem behavior. Parents may also take their children for physical examinations that include hearing and vision screenings.

When assessments are complete, the results should indicate what the child's strengths and weaknesses are and identify whether any disorders or learning disabilities are present. In addition, the results often include a report that states what the child needs to build on the strengths and compensate for the weaknesses identified by the assessment.

Teaching the Twice-Exceptional Student

Finding effective strategies to use with twice-exceptional students can present a challenge because of the variation in both the ways in which children can be gifted and the types of learning problems they can have. Teachers may need to try various strategies before discovering those that work for a particular student. Research, program evaluation, and practice show, however, that effective strategies for teaching twice-exceptional children share characteristics such as these:

- They are creative and flexible.
- They involve teamwork between gifted and special education teachers.
- They give students opportunities to interact with twice-exceptional peers.
- They lead students to a better understanding of their abilities, their limitations, and how they learn best.
- They build on the students' strengths, talents, and interests.

Teachers find that twice-exceptional students tend to learn best when given work that engages multiple senses, challenges their intellectual abilities, and offers opportunities for hands-on learning. Success often comes from project-based assignments that build on the students' interests and offer an outlet for their creative abilities. One study by Robert Sternberg showed that twice-exceptional students outperformed their brightest peers in focusing for long periods on complex projects when teachers gave assignments matched to the twice-exceptional students' particular interests and abilities.

An important requirement for success for twice-exceptional students is support. Along with encouragement, other essential forms of support are compensation strategies and accommodations in their areas of weakness. Examples of useful compensation strategies to teach twice-exceptional students are problem-solving approaches, time-management skills, organizational techniques, note-taking and study skills, and social skills training. Examples of accommodations these students might require are as follows: allowing keyboarding in place of handwriting; more time to complete schoolwork and tests; reduced homework; preferred seating; guided notes or a note-taker; and the use of assistive technology such as electronic spellers, scanning and reading software, and reading pens. In combination, these forms of support help minimize the effects of disabilities or deficits and move the students toward self-confidence and independence in learning. Such support may be given informally on an as-needed basis or may be formally put in place by means of an Individual Education Plan (IEP) or other type of plan.

Raising the Twice-Exceptional Child

Parents of twice-exceptional children face a number of challenges. Among them is the challenge to go beyond the easy explanation that a child is lazy or careless, or an underachiever or troublemaker, to discover what the underlying cause of the behaviors might be. Sometimes it takes considerable time and money to search for professionals who have the skills, experience, and insight needed to accurately assess a child's strengths and weaknesses and then provide the help the child needs.

Another challenge for parents is coming to terms with their child's twice-exceptionality. Few twice-exceptional children match the stereotypical image of a gifted child. Because their academic performance is often uneven, they tend not to be the award winners and high achievers. It may be hard for parents, as well as other relatives and twice-exceptional children themselves, to give up that traditional view of academic success.

A third challenge is finding the right learning environment for a twice-exceptional child. Public and private schools that offer programs combining the appropriate levels of challenge and support for these learners are in the minority. For this reason, a number of parents choose alternative options for educating their children, including homeschooling and virtual (Internet-based) schools.

Parents will be better able to meet these challenges by educating themselves about the following topics:

- How gifts and talents shape these children
- How learning deficits/disabilities affect them
- How these two sets of characteristics come together—the blending of the child's strengths and weaknesses.

They will also find it helpful to become knowledgeable about the following:

- Professionals who can provide the medical, therapeutic, educational, and other types of services a twice-exceptional child might need
- Laws that protect the rights of individuals with disabilities (e.g., Individuals with Disabilities Education Act and Americans with Disabilities Act)
- Educational alternatives available to their children, which might include enrichment opportunities outside of school as well as school alternatives.

Joining organizations or online groups that focus directly on the needs of twice-exceptional children provides information, resources, and much-needed support for parents. This interaction with other families facing similar challenges can open possibilities for their twice-exceptional children that parents had not considered before.

Helping Twice-Exceptional Children Find Success

Twice-exceptional children need guidance from the adults in their lives in learning to understand who they are and what they need. Essential for these children is to know that there are other people just like them, many of whom have grown up to lead happy and successful lives. Furthermore, twice-exceptional children need help in learning how to advocate for themselves, that is, how to ask for the support they need. This vital skill will help these children become independent and successful in school and later in life.

Linda C. Neumann

See also Attention Deficit Hyperactivity Disorder; Depression; Differentiation; Disabilities, Gifted; Dyslexia; Self-Efficacy/Self-Esteem; Underachievement

Further Readings

Baum, S., Cooper, C., & Neu, T. (2001). Dual differentiation: An approach for meeting the curricular needs of gifted students with learning disabilities. *Psychology in the Schools, 38*(5), 477–490.

Baum, S., & Owen, S. (2004). *To be gifted & learning disabled: Strategies for helping bright students with LD, ADHD, and more.* Mansfield Center, CT: Creative Learning Press.

Eide, B., & Fernette, E. (2006). *The mislabeled child: Looking beyond behavior to find the true sources—and solutions—for children's learning challenges.* New York: Hyperion.

Levine, M. (2002). *The myth of laziness.* New York: Simon & Schuster.

Lovecky, D. (2004). *Different minds: Gifted children with AD/HD, Asperger's syndrome, and other learning deficits.* London: Jessica Kingsley.

Nielsen, M. E. (2002). Gifted students with learning disabilities: Recommendations for identification and programming. *Exceptionality, 10*(2), 93–111.

Rivero, L. (2002). *Creative home schooling: A resource guide for smart families.* Scottsdale, AZ: Great Potential Press.

Sternberg, R. (1997). What does it mean to be smart? *Educational Leadership, 54*(6), 20–24.

Webb, J. T., Amend, E. R., Webb, N. E., Goerss, J., Beljan, P., & Olenchak, F. R. (2005). *The misdiagnosis and dual diagnoses of gifted children and adults: ADHD, bipolar, OCD, Asperger's, depression, and other disorders.* Scottsdale, AZ: Great Potential Press.

Weinfeld, R., Jeweler, S., Barnes-Robinson, L., & Shevitz, B. (2006). *Smart kids with learning difficulties: Overcoming obstacles and realizing potential.* Waco, TX: Prufrock Press.

U

Underachievement

Underachievement among intellectually gifted children would appear to be an oxymoron, yet it is reasonably common to find gifted students not working up to their abilities in school. A 1983 report prepared by the National Commission on Excellence in Education pronounced that fully half of gifted children were underachieving. Although the report did not specify how the percentage was calculated, educators agree that underachievement among highly capable children is a common phenomenon, which this entry discusses.

Definitions

Definitions of underachievement involve discrepancies between abilities and achievement, but there are multiple approaches to calculating these discrepancies. Some gifted students are not provided with opportunities to work to their abilities, but others choose not to work to their abilities even when they are given opportunities. When students choose not to work to their abilities, those choices may be conscious, unconscious, or a mixture of both. Some usual definitions of underachievement are described.

Discrepancy Between School Grades and Measures of Ability

The most common underachievement problem that frustrates parents and teachers most is caused by children who have high measured ability but do not complete assignments, homework, or put forth good effort. They rarely study or prepare for tests and seem not to be motivated to learn in school. They are characteristically disorganized and forgetful, or at least claim to be forgetful. They blame teachers, parents, or others for their problems, although some describe themselves as lazy or uninterested. Their grades may vary between A's and F's, sometimes depending on whether they prefer a teacher or subject and other times with little predictability. A nationwide study by Nicholas Colangelo and Barbara Kerr of adolescents who scored in the 95th percentile on the ACT college admission test but who were receiving below average grades in school found these young people to be predominantly boys from affluent, large schools who seemed not to blame schools or teachers for their underachievement, but were unclear about goals and seemed to lack a sense of purpose.

Discrepancies Between Test Measurements of Aptitude and Achievement

Despite students' good grades, student achievement test scores may be lower than predicted by IQ test scores. Gifted children may not be exposed to curriculum that provides them with opportunities to learn material in school that provides the challenge of which they are capable. Their test scores do not show mastery of materials that other highly intelligent students have accomplished. These students typically find their work easy, but assume the ease of curriculum is related to their giftedness, and they have become accustomed to putting forth little effort. Grades are likely very good or even excellent so that parents and teachers rarely indicate concern. When gifted children underachieve but earn excellent grades, they may confront difficult circumstances if they move to more challenging school districts or higher levels of curriculum at middle school, high school, or college because they lack experiences with academic challenge. When confronted with academic challenge, they may rise to the occasion by compensatory effort or may give up their attempts at achieving, avoid challenges, and assume they are less capable than they actually are. They can believe that their giftedness should make learning effortless.

Culturally Disadvantaged Populations

In schools where there are large populations of disadvantaged children, intellectually gifted children may go totally unrecognized. These children may do poorly on typical standardized tests of mental abilities because of differences in language and learning experiences. They may also perform poorly in school because parents and peers may not value school learning, and teachers may assume that giftedness rarely exists in such populations. Excellent logical and creative thinking, hands-on skills, unusual common sense, and rapid learning may only be exhibited outside the classroom but may be difficult to identify in school. For these students, classroom learning may seem irrelevant.

Extent

There is great variety in the extent that students underachieve. Some underachievers earn D's and F's on their report cards and underachieve so severely that unless they reverse their pattern dramatically, they are unlikely to be able to attend higher education and pursue careers commensurate with their abilities. Others only get somewhat lower grades than would be expected, but may or may not be at such high risk. With maturity and development of serious interests, it's possible for them to increase their efforts and be successful. However, depending on their career direction, their somewhat lower grades could prevent their entrance into the highly selective careers they may have preferred had they prepared well. For those who underachieved because curriculum was not appropriate but had high grades, their later accomplishments are likely to depend on their abilities to make adjustments to challenge. For those selective achievers who have achieved in some areas and underachieved in others, their later life achievement is likely to depend on the expectations of the specific career they choose. Some pay no penalty at all, but for others, career choices may be narrowed by their earlier inconsistency. For gifted underachievers who come from culturally deprived environments, many will not have the opportunities their capabilities could provide them. Others will find themselves in careers where, for the first time, their giftedness will be identified and they will be moved rapidly toward leadership positions. Their inadequate educations will, however, have served as a disadvantage for them.

School Causes

Uninteresting and undifferentiated curriculum often leads to underachievement. Curriculum that is too easy, too difficult, or unengaging can turn students away from learning. Too easy curriculum prevents students from experiencing self-efficacy and understanding how to make strong efforts. Too difficult curriculum may cause children to lose confidence in their abilities to achieve. Students who are perfectionistic or are not resilient in competition may not achieve well in highly competitive environments, but others may thrive in similar environments. Peers within the classroom also make a difference. Gifted children benefit by learning with other children who have similarly high abilities and interests and who value learning. Peer pressures that alienate good students can distract students from learning because of fears that their good grades and intellectual interests prevent their social acceptance. Thus, peer pressures can initiate students' underachievement.

Home Causes

When parents value education and respect teachers, children are much more likely to achieve in school. Parents who come from cultural or economic disadvantage may or may not have had good school experiences. The interpretation of their own learning experiences makes a difference in the educational expectations they have for their children. A more subtle problem arises when parents differ from each other with regard to their children's education. One parent may expect more effort and higher grades than the other. When parents oppose each other and give their children differing expectations regarding school effort, children who are faced with challenges and lack self-efficacy may view the parent that expects less as providing "an easy way out." Oppositional relations between parents often encourage oppositional behavior and underachievement in children.

Parent opposition with teachers can also result in underachievement. If parents lack respect for teachers and assume teachers are not teaching well, students sometimes use their parents' assumptions as reason for their lack of effort in school. Respect between parents and between parents and teachers encourages student achievement in the classroom.

Here is a dilemma. Parents of gifted children frequently must advocate for their children to be sure curriculum is sufficiently challenging. When advocacy is conducted respectfully, it is likely to be helpful for children. If advocacy is conducted disrespectfully, it can backfire and provide a message to children to only work in school when they deem curriculum to be appropriate. Students may not always be the best judge of appropriateness. For example, correct grammar and spelling may not be high on the priority list for gifted students, and it may be difficult to convince them of the relevance of routine and repetitive study for some areas of education that could be crucial in their later lives. Students are not always able to predict their educational needs for the future.

Strategies for Reversing Underachievement

In her book *Giftedness, Conflict and Underachievement,* Joanne Whitmore recommended curricular changes for successfully reversing underachievement. In 1986, Sylvia Rimm provided a model for reversing underachievement in her book then entitled *Underachievement Syndrome: Causes and Cures* and revised in 1995 as *Why Bright Kids Get Poor Grades and What You Can Do About It.* Her *trifocal model* is directed at parents, teachers, and the underachieving child. This six-step model was found to be effective at Rimm's Family Achievement Clinic, as well as in many schools, and includes (1) Assessment, (2) Communication, (3) Changing Expectations, (4) Role-Model Identification, (5) Correction of Deficiencies, and (6) Modifications at Home and School. The model provides a framework from which teachers and parents can select appropriate techniques to use for specific children who are underachieving.

Curricular changes, including subject acceleration, grade skipping, and more opportunity for choice, are helpful for both preventing and reversing underachievement. Opportunities for creativity invite students with creative minds to find curriculum more interesting. Del Siegle found that convincing students of the relevance of curriculum made a significant difference in their motivation to achieve. Carol Dweck, in her book *Mindset: The New Psychology of Success,* established that when students were told that their mind was a muscle and that using it would increase their abilities and learning, students performed better than if they were taught only study skills.

Siegle and Rimm also found that students who are active in extracurricular activities were more likely to be achievers in school. In her study of the childhood of successful women, Rimm found that these women often found their direction toward careers through their extracurricular interests and involvement. Engagement in extracurricular activities provides experiences of self-efficacy and often generalizes to school achievement.

Role models and mentors can be powerful motivators toward achievement. These role models can be parents, teachers, scout leaders, special-interest teachers, neighbors, doctors, dentists, or people they meet in chance acquaintances. Rimm also found in her survey of more than 5,000 middle schoolers that they frequently select models from the media, sports, or literature they read. Unfortunately, role models from popular culture may not always be good for student achievement. When reversing students' underachievement, pairing them with adults who are achieving role models can be helpful in motivating them. A great many successful adults have credited their teachers as having inspired their motivation.

Projections for the Future

There have always been gifted students who do not achieve to their abilities in school. Schools, families, disadvantages, as well as a media culture that negates school achievement, all contribute to increasing underachievement. Gifted educational programming can contribute to preventing and reversing underachievement. When families are involved in programming for gifted children, parents are more likely to be supportive of schools and educators can guide parents in understanding the special needs of their gifted children. Research has already provided many techniques for enhancing motivation and reversing underachievement. Dissemination of information on reversing underachievement and engaging students in learning will surely assist many students in working to their abilities in school. Because there are many types and degrees of underachievement, it will be difficult to measure progress in overcoming the underachievement of gifted students.

Sylvia Rimm

See also Diversity in Gifted Education; Family Achievement; Parenting; Resilience; Self-Efficacy/ Self-Esteem

Further Readings

Colangelo, N., & Kerr, B. A. (1993). A comparison of gifted underachievers and gifted high achievers. *Gifted Child Quarterly,* 37, 155–160.

Dweck, C. (2006). *Mindset: The new psychology of success.* New York: Random House.

Reis, S., & McCoach, B. (2000). The underachievement of gifted students: What do we know and where do we go? *Gifted Child Quarterly, 44*(3), 152–170.

Rimm, S. (2005). *Growing up too fast: The Rimm report on the secret world of America's middle schoolers.* New York: Rodale.

Rimm, S. (2007). *Keys to parenting the gifted child* (3rd ed.). Scottsdale, AZ: Great Potential Press.

Rimm, S. (2008). *Why bright kids get poor grades and what you can do about it.* Scottsdale, AZ: Great Potential Press. (Formerly *Underachievement Syndrome: Causes and Cures.* Watertown, WI: Apple Publishing, 1986.)

Rimm, S., Rimm-Kaufman, S., & Rimm, I. (1999). *See Jane win: The Rimm report on how 1,000 girls became successful women.* New York: Crown.

Siegle, D., & McCoach, B. (2006). Motivating gifted students. In F. A. Karnes & K. R. Stephens (Eds.), *The practical strategies series in gifted education.* Waco, TX: Prufrock Press.

Whitmore, J. R. (1980). *Giftedness, conflict, and underachievement.* Needham Heights, MA: Allyn & Bacon.

UNDERREPRESENTATION

Two significant events occurred in 1954 that profoundly affected the education of gifted minorities. The first was *Brown vs. Board of Education, Topeka,* which required that African Americans receive an equal education in desegregated settings. The second was the creation of the National Association for Gifted Children, the prominent advocacy organization for students identified as gifted. Both developments—one focused on diversity and equity and the other focused on giftedness and equity—represented unprecedented opportunities to meet the needs of gifted African American students, Hispanic students, and Native American students, all of whom are underrepresented in gifted education programs. This entry discusses contributing factors, recruitment and retention, and the outlook of underrepresentation of gifted.

Attention to African Americans in gifted education is riddled with controversy. Gifted education has received much criticism from both advocates and opponents. The primary criticism is that African Americans are consistently underrepresented in gifted education and advanced placement (AP) classes. At no time in the history of gifted education has their school representation matched their representation in gifted education. Gifted education has always been segregated by race. For instance, as of 2002, Black students represented approximately 17.2 percent of school districts nationally, but 8.4 percent of gifted programs—a discrepancy of more than 50 percent. Compared with Black girls, Black boys are even more underrepresented in gifted education.

Hispanics are one of the fastest growing populations, but gifted education programs do not show a parallel increase in participation. Particularly those with limited English proficiency (LEP) are neglected in programs for gifted and talented.

Andrea Bermudez and Steven Rakow surveyed highly Hispanic-populated school districts and found that very few were identifying or serving gifted LEP students, and of those districts that have developed identification procedures for this group of students, only 33 percent experienced success with the developed measures.

Finally, even in schools where Native American students are the majority, such as those serving reservation students, little attention is given to proportionate representation of Native Americans in gifted programs. Few AP classes are available to Native American students, and where available, Native American students are underrepresented.

Contributing Factors

Several factors contribute to underrepresentation. Nationally, the first step to being screened for gifted education services in most schools is teacher referral. Teachers frequently under refer minority students for gifted education services and AP classes. Lack of training in cultural diversity, low expectations and stereotypes, and lack of training in gifted education play a role in teachers not recognizing giftedness among African Americans, Hispanics, and Native Americans. Thus, teachers are the initial gatekeepers to these students accessing gifted education. Second, students are administered an intelligence or achievement test. Many times, minorities do not attain predetermined cutoff scores; this is particularly true on traditional intelligence tests, where African American students tend to score one standard deviation below White students, and Hispanic students and Native Americans score between one-half and one standard deviation below White and Asian American students. Thus, traditional tests are the second barrier. Despite concerns about using tests with culturally and linguistically diverse students, this practice continues, and so does underrepresentation.

Recruitment and Retention

How can educators increase the percentage of minority students identified as gifted and ensure that they stay in gifted programs after being recruited? Efforts must focus on both recruitment and retention.

- Instruments, policies, and procedures that have a disparate impact on African American, Hispanic, and Native American students must be changed or eliminated. Instruments (tests, checklists, nomination forms) must be selected carefully, criteria (cutoff scores, etc.) must be examined carefully, and policies and procedures (e.g., teacher referral) must be evaluated to see if they are educationally useful or harmful.
- A philosophy of inclusion rather than exclusion is necessary; it is necessary for educators to search for students to include, rather than exclude on the basis of numerical scores.
- Definitions and theories need to be developed with cultural groups in mind. Are they sensitive and responsive to the characteristics of and values of African Americans, Hispanics, and Native Americans? Educators and decision makers must understand that the notion of gifted is socially constructed, such that what is viewed as and valued as gifted in one culture may not be considered gifted in another. One cultural group may value verbal skills, another may prize social skills, and another may value creativity.
- Evaluation must be ongoing and systemic. School personnel must consistently examine patterns and trends (male vs. female representation, under-referral, ineffective tests and instruments) and eliminate barriers.
- Education, including professional development, is necessary for educators and families, as well as other decision makers and stakeholders. All parties must be given formal preparation in understanding definitions and theories of giftedness, recognizing characteristics of gifted and talented students, and understanding tests, including their purpose and limitations.
- Educators must receive formal preparation in understanding culture, including how culture affects learning and test performance. They will need to know more about culturally diverse students in terms of characteristics, learning styles, communication styles, and values, traditions, customs and norms. All school personnel require assistance in creating culturally responsive classrooms, developing multicultural curricula, and modifying their instructional styles and strategies to accommodate diverse learning and cultural styles. With such formal preparation,

educators may be less likely to view cultural differences as deficits.

Future Outlook

No group has a monopoly on being gifted. Nonetheless, the field of gifted education remains racially and culturally segregated. For change to occur, a philosophy of inclusion is essential. Instruments, definitions, theories, criteria, policies, and procedures must be selected with care and modified so that they are culturally sensitive, fair, and equitable. School personnel and families must be educated about gifted education and about cultural diversity. And educators must be diligent, assertive, and proactive about evaluating and changing gifted education and advanced placement with the focus of recruiting *and* retaining minority students.

Donna Y. Ford and Gilman W. Whiting

See also African American, Gifted; Bilingualism and Creativity; Cultural Conceptions of Giftedness; Native American, Gifted

Further Readings

Barkan, J. H., & Bernal, E.M. (1991). Gifted education for bilingual and limited English proficient students. *Gifted Child Quarterly, 35*(3), 144–147.

Bermudez, A. B., & Rakow, S.J. (1990). Analyzing teachers' perceptions of identification procedures for gifted and talented Hispanic limited English proficient (LEP) students at-risk. *Journal of Educational Issues of Language Minority Students, 7*, 21–33.

Ford, D. Y. (2006). Closing the achievement gap: How gifted education can help. *Gifted Child Today, 29*(4), 14–18.

Ford, D. Y., & Grantham, T. C. (2003). Providing access for gifted culturally diverse students: From deficit thinking to dynamic thinking. *Theory Into Practice, 42*(3), 217–225.

Ford, D. Y., & Milner, H. R. (2005). *Teaching culturally diverse gifted students*. Waco, TX: Prufrock Press.

Ford, D. Y., & Whiting, G. W. (2006). Under-representation of diverse students in gifted education: Recommendations for nondiscriminatory assessment (part 1). *Gifted Education Press Quarterly, 20*(2), 2–6.

Montgomery, D. (2001). Increasing Native American Indian involvement in gifted education in rural schools. *Psychology in the Schools, 38*(5), 467–475.

Ortiz, V., & Volloff, W. (1987). Identification of gifted and accelerated Hispanic students. *Journal for the Education of the Gifted, 11*(1), 45–53.

Tomlinson, C. A., Ford, D. Y., Reis, S. M., Briggs, C. J., & Strickland, C. A. (Eds.). (2004). *In search of the dream: Designing schools and classrooms that work for high potential students from diverse cultural backgrounds*. Washington, DC: National Association for Gifted Children.

Whiting, G. W., & Ford, D. Y. (2006). Under-representation of diverse students in gifted education: Recommendations for nondiscriminatory assessment (part 2). *Gifted Education Press Quarterly, 20*(3), 6–10.

V

VALEDICTORIANS

Most U.S. and Canadian high schools recognize the graduating student who holds the highest academic standing with the title of valedictorian. Although the naming of a valedictorian is one of the most common markers of achievement in the United States, top academic standing is largely absent from the gifted literature. There is relatively little research about valedictorians and increasing controversy about whether to continue the designation. This entry describes some of the issues relating to valedictorians and gifted.

Literally "farewell sayer," the valedictorian traditionally gives a speech at high school commencement. The first record of naming a valedictorian appeared in Harvard College presidential papers in 1759. The practice was widespread among U.S. high schools by the 1840s, serving both as public recognition of individual achievement and showcasing of bright graduates. Today, most schools award the title of valedictorian to the graduating student with the highest cumulative grade-point average. Less frequently, the student body votes for the valedictorian or holds a speaking contest to determine the recipient. In other cases, school administrators name a high-achieving student who also exemplifies some measure of outstanding character. Students with identical grade-point averages sometimes share the honor as covaledictorians. Nationally, girls outnumber boys among high school valedictorians.

Earning high academic marks across subject areas requires a particular set of abilities and motivations. In an empirical study of high school valedictorians, the Illinois Valedictorian Project, Karen Arnold and Terry Denny followed 81 high school valedictorians and salutatorians longitudinally for 15 years through a combination of periodic interviews and surveys. Arnold and Denny found that high school academic talent was a constellation of intellectual ability, enjoyment of learning, hard work, and willingness to conform to family and school expectations. Outstanding academic performance also relied on what Joseph Renzulli has labeled "schoolhouse giftedness," including sophisticated understanding of teacher requirements and superior ability in tasks such as note taking, memorization, and testing. In keeping with their well-rounded profiles, Illinois Valedictorian Project members were highly involved in extracurricular activities and friendships.

Post–high school achievements of Illinois Valedictorian Project participants reflected their generalist interests, comfort in institutional settings, and strong work ethic. Valedictorians in the study earned postsecondary degrees in much higher numbers than did their high-ability peers nationally and continued to earn high grades in college. Most entered professions, including business, law, medicine, and academia. However, occupational attainments varied far more than academic performance, and valedictorians' well-rounded, pragmatic approach to work and family life did not lend itself to career eminence or creative productivity.

Gender, race, and social class strongly influence valedictorians' professional outcomes, as shown in both the Illinois Valedictorian Project and a study of North Carolina valedictorians by Anne York. Arnold found that valedictorians of color from the class of 1981 were less likely than their White peers were to finish college and take professional jobs and that women achieved less than men when they planned their careers around family roles. Two decades later, York found that 2003–2005 female high school valedictorians in North Carolina were less likely than were male valedictorians to attend the most selective colleges and to choose highly prestigious, top-paying professions. She also found that female valedictorians were more likely to attend a prestigious college if they graduated from a high school with high-average SAT scores; male valedictorians chose colleges based mainly on their own grade-point averages.

Since the 1990s, the practice of naming a high school valedictorian has become increasingly controversial. Grade inflation has made it more difficult to distinguish among high-grade earners. Strategic students can outscore more intellectually motivated classmates by avoiding subjects that are difficult for them. Most controversial are the many grade-point-average weighting systems that make course difficulty a factor in student class rankings. Many high schools weight honors and advanced placement course grades more highly than other course grades, making it possible to earn straight A's without having the highest grade-point average in the school. Under such a grading system, the valedictorian can be decided by a thousandth of a point. Along with grade-point calculations that reward number of credits, weighted course grades lead to accusations that the valedictorian is the most strategic course taker rather than the most meritorious academic achiever. Increasingly, law suits result from these hair-splitting designations. Eligibility to become valedictorian is also controversial: Some students have sued their high schools after having been outranked by transfer or homeschooled students, or because they were eliminated by virtue of their own transfer or homeschooling status.

Some high schools and school districts around the United States have abolished class rankings for another reason: achievement pressure on students. In the context of intensely competitive admission to the most selective colleges and universities, secondary schools claim that class rankings cause unacceptably high levels of stress and competition among students. No empirical research has been conducted to test the widely held belief that class rankings (including the naming of a valedictorian) are associated with student distress. An important study of national College Board data by Paul Attewell indirectly bolstered the argument that class rankings cause high pressure. Attewell found that talented students who ranked just below the top in "star" high schools took less challenging high school classes and entered less selective colleges than did equivalent students in less elite high schools.

The National Association of Secondary School Principals conducted a 1993 survey that found 7 percent of high schools had abolished class rankings. Although no recent national data exist, a stream of popular press articles indicates a continuing trend among high schools to discontinue class rankings and cease naming a valedictorian. Despite the national controversy about rankings, the title of valedictorian remains sought after and widely recognized as a legitimate indication of academic merit.

Karen D. Arnold

See also Adolescent, Gifted; Career Counseling; College Gifted; Secondary Schools

Further Readings

Arnold, K. (1995). *Lives of promise: What happens to high school valedictorians.* San Francisco: Jossey-Bass.

Attewell, P. (2001, Oct.). The winner-take-all high school: Organizational adaptations to educational stratification. *Sociology of Education, 74*(4), 267–295.

Talbot, M. (2005, June 6). Best in class: Students are suing their way to the top. *New Yorker.*

York, E. A. (in press). Gender differences in the college and career aspirations of high school valedictorians. *Journal of Advanced Academics.*

Verbal Ability

The role of verbal ability in any discussion of giftedness is a central topic. Early intelligence tests were seen as heavily loaded in verbal components, suggesting that intelligence was often equated with high verbal ability. In more recent decades, the emphasis has begun to shift to a more balanced view of verbal ability and nonverbal ability. Nevertheless, high verbal ability persists as a basic component of giftedness because of its being a prerequisite for high-level performance in most professions for which gifted learners will prepare themselves and a basic requirement for entry to selective higher-education institutions. This entry describes aspects of verbal ability that relate to giftedness.

Characteristics of Verbal Ability

Students who are verbally advanced usually show signs of advanced verbal behaviors early. They typically learn letters and words by age 2, read at age 4 or 5, and exhibit early facility with writing and drawing. They also are strong in spoken language, fond of memorizing books or poems, for casual recitation. Choice of puzzles and games takes on a decidedly verbal cast. Preferences for Scrabble and other word games develops early. Playing with words is also a favorite pastime. Once they have unlocked the key to reading, they are voracious readers, gobbling up material in the home, whole library shelves, and other printed material available. They also are often nonstop talkers and question askers of parents and peers, seeking answers to deep questions and wanting to talk about philosophical issues such as god and the universe.

Identifying Verbal Ability

In gifted programs, verbal ability has been identified in various ways. Most prominently, it has been found through the use of group and individual intelligence tests through subsections that relate to vocabulary, analogies, and critical reading behaviors. In addition, the SAT traditionally has included sections on critical reading, analogies, sentence completion, and vocabulary. A Test of Standard Written English (TSWE) that probed usage and syntax was also included. More recent versions of the test have deleted analogies and the TSWE. The Graduate Record Exam (GRE) also contains a verbal aptitude section. The Miller Analogy Test (MAT) assesses the ability to solve 100 analogy problems in 50 minutes as a proxy for verbal intelligence. From kindergarten to graduate school, verbal tests have been widely used in selection decisions for gifted programs and advanced work.

In addition to ability measures, achievement tests, both individual and group, probe verbal capacity. Typically, two sections of such tests are devoted to vocabulary, reading comprehension, and often language arts that focus on usage. For younger students, word recognition is also featured. A student who scores at the 95th percentile and higher on one or more of these subsections is likely to be considered a candidate for gifted programs in concert with other selection criteria.

Many school districts also employ teacher recommendations, based on a checklist, to include students in programs. Verbal ability is often prominently featured on these checklists, suggesting that students who read early, show talent for writing and communication, and exhibit highly verbal skills in oral class work are strong candidates.

Verbal ability can readily be identified in specific areas of performance although it rarely is. Writing talent searches have identified writing talent as early as fourth grade. Dramatic talent can be discerned through tryouts for plays and interpretive reading competitions. Spelling ability may be found through participation in the National Spelling Bee. Grammar tests, often given in second language learning, can discern students strong in the structure of language. Only reading ability is routinely tested, with advanced reading behaviors a helpful indicator of giftedness but not a sufficient one.

Serving Students With Verbal Ability

Perhaps no group of gifted learners is easier to serve than those with verbal ability. Fascinated by words from an early age, they gravitate to books, movies, and other verbal media throughout their lives. Many of them learn to read on their own, unlocking the code in their own idiosyncratic way, often holistically rather than phonetically. They enjoy being read to as well as reading on their own. They also enjoy reading aloud for others.

Because they enjoy words so much, games and puzzles that require coming up with words or patterns of words is highly enjoyable. Scrabble, crossword puzzles, searching for synonyms, homonyms, and antonyms as well as work with analogies and metaphors is highly stimulating.

Students with verbal ability often need time to develop their writing ability although their products are usually superior to their age-mates without much effort. Using great writers as models for writing; learning the writing models of narrative, expository, and persuasive writing; and practicing form and idea with regularity all improve their written work. Learning to take criticism from peers and adults also speeds improvement as does the willingness to revise based on feedback received. Often gifted students do not receive sufficient criticism for their writing, which hinders their growth in this area of verbal aptitude.

Verbal ability also prepares students to be strong in oral skills, especially argument through formal debate competitions and clubs in addition to classroom opportunities. Specific creative outlets for oral skills include oral interpretation and drama. Young gifted learners often begin their manifestation of this ability in recitations given for real world audiences, exhibiting oral ability coupled with memory skills.

Because of their strong sensitivity to language, students with verbal ability also can benefit from second language instruction as early as they are reasonably proficient in their own language. Second language learners enjoy an advantage here as they are often bilingual from early ages and retain their capacity to speak and write in both languages across their lives. Second language instruction choices for the gifted have ranged from encouraging difficult language acquisition such as German, Latin, Chinese, and Russian to languages that are more commonly spoken in the United States and Europe such as Spanish and French. Because 60 percent of English vocabulary is derived from Latin, often one year of that language is recommended to the verbally precocious.

Often the best reading program for the gifted is one that is highly individualized, based on reading capacity, interest, and complexity of the material to challenge the intellectually gifted. Minimally, gifted learners should be provided reading material above their tested reading level to be sufficiently challenged. Exposure to great multicultural literature is also an essential ingredient of such a program to broaden student capacity for cultural understanding and empathy. Use of books as bibliotherapy has also been found to be an effective intervention for the verbally gifted child at all ages, where a protagonist shares the child's concerns and problems, and the gifted child can see the issues explored on the page, one step removed. Reference materials and books in such subject matter areas as science can also be stimulating for gifted children. Reading encyclopedias, dictionaries, and atlases can be a favorite pastime. Biography and autobiography are other genres of reading that bring great satisfaction to the verbally gifted and enhance the possibility for acquiring a role model or someone to emulate.

Yet, verbally gifted learners are likely to be most challenged and most in need of development in the area of critical reasoning. Several critical thinking ability tests can pinpoint relative strengths and weaknesses in this area as well as document growth. Consistent practice with the elements of reasoning in oral and written form can sharpen a gifted student's capacity to deal with complexity and deepen his or her knowledge of relevant issues. Formal models for teaching critical thinking have been employed to help gifted students improve in this area. The most used is the Bloom's Taxonomy of Educational Objectives, now constituting seven levels: knowledge, comprehension, application, analysis, synthesis, evaluation, and creation. Another popular model is the Paul model of reasoning, developed by Richard Paul, an educational philosopher, which posits that eight elements of reasoning are used in the real world: identifying issues or problems, purpose, point of view, assumptions, concepts, data or evidence, inferences, and consequences and implications. These models among others are explicitly taught to gifted learners and applied through questions and activities as they explore readings and current issues in various media.

Exemplary Curriculum for the Verbally Gifted

Curriculum packages have been developed to address the needs of advanced readers and verbally gifted learners. These include the Junior Great Books Program, a reading program of short stories calibrated to be intellectually challenging and highly interpretive to enable strong readers to move beyond facts and evaluative commentary into literary analysis and interpretation. Another packaged program used in both social studies and language arts is Philosophy for Children, developed to engage children in facilitated discussion of values and ethics in the context of teaching philosophical thinking. A third program in this area is the William and Mary Language Arts units of study, developed across K–12 to enable gifted learners to read more advanced selections and analyze and interpret them, to write persuasively, to develop oral communication skills, to gain linguistic competency, and to think more critically. This multifaceted program addresses multiple goals and outcomes for these learners. All these programs have evidence of effectiveness with gifted populations, with moderate to large effect sizes, suggesting that the interventions are successful if implemented faithfully in various settings.

Competitions

Just as research-based curricula can assist in developing verbal talent, so too can verbally oriented competitions. Writing contests, held in each state, are a good way for students to try out their writing skills and develop them further. Essay contests of various sorts at local, state, and national levels also provide the challenge of writing to a prompt. The *Concord Review* publication of student writing is the best high-level challenge for high school students who want to challenge themselves with a literary or social science research paper that will be considered for publication. Many other publication outlets exist for poetry, short stories, and other genres that students may want to master and experiment in.

Career Paths for the Verbally Gifted

Recent findings from a longitudinal study of advanced learners suggests that career paths for the verbally precocious can be determined as early as middle school if data are available on values and interests as well as aptitudes. Careers found in the study to be a strong match for these abilities include journalism, writing, theater, law, college professor in the humanities and social sciences, translators, and editing and publishing. Working with verbally gifted learners in schools should include a component of career counseling so their aspiration levels can be well-matched to appropriate undergraduate institutions, the programs they offer, and career clusters.

Facilitation of Verbal Talent for Creative Production

If creative production is seen as the highest level of accomplishment for gifted individuals in any field, then writing something that endures and contributes to the advancement of societal understanding is the goal of those who are verbally gifted. Studies of verbally talented writers suggest that they are autodidactic in their orientation to learning, teaching themselves what they need to know, as was the case with famous writers like Charlotte Bronte and Virginia Woolf. Yet, they also needed an audience for their work growing up, often family and close friends and tutors. Thus the education of writers is often more informal, done at home rather than at school. Their rich interior lives often require space and time for ideas to germinate and then take shape on the page. For women, this space and time issue has been acute, often leading to underproduction and lack of notable mention in the annals of famous writers. The need for a coterie of those who can appreciate the work remains a vital aspect of verbal production.

Written productivity may often come later in life for the verbally gifted. The gift for writing may be a latent talent not even tried before retirement. The law cases and their opinions may only be published close to the end of a stellar career. Novel writing may become a second career. The philosophical treatise that expounds on a particular aspect of existentialism may come even close to the end of life.

Joyce VanTassel-Baska

See also Multilingualism; Precocious Reading; Study of Mathematically Precocious Youth; Talented Readers; Talent Searches; Writers

Further Readings

Benbow, C., & Lubinski, D. (2006). The study of mathematically precocious youth after 35 years. *Perspectives on Psychological Science, 1*(4), 316–345.

Center for Gifted Education (2006). *The William and Mary Language Arts Series.* Dubuque, IA: Kendall/Hunt.

Junior Great Books. Chicago: Junior Great Books Foundation. Retrieved from http://www.greatbooks.org/programs-for-all-ages/junior.html

Reed, R., & Sharp, A. M. (Eds.). (1992). *Studies in philosophy for children: Harry Stottlemeier's discovery*. Philadelphia: Temple University Press.

VanTassel-Baska, J., & Stambaugh, T. (2006). *Comprehensive curriculum for gifted learners*. Boston: Pearson.

Very Young Creative

Paul Torrance, who extensively studied the creativity of very young children (under the age of 7), described creative behavior as, "the process of becoming sensitive to or aware of problems, deficiencies, gaps in knowledge, missing elements, disharmonies, and so on; bringing together in new relationships available information; defining the difficulty of identifying the missing elements; searching for solutions, making guesses, or formulating hypotheses about the problems or deficiencies; testing and resting them; perfecting them; and finally communicating the results" (1969, p. viii). In addition, personality traits, which may begin as inborn temperaments, can contribute greatly to the creativity of the young child, including openness to experience, independence, and nonconformity. Some creative behavior is available to everyone because it can be elicited through a variety of means, and most people are capable of everyday creativity. Unlike intelligence, research has shown that a large majority of variation seen in adult creative productivity is the result of family, school, and community environment. Further, children of high intelligence are not necessarily creative, but it is possible to be both highly intelligent and creative. This entry describes the major issues concerning creative children.

The extent to which a child is creative depends on the degree in which he or she shows novelty, displays unconventionality, diverges from what was previously accepted, and persists in exceeding previous performance. By the age of 2 or 3, children have obtained a great deal of experience in creative thinking through questioning, experimenting, and playing. Certain characteristics facilitate learning creatively: a long attention span, the capacity to organize, the ability to see things from a different perspective, and the ability to observe and listen. In addition, telling stories, creating songs, using the imagination to solve problems, observing things carefully, and exploring before formal instruction can aid in creative learning. Families that provide opportunities and resources for creative play and learning, that are open to children's risk taking, and that provide models of creative behavior can nourish creativity in young children.

Particular indicators of precocity in gifted children can be used to informally assess creativity in preschool children. Children with an unusually advanced vocabulary for their age possess a large amount of information about a variety of subjects and have an intense curiosity in something or in many things are likely to be creative. In addition, children who have a clear understanding of cause and effect relationships, strive toward perfection or excellence, are keen observers, and are interested in adult-like issues (i.e., religion, sex, race) are also likely to be creative. They are also capable of improvising with common items, engage in storytelling and highly imaginative play, have a good sense of humor, and respond to the kinesthetic or concrete. Further, they may possess exceptional abilities in creative movement and dance, visual arts, or music.

Several methods are used to identify very young creative children. Objective intelligence tests or achievement tests for specific areas are the most traditional means, but parent, peer, or professional nominations are other methods. In addition, biographical data, checklists, rating scales, observations, and performance and objective testing can be helpful. The validity and reliability of these methods vary.

Although it can be difficult to distinguish the creative among very young children, several guidelines have been created to assist in this difficult task. When very young children are tested for creativity, preschool children should be able to respond to a task that is characteristic of their development. Usually, the kinesthetic modality is most appropriate to elicit creative behavior because preschool children commonly practice skills in this area. A warm-up activity is recommended, the tests should be comprehendible to young children, and scoring and administration should be simple.

The most widely used formal assessment of creativity in very young children is the Torrance Tests of Creative Thinking. It consists of two batteries: Thinking Creatively with Words and Thinking Creatively with Pictures. The verbal tests can be administered to children as young as 3 years old, and the picture tests can be administered to children starting at age 5. The verbal tests take about 45 minutes to administer, and they provide scores for fluency, flexibility, and originality. The picture tests take about 30 minutes to administer, and they provide scores for fluency, flexibility, originality, elaboration, resistance to premature closure, and abstract thinking. In addition, picture tests also supply criterion-referenced indicators of imagery, synthesis, humor, and putting things in context.

Another method of formal assessment for creativity in very young children developed by Torrance is the Thinking Creatively in Action and Movement measure. This measure allows children to respond by movement, in words, or a combination. Words are not required because young children may not be able to best express themselves verbally. It is designed for children ages 3 to 8. The test is divided into four activities that sample the most common ways young children use their creative abilities. The first activity asks children to create multiple methods of moving. The second activity samples children's ability to imagine, empathize, fantasize, and assume different roles. In the third activity, the children are asked to describe tasks or objects in a different way. In the fourth activity, children describe other uses for objects (i.e., a different use for a paper cup or chair).

The degree of creativity varies in all children, but it is not unusual for creative skills to be unused and even ignored once children reach school age. The level of curiosity, experimentation, and creative learning in children are much greater in younger children compared with older children. Moreover, the biggest drop of creativity has been observed once children reach kindergarten. Very young children can be encouraged by preschool environments that are rich in resources, provide adequate free time for imaginative play, and tolerate unconventional questions and answers. Children's creative abilities are important for growth in a variety of areas; therefore, creating conditions that will facilitate creative development among young children is critical.

Rhea L. Owens

See also Creative Personality; Creativity, Definition; Creativity Assessment; Creativity Training; Preschool; Torrance Tests of Creative Thinking; Very Young Gifted

Further Readings

Torrance, E. P. (1969). *Dimensions of early learning series: Creativity.* Sioux Falls, SD: Adapt Press.

Torrance, E. P. (2000). Preschool creativity. In B. A. Bracken (Ed.), *The psychoeducational assessment of preschool children.* Boston: Allyn & Bacon.

VERY YOUNG GIFTED

Martha Morelock and John Feldman described gifted children as, "those showing sustained evidence of advanced capability relative to their peers in general academic skills and/or in more specific domains (music, art, science, etc.) to the extent that they need differentiated educational programming" (p. 302). To address the specific needs of gifted children and foster their development, identification and intervention for very young children (under the age of seven) is critical, as discussed in this entry.

Very young gifted children often have highly advanced verbal skills, emotional sensitivity, a cooperative play style, leadership skills, and a mature sense of humor. They are commonly curious, have a wide range of interests or demonstrate advanced skill in a single area, and are sensitive to problems with their peers. They also can be described as highly focused in their interests, persistent, divergent thinkers, and perceptive. It is not uncommon for gifted children to be precocious readers as well. Their intellectual, emotional, and motor development is often asynchronous in that although they may be advanced in one developmental area, other areas may be at the same level or below children of the same age.

Although early identification is critical with young, gifted children, it is difficult for several reasons. First, only potential giftedness is being assessed because the children are so young, and it is difficult to quantify potential. Second, young children have not had ample time to develop their talents and abilities; therefore, there is a risk for over- or underestimating giftedness. Finally, young children may have difficulty in a testing situation because it differs from the surroundings they are used to, which can lead to lower scores that do not demonstrate their true potential.

Often intelligence, ability, or achievement tests are used to measure giftedness. A score of 130 (two standard deviations above the mean) is reasonable to infer giftedness. Intelligence tests that have been used to assess for giftedness include Stanford-Binet Intelligence Scale, Form L-M; the Wechsler Preschool and Primary Scale of Intelligence; the Slosson Intelligence Test for Children and Adults; the Columbia Mental Maturity Scale; and the Pictorial Test of Intelligence. Standardized achievement/readiness tests that have been used to assess preschool children for giftedness include the Metropolitan Readiness Test, Level I; Stanford Early School Achievement Test, Level I; and Test of Basic Experiences, Level K.

Intelligence and academic achievement are not the only forms of giftedness, so other tests are used to measure children suspected of being gifted in other domains. Several standardized tests of perceptual-motor development exist that have been used to identify young children, including the following: Basic Motor Ability Test, Developmental Test of Visual-Motor Integration, Purdue Perceptual-Motor Survey, and Wechsler Preschool and Primary Scale of Intelligence. The California Preschool Competency Scale and the Vineland Social Maturity Scale are standardized tests that have been used to measure social development. The Torrance Tests of Creative Thinking and the Thinking Creativity in Action in Movement are the two tests that measure creativity.

Many other methods are helpful in identifying very young, gifted children as well. Ratings and observational checklists can be helpful in identifying behaviors and performances that may not be accessed through tests. Observations can take place in a child's natural setting, which is more comfortable for a young child. In addition, qualitative measures are especially useful in conjunction with quantitative measures. Parents and teachers are key resources when using qualitative measures because they are likely around the child most frequently and have witnessed the child in familiar and unfamiliar situations. They are also aware of what the child is interested in and how the child responds to difficulties. Actually, parents and teachers are often capable of identifying a gifted child before the child is tested.

The beginning of preschool and kindergarten can be critical times for gifted children. If gifted children are overlooked, there is a risk that they might not actualize their potential, might become underachievers, or might develop negative attitudes toward learning or school. Often, gifted children are aware of their difference from other children and can have difficulty relating to others. Gifted children may develop fear or anxiety about school and hide their gifts. In addition, finding peers with similar interests, especially at their level can be difficult; therefore, frustration or boredom may result. Other problems common in gifted children include conformity, perfectionism, extreme sensitivity, intolerance, feelings of inadequacy, or the demand for large amounts of adult attention. For these reasons, it is important to correctly identify and provide guidance and appropriate challenges in the child's areas of interest so their needs are met.

Differentiating gifted children's curriculum and early entrance into school can be beneficial in addressing their needs. Gifted children will likely benefit from a more accelerated or advanced curriculum, which incorporates the child's interests and applies abstract and complex concepts. Entering school early for gifted children can aid in the child's intellectual needs because their mental ages will likely be matched if they are ready to begin grade school. The extent and area of giftedness vary in every child, so it is key to pay attention to children's particular needs and help them cultivate their talents.

Rhea L. Owens

See also Early Entrance, Kindergarten; Early Identification; Giftedness, Definition; Identification; Preschool; Very Young Creative

Further Readings

Karnes, M. B. (1983). *The underserved: Our young gifted children.* Reston, VA: ERIC.

Morelock, M. J., & Feldman, D. H. (1992). The assessment of giftedness in preschool children. In E. V. Nuttall, I. Romero, & J. Kalesnik (Eds.), *Assessing and screening preschoolers: Psychological and educational dimensions*. Needham Heights, MA: Allyn & Bacon.

Sankar-DeLeeuw, N. (1999). Gifted preschoolers: Parent and teacher views on identification, early admission, and programming. *Roeper Review, 21*(3), 174–179.

VISUALIZATION

Whether or not they are aware of it, visualization practices of most individuals affect their behavior and emotional regulation every day. Visualization is the formation of mental images. It is a critical part of the creative process when considered in its "intentional" form because it allows the user to explore novel ways to organize and interact with facts and experiences. Creating mental images of chess pieces, for example, and probabilistic future placement, allows the player to take appropriate action offensively and defensively. This entry examines ways individuals employ visualization to creatively enhance performance, affect emotional state, and invoke visceral physical experiences.

Although the ability to visualize varies between people, the spectrums on which visualized images can be rated generally do not. Visualizations can be vivid or dull, loud or quiet, large or small. There is also a spectrum of skilled manipulating of mental images. For example, if one imagines a horse, how easily could the visualization be changed from say, a brown to blue horse? How quickly could the blue color be changed from dark to light?

An interesting by-product of intentional or unintentional visualization is affect. Emotions are often inextricably tied to images. It is challenging to separate affect from image because the biological structures used to store and retrieve memories are associated with emotional centers in the brain and an overwhelming corpus of literature supports the idea that emotions and accompanying physiological responses are also strongly associated. For example, if an individual is asked to vividly visualize the most scared she's ever been, the likelihood is that her sympathetic nervous system would be activated, increasing her heart rate, restricting blood flow from the skin and sending it to the lungs, and dilating lung bronchioles. Whereas visualizing a frightening thought can activate the sympathetic nervous system, visualizing peaceful thoughts can activate the parasympathetic nervous system, relaxing the individual and reversing sympathetic arousal, thereby also changing the individual's emotional state.

To demonstrate the immediacy and powerful effects of detailed visualization, in the following exercise, an individual is asked to imagine a perfect day. This kind of visualization is helpful for career exploration and, more importantly, to help uncover those things individuals value in their lives. Visualizers are asked to relax and close their eyes. The following is a small part of the waking up portion of the perfect day exercise.

> Imagine sometime in the future. You wake up and find yourself about to enjoy the most perfect day you can imagine. You live in a location where it is just perfect for you in a home perfectly built for you and later you will go to work that is both meaningful and fulfilling. What does your bedroom look like? Imagine it in as much detail as you can. Is there a window? What can you see through it? What time of day is it? How do you rise from bed to greet your perfect day?

The questions are asked to guide visualizers into creating a detailed, sensory-rich image of the components of their entire perfect day. The perfect day exercise exemplifies the power of visualization to reveal important personal constructs but that are sometimes ephemeral (values, emotions, etc.). It also helps create talking points for individuals intentionally working through issues to gain insight or toward reaching certain goals like career clarification, stress reduction, or performance enhancement. For example, a world champion golfer may use visualization when preparing for an important tournament: He mentally plays every hole in the course on the airline trip to the competition. He visualizes each stroke, anticipates errors, and rehearses different ways to overcome those errors. He considers what he will do if it is windy, if it rains, and if the grass is too long. He plays every hole until he has played the whole course in his mind and is confident walking off the last green holding the winner's cup.

The ability to generate and manipulate mental images seems to be associated with creativity. In one study of creativity and visualization in gifted schoolchildren, visualization and creative thinking were found to be strongly correlated but IQ and visualization were not. Interestingly, individuals who were identified as creative were no better at identifying when they were visualizing and creatively generating ideas than were those not identified as creative. The degree to which an individual can intentionally manipulate visualizations is strongly associated with their creative problem-solving ability general comprehension levels, and although visualization permeates and affects both consciousness and behavior, it is largely subliminal. Therefore, it is possible to be creative, to use visualization, and to be unaware of the use of both. Actually, many individuals are not aware of ways they use visualization creatively.

Take the example of a young child who sees a cookie jar on the countertop and recalls the emotional sensation of delicious homemade chocolate cookies on the tongue. Wanting to again experience this affect, the child subliminally visualizes the experience and feels the accompanying warm, cozy affect. Once a more satisfying emotional state is visualized, the child may create a plan to make the visualized state a realized state via creative problem solving. As the child proceeds to assemble data about the real world from memory, a plan might be devised to push a chair to the counter to allow cookie jar access. All of the imagery, sensory flooding, and actualizing planning, though serial, typically occur within milliseconds.

The child's visualized creative synthesis is little different from an attorney arguing before a jury or a couple working through problems in therapy. In each case, the visualized image (successful argument for the attorney, a happier relationship for the couple) and the accompanying positive affects significantly motivate behaviors. Without clear visualization of the respective goals, it makes little sense to work toward them. Thus, intentional, vivid visualization can be used for intentional creative problem solving, emotional control, motivation toward and away from certain outcomes, goal planning, and achievement.

Gregory Decker

See also Athletic Giftedness; Cartooning; Chess; Imagery; Imagination; Originality; Writers

Further Readings

Gilbert, J. (2008). *Visualization: Theory and practice in science education.* New York: Springer.

Lapin, J. (2007). *The art of conscious creation: How you can transform the world.* Charleston, SC: Elevate.

Webster, R. (2006). *Creative visualization for beginners.* Woodbury, MN: Llewellyn Publications.

VISUAL METAPHOR

Visual metaphor can serve as a powerful tool for learning large quantities of complex subject matter. Students can distill the most important insights from their independent study discoveries, or from a set of readings, and then translate these key insights into the form of a sketched, painted, or computer-designed visual metaphor. The image typically takes the form of a cartoon-like representation with many intricate elements or symbols, each of which illustrates one or more important ideas from the topic studied. The student usually creates a story or a bullet-point summary to explain the meaning of the symbolism in the image, showing what the various aspects of the image represent in terms of the subject matter studied.

The process of creating the visual metaphor engages the student in mode-switching, which forces the mind to transform ideas from one thought modality, usually verbal or text mode, to another mode, usually artistic representation. In terms of Howard Gardner's multiple intelligences, the process asks the student to carry many complex concepts across a thought barrier between verbal-linguistic thinking and visual-spatial thought. The difficult, creative work done during the translation process enables students to capture the essence of a large quantity of complex material, synthesizing and clarifying it while burning it into long-term memory. The process is little known and has not been extensively studied, but there are signs that it has strong potential to enhance learning, especially for gifted students with visual-spatial ability, as described in this entry.

Origin

The visual-metaphoric strategy evolved from the research of developmental psychologist Howard

Gruber who investigated the thought processes of highly creative people such as Charles Darwin and Jean Piaget. When grappling with difficult theoretic concepts and voluminous data, these eminent investigators would construct metaphorical images, or images of wide scope as Gruber designated them, to synthesize and clarify their own understandings. These images tended to congeal massive amounts of complex information into condensed form, thereby providing a basis for understanding the known and a platform for launching the search for the unknown in a field.

LeoNora Cohen adapted the cognitive processes Gruber discovered in the image of wide scope for use in the classroom. Although not as complex as the rare and lofty device used for cognitive synthesis by the geniuses Gruber studied, the visual metaphor used for instructional purposes is a highly original pedagogical tool because it relates new information to familiar ideas in metaphorical form through the mode-switching process. On rare occasions, visual metaphoric processes also have been used as conceptual research tools in scholarly publications to synthesize and illustrate complex bodies of knowledge pertinent to school reform, the implications of brain research for organizational leadership, and the intricacies of strategic planning.

Example of a Visual Metaphor Under Construction

Suppose a small group of gifted individuals decides to learn more about thoughts and actions that typify creative people. They could engage in the following process steps to create a visual metaphor that captures their findings.

Step 1. Outline or Summarize the Content

They use a linear outline, a mind map, or another favored method to capture important information pertaining to the characteristics and behaviors of creative people they read about in biographies. In this example, they might include the following attributes, among others: risk taker, purposeful, motivated, productive thinker, persistent, resilient, imaginative.

Step 2. Brainstorm Metaphorical Themes for the Drawing

They might brainstorm the following ideas as possible metaphors for the characteristics of the creative people they studied: explorer, builder, adventurer, vehicle, architect, and so on.

Step 3. Choose the Most Promising Metaphor

Here they choose the metaphor that seems most likely to incorporate the full range of concepts in the topic of study. They create some rough, preliminary sketches based on the metaphor and the set of items they listed in step 1 and then attempt to fit each of the concepts into the drawing. If they chose the vehicle as the most promising metaphor, they might sketch a futuristic all-terrain vehicle launching itself over a rocky chasm. The chasm represents risk taking, a compass on the dashboard represents purposeful direction, a sturdy frame represents resilience, a full fuel tank represents motivation, and so on.

Step 4. Sleep on It

Removing their attention from the difficult, creative task of creating a visual metaphor enables their minds to capitalize on intuitive processes, which can help them select a better metaphor, or confirm the appropriateness of the initial one. It can help them create additional, stronger connections between the symbolism in the drawing and the content. When they are satisfied with the metaphor and its symbolism, they can draw or paint a final, more elaborate and refined version of the visual metaphor.

Step 5. Write a Brief Summary Describing the Connections Between the Symbolism in the Drawing and the Content of Study

Their summary can take the form of bullet points or a short story. As a final check, they should go back through their content outline to ensure that their summary includes all of the important concepts.

Reasons to Employ Visual Metaphors in Instruction

The mode-switching process and the requirement that students build metaphorical connections with important subject matter engage students in constructing knowledge actively. The process also encourages creative and critical thinking because producing the metaphor and its symbolism is a highly creative process and ensuring that the image represents all important subject-matter content requires critical thought. More specifically, the process engages thinking skills such as imagination, intuition, metaphorical analysis, analogy, synthesis, evaluation, and divergent (original, elaborative, flexible, fluent) thinking. Finally, visual metaphors in teaching and learning comes from the ways in which they encourage integration of the arts with other curriculum areas, a much needed way of enriching the curriculum for gifted students.

Don Ambrose

See also Artistic Ability; Cartooning; Imagery; Multiple Intelligences; Visual-Spatial Learners

Further Readings

Ambrose, D. (1996). Turtle soup: Establishing innovation-friendly conditions for school reform. *Journal of Creative Behavior, 39,* 25–38.

Ambrose, D. (1998). Creative organizational vision building through collaborative visual-metaphorical thought. *Journal of Creative Behavior, 32,* 229–243.

Cohen, L. M. (1994). Mode-switching strategies. In J. Edwards (Ed.), *Thinking: International, interdisciplinary perspectives* (pp. 230–240). Melbourne, Australia: Hawker Brownlow.

Gruber, H. E. (1974). *Darwin on man: A psychological study of scientific creativity* (2nd ed.). London: Wildwood House.

Visual-Spatial Learners

Visual-spatial learners refers to students who have preferences for instructional methods that emphasize imagery and that allow manipulation of spatial elements. The theory of visual-spatial learners is based on the concept that there are two predominant learning styles: visual-spatial and auditory-sequential. Spatial information is apprehended visually. Terms such as *visuospatial, spatial visualization,* and *visual-spatial* are used to describe the inextricable connection between *visual* and *spatial.* The relationship between *auditory* and *sequential* did not become clear until insights from the field of audiology fused with brain research. These two learning styles may be related to hemispheric preferences, according to Linda Silverman, as described in this entry.

Functions of Brain Hemispheres

Recognition of the functions of the two hemispheres began more than a century ago. In the late 19th century, John Hughlings Jackson hypothesized that the processing of visual information, perception, and visual imagery are all the province of the right cerebral hemisphere, whereas the processing of auditory information, verbal expression, and propositional thinking are the domain of the left hemisphere. Other researchers have characterized the left hemisphere as more logical, analytic, linguistic, and symbolic, and the right hemisphere as more visual, visuospatial, kinesthetic, imaginative, perceptual, synthetic, and nonverbal.

People use both hemispheres for most activities—especially complex thought; however, most people do not have equal facility with both hemispheres. Just as individuals favor either their right or left hands, they tend to rely on one hemisphere more than the other. Individuals who have more powerful right hemispheric preferences perceive and organize information in a different manner that do those who have greater left hemispheric style. As IQ increases, it seems that reliance on the right hemisphere also increases. Camilla Benbow and her colleagues found evidence that highly intellectually gifted students have enhanced right hemispheric functioning. A study of gifted 4- to 6-year-olds conducted with the Kaufman Assessment Battery for Children found intellectual giftedness to be more strongly correlated with simultaneous (spatial) than with sequential processing. In highly gifted children, both types of processing were evident.

Left hemispheric reasoning is auditory-sequential; right hemispheric awareness is visual-spatial. The left hemisphere produces speech; the right communicates in images and feelings. The left hemisphere is temporal (time-oriented), whereas the right is oriented toward the manipulation of spatial patterns and relationships. It is guided by feelings, sensing, and intuition. The left hemisphere can deal well with nonmeaningful bits of information, such as phonemes, but the right hemisphere can only deal with meaningful material. As everyone has two hemispheres, everyone has access to the capacities of both hemispheres, although perhaps not equal access.

Characteristics of Visual-Spatial Learners

The theorized major scholastic differences between visual-spatial learners and auditory-sequential learners are shown here:

Visual-Spatial Learners	*Auditory-Sequential Learners*
Are whole-part learners	Learn in a step-by-step manner
Are keen observers	Are good listeners
See the "big picture"	Attend well to details
Learn concepts all at once ("Aha!")	Learn by trial and error
Think in images or feelings	Think in words or ideas
Solve problems in unusual ways	Are comfortable with one right answer
Often lose track of time	Are conscious of time
Arrive at correct solutions intuitively	Show steps of work easily
Struggle with spelling	Can sound out spelling words
Need to see relationships to learn	Excel at rote memorization
May appear disorganized	Are well organized
Learn whole words easier than phonics	Have excellent phonemic awareness
Read maps well	Follow directions well
Are good synthesizers	Are good analyzers
May have messy handwriting	Write quickly and neatly
Interweave thought and emotion	Compartmentalize thought and emotion
Learn complex concepts easily, but may struggle with easy skills	Progress sequentially from easy to difficult

Many students demonstrate both lists of attributes, but some clearly lean toward one set or the other. Tailored to auditory-sequential learners, school is often an unpleasant experience for visual-spatial learners. Gifted auditory-sequential learners are more likely to be high achievers in academic subjects, selected for gifted programs, recognized by their teachers as having high potential, and considered leaders. Gifted visual-spatial learners may more often be counted among underachievers, twice-exceptional children, dyslexics, children with attention deficit hyperactivity disorder, and creative children from minority groups. More talented children from low socioeconomic groups are identified by spatial tests than by verbal and mathematical measures.

Importance of Visual-Spatial Gifts

Success in the 21st century depends on different skills than are currently emphasized in school: grasping the big picture, multidimensional perception, problem-finding, visualization, thinking outside the box, ability to read people well, and creativity. According to Thomas West, the visual-spatial learning style may be uniquely suited for our technological world. Visual-spatial learners show promise as future surgeons, architects, engineers, pilots, mathematicians, scientists, computer programmers, designers, dentists, artists, musicians, dancers, military strategists, and so on. The importance of visual-spatial gifts cannot be overlooked. Rose Mary Webb, David Lubinski, and Camilla Benbow assert that they are vital in science, technology, engineering, and mathematics (STEM):

Carol Gohm, Lloyd Humphreys, and Grace Yao studied more than 1,000 spatially gifted high school seniors (578 boys and 511 girls) and found them to be "disenchanted with education" (p. 528). They reported that this group received less college guidance from school counselors, were less likely to go to college, and had lower career aspirations than equally intelligent students who excelled in mathematics.

Measurement of Visual-Spatial Abilities

Current intelligence tests place a greater emphasis on the assessment of visual-spatial abilities. Visual-spatial processing is one of five factors of intelligence measured in the fifth edition of the Stanford-Binet Intelligence Scale. The fourth edition of the Wechsler Intelligence Scale for Children (WISC-IV) also substantially improved its measurement of visual-spatial abilities. The Perceptual Reasoning Composite consists of Block Design and Matrix Reasoning, both excellent visual-spatial measures, and Picture Concepts, a visual similarities test. In prior versions, the Performance IQ was a mixture of spatial measures (e.g., Block Design and Object Assembly) and sequential measures (Coding and Picture Arrangement).

Several other tests of visual-spatial abilities are also in wide use. Raven's Progressive Matrices is the most popular test for identifying gifted children in various cultures worldwide; it has demonstrated a remarkable increase in spatial abilities across all cultures over the last few generations. The *Naglieri Nonverbal Abilities Test*—a series of matrices—is a group measure frequently used for identifying culturally diverse gifted children in the United States. The *Mental Rotations Test* has been employed in several studies to detect children with extraordinary visual-spatial talents.

The Gifted Development Center constructed the Visual-Spatial Identifier (VSI) during a 10-year period, with the involvement of an interdisciplinary team of psychologists, neuropsychiatrists, sociologists, reading specialists, gifted program coordinators, speech pathologists, artists, tutors, and parents. The VSI is a simple, 15-item checklist with two forms: a self-report for students and an observer report for teachers and parents. It has been validated with 750 fourth, fifth, and sixth graders in urban and rural settings. As more than 40 percent of the children at each site were Hispanic, the VSI has also been translated into Spanish.

One-third of the children in the validation studies emerged as strongly visual-spatial. An additional 30 percent showed a slight preference for the visual-spatial learning style. Added together, nearly two-thirds had a visual-spatial preference. Only 23 percent were strongly auditory-sequential. In another study conducted in Page, Arizona, under a Javits Program grant, 69 percent of predominantly Navajo children preferred the visual-spatial learning style. These findings suggest that culturally diverse students may learn better using visual-spatial methods.

Strategies for Success

To teach visual-spatial learners, it is necessary to increase emphasis on right hemisphere tasks. This can be done through humor, use of emotionally meaningful material, discovery learning, music, hands-on experiences, fantasy, and visual presentations. The following guidelines can assist teachers in adapting lessons to capitalize on visual-spatial strengths:

1. Use visual aids and visual imagery: "A picture is worth a thousand words."
2. Allow students to use a computer for written assignments. Computer instruction is also recommended because computers present information visually.

3. Avoid timed tests. Give untimed power tests.
4. Hands-on experience with manipulatives is essential.
5. Teach whole words that can be pictured before instruction in phonics.
6. Allow students to construct, draw, or otherwise create visual representations (e.g., PowerPoint slides) as a substitute for some written assignments.
7. Grade content separate from mechanics (spelling, punctuation, syntax, etc.)
8. Teach students to visualize spelling words, math problems, etc.
9. If students demonstrate consistent accuracy, allow credit for correct answers even if they cannot show their work.
10. Use inductive (discovery) techniques that encourage pattern-finding.
11. Teach students to translate what they hear into images, and record those images using webbing, mind-mapping techniques, or pictorial notes.
12. Avoid drill, repetition, and rote memorization; use more abstract conceptual approaches.
13. Teach to their strengths in visualization and imagination. Help them learn to use these powerful tools to compensate for their weaknesses.
14. Emphasize the fine arts. Art is the sanctuary of the visual-spatial learner.
15. Be emotionally supportive. Keenly sensitive to their teachers' attitudes, visual-spatial learners flourish when teachers believe in them.

With appropriate detection and classroom modifications, these children can be highly successful, particularly as they tackle more complex subject matter in high school and college. When they are placed in the right learning environment, where there is a good match between their learning styles and the way they are taught, visual-spatial learners can actualize their potential to become innovative leaders.

Linda Kreger Silverman

See also Brain Imaging; Learning Styles

Further Readings

Gohm, C. L., Humphreys, L. G., & Yao, G. (1998). Underachievement among spatially gifted students. *American Educational Research Journal, 35,* 515–531.

O'Boyle, M. W., & Benbow, C. P. (1990). Enhanced right hemisphere involvement during cognitive processing may relate to intellectual precocity. *Neuropsychologia, 28,* 211–216.

Schmidt, D. B., Lubinski, D., & Benbow, C. P. (1998). Validity of assessing educational-vocational preference dimensions among intellectually talented 13-year-olds. *Journal of Counseling Psychology, 45,* 436–453.

Silverman, L. K. (1990). *Characteristics of Giftedness Scale.* Denver, CO: Gifted Development Center. Retrieved from http://www.gifteddevelopment.com

Silverman, L. K. (1998). Personality and learning styles of gifted children. In J. VanTassel-Baska (Ed.), *Excellence in educating gifted and talented learners* (3rd ed., pp. 29–65). Denver, CO: Love Publishing.

Silverman, L. K. (2002). *Upside-down brilliance: The visual-spatial learner.* Denver, CO: DeLeon.

Silverman, L. K. (2009). The measurement of giftedness. In L. Shavinina (Ed.), *The international handbook on giftedness.* Amsterdam: Springer Science.

Springer, S. P., & Deutsch, G. (1998). *Left brain/right brain: Perspectives from cognitive neuroscience* (5th ed.). New York: W. H. Freeman.

Webb, R. M., Lubinski, D., & Benbow, C. P. (2007). Spatial ability: A neglected dimension in talent searches for intellectually precocious youth. *Journal of Educational Psychology, 99,* 397–420.

West, T. G. (1991). *In the mind's eye: Visual thinkers, gifted people with learning difficulties, computer images, and the ironies of creativity.* Buffalo, NY: Prometheus Press.

Wallace Research Symposium

Henry B. (H. B.) Wallace (1915–2005) was an exceptionally gifted individual with amazing talents. These same talents led to extraordinary success in business, which he used to translate his concern for students and the future of U.S. education into action. These concerns, coupled with a respect for the importance of research as a means to answer questions and improve life, were the impetus for the Biennial Henry B. & Jocelyn Wallace National Research Symposium on Talent Development (Wallace Research Symposium). The Wallace Research Symposium, which was initiated with an endowment from the Wallace Research Foundation in the late 1980s, was held for the first time in 1991, at the University of Iowa.

The Wallace Research Symposium, described in this entry, has been internationally acclaimed as a preeminent research conference in gifted education. The structure of the symposium, including the meeting location, quality of speakers, and presentation format, lends itself to a personal experience that represents the height of professional development. Typically conducted over 2.5 days, nearly a dozen high-profile speakers are featured at each Wallace Research Symposium. A unique combination of experts in the field of gifted education as well as outside the field leads to an intellectually stimulating experience for all in attendance.

A sample of the range of keynote presentations includes the following:

Music, the Creative Process, and the Path of Enlightenment: Guiding the Gifted Through Their "Dark Night" to the "Music of the Spheres," which was presented and performed by pianist Lorin Hollander

From "Play Partner" to "Sure Shelter": How conceptions of Friendship Differ Between Average Ability, Moderately Gifted, and Highly Gifted Children, presented by Professor Miraca Gross, University of New South Wales, Sydney, Australia

Anti-Intellectuals in Universities, Schools, and Gifted Education, presented by Professor Nicholas Colangelo, The Belin-Blank Center, The University of Iowa

Why Are We Afraid to Unleash the Academic Talent in Most Kids? presented by Jay Mathews of *The Washington Post*

Creative Giftedness, presented by Professor Robert Sternberg (formerly of Yale University)

There are five categories for presentations at Wallace Research Symposia: the Julian C. Stanley Distinguished Lecture, Keynote Presentations, Invited Presentations, Concurrent Presentations, and Poster Presentations.

In 2002, the Julian C. Stanley Distinguished Lecture was initiated in recognition of the contributions to gifted education by the late Julian C. Stanley. Those selected to deliver the Stanley Distinguished Lecture are internationally recognized scholars.

Keynote presentations, which do not have any other activities scheduled opposite them, are broad in scope and intended to encourage the participants to think innovatively about gifted education. Invited presentations are frequently scheduled two per time slot and tend to be more focused on research presentations that emphasize applications to the field. Keynote and Invited presenters are invited by the symposium's organizers.

In addition, concurrent presentations and poster presentations are selected from among the proposals submitted in response to a call for papers, which is made available several months in advance of the symposium. These presentations tend to be on specific lines of research and frequently represent cutting-edge results. The concurrent presentations are traditional (albeit shorter) in presentation format, with no more than nine sessions scheduled at the same time. Poster presentations are held in a single large room, which enables the symposium attendees to visit multiple presentations during that time.

Attendees at the Wallace Symposium come from throughout the United States as well as from a variety of countries. The 2008 Wallace Research Symposium was unique because it included 51 educators representing 46 countries (from six continents) who participated as part of a grant from the John Templeton Foundation.

Susan G. Assouline and Nicholas Colangelo

See also Belin-Blank Center; Institute for Research and Policy on Acceleration; National Association for Gifted Children

Further Readings

Belin-Blank Center: http://www.education.uiowa.edu/belinblank

Colangelo, N., & Assouline, S. G. (Eds.). (1999). *Talent development: Proceedings from the 1995 H. B. and Jocelyn Wallace National Research Symposium on Talent Development.* Scottsdale, AZ: Gifted Psychology Press.

Colangelo, N., & Assouline, S. G. (Eds.). (2001). *Talent development: Proceedings from the 1998 H. B. and Jocelyn Wallace National Research Symposium on Talent Development.* Scottsdale, AZ: Gifted Psychology Press.

Colangelo, N., Assouline, S., & Ambroson, D. (Eds.). (1992). *Talent development: Proceedings of the H. B. and Jocelyn Wallace National Research Symposium on Talent Development.* Monroe, NY: Trillium.

Colangelo, N., Assouline, S., & Ambroson, D. (Eds.). (1994). *Talent development: Proceedings from the 1993 H. B. and Jocelyn Wallace National Research Symposium on Talent Development.* Dayton, OH: Ohio Psychology Press.

Web-Based Learning

Web-based learning, or open, flexible, and virtual learning, is known or referred to by many names including *e*-learning; *a*-learning; Web-based learning, instruction, or training; Internet-based education or training; blended learning; distance learning or education; and online learning. Web-based learning is one of many tools used to deliver education or training to students. In many traditional settings, Web-based learning is located organizationally in a distance education program together with other distance delivery models such as correspondence, satellite broadcast, two-way videoconferencing, videotape, and CD-ROM/DVD delivery modalities. All such modalities try to serve learners at remote locations away from their knowledge facilitator. Many of these modalities attempt to serve the learners by interacting with them at various chronological times. Distance education is frequently referred to as those delivery modalities that try to decrease the barriers of time and location to learning—thus, the commonly used phrase *anytime, anywhere learning.* One must be cautious, however, with that correlation as not all topics or educational goals lend themselves to "anytime" as a delivery method. This entry describes aspects of Web-based learning.

Anytime, Anywhere Learning

The following definitions are used to refer to anytime, anywhere learning:

Web-based learning refers to anytime, anywhere instruction delivered via the Internet to Web-connected learners. Two common models of Web-based instruction are synchronous and asynchronous. *Asynchronous* refers to communication in which interaction between parties does not take place simultaneously. *Synchronous* refers to communication in which interaction between participants is simultaneous.

E-learning is a form of teaching and learning using electronic means of delivery, usually Web-based. E-learning uses network technologies to create, foster, deliver, and facilitate learning, anytime and anywhere.

Blended learning is the combination of multiple approaches to learning, for example, self-paced, collaborative, or inquiry-based study. Blended learning can be accomplished using blended virtual and physical resources. Examples include combinations of technology-mediated sessions, face-to-face sessions, and electronic or print materials.

Distance learning is a formal educational process in which most of the instruction occurs when a student and instructor are not in the same place. Instruction may be synchronous or asynchronous. Distance education may employ correspondence study, audio, video, and other electronic technologies.

Quality of Web-Based Learning

Web-based distance learning refers to a broad field of instruction where the faculty and student are separated geographically. The methods used for Web-based distance learning have been evolving for nearly two centuries, beginning with the use of the postal service for correspondence courses. As new technologies such as radio, television, cable, and satellite broadcasts were developed, they became transmission modes for Web-based or distance learning. Today, most distance learning takes place on the World Wide Web (WWW); making courses available anywhere and to anyone with access to an Internet-connected computer (*a*-learning). The practice of Web-based distance learning has been growing in recent years, to where the phrase is now consistently applied to a wide spectrum of activities. Web-based learning is increasingly being looked to by many institutions as a more efficient method of mobilizing their campus-based activities, expanding learning opportunities for students around the world, and making effective use of emerging new technologies.

Academic accreditation bodies recognizes that the continued development of Web-based distance learning and its worldwide acceptance depend on rigorous quality assurance, and that there are many areas in which the usual ways of doing things for on-campus provision are not necessarily appropriate in the context of Web-based learning.

Thus, the purpose for standards for *Web-based learning* means a way of providing education that involves delivering instruction using electronic and WWW technologies. There is considerable debate about appropriate terminology and a number of different terms are commonly used that refer to the same or similar sort of activity (e.g., *e-learning, distance education, distance learning*). There is also great diversity in the large number of actual arrangements—and even more in potential arrangements (how the program or courses are actually delivered)—which standards can be used to address. As the nature of institution-hosted and of collaborative, between and among institutions, provision develops and changes, and as the potential for Web-based learning is explored further, the boundaries between different forms of education are becoming less easy to recognize. Standards do not assume that Web-based learning is a separate and unique form of education around which there are clear, let alone fixed, boundaries. Nor is it assumed that all Web-based learning has uniform characteristics. However, programs and courses of Web-based learning have some basic features in common that broadly distinguish them from conventional modes of learning: physical proximity is not a requirement of study and programs made available through Web-based learning all involve some degree of geographical separation of the student from the institution responsible for providing instruction and awarding the degree. There are also a number of ways in which teaching and learning activities to support students on Web-based learning programs of study involve distinctive divisions of labor and allocations of responsibilities such as office hours, personal contact time, library resources, and so on.

Web-based standards can be arranged under the following headings, each dealing with an aspect where quality assurance is likely to require particular attention when Web-based learning is used:

1. Mission, planning, and institutional effectiveness
2. Organization, governance, and leadership
3. Public disclosure and integrity

4. Fiscal resources
5. Academic program and instruction
6. Faculty
7. Students
8. Library and other informational resources
9. Physical and technological resources

Benefits and Limitations of Web-Based Learning

Using Web-based learning, like all other delivery media, has benefits and limitations. Educators and course designers must carefully evaluate these against the use of other options on a case-by-case basis.

Benefits

Common benefits of Web-based learning when compared with conventional learning are as follows:

- Learning is typically self-paced and student directed.
- Access is available anytime, anywhere, around the globe.
- Student travel costs are reduced.
- Equipment costs for students are affordable.
- Student tracking is made easy.
- "Learning object" architecture supports on-demand, personalized learning.
- Content is easily updated.
- Students are more focused.

When compared with CD or DVD learning, the benefits of Web-based learning develop because access to the content is easy and requires no distribution of physical materials.

Limitations

Web-based learning has two genuine limitations, and both likely will be overcome in the next 5 or so years as increased high bandwidth network connections become widespread.

The first limitation is the lack of face-to-face interaction when compared with conventional classroom instruction. Web-based learning is better than CD or DVD learning in this regard. Students can use their Web connection to e-mail other students, post comments on message boards, or use chat rooms and videoconference links to communicate live. Although these methods of interaction are helpful, and an improvement over CD or DVD learning, they still do not have the impact of face-to-face interactions. With higher

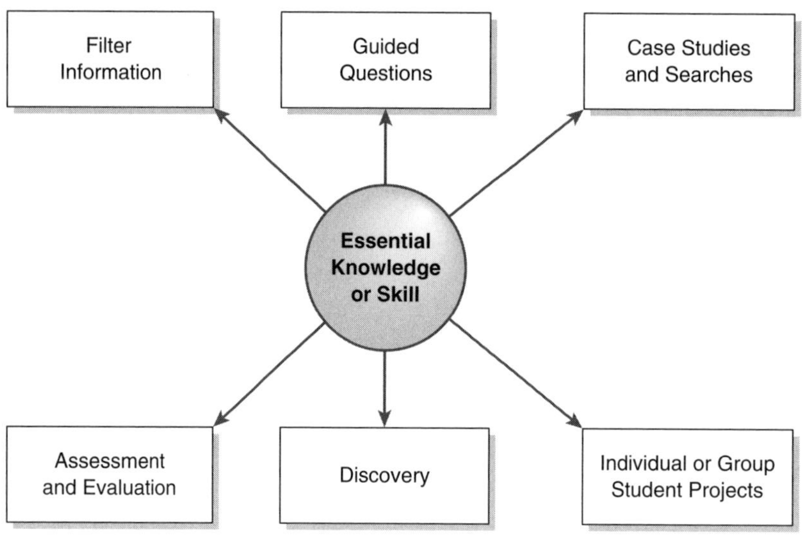

Figure 1 Web-Based Learning Design Model

bandwidth connections and improved conferencing software, students around the world will some day be able to communicate in real time with each other through full-screen video.

The second limitation is the lack of multimedia capabilities in many Web-based learning programs. Using audio and video are critical to creating persuasive descriptions, accommodating students with different learning styles, and creating realistic job simulations. Full multimedia is possible, particularly with the advent of YouTube and similar services, and many in education are using this resource. However, because large media files slow down the entire network, many information technology departments do not want such files used. The outcome is that many Web-based learning programs still comprise text and limited graphics. Once again, the bandwidth problem will likely be reduced in the future with advancements in network protocol standards and enhanced software compression.

Web-Based Learning Design Model

When starting a Web-based learning course, it is critical that the designer understand the direction the instructor wants to go and what essential knowledge and skills the instructor is trying to accomplish. The model in Figure 1 is to assist instructors in designing Web-based courses that are focused on students' understanding vital knowledge and skills and then applying them in real-world situations. The key concept is that these knowledges and skills are fluid and should be transferable to additional contexts and subjects.

Michael K. Swan

See also Online Gifted Education

Further Readings

Bruning, R. H., Horn, C. A., & PytlikZillig, L. M. (2003). *Web-based learning: What do we know? Where do we go?* Charlotte, NC: Information Age Publishing

O'Neil, H. F., & Perez, R. S. (2006). *Web-based learning: Theory, research, and practice.* Mahwah, NJ: Lawrence Erlbaum.

Wechsler Intelligence Scale for Children–Fourth Edition

Gifted children often require specialized instruction and intervention to optimize their academic performance. Before receiving individualized instruction, however, they must be identified as "gifted" through a process that typically involves the use of intelligence tests, such as the Wechsler Intelligence Scale for Children–Fourth Edition (WISC-IV), described in this entry. The first edition of the WISC was a modified version of the Wechsler-Bellevue Form II. Over the years, the WISC has been revised three additional times with the latest version being the most substantial revision of any Wechsler scale to date.

The WISC-IV represents a substantial improvement over its predecessor, the WISC-III. The many improvements made to this latest edition of the WISC have resulted in a psychometrically sound battery that is both adequate and appropriate for use in the identification of giftedness in children ages 6 to 16 years. Subtest ceilings have been raised, measures of fluid reasoning have been added, and there has been a de-emphasis on timed tasks. In addition, several excellent resources (e.g., technical reports, interpretive methods) will assist greatly in WISC-IV evaluation and interpretation, particularly for students who are gifted and who come from culturally and linguistically diverse backgrounds. A good rule of thumb when testing children for gifted and talented programming is to not rigidly adhere to a single cutoff score or criterion. Multiple data sources should always be used to make educational placement decisions.

Description

The WISC-IV is composed of 10 core-subtests that yield one global ability index, the Full-Scale Intelligence Quotient (FSIQ), and four lower-order composites: Verbal Comprehension Index (VCI), Perceptual Reasoning Index (PRI), Working Memory Index (WMI), and Processing Speed Index (PSI). Five supplementary subtests are available and can serve as substitutes for core subtests when appropriate. The clinical and psychometric features of the WISC-IV for identification of children with a variety of exceptionalities, including giftedness, have brought them to positions of dominance and popularity unrivaled in the history of intellectual assessment. Notwithstanding, the Wechsler Scales have been criticized with respect to their ability to accurately identify giftedness. These criticisms include the following: (a) difficulties in the interpretation of nontypical profiles and global ability scores, (b) lack of adequate measures of fluid reasoning, (c) overemphasis on speed of performance, (d) low test ceilings, and (e) lack of cultural fairness. The discussion that follows demonstrates, however, that these criticisms either no longer apply to the WISC-IV or have been circumvented by new interpretive procedures for the WISC-IV.

Nontypical Profiles and Global Ability Scores

Beginning with Lewis Terman, giftedness has been determined primarily by a global score from an intelligence test (i.e., IQ) that is greater than or equal to two standard deviations (SDs) above the mean. This criterion continues to be used today despite evidence that use of a global ability score may be invalid when an individual's performance on the tests comprising it is markedly variable. Because most individuals display significant variation in their cognitive ability profiles, use of a global score, such as IQ, as the sole determinant of giftedness is inappropriate. Indeed, more than 95 percent of the WISC-IV standardization sample demonstrates at least some scaled score variability. Therefore, before a global ability score, such as the FSIQ or General Ability Index (GAI), is used to make decisions regarding giftedness, the practitioner should first determine whether there is a significant difference among the scores that constitute them.

Sometimes neither the FSIQ nor the GAI is interpretable. In this situation, Betty Gridley's approach is a viable alternative. She and her colleagues proposed a method of determining giftedness that includes a "multidimensional definition of giftedness" (p. 290). Rather than relying on a global ability score, Gridley and her colleagues use the three strata of the Cattell-Horn-Carroll theory (CHC theory) as follows: superior potential or performance (top 10% of the population) in *general intellectual ability* (Stratum III); exceptional potential or performance (top 5% of the population) in *specific intellectual abilities* (Stratum II); and exceptional general or specific academic aptitudes (top 5% of the population; Strata I and II).

Fluid Reasoning Measures

Fluid Reasoning (*Gf*) refers to a type of thinking that an individual uses when faced with a relatively new task that cannot be performed automatically. This type of thinking involves, for example, forming and recognizing concepts, identifying and perceiving relationships, drawing inferences after reading a story, and reorganizing or transforming information. Overall, this ability can be thought of as a *problem-solving* type of intelligence.

In apparent response to the long-held criticism of the Wechsler Scales' lack of *Gf* measures, the fourth edition of the WISC now includes three new subtests that assess *Gf*—namely, Picture Concepts (PCn), Matrix Reasoning (MR), and Word Reasoning (WR). Dawn Flanagan and Alan Kaufman's interpretive system allows practitioners the option of generating three norm-based *Gf* clinical clusters. Given the importance of *Gf* in the identification of gifted and talented students, the WISC-IV is better suited for this purpose than were its predecessors.

Speed of Performance

The WISC-III was criticized for its inclusion of five timed tasks, all of which contributed to the FSIQ. Kaufman argued that response time would affect the performance of those gifted individuals who were either reflective, immature, or evidencing a coordination problem and suggested that the examiner pay careful attention to the examinee's behaviors during the testing session. The overemphasis on speed of performance on the WISC-III was addressed by the authors of the WISC-IV. In particular, two timed subtests were eliminated (i.e., Picture Arrangement and Object Assembly) and three were moved to supplementary status (i.e., Picture Completion, Cancellation, and Arithmetic), leaving only three timed subtests on the standard WISC-IV battery—Block Design, Coding, and Symbol Search—with the latter two contributing appropriately to the PSI.

Test Ceilings

When assessing individuals who may be intellectually gifted, practitioners should consider the age of the examinee, the age range of the test being used, and the test ceiling. Subtests with inadequate ceilings will underestimate the performance of gifted examinees because they do not include items of sufficient difficulty. As a result, the subtest will not adequately discriminate among those who score at the top of the test. For a test to have an adequate ceiling, the maximum raw score value must be equal to a standard score that is greater than two SDs above the mean of the test. However, when distinguishing among children who score in the gifted range, the maximum raw score value should be equivalent to a scaled score that is at least three SDs above the mean of the test.

All standard subtests on the WISC-IV are capable of measuring performance as many as three SDs above the mean for all ages. The *WISC-IV Technical Report Number 7* provides examiners with additional, extended norms that were developed as a result of a request from the National Association for Gifted Children to better differentiate among various degrees of intellectual giftedness. For example, whereas the WISC-IV norms show that the highest scaled score possible is 19, the norms reported in *Technical Report Number 7* extend the subtest scaled score ceilings as high as 28 in some cases to highlight the substantive and meaningful differences between scores. For older children (i.e., age 16), practitioners have the option of using the Wechsler Adult Intelligence Scale–Fourth Edition or any other intelligence battery that includes high ceilings.

Cultural Fairness

When using norm-referenced tests, practitioners should be aware of the potential concerns with fairness for different cultural groups. For example, as is the case with all current intelligence tests, the WISC-IV authors worked diligently to ensure that subtest items were not biased against any of the members of the standardization sample. The WISC-IV standardization sample was stratified across five typical demographic variables that included age, gender, geographic region, race/ethnicity, and socioeconomic status. Such sampling leads practitioners to assume that because culturally and linguistically diverse (CLD) individuals were included in the standardization sample, their performance can be compared fairly to that sample. Unfortunately, according to Samuel Ortiz, the absence of the systematic inclusion of two crucial variables, level of acculturation and degree of English language proficiency, tends to undermine the comparison of the performance of CLD individuals with the standardization sample. Creation of a truly representative sampling of *bilingual* individuals is a daunting task that faces many of the same difficulties encountered by publishers who seek to create special norm groups (e.g., deaf, learning disabilities, attention deficit disorder). As a result, the lack of a truly representative sample requires that practitioners consider the unique cultural and linguistic background histories when assessing a CLD examinee.

Dawn Flanagan and her colleagues recommend the CHC cross-battery approach, along with cultural and linguistic extensions, to provide a systematic and defensible method for greatly reducing the discriminatory aspects inherent in the use of cognitive ability tests with diverse individuals. Specifically, the use of the Culture-Language Interpretive Matrix (C-LIM), which is based on the Culture-Language Test Classifications (C-LTC), allows for the systematic interpretation of relevant cultural and linguistic characteristics that influence test performance.

Researchers have specified that an individual's familiarity with the content of the test (acculturation) and the degree to which they comprehend the language in which the test is based (proficiency) are directly related to test performance. Accordingly, tests such as the WISC-IV have been classified based on their degree of cultural loading and linguistic demand (e.g., low, medium, high). When these classifications are used in conjunction with the software program that assists in interpreting the test performances of CLD examinees (i.e., the C-LIM), this approach allows practitioners to determine whether test scores can be interpreted as valid indicators of what the test authors purport the tests to be measuring, or whether they reflect the examinee's levels of acculturation and English language proficiency.

Dawn P. Flanagan and Marlene Sotelo-Dynega

See also Intelligence; Intelligence Testing; Intelligence Theories

Further Readings

Flanagan, D. P., & Alfonso, V. C. (1995). A critical review of the technical characteristics of new and recently revised intelligence test for preschool children. *Journal of Psychoeducational Assessment, 13,* 66–90.

Flanagan D. P., & Kaufman, A. S. (2009). *Essentials of WISC-IV assessment* (2nd ed.). Hoboken, NJ: Wiley.

Flanagan, D. P., McGrew, K. S., & Ortiz, S. O. (2000). *The Wechsler intelligence scales and Gf-Gc theory: A contemporary approach to interpretation.* Boston: Allyn & Bacon.

Flanagan, D. P., Ortiz, S., & Alfonso, V. C. (2007). *Essentials of cross-battery assessment* (2nd ed.). New York: Wiley.

Gridley, B. E., Norman, K. A., Rizza, M. G., & Decker, S. L. (2003). Assessment of gifted children with the Woodcock-Johnson III. In F. A. Shrank & D. P. Flanagan (Eds.), *WJ III clinical use and interpretation: Scientist-practitioner perspectives* (pp. 285–317). Boston: Academic Press.

Kaufman, A. S. (1994). *Intelligent testing with the WISC-III.* New York: Wiley.

Ortiz, S. O. (2009). Bilingual-multicultural assessment with the WISC-IV. In D. P. Flanagan & A. S. Kaufman (Eds.), *Essentials of WISC-IV assessment* (2nd ed.). Hoboken, NJ: Wiley.

Volker, M. A., & Smerbeck, A. M. (2009). Identification of gifted students with the WISC-IV. In D. P. Flanagan & A. S. Kaufman (Eds.), *Essentials of WISC-IV assessment* (2nd ed.). Hoboken, NJ: Wiley.

Wechsler, D. (2003). *Wechsler intelligence scale for children* (4th ed.). San Antonio, TX: Psychological Corporation.

Zhu, J., Cayton, T., Weiss, L., & Gabel, A. (2008). WISC-IV extended norms (WISC-IV Technical Report No. 7). Retrieved September 16, 2008, from http://pearsonassess.com/NR/rdonlyres/C1C19227-BC79-46D9-B43C-8E4A114F7E1F/0/WISCIV_TechReport_7.pdf

Wechsler Preschool and Primary Scale of Intelligence–Third Edition

The Wechsler Preschool and Primary Scale of Intelligence–Third Edition (WPPSI-III), described in this entry, is designed to measure the general cognitive ability of young children from 2 years 6 months (2-6) to 7 years 3 months (7-3). The WPPSI-III measures verbal skills, including knowledge of words and general information, reasoning using pictorial cues, and solving problems with blocks and puzzles. The WPPSI-III also measures general language ability including receptive and expressive vocabulary.

The original Wechsler Preschool and Primary Scale of Intelligence (WPPSI) was published in 1967 in response to the development of educational programs for young children such as Head Start. These programs raised awareness of the need for accurate assessment of young children and evaluation of the effectiveness of early childhood education. The WPPSI was essentially a downward extension of the Wechsler Intelligence Scale for Children (WISC), first published in 1949. The WPPSI was revised in 1989, and the current edition was published in 2002, representing improvement of the scale to reflect input from examiners as well as research into the nature of intelligence in young children.

The WPPSI-III has been updated to measure aspects of intelligence based on Cattell-Horn-Carroll theory. Three new subtests measure fluid reasoning, which is the ability to solve problems using unfamiliar tasks or stimulus materials. Two new subtests measure processing speed, which requires timed responses on tasks requiring eye-hand coordination, and two new subtests measure expressive and receptive vocabulary.

The WPPSI-III covers two broad age groups, 2-6 to 3-11 and 4-0 to 7-3. The WPPSI-III overlaps with the Wechsler Intelligence Scale for Children–Fourth Edition (WISC-IV) at ages 6-0 to 7-3. The choice of which test to use depends on the child's estimated cognitive functioning and whether the child has previously been exposed to either test.

WPPSI-III subtests are designated as either core, supplemental, or optional. Core subtests are those that combine to form the Verbal, Performance, and Full Scale IQ scores. Supplemental subtests may be used to replace core subtests or to provide additional information. Optional subtests provide additional information but may not be used as replacements for core subtests.

At the younger age range, from 2-6 to 3-11, four core subtests are available. Receptive Vocabulary and Information form the Verbal scale. Block

Design and Object Assembly form the Performance scale. The Verbal and Performance scores are combined to determine the Full Scale IQ score. A supplemental subtest, Picture Naming, can be used as a substitute for Receptive Vocabulary or can be combined with Receptive Vocabulary to form the General Language Composite.

At the older age range, from 4-0 to 7-3, Information, Vocabulary, and Word Reasoning form the Verbal scale. Block Design, Matrix Reasoning, and Picture Concepts constitute the Performance scale. The Verbal and Performance IQ scores are used to determine the Full Scale IQ score. There are two supplemental subtests for the Verbal scale, Comprehension and Similarities, and two supplemental subtests for the Performance scale, Picture Completion and Object Assembly. The supplemental subtests may be used as replacements for other subtests in the same scale. A third scale for this age group, Processing Speed, consists of one core subtest, Coding, and one supplemental subtest, Symbol Search. The General Language Quotient consists of two tests that are optional at this age range, Receptive Vocabulary and Picture Naming.

Many WPPSI-III subtests are similar to subtests of the same name on the WISC-IV. Performance subtests include Block Design, which requires the child to reproduce designs using blocks with either one or two colors. Object Assembly asks the child to assemble puzzles of common objects. In Picture Concepts, the child must choose pictures that go together from two or three rows of pictures. Picture Completion requires the child to locate the missing element in an incomplete picture. Matrix Reasoning asks the child to solve visual puzzles by selecting the missing piece from several alternatives.

Verbal subtests include Information, which requires the child to answer questions about everyday subjects. The Vocabulary subtest asks the child to define words. For Word Reasoning, the child identifies an object or concept based on verbal clues. On Similarities, the child must describe how two objects are alike. Comprehension asks the child to provide solutions to problems involving common social situations.

Coding is a Processing Speed subtest that asks the child to copy symbols that are paired with other symbols. In Symbol Search, the child scans a row of symbols to determine if a target symbol is present or not.

Unique WPPSI-III subtests are those that form the General Language Composite. For Receptive Vocabulary the child points to one picture out of four that shows the meaning of a word. Picture Naming asks the child to name the item shown in a picture.

The WPPSI-III was standardized on 1,700 children representing the population of the United States in age, sex, race and ethnicity, geographic region, and parental education level. The test has good psychometric properties, including reliability, stability, and validity. The manuals and testing materials are interesting for children and provide excellent directions and scoring instructions for examiners.

The WPPSI-III can be used to identify intellectual giftedness and cognitive delay, and as a guide for placement in special programs. Because of the composite scores that are available, it provides some diagnostic information about cognitive strengths and weaknesses as well as the opportunity for the examiner to observe the child's responses to various materials and tasks. The General Language Quotient offers information about overall language skills, and this composite as well as the Verbal scale can be administered to children with motor impairments.

Weaknesses include the fact that only four core subtests are available at the younger age range, making the WPPSI-III more suitable as a screening instrument than as a comprehensive test of general intellectual ability. There is little continuity between the younger and older age ranges because of the different combinations of subtests used to obtain the IQ scores. There are a limited number of test items for children who are extremely low or high functioning, so it is difficult or impossible to distinguish performance at the extremes. Furthermore, because of the option to substitute supplemental subtests for core subtests, many different combinations of subtests may be used to determine the Full Scale IQ, especially at the older age range. This feature of the WPPSI-III is raises the potential for misuse as well as misunderstanding what the Full Scale IQ means for a particular child.

Julia Shaftel

See also IQ; Wechsler Intelligence Scale for Children–Fourth Edition

Further Readings

Lichtenberger, E. O., & Kaufman, A. S. (2004). *Essentials of WPPSI-III assessment.* Hoboken, NJ: Wiley.

Sattler, J. M., & Dumont, R. (2004). *Assessment of children: WISC-IV and WPPSI-III supplement.* San Diego, CA: Jerome M Sattler.

Wechsler, D. (2002). *WPPSI-III administration and scoring manual.* San Antonio, TX: Psychological Corporation.

WILLIAMS SYNDROME

Williams syndrome, described in this entry, is a rare, genetically based neurodevelopmental disorder characterized by a complex profile of impairments and abilities, and a host of serious cardiac, digestive, metabolic, and other medical problems. Especially common are a supravalvular aortic stenosis (narrowing of the aorta), accompanied by mild-to-moderate mental retardation as measured by standard IQ tests, as well as characteristic craniofacial features and heightened musical and narrative abilities. The prevalence of Williams syndrome is estimated at 1 in 20,000 births.

The disorder was named after a New Zealand cardiologist, J. C. P. Williams, who first described in 1961 four cases of young children who shared similar health problems and unusual facial features. This condition was also independently recognized as a syndrome in 1962 by German cardiologist Alois J. Beuren and is sometimes called Williams-Beuren syndrome.

Overview

People affected by Williams syndrome have distinctive facial features that make them look much more like others with this condition than like members of their own families. These facial features include a broad forehead, full cheeks, a wide mouth, an upturned nose, and prominent eyes, which results in their faces being described as "elfin" or "pixie-like." Because they are often perceived as attractive and lovable, children with Williams syndrome usually evoke positive responses from family members, teachers, and therapists.

In 1993, Williams syndrome was determined to be caused by a microdeletion of DNA in a single copy region of chromosome 7, 7q11.23. The first deleted gene identified as responsible for Williams syndrome was the elastin gene (ELN), which causes supravalvular aortic stenosis in those both with and without Williams syndrome. In the adjacent area of the chromosome 7q11.23 between 16 and 20 other genes have been linked to behavioral and physical phenotype of Williams syndrome: characteristic behavioral and cognitive profile, heightened sociability, visuospatial and visuomotor integrative deficits, and physical appearance.

Children with Williams syndrome are often born with serious, even life-threatening cardiac, digestive, and other medical problems that require surgical interventions. Small stature and slight built in combination with skeletal problems such as progressive joint limitations and subsequent contractures, depression of the chest, and angulation of the big toe are also symptoms of Williams syndrome.

Most children with Williams syndrome show delays in most areas of development. They are late to speak, walk, run, read, and write. By late childhood, they often make up for the initial language delay but the visuospatial and visuomotor integrative challenges endure throughout their lifetime. They show a marked unevenness across subtests of most IQ tests achieving relatively high scores on verbal tests and low scores on performance tests. In general, such tests are considered a challenge because of distractibility, impulsiveness, and rigidity of these children. Because of these behavioral characteristics, a secondary diagnosis of attention deficit disorder with (ADHD) or without (ADD) hyperactivity is sometimes given.

Giftedness and Talent

Five areas of unusual aptitude have been identified in Williams syndrome: language, sociability, curiosity, memory, and musicality. These areas of considerable skills stand in contrast with the relatively low levels of overall functioning including cognitive limitations and behavioral challenges.

Children with Williams syndrome possess auditory hypersensitivity to certain sounds, along with giftedness in music and heightened phonological memory. The powerful relationship with the auditory world is central to the Williams syndrome profile. Most children with Williams syndrome are fascinated by auditory stimuli and are able to detect nearly imperceptible sounds in noisy environments. Some of the usual sounds, such as vacuum cleaner, lawn mower, and thunder are perceived as unbearable and aversive, and the children often attempt to protect themselves by putting their hands over their ears. However, children with Williams syndrome have an exaggerated ability to attend to, identify, interpret, and remember auditory information. This ability is linked to their highly developed vocabulary, an excellent phonological memory, and an unusual aptitude for music, storytelling, and foreign languages.

Perfect pitch is a rare ability possessed by one in 10,000 people in the general population, yet it has been attributed to persons with Williams syndrome by clinicians, researchers, and musicians alike. Both absolute pitch, the ability to identify natural and accidental (sharps and flats) notes from several octaves, and relative pitch, the relation between pitches, have been identified as areas of talent in Williams syndrome. Brain imaging studies suggest that language and musical ability in Williams syndrome are related neuroanatomically. Musically gifted individuals with Williams syndrome are similar to professional musicians with absolute pitch in that they show leftward asymmetry of the planum temporal area in the auditory cortex, an area also associated with language processing.

Parents of individuals with Williams syndrome must be credited for recognizing and developing their children's musical talent and flair for musical performance, as well as for using these talents to support development in other areas. In addition, because of parental efforts, musicality in Williams syndrome has become a major area of research. Musicality is a well-documented area of giftedness in Williams syndrome, and researchers have now confirmed what parents have known all along: Individuals with Williams syndrome are more engaged in musical activities than any other people with a disability. Like musical talent of unaffected individuals, the extraordinary musical talent of those with Williams syndrome requires family and professionals' commitment to support and cultivate their musical skills.

Talent development approaches usually implemented in programs for the gifted and talented also show promise for children and youth with Williams syndrome. "Music and Minds," a residential summer camp program at the University of Connecticut in Storrs, offers young adults with Williams syndrome enrichment programs based on each participant's learning style, patterns of talent development, and past experiences. Belvoir Terrace in Lenox, Massachusetts, is another successful program where musically talented individuals with Williams syndrome develop and demonstrate their remarkable musicality in singing, performing, and composing. Throughout the past decade, musical talent in Williams syndrome was repeatedly recognized on radio and television programs such as *All Things Considered, 60 Minutes, Inside Edition, Nightline,* and the Nova documentary *The Mind Traveler.*

Williams syndrome is a disorder that transcends existing theories of intelligence, cognitive impairment, giftedness, and talent. It offers a unique opportunity to move beyond categorizing a group of people as "disabled" and to develop educational programs that support and nurture their unique interests and talents. It also provides an opportunity to re-think traditional approaches to special needs programs for children and youth with other neurodevelopmental conditions and to develop educational environments that support their interests and talents to the fullest.

Olga Solomon

See also Twice Exceptional; Verbal Ability

Further Readings

Bellugi, U., & St. George, M. I. (Eds.). (2001). *Journey from cognition to brain to gene: Perspectives from Williams syndrome.* Cambridge: MIT Press.

Morelock, M. J., & Feldman, D. H. (2003). Prodigies, savants and Williams syndrome: Windows into talent and cognition. In K. A. Heller, F. J. Monks, R. J. Sternberg, & R. Subotnik (Eds.), *International handbook for research on giftedness and talent* (2nd ed., pp. 227–242). Oxford, UK: Elsevier.

Morris, C., Lenhoff, H. M., & Wang, P. P. (Eds.). (2006). *Williams-Beuren syndrome: Research, evaluation, and treatment.* Baltimore: John Hopkins University Press.

Semel, E., & Rosner, S. R (2003). *Understanding Williams syndrome: Behavioral patterns and interventions.* Mahwah, NJ: Lawrence Erlbaum.

Sforza, T., Lenhoff, H. M., & Lenhoff, S. (2006). *The (strangest) song: One father's quest to help his daughter find her voice.* Amherst, NY: Prometheus Books.

Women, Gifted

Research on gifted women in various domains illustrates the complex and diverse paths they choose. Some have partners and some do not. Some have children and some do not. Some live fast-paced lives characterized by restless energy and a constant need to work. Others work more peacefully and carefully, living quieter lives while achieving similar or even higher levels of productivity. The processes of developing their talents also vary. Many gifted women evolved their talents over decades, drawing from a backdrop of earlier varied life experiences that helped them to prepare for their future life accomplishments. This entry describes theories of talent development in gifted women and the challenges facing gifted women.

Theories About Talent Development in Gifted Women

Although many articles have been published on gifted women, few researchers have proposed theories about the process of women's talent development that span various domains, and that can be widely applied under a variety of circumstances. Three such theories have been offered by researchers, including Sally Reis' theory of talent development, Karen Arnold, Kate Noble, and Rena Subotnik's theory of "remarkable women," and Barbara Kerr's work and themes about "smart girls and women."

Reis's Theory of Women's Talent Development

In research with gifted women who achieved eminence, Reis drew on research about this topic spanning two decades of work, proposing a new theory of women's talent development that suggested that the cumulative and contextual experiences of women of accomplishment differ from those of men in intellectual, moral, personal, and work perceptions. In studying the life experiences of an award-winning children's writer, for example, Reis found the writer wove memories of her Hispanic heritage and parenting into her literary work, incorporating the insights and creative experiences she had gained as a mother and through reflections on her own childhood. Other gifted women in Reis's study of eminent women made careful choices about the development of their talents, achieving at high levels through working steadily and slowly, though acknowledging and sometimes even celebrating the detours that occurred in their lives, such as raising family, helping others, and working in service for the betterment of others at home or in the community. All felt a certain intensity in their lives, characterized by a need and sense of obligation to pursue their talents in an active way. Many compared their own lives with the lives of their contemporaries—other equally talented women who did not attain the same level of eminence, but who appeared to live much calmer, and in some cases, happier lives.

Based on this research with gifted women, Reis proposed the following definition about the process of talent development in women:

Feminine talent development occurs when women with high intellectual, creative, artistic or leadership ability or potential achieve at high levels in an area they choose and when they make contributions that they consider meaningful to society; these contributions are enhanced when the women develop personally satisfying relationships and pursue what they believe to be significant and consequential work. (2005, p. 222).

Remarkable Women by Arnold, Noble, and Subotnik

Arnold, Noble, and Subotnik suggest that talent development in women may differ from that of men because of differences in psychological needs and drives, in issues faced at home and at work, and in access to resources that encourage the development of gifts. Arnold, Noble, and Subotnik's model of talent development defines gifted behavior differently than traditional models do. Most striking is their inclusion of the personal sphere as an outlet for gifted behavior. They note, for example, that there is talent in nurturing children well, building strong primary relationships, and making a home—particularly for the many women worldwide whose pasts are marked by dysfunction, lack of health services and other obstacles. In addition to the personal sphere, Arnold, Noble, and Subotnik recognize giftedness more traditionally, stating, "The widest sphere of influence lies in the creation of ideas or products that change the course of a domain or a social arena" (p. 435). Success in the public sphere is characterized as "leadership" or "eminence." The model also heavily stresses context, however, suggesting that what qualifies as gifted behavior depends on a woman's individual background. Women with many opportunities and fewer obstacles may be seen as gifted if they become eminent for outstanding contributions to a field, whereas an Indian woman of low caste may be seen as demonstrating gifted behavior if she overcomes obstacles to receive a degree or obtain a career.

An emphasis on context in women's lives is seen throughout the talent development model offered by Arnold, Noble, and Subotnik. Central to the model is the idea that women's relative position in relation to "the mainstream of their societies' achievement centers" has a powerful effect on whether and to what degree they will develop their talents. Thus, demographic variables such as race, wealth, and geographic location are key facilitators/inhibitors of talent development. In this model, adversity may either help or hinder development of women's gifts—depending on the woman and the circumstances. Other factors include desire to achieve and the support and validation of at least one other person.

As described by Arnold, Noble, and Subotnik, the characteristics of achieving women are those that allow them to overcome cultural and gender discrimination in whatever form they take. Thus, "cognitive and emotional flexibility," willingness to take risks and aim high, tolerance for making mistakes, persistence in the face of adversity, and the ability to resist the tendency to internalize limiting messages from the outside world may all play a role in women's talent development. Talent is important, according to this model, but it certainly is not the only factor that influences women's achievement, for as the authors state, a high level of innate ability is insufficient to withstand cultural pressures that have caused untold numbers of women to discount or deny their gifts.

Kerr's Smart Girls and Women

Kerr's writings on eminent women differ from other work discussed in this entry in that Kerr conducted biographical research. Kerr studied the lives of 33 eminent women in various domains, including Margaret Meade, Eleanor Roosevelt, Marie Curie, Maya Angelou, Katherine Hepburn, and Rigoberta Menchú, in an attempt to draw some conclusions about how women's talent develops. In this review of the lives of successful actors, scientists, activists, writers, and more, she found several themes, detailed in the following sections.

One of the unique factors identified in Kerr's analysis of women's talent development is time alone during girlhood. For some of these girls who later became eminent women, time alone was a choice; for others, a state forced on them by circumstance. Kerr suggests that, regardless of the cause of isolation, periods of aloneness provided these girls with time for reflection and an appreciation for individual work. Individualized instruction likewise was common across this group. Kerr notes that, for these girls, being able to move through material at their own paces probably prevented boredom and allowed advancement of skills in areas of particular talent. This individualized instruction was often provided within the larger environment of same-sex education, allowing for attention beyond that which might have been found within mixed-gender classrooms. Finally, most of the women Kerr studied had mentors—and they had mentors who had access at the highest level of their professions. Kerr cautions that one should not draw the conclusion that these eminent women owed their success to their relationships with influential people but, rather, that their talent was significant enough to impress those at the peak of their individual fields.

In addition to the variety of external factors, Kerr found a number of internal characteristics common to eminent women. First, almost all the women she studied were talented and insatiable readers as girls, which may have facilitated their learning and provided fodder for new ideas. Many also felt that they were "different" or "special" from a young age, either because of their gifts, or for other reasons, including the feeling that they were physically unattractive. All but one found adolescence painful and troublesome, increasing the time they spent alone and providing direct experience of the costs and benefits of standing apart. As they grew toward adulthood, each of the women Kerr studied formed identities relating to their ideas and work, rather than defining themselves primarily by relationships with others.

Likewise, most of the women were able to avoid seeing themselves primarily in terms of their membership in a couple or group. Instead, Kerr's eminent women were able to connect with others such as mentors or partners without losing their own identities or goals. Finally, in keeping with the idea that work was a huge part of the lives and relationships of these women, Kerr found that many joined work and love by marrying or partnering others who shared their passions. Georgia O'Keeffe and Alfred Steiglitz, Marie and Pierre Curie, and Gertrude Stein and Alice B. Toklas are provided as examples of just a few such couples.

The Challenges Facing Gifted Women

Different research studies on gifted women who have not achieved at high levels in their adult lives tell a similar story. The gifted women who did not achieve were extremely bright in school, but as they grew up, they began to feel ambivalent about their future and their responsibilities to loved ones. Their dreams for future high-profile careers and important work wavered and diminished, and they began to doubt what they previously believed they could accomplish. Their beliefs about their abilities as well as their self-confidence may have been undermined during childhood or adolescence. Some acquired various levels of "feminine modesty," leading to changes in self-perceptions of ability and talent, which subsequently affected others' perceptions of their potential. Some fell in love in college and suddenly and unexpectedly, the dreams of the person they loved became more important to them than their own dreams and they lowered their aspirations to pursue the relationship. Some decided to become nurses instead of doctors, and some completed a bachelor's degree instead of a Ph.D. Some accepted less challenging work that was different from what they had dreamed about doing a decade earlier, but that enabled them sufficient time to raise their families and support their partner's work. Some talented women born after the women's movement were surprised to find that they had to make choices that benefited those they loved, after being consistently told that they could "have and do it all." They learned, often to their surprise, that they could not.

The reasons for the successful accomplishments of some highly talented girls and women and the failure of others to realize their high potential in meaningful work is complex and depends on many factors, including values, personal choices, and social-cultural forces. Some gifted women have a sense of destiny about their own potential to produce meaningful work that makes a difference. Reis's research suggests that gifted women made active choices to pursue their talents because they had a sense of destiny about the importance of their work. Many personal choices and barriers faced this diverse group, and some of their motivation and determination emerged in overcoming and successfully negotiating these obstacles. The development of a creatively productive life and the attainment of eminence is complex and decidedly personal. What one participant regarded as an obstacle, another perceived as an intriguing challenge. Although some were negatively influenced by their parents' lack of support and withdrew from relationships, others used this anger and rebelled, and eventually became eminent in their selected area of endeavor. The ways in which the same barriers differentially affect talented women provides the fascination about conducting research on the individual paths they follow to achieve high levels of accomplishment. Not all gifted women experience the same barriers, but research that has been conducted suggests a combination of the following that occur across the life span and differentially affect productivity at different ages and stages: personality characteristics such as modesty, dilemmas about abilities and talents, personal decisions about family, decisions about duty and caring (putting the needs of others first) as opposed to nurturing personal needs, religious beliefs, and social issues. Some of these dilemmas cannot be resolved to the satisfaction of everyone involved. Rather, they shift or are eliminated when changes occur in a woman's life, such as when her children grow up, her marriage ends, a new relationship starts, or she changes a home or work environment. If our society is to more actively help talented girls and adult women to realize their abilities and potential, expectations about women's personal choices and work process and environments must be altered, and our society must support diversity of life choices.

Sally M. Reis

See also Creative Productivity; Eminence; Gifted Education Centers; Girls, Gifted; Talent Development

Further Readings

Arnold, K. D., Noble, K. D., & Subotnik, R. F. (1996). *Remarkable women: Perspectives on female talent development.* Cresskill, NJ: Hampton Press.

Kerr, B. A. (1985). *Smart girls, gifted women.* Columbus, OH: Ohio Psychology Publishing.

Kerr, B. A. (1997). *Smart girls: A new psychology of girls, women, and giftedness* (Rev. ed.). Scottsdale, AZ: Great Potential Press.

Reis, S. M. (1998). *Work left undone.* Mansfield Center, CT: Creative Learning Press.

Reis, S. M. (2005). Feminist perspectives on talent development: A research based conception of giftedness in women. In R. J. Sternberg & J. Davidson (Eds.), *Conceptions of giftedness* (2nd ed.). New York: Cambridge University Press.

World Conferences

Conferences on Gifted and Talented Children, described in this entry, are held every 2 years in a different country. These are presented by the World Council for Gifted and Talented Children. This council was organized in the mid-1970s by a group of educators from the United States and England who were dedicated to the challenge of providing the best for the world's brightest children. The council has members from more than 50 countries, so the conferences are truly international events. They are one of the most multicultural conference events held in the world today. To date, they have been held in London, San Francisco, Jerusalem, Montreal, Manila, Hamburg, Salt Lake City, Sydney, La Hague, Toronto, Hong Kong, Seattle, Istanbul, Barcelona, Adelaide, New Orleans, and Warwick.

The themes for the conferences have evolved from "New Thinking for the Future" in 1985, "The Challenge of Excellence" in 1989, "Talent for the Future—Social and Personality Development" in 1991, "A Gifted Globe" in 1993, "Maximizing Potential—Lengthening and Strengthening our Stride" in 1995, "Connecting the Gifted Community Worldwide" in 1997, "Challenge for the New Millennium" in 1999, "Celebrating the Gifted Children of the World" in 2005, to "Promoting the Dream" in Canada's 2009 conference. The progression of themes is an indication of the changes in the world, the development of new roles and dimensions in education and the ever-changing political scene worldwide.

Educational groups in interested countries submit a bid to host a conference, in a similar manner to the Olympic bids. These are evaluated by the executive of the World Council and a decision is made. This is done at least 4 years in advance. The decisions are made according to a published criteria available from the council's headquarters. A critical element in the decision is to move the conferences around to different parts of the world and to be cognizant of the world political situations at the time.

The purpose of the World Council is to focus world attention on gifted and talented children in many ways. It facilitates worldwide communication of information, creates an atmosphere of acceptance of all types of giftedness from any background and any country, supports and disseminates research, provides opportunities for sharing and exchange of ideas, supports national groups and international programs, and importantly, supports and enhances parent and family groups. To this end, the conference is appealing and valuable for all types and levels of educators, psychologists, social workers, researchers, and parents.

Informal events including families also are planned. These include events such as sports games, shows, dinner cruises, special feasts, and cultural experiences unique to the host country.

The program schedule varies from one conference to another but they all include a variety of keynote speakers, specific topic speakers, panels, workshops, and poster and round-table sessions.

Anyone is welcome to submit a proposal to hold any type of session, other than main speaker. The keynote speakers are carefully chosen from the gifted and talented people around the world—Peter Ustinov being an example, as in Toronto he discussed his work with children of the world through the United Nations. The hope is to have speakers who will inspire, excite, and challenge the conference audience.

Throughout the conference, local student groups usually present musical interludes, band numbers, and various other entertaining bits. In 1993, in Toronto the idea of a Youth Summit was developed and created by Norah Maier, Edna McMillan, and Julien Kitchen. Young gifted students from around the world came together in Toronto for a program running parallel to the conference that had its own goals and activities as well as being integrated with the adult conference for a variety of events. With 80 students from 15 countries, this initial event was so successful that it has been a component of most of the world conferences since. The interaction with students from such a variety of countries and backgrounds is often a memorable and life-changing event for these young people as they forge new and lasting friendships.

Edna Marie McMillan

See also World Council for Gifted and Talented Children

Further Readings

World Council for Gifted and Talented Children: http://www.world-gifted.org

World Council for Gifted and Talented Children

The World Council for Gifted and Talented Children (WCGTC), described in this entry was founded in London, England in 1975 at an international conference for gifted and talented children, chaired by Henry Collis, a prominent educator of the gifted and director of the National Association for Gifted Children in England. His vision evolved into a nonprofit organization of educators in the field of gifted education that spans the globe today.

The First Conference

The first conference was attended by more 500 people from 53 countries. Here, Harold C. Lyon, director of the Office of Gifted and Talented, from the United States, proposed that the participants join in a worldwide initiative to form a permanent organization to advocate for the gifted children of the world. In response, 150 educators in the field became members of the founding organization. This first conference was, subsequently, included in the numerical designation of the biennial world conferences of the WCGTC.

The First Executive

At the London conference, the first executive was elected. The first president was Dan Bitan, director of Gifted Education in Israel, and the first vice-president was Henry Collis. The remaining elected officers were from the United States: Alexis DuPont DeBie as executive vice-president, Dorothy Sisk as secretary, and Elizabeth Neuman and Marjorie Craig as co-treasurers.

The Incorporation

The World Council was officially incorporated and registered in the state of Delaware as a nonprofit organization on March 30, 1976. The officers at the time were representatives from three nations: from Israel, President Dan Bitan; from the United Kingdom, Vice-President Henry Collis; and from the United States, Executive Vice-President Alexis DuPont DeBie, joint Secretaries Dorothy Sisk and Elizabeth Neuman, and Treasurer Bob Swain.

The Second and Third Conferences

Bob Swain's proposal brought the second World Conference to San Francisco in 1977. Representation in the new seven-member executive expanded to seven nations: President Iraj Broomand of Iran, Vice-President Dorothy Sisk of the United States, Marie Schmidt of Venezuela, Levcho Zdravchev of Bulgaria, Warren Lett of Australia, Henry Collis of the United Kingdom, and Dan Bitan of Israel.

In 1978, with the Iranian conflict disrupting the ability of President Iraj Broomand to continue to serve as president of the World Council, Vice President Dorothy Sisk assumed the presidency until Henry Collis was elected as president at the third conference held in Jerusalem in 1979. He held the post until 1981.

A Developing Organization

As a requirement of incorporation, a constitution for the World Council was drafted by a subcommittee consisting of Sisk, representing the board, and two other founding members, DuPont DeBie and Neuman.

A major undertaking discussed at the San Francisco meeting was the creation of a journal. Levcho Zdravchev agreed to edit and publish the journal for the WCGTC, which was named *GATE: Gifted and Talented Education.* He published three issues of *GATE,* absorbing the cost of the journal at his Bulgarian office.

At the Jerusalem conference, Dorothy Sisk became the editor of the journal, now to be named *Gifted International,* and she held the post until 1993. During this time, Tom Kemnitz, owner of Trillium Press, published and distributed the journal at his expense. In the 1990s, under the editorship of John Feldhusen, the name was changed to *Gifted and Talented International.* Subsequent editors have been Joyce VanTassel-Baska and Maria McCann. The current editor is Taisir Subhi Yamin.

A third development, in 1979, was the creation of a permanent secretariat, today known as the headquarters, established at Teachers College, Columbia University, New York, with Milton Gold as executive administrator and A. Harry Passow as honorary director.

A further undertaking was the development of a newsletter. In 1980, *World Gifted* was produced by Dorothy Sisk and published by Milton Gold, assisted by Beverly Goodloe Kaplan. The newsletter has customarily been published by the hosting institution.

Successive Conferences and Presidents

Successive conferences took place upon the initiative and successful bidding of various leaders in the field. Bitan proposed Jerusalem as the site for the 1979 conference. Bruce Shore bid for the 1981 Montreal, Canada, conference, attended by 1,200 participants, with 350 presenting. In Montreal, James Gallagher assumed the presidency for a 4-year term.

Aurora Roldan's bid for Manila brought the next conference to the Philippines in 1983 and spawned the South East Asian organization.

The sixth biennial conference in Hamburg, Germany, in 1985, was proposed by Klaus Urban, which moved the event to Europe. The conference drew 1,200 participants from 47 different countries and 500 presentations. In Hamburg, A. Harry Passow became the president.

Calvin Taylor's proposal brought the next conference to Salt Lake City, Utah, in 1987. The organization had grown, as evidenced by its 1,756 participants and 400 presentations involving 775 presenters.

The next conference, proposed by Ken Imison, was held in Sydney, Australia, in 1989. Norah Maier was elected president. Vice-President Franz Mönks brought the next conference in 1991 to The Hague, Netherlands. Norah Maier, who had successfully proposed Toronto for the 1993 site, retired as president that year and was succeeded by Wu Tien-Wu from Taiwan, who had been responsible for the bringing the first strong delegation from Taiwan to the world conference in Montreal.

Between the 9th and 10th conferences, the Vienna Summit was held to examine new ways of reaching the goals of the World Council in the domains of teacher education, research, organization and planning, and policy issues.

Biennial conference sites after Toronto were Hong Kong in 1995, Seattle in 1997, Istanbul in 1999, Barcelona in 2001, Adelaide in 2003, New Orleans in 2005, Warwick in 2007, and Vancouver, Canada, in 2009.

The 4-year terms of the presidency during these years were held by Barbara Clark, from 1997 to 2001, by Klaus Urban, from 2001 to 2005, and by Den-Mo Tsai of Taiwan, from 2005 to 2009.

Affiliated Organizations and Federations

The World Council, whose membership consists of educators, graduate students, parents, educational institutions, and interested members in the international community, serves as a unifying organization globally. National associations and federations have joined as affiliated members to take advantage of the additional visibility and support they achieve, helping to further the mission of working for the welfare of gifted and talented children everywhere.

Headquarters

In 1983, for various reasons, the secretariat was transferred from New York to Tampa, at the University of South Florida, with Dorothy Sisk as executive secretary. Five years later, it was moved to Lamar University in Beaumont, Texas, with Sisk now as executive administrator. At both of these sites, all World Council expenses were covered by the hosting institutions. In 1993, the secretariat was moved to Purdue University in West Lafayette, Indiana, and administered by the graduate students of John Feldhusen. Partly because of a financial incentive from David Belin, the office was moved to the Belin-Blank Center for Gifted and Talented Development at the University of Iowa in Iowa City in 1995, with Nicholas Colangelo serving as the executive director for 2 years. Subsequently, the headquarters was moved to Northridge, California, to the consulting company of Sheila Madsen and Dennis Stevens. In May 2005, the headquarters located at the University of Winnipeg. It is supported by the Faculty of Education, with Cathrine Froese Klassen as executive administrator. At present, the main thrusts of the WCGTC are communicated to its members and the general public through the its Web site.

Continuing Mission

The World Council continues to focus world attention on gifted and talented children to ensure the realization of their valuable potential to the benefit of humankind. This original and overriding purpose continues to guide the World Council in the 21st century. The organization has benefited from the vision and energy of its founders and their successors in office, from its dedicated and hardworking executive committees, from its support from elected delegates worldwide, from its generous donors and hosting institutions, and from its members across the globe, now numbering more than 700 and continuing to grow.

Cathrine Froese Klassen

See also National Association for Gifted Children

Further Readings

World Council for Gifted and Talented Children: http://www.world-gifted.org

World Views

Profound disagreements abound within most academic fields, including gifted education. Practitioners and scholars in the field of gifted education can become trapped within competing sets of implicit assumptions about the nature of intelligence, giftedness, creativity, and talent. Many arguments in this field, or in any academic field for that matter, arise from the incompatibility of philosophical assumptions held by differing groups of professionals. These assumptions are framed by several competing philosophical world views, which are based on a set of world hypotheses articulated by philosopher Stephen Pepper and elaborated by others since. World views are deep-rooted metaphors that guide our assumptions about the nature of reality. For example, some theorists denigrate the notion that a gifted person's intelligence can be captured by an IQ score, but others embrace IQ as an important measure of intellect. This dispute is rooted in the ways in which opposing world views frame our assumptions about the human mind. The world views include mechanism, contextualism, organicism, and formism.

These four competing world views implicitly shape scholars' beliefs about the nature of appropriate theories and investigative methodologies while guiding and confining practitioners' beliefs about the nature of appropriate instructional strategies and curriculum design. Strong adherence to a particular world view often gives rise to dogmatic insularity, which is the tendency to despise and dismiss viewpoints that differ from one's own. The problem of dogmatic insularity slows progress in a field or profession because the disciples of competing belief systems, or paradigms, have great difficulty finding common ground for progress. This entry provides descriptions of the world views and examples of world-view influence.

Descriptions of the World Views

Each world view is based on a root metaphor, which frames a professional's basic assumptions about important phenomena. The *mechanistic world view* is based on the metaphor of a machine and encourages the belief that reality is machine-like at its essence. Mechanism prompts us to reduce phenomena, breaking them into their component parts to predict and control events through discovery of cause-effect relationships. For example, researchers who employ experimental-quantitative research methods to search for predictable mechanisms of thought are guided by mechanistic beliefs.

The *contextualist world view* is based on the metaphor of an ongoing event within its context, such as a canoe trip down a set of rapids, and emphasizes social interaction, shared meanings, and the unpredictably evolving, contextually shaped, nature of events. For example, researchers are guided by contextualism when they employ qualitative-ethnographic methods, embedding themselves in a classroom context to investigate the contextually influenced, unpredictably unfolding dynamics of students' experiences.

The *organicist world view* is based on the metaphor of a growing, well-integrated organism developing through predictable stages toward a particular end, such as a tree growing in a forest. Organicism emphasizes the whole system, not just the parts. It also highlights the ways in which the systems ties together by revealing integrative connections among its elements as well as the integration of subsystems into larger systems with different properties emerging at higher levels. Piaget's stage theory of development is an example of organicist thinking.

The *formist world view* is based on the root metaphor of similarity and emphasizes the intriguing recurrence of patterns in diverse phenomena. For example, interdisciplinary groups of complexity theorists at the Santa Fe Institute are discovering patterns of similarity in the behavior of chemical reactions, human thought patterns, animal populations in specific ecological niches, the dynamics of national economies, and other complex, adaptive systems.

According to prominent philosophers, adherence to a single world view can provide effective guidance for investigation up to a point; however, no single world view provides a complete or even an adequate portrayal of complex phenomena. Consequently, investigators and practitioners who become trapped dogmatically within the tenets of a single world view limit their effectiveness and cannot claim comprehensive understanding of the more complex phenomena in their field. Gifted education entails the study of exceptionally complex phenomena because the human mind is one of the most complex systems in the universe. In view of this complexity, investigations and theoretic interpretations from multiple world views are needed if more comprehensive understanding of high ability is to be grasped. Taken together, investigations from several different world-view vantage points can provide broader and deeper understandings. The more complex the phenomena of interest, the more necessary it is to consider contributions from multiple world views.

However, communication among adherents to opposing world views is difficult because the world-view frameworks tend to be incommensurable, and this promotes dogmatic insularity. That is, they lack common standards for comparison, and agreement on terminology. Very bright people adhering to differing world views and discussing the same phenomenon often talk past each other because their fundamental conceptual frameworks are so different. During the infrequent periods when they do understand each other, they tend to launch into vehement intellectual conflict, again because of their fundamentally opposing assumptions.

Examples of World-View Influence

World-view conflicts abound in fields related to high ability. For instance, some mechanistic cognitive scientists such as Steven Pinker believe that the human brain is a machine made of meat and consciousness arises solely from the electrochemical mechanisms within the cranium. Organicist-contextualist cognitive scientists vehemently disagree, arguing that consciousness is constructed largely from social interaction and the influences of sociopolitical and ideological contexts. From within each of the warring camps, the preferred position appears logical and comprehensive, but the opposing position appears to be ill conceived at best. Nevertheless, from the macro-perspective of philosophical world-view analysis, both camps are partially on target and contributions from both are needed to glean a more comprehensive view of the mind.

The following is another example of how world view directly and powerfully influences gifted education. The federal No Child Left Behind legislation's emphasis on testing for accountability to predict and control learning outcomes marks it as dogmatically mechanistic. In assuming that all children and all schools can achieve its standards, it tends to ignore the contextual influences on learning such as child poverty and inequality of opportunity.

In essence, no single world view has a monopoly on the truth, and one world view is not necessarily better or worse than another. All four world views are extremely broad in scope but each has its strengths and weaknesses. Mechanism offers us the advantage of precision but it tends to ignore the important influences of context, the integrative, holistic nature of many phenomena, and difficult to discern, far-flung similarities. Contextualism reveals the unpredictable influences of context, organicism sheds light on integrative interconnections, and formism reveals similarities, but these three world views lack the precision of mechanism. The inability of a single world view to encompass the entirety of a complex phenomenon, and the tendency of professionals to trap themselves within a particular world view indicate that open-minded dialogue is crucial for understanding high ability.

Don Ambrose

See also Cognition; Controversies in Gifted Education; High-Stakes Testing; IQ; No Child Left Behind; Research, Qualitative; Research, Quantitative

Further Readings

Ambrose, D. (1996). Unifying theories of creativity: Metaphorical thought and the unification process. *New Ideas in Psychology, 14*, 257–267.

Ambrose, D. (1998). Comprehensiveness of conceptual foundations for gifted education: A world-view analysis. *Journal for the Education of the Gifted, 21*, 452–470.

Ambrose, D. (2000). World-view entrapment: Moral-ethical implications for gifted education. *Journal for the Education of the Gifted, 23*, 159–186.

Overton, W. F. (1984). World views and their influence on psychological thoughts and research: Khun-Lakatos-Laudan. In H. W. Reese (Ed.), *Advances in child development and behavior* (Vol. 18, pp. 91–226). New York: Academic Press.

Pepper, S. C. (1942). *World hypotheses*. Berkeley: University of California Press.

Writers

The playwright, the poet, the novelist, the memoirist, the screenwriter, and the journalist are the varieties of writers discussed in this entry. What is creativity in writing, and how is it judged? How does creativity in writing relate to creativity in general? A small number of researchers, mostly educators and psychologists, have been asking these questions. Conventionally, the "creative" writer is defined as the writer who writes poetry, fiction, plays, song lyrics, screenplays, or essays that usually don't have footnotes (except for the novels of such postmodern fiction writers as David Foster Wallace). If the writer uses footnotes and other sources, he or she is a scholarly writer but not a creative writer.

A surge in research on creativity began in the late 1940s, after World War II, when the Institute for Personality Assessment and Research (IPAR) at the University of California at Berkeley, and the Army Aptitudes Project in the Structure of Intellect (SOI) at the University of California at Los Angeles began to develop tests, checklists, and other devices and instruments to help the country find and describe people who are most effective. Those who wrote on the psychology of creative writers included psychologist Frank Barron, who studied eminent, popular, and student writers. Social psychologist Dean Keith Simonton also studied writers according to genre, geographical location of residence, and eminence. Howard Gardner did a case study of T. S. Eliot using Gardner's concept of linguistic intelligence. Psychotherapists Nancy Andreason, Kay Jamison, and Albert Rothenberg studied writers with regard to their psychopathology. Scott Kaufman and James Kaufman edited a book on the psychology of creative writing. Jane Piirto did a study of 180 contemporary U.S. creative writers.

Such research has shown that creative writers were often early readers. They used early reading and writing to escape. They have high conceptual intelligence and high verbal intelligence. They are independent, nonconforming, and not interested in joining groups. They value self-expression and are productive. They are often driven, able to take rejection, and like to work alone for long periods.

In addition, writers often have difficulty with alcohol or substances. They prefer writing as their mode of expression of emotions and feelings. Creative writers are not immune to great ambition and envy, probably because they are often rejected by publishers, editors, and agents, and when one of their number succeeds, they wonder, "Why not me? What is the difference between my writing and his?" Their conceptual intelligence allows them to focus on philosophical matters, but they are able to convey the concepts concretely, so that the average reader can apprehend them. The concern with philosophical matters may take an almost religious, and certainly a spiritual tone. Writers are often politically active, most often left-leaning. They experience a higher rate of psychopathology and suicide than does the general population. Depression is more common than in the normal population, and writers are 10 times more likely to experience bipolar spectrum disorders than is the general population. Writers have often experienced childhood trauma. Poets have the highest rate of suicide among writers; journalists have the lowest. Writers seem to empathize with the underdog and with the oppressed. Of people imprisoned worldwide for their convictions, journalists rank highest. Writers' verbal talent is often shown in their odd senses of humor. Studies with psychological instruments such as the Myers Briggs Type Indicator (MBTI) show that writers prefer intuition as a learning style.

In their creative process, writers have said that (a) they seem to have rituals; for example, they like to walk; (b) they crave silence; (c) they go to retreats and colonies; (d) they are inspired by travel; (e) they use imagination; (f) they trust their dreams; (g) they seek solitude so they may go into a state of reverie (or flow); (h) they meditate; (i) they get inspiration from the muse (desire or love); (j) they are inspired by others' works of art and music; (k) they use substances to help their inspiration, or to "come down" after working, because they have explored deep places of their psyches; (l) they improvise (automatic writing, free writing).

Piirto found 16 themes in the lives of 180 contemporary U.S. creative writers, and arranged them according to the Environmental Suns in the Piirto Pyramid of Talent Development:

The Sun of Home

Theme 1: Unconventional families and family traumas

Theme 2: Extensive early reading

Theme 3: Early publication and interest in writing

Theme 4: Incidence of depression or acts such as use of alcohol, drugs, or the like

Theme 5: Being in an occupation different from their parents

The Sun of Community and Culture

Theme 6: Feeling of marginalization or being an outsider, and a resulting need to have their group's story told (e.g., minorities, lesbians, regional writers, writers from lower socioeconomic class, writers of different immigration groups)

Theme 7: Late career recognition

The Sun of School

Theme 8: High academic achievement and many writing awards

Theme 9: Nurturing of talents by both men and women teachers and mentors

Theme 10: Attendance at prestigious colleges, majoring in English literature but without attaining the Ph.D.

The Sun of Chance

Theme 11: Residence in New York City at some point, especially among the most prominent

Theme 12: The accident of place of birth and of ethnicity forms their subject matter

The Sun of Gender

Theme 13: Conflict with combining motherhood and careers in writing

Theme 14: Societal expectations of "femininity" incongruent with their essential personalities

Theme 15: History of divorce more prevalent in women

Theme 16: Military service more prevalent in men

Jane Piirto

See also Creative Personality; Literary Creativity; Playwrights; Verbal Ability

Further Readings

Andreason, N. (1987). Creativity and mental illness: Prevalence rates in writers and their first-degree relatives. *American Journal of Psychiatry, 144,* 1288–1292.

Barron, F. (1969). The psychology of the creative writer. *Explorations in Creativity, 43*(12), 69–74.

Gardner, H. (1994). *Creating minds.* New York: Basic Books.

Jamison, K. R. (1993). *Touched with fire: Manic-depressive illness and the artistic temperament.* New York: Free Press.

Kaufman, S., & Kaufman. J. (2009). *The psychology of creative writing.* Cambridge, UK: Cambridge University Press.

Piirto, J. (2002). *"My teeming brain": Understanding creative writers.* Cresskill, NJ: Hampton Press.

Rothenberg, A. (1990). *Creativity and madness.* Baltimore: Johns Hopkins University Press.

Simonton, D. K. (1994). *Greatness: Who makes history and why?* New York: Guilford Press.

Index

Entry titles and their page numbers are in **bold**.